◆

RESEARCH
METHODS IN
ANTHROPOLOGY

ALTAMIRA
PRESS
A Division of Sage Publications, Inc.

RESEARCH METHODS IN ANTHROPOLOGY

SECOND EDITION

Qualitative and Quantitative Approaches

H. Russell Bernard

ALTAMIRA
PRESS

A Division of Sage Publications, Inc.
Walnut Creek   London   New Delhi

For information address:

AltaMira Press
1630 North Main Street, Suite 367
Walnut Creek, CA 94596

SAGE Publications Ltd.
6 Bonhill Street
London EC2A 4PU
United Kingdom

SAGE Publications India Pvt. Ltd.
M-32 Market
Greater Kailash I
New Delhi 110 048 India

Printed in the United States of America

Library of Congress Cataloging-in-Publication Data

Bernard, H. Russell (Harvey Russell), 1940-
    Research methods in anthropology: qualitative and quantitative
approaches / H. Russell Bernard.—2nd ed.
        p.   cm.
    Includes bibliographical references and index.
    ISBN 0-8039-5244-9.—ISBN 0-8039-5245-7 (pbk.)
    1. Ethnology—Methodology.   I. Title.
GN345.B36   1994
306'.072—dc20   93-43670

98 99 00 01 10

Originally published by Sage Publications, Inc.

Contents

Preface

S ince 1988, when I wrote the first edition of this book, I've heard from
many colleagues that their departments are offering courses in research
methods. This is very encouraging. Anthropologists of my generation, trained
in the 1950s and 1960s, were hard pressed to find courses we could take on
how do research. There was something rather mystical about the how-to of
fieldwork; it seemed inappropriate to make the experience too methodical.

The mystique is still there. Anthropological fieldwork is fascinating and
a bit dangerous. Seriously: Read Nancy Howell's 1990 book on the
physical hazards of fieldwork if you think this is a joke. But many
anthropologists have found that participant observation loses none of its
allure when they collect data systematically and according to a research
design. Instead, they learn that having lots of reliable data when they return
from fieldwork makes the magic of the experience all the more magical.

I wrote this book to make it easier for students to collect reliable data
from their first fieldwork experience. We properly challenge one another's
explanations for why Hindus don't eat cattle and why in some cultures
mothers are more likely than fathers to abuse their children. That's how
knowledge grows. Whatever our theoretical orientation, though, all of us
need data on which to test explanations. The methods for collecting and
analyzing data belong to all of us.

The book begins with a chapter about where I think cultural anthropology fits in the history of science. I discuss the philosophical position
known as *positivism* and lay out my perspective on quantitative and
qualitative methods in anthropology. As you read that chapter, think about
your own position on these issues. It is not necessary to agree with my
ideas on epistemological issues to profit from the later chapters on how to
select informants, how to choose a sample, how to do questionnaire
surveys, how to write and manage field notes, and so on.

Chapter 2 introduces the vocabulary of social research. There's a lot of jargon, but it's the good kind. Important concepts deserve words of their own, and Chapter 2 is full of important concepts like reliability, validity, levels of measurement, operationism, and covariation.

Chapter 3 is about research design and the experimental method. You should come away from Chapter 3 with a tendency to see the world as a series of natural experiments waiting for your evaluation.

Chapter 4 deals with sampling. It's a tough chapter, and it will take you a little time and effort to get through it. If you've had a course in statistics before, the concepts in Chapter 4 will be familiar to you. If you haven't had any stats before, read the chapter anyway.

Trust me. There is almost no math in Chapter 4. There is one square root sign, used in calculating the standard error of the mean. If you don't understand what the standard error is, you have two choices. You can ignore it and concentrate on the concepts that underlie good sampling or you can study Chapter 18 on univariate statistics and return to the sampling chapter later.

I've placed the sampling chapter early in the book because the concepts in that chapter are so important. The validity of research findings depends crucially on measurement, but your ability to generalize from valid findings depends crucially on sampling. Read Chapter 4 several times, if you need to. It will pay off.

Chapter 5 is about how to choose a research problem. We always want our research to be theoretically important, but what does that mean? After you study this chapter, you should know what theory is and how to tell if your research is likely to contribute to theory or not. Chapter 5 is the first of several places in the book where I deal with ethics. I don't have a separate chapter on ethics. The topic is important in every phase of research, even in the beginning phase of choosing a problem to study.

Chapter 6, on conducting a search of the literature, is the last of the preliminary chapters before we get to the chapters on fieldwork and data collection. Don't skip this chapter. You'll be amazed at how rich the library resources are these days. And if you're fortunate enough to be at a school that has the latest in electronic library resources, don't fail to take advantage of those resources. Several of the most important library tools are described in Chapter 6.

Chapters 7-15 deal with fieldwork and methods for collecting data. All field research methods in anthropology depend, ultimately, on participant observation, the subject of Chapter 7.

Chapter 8 is about selecting and working with informants. I've never been comfortable with the word "informant." I suppose it sounds too much like "informer." Psychologists call the people they study "subjects," and sociologists refer to their "respondents." Some anthropologists today refer to their "consultants" or their "collaborators." None of those words sound any better to me than "informant."

Chapter 9 describes how to write and how to manage field notes. These days, managing field notes (and other texts) is a chore easily done by computer.

Chapter 10 is titled "Unstructured and Semistructured Interviewing." All data gathering in fieldwork boils down to two broad kinds of activities: watching and listening. You can observe people and the environment, and you can talk to people and get them to tell you things. Most data collection in anthropology is done by just talking to people. This chapter is about how to do that effectively.

Increasingly, anthropologists are using highly structured interviewing techniques, including questionnaires, to gather data. Chapter 11 describes pile sorts, triad tests, free listing, frame eliciting, ratings, rankings, and paired comparisons—that is, everything *but* questionnaires. Chapter 12 is devoted to questionnaire research, including such topics as how to train interviewers, how to write useful questions, and the relative merits of face-to-face, telephone, and mail surveys.

One topic not covered in Chapter 12 is how to build and use scales to measure concepts. Chapter 13 deals with this topic in depth, including sections on Likert scales and semantic differential scales, two of the most common scaling devices in social research.

Chapters 14 and 15 are about watching. Watching people can be done obtrusively (standing around with a stopwatch and a note pad) or unobtrusively (lurking out of sight, or getting hold of the paper trail—phone bills, marriage contracts, office memos—that so much behavior leaves behind these days).

Chapter 14 discusses the two major forms of direct observation, continuous monitoring and spot sampling. This chapter includes new material on how to sample behavior in time allocation research.

Chapter 15 deals with unobtrusive research, including behavior trace studies. Archeologists do behavior trace studies all the time; you may be surprised at how much you can learn from studying the traces of current behavior. Your credit rating, after all, is based on other people's evaluation of the traces of your behavior.

Naturalistic experiments are mentioned first in Chapter 3, as part of the discussion of the experimental method. In Chapter 15 I describe this method in some detail. I also discuss disguised observation, the method that poses the most serious ethical problems in social research.

Chapters 16-20 deal with data analysis. Data do not "speak for themselves." You have to process data, pore over them, sort them out, and produce an analysis. The canons of science that govern data analysis and the development of explanations apply equally to qualitative and quantitative data.

Chapter 16 is about the analysis of qualitative data. Some methods discussed in this chapter include the building of taxonomies, ethnographic decision-tree modeling, and the presentation of theme matrices. I also discuss the judicious use of quotes in ethnographic reportage as a method of data analysis.

Chapter 17 lays out the steps for creating a codebook. This is a critical, often-overlooked, but vital step in statistical data analysis.

Chapters 18-20 present the basic concepts of the most common statistical techniques used in the social sciences. If you want to become comfortable with statistical analysis, you need more than a basic course; you need a course in regression and applied multivariate analysis and a course (or a lot of hands-on practice) in the use of statistical packages, such as SPSS, SAS, or SYSTAT. Neither the material in this book nor a course in the use of statistical packages is a replacement for taking statistics from professional instructors of that subject.

Nevertheless, after working through the materials in chapters 18-20 you will be able to use basic statistics to describe "what's going on" in your data. You'll also be able to take your data to a professional statistical consultant and understand what she or he suggests.

Chapter 18 deals with univariate statistics; that is, statistics that describe a *single variable*, without making any comparisons among variables. Chapters 19 and 20 are discussions of bivariate and multivariate statistics that describe *relationships among variables* and that let you test hypotheses about what causes what.

I don't provide exercises at the end of chapters. Instead, throughout the book, you'll find dozens of examples of real research that you can replicate. One of the best ways to learn about research is to repeat someone else's successful project. The best thing about replicating previous research is that *whatever* you find out has to be significant. Whether you corroborate or falsify someone else's findings, you've made a serious contribution to the store of knowledge. If you repeat any of the research projects described in this book, write and tell me about what you found.

Acknowledgments

I could not have written the book without the help and encouragement of many students, colleagues, and friends. As I wrote the first edition of this book, many students offered me the benefit of their advice, both on the subject of research methods in anthropology and on my treatment of that topic. Domenick Dellino, Michael Evans, Camilla Harshbarger, Fred Hay, Robinette Kennedy, Christopher McCarty, and David Price were very helpful.

Among colleagues, Carole Hill, Aaron Podolefsky, and Roger Trent provided detailed, helpful criticisms of drafts of the first edition. Jeffrey Johnson used a draft of the first edition in his research methods class. He and his students, especially Dawn Parks, provided valuable comments.

Since the first edition of this book came out in 1988, several colleagues who have used this book have shared with me their wisdom on how to teach research methods. In particular, I thank Penn Handwerker, Jeffrey Johnson, Willett Kempton, Paula Sabloff, and Alvin Wolfe. Douglas Raybeck reviewed the prospectus for the second edition and gave excellent guidance.

Students at the University of Florida have been keen critics of the first edition and helped me all along the way. My thanks in particular to Holly Williams, Gery Ryan, Gene Ann Shelley, Barbara Marriott, Kenneth Adams, Susan Stans, Bryan Byrne, and Louis Forline.

Over the past 27 years of teaching research methods, I have benefited from the many textbooks on the subject in psychology (e.g., Murphy et al., 1937; Kerlinger, 1973), sociology (e.g., Goode & Hatt, 1952; Lundberg, 1964; Nachmias & Nachmias, 1976; Babbie, 1983), and anthropology (e.g, A. Johnson, 1978; Pelto & Pelto, 1978). The scholars whose works have most influenced my thinking about research methods have been Paul Lazarsfeld (1954, 1982; Lazarsfeld & Rosenberg, 1955; Lazarsfeld et al., 1972) and Donald Campbell (1957, 1974, 1975; Campbell & Stanley, 1966; Cook & Campbell, 1979).

Over those same 27 years, I've profited from lengthy discussions about research methods with Michael Agar, Stephen Borgatti, James Boster, Ronald Cohen, Roy D'Andrade, Linton Freeman, Sue Freeman, Christina Gladwin, Marvin Harris, Jeffrey Johnson, Pertti Pelto, the late Jack Roberts, A. Kimball Romney, Douglas White, Lee Sailer, Thomas Schweizer, Susan Weller, and Oswald Werner. Other colleagues who have had a personal influence on my thinking about research methods include Ronald Burt, Michael Burton, Carol Ember, Melvin Ember, Eugene Hammel, Allen Johnson, Maxine Margolis, Ronald Rice, Peter Rossi, James Short, Harry Triandis, the late Charles Wagley, and Alvin Wolfe. Most of them knew that they were helping me talk and think through the issues presented in this book, but some may not have, so this seems like a good time to say thank you to all of them.

I also thank my colleagues at the Museum of Ethnology in Osaka, Japan, for their hospitality and support from March-June, 1991 when I began the research for this edition. Particular thanks to Kazuko Matsuzawa, Paul Eguchi, Etsuko Kuroda, and Takashi Nakagawa.

Since 1988, Pertti Pelto, Stephen Borgatti, and I have taught at the National Science Foundation Summer Institute on Research Methods in Cultural Anthropology. Pertti Pelto, of course, wrote the pioneering methods text in cultural anthropology (1970); my intellectual debt to him cannot be exaggerated. In particular, I've been influenced by Pelto's sensible combination of ethnographic and numerical data in field research.

Stephen Borgatti has tutored me on the measurement of similarities and dissimilarities and has profoundly influenced my thinking about the formal study of emically defined cultural domains. Readers will see many references in this book to Borgatti's suite of computer programs, called ANTHROPAC. That package and the advent of very lightweight computers has made it possible for anthropologists to do multidimensional scaling, hierarchical clustering, Likert scaling, Guttman scaling, and other computationally intensive data analysis tasks *in the field*.

My closest colleague, and the one to whom I am most intellectually indebted, is Peter Killworth, with whom I have worked for the past 22 years. Peter is a geophysicist at Oxford University and is accustomed to working with data that have been collected by deep-sea current meters, satellite weather scanners, and the like. But he shares my vision of an effective science of humanity, and he has shown an appreciation for the difficulties a naturalist like me encounters in collecting real-life data, in the field, about human behavior and thought.

Most importantly, he has helped me see the possibilities for overcoming those difficulties through the application of scientific research practices. The results are never perfect, but the process of trying is always exhilarating. That's the central lesson of this book, and I hope it comes through.

Carole Bernard copyedited this book and saved me from many embarrassing infelicities of phrase. Much more importantly, she has lived through my writing this book—twice. No one can possibly know, without firsthand experience, what it's like to live with someone who is writing a book. I only know that I wouldn't want to do it.

Mitch Allen, my editor at Sage Publications, read drafts and made cogent suggestions for improving the prose, the epistemological arguments, and the organization of the material. Mitch is a treasure in the editing profession.

H.R.B.
Gainesville, Florida
June 1, 1993

1

Cultural Anthropology
and Social Science

This book is about research methods in cultural anthropology. The theme of this book is that methods belong to all of us in the discipline—indeed, in all of social science. Whatever our theoretical orientation, a sound mix of qualitative and quantitative data is inevitable in any study of human thought and behavior. Whether we do words or numbers, we might as well do them right.

The problem with trying to write a book about research methods (besides the fact that there are so *many* methods) is that the word "method" itself has at least three meanings. At the most general level, it means *epistemology* or the study of how we know things. At a still-pretty-general level, it's about strategic choices, like whether to do participant observation fieldwork, a library dissertation, or an experiment. At the specific level, it's about what kind of sample you select, whether you do face-to-face interviews or use the telephone, whether you use an interpreter or learn the local language well enough to do your own interviewing, and so on.

When it comes to epistemology, there are several key questions. One is whether you subscribe to the philosophical principles of *rationalism* or *empiricism*. Another is whether you buy the assumptions of the scientific method, often called *positivism* in the social sciences, or favor the competing method, often called *humanism* or *interpretivism*. These are tough questions, with no easy answers. I discuss them in turn.

Rationalism, Empiricism, and Kant

The clash between rationalism and empiricism is at least as old as ancient Greek philosophy. It is still a hotly debated topic in the philosophy of knowledge.

Rationalism is the idea that human beings achieve knowledge because of their capacity to reason. That is, there are a priori truths, and if we just prepare our minds adequately those truths will become evident to us. From the rationalist perspective, progress of the human intellect over the centuries has resulted from reason. Many great thinkers, from Plato to Leibnitz, subscribed to the rationalist principle of knowledge. "We hold these truths to be self-evident . . ." is an example of assuming a priori truths.

The competing epistemology is empiricism. For empiricists, the only knowledge that human beings acquire is from sensory experience. David Hume (1711-1776), for example, held that human beings are born with empty boxes for minds and that the boxes are filled with experiences throughout life. We see and hear and taste things and, as we accumulate experience, we make generalizations; we come to understand what is true from what we are exposed to. (For a review of the rationalism-empiricism issue, see De Santillana & Zilsel, 1941.)

Immanuel Kant (1724-1804) proposed a third alternative. A priori truths exist, he said, but if we see those truths it's because of the way our brains are structured. The human mind, said Kant, has a built-in capacity for ordering and organizing sensory experience. This was a powerful idea that led many scholars to look to the human mind itself for clues about how human behavior is ordered.

Noam Chomsky, for example, proposed that human beings can learn any language because they have a universal grammar already built into their minds. This would account, he said, for the fact that material from one language can be translated into any other language. A competing theory was proposed by B. F. Skinner. Humans learn their language, Skinner said, the way they learn everything else—by operant conditioning, or reinforced learning. Babies learn the sounds of their language, for example, because people who speak the language reward babies for making the "right" sounds (see Skinner, 1957; Chomsky, 1972; Stemmer, 1990).

The intellectual clash between empiricism and rationalism creates a dilemma for anthropologists. Empiricism holds that people learn their values and that values are therefore relative. I consider myself an empiricist, but I accept the rationalist idea that there are universal truths about right and wrong.

I'm not in the least interested, for example, in transcending my disgust with, or becoming empirically objective about genocide. No one has ever found a satisfactory way out of this dilemma. As a practical matter, I recognize that both rationalism and empiricism have contributed to our current understanding of the diversity of human cultures.

Modern social science has its roots in the empiricists of the French and Scottish Enlightenment periods. The early empiricists of the period, like Hume, looked outside the human mind, to human behavior and experience, for answers to questions about human differences. They made the idea of a mechanistic science of humanity as plausible as the idea of a mechanistic science of other natural phenomena.

In the rest of this chapter, I outline the assumptions of the scientific method and how they apply to the study of human thought and behavior in general, and to anthropology in particular.

The Norms of Science

The norms of science are clear. Science is "an objective, logical, and systematic method of analysis of phenomena, devised to permit the accumulation of reliable knowledge" (Lastrucci, 1963:6). Three words in Lastrucci's definition, "objective," "method," and "reliable," are especially important.

1. Objective. The idea of truly objective inquiry has long been understood to be a delusion. Scientists do hold, however, that *striving* for objectivity is useful. In practice, this means constantly trying to improve measurement (to make it more precise and more accurate) and submitting our findings to peer review, or what Robert Merton called the "organized skepticism" of our colleagues.
2. Method. Each scientific discipline has developed a set of techniques for gathering and handling data, but there is, in general, a single scientific method. The method is based on three assumptions: (a) that reality is "out there" to be discovered; (b) that direct observation is the way to discover it;

and (c) that material explanations for observable phenomena are always sufficient, and that metaphysical explanations are never needed.

3. Reliable. Something that is true in Detroit is just as true in Vladivostok and Nairobi. Knowledge can be kept secret by nations, but there can never be such a thing as "Venezuelan physics," "American chemistry," or "Kenyan geology."

Not that it hasn't been tried. From around 1935 to 1965, T. D. Lysenko, with the early help of Josef Stalin, succeeded in gaining absolute power over biology in what was then the Soviet Union. Lysenko developed a Lamarckian theory of genetics, in which human-induced changes in seeds would, he claimed, become inherited. Despite public rebuke from the entire non-Soviet scientific world, Lysenko's "Russian genetics" became official Soviet policy—a policy that nearly ruined agriculture in the Soviet Union and its European satellites well into the 1960s (Zirkle, 1949; Joravsky, 1970; also see Storer, 1966, on the norms of science).

The Development of Science

Early Ideas

The scientific method is barely 400 years old and its systematic application to human thought and behavior just 150. Aristotle insisted that knowledge should be based on experience and that conclusions about general cases should be based on the observation of more limited ones. But Aristotle did not advocate disinterested, objective accumulation of reliable knowledge. Moreover, like Aristotle, all scholars until the seventeenth century relied on metaphysical concepts, like the soul, to explain observable phenomena. Even in the nineteenth century, biologists still talked about "vital forces" as a way of explaining the existence of life.

One ancient scholar stands out as a forerunner of modern scientific thinking—the kind of down-to-earth explanations for things that would eventually divorce science from studies of mystical phenomena. Titus Lucretius Carus (first century BC) is a scholar whose work has been little appreciated in the social sciences (but see Harris, 1968, for an exception). In his single surviving work, a poem entitled *Nature of Things*, Lucretius suggested that everything that existed in the world had to be made of some material substance. Consequently, if the soul and the gods were real, they had to be material, too (see Minadeo, 1969).

But Lucretius' work did not have much impact on the way knowledge was pursued.

Exploration, Printing, and Modern Science

Skip to around 1400, when a series of revolutionary changes began in Europe—some of which are still going on—that transformed Western society and other societies around the world. In 1413, the first Spanish ships began raiding the coast of West Africa, hijacking cargo, and capturing slaves from Islamic traders. New tools of navigation (the compass and the sextant) made it possible for adventurous plunderers to go farther and farther from European shores in search of booty.

These breakthroughs were like those in architecture and astronomy by the ancient Mayans and Egyptians. They were based on systematic observation of the natural world, but they were not generated by the social and philosophical enterprise we call science. That required several other revolutions.

Johannes Gutenberg completed the first edition of the Bible on his newly invented printing press in 1455. (Printing presses had been used earlier in China, Japan, and Korea but lacked movable type.) By the end of the fifteenth century, every major city in Europe had a press. Printed books provided a means for the accumulation and distribution of knowledge. Eventually, printing would make organized science possible, but it did not by itself guarantee the objective pursuit of reliable knowledge any more than the invention of writing had done four millennia before (Eisenstein, 1979; N. Davis, 1981).

Martin Luther was born just 15 years after Gutenberg died, and the Protestant Reformation, beginning in 1517, added much to the history of modern science. It challenged the authority of the Roman Catholic church to be the sole interpreter and disseminator of theological doctrine. The Protestant affirmation of every person's right to interpret scripture required literacy on the part of everyone, not just the clergy. The printing press lowered the price of books and made it possible for every family of some means to own (and read) its own Bible. In turn, widespread literacy furthered the development of science as an organized activity.

Galileo

The direct philosophical antecedents of modern science came at the end of the sixteenth century. If I had to pick a single figure on whom to bestow the honor of founding modern science, it would be Galileo Galilei. His best-known achievement, of course, was his thorough refutation of the Ptolemaic geocentric (Earth-centered) theory of the heavens. But he did more than just insist that scholars *observe* things rather than rely on metaphysical dogma to explain them. He developed the idea of the experiment by causing things to happen (rolling balls down differently inclined planes, for example, to see how fast they go) and measuring the results.

Galileo was born in 1564 and became professor of mathematics at the University of Padua when he was 28. He developed a new method for making lenses and used the new technology to study the motions of the planets. He concluded that the sun (as Copernicus claimed), not the Earth (as the ancient scholar Ptolemy had claimed), was at the center of the solar system.

This was one more threat to their authority that Roman church leaders didn't need at the time. They already had their hands full, what with breakaway factions in the Reformation and other political problems. The church reaffirmed its official support for the Ptolemaic theory, and in 1616 Galileo was ordered not to espouse either his refutation of it or his support for the Copernican heliocentric (sun-centered) theory of the heavens.

Galileo waited 16 years and published the book that established science as an effective method for seeking knowledge. The book's title was *Dialogue Concerning the Two Chief World Systems, Ptolemaic and Copernican*, and it still makes fascinating reading (Galilei, 1967). Between the direct observational evidence that he had gathered with his telescopes and the mathematical analyses that he developed for making sense of his data, Galileo hardly had to espouse anything. The Ptolemaic theory was simply rendered obsolete.

The Inquisition convicted Galileo in 1633 for heresy and disobedience. It ordered him to recant his sinful teachings and confined him to house arrest until his death in 1642. Galileo nearly published *and* perished. (See Drake, 1978, and Fermi & Bernardin, 1961, for reviews of Galileo's life and work.)

Descartes and Bacon

Two other figures are often cited as founders of modern scientific thinking: René Descartes (1596-1650) and Francis Bacon (1561-1626). Bacon is known for his emphasis on *induction*, the use of direct observation to confirm ideas, and the linking together of observed facts to form theories or explanations of how natural phenomena work. Bacon correctly never told us how to get ideas or how to accomplish the linkage of empirical facts. Those activities remain essentially humanistic—you think hard. (See Paterson, 1973, Vickers, 1978, and Weinberger, 1985, for reviews of Bacon's contribution to modern scientific thought.)

To Bacon goes the honor of being the first "martyr of empiricism." In March 1626, at the age of 65, Bacon was driving through the rural area north of London. He had an idea that cold might delay the biological process of putrefaction, so he stopped his carriage, bought a hen from a local resident, killed the hen, and stuffed it with snow. He caught bronchitis and died a month later (Lea, 1980).

Descartes didn't make any systematic, direct observations—he did neither fieldwork nor experiments—but in his *Discourse on Method* (1960), he distinguished between the mind and all external material phenomena. He also outlined clearly his vision of a universal science of nature based on direct experience and the application of reason—that is, observation and theory (Schuster, 1977; Markie, 1986).

Newton

Isaac Newton (1643-1727) pressed the scientific revolution at Cambridge University. He invented calculus and used it to develop celestial mechanics and other areas of physics. Just as important, he devised the hypothetico-deductive model of science that combines both induction (empirical observation) and deduction (reason) into a single, unified method (Toulmin, 1980).

In this model, which more accurately reflects how scientists actually conduct their work, it makes no difference where you get an idea: from data, from a conversation with your brother-in-law, or from just plain, hard, reflexive thinking. What matters is whether or not you can *test* your idea against data in the real world. This model seems rudimentary to us now, but it is of fundamental importance and was quite revolutionary in the late seventeenth century. (See Christiansen, 1984, and Westfall, 1980, for reviews of Newton's life and his contribution to the establishment of modern scientific thought and practice.)

Science, Money, and War

The scientific approach to knowledge was established just as Europe began to experience the growth of industry and the development of large cities. Those cities were filled with uneducated factory laborers. Fewer and fewer farmers had to produce more and more food for the growing urban population.

As a new method for acquiring knowledge about natural phenomena, science promised bigger crops, more productive industry, and more successful military campaigns. Optimism ran high. The organizing mandate for the French Academy of Science (1666) included a modest proposal to study "the explosive force of gunpowder enclosed (in small amounts) in an iron or very thick copper box" (Easlea, 1980:216).

As the potential benefits of science became evident, political support increased across Europe. More scientists were produced; more university posts were created for them to work in; more laboratories were established at academic centers. Journals and learned societies developed as scientists sought more outlets for publishing their work.

Sharing knowledge through journals made it easier for scientists to do their own work and to advance through university ranks. Publication and knowledge sharing became a material benefit, and the behaviors were soon supported by a value, a norm.

The norm was so strong that European nations at war allowed enemy scientists to cross their borders freely in pursuit of knowledge. In 1780, Reverend Samuel Williams of Harvard University applied for and received a grant from the Massachusetts legislature to observe a total eclipse of the sun predicted for October 27. The perfect spot, he said, was an island off the coast of Massachusetts.

Unfortunately, Williams and his party would have to cross Penobscot Bay. The American Revolutionary War was still on, and the bay was controlled by the British. The speaker of the Massachusetts House of Representatives, John Hancock, wrote a letter to the commander of the British forces, saying "though we are politically enemies, yet with regard to Science it is presumable we shall not dissent from the practice of civilized people in promoting it" (Rothschild, 1981, quoted in Bermant, 1982:126). The appeal of one "civilized" person to another worked. Williams got his free passage.

The Idea of a Social Science

Newton and Locke

It is fashionable these days to say that social science should not imitate physics. As it turns out, physics and social science were developed at about the same time, and on the same philosophical basis, by two friends, Isaac Newton and John Locke (1632-1704). It would not be until the nineteenth century that a formal program of applying the scientific method to the study of humanity would be proposed by Auguste Comte, Claude-Henri de Saint-Simon, Adolphe Quételet, and John Stuart Mill. But Locke understood that the rules of science applied equally to the study of celestial bodies (what Newton was interested in) and to human behavior (what Locke was interested in).

Locke reasoned that since we can not see everything, and since we can not even record perfectly what we do see, some knowledge will be closer to the truth than other knowledge. Prediction of the behavior of planets might be more accurate than prediction of human behavior, but both predictions should be based on better and better observation, measurement, and reason (see Nisbet, 1980).

Voltaire, Condorcet, and Rousseau

The legacy of Descartes, Galileo, and Locke was crucial to the eighteenth-century Enlightenment and to the development of social science. Voltaire (François Marie Arouet, 1694-1778) was an outspoken proponent of Newton's nonreligious approach to the study of all natural phenomena, including human behavior. In his *Essay on the Customs and Spirit of Nations*, Voltaire introduced the idea of a science to uncover the laws of history. This was to be a science that could be applied to human affairs and that *enlightened* those who governed so that they might govern better.

Other Enlightenment figures had quite specific ideas about the progress of humanity. Marie Jean de Condorcet (1743-1794) described all of human history in 10 stages, beginning with hunting and gathering, and moving up through pastoralism, agriculture, and several stages of Western states. The 9th stage, he reckoned, began with Descartes and ended with the French Revolution and the founding of the republic. The last stage was the future, reckoned as beginning with the French Revolution.

Jean-Jacques Rousseau (1712-1778), by contrast, believed that humanity had started out in a state of grace, characterized by equality of relations, but that the rise of the state had corrupted all that and had resulted in slavery, taxation, and other evils. Rousseau was not, however, a raving romantic, as is sometimes supposed. He did not advocate that modern people abandon civilization and return to hunt their food in the forests. Instead, in his classic work *The Social Contract*, Rousseau laid out a plan for a state-level society based on equality and agreement between the governed and those who govern.

The Enlightenment philosophers, from Bacon to Rousseau, produced a philosophy that focused on the use of knowledge in service to the improvement of humanity, or, if that weren't possible, at least to the amelioration of its pain. The idea that science and reason could lead humanity toward perfection may seem a rather naive notion these days, but it was built into the writings of Thomas Paine and Rousseau and incorporated into the rhetoric surrounding rather sophisticated events like the American and French revolutions.

Quételet, Saint-Simon, Comte, and Early Positivism

The person most responsible for laying out a program of mechanistic social science was Auguste Comte (1798-1857). In 1824, he wrote: "I believe that I shall succeed in having it recognized . . . that there are laws as well defined for the development of the human species as for the fall of a stone" (quoted in Sarton, 1935:10).

Comte could not be bothered with the empirical research required to uncover the Newtonian laws of social evolution that he believed existed. Comte was content to deduce the social laws and to leave "the verification and development of them to the public" (1875-1877, III:xi; quoted in Harris, 1968).

Not so Adolphe Quételet (1796-1874), a Belgian astronomer who turned his skills to both fundamental and applied social research. He developed life expectancy tables for insurance companies and, in his book *A Treatise on Man* (1842), he presented statistics on crime and mortality in Europe. The first edition of that book (1835) carried the audacious subtitle "Social Physics," and, indeed, Quételet extracted some very strong generalizations from his data. He showed that, for the Paris of his day, it was easier to predict the proportion of men of a given age who would be in prison than the proportion of those same men who would die in a given year. "Each age [cohort]," said Quételet, "paid a more uniform and constant tribute to the jail than to the tomb" (1969:viii).

Despite Quételet's superior empirical efforts, he did not succeed in building a following around his ideas for social science. But Claude-Henri de Saint-Simon (1760-1825) did, and he was apparently quite a figure. He fought in the American Revolution, became a wealthy man in land speculation in France, was imprisoned by Robespierre, studied science after his release, and went bankrupt living flamboyantly.

Saint-Simon had the audacity to propose that scientists become priests of a new religion that would further the emerging industrial society and would distribute wealth equitably. The idea was taken up by industrialists after Saint-Simon's death in 1825, but the movement broke up in the early 1830s, partly because its treasury was impoverished by paying for some monumental parties (see Durkheim, 1958).

Saint-Simon was the originator of the so-called positivist school of social science, but Auguste Comte developed the idea in a series of major books. Comte tried to forge a synthesis of the great ideas of the Enlightenment—the ideas of Kant, Hume, and Voltaire—and he hoped that the new science he envisioned would help to alleviate human suffering. Between 1830 and 1842, Comte published a six-volume work, *The System of*

Positive Philosophy, in which he proposed his famous "law of three stages" through which knowledge developed.

In the first stage of human knowledge, said Comte, phenomena are explained by invoking the existence of capricious gods whose whims can't be predicted by human beings. Comte and his contemporaries proposed that religion itself evolved, beginning with the worship of inanimate objects (fetishism) and moving up through polytheism to monotheism. But any reliance on supernatural forces as explanations for phenomena, said Comte, even a modern belief in a single deity, represented a primitive and ineffectual stage of human knowledge.

Next came the metaphysical stage, in which explanations for observed phenomena are given in terms of "essences" like the "vital forces" commonly invoked by biologists of the time. The so-called positive stage of human knowledge is reached when people come to rely on empirical data, reason, and the development of scientific laws to explain phenomena. Comte's program of positivism, and his development of a new science he called "sociology," is contained in his four-volume work *System of Positive Polity*, published between 1875 and 1877 (see Comte, 1974, for an overview).

I share many of the sentiments expressed by the word "positivism," but I've never liked the word itself. I suppose we're stuck with it. Here is John Stuart Mill in 1866 explaining the sentiments of the word to an English-speaking audience: "Whoever regards all events as parts of a constant order, each one being the invariable consequent of some antecedent condition, or combination of conditions, accepts fully the Positive mode of thought" (p. 15), and "All theories in which the ultimate standard of institutions and rules of actions was the happiness of mankind, and observation and experience the guides . . . are entitled to the name Positive" (p. 69).

Mill thought that the word "positive" was not really suited to English, and would have preferred to use "phenomenal" or "experiential." I wish he'd trusted his gut on that one.

Comte's Excesses

Comte wanted to call the new positivistic science of humanity "social physiology," but Saint-Simon had used that term. Comte also used the term "social physics," but apparently dropped it when he found that Quételet was using it, too. The term "sociology" became somewhat controversial; language puritans tried for a time to expunge it from the literature on the grounds that it was a bastardization—a mixture of both Latin (societas) and Greek (logo) roots. Despite the dispute over the name of the discipline,

Comte's vision of a scientific discipline that both focused on and served society found wide support. (For an overview of Comte's major works, see Comte, 1974.)

Unfortunately, Comte, like Saint-Simon, had more in mind than just the pursuit of knowledge for the betterment of humankind. Comte envisioned a class of philosophers who, with support from the state, would direct all education. They would advise the government, which would be composed of capitalists "whose dignity and authority," explained John Stuart Mill (1866), "are to be in the ratio of the degree of generality of their conceptions and operations—bankers at the summit, merchants next, then manufacturers, and agriculturalists at the bottom" (p. 122).

It got worse. Comte proposed his own religion; condemned the study of planets that were not visible to the naked eye; advocated burning most books except for a hundred or so of the ones that people needed in order to become best educated. "As his thoughts grew more extravagant," Mill tells us, Comte's "self-confidence grew more outrageous. The height it ultimately attained must be seen, in his writings, to be believed" (ibid.:130).

Comte attracted a coterie of admirers who wanted to implement the master's plans. Mercifully, they are gone (we hope), but for many scholars, the word "positivism" still carries the taint of Comte's ego.

Despite Comte's excesses, the idea that the scientific method is the surest way to produce effective knowledge (knowledge for control of events), and the idea that effective knowledge could be brought to bear to bring about social reform, captured the imagination of many scholars. These ideas continue to motivate many social scientists, including me.

Later Positivism

Positivism has taken some interesting turns since Comte. Ernst Mach (1838-1916), an Austrian physicist, took Hume's arch-empiricist stance further than Hume might have done himself: If you could not verify something, insisted Mach, then you should question its existence. If you can't see it, then it isn't there. This extreme stance led Mach to reject the atomic theory of physics because, at the time, atoms could not be seen!

The discussion of Mach's ideas was the basis for the foundation of a seminar group that met in Vienna and Berlin during the 1920s and 1930s. The group, composed of mathematicians, philosophers, and physicists, came to be known as the Vienna Circle of logical positivists. They were also known as logical empiricists, and when social scientists today discuss positivism, it is almost always this particular brand that they have in mind (see Mach, 1976).

The term *logical empiricism* better reflects the philosophy of knowledge of the members of the Vienna Circle than does *logical positivism*. Unfortunately, Feigl and Blumberg used "logical positivism" in the title of their 1931 article in the *Journal of Philosophy* in which they laid out the program of their movement, and the name stuck—again (L. Smith, 1986).

The fundamental principles of the Vienna Circle were that knowledge is based on experience and that metaphysical explanations of phenomena were incompatible with science. Science and philosophy, they said, should attempt to answer only answerable questions. A question like "Is green or red a more beautiful color?" can only be addressed by metaphysics and should be left to artists.

In fact, the logical positivists of the Vienna Circle did not see art—painting, sculpture, poetry, music, literature, and literary criticism—as being in conflict with science. The arts, they said, allow people to express personal visions and emotions and are legitimate unto themselves. Since poets do not claim that their ideas are testable expressions of reality, their ideas can be judged on their own merits as either evocative and insightful, or not. Therefore, any source of wisdom (like poetry) that generates ideas, and science, which tests ideas, are mutually supportive and compatible (Feigl, 1980).

I find this to be eminently sensible. The way I see it, the search for understanding is a human activity, no matter who does it and no matter what epistemological assumptions they follow. Understanding begins with questions and with ideas about how things work. What makes people practice infanticide? Why do women earn less than men for the same work? What causes such a high rate of alcoholism among Native Americans? Why do just 3.5% of the world's cultures practice dowry while 30% practice bride price? Why do nation states almost universally try to wipe out minority languages?

Humanism, Hermeneutics, and Phenomenology

No epistemological tradition has a patent on interesting questions like these or on good ideas about the answers to such questions.

Humanism is an intellectual tradition that traces its roots to Protagoras' (485-410 BC) dictum that "Man is the measure of all things." Humanism has been historically at odds with the philosophy of knowledge represented by science.

Ferdinand C. S. Schiller (1864-1937), for example, was a leader of the European humanist revolt against positivism. He argued that since the method and contents of science are the products of human thought, reality and truth could not be "out there" to be found, as positivists assume, but must be made up by human beings (Schiller, 1969). (See W. Jones, 1965, and Snow, 1964, for discussions of the relation between the sciences and the humanities today.)

Humanists do not deny the effectiveness of science for the study of nonhuman objects, but emphasize the uniqueness of humanity and the need for a different (that is, nonscientific) method for studying human beings. Similarly, scientists do not deny the inherent value of humanistic knowledge. To explore whether King Lear is a pathetic character (to be pitied) or a successful leader (to be admired) is an exercise in seeking humanistic knowledge. The answer to the question can not possibly be achieved by the scientific method. In any event, the answer to the question is not important. Carefully examining the question of Lear, however, leads to insight about the human condition—and that *is* important.

Hermeneutics refers to the close study of the Bible. In traditional hermeneutics, it is assumed that the Bible contains truths and that human beings can extract those truths through careful study and exegesis. In recent years, the hermeneutic tradition has come into anthropology with the close and careful study of free-flowing native texts, such as myths or other stories. The hermeneutic approach stresses that myths contain some underlying meaning, at least for the people who tell the myths, and it is our job to discover that meaning.

By extension, the term hermeneutics is now used to cover the study of free-flowing acts of people, construing those acts as if they were texts whose internal meaning can be discovered by proper exegesis. Portable camcorders should promote much more hermeneutic scholarship in the future, as anthropologists record people dancing, singing, telling stories, and participating in events. (See Agar, 1982, and Biesele & Tyler, 1986, for discussions of hermeneutics in modern cultural anthropology.)

Like positivism, *phenomenology* is a philosophy of knowledge that emphasizes direct observation of phenomena. Unlike positivists, however, phenomenologists seek to *sense* reality and to describe it in words, rather than numbers—words that reflect consciousness and perception. Phenomenology is part of the humanistic tradition that emphasizes the common experience of all human beings and our ability to relate to the feelings of others (see Veatch, 1969).

The philosophical foundations of phenomenology were developed by Edmund Husserl (1859-1938), who argued that the scientific method, appropriate for the study of physical phenomena, was inappropriate for the study of human thought and action (see Husserl, 1970). Husserl's ideas were elaborated by

Alfred Schutz, and Schutz's version of phenomenology had a major impact in social science, particularly in psychology, but also in anthropology.

When you study molecules, Schutz said, you don't have to worry about what the world "means" to the molecules (1962:59). But when you try to understand the reality of a human being, it's a different matter entirely. The only way to understand social reality, Schutz maintained, was through the meanings that people give to that reality. In a phenomenological study, the researcher tries to see reality through an informant's eyes.

Phenomenologists try to produce convincing descriptions of what they experience rather than provide explanations and causes. Good ethnography—a narrative that describes a culture or a part of a culture—is usually good phenomenology, and there is still no substitute for a good story, well told—especially if you're trying to make people understand how the people you've studied think and feel about their lives.

About Numbers

The split between the positivistic approach and the interpretive-phenomenological approach pervades the human sciences. In psychology, most research is in the positivistic tradition, while interpretivism flourishes in clinical work because, as its practitioners cogently point out, it works. In sociology, there is a growing minority tradition of interpretive research, but the field is mostly dominated by the positivistic approach.

In cultural anthropology, the debate between positivists and interpretivists is often tied to the issue of qualitative versus quantitative data. Most anthropological research, in fact, is based on qualitative data, but much of that research is also squarely in the positivist tradition. It is important to keep the concepts of quantification and science separate.

Quantification in Anthropology

The most articulate spokesman against the idea that cultural anthropology could ever be a quantified science was Paul Radin. In a brilliantly written book, *The Method and Theory of Ethnology* (1966, orig. 1933), with which I have always thoroughly disagreed, Radin attacked both his professor (Franz Boas) and his contemporaries (Clark Wissler, Alfred Kroeber, Edward Sapir, Robert Lowie, and Margaret Mead) for abandoning the humanistic, historical study of culture and for trying to make ethnology a comparative, ultimately quantitative, science.

Radin was right: That's exactly what they had in mind. Lowie, for example, recognized that meteorology and genetics were probabilistic sciences—that is, we say there is a 40% chance of rain tomorrow, or that someone's children have a 25% chance of having blue eyes—and ho envisioned cultural anthropology becoming one, too (1914:95). Sapir (1968:4, orig. 1916) talked of adding a "quantitative correction" to the qualitative, historical studies that anthropologists were doing on aboriginal peoples at that time.

For Radin, the scientific approach was a tragedy because quantitative studies focused attention on aggregates rather than on individuals. It's really too bad that the genuine intellectual debate between humanism and positivism has gotten tangled up in the issue of quantification. Quantification is important in anthropology, as it is in any science (see A. Johnson, 1978, for a discussion), but all quantification is not science, and all science is not quantified.

Searching the Bible for statistical evidence to support the subjugation of women doesn't turn the enterprise into science. By the same token, at the early stages of development, any science relies primarily on qualitative data. Long before the application of mathematics to describe the dynamics of avian flight, qualitative, fieldworking ornithologists did systematic observation and recorded (in words) data about such things as wing movements, perching stance, hovering patterns, and so on. Qualitative description is a kind of measurement, an integral part of the complex whole that comprises scientific research.

As sciences mature, they come naturally to depend more and more on quantitative data and on quantitative tests of qualitatively described relations. For example, qualitative research might lead us to say that "most of the land in Xakaloranga is controlled by a few people." Later, quantitative research might result in our saying "76% of the land in Xakaloranga is controlled by 14% of the inhabitants." The first statement is not wrong. But the second statement confirms the first and carries more information as well. If it turned out that "46% of the land is controlled by 31% of the inhabitants," then the first, qualitative statement would be rendered weak by the quantitative observations.

For those anthropologists whose work is in the humanistic, phenomenological tradition, quantification is inappropriate. And for those whose work is in the positivist tradition, it is important to remember that numbers do not automatically make any inquiry scientific.

Above all, remember: The term "ethnography" does not mean "qualitative." As a noun, it means a description of a culture, or a piece of a culture. As a verb (doing ethnography), it means the collection of data that describe a culture. In the rest of this book, you'll read about methods that will let you build an ethnographic record. Some of those methods involve field-work, some involve library work. Some methods for building an ethnographic record involve watching, others involve listening. Some result in words, others result in numbers.

Ethics and Social Science

The biggest problem in conducting a science of human behavior is not methodological but ethical. For while scholars argue about whether a true science of human behavior is possible, it is being done all the time, and with rather spectacular, if sometimes disturbing, success.

In the mid-nineteenth century, when Quételet and Comte were laying down the program for a science of human affairs, no one could predict the outcome of elections, or engineer the increased consumption of a particular brand of cigarettes, or help people through crippling phobias with behavior modification. We can do those things now. We can predict accurately the reduction in highway carnage of increasing the drinking age by 1, 2, or 3 years. We can predict the number of additional suicides that result from each percentage point of unemployment.

For all the jokes cracked about the mistakes made by economists, or about the wisdom of engineering cigarette purchases in the first place, the fact remains: We can do these things. And we're getting more and more accurate all the time. Since the eighteenth century, every phenomenon (including human thought and behavior) to which the scientific method has been systematically applied, over a sustained period of time, by a large number of researchers, has yielded its secrets, and the knowledge has been turned into more effective human control of events.

It hardly needs to be pointed out that the increasing effectiveness of science over the past few centuries has also given human beings the ability to cause greater environmental degradation, to spread tyranny, and even to cause the ultimate planetary catastrophe. This makes a science of humanity even more important now than it has ever been before.

Consider this: Marketers in a midwestern city, using the latest super-computers, found that if someone bought disposable diapers at 5 p.m. the next thing he or she was likely to buy was a six-pack of beer. So the marketers set up a display of chips next to the disposable diapers and increased snack sales by 17% (Wilke, 1992). We need to turn our skills in the production of such effective knowledge to other important problems: hunger, disease, poverty, war, environmental pollution, family and intergroup violence, and racism, among others. Social science can play an important role in social change by predicting the consequences of ethically mandated programs and by refuting false notions (such as various forms of racism) that are inherent in most popular ethical systems. In the rest of this book, I deal with some of the methods we can use to make those contributions.

2

The Foundations
of Social Research

This chapter is about the fundamental concepts of research: *variables, measurement, validity, reliability, cause and effect*, and *theory*. When you finish this chapter you should understand the mutually supportive roles of data and ideas in the development of theory, along with the crucial role of measurement in science.

You should also have two new skills:

1. You should be able to reduce any complex human phenomenon, like "being modern" or "anomie" or "alienation" or "readiness to learn research methods," to a set of measurable traits.
2. You should become hypercritical of your new ability. Just because you *can* make up measurements doesn't guarantee that they're useful or meaningful. However, the better you become at concocting clever measurements for complex things, the more critical you'll become of your own concoctions and those of others.

Variables

A *variable* is something that can take more than one value, and *values can be words or numbers*. If you ask someone how old they are, the response might be 18 or 78. If you ask them their religion, the response might be "Methodist" or "Buddhist." The most common variables in social research are age, sex, ethnic affiliation, education, income, marital status, and occupation. Others that you might see, particularly in anthropological research, include blood pressure, number of children, number of times married, distance from an airport (or a well or a road or a market), or level of support for rebels fighting in Eritrea.

All social research is based on defining variables, looking for associations among them, and trying to understand whether one variable causes another. Social science research, then, is about variables, not about people. Research can affect people, though, so all research has an ethical component. I'll have more to say about this throughout the book.

Dimensions

Variables can be *unidimensional* or *multidimensional*. The distance from Boston to Denver can be expressed in driving time or in miles, but no matter which measure you use, you can express distance in just one dimension, with a straight line. You can see this in Figure 2.1.

If we add Miami, we have three distances: Boston-Miami, Boston-Denver, Denver-Miami. To express the relationship among three cities, we have to use two dimensions. Look at Figure 2.2.

The two dimensions in Figure 2.2 are up-down and right-left, or north-south and east-west. If we add Nairobi to the exercise, we'd either have to add a third dimension (straight through the paper at a slight downward angle from Denver) or do what Gerardus Mercator (1512-1594) did to force a three-dimensional object (the Earth) into a two-dimensional picture.

Unidimensional variables, like height, weight, birth order, age, and marital status are relatively easy to measure. Stress, wealth, and political orientation, by contrast, are all multidimensional and are more difficult to measure. To measure the wealth of various Americans, for example, you may have to account for salaries, social security, private pension funds, gifts, gambling winnings, tax credits, interest on savings, tips, food stamps, contributions from extended kin, and so on.

In Chapter 13, on constructing scales, we'll look at how to test for unidimensionality of variables.

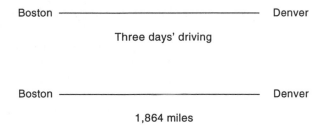

Figure 2.1. Two ways to measure distance.

Race and Gender

Race and gender are examples of variables that are complex but appear simple. Their complexity is hard to measure so we measure them simply, as *dichotomous variables*, with two values each: black/white, female/male.

We have learned a lot about the effects of racial discrimination by reducing the variable "race" to just two values. Anyone in the United States who is labeled "black" is more likely to be the victim of a violent crime than anyone labeled "white," more likely to die in infancy, and more likely to be poor.

Still, there are many gradations of skin color besides black and white, so it's reasonable to ask whether people who are *more* black are *more* likely to be a victim of a violent crime, to die in infancy, to be poor, and so forth. Around 1970, medical researchers began to find a relationship in the United States between darkness of skin color and blood pressure among

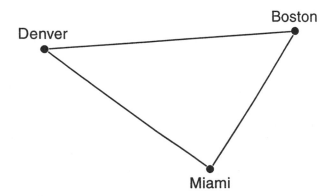

Figure 2.2. Three points create two dimensions.

people labeled "blacks" (see E. Boyle, 1970; Harburg et al., 1978). The darker the skin, the higher blood pressure was likely to be.

Later, researchers began to find that education and social class were more important predictors of high blood pressure among blacks than was darkness of skin color (see Keil et al., 1977, 1981). This probably meant that darker-skinned people were more likely to be the victims of discrimination: uneducated and poor. Poverty causes stress and poor diet, both of which are direct causes of high blood pressure.

This leads us to think about what we might learn if skin color were treated as a continuous variable rather than as a dichotomous one. Suppose that instead of coding people as "black" or "white" we measured skin color with a photospectrometer or some other device, like a set of color chips. We'd learn whether white schoolteachers react more negatively to darker-skinned black children than to lighter-skinned black children. We'd learn whether lighter-skinned blacks live longer than do darker-skinned blacks.

Findings like these would illuminate the dynamics of racism: how it plays out, not just its consequences. We might be able to account for some of the variation in black children's school scores as a function of teacher reaction to skin color. We might learn that skin color leads to discrimination and poverty and, finally, to lowered life expectancy.

If the benefits of such research are attractive, though, consider the risks. Racists might claim that our findings support their hateful ideas about the genetic inferiority of African-Americans. Life insurance companies might start charging people premiums based on amount of skin pigmentation. Even if the Supreme Court ruled against this practice, how many people would be hurt before the matter were adjudicated?

Gender is another dichotomous variable (male and female) that is more complex than it seems. We usually measure gender according to the presence of male or female sexual characteristics. Then we look at the relationship between the presence of those characteristics and things like income, education, amount of labor migration, or child-rearing activities, math aptitude, market success, likelihood of divorce, or IQ.

If you think about it, we're not interested in biological gender in most social research. What we really want to know is how being *more* male or *more* female (socially and psychologically) predicts things like income, labor migration, and so on. Sandra Bem (1974) once developed an "androgyny scale" that does this. Twenty years later, we're beginning to learn about sex roles from research that assumes that differences between men and women are more complex than a biological dichotomy would make them appear.

Dependent and Independent Variables

When you buy life insurance, the company predicts how long you will live, given your sex, age, education, weight, blood pressure, and a few other variables. They bet you that you will not die this year. You take the bet. If you lose (and remain alive), the company takes your annual premium and banks it. If you win the bet (and die), the company pays your beneficiary.

For insurance companies to turn a profit, they have to win more bets than they lose. They can make mistakes at the individual level, but in the *aggregate* (that is, averaging over all people) they have to predict longevity from things they can measure.

Longevity, then, is called the *dependent variable*, because it *depends on* height, sex, education, occupation, and so on. These are called the *independent variables*. In our earlier example, blood pressure was the dependent variable. There is no way skin color depends on a person's blood pressure.

It's not always easy to tell whether a variable is independent or dependent. Is high female infant mortality among Amazonian tribal people dependent on high levels of warfare, or vice versa? Is high income dependent on large landholding, or vice versa?

A lot of mischief is caused by failure to understand which of two variables depends on the other. Oscar Lewis (1961, 1965) described what he called a "culture of poverty" among slum dwellers in cities around the world. One of the things that characterizes this culture, said Lewis, is a low level of orientation toward the future, as indicated by poor people shopping every day for food and never buying large economy sizes of anything. Lewis's point was that truly poor people can't invest in soap futures by buying large boxes of it. He saw a low level of expressed orientation toward the future, then, as *dependent on* poverty.

Many people concluded from Lewis's work that poverty was dependent on a low level of future orientation. According to this topsy-turvy, victim-blaming reasoning, if poor people would just learn to save their money and invest in the future, then they could break the poverty cycle. Such reasoning may serve to create pointless programs to teach poor people how to save money they don't have, but it doesn't do much else.

The *educational model* of social change is another lesson in confusion about dependent and independent variables. The model is based on the idea that thought causes behavior. If you want to change people's behavior, the reasoning goes, then you have to change how they think: Teach men to use condoms, teach women to use birth control devices, teach everyone to wash their hands after defecating.

The educational model of social change creates a lot of employment for researchers and development project workers, but it doesn't produce much in the way of desired change. This is because behavioral change (the supposed dependent variable) often doesn't depend on education (the supposed independent variable). In fact, it's sometimes the other way around. When women have access to well-paying jobs outside the home, they tend to lower their fertility. Once that happens, an antinatality culture develops.

Measurement and Concepts

Variables are measured by their *indicators*, and indicators are defined by their *values*. Some variables, and their indicators, are easily observed and measured. Others are more conceptual. The difference is important.

Consider the variables race and gender again. If skin color can take one of two values (black or white), then to *measure* race you simply look at a person and decide which value to record. If you use secondary sexual characteristics as an indicator of gender, then to *measure* gender you look at a person and decide whether they are female or male.

In other words, *measurement is deciding which value to record*. That decision is prone to error. Many people have ambiguous secondary sexual characteristics and many women wear clothes traditionally worn by men. Is Pat a man or a woman's name? What about Chris? Leslie? Any of these indicators may mislead you into making the wrong measurement—marking down a male as female, or vice versa. *Improving measurement in science means lowering the probability of and the amount of error*. Light-skinned African-Americans who cease to identify themselves ethnically as black persons count on those errors for what they hope will be upward economic mobility. Dark-skinned "whites," like some Americans of Mediterranean descent, sometimes complain that they are being "mistaken for" blacks and discriminated against.

Race and gender are *concepts*, or mental creations. In fact, all variables are concepts, but some concepts, like height and weight, are easier to measure than others. Concepts like religious intensity, dedication to public service, willingness to accept new agricultural technologies, tolerance for foreign fieldwork, desire for an academic job, compassion, and jealousy are more difficult to measure. Our belief in the existence of such variables is based on our experience: Some people just seem more religiously intense than others, or more tolerant of foreign fieldwork than others, etc.

We verify our intuition that conceptual variables exist by measuring them, or by measuring their results. Suppose you put an ad in the paper that says: "Roommate wanted. Easy-going, nonsmoker preferred." When people answer the ad you can look at their fingers and smell their clothes to see if they smoke. But you have to ask people a series of indicator *questions* to gauge their easy-goingness.

Similarly, if you are doing fieldwork in a Peruvian highland village, and you want to predict who among the villagers is predisposed to migrate to the coast in search of work, you will want to measure that predisposition with a series of indicators. In this case, the indicators can be answers to questions ("Have you ever thought about migrating?"). Or they might be observable facts (Does a person have a close relative who has already migrated?). Or they might be a combination of these.

It is easier to measure some concepts than others, but all measurement is difficult. People have worked for centuries to develop good instruments for measuring things like temperature. And if it's difficult to measure temperature, how do you measure worker alienation or machismo? Measuring variables like these—ones that lack concrete indicators—is our greatest challenge in social science because they comprise most of the variables we're interested in.

One of the most famous variables in social science is "socioeconomic status" (SES). Measuring it is no easy task. You can use income as one indicator, but there are many wealthy people who have low status, and many relatively low-income people who have high status. You can add "level of education" to income as an indicator, but that still won't be enough in most societies of the world to get at something as multidimensional as SES. You can add occupation, father's occupation, number of generations in a community, and so on, depending on the culture you are studying, and you're still likely to be dissatisfied with the result.

Indicators of any concept may vary from culture to culture. The androgyny scale developed by Bem seems to be useful in our own culture. It helps predict things about people that are not measured by the scale itself. But the Bem scale is based on assumptions about maleness and femaleness that are appropriate to our culture and may be inappropriate to people in other cultures.

Conceptual and Operational Definitions

While most of the interesting variables in social science are concepts, some of our most important concepts are not variables. The concept of culture, for example, is not a variable. The *particular* culture of particular groups does vary, of course. The concept of *"a* culture," then, *is* a variable. The concept of "positivism" is *not* a variable; the concept of "philosophies of science" *is* a variable.

Conceptual Variables

There are two ways to define variables—conceptually and operationally. *Conceptual definitions* are abstractions, articulated in words, that facilitate understanding. They are the sort of definitions we see in dictionaries, and we use them in everyday conversation to tell people what we mean by some term or phrase. *Operational definitions* consist of a set of instructions on how to measure a variable that has been conceptually defined.

Suppose I tell you that "Alice and Fred just moved in to a spacious house." Nice concept. You ask: "What do you mean by 'spacious?' " and I say "You know, it has lots and lots of space; the rooms are big and the ceilings are high."

If that isn't enough for you, we'll have to move from a conceptual definition of "spacious" to an operational one. We'll have to agree on what to measure: Do we count the screened-in porch and the garage or just the interior living space? Do we count the square footage or the cubic footage? That is, do we get a measure of the living surface, or some measure of the "feeling of spaciousness" that comes from high ceilings? Do we measure the square footage of open space before or after the furniture and appliances go in? If we had to agree on things like this for every concept, ordinary human discourse would come to a grinding halt.

Science is not ordinary human discourse, however, and this, in my view, is the most important difference between the two main styles of cultural anthropology. Humanistic anthropologists seek to maintain the essential feel of human discourse. Scientific anthropologists focus more on specific measurement. I do not see these two styles as inimical to one another, but as complementary.

To get a feel for how complementary the two styles can be, ask some 50-year-old and some 20-year-old women and men to tell you how old you have to be in order to be middle aged. You'll see immediately how volatile the conceptual definition of "middle age" is. If you ask your informants about what it means to "be middle aged," you'll get plenty of material for an interesting paper on the subject. If you want to *measure* the differences between men and women and between older and younger people on this variable, you may have to do more than just ask them. Figure 2.3 shows an instrument for measuring this variable.

Many concepts that we use in anthropology have volatile definitions: "power," "social class," "machismo," "alienation," "willingness to change,"

1 5 10 15 20 25 30 35 40 45 50 55 60 65 70 75 80 85 90 95 100

Here is a line that represents age. Obviously, a person 1 year old is a baby,
and a person 100 years old is old. Put a mark on the line where you think
middle age begins and another mark where you think middle age ends.

Figure 2.3. An instrument for measuring what people think "middle age" means.

and "fear of retribution." If we are to talk sensibly about such things, we
need clear, *intersubjective* definitions of them. In other words, while there
can be no objective definition of "middle age," we can at least agree on what
we mean by "middle age" for a particular study and on how to measure the
concept.

Complex variables are conceptually defined by reducing them to a series
of simpler variables. Saying that "the people in this village are highly
acculturated" can be interpreted in many ways. But if you state clearly that
you include "being bilingual," "working in the national economy," and
"going to school" in your conceptual definition of acculturation, then at
least others will understand what you're talking about when you say that
people are "highly acculturated."

Similarly, "machismo" might be characterized by "a general feeling of
male superiority," accompanied by "insecure behavior in relationships
with women." Intelligence might be conceptually defined as "the ability
to think in abstractions and to generalize from cases." These definitions
have something important in common: They have no external reality
against which to test their truth value.

Conceptual definitions are at their most powerful when they are linked
together to build theories that explain research results. "Dependency
theory," for example, links the concept of "control of capital" with concepts of "mutual security" and "economic dependency." The linkage helps
explain why economic development often results in some groups winding
up with less access to capital than they had prior to a development program.
It is a theory, in other words, to explain why the rich get richer and the
poor get poorer. Conceptual definitions are at their weakest in the conduct
of research itself, because concepts have no empirical basis—they have to
be made up in order to study them.

There is nothing wrong with this. There are three things one wants to do
in any science: (a) describe a phenomenon of interest, (b) explain what
causes it, and (c) predict what it causes. The existence of a conceptual
variable is inferred from what it predicts—how well it makes theoretical
sense out of a lot of data.

The Concept of Intelligence

The classic example of a conceptual variable is intelligence. Intelligence is anything we say it is. There is no way to tell whether it is really: (a) the ability to think in abstractions and to generalize from cases, or (b) the ability to remember long strings of unconnected facts. In the last analysis, the value of the concept of intelligence is that it allows us to predict, with varying success, things like job income, grade-point average, likelihood of having healthy children, and the possibility of being arrested for a felony.

The key to understanding the last statement is the phrase "with varying success." It is by now well known that measures of intelligence are culture bound; the standard U.S. intelligence tests are biased in favor of whites and against African-Americans because of differences in the test takers' access to education and differences in their life experiences. Further afield, intelligence tests for Americans don't have any meaning at all to people in radically different cultures.

There is a famous, perhaps apocryphal, story about some American researchers who determined to develop a culture-free intelligence test based on manipulation and matching of shapes and colors. With an interpreter along for guidance, they administered the test to a group of Bushmen in the Kalahari Desert of South Africa. The first Bushman they tested listened politely to the instructions about matching the colors and shapes and then excused himself.

He returned in a few minutes with half a dozen others, and they began an animated discussion about the test. The researchers asked the interpreter to explain that each man had to take the test himself. The Bushmen responded by saying how silly that was; they solve problems together and they would solve this one, too. So, although the content of the test might have been culture free, the testing procedure itself was not.

This critique of intelligence *testing* in no way lessens the importance or usefulness of the *concept* of intelligence. The concept is useful, in certain contexts, because its measurement allows us to predict other things we want to know. And it is to measurement that we now turn.

Operational Definitions

Conceptual definitions are limited because they do not allow us to measure anything, and without measurement we can not make strict comparisons. We can not tell whether Spaniards are more flamboyant than the

British, or whether Zunis are more or less Apollonian than Navahos. We can not tell whether Catholicism is more authoritarian than Buddhism. We can not evaluate the level of anger in a peasant village over land reform, or compare the level of anger to that found in another village.

Operational definitions specify exactly what you have to do in order to measure something that has been defined conceptually. Here are four examples of operational definitions:

1. Intelligence: Take the Stanford-Binet Intelligence Test and administer it to a person. Count up the score. Whatever score the person gets is his or her intelligence.
2. Machismo: Ask a man if he approves of women working outside the home, assuming the family doesn't need the money; if he says "no," then give him a score of 1, and if he says "yes," then score him 0. Ask him if he thinks women and men should have the same sexual freedom before marriage; score 1 if he says "no" and score 0 for "yes." Ask him if a man should be punished for killing his wife and her lover; if he says "no," score 1; score 0 for "yes." Add the scores. A man who scores 3 has more machismo than a man who scores 2, and a man who scores 2 has more machismo than a man who scores 1.
3. Tribal identity: Ask American Indians if they speak the language of their ancestors fluently. If "yes," score 1. If "no," score 0. Ask them if they attend at least one pow-wow each year. Score 1 for "yes," and 0 for "no." Ask them eight other questions of this type, and give them a score of 1 for each answer that signifies self-identification with their tribal heritage. Anyone who scores at least 6 out of 10 is an "identifier." Five or less is a "rejecter" of tribal heritage or identity.
4. Support for trade barriers against Japan: Ask workers in a factory to complete the Arlenberger Scale for Support of Trade Barriers Against Japan. Add the four parts of the scale together to produce a single score. Record that score.

These definitions sound pretty boring, but think about this: If you and I use the same definitions for variables, *and if we stick to those definitions in making measurements*, then our data are strictly comparable:

> We can tell if people in tribe A have higher cultural identity scores than do people in tribe B.
> We can tell if children in city A have higher intelligence scores than do children in city B.
> We can tell if older men in Huehuetenango have higher machismo scores than do younger men in that village.
> We can tell whether the average scores indicating level of support for trade barriers against Japan is greater among workers in the factory you studied than it is among workers in the factory I studied.

I find the ability to make such comparisons exciting, and not boring at all. But did you notice that I *never* said anything in those comparisons about cultural identity per se, or intelligence per se, or machismo or support for trade barriers per se. In each case, all I said was that we could tell if the *scores* were bigger or smaller.

Operational definitions are *strictly limited to the content of the operations specified.* If the content of an operational definition is bad, then so are all conclusions you draw from using it to measure something.

This is *not* an argument against operationism in science. Just the opposite. Operationism is the best way to expose bad measurement. By defining measurements operationally, we can tell if one measurement is better than another.

Adhering to bad measurements is bad science and can have some bad consequences for people. I was once a consultant on a project that was supposed to help Chicano high schoolers develop good career aspirations. Studies had been conducted in which Chicano and Anglo-American high schoolers were asked what they wanted to be when they reached 30 years of age. (White, non-Hispanic Americans are called *Anglo-Americans* or just *Anglos* in the American Southwest.) Chicanos expressed, on average, a lower occupational aspiration than did Anglos. This led some social scientists to advise policy makers that Chicano youth needed reinforcement of career aspirations at home. (There's that educational model again.)

Contrary to survey findings, ethnographic research showed that Chicano parents had very high aspirations for their children. The parents were being frustrated by two things: (a) despair over the cost of sending their children to college, and (b) high school counselors who systematically encouraged young Chicana women to become housewives and young Chicano men to learn a trade or go into the armed services.

The presumed relationship between the dependent variable (level of career aspiration) and the independent variable (level of aspiration by parents for the careers of their children) was backward. Even worse, the operational definition of the variable "career aspiration" was useless. Asking Chicano youth what they wanted to be when they were 30 years old, and using their answers as the operational definition of "career aspiration," did not reflect reality.

Here's the operational definition that should have been used in the study of Chicano parents' aspirations for their children's careers:

Go to the homes of the respondents. Using the native language of the respondents (Spanish or English, as the case may be), talk to parents about what they want their high-school-age children to be doing in 10 years. Explore each answer in depth and find out why parents give each answer.

Ask specifically if the parents are telling you what they think their children *will* be doing or what they *want* their children to be doing. If parents hesitate, say "Suppose nothing stood in the way of your [son] [daughter] becoming anything they wanted to be, what would you like them to be doing 10 years from now?"

Write down what the parents say and code it for the following possible scores: 1 = unambivalently in favor of children going into high-status occupations; 2 = ambivalent about children going into high-status occupations; 3 = unambivalently in favor of children going into low- or middle-status occupations.

Use Nakao's occupation scale to decide whether the occupations selected by parents as fitting for their children are high, middle, or low status. Be sure to take and keep notes on what parents say are the reasons for their selections of occupations.

Notice that taking an ethnographic approach did not stop us from being operational.

The Problem with Operationism

Strict operationism creates a knotty philosophical problem. Measurement turns abstractions (concepts) into reality. Since there are many ways to measure the same abstraction, the reality of any concept hinges on the device you use to measure it. So, temperature is different if you measure it with a thermocouple or a thermometer; intelligence is different if you measure it with a Stanford-Binet test or an MMPI test. If you ask an informant "How old are you?" or "How many birthdays have you had?" you will probably retrieve the same number. But the very concept of age in the two cases is different because different "instruments" (queries are instruments) were used to measure it.

This principle was articulated in 1927 by Percy Bridgman in *The Logic of Modern Physics*, and has become the source of an enduring controversy. The bottom line on strict operational definitions is this: No matter how much you insist that intelligence is really more than what is measured by an intelligence test, that's all it can ever be. Whatever you think intelligence is, it is exactly and only what you measure with an intelligence test and nothing more.

If you don't like the results of your measurement, then build a better test, where "better" means that the outcomes are more useful in building theory, in making predictions, and in engineering behavior.

I see no reason to waffle about this, or to look for philosophically palatable ways to soften the principle here. The science that emerges from a strict operational approach to understanding variables is much too powerful to water down with backtracking. It is obvious that "future orientation" is more than my asking an informant "Do you buy large or small boxes of soap?" The problem is, *you* might not include that question in your interview of the same informant, unless I specify that I asked that question in that particular way.

Operational definitions permit scientists to talk to one another using the same language. They permit replication of research and the unlimited redefinition of concepts by refining of instruments. As operational definitions get better and better, our ability to test theory gets better, too.

Robert Hunt (1988) wanted to run an empirical test of the old anthropological idea that large canal irrigations systems must have centralized authority for management. He collected data on irrigation systems around the world to test this idea, but he found that all the central concepts in the theory were fuzzy. Concepts like "large," "centralized authority," and even "irrigation system" were poorly conceived and unoperationalized in the literature.

By operationalizing these concepts, Hunt was able to run a test on data about many irrigation systems. It turns out that at about 50 hectares, it's a toss-up whether an irrigation system is unified under a central authority. At 100 hectares there is a good chance that centralization will emerge. At about 3,000 hectares, centralization is assured.

Levels of Measurement

Whenever you define a variable operationally, you do so at some *level of measurement*. There are, in ascending order, four levels of measurement: nominal, ordinal, interval, and ratio. The general principle in research is: Always use the highest level of measurement that you can.

Nominal Variables

A *nominal variable* is an exhaustive list of things, each of which is mutually exclusive. Religion is an example of a nominal variable. If you were doing a study in India, you might classify your informants according to whether they were Hindus, Moslems, Buddhists, Jains, or Christians. Each of those categories is mutually exclusive, but they do not exhaust the possibilities. There are many other religions represented in India. If you only want to know whether your informants are *not* in the paramount religions in India, you would include a category called "other." The famous "other" category in nominal-level variables is the way we achieve exhaustiveness in questionnaires. (See Chapter 12 for a discussion of questionnaire design.)

If you are doing a study of a coastal peasant village in Nigeria, you might want to know the occupations of your informants. The list of occupations in the village is a measuring instrument at the nominal level. You hold each informant up against the list and see which occupation(s) he or she has. An informant might have more than one nominal attribute on the variable "occupation." She might be a produce seller in a market and a basket weaver as well.

Nominal measurement is *qualitative*. It involves naming things and putting them into mutually exclusive and exhaustive categories. When you assign the numeral 1 to males and 2 to females, all you are doing is substituting one kind of name for another. Calling males "1" and females "2" does not make the variable quantitative. Though the number 2 is twice as big as the number 1, this fact is meaningless with nominal variables. Assigning numbers to categories of things makes it easier to do certain kinds of statistical analysis on qualitative data (this will be discussed further in Chapter 19), but it doesn't turn qualitative variables into quantitative ones.

Ordinal Variables

Like nominal-level variables, *ordinal variables* are exhaustive and mutually exclusive, but they have one additional property: Their values can be rank ordered. Any variable measured as high, medium, or low, like socioeconomic class, is ordinal. The three classes are, in theory, mutually exclusive and exhaustive. But, in addition, a person who is labeled "middle class" is lower in the hierarchy than one labeled "high class" and higher in the same hierarchy than one labeled "lower class."

Similarly, the variable "level of acculturation" might be divided into three steps: completely traditional, somewhat acculturated, and totally assimilated. Chiefdoms are *more* complex than bands, but less complex than states. Swidden horticulturists are *more* settled than hunter-gatherers and less settled than plow agriculturalists. What ordinal variables do not tell us is *how much* more.

This is the most important characteristic of ordinal measures: There is no way to tell how far apart the attributes are from one another. A person who is middle class might be twice as wealthy and three times as educated as a person who is lower class—or three times as wealthy and four times as educated. The distances between the values of the variable (lower, middle, upper, or bands, chiefdoms, states) have no meaning.

Interval Variables

Interval variables have all the properties of nominal and ordinal variables. They are an exhaustive and mutually exclusive list of attributes, and the attributes have a rank-order structure. They have one additional property as well: The distances between the attributes are meaningful.

The difference between 30° centigrade and 40° is the same 10° as the difference between 70° and 80°, and the difference between an IQ score of 90 and 100 is (assumed to be) the same as the difference between one of 130 and 140. On the other hand, 80° is not twice as hot as 40°, and a person who has an IQ of 150 is not 50% smarter than a person who has an IQ of 100.

Ratio Variables

Ratio variables are interval variables that have a zero point. A person who is 40 years old is 10 years older than a person who is 30, and a person who is 20 is 10 years older than a person who is 10. The 10-year intervals between the attributes (years are the attributes of age) are identical. Furthermore, a person who is 20 is twice as old as a person who is 10, and a person who is 40 is twice as old as a person who is 20. These, then, are true ratios.

There are few interval variables that are not also ratio variables. Temperature and intelligence are nonratio, interval variables. The difference between 50° and 60° Celsius is the same as the difference between 150° and 160°. But 150° is not three times as hot as 50°.

It is common practice in the social sciences to refer to ratio variables as interval variables. Some examples include age, number of years of education, number of times a person has changed residence, income in dollars or other currency, years spent migrating, population size, distance in meters from a house to a well, number of violent crimes per hundred thousand population, number of dentists per million population, number of months since last employment, number of kilograms of fish caught per week, and number of hours per week spent in subsistence activities.

In general, concepts (like acculturation) are measured at the ordinal level. Informants get a high score for being "very acculturated," a low score for being "unacculturated," and a medium score for being "somewhat acculturated." When a concept variable like intelligence or level of modernization is measured at the interval level, it is likely to be the focus of a lot of controversy regarding the validity of the measuring instrument.

Concrete, observable things are often measured at the interval level. But not always. Observing whether a man hunts or not is a nominal, qualitative measurement based on direct observation.

Remember this rule: Always measure things at the highest level of measurement possible. Don't measure things at the ordinal level if you can measure them intervally. If you want to know the price that farmers have paid for their land, then ask the price. Don't ask them whether they paid "between 1 million and 2 million pesos, 2 million and 5 million, 5 and 10 million, above 10 million."

If you want to know how much education people have had, ask them how many years they went to school. Don't ask "Have you completed grade school, high school, some college, four years of college?" These kinds of questions simply throw away information by turning interval-level variables into ordinal ones.

During data analysis you can lump interval-level data together into ordinal or nominal categories. If you know the ages of your informants, you can divide them into "old" and "young"; if you know the number of calories consumed per week for each family in a study, you can divide the data into low, medium, and high. But you can not do this trick the other way around. If you collect data on income by asking people whether they earn "less than a million drachmas per year" or "more than a million drachmas," you can not go back and assign actual numbers of drachmas to each informant.

Notice that "less than a million drachmas" and "more than a million" is an ordinal variable that looks like a nominal variable because there are only two attributes. If the attributes are rankable, then the variable is ordinal. "A lot of fish" is more than "a small amount of fish," and "highly educated" is greater than "poorly educated." Ordinal variables can have any number of ranks. For purposes of statistical analysis, though, ordinal scales with five or more ranks are often treated as if they were interval-level variables.

Units of Analysis

One of the very first things to do in any research project is decide on the *unit of analysis*. In an ethnographic case study, there is exactly one unit of analysis—the community or village or tribe. Research designed to test hypotheses requires many units of analysis, usually a sample from a large population—farmers, Navahos, Chicano migrants, Yanomami warriors, women in trade unions in Rio de Janeiro.

Although most research in anthropology is about populations of people, many other things can be the units of analysis. You can focus on farms instead of farmers; or on trade unions instead of trade unionists; or on wars instead of warriors. You can study marriage contracts, folk tales, songs, myths, and even whole countries or cultures.

Paul Doughty (1979) surveyed demographic data on 134 countries in order to make a list of "primate cities." A country is said to have a primate city if its most populous city is at least three times larger than the next two cities combined. In Doughty's study, the units of analysis were countries rather than cities.

For each country, Doughty did the sums on the population of the three largest cities and coded whether the country had a primate city or not. He discovered that this characteristic of extreme concentration of population is associated with Latin America more than with any other region of the world.

Mathews (1985) did a study of how men and women in a Mexican village tell a famous folktale differently. The tale is called *La Llorona* (The Weeping Woman) and is known all over Mexico. Mathews's research had to do with the problem of intracultural variation—different informants telling the same story in different ways. She studied a sample of the population of *La Llorona* stories in the village where she was working. Each story, as told by a different informant, had characteristics that could be compared across the sample of stories. One of the characteristics was whether the story was told by a man or a woman, and this turned out to be the most important variable associated with the stories, which were the units of analysis.

Berlin and Kay (1991) studied over a hundred languages of the world regarding how people name different colors. The physical spectrum of color in the world is fixed, but different languages mark the boundaries between colors differently. Berlin and his associates showed informants a large set of color chips that nearly replicates the continuous color spectrum and asked everyone to name the colors they recognized.

From these data, the researchers were able to relate color terms to other data on the sociocultural evolutionary level of each society in the sample, and they have come up with a theory of how color terminology has evolved for the world's languages. Although individual informants were asked to take the color chip tests, the units of analysis in this landmark study were languages.

Remember this rule: No matter what you are studying, always collect data on the lowest level unit of analysis possible.

Collect data about individuals, for example, rather than about households. If you are interested in issues of production and consumption (things that make sense at the household level), you can always package your data about individuals into data about households during analysis. But if you want to examine the association between female income and child spacing and you collect income data on households in the first place, then you are locked out. You can always aggregate data collected on individuals, but you can never *disaggregate* data collected on groups.

The Ecological Fallacy

Once you select your unit of analysis, remember it as you go through data analysis, or you're likely to commit the dreaded "ecological fallacy." This fallacy is also known as the Nosnibor effect, after Robinson (1950), who identified and described it. It comes from drawing conclusions about the wrong units of analysis—usually making generalizations about people from data about groups.

Suppose you do a survey of villages in a region of southern India. For each village you have data on such things as the number of people, the average age of men and women, and the monetary value of a list of various consumer goods in each village. That is, when you went through each village, you noted how many refrigerators and kerosene lanterns and radios there were, but you do not have these data for each person or household in the village because you were not interested in that when you designed your study. (You were interested in characteristics of villages as units of analysis.)

In your analysis, you notice that the villages with the population having the lowest average age also have the highest average dollar value of modern consumer goods. You are tempted to conclude that young people are more interested in (and purchase) modern consumer goods more frequently than older people.

But you might be wrong. Villages with greater employment resources (land and industry) will have lower levels of labor migration by young people. Because more young people stay there, this will lower the average age of wealthier villages. Though *everyone* wants household consumer goods, only older people can afford them, having had more time to accumulate the funds.

It might turn out that the wealthy villages with low average age simply have wealthier older people than villages with higher average age. It is not valid to take data gathered about villag*es* and draw conclusions about villag*ers*, and this brings us to the crucial issue of validity.

Validity, Reliability, Precision, and Accuracy

Validity refers to the accuracy and trustworthiness of instruments, data, and findings in research. Nothing in research is more important than validity.

Instrument Validity

1. Are the instruments that were used to measure something valid? Are SAT and GRE scores, for example, valid instruments for measuring the ability of students to get good grades? If they are, then are grades a valid measure of how smart students are? Is the question "Do you practice polytheistic fetishism?" a valid instrument for measuring religious practices? The validity of data is tied to the validity of instruments. If questions asking people to recall their behavior are not valid instruments for tapping into informants' past behavior, then the data retrieved by those instruments are not valid, either.

Data Validity

2. Assuming that data are valid, then are the findings and conclusions from those data valid, too? For example, is it valid to conclude that firemen cause fires just because fires and firemen are always seen together? Is it valid to conclude that poor people have no ambition just because they say they don't? Is it valid to conclude that Asian-Americans in U.S. schools do better in math than other ethnic groups? And if this *is* the case, then is it valid to conclude that Asian-Americans are simply better at math than other people are?

Finding Validity

3. Assuming that data are valid, and that the findings are valid also, then are the explanations that are offered to account for the findings valid? Since Asian-Americans actually do better in math than other ethnic groups in U.S. schools, why is this the case? Is the fact that Asian-American children come from homes with lower divorce rates a valid explanation for their higher math scores? (They do, and it isn't.)

Reliability refers to whether or not you get the same answer by using an instrument to measure something more than once. If you insert a thermometer into boiling water at sea level, it should register 212° Fahrenheit each and every time. "Instruments" can be things like thermometers and scales, or questions that you ask informants. If you ask 10 informants "Do the ancestors take revenge on people who don't worship them?" would you get the same answer from each of them? What about if you asked "Does it rain a lot around here?"

Precision is another matter. Suppose your bathroom scale works on a spring mechanism. When you stand on the scale, the spring is compressed. As the spring compresses, it moves a pointer to a number that signifies how much weight is being put on the scale. Now, assume that there exists some true value, in pounds, representing your weight. Let's say that you really, truly weigh 156.625 pounds, to the nearest thousandth of a pound.

If your bathroom scale is like mine, there are five little marks between each pound reading; that is, the scale registers weight in fifths of a pound. In terms of precision, then, your scale is somewhat limited. The best it could possibly do would be to inform you that you weigh "somewhere between 156.6 and 156.8 pounds, and closer to the former figure than to the latter." In this case, you might not be too concerned about the error introduced by lack of precision.

Whether you care or not depends on the needs you have for data. If you are concerned about losing weight, then you're probably not going to worry too much about the fact that your scale is only precise to the nearest fifth of a pound. But if you're measuring the weights of pharmaceuticals, and someone's life depends on your getting the precise amounts into a compound, well, that's another matter.

Finally, assume that you are satisfied with the level of precision of the scale. What if the spring were not calibrated correctly (there was an error at the factory where the scale was built, or last week your overweight house guest bent the spring a little too much) and the scale were off? Now we have the following interesting situation: The data from this instrument are valid (it has already been determined that the scale is measuring weight—exactly what you think it's measuring); the data are reliable (you get the same answer every time you step on it); and they are precise enough for your purposes. But they are not *accurate*. What next?

You could see if the scale were always inaccurate in the same way. You could stand on it 10 times in a row, without eating or doing exercise in between. That way, you'd be measuring the same thing 10 different times with the same instrument. If the reading were always the same, then the instrument would at least be reliable, even though it wasn't accurate. Suppose it turned out that your scale were always incorrectly lower by 5 pounds (this is called *systematic bias*), then a simple correction formula would be all you'd need in order to feel confident that the data from the instrument were pretty close to the truth. The formula would be:

$$\text{True Weight} = \text{Your Scale Weight} + 5 \text{ pounds}$$

The scale might be off in more complicated ways, however. It might be that for every 10 pounds of weight put on the scale, an additional half-pound correction has to be made. Then the recalibration formula would be

$$\text{True Weight} = (\text{Your Scale Weight}) + (\text{Scale Weight}/10) (.5)$$

or

$$(\text{Your Scale Weight}) \times (1.05)$$

That is, take the scale weight, divide by 10, multiply by half a pound, and add the result to the reading on your scale.

If an instrument is not precise enough for what you want to do with the data, then you simply have to build a more precise one. There is no way out. But if it is precise enough for your research and reliable, but inaccurate in known ways, then a formula can be applied to correct for the inaccuracy.

Determining Validity

You may have noticed that I just casually slipped in the statement that the scale had already been determined to be a valid instrument. How do we know that the scale is measuring weight? Maybe it's measuring something else. How can we be sure? In fact, there is no direct way to evaluate the validity of a measurement instrument. Ultimately, we are left to decide, on the basis of our best judgment, whether an instrument is valid or not. There are several things to look for in making that judgment.

Face Validity

Face validity is simply looking at the operational indicators of a concept and deciding whether or not, on the face of it, the indicators make sense. For example, Boster (1985) studied how well the women of the Aguaruna Jívaro in Peru understood the differences among manioc plants. He planted some fields with different varieties of manioc and asked women to identify the varieties. This technique, or instrument, for measuring cultural competence has great face validity; most researchers would agree that being able to identify more varieties of manioc is a valid indicator of cultural competence in this domain.

Boster might have simply asked women to list as many varieties of manioc as they could. This instrument would not have been as valid, on the face of it, as having them identify actual plants that were growing in the field. There are just too many things that could interfere with a person's memory of manioc names, even if they were supercompetent regarding the planting of the roots, harvesting them, cooking them, trading them, and so on.

Criterion Validity

Some concepts are too complex to be measured by simple indicators. "Life satisfaction," for example, is a complex variable, or construct, that might be composed of the concepts "sufficient income," "general feeling of well-being," and "satisfaction with level of personal control over one's life." Other complex constructs are "quality of life," "socioeconomic class," "small-holder farm productivity," "access to forest biomass," and so on. Complex instruments are used to measure complex constructs and are judged by what is called *criterion validity*. The data from an instrument that *purportedly* measures a construct are compared against some criterion that is already *known* to be valid.

A tape measure, for example, is known to be an excellent instrument for measuring height. If you knew that a man in our culture wore shirts with 35" sleeves, and pants with 34" cuffs, you could bet that he was over 6' tall and be right more than 95% of the time. On the other hand, you might ask "Why should I measure his cuff length and sleeve length in order to know *most of the time, in general*, how tall he is, when I could use a tape measure and know *all of the time, precisely* how tall he is?"

Indeed. If you want to measure someone's height, then use a tape measure. Don't substitute a lot of fuzzy proxy variables for something that's directly measurable by known, valid indicators. But if you want to measure things like quality of life and socioeconomic class that don't have well-understood, valid indicators, then a complex measure will just have to do until something simpler comes along.

The preference in science for simpler explanations and measures is called "the principle of *parsimony*." (It is also known as *"Ockham's razor,"* after William of Ockham [1285-1349], a medieval philosopher who coined the dictum "non sunt multiplicanda entia praeter necessitatem," or "don't make things more complicated than they need to be.")

Besides parsimony, another test of criterion validity is the *known group* comparison technique. Suppose that you are interested in measuring attitudes of men in Japan toward women working outside the home. From previous research, you know that people with very little education, as well as people with a lot of education, are more conservative on this issue than people with a median education.

If you are testing the validity of an instrument that you've devised to measure liberalism or conservatism regarding gender roles, then you should pick some informants who are poorly educated, others who are highly educated, and others who have a median education. Your test should show what you already know to be the case from previous research with other instruments. The "known group" score is your criterion for the validity of your instrument.

In my view, the best test for the validity of an instrument is whether it lets you predict something else you're interested in. Remember the life insurance problem? You want to predict whether someone is likely to die in the next 365 days in order to know how much to charge them in premiums. Age and sex tell you a lot. But if you know someone's weight, whether they smoke, whether they exercise regularly, what their blood pressure is, whether they have ever had any of a list of diseases, and whether they test-fly experimental aircraft for a living, then you can predict, with a higher and higher degree of accuracy, whether they will die within the next 365 days. Each piece of data is a valid indicator of some independent variable, each of which adds to your ability to predict something of interest.

The bottom line on all this is that validity is never demonstrated, only made more likely. We are never dead sure of anything in science. We try to get closer and closer to the truth by better and better measurement. All of science relies on constructs, the existence of which must ultimately be demonstrated by their effects. You can ram a car against a cement wall at 50 miles an hour and account for the amount of mangling done to the radiator by referring to a concept called "force." The greater the force, the more crumpled the radiator. You demonstrate the existence of intelligence by showing how it predicts school achievement or monetary success.

The Problem with Validity

If you suspect that there is something deeply, desperately wrong with all this, especially in social science where we can't manipulate the concepts or underlying forces that we're trying to demonstrate, you're right.

The whole argument for the validity (indeed, the very existence) of something like intelligence is, frankly, circular: How do you know that intelligence exists? Because you see its effects in achievement. And how do you account for achievement? By saying that someone has achieved highly because they're intelligent. How do you know machismo exists? Because men dominate women in some societies. And how do you account for dominance behavior, like wife beating? By saying that wife beaters are acting out their machismo.

In the hierarchy of construct reality, then, force ranks way up there, while things like intelligence and machismo are pretty weak by comparison. Ultimately, the validity of a concept depends on two things: the utility of the device that measures it and the collective judgment of the scientific community that a construct and its measure are valid. In the end, we are left to deal with the effects of our judgments, which is just as it should be. Valid measurement makes valid data, but validity itself depends on the collective opinion of researchers.

Cause and Effect

If your measurements of a conceptual or observable variable are valid, then you can be reasonably confident that one variable causes another if four conditions are met.

1. The two variables must be *associated* with one another.
2. The association must not be *spurious*.
3. The presumed causal variable must always precede the other in *time*.
4. Finally, a mechanism must be available that explains *how* an independent variable causes a dependent variable. There must be a *theory*.

Condition 1: Association

When two variables are related they are said to *covary*. Covariation is also called *correlation* or simply *association*. Association is not a *sufficient* condition for claiming a causal relationship between two variables, but it is a *necessary* one. Whatever else may be needed to establish cause and effect, you can't claim that one thing causes another if they aren't related in the first place.

Here are a few interesting covariations taken from recent literature: (a) Many desert folk have taboos against eating seafood. (b) Polygyny seems to disappear under conditions of urbanization. (c) Prestige covaries with hunting prowess among band-level peoples. (d) In the industrialized nations of the world, the number of suicides per 100,000 population rises and falls rather predictably with the unemployment rate. (e) Sexual freedom for women tends to increase with the amount that women contribute to subsistence, whether measured in terms of money or labor.

It is *usually* better, for establishing cause and effect, if variables are *strongly* and *consistently* related, but this is not always the case. Regarding strength of relationship, consider the following example. Farmers in the Third World make decisions about acceptance of new technologies (fertilizers, cropping systems, hybrid seeds, credit, and so on), but these decisions might be made on the basis of many simultaneous factors, all of which are weakly, but causally related to the final decision.

Some factors might be: the personal leadership qualities of the individual farmer; the personal economic situation of a farmer; the prior acceptance of innovations by others close to the farmer (the so-called contagion factor); the farmer's personal acquaintance with technology brokers (the "network" factor); the farmer's level of education; and so forth. Each independent variable may contribute only a little to the outcome of the dependent variable (the decision that is finally made), but the contribution may be quite direct and causal in nature.

Even consistency of relationship is not always a good sign. In recent years, many consistent relationships have been challenged in the social sciences. In the study of East African agriculture, for example, studies once showed consistently that men make the decision regarding whether or not to apply fertilizer to fields. Based on the evidence, agricultural economists (including East Africans) contacted men when they wanted to get the word out about a new fertilizer. Someone noticed that the application of fertilizer was erratic; it appeared on some plots, and not on others, even within a single household.

The question became: What are the multiple decision factors that influence a man to apply fertilizer to a particular field? Eventually, of course, the enigma was resolved: Some plots are controlled by women (Art Hansen, personal communication). It is easy to laugh at this sort of thing, but remember, everything is simple *after* you understand it.

Condition 2: Lack of Spuriousness

Two variables may appear related even though they are independent of one another, in the sense that increasing the independent variable does not lead to a change in the dependent one. When that happens the covariation is said to be *spurious*. A spurious correlation can occur when the scores on two variables are caused by a third variable. The per-person consumption of ice cream covaries rather dramatically with the number of miles driven per day in the United States. Both increase during the summer, but ice cream consumption and driving miles are independent of one another. There is a high correlation between the number of fire fighters at a fire and the amount of damage done. It would be easy to conclude that fire fighters *cause* fire damage, but we know better: Both the amount of damage and the number of fire fighters is caused by the size of the blaze.

When you *control for* the third variable, the original bivariate relation is weakened. There is a correlation between the number of cups of coffee drunk each day by men in the United States 40 to 50 years of age and the likelihood that they will have a heart attack during those years. It is tempting to conclude that caffeine causes heart attacks. But it turns out that American men reach the peak of their economic and executive power between 40 and 50 years of age. Among those with higher executive power, there is a tendency to drink more coffee, *and* there is also a greater likelihood of their having a heart attack. We suspect, then, that a third variable, perhaps the stress of executive-level jobs, contributes to both coffee drinking and heart attacks, and that this might account for the association between those two variables.

There are many examples of spurious covariations in anthropology. The longer a society requires that women not engage in sexual intercourse after giving birth, the more likely the society is to support polygynous marriage. But when high male mortality in warfare is held constant, the original relationship vanishes (M. Ember, 1974). Marchione (1980) found a strong relationship between rural versus urban residence and the weight status of 1-year-olds in Jamaica. By controlling for food expenditures of rural and urban households (rural households grew more of their own food), the correlation practically disappeared. Mwango (1986) found that illiterates in Malawi were much more likely than literates to brew beer for sale from part of their maize crop. The covariation was rendered insignificant when he controlled for wealth, which causes both greater education (hence, literacy) and the purchase, rather than the brewing, of maize beer.

Spurious covariations sometimes occur simply because there are thousands and thousands of things that vary in the world and some of them are bound to covary by chance alone. Or spurious relations may be artifacts of the analysis. Dellino (1984) found an inverse relation between perceived quality of life and involvement with the tourism industry on the island of Exuma in the Bahamas. When he controlled for the size of the community (he studied several on the island), the original correlation disappeared.

People in the more congested areas were more likely to score low on the perceived-quality-of-life index whether or not they were involved with tourism, while those in the small, outlying communities were more likely to score high on the index. In addition, people in the congested areas were also more likely to be involved in tourism-related activities, because that's where the tourists go.

The list of spurious relations is endless, and it is not always easy to detect them for the frauds that they are. A higher percentage of men get lung cancer than women, but when you control for the length of time that people have smoked, the gender difference in carcinomas vanishes. Pretty consistently, young people accept new technologies more readily than older people. But in many societies, the relation between age and readiness to adopt innovations disappears when you control for level of education. Urban migrants from tribal groups often give up polygyny, but both migration and abandonment of polygyny are often caused by a third factor, lack of wealth.

Your only defense against spurious covariations is vigilance. No matter how obvious a covariation may appear, discuss it with a disinterested colleague, or with several colleagues. Be sure that they are people who have no stake whatsoever in telling you what you'd like to hear. Present your initial findings in open colloquia and in class seminars at your university or where you work. Beg people to find potentially spurious relations in your work. You'll thank them for it if they do.

Condition 3: Precedence, or Time Order

Besides a nonspurious association between variables, one other thing is required in order to establish a cause-and-effect relationship between two variables: a logical time order. Skin color comes before blood pressure in time; low aptitude for mathematics comes after gender; religion comes before political orientation (that is, being a political conservative does not generally cause people to profess one religion over another). Fire fighters do not cause fires; they show up after the blaze starts.

Unfortunately, things are not so clear cut in actual research. Does adoption of new technologies cause wealth, or is it the other way around? Does urban migration cause dissatisfaction with rural life, or the reverse? Does consumer demand cause new products to appear, or vice versa? Does the growth in the number of lawsuits in this country cause more people to study law so that they can cash in, or did overproduction of lawyers cause more lawsuits?

What about elective surgery? Does the increased supply of surgeons cause an increase in elective surgery, or does the demand for surgery create a surfeit of surgeons? Or are both caused by one or more external variables, like an increase in discretionary income in the upper middle class, or the fact that insurance companies pay more and more of Americans' medical bills?

Condition 4: Theory

Finally, even when you have established nonspurious, consistent, strong covariation, as well as a time sequence for two variables, you need a theory that explains the association. Theories consist of good ideas about how things work.

One of my favorite good ideas in social science about how things work is called "cognitive dissonance theory" (Festinger, 1957). It is based on the insight that people can tell the difference when their beliefs about what *ought* to be don't match their perception of how things really are, and that the dissonance is uncomfortable. People then have a choice: They can live with the dissonance (be uncomfortable); change the external reality (fight city hall); or change their beliefs (the easy way out).

Dissonance theory helps explain why some people accept new technologies that they initially reject out of fear for their jobs: Once a technology is entrenched, and there is no longer any chance of getting rid of it, it becomes easier to change one's ideas about what's good and bad than it is to live with dissonance. It explains why some men change their beliefs about women working outside the home: Economic necessity drives women into the work force, and it becomes painful to hold onto the idea that that's the wrong thing for women to do.

On the other hand, some people leave their jobs rather than accept new technologies, and some men still are not supportive of women working outside the home—even when those men depend on their wives' income to make ends meet. This is an example of a general theory that fails to predict local phenomena. It leads us to seek more data and more understanding to predict when cognitive dissonance theory is insufficient as an explanation.

Many theories are developed to explain a purely local phenomenon and then turn out to have wider applicability. We notice, for example, that when men from polygynous African societies move to cities, they often give up polygyny. This consistent covariation is explained by the fact that men who move away from tribal territories in search of wage labor must abandon their land, their houses, and the shared labor of their kinsmen. Under those conditions, they simply can not afford to provide for more than one wife, much less the children that multiple wives produce. The relation between urbanization and changes in marriage customs is explained by *antecedent* and *intervening* variables.

Mwango (1986) found that Malawian farmers who own more land are more likely to adopt hybrid maize than farmers with less land. Farmers saw the economic benefits of the hybrid, but they did not want to be without local maize. They said the latter tasted better in traditional porridge. Besides, what if the hybrids failed, or there wasn't enough rain? At a certain level of land ownership, of course, farmers also had sufficient storage facilities to permit experimentation with hybrids, while holding on to a supply of local maize. Conclusion: Land holding is related to adoption of hybrids if adequate storage of local crops is present first.

As you read the literature in social science, you'll see references to lots of theories. "Contagion theory" invokes a "copycat mechanism" to explain why suicides are more likely to come in batches when one of them is widely publicized in the press. "Relative deprivation theory" is based on the insight that people compare themselves to specific peer groups, not to the world at large. It explains why anthropology professors don't feel all that badly about engineering professors earning a lot of money, but hate it if sociologists in their university get significantly higher salaries.

All such theories start with one or two primitive axioms—things you have to take at face value. The idea that cognitive dissonance is uncomfortable and that people strive naturally toward cognitive consonance doesn't get explained. It's a primitive axiom. The idea that people compare themselves to reference groups doesn't get explained. It, too, is a primitive axiom, an assumption, from which you deduce some results. The results are predictions, or hypotheses, that you then go out and test.

The ideal in science is to deduce a prediction from theory and to test the prediction. That's the culture of science. The way social science really works much of the time is that you don't predict results, you "postdict" them. You analyze your data, come up with findings, and explain the findings after the fact.

There is nothing wrong with this. Knowledge and understanding can come from good ideas before or after you collect data. You must admit, though, there's a certain panache in making a prediction, sealing it in an envelope, and testing it. Later, when you take the prediction out of the envelope and it matches your empirical findings, you get a lot of points.

The Kalymnian Case

Here's an example of explaining findings after the fact. In my experience, it's pretty typical of analysis in anthropology.

In my fieldwork in 1964-1965 on the island of Kalymnos, Greece, I noticed that young sponge divers (in their 20s) were more likely to get the bends than were older divers (those over 30). (The "bends" is a crippling malady that affects divers who come up too quickly after a long time in deep water.) I also noticed that younger divers were more productive than very old divers (those over 45), but not more productive than those in their middle years (30 to 40).

As it turned out, younger divers were subject to much greater social stress to demonstrate their daring and to take risks with their lives—risks that men over 30 had already put behind them. The younger divers worked longer under water (gathering more sponges), but they came up faster and were consequently at higher risk of bends. The middle group of divers made up in experience for the shortened time they spent in the water, so they maintained their high productivity at lower risk of bends. The older divers were feeling the effects of infirmity brought on by years of deep diving, hence their productivity was lowered, along with their risk of death or injury from bends. Of course, the real question was: What *caused* the young Kalymnian divers to engage in acts that placed them at greater risk?

My first attempt at explaining all this was pretty lame. I noticed that the men who took the most chances with their lives had a certain rhetoric and swagger. They were called *levedhis* by other divers and by their captains. I concluded that somehow these men had more *levedhia* and that made them higher risk takers. In fact, this is what many of my informants told me. Young men, they said, feel the need to show their manhood, and that's why they take risks by staying down too long and coming up too fast.

The problem with this cultural explanation was that it just didn't explain anything. The mistake I made was that I tried to use something I couldn't see (the mystic levedhia) to explain something I saw. I had to postulate the existence of something (a value) in order to explain something that manifestly existed, variation in diving behavior.

Yes, the high-risk takers swaggered and exhibited something we could label "machismo." But what good did it do to say that lots of machismo caused people to dive deep and come up quickly? Where did young men get this feeling, I asked. That's just how young men are, my informants told me. I supposed that there could be something to this testosterone-poisoning theory, but it didn't seem adequate.

Eventually I understood that the swaggering behavior and the values voiced about manliness were cultural ways to ratify, not explain, the high-risk diving behavior. Both the diving behavior and the ratifying behavior were the product of a third variable, called *platika*.

Divers traditionally took their entire season's expected earnings in advance, before shipping out in April for the 6-month sponge fishing expedition in North Africa. By taking their money (platika) in advance, they placed themselves in debt to the boat captains. Just before they shipped out, the divers would pay off the debts that their families had accumulated during the preceding year. By the time they went to sea, the divers were nearly broke and their families started going into debt again for food and other necessities.

In the late 1950s, synthetic sponges began to take over the world markets, and young men on Kalymnos left for overseas jobs rather than go into sponge fishing. As divers left the island, and as living costs escalated, the money that the remaining divers commanded in advance went up. But with the price of sponge stable or dropping, due to competition with synthetics, the boat captains kept losing profits. Consequently, they put more pressure on the divers to produce more sponge, to stay down longer, and to take greater risks. This resulted in more accidents on the job (Bernard, 1967, 1987).

Note that in all the examples of theory I've just given, the predictions and the post hoc explanations, I didn't have to quote a single statistic— not even a percentage score. That's because theories are qualitative. Ideas about cause and effect are based on insight, are derived from either qualitative or quantitative observations, and are initially expressed in words. *Testing* causal statements—finding out *how much* they explain rather than *whether* they seem to be plausible explanations—requires quantitative observations. But theory construction—explanation itself— is the quintessential qualitative act.

3

Anthropology and Research Design

Early in this century, F. C. Bartlett went to Cambridge University to study anthropology with W. H. R. Rivers. When Bartlett got to Cambridge, he asked Rivers for some advice. "The best training you can possibly have," Rivers told Bartlett," "is a thorough drilling in the experimental methods of the psychological laboratory" (Bartlett, 1937:416).

Bartlett found himself spending hours in the lab, "lifting weights, judging the brightness of lights, learning nonsense syllables, and engaging in a number of similarly abstract occupations" that seemed to be "particularly distant from the lives of normal human beings." In the end, though, Bartlett concluded that Rivers was right. Training in the experimental methods of psychology, said Bartlett, gives one "a sense of evidence, a realization of the difficulties of human observation, and a kind of scientific conscience which no other field of study can impart so well" (ibid.:417).

It would be useful if we could take advantage of the power of the experimental method in anthropology. In this chapter I discuss how experimental thinking can help us design better research and better understand the sorts of natural events that we study in anthropology.

There are four kinds of experiments: *true experiments, quasi-experiments, natural experiments,* and *naturalistic experiments*. The difference is in how much control you have over the design of the intervention and the assignment of individuals to groups.

True Experiments with People

There are five steps to follow in conducting true experiments with people.

1. You need at least two groups, called the *treatment group* (or the *intervention group* or the *stimulus group*) and the *control group*. One group gets the intervention (a new drug, for example), and the other group (the control group) doesn't.
2. Individuals must be *randomly assigned* either to the intervention group or to the control group to ensure that the groups are equivalent. Some individuals in a population may be more religious, or more wealthy, or less sickly, or more prejudiced than others, but random assignment ensures that those traits are randomly distributed through the groups in an experiment. The degree to which randomization ensures equivalence, however, depends on the size of the groups created. With random assignment, two groups of 50 are more equivalent than four groups of 25. The principle behind random assignment will become clearer after you work through Chapter 4 on sampling.
3. The groups are measured on one or more dependent variables (income, infant mortality, attitude toward abortion, knowledge of curing techniques, or other things you hope to change by the intervention); this is called the *pretest*.
4. The intervention (the independent variable) is introduced.
5. The dependent variables are measured again. This is the *posttest*.

Here's a made-up example of a true experiment: Take 100 19-year-old college sophomore women and randomly assign 50 of them to each of two groups. Bring each woman to the lab and show her a series of flash cards. Let each card contain a single three-digit random number. Measure how many three-digit numbers people can remember. Let the 50 members of one group hear the most popular rock song of the week playing in the background as they take the test. Let the other group of 50 hear nothing.

Measure how many three-digit numbers people can remember and whether rock music improves or worsens performance on the task.

Notice how only people of the same age, gender, and level of education were selected, and how everyone in the experimental group hears the same tune. Suppose that the rock-music group does better on the task. We want to be sure that it's not because of their gender or their age or their education, but because of the music. Putting in more independent variables (like males, graduate students, and different tunes) creates what are called *confounds*. They confound the experiment and make it impossible to tell if the intervention is what really caused any observed differences in the dependent variable.

True Experiments: In the Lab

True experiments with people are common in laboratory psychology and in the testing of new medicines. Laboratory experiments often produce results that beg to be tested in the natural world by anthropologists. Aaronson and Mills (1959) demonstrated in a lab experiment that people who go through severe initiation to a group tend to be more positive toward the group than are people who go through a mild initiation. They reasoned that people who go through tough initiation rites put a lot of personal investment into getting into the group. Later, if people see evidence that the group is not what they thought it would be, they are reluctant to admit the fact because of the investment.

Aaronson and Mills's findings were corroborated by Gerard and Mathewson (1966) in an independent experiment. Those findings could now be the basis for a cross-cultural test of the original hypothesis.

Similarly, events in the real world can stimulate laboratory experiments. In 1963, in Queens, New York, Kitty Genovese was stabbed to death in the street one night. There were 38 eyewitnesses who saw the whole grisly episode from their apartment windows, and not one of them called the police. The newspapers called it "apathy," but Bib Latané and John Darley (1968) had a different explanation. They called it "diffusion of responsibility," and they did an experiment to test their idea.

Latané and Darley invited ordinary people to participate in a "psychology experiment." While the subjects were waiting in an anteroom to be called for the experiment, the room filled with smoke. If there was a single subject, 75% reported the smoke right away. If there were three or more subjects waiting together, they reported the smoke only 38% of the time. People in groups just couldn't figure out whose responsibility it was to do something. So they did nothing. Thus, lab experiments can test things in the real world and can generate things to test in the real world.

True Experiments: In the Field

When they are done outside the lab, experiments are called *field experiments*. Janet Schofield and her colleagues did a 3-year ethnographic study of a middle school. During the first year they noticed that African-American and white children seemed to react differently to "mildly aggressive acts"—things like bumping in the hallway, poking one another in the classroom, asking for food, or using another student's pencil without permission. There appeared to be no overt racial conflict in the school, but during interviews white students were more likely to report being intimidated by their African-American peers than vice versa (Sagar & Schofield, 1980:593).

To test their impression, Schofield and her colleagues did a field experiment. They randomly chose 40 black and 40 white male students. Each student looked at a series of sketches depicting some mild aggressive act. One sketch, for example, showed a student poking another with a pencil in class. All the students saw the same sketches except that the race of the perpetrator and the race of the victim varied. After looking at the sketches, the students rated how well adjectives like playful, friendly, mean, and threatening described the behavior of the perpetrator in the sketch (ibid.:594).

The result: The white children read more threat into the behaviors of black children than vice versa. Schofield and Anderson concluded that, for subjects of this experiment, in this school, the stereotype of the threatening black male is already ingrained in whites by middle school (1987:272).

Field experiments can produce powerful evidence for applications projects. Ronald Milliman (1986) conducted an experiment to test the effects of slow and fast music on the behavior of customers in a restaurant. First, Milliman played a number of instrumental pieces as background music. He asked 227 randomly chosen customers "Do you consider the music playing right now as slow tempo, fast tempo, or in between?" From these data he identified slow music as 72 beats per minute or fewer and fast music as 92 beats per minute or more.

Then, for eight consecutive weekends, Milliman played slow music and fast music on alternating nights. The first weekend, he played slow music on Friday night and fast music on Saturday night. The next weekend he reversed the order. He used instrumental music so as not to confound the experiment with *exogenous variables* like gender of vocalist, popularity of vocalist, and so on.

Milliman looked at the effect of the two music tempos on six dependent variables. Music tempo had no effect on the time it took for employees to take, prepare, and serve customers' orders. It had no effect on the number of people who decided to leave the restaurant before being seated (it was a popular restaurant, and there was usually a wait on weekends for a table). And it had no effect on the total dollar amount of food purchased.

The music tempo had a significant effect, however, on the amount of time that customers spent at their tables. With slow music, customers spent 56 minutes eating; with fast music, they spent only 45 minutes. During those extra 11 minutes, the average bar tab was $30.47 per table, about $9 more than the average bar tab per table in the fast-music treatment. Since the amount of food purchased was the same under both conditions, and since profits are higher on bar purchases, the total profit margin per table was dramatically higher in the slow music treatment.

True field experiments are rare in anthropology, but not unprecedented. Marvin Harris (in press) conducted an experiment in Brazil to test the effect of substituting one word in the question that deals with race on the Brazilian census. The demographers who designed the census decided that the term *parda* was a more reliable gloss than the term *morena* for what English speakers call "brown"—despite overwhelming evidence that Brazilians prefer the term morena. Harris wanted to know what the effect was of substituting the word parda for morena on the Brazilian census.

In the town of Rio de Contas, he assigned 505 houses randomly to one of two groups and interviewed one adult in each house. All respondents were asked to say what *cor* (color) they thought they were. This was the "free-choice option." Then they were asked to choose one of four terms that best described their cor. One group (with 252 respondents) was asked to select among *branca* (white), parda (grey or brown), *preta* (black), and *amerela* (yellow). This was the "parda option" and is the one used on the Brazilian census. The other group (with 253 respondents) was asked to select among branca, morena (brown), preta, and amerela. This was the "morena option," and is the intervention, or "treatment" in Harris's experiment.

Among the 252 people given the parda option, 131 (52%) identified themselves as morena when given a free choice. But when given the parda option, only 80 (32% of the 252) said they were parda and 41 said they were branca. Presumably, those 41 people would have labeled themselves "morena" if they'd had the chance; not wanting to called themselves "parda," they said they were branca. The parda option, then, produces more "whites" (brancas) in the Brazilian census and fewer "browns" (pardas).

Of the 253 people who responded to the morena option, 160 (63%) said they were morena. Of those 160, only 122 had chosen to call themselves morena in the free-choice option. So, giving people the morena option increases the number of "browns" (morenas) and decreases the number of "whites" (brancas) in the Brazilian census.

Does this difference make a difference? Social scientists who study the Brazilian census have found that those labeled "whites" are likely to live longer than those in other categories. But, Harris asked, who are the whites? If 41% of the self-identified morenas say they are whites when forced to label themselves parda, what does this do to all the social and economic statistics about racial groups in Brazil?

Quasi-Experiments

Quasi-experiments are most often used in evaluating social programs. Suppose a researcher has invented a technique for improving reading comprehension among third graders. She selects two third-grade classes in a school district. One of them gets the intervention and the other doesn't. Students are measured before and after the intervention to see whether their reading scores improve. This design contains many of the elements of a true experiment, but the participants are not assigned randomly to the treatment and control groups.

Campbell and Boruch (1975) show how this lack of random assignment leads to problems. Suppose the children in one class are, by chance, from wealthier homes, on average, than the children in the other class, and suppose that the wealthier children test higher in reading comprehension than do the poorer children at the end of the year. Would you be willing to bet, say, $300,000 on implementing the new reading comprehension program in all classes in the school district? Would you bet that it was the new program and not some *confound*, like socioeconomic class, that caused the differences in test scores?

If all the children, one at a time, were assigned randomly to the two groups (those who got the program and those who didn't), then this confound would disappear—not because socioeconomic status (SES) stops being a factor in how well children learn to read, but because children from poor and rich families would be equally likely to be in the treatment group or in the control group. Any bias that SES causes in interpreting the results of the experiment would be distributed randomly and would, in theory, wash out.

Natural Experiments

True experiments and quasi-experiments are *conducted*, and the results are *evaluated* later. Natural experiments, by contrast, are going on around us all the time. They are not conducted by researchers at all—they are simply evaluated.

Here are four examples of common natural experiments: (a) Some people choose to migrate from villages to cities, while others stay put. (b) Some villages in a region are provided with electricity, while some are not. (c) Some middle-class Chicano students go to college, some do not. (d) Some cultures practice female infanticide, some do not.

Each of these situations constitutes a natural experiment that tests *something* about human behavior and thought. The trick is to ask "What hypothesis is being tested by what's going on here?"

To evaluate natural experiments—that is, to figure out what hypothesis is being tested—you need to be alert to the possibilities and collect the right data. There's a really important natural experiment going in an area of Mexico where I've worked over the years. A major irrigation system has been installed over the last 30 years in parts of a valley. Some of the villages affected by the irrigation system are populated entirely by Ñähñu Indians; other villages are entirely mestizo.

Some of the Indian villages in the area are too high up the valley slope for the irrigation system to reach. I could not have decided to run this multimillion dollar irrigation system through certain villages and bypass others, but the instant the decision was made by others, a natural experiment on the effects of a particular intervention was set in motion. There is a treatment (irrigation), there are treatment groups, and there are control groups. (See Finkler, 1974, for an ethnographic study of the effects of irrigation on an Indian village.)

Unfortunately, I can't evaluate the experiment because I failed to see the possibilities early enough. I did not do the necessary pretesting on a variety of dependent variables (village and personal wealth, migration rates, alcoholism, etc.) that I believe have been affected by the coming of irrigation. Had I done so, I would now have *baseline data* and be in a better position to ask "What hypotheses about human behavior are being tested by this experiment?" I can't reconstruct variables from 20 or 30 years ago. The logical power of the experimental model for establishing cause and effect between the intervention and the dependent variables is destroyed.

Some natural experiments, like the famous 1955 Connecticut speeding law, produce terrific data for evaluation.

In 1955, the governor of Connecticut ordered strict enforcement of speeding laws in the state. The object was to cut down on the alarming number of traffic fatalities. Anyone caught speeding had their driver's license suspended for at least 30 days. Traffic deaths fell from 324 in 1955 to 284 in 1956. A lot of people had been inconvenienced with speeding tickets and suspension of driving privileges, but 40 lives had been saved.

The question, of course, was whether the crackdown was the cause of the decline in traffic deaths. Campbell and Ross (1968) evaluated the experiment. They plotted the traffic deaths for all the years from 1951 to 1959 in Connecticut, Massachusetts, New York, New Jersey, and Rhode Island. Each of those states has more or less the same weather, and they all produced a lot of data on traffic fatalities.

As it turned out, four of the five states experienced an increase in highway deaths in 1955, and all five states had a decline in traffic deaths the following year, 1956. If that were all you knew, you couldn't say that the governor's crackdown in Connecticut had had any effect. However, traffic deaths continued to decline steadily in Connecticut for the next three years (1957, 1958, 1959). They went up in Rhode Island and Massachusetts, went down a bit and then up again in New Jersey, and remained about the same in New York.

Connecticut was the only state that showed a consistent reduction in highway deaths for four years after the stiff penalties were introduced. Campbell and Ross treated these data as a series of natural experiments, and the results were convincing: Stiff penalties for speeders saves lives.

If you think like an experimentalist, you eventually come to see the unlimited possibilities for research going on all around you. The number of plays in a football game is highest in the second quarter, next highest in the fourth quarter, and lowest in the first and third quarter. Webb and Weick (1983) figured out that this was a test of the "deadline hypothesis" in psychology—that people perform most when they face a deadline. They supported their idea with the observation that trading goes up in the last 2 hours of the day at the New York Stock Exchange. When the trading day was extended from 3:00 p.m. to 3:30 p.m. in the 1970s, the rise in trading volume was *still* during the last 2 hours.

Cialdini et al. (1976) evaluated the natural experiment that is conducted at most big universities every Monday during football season. Over a period of eight weeks, professors at Arizona State, Louisiana State, Ohio State, Notre Dame, Michigan, the University of Pittsburgh, and the University of Southern California recorded the percentage of students in their introductory psychology classes who wore school insignias (buttons, hats, T-shirts, etc.) on the Monday after Saturday football games. For 177 students per week, on average, over 8 weeks, 63% wore some school insignia after wins in football versus 44% after losses or ties. The difference is statistically significant.

Naturalistic Experiments

In a *naturalistic* experiment, you *contrive* to collect experimental data under natural conditions. You make the data happen, out in the natural world (not in the lab), and you evaluate the results.

Consider this: You're having coffee near the Trevi Fountain in Rome. You overhear two Americans chatting next to you and you ask where they're from. One of them says he's from Sioux City, Iowa. You say you've got a friend from Sioux City, and it turns out to be your new acquaintance's cousin. The culturally appropriate reaction at this point is for everyone to say, "Wow, what a small world!"

Stanley Milgram (1967) contrived an experiment to test how small the world really is. He asked people in the midwestern United States to send a folder to a divinity student at Harvard University, but only if people *knew* the divinity student personally. Otherwise, he asked them to send the folders to an acquaintance of theirs whom they thought had a chance of knowing the "target" at Harvard.

The folders got sent around from acquaintance to acquaintance until they wound up in the hands of someone who actually knew the target—at which point the folders were sent, as per the instructions in the game, to the target. The average number of links between all the "starters" and the target was about five.

Now, no one expects this experiment to actually happen in real life. It's contrived as can be and lacks control. On the other hand, it's compelling because it says *something* about how the natural world works. Tell people about Milgram's experiment and ask them to guess how many links it takes to get a folder between any two randomly chosen people in the United States. Most people will guess a much bigger number than five. It really *is* a small world.

I'll have a lot more to say about naturalistic experiments in Chapter 15 on unobtrusive observation.

Internal and External Validity

In evaluating the logical power of natural experiments, we can learn a lot from the demands that are placed on the conduct of true experiments. When a true experiment (with full control by the researcher) is carried out properly, the results have high *internal validity*. This means that changes in the dependent variables were *caused by*—not merely related to or correlated with—the treatment. This is why the experimental method is so powerful.

Consider the following true experiment, designed to test whether offering people money produces fewer errors in an arithmetic task. Take two groups of individuals and ask them to solve 100 simple arithmetic problems. Tell one group that they will be given a dollar for every correct answer. Tell the other group nothing. Be sure to assign participants randomly to the groups to ensure equal distribution of skill in arithmetic. See if the treatment group (the one that gets the monetary rewards) does better than the control group.

This experiment can be embellished to eliminate confounds that threaten internal validity. Conduct the experiment a second time, reversing the control and treatment groups. In other words, tell the treatment group that this time they will not receive any financial reward for correct answers, and tell the control group that they will receive a dollar for every correct answer. (Of course, give them a new set of problems to solve.)

Or conduct the experiment many times, changing or adding independent variables. In one version of the experiment, you might keep the groups from knowing about each other. In another iteration, you might let each group know about the other's efforts and rewards (or lack of rewards). Perhaps when people know that others are being rewarded for good behavior and they themselves are not rewarded they will double their efforts to gain the rewards (this is called the "John Henry effect"). Or perhaps they just become demoralized and give up. By controlling the interventions and the group membership you can build up a series of conclusions regarding cause and effect between various independent and dependent variables.

Controlled experiments have the virtue of high internal validity, but they have the liability of low *external validity*. It may be true that a reward of a dollar per correct answer results in significantly more correct answers for the groups you tested in your laboratory. But you can't tell whether a dollar is sufficient reward for all groups, or whether a quarter would be enough to create the same experimental results in some groups. Worst of all, you don't know whether the laboratory results explain *anything* you want to know about in the real world.

To test external validity, you might propose some kind of monetary reward for teaching children to do arithmetic. Perhaps a penny per correct answer might be enough. You'll probably run afoul of strongly held values in communities against doing this sort of thing, but the point is that the laboratory experiment, with high internal validity, would suggest research that *tests* external validity. In this regard, controlled laboratory experiments are very much like ethnography: They have an elegant ring of internal truth, but they may have low generalizability. (Controlled experiments in classrooms, on the other hand, where conditions are, in fact, natural, tend to have good external validity.)

It is easier to control threats to validity in true experiments than in quasi-experiments and in naturalistic experiments; it is impossible to control them in natural experiments. For the third-grade reading-skills experiment, internal validity means that a researcher can tell whether changes in reading comprehension are due to the treatment program. If they are, then the next questions are: How far do the results generalize? Just to the third graders in the experiment? To all third graders in the school district? To all third graders in the state? In the country?

It is impossible to establish internal validity for the Mexican irrigation experiment. Suppose infant mortality goes down in the villages that get irrigation. Is that the result of the irrigation? It turns out that villages that get irrigation have more stable populations (lower rural-urban migration) than villages that are bypassed. The government is more likely to spend money in stable villages on such things as clinics and other facilities that improve infant care.

Kinds of Confounds: Threats to Validity

It's pointless to ask questions about external validity until you establish internal validity. In a series of influential publications, Donald Campbell and his colleagues have identified the threats to internal validity of experiments (see Campbell, 1957, 1979; Campbell & Stanley, 1966; Cook & Campbell, 1979). Here are seven confounds that are most likely to affect anthropological data.

1. History. The *history confound* refers to any independent variable, other than the treatment, that occurs between the pretest and the posttest in an experiment and that affects the experimental groups differently.

Suppose you are doing a laboratory experiment with two groups (experimental and control), and there is a power failure in the building. So long as the lights go out for both groups, there is no problem. But if the lights go out for one group and not the other, it's difficult to tell whether it was the treatment or the power failure that causes changes in the dependent variable.

In a laboratory experiment, history is controlled by isolating subjects as much as possible from outside influences. When we do experiments outside the laboratory, it is almost impossible to keep new independent variables from creeping in and confounding things.

Recall that example of introducing a new reading program into third-grade classes. Suppose that right in the middle of the school term during which the experiment was being conducted, the Governor's Task Force on Elementary Education issues its long-awaited report, and it contains the observation that reading skills must be emphasized during the early school years. Furthermore, it says, teachers whose classes make exceptional progress in reading should be rewarded with 10% salary bonuses.

The governor accepts the recommendation and announces a request for a special legislative appropriation. Elementary teachers all over the state start paying extra attention to reading skills. Even supposing that the students in the treatment classes do better than those in the control classes, how can we be certain that the magnitude of the difference would not have been greater had this historical confound not occurred?

In the Mezquital Valley irrigation experiment, the historical confounds are much greater. Over the last 30 years, roads have been paved, clinics and schools have been built, additional Protestant missionaries have arrived. All these things, irrigation included, may be caused by some common force (like modernization throughout the Third World), or they may be linked in a complex pattern of cause and effect. The history confound in natural experiments is really messy.

2. Maturation. The *maturation confound* refers to the fact that people in any experiment grow older or get more experienced while you are trying to conduct an experiment.

Consider the following experiment: Start with a group of teenagers on an American Indian reservation and follow them for the next 60 years. Some of them will move to cities, some will go to small towns, and some will stay on the reservation. Periodically, test them on a variety of dependent variables (their political opinions, their wealth, their health, their family size, and so on). See how the various experimental treatments (city versus reservation versus small-town living) affect these variables.

Here is where the maturation confound enters the picture. The people you are studying get older. Older people in many societies become more politically conservative. They are usually wealthier than younger people. Eventually, they come to be more illness-prone than younger people. Some of the changes you measure in your dependent variables will be the result of the various treatments and some of them may just be the result of maturation.

3. Testing and Instrumentation. The *testing confound* occurs in laboratory and field experiments, when subjects get used to being tested for indicators on dependent variables. This quite naturally changes their responses. Asking people the same questions again and again in a long field study can have this effect.

The *instrumentation confound* results from changing measurement instruments. If you do a set of observations in the field, and later send in someone else to continue the observations, you have changed instruments. This will threaten the internal validity of your study. It will be difficult to know which observations are closer to the truth: yours or those of the substitute instrument (the new field researcher). In multiresearcher projects, this problem is usually dealt with by training all investigators to see and record things in more or less the same way. This is called increasing *interrater reliability*. (See the section on *Using Interviewers* in Chapter 12.)

4. Regression to the Mean. *Regression to the mean* is a confound that occurs when you deal with two groups that show extreme scores on a dependent variable. No matter what the treatment is, over time you'd expect the scores to become more moderate. This is one of the most common and most overlooked threats to internal validity. If men who are taller than 6'7" marry women who are taller than 6'3", then their children will be (a) taller than average, *and* (b) closer to average height than either of their parents are. The dependent variable, height of children, should be expected to regress toward the mean since it really can't get more extreme than the height of the parents.

Many social intervention programs make the mistake of using people with extreme values on dependent variables as subjects. Suppose that the bureaucrats who selected the route of the irrigation canals in the Mexican experiment, wanting to ensure that the experiment succeeded, selected a route that ran through the poorest villages. Whether those villages got irrigation or not, their income would probably have gone up, if for no other reason than it couldn't have gone down very much, no matter what opportunities people did or didn't have.

5. Selection of Experimental Subjects. *Selection bias* in choosing subjects is a major confound to validity in quasi-experiments and in natural experiments. In laboratory experiments, you assign subjects at random, from a single population, to treatment groups and to control groups. This distributes any differences among individuals in the population throughout the groups, making the groups equivalent. It is not likely, therefore, that differences among the groups will cause differences in outcomes on the dependent variables, so selection is not a threat to the internal validity of the experiment.

In natural experiments, however, we have no control over assignment of individuals to groups. Question: Do victims of violent crime have less stable marriages than do persons who have not been victims? Obviously, researchers can not randomly assign subjects to the treatment (violent crime). It could turn out that people who are victims of this treatment are more likely to have unstable marriages anyway, even if they never experienced violence.

Question: Do rural-urban migrants in the Third World engage in more entrepreneurial activities than do rural stay-at-homes? If we could assign rural people randomly to the treatment group (those engaging in urban migration), we'd have a better chance of finding out. Since we can not, selection is a threat to the internal validity of the experiment. Suppose that the answer to the last question were "yes." We could not know whether the treatment (migration) caused the outcome (greater entrepreneurial activity), or whether the outcome is the result of self-selection for migration by entrepreneurial personalities.

6. Mortality. The *mortality confound* refers to the fact that individuals may not complete their participation in an experiment. Suppose we follow two sets of Mexican villagers—some who receive irrigation and some who do not—for 5 years. During the 1st year of the experiment we have 200 villagers in each group. By the 5th year, 170 remain in the treatment group, and only 120 remain in the control group. One conclusion is that lack of irrigation caused those in the control group to leave their village at a faster rate than those in the treatment group. But what about those 30 people in the treatment group who left? Mortality can be a serious problem in natural experiments if it gets to be a large fraction of the group(s) under study.

7. Diffusion of Treatments. The *diffusion confound* occurs when a control group can not be prevented from receiving the treatment in an experiment. This is particularly likely in quasi-experiments where the independent variable is an information program.

In a recent project with which I was associated, a group of black people were given instruction on modifying their diet and exercise behavior. The object was for them to lower their blood pressure. Another group was randomly assigned from the population to act as controls—that is, they would not receive instruction. The evaluation team measured blood pressure in the treatment group and in the control group before the program was implemented. But when they went back after the program was completed, they found that control group members had also been changing their behavior. People in the control group had learned of the new diet and exercises from the members of the treatment group.

Thought Experiments

As you can see, it is next to impossible to eliminate threats to validity in natural experiments. However, there is a way to understand those threats and to keep them as low as possible: Think about research questions as if it were possible to test them in *true* experiments. These are called "thought experiments."

Suppose your research question were whether small farms are more productive than large farms for agricultural development in the Third World. Suppose further that you could conduct a true experiment on this topic. What would that experiment look like? You might select some countries with similar populations and economies and have some of them use small farms while others used big farms for purposes of development. Then, after a while, you'd measure some things about the countries' development and see which of them did better.

How could you be sure that small farms or big farms made any difference? Perhaps you'd need to control for population density, or for number of years under colonial rule, or per capita income. Obviously, you can't do a true experiment on this topic, randomly assigning countries to a large-farm or small-farm "treatment." But you *can* consider postcolonial Third World countries that rely primarily on large farms as a control group and those that are instituting new small-farm programs as a "treatment" group.

Or suppose you want to investigate whether warfare leads to female infanticide. It is obvious what kind of macabre experiment you'd have to set up. Nevertheless, do the thought experiment (and rest assured that no ethical issues are at stake in thinking!). What experimental conditions would be required for you to be sure that both infanticide *and* warfare were not caused by some third factor, like high population densities and low levels of environmental resources?

When you've itemized the possible threats to validity in your experiment, go out and look for natural experiments (societies) in the world that conform most closely to your ideal experiment. Then evaluate those natural experiments.

Controlling for Threats to Validity

In what follows, I want to show you how the power of experimental logic can be applied to many fieldwork problems, even if random assignment is out of the question. We begin with the design that does the best job of controlling for all threats to validity in true experiments. It is called the *Solomon Four-Group Design*, shown in Figure 3.1(a). In that figure, *R* means that participants in the experiment are assigned randomly to one of four groups. The letter *O* refers to an observation of some dependent variable(s), and *X* signifies some intervention, stimulus, or treatment in a group.

	Time 1		Time 2	
	Assignment	Pretest	Intervention	Posttest
3.1(a) The Solomon Four-Group Design				
Group 1	R	O_1	X	O_2
Group 2	R	O_3		O_4
Group 3	R			
Group 4	R			
3.1(b) The Campbell and Stanley Posttest Only Design				
Group 1	R		X	O_1
Group 2	R			O_2
3.1(c) The One-Shot Case Study Design				
			X	O
3.1(d) The Two-Group Posttest Only Design				
			X	O_1
				O_2
3.1(e) The One-Group Pretest-Posttest Design				
		O_1	X	O_2
3.1(f) The Static Group Comparison Design				
		O_1	X	O_2
		O_3		O_4

Figure 3.1. Some research designs.

From a population of potential participants, some people have been assigned randomly to the four groups represented by the rows of Figure 3.1. Read across the top row of the figure. An observation (measurement) of some dependent variable(s) is made at time 1 on group 1. That is O_1. Then an intervention is made (the group is exposed to some treatment) and another observation is made at time 2 (O_2).

Now look at the second row of the figure. A second group of people are observed, also at time 1. Measurements are made of the same dependent variable(s) that were made for the first group. The observation is labeled O_3, but it takes place at the same time as O_1. No intervention is made on this group of people. They remain unexposed to the independent variable in the experiment. Later, at time 2, after the first group has been exposed to the intervention, the second group is observed again (O_4).

Random assignment of participants ensures equivalent groups, and the second group, without the intervention, ensures that several threats to internal validity are taken care of. Most importantly, you can tell whether any differences between the pretest and posttest scores for the first group would have happened anyway, even if the intervention hadn't taken place.

The addition of the third and fourth groups attacks other validity problems. Very importantly, it controls for testing biases. Maybe the differences between variable measurements at times 1 and 2 are just the result of people getting savvy about being watched and measured. Since there are no measurements at time 1 for groups 3 and 4, this problem is controlled for.

The Posttest Only Design

Look at Figure 3.1(b). It is the second half of the Solomon four-group design and is called the *posttest-only* design. It retains the random assignment of participants in the Solomon four-group design, but eliminates the pretesting. Except for the fact that researchers like to do it (because they feel like they're more in control), there really is no need for pretesting at all, *so long as participants in the experiment are assigned randomly to the groups*. With random assignment, the assumptions of the statistical tests that are generally used in the evaluation of experiments are satisfied, so pretesting is unnecessary (Cook & Campbell, 1979).

The Experimental Model and Anthropology

Now, of course, random assignment is just not possible in anthropological fieldwork where we are evaluating the outcomes of natural experiments. The experimental designs generally used in anthropology are known as the *one-shot case study* (also known as the *one-group posttest only* design), the *one-group pretest-posttest* design, and the *untreated control group* design (also called *static-group comparison*).

The One-Shot Case Study, or One-Group Posttest Only Design

The *one-shot case study* design is shown in Figure 3.1(c). Here, a single group of individuals is measured on some dependent variable *after* an intervention has taken place. This is the design used in many culture change studies. An anthropologist arrives in a community and notices that something important has taken place. Tourism has begun to be exploited, or independence from colonial rule has been achieved. The researcher tries to evaluate the experiment by interviewing people (O) and trying to assess the impact of the intervention (X). The problem, of course, is that you can't be sure that what you observe is the result of some particular intervention.

In the 1950s, physicians began general use of the Pap Test, a simple procedure for determining the presence of cervical cancer. Following the introduction of the Pap Test, measurements were made for several years to see if there was any effect. Sure enough, cervical cancer rates dropped and dropped. Later, it was noticed that cervical cancer rates had been dropping steadily since the 1930s. Of course, early detection of any cancer is important in fighting the disease. But the data from the 1930s and 1940s show that, initially at least, the Pap Test was not responsible for lower rates of cervical cancer (Williams, 1978:16).

Moral: Never use a design of less logical power when one of greater power is feasible. Though pretest data were available, researchers treated the situation as if it were a one-shot case study. On the other hand, a one-shot case study is often the best you can do (virtually all ethnography falls in this category), and as I have said before, there is nothing that beats a good story, well told.

The Two-Group Posttest Only Design

This design, 3.1(d), improves on 3.1(c) by adding an independent case that is evaluated at time 2. Consider two villages in the same cultural region; one village has experienced a major intervention (tourism, a factory, an irrigation system) while the other village has not. You measure a series of variables (income, attitudes toward the national government, the amount of time women spend in child-rearing activities) in both villages. These are O_1 and O_2.

If the differences between O_1 and O_2 are small, you can't tell if the intervention, X, caused those differences. This design is quite convincing, though, when the differences between O_1 and O_2 are large and where you have lots of participant observation data to back up the claim that the intervention is responsible for those differences.

The One-Group Pretest-Posttest Design

The one-group pretest-posttest design is shown in Figure 3.1(e). Some variables are measured (observed), then the intervention takes place, and then the variables are measured again. This takes care of some of the problems associated with the one-shot case study, but it doesn't eliminate the threats of history, testing, maturation, selection, and mortality. Most importantly, if there is a significant difference in the pretest and posttest measurements, we can't tell if the intervention made that difference happen.

The Untreated Control Group,
or Static Group Comparison Design

To take care of this problem, a control group is added in the *untreated control group*, or *static-group comparison* design. This is represented in Figure 3.1(f). This design looks a bit like the posttest-only control group design, with pretesting added. The difference, however, is much greater than that, and very important for anthropology.

In the posttest-only design, participants are assigned at random to either the intervention or control group. In the static group comparison design, the researcher has no control over assignment of participants. This leaves the static-group comparison design open to an unresolvable validity threat. There is no way to tell whether the two groups were comparable at time 1, before the intervention, even with a comparison of observations 1 and 3. Therefore, you can only guess whether the intervention caused any differences in the groups at time 2.

Despite this, the static-group comparison design is the best one for evaluating natural experiments, where you have no control over the assignment of participants anyway. You can compare the dependent variables (longevity, number of Western material artifacts found in someone's home, use of alcohol, consumption of beef, income, morbidity, average age at menarche, or whatever) in both groups at time 1 to see whether the groups are comparable. This is the comparison of observations 1 and 3.

You can also compare observations 1 and 2 to see if there is a difference in the dependent variables after the intervention. You can compare observations 3 and 4 against observations 1 and 2. If the intervention made a difference, then there should be a greater difference between 1 and 2 than between 3 and 4.

Because of all these analytic possibilities, it is better to split your time in any culture change study and do two static-group comparison studies than to spend all your time on a one-shot case study, or even on a one-group pretest-posttest study. You may not get the logical power of the posttest-only design (with its random assignment), but you'll come a lot closer than if you study one group, no matter how in-depth your study is.

Lambros Comitas and I wanted to find out if the experience abroad of Greek labor migrants had any influence on men's and women's attitudes toward gender roles when they returned to Greece. The best design would have been to survey a group before they went abroad, then again while they were away, and again when they returned to Greece. Since this was not possible, we chose two samples, each half the size of the sample we could afford to study. One group consisted of persons who had been abroad, and the other consisted of persons who had never left Greece. We treated these two groups as if they were part of a static-group comparison design (Bernard & Comitas, 1978).

From a series of life histories with migrants and nonmigrants, we learned that the custom of giving dowry was under stress (Bernard & Ashton-Vouyoucalos, 1976). Our survey confirmed this: Those who had worked abroad were far less enthusiastic about providing expensive dowries for their daughters than were those who had never left Greece. We concluded that this was in some measure due to the experiences of migrants in West Germany.

Of course, there were threats to the validity of this conclusion: Perhaps migrants were a self-selected bunch of people who held the dowry and other traditional Greek customs in low esteem to begin with. But we had those life histories to back up our conclusion. Surveys are weak compared to true experiments, but their power is improved if they are conceptualized in terms of testing natural experiments and if their results are backed up with ethnographic data.

4

Sampling

In this chapter I deal with the following questions:

Why are samples taken?
What kinds of samples are there?
How big should a sample be?

Along the way, I will offer examples of how anthropologists can take good samples under fieldwork conditions.

Why Are Samples Taken?

Scientific samples are *not* needed in research where the subject of inquiry is homogeneous. A vial of blood from your arm is as good a sample as a vial from your leg if you want to measure your cholesterol level. And there is no need for scientific sampling in phenomenological research, where the object is to understand the meaning of expressive behavior or to understand how things work.

But if you are studying variables in a population of diverse elements, then a scientifically drawn sample is a must. Whether the population consists of all 1,800 people in a village, or all the thousands of property exchange agreements in a courthouse, it takes less time and less money to study a sample of them than it does to study all of them. Since most anthropological fieldwork is done by a single researcher on a tight budget, sampling is generally an economic necessity for scientific research.

If samples were just easier and cheaper to study but failed to produce useful data, there wouldn't be much to say for them. A study based on a representative sample, however, is often *better* than one based on the whole population. That is, sample data may have greater *internal validity* than data from the whole population.

The U.S. Constitution requires that the government conduct a count of the population every 10 years. In 1980, the Bureau of the Census failed to count at least 4 million people, mostly African-Americans and Hispanics. The bureau suggested adjusting the census figures with data from samples. The samples, they said, would make the counts more accurate.

It's next to impossible to interview more than a few hundred people in any field study if you're trying to do all the work yourself. Even in a community of just 1,000 households, you'd need several interviewers to reach everyone. Interviewers may not use the same wording of questions; they may not probe equally well on subjects that require sensitive interviewing; they may not be equally careful in recording data on field instruments and in coding data for analysis. The more personnel there are on any project, the greater the instrumentation threat and the more risk to the validity of the data.

Most importantly, you have no idea how *much* error is introduced by these problems. If a well-chosen sample of people are interviewed by researchers who have similarly high skills in getting data, there is a known chance of being incorrect on the estimate for any variable. We often hear the results of opinion polls reported as having "a margin of error of plus or minus 3 points," for example. (Careful, though: If you have a project that requires multiple interviewers and you try to skimp on personnel, you run a big risk. Overworked or poorly trained interviewers will cut corners; see Chapter 12.) Furthermore, studying an entire population may pose a "history threat" to the internal validity of your data. If you *don't* add interviewers, you may take so long to complete your research that events intervene that make it impossible to interpret your data.

Suppose you are interested in how a community of Hopi people feel about certain aspects of the relocation agreement being forged in their dispute with the Navaho. You decide to interview *all* 210 adults in the community. It's difficult to get some people at home, but you figure that you'll just do the survey, a little at a time, while you're doing other things during your year in the field.

About 6 months into your fieldwork, you've gotten 160 interviews on the topic—only 50 to go. Just about that time, the courts adjudicate a particularly sore point that has been in dispute for a decade regarding access to a particular sacred site. All of a sudden, the picture changes. Your "sample" of 160 is biased toward those people whom it was easy to find, and you have no idea what *that* means. And even if you could now get those remaining 50 informants, their opinions may have been radically changed by the court judgment. The opinions of the 160 informants who already talked to you may have also changed.

Now you're really stuck. You can't simply throw together the 50 and the 160, because you have no idea what that will do to your results. Nor can you compare the 160 and the 50 as representing the community's attitudes before and after the judgment. Neither sample is representative of the community.

If you had taken a representative sample of 52 people in a single week early in your fieldwork, you'd now be in much better shape because you'd know the potential sampling error in your study. (I'll discuss how you know this later on in this chapter.) When historical circumstances (the surprise court judgment, for example) require it, you could interview the same sample of 52 again (in what is known as a *panel study*), or take another representative sample of the same size and see what differences there are before and after the critical event. In either case, *you are better off with the sample than with the whole population*. By the way, there is no guarantee that a week is quick enough to avoid the problem described here. It's just less likely to be a problem.

What Kinds of Samples Are There?

There are seven major kinds of samples. Three of them—simple random, stratified random, and cluster samples—are based on the principles of probability theory. The other four—quota, purposive, snowball, and haphazard samples—are not. Probability samples are *representative* of larger populations, and they increase external validity in any study. The general rule is this: Use representative, probability sampling whenever you can and use nonprobability sampling methods as a last resort.

Probability Samples

Probability samples are based on taking a given number of units of analysis from a list, or *sampling frame*, which represents some *population* under study. In a probability or representative sample, each individual must have exactly the same chance as every other individual of being selected.

There are two ways to make a sample more representative of a population: (a) Make sure that every element has an equal chance of winding up in the sample, and (b) increase the sample size.

The first way is by far the more important. In 1970, while the United States was engaged in an unpopular war in Vietnam, men were selected by supposedly random draw for the draft. Three hundred and sixty-six capsules (one for each day of the year, including leap year) were put in a drum, and the drum was turned to mix the capsules. Then dates were pulled from the drum, one at a time. All the men whose birthdays fell on the days that were selected were drafted.

When enough men had been selected to fill the year's quota, the lottery stopped. Men whose birthdays hadn't been pulled were safe for the year. It turned out that men whose birthdays were in the later months had a better chance of being drafted than men whose birthdays were earlier in the year. This happened because the drum wasn't rotated enough to thoroughly mix the capsules (Williams, 1978). Not a good technique.

How Big Should a Sample Be?

The proper size of a sample depends on many things: (a) the heterogeneity of the population or chunks of population (strata or clusters) from which you choose the elements; (b) how many population subgroups you want to deal with simultaneously in your analysis; (c) how accurate you want your sample statistics (or parameter estimators) to be; (d) the size of the phenomenon that you're trying to detect; and (e) how much money and time you have.

It will take the rest of this chapter to deal with the first four of these. Let's get the practical issue of money out of the way first because, frankly, everything depends on it.

There is always going to be a trade-off between greater accuracy and greater economy in sampling. In a study of households in a county, you *should* take a few households from each community (cluster), rather than study many households in a few randomly chosen communities. The problem is that this may force you to spend more in both time and money on travel than your budget will allow. So the rule actually becomes: Study all the highest-level clusters that you can afford.

This tension between economy and accuracy in sampling is especially acute in anthropological research, where the investigator often has to collect the data personally, or with the help of a very few local assistants, usually on a budget of a few thousand dollars. The practical limit for samples where you collect the data yourself is around 400 elements, whether you are doing an attitude survey, or a survey of material household wealth, or a behavioral survey (as in studies of health care, nutrition, or agricultural practices).

Fortunately, this is adequate for samples of most populations that anthropologists study and for many questions that anthropologists ask of their data. In the next two sections I'll explain why.

Sampling Theory

Suppose you want to know the average height of men in a community. You could measure them all and divide by the number of men, or you could take a sample, measure *them*, and divide by the number in the sample. The average height for the sample is the *sample statistic*. It is an *estimate* of the true average height—the *parameter*—of all the men in the community. We observe samples, calculate statistics, and estimate parameters. The trick is to get a precise idea of the likelihood that the sample statistic is correct and how far off the mark it's likely to be. That's what sampling theory is about.

Consider a population of just five households, shown in Table 4.1. Household #1 has 5 people; #2 has 6 people; #3 has 4 people; #4 has 8 people; and #5 has 5 people. There are 28 people all together in the five households, with a mean of 5.6 per household.

If you took a sample of one household, you might get a sample statistic of 4 or a statistic of 8 for this population of households. How about a sample of 2? Well, there are 10 unique samples of 2 in a population of 5 elements. Here they are:

The mean of the means for all 10 samples (that is, the mean of the *sampling distribution*) is 5.6. The data on the five households in Table 4.1 show that this is also the actual mean of the variable in the population.

The standard deviation is a measure of how much the scores in a distribution vary from the mean score. The larger the standard deviation, the more dispersion. (If you are unfamiliar with the concept of standard

TABLE 4.1

All the Samples of 2 in a Population of 5 Households

Sample	Mean	Household	Size
1 & 2	$5 + 6 \div 2 = 5.5$	1	5
1 & 3	$5 + 4 \div 2 = 4.5$	2	6
1 & 4	$5 + 8 \div 2 = 6.5$	3	4
1 & 5	$5 + 5 \div 2 = 5.0$	4	8
2 & 3	$6 + 4 \div 2 = 5.0$	5	5
2 & 4	$6 + 8 \div 2 = 7.0$		$28 \div 5 = 5.6$
2 & 5	$6 + 5 \div 2 = 5.5$		
3 & 4	$4 + 8 \div 2 = 6.0$		
3 & 5	$4 + 5 \div 2 = 4.5$		
4 & 5	$8 + 5 \div 2 = 6.5$		
	$56 \div 10 = 5.6$		

deviation, it is described in detail in Chapter 18.) The standard deviation of the mean of the sampling distribution is the *standard error* of the mean. This is shown in Table 4.2.

In our example, the sample mean is 5.6 and the standard deviation, or standard error, is .83. About 68% of the time, sample means will fall within one standard deviation of the true mean for a variable; 95% of the time they will fall within two standard deviations; and virtually all sample

TABLE 4.2

Standard Deviation of the Sampling Distribution in Table 4.1

Sample	Sample Mean	(Sample Mean − Actual Mean)^2
1 & 2	5.5	$(5.5 - 5.6)^2 = .01$
1 & 3	4.5	$(4.5 - 5.6)^2 = 1.21$
1 & 4	6.5	$(6.5 - 5.6)^2 = .81$
1 & 5	5.0	$(5.0 - 5.6)^2 = .36$
2 & 3	5.0	$(5.0 - 5.6)^2 = .36$
2 & 4	7.0	$(7.0 - 5.6)^2 = 1.96$
2 & 5	5.5	$(5.5 - 5.6)^2 = .01$
3 & 4	6.0	$(6.0 - 5.6)^2 = .16$
3 & 5	4.5	$(4.5 - 5.6)^2 = 1.21$
4 & 5	6.5	$(6.5 - 5.6)^2 = .81$
		6.90

$$\text{Standard Deviation of the Mean of the Sampling Distribution} = \sqrt{\frac{6.9}{10}} = .83$$

means (99.7%) will fall within three standard deviations of the parameter. In our example, two standard errors is

$$.83 \times 2 = 1.66$$

so, we can be 95% confident that the true value for the variable in which we are interested lies between

$$5.6 + 1.66 = 7.26$$

and

$$5.6 - 1.66 = 3.94$$

Unfortunately, the actual range of possible means in our example was only 4.5-7.0. In a small population, a small sample doesn't tell us very much about the true means.

Furthermore, in this last exercise I *gave* you the actual mean of the population. In real research, that's what you want to estimate, and you won't have the luxury of taking 100 samples to get the mean of the sampling distribution either. You'll get one shot at estimating parameters. That's why sample size is so critical.

Assuming that you maximize the representativeness of samples, sample size determines (a) the risk you take of your sample statistics being incorrect—that is, its *probability value*, and (b) *how* incorrect a sample statistic might be—that is, its *confidence interval*. If you have a sample statistic that is significant at the .05 level (which we'll discuss in Chapter 19), with a 3% confidence interval, that means that 95% of the time (1.0 − .05) your statistic for a variable would be correct to within 3%, plus or minus, of the true value of the variable in the population.

Sample Size Is More or Less Independent of Population Size

Here is a formula for determining sample size (Krejcie & Morgan, 1970). It contains a built-in correction for taking samples from small populations—the kind that anthropologists usually work with.

$$\text{Sample size} = \frac{\chi^2 NP(1-P)}{C^2(N-1) + \chi^2 P(1-P)}$$

where χ^2 is the chi-square value for 1 degree of freedom at some desired probability level; N is the population size (which gets more important as N gets smaller); P is the population parameter of a variable; and C is the confidence interval you choose. (Chi-square is described in Chapter 19. The concept of degrees of freedom is described in Chapter 18 in the section on t-tests.)

Since P is what we want to estimate with a sample, we will always set P to 0.5 in this formula. In a perfectly homogeneous population (where $P = 0\%$ or $P = 100\%$), a sample of one element gives you a probability of 1 of being correct in your estimation of the parameter for a variable (since the "variable" doesn't vary at all). As any population becomes maximally heterogeneous (as P approaches 0.5) the sample size must increase in order to maintain any given confidence interval and probability level of being on the mark.

The assumption that $P = 0.5$ in the formula is therefore the worst possible case; by setting P to 0.5 you will always err on the safe side in determining the appropriate size of your sample.

Let's take an example. You are sampling a Mexican village of 540 resident adult men to determine how many have ever worked illegally in the United States. How many of those men do you need to interview to ensure a 95% probability sample, with a 5% confidence interval? The chi-square value for 1 degree of freedom at the .05 level of probability (95%) is 3.841 (see Chapter 19). The sample size required, then, is

$$(3.841)(540)(.5)(.5)/[(.05)^2(539) + (3.841)(.5)(.5)] = 225$$

For a small population like this one, we need a pretty large percentage of the group ($225/540 = 42\%$) to ensure a 95% probability sample, with a 5% confidence interval—that is, to be 95% confident that the true proportion of illegal migrants in the village lies within 5% of our sample mean.

If we were willing to settle for a 10% confidence interval, we'd need only 82 people in our sample, but the trade-off would be substantial. If 65 out of 225, or 29%, reported that they had worked in the United States, we would be 68% confident that from 24% to 34% really did, and 95% confident that 19% to 39% did. But if 24 out of 82 (the same 29%) reported having worked in the United States as labor migrants, we'd be just 68% sure that the true figure was between 19% and 39%, and 95% confident that it was between 9% and 39%. With a possible spread like that, you wouldn't want to bet much on the sample statistic of 29%.

If it weren't for ethnography, this would be a major problem in taking samples from small populations—the kind we often study in anthropology. If you've been doing ethnography in a community of 1,500 people for 6 months,

TABLE 4.3

Size of the Sample Required for Various Population Sizes
at 5% Confidence Interval

Population Size	Sample Size
50	44
100	80
150	108
200	132
250	152
300	169
400	196
500	217
800	260
1,000	278
1,500	306
2,000	322
3,000	341
4,000	351
5,000	357
10,000	370
50,000	381
1,000,000	384

SOURCE: Krejcie and Morgan (1970), reproduced with permission.

however, you may feel comfortable taking a confidence interval of 10% because you are personally (not statistically) confident that your intuition about the group will help you interpret the results of a small sample.

Table 4.3 shows the results of applying the chi-square-adjusted formula to various size populations for 5% confidence intervals. By the time the population reaches 400, the sample size is down to 196 (less than half). At 1,000, it's 278 (about 28%); at 2,000, it's 322 (16%). At 5,000, it's only 357 (7%), and then it levels off rather dramatically. Sample size, in fact, is almost independent of population size once populations exceed about 100,000.

Thus, only 384 elements are required to estimate, with 95% probability and a confidence interval of 5%, the proportion of a dichotomous (yes-no) variable in a population of a million. This is why a sample of 400 is such a good bet.

The Catch

The catch is, you won't want to measure just dichotomous variables, but complex things like indexes of acculturation. You may want to test for the *interaction* among variables, or you may want to test for the presence of small differences between populations. Suppose you suspect that blacks and whites in a prison system receive different sentences for the same crime. Henry (1990:121) shows that a difference of 16 months in sentence length for the same crime would be detected with a sample of just 30 in each racial group (if the members of the sample were selected randomly, of course). To detect a difference of 3 months, however, you need 775 in each group.

The sample size produced by the formula above is thus a *minimum*. Sampling is one of the trickiest parts of social research. I recommend strongly that you consult an expert in sampling if you are going to do complex tests on your data. (For excellent coverage of all the basics in sampling theory and sample design, see Sudman, 1976, and Jaeger, 1984.)

The Bottom Line

The bottom line on sample size for most fieldwork situations is this: (a) In a large population (anything over 5,000), a representative sample of 400 will be sufficient for estimating proportions or means (like what percent of the men in that Mexican village have worked illegally in the United States, given a 5% confidence interval). (b) In order to halve the confidence interval you have to quadruple the sample size. (c) Don't worry about how big a percentage your sample is of a population; worry about taking good (representative) samples.

Sampling Frames—Always Get or Take a Census

The first thing you need for a good sample is a sampling frame. It may be a telephone directory, or the tax rolls of a community, or a census of a village that you did yourself. In the United States, the city directories (published by R. L. Polk and Company) are often adequate sampling frames. The directories are available for many small towns at the local library or Chamber of Commerce. Professional survey researchers in the United States often purchase samples from firms that keep up-to-date databases just for this purpose.

In most fieldwork situations, however, sampling frames are not so easy to come by. One of the first things any field worker should do in studying a small community (up to about 3,000 people, for practical reasons) is take a census, even if a recent one already exists.

A census gives you the opportunity to walk around a community and to talk with most of the members at least once. It lets you be seen by others, and it gives you an opportunity to answer questions, as well as to ask them. It allows you to get information that official censuses don't retrieve (migration history, for example, or household material inventory). Most importantly, it gives you a sampling frame from which to take samples throughout your research in the field and it gives you baseline data for comparison when you go back to the same community years later.

Simple Random Samples

To achieve a simple random sample of 200 out of 640 adults in a village, you number everyone from 1,640 and then take a random grab of 200 out of the numbers from 1 to 640. You can do this with a table of random numbers, like the one in Appendix A, taken from the Rand Corporation's volume called *A Million Random Digits with 100,000 Normal Deviates* (1965). The book has no plot or characters, just a million random numbers—a few of which have been reprinted in Appendix A. You can use Appendix A in the field for most projects you'll ever do.

Just enter the table anywhere. Since the numbers are random, it makes no difference where you start. (Of course, if you always enter the table at the same spot, the numbers cease to be random! But I'll assume that you always enter the table more or less haphazardly, which is good enough.) Read down a column or across a row. The numbers are in groups of five, in case you ever want to take samples up to 99,999 units. If you are sampling fewer than 10 units in a population, then look just at the first digit in each group. If you are sampling from 1 to 99 units, then look just at the first two digits, and so on.

Throw out any numbers that are too big for your sample. Say you are taking 300 sample minutes from a population of 5,040 daylight minutes in a week during November in Atlanta. (You might do this if you were trying to describe what a family did during that week.) Any three-digit number larger than 300 is automatically ignored. Just go on to the next number in the table. Ignore duplicate numbers, too.

If you go through the table once (down all the columns) and still don't have enough numbers for your sample, then go through it again, starting with the second digit in each group, and then the third. If you began by taking numbers in the columns, take them from rows. You probably won't run out of random numbers for rough-and-ready fieldwork samples if you use Appendix A for the rest of your life. (If you have a microcomputer with you in the field, you can use programs like MYSTAT or KWIKSTAT to generate lists of random numbers. Details on how to get these programs are in Appendix G.)

When you have your list of random numbers, then whoever goes with each one is in the sample. Period. If there are 1,230 people in the population, and your list of random numbers says that you have to interview person #212, then do it. No fair leaving out some people because they are members of the elite and probably wouldn't want to give you the time of day, or leaving out the town drunk because you don't want to have to deal with him if he turns up in your sample. None of that. Tampering with a random sample because you think you have good reason to do so is pernicious, so don't do it—at least not unless you're willing to say exactly how you tampered with it when you publish your results.

In the real world of research, of course, random samples are tampered with all the time. The most common form of meddling is when interviewers find a sample selectee is not at home and they go to the nearest house for a replacement. This can have dramatically bad results. Suppose you go out to interview between 10 a.m. and 4 p.m. People who are home between 10 a.m. and 4 p.m. are more likely to be elderly or sick or mothers with several small children. Of course, those same people are home in the evening, too, but then they're joined by all the single people back from work, so the *average family size* goes down after 6 p.m. If you don't go back at night to find respondents who were absent during the day, you'll conclude that average family size is larger than it really is.

Any expedient tampering with a random sample should be noted at every turn and mentioned in methodological footnotes in your publications. A random sample is only representative of a population if you don't tinker with it. If you suspect that, say, 25% of your sample won't be reachable, then increase your sample size by 25% from the beginning so the final sample will be both the right size and representative. And report this ploy, too.

Systematic Random Sampling

Most people don't actually do *simple* random sampling these days; instead they do something very closely related, called *systematic* random sampling because it is much, much easier and more economical to do. If you are dealing with an unnumbered sampling frame of 36,240 (the current student population at the University of Florida), then simple random sampling is nearly impossible. You would have to number all those names first. In doing systematic random sampling, you need a random start and a *sampling interval*, N. You enter the sampling frame at a randomly selected spot (using Appendix A again) and take every Nth person (or item) in the frame.

In choosing a random start, you only need to find one random number in your sampling frame. This is usually easy to do. If you are dealing with 36,240 names, listed on a computer printout, at 400 to a page, then number 9,457 is 257 names down from the top of page 24.

The sampling interval depends on the size of the population and the number of units in your sample. If there are 10,000 people in the population, and you are sampling 400 of them, then after you enter the sampling frame (the list of 10,000 names) you need to take every 25th person (400 × 25 = 10,000) to ensure that every person has at least one chance of being chosen. If there are 640 people in a population, and you are sampling 200 of them, then you would take every 4th person. If you get to the end of the list and you are at number 2 in an interval of 4, just go to the top of the list, start at 3, and keep on going.

Periodicity and Systematic Sampling

Whenever you do systematic random sampling, you need to be aware of the *periodicity* problem. Suppose you're studying a big retirement community in South Florida. The development has 30 identical buildings. Each has six floors, with 10 apartments on each floor, for a total of 1,800 apartments. Now suppose that each floor has one big corner apartment that costs more than the others and attracts a slightly more affluent group of buyers. If you do a systematic sample of every 10th apartment, then, depending on where you entered the list of apartments, you'd have a sample of 180 corner apartments or no corner apartments at all.

David and Mary Hatch (1947) studied the Sunday society pages of the *New York Times* for the years 1932 to 1942. They found only stories about weddings of Protestants and concluded that the elite of New York must therefore be Protestant. Cahnman (1948) pointed out that the Hatches had studied only June issues of the *Times*. It seemed reasonable. After all, aren't most society weddings in June? Well, yes. Protestant weddings. Upper-class Jews married in other months, and the *Times* covered those weddings.

Sampling frames with periodicity problems may be rare, but how do you know yours isn't one of them? It takes a lot of luck just to see some of these hidden periodic features and a lot more trouble to work out a systematic sampling device that doesn't fall into the periodicity trap. You can avoid these hidden problems by doing simple random sampling.

Another solution is to make two systematic passes through the population using different sampling intervals, and then compare the two samples. Any differences should be easily attributable to sampling error.

Sampling from a Telephone Book

All this is fine if you know that the sampling frame has 36,240 elements. What do you do when the size of the sampling frame is unknown? If you are using a big telephone book (an unnumbered sampling frame of unknown size), first calculate the number of pages that actually contain listings. To do this, jot down the number of the first and last pages on which listings appear. (Most phone books begin with a lot of pages that do not contain listings.) Suppose the listings begin on page 30 and end on page 520. Subtract 30 from 520 and add 1 (520 − 30 + 1 = 491) to calculate the number of pages that carry listings.

Then note the number of columns per page and the number of lines per column (count all the lines in a column, even the blank ones). Suppose the phone book has three columns and 96 lines per column (this is quite typical).

To take a random sample of 200 nonbusiness listings from this phone book, take a random sample of 300 page numbers (yes, 300) out of the 491 page numbers between 30 and 520. Just think of the pages as a numbered sampling frame of 491 elements. Next, take a sample of 300 column numbers. Since there are three columns, you want 300 random choices of the numbers 1,2,3. Finally, take a sample of 300 line numbers. Since there are 96 lines, you want 300 random numbers between 1 and 96.

Match up the three sets of numbers and pick the sample of listings in the phone book. If the first random number between 30 and 491 is 116, go to page 116. If the first random number between 1 and 3 is 3, go to column 3. If the first random number between 1 and 96 is 43, count down 43 lines. Decide if the listing is eligible. It may be a blank line or a business. That's why you generate 300 sets of numbers to get 200 good listings.

Stratified Sampling

Stratified sampling is done whenever it is likely that an important subpopulation will be underrepresented in a simple random sample. Suppose you are doing a study of factors affecting grade-point averages among college students. You suspect that the independent variable called "race" has some effect on the dependent variable.

Suppose further that just 10% of the student population is African-American and that you have time and money to interview 400 students out of a population of 8,000. If you took 10,000 samples of 400 each from the population (replacing the 400 each time, of course), then the average number of African-Americans in all the samples would approach 40—that is, 10% of the sample.

But you are going to take *one* sample of 400, and there is a substantial probability that *that* particular sample will contain only 10 African-Americans. Given this, it is difficult to trust a simple random sample. Instead, you put the African-Americans into separate *stratum*, or subpopulation, before you draw the sample. Then you draw two random samples, one of 360 from the white population, and one of 40 from the African-American population. That way, the strata are represented in the sample in the same proportion as they are in the population under study.

Stratifying a population is very attractive because the items in each subframe are more like each other than they are like the items in other subframes. As the subframes get smaller and smaller, the items in those subframes get more and more homogeneous and the difference between the subframes gets greater and greater. This is called maximizing the *between-group variance* and minimizing the *within-group variance* for the independent variables in a study. It's what you want to do in building a sample. But there are costs.

Disadvantages of Stratified Sampling

Despite its attractiveness, there are four problems associated with stratifying samples.

1. To stratify a sample you must *know* the relevant independent variables on which to stratify. What if you are wrong in your assumption that "race" is related to grade-point averages? Separating the population into racial strata would not just be silly, it would introduce error of an unknown kind into the sample.

Remember this rule: Unless you are certain about the independent variables that could be at work in affecting your dependent variable, leave well enough alone and don't stratify.

2. Even if you are correct about the independent variable (or variables), you must know the proportions of the variable(s) in the population to replicate the distribution fairly in the sample. Of course, if your sampling

frame is a list of students (or whatever), with lots of information already included (race, religion, family income, gender, etc.), you can simply count the occurrences of the independent variable. In anthropological research you don't often have this luxury.

So, remember this rule also: If you think you know the independent variables that make a difference in your dependent variable, but you can't be sure of their proportionate distribution in the population, then leave well enough alone and do a simple random or systematic random sample.

3. For anthropologists, stratifying takes time (and often money) to do properly. There are cases where sampling frames are available and where all the strata in which you are interested are broken out, but those cases are rare. In fieldwork, *you* will probably have to do the stratifying. You'll have to develop a master sampling frame, identify the variables, and mark each element in the master frame that exhibits each variable on which you want to stratify.

4. Finally, each stratum is subject to its own sampling error. In an African village, you may have Christians, Muslims, and animists. If you want to compare these groups, as well as males and females, then you've got six strata (Muslim males, Muslim females, Christian males, etc.). If your resources let you study 400 people, then each stratum will contain just 67 elements. With 67 elements, you risk getting an unrepresentative sample of any particular stratum.

Disproportionate Sampling

There are times when you *must* stratify a population to guarantee that subpopulations of interest will be represented in your study. The strata in a stratified sample should be the same size to maximize the reduction of sampling error. Quite often, though, the strata of interest are only 10% of the population, or even less. In this event, many researchers prefer to do *disproportionate* stratified sampling.

Suppose you have a tribal group of 800 Xingu Amazon Indians, of whom 20 are known shamans. You decide to watch a sample of the group and study their subsistence behavior, and you are particularly interested in the difference between shamans and others. Your ethnographic efforts lead you to believe that there is very low variability in subsistence behavior among the nonshaman population, so that a sample of only 63 will be sufficient. Your ethnography, in other words, makes you satisfied with an overall probability of 68% and a confidence interval of 10% on most variables.

The chance, however, of your choosing *one* of the 20 shamans among the 63 elements selected from the population of 800 is just 2.5% (20/800 = 2.5%). Given the purpose of your study, you decide not to risk choosing a random sample of 63 persons, only 3 or 4 of whom are shamans. In this case, it is better to stratify the sample and take 61 nonshamans along with 16 shamans. This is a slight increase in effort (you have increased the sample from 63 to 77), but it results in a massive increase in the usefulness of your sample.

Here's another example. You are studying child rearing in a Malay village of 2,600 people. From your ethnography you have concluded that there are basically three strategies employed by parents: strict, lax, and mixed. That is, some parents are consistently strict in the way they interact with their children; others are rather forgiving; and others exhibit a mixture of both behaviors. We'll assume that you have conceptualized and operationalized these behavioral strategies clearly and can recognize them in each set of parents that you interview.

You suspect that a key independent variable in this study is the number of children above toddler age in the household. You have done a census of the 460 households and are about to choose a sample of 60 of them for your survey (whether by interview or observation or both) of child-rearing practices. Unfortunately, only 50 households (about 11%) have just one child, and in 32 of them the child is less than 3 years of age. You only have 18 households out of 460 (4%) in which there is one child above toddler stage.

If you took those proverbial 10,000 samples of 60 each from the 460 households, then the average number of households with only-children over 3 years of age would be 4% of 60, or about 2.5. You have about a 9% chance, on any draw of 60 elements out of 460, that any stratum of 4% will not be represented at all—that is, there will be zero units of that type in the sample.

Even if random samples always produced true representations of a population, your sample would still have just two families with a single child, where that child is over 3 years of age. That is hardly a sufficient number for you to be able to make any statistical comparisons between families that exhibit the different styles of child rearing that you have identified by ethnography. What to do?

The answer is: Interview 14 of those families, thus creating a disproportionate stratified sample in which 77% of one stratum is observed, while only a fraction of the other strata are selected for observation.

Weighting Results

Later on, in the analysis portion of the research, this decision may have to be dealt with by "weighting" the results when making comparisons among strata. The 14 cases of only-children over 3 years of age comprise 3% of the 460 households in the village, but they are 14/60, or 23% of your sample, or seven times the expected number (3% of 60 = 2) in a perfectly representative random sample.

Now, as long as you are looking at the two subsamples separately or comparing the subsamples against one another, you are all right. If you say "54% of the families with only-children over 3 years of age have combined cash incomes of over $800 per year, while 71% of those families with at least two children under 3 have combined annual cash incomes of less than $400," then there is no problem with the fact that those 14 families with only-children over 3 years of age constitute just 3% of the village households. On the other hand, if you wanted to combine the subsample into one large sample, to compare, say, all men with all women with regard to their attitude on spanking children, then the disproportionate nature of your sample has to be considered.

To do this, *weight* your results: Multiply by 7 all the data from the 446 families that have *not* been disproportionately sampled. That will put into perspective the data from the 14 families that have been sampled at seven times their representation.

This is a case where the probability of selection to a sample is unequal. You should also weight your data when you have unequal response rates in a stratified sample. Suppose you sample 200 farmers and 200 herders in a rural African community. Of the 400 potential informants, 178 farmers and 163 herders respond to your questions. The weight of each farmer's data is 178/163 = 1.09 times the weight of each herder's data. When you do your analysis, multiply the data from farmers by 12 and multiply the data from herders by 11 so that each farmer's case is 1/11th (1.09) times each herder's case.

Weighting is a simple procedure these days with canned statistical analysis packages like SPSS, SAS, and SYSTAT. Before all these programs were available, researchers thought twice about disproportionate sampling because they knew what a nuisance it was going to be during analysis. More researchers choose disproportionate sampling these days just because there is no nuisance penalty for doing so.

As you can see, stratifying samples has its costs as well as its benefits. It is worth repeating that, unless you have a really good reason to do so, don't try to improve on a simple (or systematic) random sample. The example just given of the need for disproportionate sampling is a good reason. Another good reason is that you do not have a sampling frame, a single list, from which to draw a simple random sample. That happens *very* frequently in anthropology, and it brings us to the use of cluster samples and nonrandom samples.

Cluster Sampling and Complex Sampling Designs

Cluster sampling is a way to sample populations for which there are no convenient lists or frames. It's also a way to minimize travel time in reaching scattered units of data collection. Cluster sampling is based on the fact that people act out their lives in more or less natural groups, or "clusters." They live in geographic areas (like counties, precincts, states, and so on), and they participate in the activities of institutions (like schools, churches, brotherhoods, credit unions, etc.). Even if there are no lists of people whom you want to study, you can sample areas or institutions and locate a sample within those clusters.

For example, there are no lists of schoolchildren in large cities, but children cluster in schools. There *are* lists of schools, so you could take a sample of them, and then sample children within each school selected. The idea in cluster sampling is to narrow the sampling field down from large, heterogenous chunks to small, homogeneous ones that are relatively easy to sample directly.

Earlier, I mentioned a study that Lambros Comitas and I did comparing Greeks who had returned from West Germany as labor migrants with Greeks who had never left their country (Bernard & Comitas, 1978). There were no lists of returned migrants, so we decided to locate the children of returned migrants in the Athens schools and use them to select a sample of their parents. The problem was, we couldn't even get a list of schools in Athens.

So we took a map of the city and divided it into small bits by laying a grid over it. Then we took a random sample of the bits and sent interviewers to find the school nearest each bit selected. The interviewers asked the principal of each school to identify the children of returned labor migrants. (It was easy for the principal to do: He said that all the returned migrant children spoke Greek with a German accent.) That way, we were able to make up two lists for each school: one of children who had been abroad, and one of children who had not. By sampling children randomly from those lists at each school, we were able to select a representative sample of parents. This two-stage sampling design combined a cluster sample with a simple random sample to select the eventual units of analysis.

Anthony and Suely Anderson (1983) wanted to compare people in Bacabal County, Brazil, who exploited the babassu palm with those who didn't. There was no list of households, but they did manage to get a list of the 344 named hamlets in the county. They divided the hamlets into those that supplied whole babassu fruits to new industries in the area and those that did not. Only 10.5% of the 344 hamlets supplied fruits to the industries, so the Andersons selected 10 hamlets randomly from each group for their survey. In other words, in the first stage of the process they stratified the clusters and took a disproportionate random sample from one of the clusters.

Next, they did a census of the 20 hamlets, collecting information on every household and particularly whether the household had land or was landless. At this stage, then, they created a sampling frame (the census) and stratified the frame into landowning and landless households. Finally, they selected 89 landless households randomly for interviewing. This was 25% of the stratum of landless peasants. Since there were only 61 landowners, they decided to interview the entire population of this stratum.

Sampling designs can involve several stages. Suppose you want to study Haitian refugee children in Miami. If you take a random sample of schools, you'll probably select some in which there are no Haitian children. A three-stage sampling design is called for. In the first stage, you would make a list of the neighborhoods in the city, find out which ones are home to a lot of refugees from Haiti, and sample those districts. In the second stage, you would take a random sample of schools from each district. Finally, in the third stage of the design, you would develop a list of Haitian refugee children in each school and draw your final sample.

Maximizing Between-Group Variance: The Wichita Study

Whenever you do multistage cluster sampling, be sure to take as large a sample as possible from the largest, most heterogeneous clusters. The larger the cluster, the larger the *between-group variance*; the smaller the cluster, the higher the *within-group variance*. Counties in the United States are more like each other on any variable (income, race, average age, whatever) than states are; towns within a county are more like each other than counties are; neighborhoods in a town are more like each other than towns are; blocks are more like each other than neighborhoods are. In sampling, the rule is: Always maximize between-group variance.

What does this mean in practice? Following is an actual example of multistage sampling from John Hartman's study of Wichita, Kansas (Hartman,

1978; Hartman & Hedblom, 1979:160ff). At the time of the study, in the mid-1970s, Wichita had a population of about 193,000 persons over 16. This was the population to which the study team wanted to generalize. The team decided that they could afford only 500 interviews. There are 82 census tracts in Wichita, from which they randomly selected 20. These 20 tracts then became the actual population of their study. We'll see in a moment how well their actual study population simulated (represented) the study population to which they wanted to generalize.

Hartman and Hedblom added up the total population in the 20 tracts and divided the population of *each tract* by the total. This gave the percentage of people that each tract, or cluster, contributed to the new population total. Since the researchers were going to do 500 interviews, each tract was assigned that percentage of the interviews. If there were 50,000 people in the 20 tracts, and one of the tracts had a population of 5,000, or 10% of the total, then 50 interviews (10% of the 500) would be done in that tract.

Next, the team numbered the blocks in each tract and selected blocks at random until they had enough for the number of interviews that were to be conducted in that tract. When a block was selected it stayed in the pool, so that in some cases more than one interview was to be conducted in a single block. This did not happen very often, and the team wisely left it up to chance to determine it.

This study team made some excellent decisions that maximized the heterogeneity (and hence the representativeness) of their sample. As clusters get smaller and smaller (as you go from tract to block to household, or from village to neighborhood to household), the homogeneity of the units of analysis within the clusters gets greater and greater. People in one census tract or village are more like each other than people in different tracts or villages. People in one census block or barrio are more like each other than people across blocks or barrios. And people in households are more like each other than people in households across the street or over the hill.

This is very important. Most researchers would have no difficulty with the idea that they should only interview one person in a household because, for example, husbands and wives often have similar ideas about things and report similar behavior with regard to kinship, visiting, health care, child care, and consumption of goods and services. Somehow, the lesson becomes less clear when new researchers move into clusters that are larger than households.

But the rule stands: Maximize heterogeneity of the sample by taking as many of the biggest clusters in your sample as you can, as many of the next biggest, and so on, always at the expense of the number of clusters at the bottom where homogeneity is greatest. Take more tracts or villages and fewer blocks per tract or barrios per village. Take more blocks per tract or barrios per village and fewer households per block or barrio. Take more households and fewer persons per household.

Many survey researchers say that, as a rule, you should have no fewer than five households in a census block. This rule is based on the notion that there should be no fewer than five of the smallest clusters before reaching the individual unit of analysis. It is an extension of the principle that no cell in any statistical analysis should have fewer than five things in it. The Wichita group did not follow this rule and they were correct not to. They only had enough money and person power to do 500 interviews and they wanted to maximize the likelihood that their sample would represent faithfully the characteristics of the 193,000 adults in their city.

The Wichita study group did something else that was clever. They drew two samples, one main sample and one alternate sample. Whenever they could not get someone on the main sample, they took the alternate. That way, they maximized the representativeness of their sample because the alternates were chosen with the same randomized procedure as the main respondents in their survey. They were not forced to take next-door neighbors when a main respondent wasn't home. As I noted earlier, that kind of "winging it" in survey research has a tendency to clobber the representativeness of samples. In the United States, at least, interviewing only people who are at home during the day produces data that represent women with small children, shut-ins, and the elderly—and little else.

Next, the Wichita team randomly selected the households for interview within each block. This was the third stage in this multistage cluster design. The fourth stage consisted of flipping a coin to decide whether to interview a man or a woman in households with both. Whoever came to the door was asked to provide a list of those in the household over 16 years of age. If there was more than one eligible person in the household, the interviewer selected one at random, conforming to the decision made earlier on sex of respondent.

Table 4.4 shows how well the Wichita team did.

All in all, they did very well. In addition to the variables shown in the table here, the Wichita sample was a fair representation of marital status, occupation, and education, although on this last independent variable there were some pretty large discrepancies. For example, 8% of the population of Wichita, according to the 1970 census, had less than 8 years of schooling, while only 4% of the sample had this characteristic. Only 14% of the general population had completed 1 to 3 years of college, while 22% of the sample had that much education.

TABLE 4.4

Comparison of Survey Results and Population Parameters
for the Wichita Study by Hartman and Hedblom

	Wichita	Their Sample for 1973
	(in percentages)	
White	86.8	82.8
Black	9.7	10.8
Chicano	2.5	2.6
Other	1.0	2.8
Male	46.6	46.9
Female	53.4	53.1
Median age	38.5	39.5

SOURCE: John J. Hartman and Jack H. Hedblom, *Methods for the Social Sciences: A Handbook for Students and Non-Specialists.* (Contributions in Sociology, No. 37, Greenwood Press, an imprint of Greenwood Publishing Group, Inc., Westport, CT, 1979), p. 165. Copyright, 1979 by John J. Hartman and Jack Hedblom. Reprinted with permission.

All things considered, though, the sampling procedure followed in the Wichita study was a model of technique, and the results show it. Whatever they found out about the 500 people they interviewed, the researchers could be very confident that the results were generalizable to the 193,000 adults in Wichita.

The Wichita study may seem remote from anthropological research, but more and more anthropologists are participating in team studies of urban populations where cluster designs are called for. Winter (1991) and Winter et al. (1989) studied the daily food expenditures of women in the city of Oaxaca, Mexico. They did a two-stage cluster sample of the whole city, with a goal of getting 600 interviews.

Oaxaca is divided into 54 "fiscal sectors." In the first stage, Winter et al. selected a random sample of the blocks within the fiscal sectors. Then, in the second stage, they selected 800 of the 3,600 households in the sectors. Households that had a male head and no spouse were ineligible for the study. The team also had some refusals and some absences; in the end, though, they got 630 interviews.

All the lessons of multistage cluster sampling apply to anthropologists working in deserts, in jungles, and in cities. There may not be a sampling frame of Ñähñu Indians in the Mezquital Valley in Mexico, but there *is* a list of counties in the valley, and within each county there *is* a list of communities. Within each community, it turns out, there is a census done by the local schoolteachers. From such a census, one may draw a random sample and conduct research.

In sum: If you don't have a sampling frame for a population, try to do a multistage cluster sample, narrowing down to natural clusters that do have lists. Sample heavier at the higher levels in a multistage sample and lighter at the lower stages.

Nonprobability Sampling

Despite our best efforts, it is often impossible to do strict probability sampling in the field. There are a number of alternatives that are appropriate under different circumstances. These include *quota* sampling, *purposive* sampling, *haphazard* sampling, and *snowball* sampling. The disadvantage of these techniques is that studies based on them have very low external validity. You can't generalize beyond your sample. On the other hand, when backed up by ethnographic data, studies based on these sampling techniques are often highly credible.

Quota Sampling

In quota sampling, you decide on the subpopulations of interest and on the proportions of those subpopulations in the final sample. If you are going to take a sample of 400 adults in a small town in Japan, you might decide that, since gender is of interest to you as an independent variable, and since women make up about half the population, then half your sample should be women and half should be men. Moreover, you decide that half of each gender quota should be older than 40 and half should be younger, and that half of each of those quota should be self-employed and half should be salaried.

When you are all through designing your quota sample, you go out and fill the quotas. You look for, say, five self-employed females who are over 40 years of age and who earn more than 160,000 yen a month and for five salaried males who are under 40 and who earn less than 150,000 yen a month. And so on.

Commercial polling companies use quota samples that are finely tuned on the basis of decades of research and many costly mistakes. The most famous of those mistakes happened in 1948 when pollsters predicted that Thomas Dewey would beat Harry Truman in the U.S. presidential election. The *Chicago Tribune* was so confident in those predictions that it printed an edition announcing Dewey's victory—while the votes were being counted that would make Truman president.

Quota sampling resembles stratified probability sampling with an important difference: The interviewers choose the sample on the spot. Over the years, organizations like Gallup, Roper, Harris, and others have learned how to train interviewers *not* to choose biased samples in filling their quotas—that is, not to choose respondents who are pretty much like themselves, but to choose respondents who really represent the range of variables in a population.

If you decide to do a quota sample, be careful that you don't select only people whom you would enjoy interviewing and that you don't avoid people whom you would find obnoxious or hostile. Don't avoid interviewing people who are hard to contact (busy people who are hardly ever home, or people who work nights and sleep days). Be particularly careful not to select only those people who are eager to be interviewed.

Purposive or Judgment Sampling

In judgment sampling, you decide the purpose you want an informant (or a community) to serve and you go out to find one. This is somewhat like quota sampling, except that there is no overall sampling design that tells you how many of each type of informant you need for a study.

Moreover, in judgment sampling it's not even necessary to decide up front what *kinds* of units of analysis to study. I used purposive sampling in my study of the Kalymnian (Greek) sponge fishing industry (1987). I knew I had to interview sponge merchants, boat owners, and divers, but my first interviews taught me that I had to interview people whom I had never considered: men who used to be divers but who had quit, gone to Australia as labor migrants, and returned to their island.

Purposive samples emerge from your experience in ethnographic research. You learn *in the field*, as you go along, to select the units of analysis (people, court records, whatever) that will provide the information you need. This is what Russell Belk and his colleagues (1988) did in their detailed ethnographic study of buyers and sellers at a swap meet. They argue that purposive sampling is particularly suited to naturalistic inquiry—just the sort that anthropologists do a lot of.

That argument feels good, but be careful. We can learn a lot from nonrepresentative samples, but they must not be elevated to a status they can not achieve. Ethnography is the surest method to achieve understanding of how things work in a group of people we have talked to and observed. Representative sampling is the only way to take that understanding and extend it to people whom we *haven't* studied—people in the rest of the community who we didn't talk to or observe.

There are several good reasons for using nonprobability samples. Judgment sampling is often used in pilot studies before testing a hypothesis with a representative sample. It is also used in the selection of a few cases for intensive study. You wouldn't select a research community by chance, but would rely on your judgment to find one that reflects the things you are interested in. Life history research and qualitative research on special populations (drug addicts, trial lawyers, shamans) rely on judgment sampling.

Judgment sampling is also used in studying critical cases. Polling companies try to identify communities across the United States that have voted for the winner in the past, say, six presidential elections. Then they poll those few communities that meet the criterion.

Choosing key informants in fieldwork is a kind of critical-case sampling. It would be pointless to select a handful of people randomly from a population and try to turn them into trusted key informants.

Haphazard or Convenience Sampling

Haphazard sampling is useful for exploratory research, to get a feel for "what's going on out there," and for pretesting questionnaires to make sure that the items are unambiguous and not too threatening. In other situations, however, haphazard sampling is just plain dangerous. It involves nothing more than grabbing whoever will stand still long enough to answer your questions.

Studies of the homeless in America are usually done with convenience samples, but Burnham and Koegel (1988) showed that (for Los Angeles, at least) probability samples are much better than convenience samples for estimating parameters like how many people actually sleep on the street.

If you ask students at the library how they feel about some current campus issue, you may get different answers than if you ask students who are playing cards in the cafeteria. If you only do interviews around noon, when it is convenient for you, you'll miss all those people for whom noon is not a convenient hour. If you want to know the effect of a new road on some peasants and you only interview people who come to town on the road, you'll miss all the people who live too far off the road for it to do them any good.

It is not necessary to list all the ways that your own prejudices can inflict fatal damage on a convenience sample. All samples are representative of *something*. The trick is to make them representative of what *you* want them to be.

Snowball Sampling

In snowball sampling you locate one or more key individuals and ask them to name others who would be likely candidates for your research. If you are dealing with a relatively small population of people who are likely to be in contact with one another, then snowball sampling is an effective way to build an exhaustive sampling frame. But in a large population, people who are better known have a better chance of being named in a snowball procedure than people who are less well known. In large populations, then, every person does not have the same chance of being included in a snowball sample.

Snowball sampling is very useful, however, in studies of social networks, where the object is to find out who people know and how they know each other. It is also useful in studies of small, bounded, or difficult-to-find populations, like members of elite groups, women who have been recently divorced, urban migrants from a particular tribal group, and so on.

Ostrander (1980), for example, used snowball sampling to locate informants in her study of class consciousness among upper-class women in a midwestern U.S. city. She selected her first informant by looking for someone who had graduated from an elite women's college, was listed in the social register, was active in upper-class clubs—and who would talk to her. At the end of the interview, she asked the informant to "suggest another woman of your social group, with a background like yours, who might be willing to talk to me."

David Griffith and his colleagues used *two* snowball samples in their anthropological study of food preferences in Moberly, Missouri. They chose an initial "seed" household in a middle-income neighborhood and asked the informant to name three people in town with whom he interacted on a regular basis. The first person cited by the informant lived in a lower-income neighborhood across town. That person, in turn, named other people who were in the lower-income bracket.

After a while, the researchers realized that, though they'd started with a middle-income informant who had children at home, they were getting mostly lower-income, elderly people in the snowball sample. So they started again, this time with a seed from an elite, upper-middle-income neighborhood. By the time they got through, Griffith et al. had a well-balanced sample of 30 informants with whom they did in-depth interviews. (This study is reported by J. Johnson, 1990:78.)

Snowball sampling is widely used in community studies. Sanjek (1978) used this method in his study of migrants to Accra; Laumann and Pappi (1974) used it in their network study of the elite in a town in Germany;

and E. Miller (1986) used the method to locate female petty criminals and prostitutes in her study of street women.

Probability Proportionate to Size

The best estimates of a parameter are produced in samples taken from clusters of equal size. When clusters are not equal in size, then samples should be taken PPS—with probability proportionate to size. This is easy to do in countries where you have neat clusters, such as census tracts and blocks.

Suppose you had money and time to do 800 household interviews in a city of 50,000 households. You intend to select 40 blocks, out of a total of 280, and do 20 interviews in each block. You want each of the 800 households in the final sample to have exactly the same probability of being selected.

Should each block be equally likely to be chosen for your sample? No, because census blocks never contribute equally to the total population from which you will take your final sample. A block that has 100 households in it *should* have twice the chance of being chosen for 20 interviews as a block that has 50 households, and half the chance of a block that has 200 households. When you get down to the block level, each household on a block with 100 residences has a 20% (20/100) chance of being selected for the sample; each household on a block with 300 residences has only a 6.7% (20/300) chance of being selected.

PPS sampling is called for under three conditions: (a) when you are dealing with large, unevenly distributed populations (such as cities that have high-rise and single-family neighborhoods); (b) when your sample is large enough to withstand being broken up into a lot of pieces (clusters) without substantially increasing the sampling error; and (c) when you have data on the population of many small blocks in a population and can calculate their respective proportionate contributions to the total population.

These are luxury conditions for most anthropologists. More often than not you'll be working in a rural area, where there are no census materials and fairly large territories to cover. Even in urban areas, you may have no access to accurate census material. But if you suspect you are dealing with very unevenly distributed populations, what do you do?

PPS Samples in the Field

In this most typical situation for anthropologists—when you don't have neat strata, when you don't have neat clusters, when you don't have

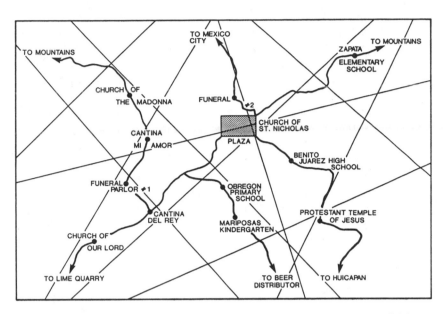

Figure 4.1. Creating maximally heterogeneous sampling clusters in the field.

sampling frames printed out on a computer by a reliable government agency—place your trust in randomness and *create* maximally heterogeneous clusters from which to take a random sample.

Draw or get a map of the area you are studying. Place 100 numbered dots around the edge of the map. Try to space the numbers equidistant from one another, but don't worry if they are not. Select a pair of numbers at random and draw a line between them. Now select another pair of numbers (be sure to replace the first pair before selecting the second), and draw a line between them. In the unlikely event that you choose the same pair twice, simply choose a third pair. Keep doing this, replacing the numbers each time. After you've drawn about 50 lines, you can begin sampling.

Notice that the lines drawn across the map (see Figure 4.1) create a lot of wildly uneven spaces. Since you don't know the distribution of population density in the area you are studying, this technique maximizes the chance that you will properly survey the population, more or less PPS. By creating a series of (essentially) random chunks of different sizes, you distribute the error you might introduce by not knowing the density, and that distribution lowers the possible error.

Number the uneven spaces created by the lines and choose some of them at random. Go to those spaces, number the households, and select an appropriate number at random. Remember, you want to have the same number of households from each made up geographic cluster, no matter what its size. If you are doing 400 interviews, you would select 20 geographic chunks and do 20 interviews or behavioral observations in each.

Penn Handwerker (1993a) used a variation of this method in his study of sexual behavior on Barbados. In Handwerker's variation of map sampling, you generate 10 random numbers between 0 and 360 (the degrees on a compass). Next, put a dot in the center of a map that you will use for the sampling exercise and use a protractor to identify the 10 randomly chosen compass points. You then draw lines from the dot in the center of the map through all 10 points to the edge of the map and interview people (or observe houses, or whatever) along those lines. If you use this technique, you may want to establish a sampling interval (like every seventh house). If you finish interviewing along the lines and don't have enough cases, you can take another random start, with the same or a different interval and start again. Be careful of periodicity, though.

Camilla Harshbarger (1994) used another variation of map sampling in her study of farmers in North West Province, Cameroon. To create a sample of 400 farmers, she took a map of a rural community and drew 100 dots around the perimeter. She used a random number table to select 50 pairs of dots and drew lines between them. She numbered the points created by the crossing of lines, and chose 80 of those points at random. Then, Harshbarger and her field assistants interviewed one farmer in each of the five compounds they found closest to each of the 80 selected dots. (If you use this dot technique, remember to include the points along the edges of the map in your sample, or you'll miss households on those edges.)

Of course, there are times when a random, representative sample is out of the question. After she did those interviews with 400 randomly selected farmers in North West Province, Cameroon, Harshbarger set out to interview Fulani cattle herders in the same area. Here's what Harshbarger wrote about her experience in trying to interview the herders:

> It was rainy season in Wum and the roads were a nightmare. The graziers lived very far out of town and quite honestly, my research assistants were not willing to trek to the compounds because it would have taken too much time and we would never have finished the job. I consulted X and he agreed to call selected people to designated school houses on certain days. We each took a room and administered the survey with each individual grazier.

Not everyone who was called came for the interview, so we ended up taking who we could get. Therefore, the Wum grazier sample was not representative and initially that was extremely difficult for me to accept. Our team had just finished the 400-farmer survey of Wum that *was* representative, and after all that work it hit me hard that the grazier survey would not be. To get a representative sample, I would have needed a four-wheel drive vehicle, a driver, and more money to pay research assistants for a lengthy stay in the field. Eventually, I forgave myself for the imperfection. (personal communication)

The lessons here are clear. (a) If you are ever in Harshbarger's situation, you, too, can forgive yourself for having a nonrepresentative sample. (b) Until then, like Harshbarger, you should feel badly about it.

5

Choosing Research Problems, Sites, and Methods

The Ideal Research Process

Despite all the myths about how research is done, it's actually a messy process that is cleaned up in the reporting of results. Here is how the research process is supposed to work in the ideal world:

1. First, a theoretical problem is formulated.
2. Next, an appropriate site and method are selected.
3. Then, data are collected and analyzed.
4. Finally, the theoretical proposition with which the research was launched is either challenged or supported.

In fact, all kinds of practical issues get in the way. In the end, research papers are written so that the chaotic aspects of research are not emphasized, and the orderly inputs and outcomes are.

102

I see nothing wrong with this: It would be a monumental waste of precious space in books and journals to describe the *real* research process for every project that is reported. Besides, every seasoned researcher knows just how messy it all is, anyway. On the other hand, you shouldn't have to become a highly experienced researcher before you're let into the secret of how it's done.

A Realistic Approach

There are five questions to ask yourself about every research question you are thinking about pursuing. Most of these questions can also be asked about potential research sites and research methods. If you answer these questions honestly (at least to yourself), chances are you'll do good research every time. If you cheat on this test, even a teeny bit, chances are you'll regret it. The questions are:

1. Does this topic (village, data collection method) really interest me?
2. Is this a problem that is amenable to scientific inquiry?
3. Are adequate resources available to investigate this topic? (to study this population? to use this particular method?)
4. Will my research question, or the methods I want to use, lead to unreasonable ethical problems?
5. Is the topic of theoretical interest?

Personal Interest

The first thing to ask about any potential research question is: Am I really excited about this? Researchers do their best work when they are genuinely having fun, so don't do boring research when you can choose any topic you like.

Of course, you can't always choose any topic you like. In contract research you may sometimes have to take on a research question that a client finds interesting, but that you find deadly dull. The most boring research I've ever done was on a contract where my co-workers and I combined ethnographic and survey research of rural homeowners' knowledge of fire prevention and their attitudes toward volunteer fire departments.

By comparison, I *was* interested in a contract study of the effects of coeducational prisons on homosexuality among male and female inmates.

It is no accident that I never published the results of the former study, but did write up the results of the latter (Killworth & Bernard, 1974).

I've caught many students doing research for term projects, MA theses, and even doctoral dissertations simply out of convenience and with no enthusiasm for the topic. If you are not interested in a research question, then no matter how important other people tell you it is, don't bother with it. If others are so sure that it's a dynamite topic of great theoretical significance, let *them* study it.

The same goes for research populations. If you select a topic of interest, and then try to test it on a population in which you have no interest, your research will suffer. It's really hard to conduct penetrating, in-depth interviews over a period of a year if you aren't interested in the lives of the people you're studying.

This doesn't mean that anthropologists and the people they study have to *like* one another, but both are well served if they find each other interesting. The anthropologist needs to sustain his or her interest in order to go out every day and collect data. The studied group needs to be able to gossip about the anthropologist's antics with interest in order to tolerate the intrusion. When Colin Turnbull went to study the Ik, he had a hunch he wouldn't like them. In fact, he was repulsed by much of what he saw in his study of those mountain people. Still, he was fascinated by the Ik and how they survived under such harsh conditions (personal communication; see Turnbull, 1972).

You don't need any justification for your interest in studying a particular group of people. Personal interest is . . . well, personal. A colleague once told me that he had wanted to go to a particular community, but that someone had beat him to it. He was interested in the community because it was known for its super-macho culture of men who risked their lives doing very dangerous work. He wound up going to another community, known for its vendetta culture, because, he said, it suited his own need to study people who live dangerously.

The point is, when you are about to go to the field, ask yourself: Will my interest be sustained there? If the answer is "no," then reconsider going. Accessibility is not enough to make good research happen.

Science Versus Nonscience

If you're really excited about a research topic, then the next question is: Is this a topic that can be studied by the methods of science? If the answer is "no," then no matter how much fun it is, and no matter how important it seems, don't even try to make a scientific study of it. Either let someone else do it, or use a humanistic approach. For example, consider a biblical scholar who asks the empirical question: How often do derogatory references to women occur in the Old Testament? So long as the concept of "derogatory" has been well defined (and your colleagues agree with high intersubjectivity), this question can be answered by applying the scientific method. You simply look through the corpus of data and count the instances that turn up. (Recall that intersubjectivity means that researchers agree on what constitutes an instance of some variable. Intersubjectivity is a useful concept because it eliminates the need for "objectivity," which everyone knows is impossible when dealing with conceptual variables like "derogatoriness.")

But suppose the researcher asks: Does the Old Testament offer support for unequal pay for women today? In that case, the query is simply not answerable by the scientific method. It is no more answerable than the question: Is Rachmaninoff's music more melancholy than that of Tchaikovsky? Or: Is it morally correct to mainstream slightly retarded children in grades K-6? Or: Should the remaining hunting and gathering bands of the world be preserved just the way they are and kept from being spoiled by modern civilization? Whether or not a study is a scientific one depends first on the nature of the question being asked and *then* on the methods used.

If you've been reading this book straight through from the beginning, you know that when I talk about using the scientific method I'm *not* talking about numbers. In science, whenever a research problem can be investigated with quantitative measurement, numbers are more than just desirable, they're required. On the other hand, there are many intellectual problems in anthropology for which quantitative measures are not yet available. Those problems require qualitative measurement.

First-pass descriptions of processes (like beer making, for example), or of events (like fiestas), or of systems of nomenclature (like kinship terms, disease terms, and ethnobotanical terms) require words, not numbers. Remember that you can use words to measure things, too. Suppose you get a list of plant names—a bunch of words. Suppose that you ask informants, for each plant, "Is it edible?" The yes-no answers are nominal—that is, qualitative—measurement. Suppose you ask informants to tell you which of two plants is *more* nutritious. The result is an ordinal measure of "perception of nutritiousness."

We'll get back to this kind of systematic, qualitative data collection in Chapter 11.

Resources

The next question to ask is whether adequate resources are available for you to conduct your study. There are three major kinds of resources: time, money, and people. What may be adequate for some projects may be inadequate for others. Be totally honest with yourself about this issue.

Time

To write a book based on solid ethnographic understanding takes a year or more just for the field research. By contrast, the data collection phase of some hypothesis-testing research, based on field surveys, might be completed in a matter of weeks. A lot of applied anthropological research is now done in weeks or months, rather than in years, using rapid assessment methods. Rapid assessment methods are the same ones that everyone else uses but are done quickly (see Chapter 7).

If you are doing research for a term project, the topic has to be something you can look at in a matter of a few months—and squeezing the research into a schedule of other classes, at that. It makes no sense to select a topic that requires two semesters' work when you have one semester in which to do the research. This effort to cram 10 gallons of water into a 5-gallon can is futile and quite common. Don't do it.

Money

Many things come under the umbrella of money. Equipment is essentially a money issue, as is salary or subsistence for you and other persons involved in the research. Funds for field assistants, computer time, supplies, and travel all have to be calculated before you go out and try to actually conduct research. No matter how interesting it is to you, and no matter how important it may seem theoretically, if you haven't got the resources to use the right methods, skip it for now.

Naturally, most people do not have the money it takes to mount a major research effort. That's why there are granting agencies. Writing proposals is a special craft. It pays to learn it early. Research grants for MA research are typically between $1,000 and $3,000. Most grants for doctoral research are between $5,000 and $15,000. If you spend 100 hours working on a grant proposal that brings you $5,000 to do your research, that's $50/hour for your time.

If your research requires comparison of two groups over a period of 12 months, and you only have money for 6 months of research, can you accomplish your research goal by studying one group? Can you accomplish it by studying two groups for 3 months each? Ask yourself whether it's worthwhile pursuing your research if it has to be scaled down to fit available resources. If the answer is "no," then consider other topics.

People

"People" includes you and other persons involved in the research, as well as those whom you are studying. Does the research require that you speak Papiamento? If so, then are you willing to put in the time and effort to learn that language? Can the research be done effectively with interpreters? If so, are such people available at a cost that you can handle?

Does the research require access to a particular village? Can you gain access to that village? Will the research require that you interview elite members of the society you are studying? Will you be able to gain their cooperation? Or will they tell you to get lost or, even worse, lead you on with a lot of platitudes about their culture?

Ethics

I wish I could give you a list of criteria against which you could measure the "ethicalness" of every research idea you ever come up with. Unfortunately, it's not so simple. The fact is, what is ethical research today may become unethical tomorrow, and vice versa. During World War II, many anthropologists (Margaret Mead and Ruth Benedict among them) worked for what would today be called the Department of Defense, and they were applauded as patriots for lending their expertise to the war effort. During the Vietnam War, anthropologists who worked for the Department of Defense were excoriated. Today, anthropologists are again working for the Department of Defense, as well as for multinational corporations. Is this simply because that's where the jobs are? Perhaps. Times and views about ethics change.

Stanley Milgram did a famous experiment on obedience (1963). He duped people into thinking that they were taking part in an experiment on how well human beings learn under conditions of punishment. The subjects in the experiment were "teachers." The "learners" were Milgram's accomplices. They sat behind a wall, where they could be heard by subjects, but not seen. Each time the learner made a mistake on a test, the subject was told to turn up an electric shock meter that was clearly marked "mild shock," "medium shock," and so on, all the way up to "DANGER."

As the learners made mistakes, they feigned greater and greater discomfort with the increasing electric shock level that they were supposedly enduring. At the danger level, they screamed and pleaded to be let go. The experimenter kept telling the subject to administer the shocks. A third of the subjects obeyed orders and administered what they thought were lethal shocks. Many subjects protested, but were convinced by the researchers in white coats that it was all right to follow orders.

Until Milgram did that troubling experiment, it had been easy to scoff at Nazi war criminals, whose defense was that they were "just following orders." Milgram's experiment taught us that perhaps a third of Americans had it in them to follow orders until they killed innocent people.

Was Milgram's experiment unethical? Some subjects reportedly experienced emotional trauma for years afterward, whenever they contemplated what they had done. Plenty of people worried at the time about the ethics of Milgram's experiment, but no one stopped him.

Milgram's experiment could never get by a Human Subjects Review Committee at any university in the United States today. As I said, views of ethics change. Still, it was less costly, and more ethical, than the natural experiments carried out at My Lai or Chatilla—the Vietnamese village and Lebanese refugee camps—whose civilian inhabitants were wiped out by U.S. and Lebanese soldiers, respectively, "under orders." Those experiments, too, showed what ordinary people are capable of doing, except in those cases, real people really got killed.

Just because times and ideas about ethics seem to change does not mean that anything goes. Appendix B contains the *Statement of Professional and Ethical Responsibilities* (sometimes called the "Code of Ethics") of the Society for Applied Anthropology. This document is not perfect, but it covers a lot of ground and is based on the accumulated experience of thousands of researchers like yourself who have grappled with ethical dilemmas over the past 50 years. Look at the statement regularly during the course of a research project, both to get some of the wisdom that has gone into it and to develop your own ideas about how the document might be improved (see Fluehr-Lobban, 1991, for a thorough discussion of current issues on ethics and anthropological research.)

Nor is everything "relative." Cultural and ethical relativism is an excellent antidote for overdeveloped ethnocentrism. But cultural relativism is a poor philosophy to live by, or on which to make judgments about whether to participate in particular research projects. Can you imagine any anthropologist today defending the human rights violations of Nazi Germany as just another expression of the richness of culture? Would you feel comfortable defending, on the basis of relativism, the Aztec practice of tearing out human hearts to appease their gods? Or the practice of so-called ethnic cleansing? Or countless other horrible events in humanity's history?

There is no value-free science. Everything that interests you as a potential research focus will come fully equipped with risks to you and to your informants. In each case, all you can do (and what you *must* do) is assess the potential human costs and the potential benefits—to you, personally, and to humanity through the accumulation of knowledge.

Don't hide from the fact that you are interested in your own glory, your own career, your own advancement. It's a safe bet that your colleagues are interested in their career advancement, too. We have all heard of cases in which a scientist put his or her own career aggrandizement above the health and well-being of others. This is devastating to science, and to scientists; it can only happen when otherwise good, ethical people (a) convince themselves that they are doing something noble for humanity, rather than for themselves, and (b) consequently fool themselves into thinking that that justifies hurting others.

When you make these assessments of costs and benefits, be prepared to come to decisions that may not be shared by all your colleagues. For example, remember the problem of the relationship between darkness of skin color and various measures of life success (including wealth, health, and longevity)? Would you, personally, be willing to participate in a study of this problem? Some readers would, while others would not.

Suppose the study was likely to show that a small, but significant percentage of the variance in earning power in the United States was predictable from darkness of skin color. Some would argue that this would be useful evidence in the fight against racism and would therefore jump at the chance to do the investigation. Others would say that the evidence would be used by racists to do further damage in our society; they would argue that such a study ought never be done in the first place, lest it fall into the wrong hands.

There is no answer to this dilemma. Above all, be honest with yourself. Ask yourself: Is this ethical? If the answer to yourself is "no," then skip it; find another topic. Once again, there are plenty of interesting research questions that meet the criteria above and will not put you into a moral bind.

Theory

All research is specific. Whether you conduct ethnographic or questionnaire research, the first thing you do is *describe a process* or *investigate a relationship* among some variables in a population. To get from description to theory is a big leap and involves asking "What causes the phenomenon to exist in the first place?"

Theory comes in two basic sizes: elemental or *idiographic* theory and *nomothetic* theory. An idiographic, or elemental, theory accounts for the facts in a single case. A nomothetic theory accounts for the facts in many cases. The more cases that a theory accounts for, the more nomothetic it is.

Idiographic Theory

Most theory in anthropology is idiographic. Here are four examples.

1. Anthony Paredes has been doing research on the Poarch Band of Creek Indians in Alabama since 1971. When he began his research, the Indians were a remnant of an earlier group. They had lost the use of the Creek language, were not recognized by the U.S. government as a tribe, and had little contact with other Indians for decades. Yet, the Poarch Creek Indians had somehow maintained their identity.

Paredes wanted to know how the Indians had managed this. He did what he called "old-fashioned ethnography," including key-informant interviewing, and learned about a cultural revitalization movement that had been going on since the 1940s. That movement was led by some key people whose efforts over the years had made a difference. Paredes's description of how the Poarch Creek Indians held their cultural identity in the face of such odds is an excellent example of elemental, idiographic theory. As you read Paredes's account you feel you understand how it worked (see Paredes, 1974, 1992).

2. Next, consider the case of the kitchen fires in India. In 1977, the New Delhi police reported 311 deaths by kitchen fires of young women. In 1983, there were 690 kitchen fire deaths (Claiborne, 1984). How to explain this phenomenon?

It turned out that in most cases, the women were young brides. The variables of interest, then, were "likelihood to die in a kitchen fire" and "being a young bride." Gross (1992) explains the phenomenon as a consequence of female hypergamy and dowry. Families that can raise a large dowry can marry off their daughter to someone of greater means. This created a bidding war as the families of wealthier sons demanded more and more for the privilege of marrying into their families.

Apparently, many families of daughters went into debt to accumulate the dowries. When they couldn't pay off the debt, some of the families of the grooms murdered the brides in faked "kitchen accidents" where kerosene stoves purportedly blew up. That gave the grooms' families a chance to get another bride whose families could deliver.

This, too, is an elemental or idiographic theory. You notice a phenomenon and a relationship of interest that begs to be explained. You do your homework at the local level and you explain the cause of the phenomenon.

3. Next, consider the well-known case of fraternal polyandry. Hiatt (1980) noticed that among the Sinhalese of Sri Lanka, there was a shortage of women among those groups that practiced polyandry. He theorized that the shortage of women accounted for the practice of polyandry.

Earlier, Goldstein (1971) observed that in Tibet, polyandry was practiced only among people who didn't own land. It turns out that in feudal times, some peasants were given a fixed allotment of land which they could pass on to their sons. In order not to break up the land, brothers would take a single bride into one household.

4. Finally, Michael Smith (1986) reexamined the forces that held together the Aztec empire. Previous theorists had argued that military coercion was the main force integrating the empire. Smith's data support a theory in which the main integrative force was "collusion between rulers of the core states and the nobility of the provinces who gained economic rewards for their participation in the tribute empire" (1986:70).

Paredes's theory of how the Poarch Creeks maintained their cultural identity does not tell us how other Native American groups managed to do this or why some groups did *not* manage it. Gross's explanation for the kitchen fires in India rings true, but it does not explain why other societies that have escalating dowry fail to have kitchen fires. Neither Hiatt's nor Goldstein's theory tells us why other societies practice polyandry, or why polyandry is so rare among societies of the world. And Smith's theory does not tell us when we should expect collusion between central rulers and feudal nobility to replace military coercion as the principal means of holding a state together.

This does not diminish at all the usefulness of these idiographic theories. In anthropology, at least, a lot of the best work is at this level of theory making.

Nomothetic Theory

Nomothetic theories are a step up in generalizability from elemental theories. Nomothetic theories address questions like "Why are so few societies polyandrous?" or "What accounts for the existence of dowry?"

Dowry is found in just 7.5% of the world's societies, and several anthropologists have tried to account for it. Boserup (1970) hypothesized that dowry should occur in societies where a woman's role in subsistence production is low. She was right, but many societies where women's productive effort is of low value do *not* have dowry. Gaulin and Boster (1990) offered a theory that predicts dowry in stratified societies that have monogamous or polyandrous marriage. Their theory works better than Boserup's—it misclassifies fewer societies—but still makes some mistakes. Fully 77% of dowry societies are, in fact, stratified and have monogamous marriage, but 63% of all monogamous, stratified societies do *not* have dowry.

Harris (1980), building on Boserup's model, hypothesized that dowry should occur in societies where women's role in subsistence production is low *and* where their value in reproduction is also low. In other words, if women are a liability in both their productive and reproductive roles, one should expect dowry as a compensation to the groom's family for taking on the liability represented by a bride who marries into a groom's family.

Adams (1993) operationalized this idea. He reasoned that, since women are less suited physically to handling a plow, societies with plow agriculture and high-quality agricultural land should find women's labor of low value. If those societies have high population density, then women's reproductive role should be of low value. Finally, in societies with both these characteristics, patrilocal residence would make accepting a bride a real liability and would lead to demand for compensation—hence, dowry.

Adams tested his idea on the same sample of 186 societies that Gaulin and Boster used to test their theory, and Adams's theory makes about 25% fewer errors than Gaulin and Boster's in predicting which societies have dowry. There has been a succession of theories to account for dowry; each theory has done a bit better than the last and each has been based on reasoning from common-sense principles. That's how nomothetic theory grows.

Contrary to popular opinion, there is a *lot* of nomothetic theory around in anthropology. James Dow (1986) asked "What is the common structure that can describe and explain the organization of all forms of symbolic healing, regardless of the culture in which they occur?" (1986:56). The data organized by Dow support a theory that successfully incorporates both magical healing and Western psychotherapy.

William Keegan (1986) examined horticultural production in light of what is known as "optimal foraging theory." This nomothetic theory deals with how people maximize their caloric and protein gains in the search for food. On the principle that "protein is the currency on which subsistence decisions are based," Keegan predicted how horticulturists select garden plots and decide what to plant. He used data from the Machiguenga of the Peruvian Amazon region to test his predictions.

Finally, Alice Schlegel and Herbert Barry (1986) looked at the consequences of female contribution to subsistence. Their nomothetic theory predicts that women will be more respected in societies where they contribute a lot to subsistence than in societies where their contribution is low.

In societies where women contribute a lot to subsistence, Schlegel and Barry's theory predicts that women will be spared some of the burden of pregnancy "through the attempt to space children" more evenly (ibid.:46). In such societies, women will be subjected to rape less often; they will have greater sexual freedom; they will be worth more in bride wealth; and they will have greater choice in selection of a spouse. Schlegel and Barry examined data from 186 societies (the Standard Cross-Cultural Sample given in Murdock and White, 1969; see Chapters 9 and 15 and Appendix C), and their predictions were supported.

There is no "list" of research topics. You have to use your imagination and your curiosity about how things work and follow hunches. Above all, never take anything at face value. Every time you read an article, ask yourself: "What would a study look like that would test whether the major assertions and conclusions of this article are really correct?" Whenever anyone says something like "The only things students really care about these days are drugs, sex, and rock-and-roll," the proper response is "We can test that."

A Guide to Research Topics, Anyway

There may not be a list of research topics, but there are some useful guidelines. Look at Table 5.1. I have divided all research topics into 15 varieties, based on the relationships among five major kinds of social science variables. Once you become familiar with these 15 kinds of relationships between variables, you'll find it much easier to generate ideas for research topics.

The five kinds of variables are:

1. Internal states. These include attitudes, beliefs, values, and perceptions. Cognition is an internal state.
2. External states. These include characteristics of people, such as age, wealth, health status, height, weight, gender, and so on.

TABLE 5.1

Types of Studies

	Internal States	External States	Behavior Reported	Behavior Observed	Artifacts	Environment
Internal states	I	II	IIIa	IIIb	IV	V
External states		VI	VIIa	VIIb	VIII	IX
Behavior reported observed			Xa	Xb Xc	XIa XIb	XIIa XIIb
Artifacts					XIII	XIV
Environment						XV

3. Behavior. This covers what people eat, who they communicate with, how much they work and play—in short, everything that people do and much of what social scientists are interested in understanding in the first place.

4. Artifacts. This includes all the physical residue from human behavior—radioactive waste and sludge, tomato slicers, arrowheads, computer diskettes, penis sheaths—everything.

5. Environment. This category includes both physical and social environmental niches and characteristics. Amount of rainfall, amount of biomass per square kilometer, presence of socioeconomic class indicators, location on a river or ocean front, political "climate," and so on.

Keep in mind that category (3) includes both reported behavior and actual behavior. A great deal of research has shown that about a third to a half of everything informants report about their behavior is not true. If you ask people what they eat, they'll tell you, but it may have no useful resemblance to what they actually eat. If you ask people how many times a year they go to church, you're likely to get data that do not reflect behavior but something else. (See Bernard, Killworth et al., 1984, for a review of the literature on this problem, and Freeman et al., 1987, for useful indications of how to study and control for this problem.)

Some of the difference between what people say they do and what they do is the result of out-and-out lying; most of it is the result of the fact that people simply can't hang on to the level of detail about their behavior that is called for when they are confronted by social scientists asking them how often they go to church, or eat beef, or whatever. Of course, what people *say* about their behavior may be precisely what you're interested in, but that's a different matter.

Most anthropologists focus their attention on internal states and on reported behavior. But the study of humanity can be much richer, once you get the hang of putting together these five kinds of variables and conjuring up potential relationships. Here are some examples of possible studies for the cells in Table 5.1

Cell I:

Religious beliefs and attitudes toward gun control in the United States.

Disposition toward illegal labor migration and attitudes toward family size among Mexican migrants.

Attitudes toward participation in modern commerce and strength of value of cattle among Masai men.

Cell II:

Relationship between age and attitude toward premarital chastity for women or/and men.

Health status and willingness to plan for the future.

Wealth and political orientation.

Cell IIIa

Attitude toward corporal punishment for children and reported frequency of physical abuse by spouse.

Belief in the power of the local chief to settle disputes and reported use of government services.

Cell IIIb

An example of a study in this cell that simply could not be conducted using reported behavior would be an examination of the attitudes of Muslims, Jews, and Hindus regarding pork and beef, and their behavior when confronted by these meats during social events outside the home.

Cell IV:

Political orientation of an informant and magazines seen in his or her home.

Attitude toward the government and presence or absence of radio or TV in the home.

Belief in energy conservation and ownership of a bicycle.

Cell V:

Attitude toward use of wood for building houses, and the level of forestation in a region.

Belief in obedience toward authority, and the level of authoritarian enforcement by local regimes.

Cell VI:

Covariation between gender and income, health status and political power, marital status and health status, etc.

Cells VIIa and b:

Gender and reported (VIIa) or observed (VIIb) frequency of church attendance.

Marital status and reported or observed level of interaction with kin, as opposed to friends.

Cell VIII:

Covariation between age, marital status, wealth, or health status and the value of certain key possessions.

Cell IX:

Relationship between health status of populations and their exposure to various kinds of environmental factors.

Cell Xa:

Are people who report having been labor migrants more or less likely to report that they engage in polygyny? Comparisons of informant reports and direct observations are in cell Xb; comparisons of direct observations on two different variables fall into cell Xc.

Cells XIa and b

Relation between the number of hours worked (reported or observed) and the presence or absence of certain material symbols of wealth.

Cells XIIa and b

Relation between reported or observed consumption of meat and the amount of protein biomass per square kilometer.

Cell XIII:

Does the presence of a refrigerator also predict the presence of screened windows (or other artifacts) in an economically developing peasant community?

Cell XIV:

Are certain artifacts (relating, for example, to subsistence), more or less likely to be found in rainforests, or deserts, or shoreline communities?

Cell XV:

Are certain physical/geographic environments more likely to exhibit certain social environmental qualities? Are tropical areas more likely to be poverty areas, for example?

The above list is only meant to give you an idea of how to think about potential covariations and, consequently, about potential research topics. Always keep in mind that covariation does not mean cause. Covariation can be spurious, the result of an antecedent or an intervening variable. (Refer again to Chapter 2 for a discussion of causality, spurious relationships, and antecedent variables.)

6

The Literature Search

The first thing to do after you get an idea for a piece of research is to find out what has been done. It is impossible to overemphasize the importance of a thorough literature search. Without a truly heroic effort to uncover sources, you risk two things: wasting a lot of time going over already covered ground, and having your colleagues ignore your work because you didn't do your homework.

This chapter is about how to make the heroic effort relatively painless and avoid those undesirable outcomes. It's about using the main "documentation resources" in your library. In the jargon of library science, a documentation resource is anything that helps you find literature, published or unpublished.

There are three main documentation resources: (a) people, (b) review articles, and (c) bibliographic search tools.

People

There is nothing useful, or prestigious, or exciting about discovering literature on your own. Reading it is what's important, and you should not waste any time in finding it. Experts are great documentation resources. Begin by asking everyone and anyone whom you think has a remote chance of knowing something about the topic you're interested in if they can recommend some key articles or books that will get you into the literature on your topic.

Use a snowball sample to conduct this first stage of your literature review. If the people you know are not experts in the topic you're studying, ask them if they know personally any people who *are* experts. Then contact the experts by phone.

Yes, by phone. Letters demand a written response, and most people don't have the time to do that. But most people *will* talk to you on the phone. A knowledgeable person in the field can give you three or four key citations over the phone right on the spot. As you'll see a little later in this chapter, that's enough to get you straight into the literature.

Review Articles

The *Annual Review of Anthropology* is a good place to start reading. It has been published since 1959 (between 1959 and 1969 it was published every 2 years and was called the *Biennial Review of Anthropology*) and now contains several hundred review articles. Many review articles of interest to anthropologists are also published in the *Annual Review* series volumes on sociology, psychology, and economics. Authors who are invited to publish in the series are experts in their fields; they have digested a lot of information and have packaged it in a way that gets you right into the middle of a topic in a hurry.

Don't worry about review articles being out of date. The *Social Science Citation Index* (SSCI) and other documentation resources have virtually eliminated the problem of obsolescence in bibliographies and review articles. More about the SSCI below.

Bibliographic Search Tools

The overwhelming majority of the research in any discipline, especially one as large and as international as anthropology, is published in hundreds upon hundreds of independent journals, some of which are short lived. Journals in sociology, psychology, geography, political science, criminal justice, and other social science disciplines publish a lot of the information that anthropologists need in their own studies of social problems and of modern societies around the world.

But not all research of interest to anthropologists is published in journals or books. Much of the descriptive data on social issues and on peoples of the world are published in a variety of reports from governments, industries, and private research foundations. No research project should be launched (and certainly no request for funding of a research project should be submitted) until you have thoroughly searched these potential sources for published research on the topic you are interested in.

As formidable as the amount of information being produced in the world is, there is an equally formidable set of documentation resources for handling that information. The human and physical resources required to document and index the social science information being produced today are quite extraordinary.

Suppose you just want to look up "Cameroon," or "family violence," or "Pushtun," or "Mayan," and find all the books and articles published anywhere in 1994 on any of those topics. To be able to do that, someone would have to read through all the material produced on thousands of topics, published in thousands of journals and reports, and would have to index all that information. This is exactly what's done at the Institute for Scientific Information (ISI) in Philadelphia.

The Social Sciences Citation Index

ISI is the corporation that produces a set of citation indexes, including the *Science Citation Index* (SCI), the *Social Sciences Citation Index* (SSCI), and the *Arts and Humanities Citation Index* (A&HCI). These indexes are available in every major university library, and in many small college libraries, too, and are the most important documentation resources available to researchers in all scholarly disciplines. They are not the only tools you need to consult when doing a literature search, but they should be the first ones you use.

The citation indexes are produced by a staff of over 500 people who go through thousands of journals each year, entering into a computer the title, author, and reference for every article, book review, editorial, obituary, and comment in each journal. The SSCI is based on a survey of more than 4,600 journals, including publications in 35 languages other than English.

Of these, 1,400 journals are covered fully: every single article, research report, obituary, book review, editorial, and letter to the editor is indexed. The other 3,200 journals are covered selectively, principally for their major research articles and research reports.

The ISI staff also enters into the computer the *citations* in each article indexed—that is, they note all the references cited by each author of each article in each journal surveyed. The citations are alphabetized by author's last name. So, if you know the name of an author whose work *should* be cited by anyone working in a particular field, you can find out, for any given year, who cited that author, and where.

This allows you to search the literature *forward* in time rather than backward. Before the citation indexes were developed, all you could do was search backward. If you knew of an article published in 1985, then you could look at the references cited by its author. Those references would be no later than, say, 1984. Each of those references would also have a bibliography going back in time. But with the citation indexes, if you know of a single, classic article written in, say, 1978, you can find all the articles in which that article was cited in 1994 and work backward from those.

This means that older bibliographies, like those in the early issues of the *Annual Reviews of Anthropology* series, are no longer out of date. If you find a 1966 bibliography dealing with Melanesia, you can use it to determine the handful of classic references up to that time, and then go to the SSCI to find out who has cited those references since 1966. You would start with the current volume of the SSCI, because chances are that anyone citing a pre-1966 reference in a 1994 paper has also cited papers of interest to you that were published between 1966 and 1993.

The more science oriented of the 3,200 selectively covered journals in the SSCI are fully covered in SCI, and the humanities journals are covered in the AHCI. You need to supplement your literature search by referring to several other documentation resources, but you start with the citation indexes. The data from the 1,400 fully covered journals are on CD-ROM going back to 1987. The CD-ROM is very easy to use, but if you're going to search the SSCI before 1987, be prepared to spend time at it.

How much time? That depends on your research problem and whether you can afford to use a computer service to do the literature search for you. All the citation indexes, and a host of other documentation publications, are available for what is called "on-line interrogation." Most college and university libraries have computer terminals that you can use to do on-line literature searches. You simply interrogate the database of citation indexes and ask for a list of, say "all articles published in the last 20 years that cited Frank Cancian's 1965 book on *Economics and Prestige in a Mayan*

Community" or "all articles in the last 15 years with the words 'mental health' and 'migration' in the title," and so on.

These kinds of searches take only minutes, but can cost $100 if they find hundreds of references, which they will do if you phrase your question broadly (like "What are all the articles on refugee resettlement in the last 10 years?). Typically, however, on-line searches cost a lot less—more like $30, especially if you can phrase your question to home in on your topic of interest. Of course, if you're just shopping, you'll get exactly what you ask for: a shopping list.

You can do your search of the citation indexes without a computer by just spending time in the library. A typical search for a term paper in a senior or graduate course in anthropology takes about 3 or 4 hours with the SSCI. If you are doing a literature search for your MA or Ph.D thesis, plan on spending more like 15 or 20 hours with the SSCI. (Of course, this doesn't count the time it takes you to look up the references in the library, once you locate them.)

How to Use the SSCI

Full instructions for using the SSCI are given in each year's volumes, so I will only give you the outline here. You should be able to start using the SSCI immediately, though, from just the information in this chapter.

The SSCI is issued three times a year, with an annual issue that combines all the information into one set of six volumes. The set contains three main parts: a citation index, a source index, and a subject index. The subject index (called the *Permuterm*) consists of a list of all *pairs of words* in the titles of all articles surveyed (including book reviews, comments, etc.).

So, for example, if you were interested in studies of religion in Mexico, you could look up "Mexico" and go down the list until you got to "religion," or you could look up "religion" and go down the list until you got to "Mexico"—provided that authors of articles in which you might be interested had the good sense to give their work descriptive titles. (If you use the CD-ROM SSCI, you just give the computer pairs of words, one pair at a time, and the computer gives you a list of all the articles that contain the pair of key words in the title.)

Cute titles on scientific articles just hide them from people who want to find them in the SSCI or other indexing tools. If you write an article about illegal Mexican labor migration to the United States and call it something like "Whither Juan? Mexicans on the Road," it's a sure bet to get lost immediately, unless (a) you happen to publish it in one of the most widely read journals, and (b) it happens to be a blockbuster piece of work that everyone talks about and cites in articles that they write that *do* have descriptive titles. Since most scientific writing is not of the blockbuster variety, you're better off putting words into the titles of your articles that describe what the articles are about.

The actual citation index is an alphabetical listing of the last names of all the people who were cited in the journal articles surveyed during that year. Each citation also carries the year of the article cited (because many authors are cited for more than one of their works in any given year), along with the last name of the person who cited the article or book.

The source index is an alphabetical listing, by last name, of the primary authors who wrote the articles surveyed for the citation index. The full reference of the work is given, and each entry is identified as an article, book, review, letter, etc. *All referenced citations are listed for each work in the source index.* This is very important because it lets you tell whether an article is likely to be of use to you or not.

The source index even contains the address of the author, if it were provided in the article. This allows you to contact the author in case you can not get hold of the publication, or if you want to follow up with some questions or comments. Many sources are anonymous. The source index lists thousands of such items at the beginning of the volume, including book reviews in *Scientific American*, bibliographies in *Lancet*, and so on.

A search in the SSCI can begin with the name of an author whose work you already know (in which case you want to know who cited that work in any given year since 1956, the earliest year available); or it can begin with a topic. Suppose you are interested in race relations in Brazil. Except for the current volumes, the hard-copy version of the SSCI is organized in 5-year chunks: 1986-1990, 1981-1985, and so on.

You can take a current volume of the Permuterm Index, like 1991, and look up Brazil. You'll find articles published in 1991 that also contain the word "race" in their titles. Moving back through the volumes, you'll find dozens of articles that have those two words in their titles. In fact, if you go down the list of title words that co-occur with the word "Brazil" you'll also find things like "inequality" and "social mobility." These are all good possibilities.

In the 1981-1985 volume, there is a 1984 article under "race" by L. Culpi. If you look up L. Culpi in the source index, you'll find that the article is jointly written with F. M. Salzano, is entitled "Migration, Genetic-Markers, and Race Admixture in Curitiba, Brazil," and is published in the *Journal of Biosocial Studies*. Another article from the Permuterm for 1981-1985 was by C. A. A. Barbosa. It is with several other authors and is on "Race, Height, and Blood Pressure in Northeastern Brazil." It was published in *Social Biology*.

These articles seem somewhat peripheral to your search, but there are many articles in the 1981-1985 Permuterm that have "Brazil" and "inequality" in the title. One, by D. B. Bills, is a review of a book by J. Pastore entitled *Inequality and Social Mobility in Brazil*. The review was published in the 1984 volume of *Rural Sociology*.

The source index also tells you that, in 1984 at least, Bills was at the Illinois Institute of Technology, Department of Social Science, Chicago, IL 60616. You can check Bills's address by looking in the source index for recent years. If he's published anything recently in one of those 5,270 journals that the SSCI covers, a citation to it will turn up in the source index along with the author's address. The CD-ROM version of the SSCI, by the way, also contains this information.

Some topics are easier to study than others. There are dozens of unique references in the 1991 source index of the SSCI with the word "Nicaragua" in the title. On the other hand, there is very little in either the source or Permuterm indexes on the Maldive Islands. There are three sources dealing with the Maldives in 1982, all reviews of the same book, *People of the Maldive Islands* by C. Maloney, published in 1980. Apparently, very little work is being done on the Maldives. Perhaps the SSCI is just missing a lot of published research on the Maldives? Well, between 1981 and 1985, the SSCI indexed 2,401 journals fully (every book review, editorial, etc.), and another 2,869 journals selectively (just the major articles). Those journals yielded 617,156 source items (mostly full-length articles), and those source items produced 7,207,090 citations to 3,777,166 unique items by 884,249 unique authors. Think of it: citations to nearly 4 million different items, mostly books and articles (SSCI, 1981-1985, Vol. 1:25).

Now, 617,156 sources is only a good-sized fraction of all the significant social science papers published in the world in 5 years. But 3.77 *million* citations means that over the 5-year period, much of the significant literature on almost any topic is likely to be indexed.

The 5,270 journals covered by the SSCI between 1981 and 1985 might miss some papers that are important to your research, but the *authors* of all the papers in those journals are likely to have read, and cited, the available work that you need. All it takes is systematic effort on your part to run that work down.

Obscure and "Grey" Literature

But what about all those other journals—the ones that social scientists *don't* usually run across? What about articles that no one bothers to cite, especially articles in journals that are not covered by the SSCI? And what about government reports and other literature that are not published in journals and books? To ensure that your literature search is complete, you need to use several other documentation tools besides the citation indexes.

The most important are *Anthropological Index*; the *International Bibliography of Social and Cultural Anthropology*; the *Catalog of the Peabody Museum Library* and its continuing publication, *Anthropological Literature*; *Abstracts in Anthropology*; the various publications of the Congressional Information Service, Inc.; and *Geographical Abstracts*. There are also indexing and abstracting resources in fields such as sociology, psychology, women's studies, race relations, education, and criminology. All of them provide information of importance to anthropologists.

Anthropological Index (AI)

The AI is the index to the periodicals in the Museum of Mankind library, in the British Museum. It appears quarterly, from the Royal Anthropological Institute in London (RAI), and is up to date. The AI covers a lot of journals and papers that the SSCI does not cover, especially esoteric publications from Third World nations and from Eastern Europe. The 1983 volume contained over 8,000 items and listed 69 items under "South Asia, Ethnography," from sources such as the *Journal of the Indian Anthropological Society*, the *UNESCO Courier*, and the *Bulletin of the National Museum of Ethnology* in Osaka, Japan.

Abstracts in Anthropology (AIA)

AIA is a quarterly journal, published since 1970, that selectively covers current literature on archeology, cultural anthropology, physical anthropology, and linguistics. Indexing journals simply list all the items and cross-index them by author, title, and subject heading. An abstracting journal summarizes the articles it covers by publishing abstracts of anywhere from 50 to 200 words.

Indexing journals cover more ground; abstracting journals provide more depth. AIA publishes 150-word abstracts of the research articles in each of about 130 journals in each issue. AIA publishes the abstracts to all the research articles in the 7 most important journals for cultural anthropologists, so browsing through AIA from time to time is a good way to keep up with the leading edge of the discipline. The 7 top journals, in alphabetical order, are *American Anthropologist, American Ethnologist, Current Anthropology, Ethnology, Human Organization, Journal of Anthropological Research*, and *Man*.

AIA covers some journals not covered by other publications—journals like *Oral History* (published by the Institute of Papua New Guinea) and *Caribbean Studies* (published by the Institute of Caribbean Studies at the University of Puerto Rico). The SSCI does not cover the *Papers in Anthropology* series of the University of Oklahoma, now in its 28th volume, but AIA did cover it for 1983.

One of the papers abstracted that year was by G. Agogino and B. Ferguson on an Indian-Jewish community in the state of Hidalgo, Mexico, very close to the Ñähñu Indian communities I've studied.

Of course, I would have located the paper through the SSCI had anyone *cited* it in one of the 4,600 journals that the SSCI covered in 1984 and 1985; but a check revealed that no one did cite it, so looking through AIA was probably the only way I could have run into that particular piece of work. Just browsing through AI and AIA is a great way to keep up with what's going on in anthropology.

The International Bibliography of Social and Cultural Anthropology (IBSCA)

The *International Bibliography of the Social Sciences* (IBSS) is published by Tavistock Press under the auspices of the International Committee on Social Science Information and Documentation (ICSSID), a UNESCO-funded body. Every year since 1952, ICSSID has published IBSS in four volumes, one each on sociology, political science, economics, and anthropology. These volumes are based on data submitted by librarians around the world (from Thailand, Haiti, Zambia, Hungary, Argentina, etc.) who document the social science information being produced in their countries.

This information flows into the Paris headquarters of the ICSSID, is entered into a computer by a full-time indexing specialist, and is sorted and selected for inclusion in each year's volumes. IBSCA is the best source for locating materials published by national and regional journals in the Third World and in the Eastern European countries.

One of the important functions of ICSSID has been to develop a standard set of indexing terms for the four social science disciplines represented by the IBSS. The result of over 30 years of effort has been a systematic, thorough, and easy-to-follow indexing system. Under applied anthropology, for example, articles are indexed for community development, labor problems, housing, etc. The 1981 volume indexed 7,782 items from almost 600 different journals, and the subject index ran to more than 150 pages.

The Catalog of the Peabody Museum Library and Anthropological Literature (AL)

The library of the Peabody Museum of Archaeology and Ethnology, called the Tozzer Library, is the largest collection of anthropological literature in the world. The card catalog of the Tozzer collection identifies all the books, manuscripts, letters, periodicals, and articles in periodicals in the library's holdings.

That catalog, which contained 275,000 items, was published in 1963 in a set of 52 huge volumes, including 26 volumes of author cards and 26 volumes of subject cards. Four supplements were published; the last, published in 1979, added over 100,000 items. In 1979, the Tozzer Library began publishing a quarterly journal, called *Anthropological Literature* (AL), in which it indexes its acquisitions (much as *Anthropological Index* indexes the acquisitions of the Museum of Mankind Library in London).

All the indexing to the Tozzer Library's holdings since 1986 are in an on-line database called HOLLIS. If you have access to electronic mail at a major university, you can log into HOLLIS via Telenet to HOLLIS.HARVARD.EDU (Hay, 1992).

The original catalog of the Peabody Library, its supplements, and AL are particularly good for finding older materials in North American, Middle American, and South American archeology and ethnology. The Tozzer Library was founded in 1866, and many of the periodicals received by the library have been indexed since before World War I. You can use its published catalog, then, as a complete index to major journals such as the *American Anthropologist, American Antiquity*, and the like.

The Congressional Information Service (CIS)

The term "grey literature" refers to publications put out by government agencies, private foundations, and industries. A lot of this information is useful to anthropologists, but is hard to locate. The documentation tools that allow you to scour these sources are the *CIS Annual*, the *American Statistical Index* (ASI), the *Statistical Reference Index* (SRI), and the *Index to International Statistics* (IIS). All of them are products of the Congressional Information Service, Inc., or CIS.

These annual publications provide information on health care, housing, transportation, agriculture, protection of the environment, nutrition, compensatory education, rural-urban migration, and many other social issues. They will also help you locate research papers and primary data sources on the demographics of U.S. ethnic groups as well as basic demographic and economic data on other countries.

Each yearly issue of the CIS publications consists of two volumes: an index and abstracts. The abstracts volume provides source information and short abstracts for all the references covered in any given year. The index allows you to find the sources by looking up subject headings. The subject indexing system is extremely thorough. An item in the abstracts volume may be cross-listed under a dozen or more subject headings.

The *CIS Annual* volumes are a guide to publications of the U.S. Congress since 1970. In addition to congressional publications, the *CIS Annual* also references House and Senate hearings, joint hearings, reports entered into public access by submission to Congress, and testimony before congressional committees. All of these, of course, are in print and are available to the public. Some typical titles of reports referenced in the 1984 issue of the *CIS Annual* include "Alcohol and the Elderly," "Disposition of Judgment Funds Awarded the Creek Nation," "Indian Health Care: An Overview of the Federal Government's Role," "Navaho-Hopi Land Exchange," and "U.S.-Mexico Border Issues and the Peso Devaluation."

The *American Statistical Index* (ASI) has been published since 1973. It covers federal government publications, other than those issued by Congress, and not including government agency journals, which are covered by the *Index to U.S. Government Periodicals*. Even if you are at one of the universities that act as repositories for federal publications (and every state has at least one such library), that is no guarantee that you will find what you are looking for.

In fact, many publications of the federal government are neither listed by the Government Printing Office, nor available through them. They are not even available in repositories, even if they are listed in the master index, the *U.S. Superintendent of Documents Monthly Catalog*. Quite often, government publications of interest to scholars are only available through the agencies that issued them.

Fortunately, they are also available on microfiche in libraries that subscribe to the ASI. The ASI is the master guide, then, to all statistical publications of the U.S. government. It does not index technical materials, such as technical reports on contracts that are issued for research by federal agencies. Those are available through NTIS (the National Technical Information Service), NASA, the National Library of Medicine, and ERIC (the Educational Resources Information Center). The ASI also doesn't index congressional publications. Those are covered by *CIS Annual*.

The ASI lets you search for statistical reports on particular cities, regions, countries, applications topics, and ethnic groups. In going through the 1984 issue of the ASI, I found a report on the amount and value of U.S. Postal Service money orders sent to various countries in Latin America during 1983. This was an excellent source for estimating the importance of remittances by migrants to Latin American economies.

I also found reports on agricultural production in sub-Saharan Africa, by country, 1982-1983; food supply policies of 21 developing countries, with farm sector data, tariff income, and price and import amounts of five types of grain, 1960-1981; employment and training programs for Indians and Alaskan Natives, including funding allocations, by tribe and group; and so on. The ASI is *the* place to start if you are looking for basic demographic reports on ethnic segments of the U.S. population, including Micronesians, Indians, Alaskan Natives, Puerto Ricans, and Virgin Islanders.

The *Statistical Reference Index* (SRI), published since 1980, is a selective guide to U.S. statistical publications from private and state government sources. The SRI is a good place to look for data on U.S. ethnic populations. *Sales and Marketing*, for example, published tables in 1984 showing the distribution of Hispanics by state and by country of origin. The wages of Arizona farm workers and their hours of labor, quarterly, from 1979 to 1981, are given in a report from the Crop and Livestock Reporting Service of the University of Arizona. *Maine Educational Facts 1982-1983* published data on the number of Indians attending public school in Maine, by grade.

Many statistical reports generated by U.S. state and private agencies deal with other nations. The SRI volume for 1984 documented reports and articles on the population characteristics of Bangladesh; the living arrangements of young (15 to 24) Western Europeans; the distribution of telephones by country in 1982; refugee populations and resettlements, by country; bank loans to South African countries; and visitor arrivals in Pacific area countries, by country of origin, travel mode, visitor gender, expenditures, and types of lodging for 1982.

The documents cited in the SRI are all on microfiche. Larger libraries subscribe to the microfiche collection, along with the SRI. If your library doesn't have the microfiche collection, you can write to the agency or corporation that issued a particular listed report and get a copy.

Finally, CIS introduced the *Index to International Statistics* (IIS) in 1983. The 10 years of these volumes are an absolute treasure trove for anthropologists. You can look up statistical reports on applications topics (health care, development, migration, refugees, etc.), or on particular countries or cities.

If you are doing research on Hong Kong, for example, you might want to see the report on educational enrollments there, with trends predicted to the year 2000 (from UNESCO), or the one on health conditions and services, 1970-2004 (from WHO), or the one on income distribution and its relation to economic development and government policy (from ILO). Your research might benefit from the UN report on infant deaths, by country, or from the WHO report on diarrhea incidence and death among children under age 5 in 11 African and Asian countries.

Like the ASI and the SRI, the IIS also comes with an optional microfiche collection of the actual documents indexed and abstracted in the master volumes. The CIS publications are indispensable tools for anthropologists who really want to find out what's out there.

Geographical Abstracts (GA)

Since 1966, GA has published yearly volumes on social and historical geography, economic geography, and regional and community planning. I consider these volumes essential documentation resources for cultural anthropologists.

The volume on social and historical geography, for example, includes sections on migration, human relations to the environment, medical geography, cultural geography, and historical documentary evidence. In the 1982 volume I located a government manuscript by Henry Selby and A. I. Murphy on "The Role of the Mexican Urban Household in Decisions About Migration to the U.S." The citation was taken from the 1981 volume of the *U.S. Government Reports Announcements* bulletin. I went to the *American Statistical Index* but was not able to locate the document; the listing in the *Announcements* bulletin, however, made the report accessible, so without *Geographical Abstracts* I'd have missed Selby and Murphy's work.

GA has very good international coverage. I found an article by J. G. Velásquez, published in *Amazonia Peruana*, which looks at migrations of families along several rivers in the Amazon. This article, in Spanish, was abstracted in English in GA, but there was no reference to the article in any of the other documentation sources. Of particular interest to me was an article on "Tourism as a Development Factor in Tropical Countries: A Case Study of Cancún, Mexico," by E. Gormsen, published in *Applied Geography and Development* in 1982. This article was not in the SSCI source index.

Current Index to Journals in Education

The *Current Index to Journals in Education* (CIJE), is a monthly guide, covering 780 major social science journals, published since 1969. You can find a lot of things in the CIJE that you can't find in the SSCI, because of the CIJE's thorough subject index. For example, in the January-June 1985 issue, I looked up the subject heading "Belize" and found an article entitled "Gender Understanding and Sex Role Preference in Four Cultures" by R. H. Munroe et al., published in *Developmental Psychology*, 1984. The article describes the results of a study using both a scale of gender understanding and a measure of sex-role preference among 3- to 9-year-olds in Belize, Kenya, Nepal, and American Samoa.

Since none of the countries' names appears in the title, you won't find this article in the subject index of the SSCI—which you'll recall is based on all pairs of significant title words—unless you look under gender, or sex role, or understanding, or preference. If Munroe's article is cited by others since 1985, then you will find those citations in the SSCI under R. H. Munroe in the citation index for those years—but only if you already know about the article and the author's name.

Other Important Documentation Resources

Students of American Indian cultures should become familiar with the catalog of manuscripts at the National Anthropological Archives (NAA). The archives are housed in the Department of Anthropology, National Museum of Natural History, Smithsonian Institution. The original purpose of the archive was to aid Bureau of American Ethnology (BAE) staff in their studies of American Indians between 1879, when the BAE was founded, and 1965, when it and the National Museum's Department of Anthropology were combined into the Smithsonian's Office of Anthropology.

The *Bibliographic Index*, published continuously since 1937, indexes over 2,600 scholarly periodicals for substantial bibliographies. It also lists separate, published bibliographies by subject. The subject index allows you to find reference lists in many topical specialties within cultural anthropology, archeology, and physical anthropology. This is a very good place to start if you are looking for some basic leads into the citation index of the SSCI.

Anyone interested in peasant peoples will find the *World Agricultural Economics and Rural Sociology Abstracts* (WAERSA, since 1959) an indispensable resource. WAERSA covers journals published in 48 languages. It has a thorough subject index and abstracts over 7,000 items a year, including many articles and symposium proceedings on adoption of agricultural innovations, farming systems research, rural development, and collectives.

Sociological Abstracts (SA, since 1952) has excellent coverage of research methodology, the sociology of language, occupations and professions, health, family violence, poverty, and social control. It covers the sociology of knowledge and the sociology of science, as well as the sociology of the arts, religion, and education. SA also has good coverage of Marxist sociology.

If you are working in the area of criminal justice, you will want to consult the *Criminal Justice Periodical Index* (CJPI), as well as *Criminology and Penology Abstracts* (CPA) and *Criminal Justice Abstracts* (CJA). *Sociological Abstracts* handles some of the work indexed in these two publications, but the CJPI, CPA, and CJA provide much more in-depth coverage of these fields.

Medical and nutritional anthropologists should consult the *Index Medicus* (IM). In addition to the clinical literature, IM indexes studies on alcoholism and drug abuse, cultural factors in disease formation and control, cultural factors in nutrition, and ethnopharmacology.

Anthropologists interested in cognition, culture and personality, learning and perception, growth and development, or cross-cultural psychology should become familiar with *Psychology Abstracts* (PA). The 1984 subject index of PA listed 68 references to Mexican-Americans, for example. It also listed 42 articles dealing with Mexico, 57 dealing with Nigeria, and 11 dealing with Thailand.

There were 33 references to cultural assimilation in the 1984 PA, some of which overlap with the references to Mexican-Americans. I found 40 indexed articles on cultural bias in testing and over 300 articles reporting tests of cross-cultural differences in such things as reticence, perception of women's roles, alienation, and so on. PA indexed and abstracted more than 33,000 articles in 1984. Learning and perception are also covered in *Child Development Abstracts and Bibliography* (since 1927).

Linguistic anthropologists should become familiar with *Language and Language Behavior Abstracts* (since 1967); *Linguistic Bibliography* (since 1948); and *Communications Abstracts* (since 1978).

If you are interested in political anthropology, you should start browsing through the *International Political Science Abstracts*. It has appeared annually since 1951 and is a good source of information on political movements. Of related interest, and quite useful, are the *Gallup Reports*, which, since 1935, have published the results of all the Gallup polls. The *Index to International Public Opinion Research* (since 1978) provides similar data for other countries, mostly in Western Europe and Japan. Political anthropologists will also find the *Peace Research Abstracts Journal* (since 1970), and the *Sage Public Administration Abstracts* of value.

Urban anthropologists should consult the *Sage Urban Studies Abstracts*. Those interested in demography should look at the *Population Index* for references to studies on migration, fertility, natality, health and welfare, and mortality. The *Population Index* is a critical resource for basic demographic information about any country in which you are conducting research.

The *Poverty and Human Resources Abstracts* (since 1966) are particularly useful for finding research on immigration, ethnic and minority groups, aging and retirement, poverty and public policy, women's health and minority health, labor force participation, and similar social issues. Other documentation resources for social issues include *Sage Race Relations Abstracts*, *Inventory of Marriage and Family Literature*, and *Sage Family Studies Abstracts*. The quarterly *Women's Studies Abstracts* is an international journal that abstracts articles on women's roles. Many entries are historical, or deal with non-Western cultures.

The *British Humanities Index* (since 1962) has good coverage of international folklore and ethnic minority studies and provides coverage of British journals that are not indexed in other publications.

The *Film Literature Index* is an international quarterly journal that documents films, including ethnographic films and film reviews.

Scholars in all fields should be familiar with the weekly journal called *Current Contents* (CC), founded in 1961. CC simply reproduces the tables of contents of journals. There are a number of versions of CC: one on the life sciences, one on mathematics, one on physics, and so on. The one on social and behavioral and social sciences lists the tables of contents of 1,300 journals from around the world. Each issue carries a key-word index, taken from the titles of the articles, as well as an author index. If you are interested in keeping on top of a fast-breaking field, CC is *the* publication to consult.

Finally, medical anthropologists should become familiar with the on-line database services BIOSIS PREVIEWS, LIFE SCIENCES COLLECTION, MEDLINE, and EMBASE (computer programs and databases are customarily written in capital letters). Droessler and Wilke (1984) reviewed all these databases and found EMBASE to be the overall best value for physical anthropologists.

Whether or not you use an on-line service, there is no way to overemphasize the importance of using the documentation tools described here when you are starting out on a research project. The indexes and abstracting journals will help you do that.

CD-ROM and On-Line Databases

Many of the documentation resources I've reviewed here are available in CD-ROM. These handy disks are very expensive, but most college libraries now subscribe to at least some of the important CD-ROM products. Besides the *Social Science Citation Index*, all the Congressional Information Service resources are available on CD-ROM. The CIS index is available all the way back to 1789. The *American Statistical Index on CD-ROM* goes back to 1973. The *Statistical Reference Index* on disk goes back to 1980; and the *Index to International Statistics* goes back to 1983. These resources make it very, very easy to hunt through masses of literature.

Below are some other CD-ROM resources of interest to anthropologists.

Cumulative Index to Nursing and Allied Health

This product indexes over 300 journals, plus books and dissertations. The index goes back to 1983 and is updated monthly. A must for medical anthropologists.

ERIC

The CD-ROM version of ERIC contains the *Current Index to Journals in Education* (CIJE—see above) and the *Resources in Education* file, which covers citations to conference proceedings, reports, and other hard-to-find literature. This database begins with 1966 and is updated quarterly.

MLA International Bibliography on Wilsondisc

The Modern Language Association's *International Bibliography* indexes over 3,000 journals from all over the world. In addition to literature and language, the source journals cover linguistics and folklore. This is a particularly good resource for many cultural anthropologists. The database begins with 1981 sources and is updated quarterly.

NTIS

The National Technical Information Service indexes and abstracts federally funded research reports in all areas of science. If you want to find archeological site reports from federally funded projects, this is the place to look. The database goes back to 1983 and is updated quarterly.

PSYCLIT

This is an absolutely massive database that indexes and abstracts books and journals in psychology and related fields. Many of the journals covered in *PSYCLIT* are of interest to anthropologists. Because the database contains abstracts as well as citations, this is one of the most popular CD-ROM products among social science researchers. The database goes back to 1974 and is updated quarterly.

SOCIOFILE

This has a selection of abstracts from *Sociological Abstracts* (see above) and from the *Social Planning/Policy and Development Abstracts* (SOPODA) database. This is another very popular database among social researchers, with journal indexing going back to 1974. The database is updated every 4 months.

LEXIS/NEXIS

If your library has *LEXIS/NEXIS*, don't consider any literature search complete until you've used this system. This database contains the actual text of articles from the major English-language newspapers and magazines.

OCLC

The Online Computer Library Center, or OCLC, is the world's largest library database. Nearly 5,000 libraries catalog their holdings in OCLC, and in 1992 the OCLC had 25 million bibliographic records (Hay, 1993). While all major libraries (and thousands of minor libraries) throughout the industrialized world have OCLC, they don't give their patrons direct access to the system. But if your library allows direct access to OCLC, then this is the place to start.

7

Participant Observation

"Once the field worker has gained entry, people tend to forget he is there, and let down their guard, but he does not; however much he seems to participate, he is really there to observe and even to watch what happens when people let down their guard" (Gans, 1968:314).

What Is Participant Observation?

Participant observation, or ethnographic fieldwork, is the foundation of cultural anthropology. It involves getting close to people and making them feel comfortable enough with your presence so that you can observe and record information about their lives. If this sounds a bit crass, I mean it to come out that way. Only by confronting the truth about participant observation—that it involves a certain amount of deception and impression

136

management—can we hope to conduct ourselves ethically in fieldwork. I'll have a lot more to say about this in Chapter 15.

Some participant observers advocate "going native" and "becoming the phenomenon" (Jorgensen, 1989), but most anthropologists advocate maintaining some distance and objectivity. Later in this chapter, I'll discuss this issue in some detail.

The thing to remember about participant observation is that it is belongs to everyone, interpretivists and positivists alike. Anthropologists of both epistemological persuasions do participant observation fieldwork to collect life-history documents, attend sacred festivals, and talk to people about sensitive topics. Others use it to do time allocation studies or to make detailed counts of calorie budgets. Whether your data consist of numbers or words, participant observation lets you in the door so you can do research.

Participant observation involves establishing rapport in a new community; learning to act so that people go about their business as usual when you show up; and removing yourself every day from cultural immersion so you can intellectualize what you've learned, put it into perspective, and write about it convincingly.

If you are a successful participant observer you will know when to laugh at what your informants think is funny; and when informants laugh at what you say, it will be because you *meant* it to be a joke.

Participant Observation and Fieldwork

All participant observation is fieldwork, but not all fieldwork is participant observation. If you make up a questionnaire in your office, send it out, and wait for the mail to bring your data in, that's not field research. If you take a random sample of a community, go door to door, and do a series of face-to-face interviews, that *is* field research—but it's not participant observation. If you go to a native market in a community that you've never visited before and monitor the behavior of patrons and clients as they go through their transactions, that, too, is field research, but it isn't participant observation. It's just plain observation.

Participant observation fieldwork can involve an array of data collection methods. These include observation, natural conversations, various kinds of interviews (structured, semistructured, and unstructured), checklists, questionnaires, and unobtrusive methods. We'll look at all of these and more in the other chapters in this section of the book.

Fieldwork Roles

Fieldwork can involve two quite different roles—that of participating observer and that of observing participant. By far, most anthropological research is based on the first role, that of participating observer.

In 1965 I went to sea with a group of Greek sponge fishermen in the Mediterranean. I lived in close quarters with them, ate the same awful food as they did, and generally participated in their life—as an outsider. I did not dive for sponges, but spent most of my waking hours studying the behavior and the conversation of the men who did. The divers were curious about what I was writing in my notebooks, but they went about their business and just let me take notes, time their dives, and shoot movies (Bernard, 1987). I was a participating observer.

Gene Shelley (1992) studied people who suffer from end-stage kidney disease. She spent hundreds of hours in a dialysis clinic, observing, listening, chatting, interviewing, and taking notes on all aspects of the patients' lives. She did not pretend she was a nurse. Nor did she go through dialysis herself. She, too, assumed the first role: participating observer.

Circumstances can sometimes overtake the role of mere participating observer. William Kornblum was doing fieldwork with a group of Boyash (gypsies) in France. One night, the camp was attacked by a rival group and Kornblum found himself on the front line. The woman of the house where he was living "had no sympathy for the distinction between participant and observer. She thrust a heavy stick in my hand shoved me toward the door" (1989:1).

Mark Fleisher (1989) took the second role, that of observing participant. Senior researchers at the U.S. Bureau of Prisons asked Fleisher to do an ethnographic study of job pressures among correctional officers ("guards" in plain English) in a maximum-security federal penitentiary. Fleisher said he'd be glad to do the research and asked when he could start "walking the mainline" with the guards—that is, accompany them on their rounds through the prison. He was told that he'd be given an office at the prison and that the guards would come to the office to be interviewed.

Fleisher said he was sorry, but he'd have to have the run of the prison. He was told that only sworn correctional officers could walk the prison halls. So Fleisher went to training camp for 6 weeks and became a sworn federal correctional officer. *Then* he began his yearlong study of the penitentiary at Lompoc, California. He became an observing participant in the culture he was studying. Note, though, that Fleisher never hid what he was doing. When he went to USP-Lompoc, he told everyone that he was an anthropologist doing a study of prison life.

Barbara Marriott (1991) studied how the wives of U.S. Navy male officers contributed to their husbands' careers. Marriott was herself the wife of a retired captain. She was able to bring the empathy of 30 years' full participation to her study. She, too, took the role of observing participant and, like Fleisher, she told her informants exactly what she was doing.

Some field workers start out as participating observers and find that they are drawn completely into their informants' lives. This happened to Kenneth Good when he went to study the Yanomami in the Amazon. He learned Yanomami, married a Yanomami woman, and wound up staying in the forest for 13 years (Good, 1991). Marlene Dobkin de Rios did fieldwork in Peru and married the son of a Peruvian folk healer, whose practice she studied (Dobkin de Rios, 1981). There are many examples of anthropologists "going native," and sometimes it leads to interesting books. It can also lead to just dropping out of research. This is a personal decision.

Note that I don't count the "uninvolved, fly-on-the-wall observer" as one of the types of participant observation. Direct observation is a potent method for gathering data, though. John Roberts did a landmark direct observation study. In 1949, he and a Zuni interpreter took turns sitting in one of the rooms of a Zuni house and simply dictating their observations into a tape recorder. This went on for 5 days and the data produced an entire book, rich in detail about Zuni life at the time. People let Roberts park in their homes for 5 days because Roberts was a participant observer of Zuni life and had gained his informants' confidence.

How Much Time Does It Take?

Most basic anthropological research is done over a period of about a year, but a lot of participant observation studies are done in a matter of weeks. Applied anthropologists may not have the luxury of doing long-term participant observation fieldwork and may use rapid assessment procedures instead. Rapid assessment of agricultural or medical practices may include participant observation.

Basically, rapid assessment means going in and getting on with the job of collecting data without spending months developing rapport. This means going into a field situation armed with a list of questions that you want to answer and perhaps a checklist of data that you need to collect. Chambers (1991) advocates what he calls participatory rural appraisal. In participatory mapping, for example, he asks people to draw maps of villages and locate key places on the maps.

In participatory transects, he borrows from wildlife biology and systematically walks through an area, with key informants, observing and asking for explanations of everything he sees along the transect. He engages people in group discussions of key events in a village's history, and asks people to identify clusters of households according to wealth.

In other words, as an applied anthropologist, Chambers is called on to do rapid assessment of rural village needs, and he takes the people fully into his confidence as research partners. (For an introduction to rapid assessment in medical anthropology, see Scrimshaw & Hurtado, 1987; for rapid assessment procedure in agricultural research, see Shaner et al., 1982.)

At the extreme low end it is possible to do useful participant observation in just a few days. Assuming that you've wasted as much time in laundromats as I did when I was a student, you could conduct a reasonable participant observation study of one such place in a week. You'd begin by bringing in a load of wash and paying careful attention to what's going on around you.

After two or three nights of observation, you'd be ready to tell other patrons that you were conducting research and that you'd appreciate their letting you interview them. The reason you could do this is because you already speak the native language and have already picked up the nuances of etiquette from previous experience. Participant observation would help you intellectualize what you already know.

The amount of time that you spend in the field doing participant observation research does make a difference, however, in what you are likely to find. Raoul Naroll (1962) compared ethnographies that were based on a year or more in the field with those based on less than a year. He found that anthropologists who stayed in the field for at least a year were more likely to report on sensitive issues like witchcraft, sexuality, political feuds, etc. Also, anthropologists who have done very long-term participant observation, in a series of studies over several decades, find that they eventually get data about social change that is simply not possible to get in any other way (Foster et al., 1979).

Validity—Again

There are at least five reasons for insisting on participant observation in the conduct of scientific research about cultural groups.

1. First, as I've stressed, participant observation makes it possible to collect different kinds of data. Anthropologists have witnessed births,

interviewed violent men in maximum-security prisons, stood in fields noting the behavior of farmers, trekked with hunters through the Amazon forest in search of game, and pored over records of marriages, births, and deaths in village churches around the world.

It is impossible to imagine a complete stranger walking into a birthing room and being welcomed to watch and record the event, or being allowed to examine a community's vital records at whim. It is impossible, in fact, to imagine a total stranger doing *any* of the things just mentioned, or the thousands of other intrusive acts of data collection that anthropologists engage in. What makes all this possible is participant observation.

2. Second, participant observation reduces the problem of reactivity— i.e., people changing their behavior when they know that they are being studied. As you become less and less of a curiosity, people take less and less interest in your comings and goings. They go about their business and let you do such bizarre things as conduct interviews, administer questionnaires, and even walk around with a stopwatch, clipboard, and camera. Lower reactivity means higher validity of data.

Nothing is guaranteed in fieldwork, though. When Le Compte told children at a school that she was writing a book about them, they started acting out in "ways they felt would make good copy" by mimicking characters on popular TV programs (Le Compte et al., 1993).

3. Third, participant observation helps you formulate sensible questions, in the native language. Have you ever gotten a questionnaire in the mail and said to yourself "What a dumb set of questions"? If a social scientist who is a member of your own culture can make up what you consider to be "dumb" questions, imagine the risk *you* take in making up a questionnaire in a culture very different from your own. Remember, too, that it's just as important to ask sensible questions in a face-to-face interview as it is on a survey instrument.

4. Fourth, participant observation gives you an intuitive understanding of what's going on in a culture and allows you to speak with confidence about the meaning of data. It lets you make strong statements about cultural facts that you've collected. It extends both the internal and the external validity of what you learn from interviewing and watching people. In short, participant observation helps you understand the *meaning* of your observations. Here's a classic example.

In 1957, N. K. Sarkar and S. J. Tambiah published a study, based on questionnaire data, about economic and social disintegration in a Sri

Lankan village. They concluded that about two-thirds of the villagers were landless. The British anthropologist, Edmund Leach, did not accept that finding (Leach, 1967). He had done participant observation fieldwork in the area and knew that the villagers practiced patrilocal residence after marriage. By local custom, a young man might receive use of some of his father's land even though legal ownership might not pass to the son until the father's death.

In assessing land ownership, Sarkar and Tambiah asked whether a "household" had any land, and if so, how much. They defined an independent household as a unit that cooked rice in its own pot. Unfortunately, all married women in the village had their own rice pots. So, Sarkar and Tambiah wound up estimating the number of independent households as very high, and the number of those households that owned land as very low. Based on these data, they concluded that there was gross inequality in land ownership and that this characterized a "disintegrating village" (the title of their book).

You should not conclude from Leach's critique that questionnaires are "bad" while participant observation is "good." Participant observation makes it possible to collect both quantitative survey data and qualitative interview data from a representative sample of a population. Qualitative and quantitative data inform each other and produce insight and understanding in ways that can not be duplicated by either approach alone. Whatever data collection methods you choose, participant observation maximizes your chances for making valid statements.

5. Fifth, many research problems simply can not be addressed adequately by anything except participant observation. If you want to understand how a local court works, you can't very well disguise yourself and sit in the court room unnoticed. The judge would soon spot you as a stranger, and after a few days you would have to explain yourself. It is better to explain yourself at the beginning and get permission to act as a participant observer. In this case, your participation consists of acting like any other local person who might sit in on the court's proceedings.

After a few days, or weeks, you would have a pretty good idea of how the court worked: what kinds of crimes are adjudicated, what kinds of penalties are meted out, and so forth. You might develop some specific hypotheses from your qualitative notes—hypotheses regarding covariations between severity of punishment and independent variables other than severity of crime. Then you could test those hypotheses on a sample of courts.

If you think this is unrealistic, try going down to your local traffic court and see whether defendants' dress or manner of speech predict variations in fines for the same infraction. The point is, getting a general understanding of how any social institution or organization works—the local justice system, a hospital, a ship, or an entire village—is best achieved through participant observation.

Entering the Field

Perhaps the most difficult part of actually doing participant observation fieldwork is making an entry. There are five rules to follow.

1. First of all, there is no reason to select a site that is difficult to enter when equally good sites are available that are easy to enter (see Chapter 5). In many cases, you *will* have a choice—among equally good villages in a region, or hospitals, or political precincts, or cell blocks. In those cases, choose the field site that promises to provide easiest access to data.

2. Go into the field with plenty of written documentation about yourself and your project. You need one or more letters of introduction from your university, your funding agency, or your client if you are doing contract research. Letters from universities should spell out your affiliation, who is funding you, and how long you will be at the field site. Be sure that any such letters are in the language spoken where you will be working, and that they are signed by the highest academic authorities possible.

Letters of introduction should not go into detail about your proposed research. If you are going to do research on a modern institution, prepare a separate document, in the native language of the field site, describing your proposed work, and present it to gatekeepers along with your letters of introduction.

3. Don't try to wing it, unless you absolutely have to. There is nothing to be said for "getting in on your own." Use personal contacts to help you make your entry into a field site. When I went to the island of Kalymnos, Greece, in 1964, I carried with me a list of people to look up. I collected the list from people in the Greek-American community of Tarpon Springs, Florida, who had relatives on Kalymnos.

If you are studying modern institutions (hospitals, police departments, universities, etc.), it is usually best to start at the top and work down. Find out the names of the people who are the gatekeepers and see them first. Assure them that you will maintain strict confidentiality and that no one in your study will be personally identifiable. In some cases, starting at the top can backfire, though. If there are warring factions in a community or organization, and if you gain entry to the group at the top of *one* of those factions, you will be asked to side with that faction.

Another danger is that top administrators of institutions may try to enlist you as a kind of spy. They may offer to facilitate your work if you will report back to them on what you find out about specific individuals. This is absolutely off limits in research. If that's the price of doing a study, you're better off choosing another institution. In my 2 years as a consultant to the Federal Bureau of Prisons, no one ever asked me to report on the activities of specific inmates. But other applied researchers have reported experiencing this pressure, so it's worth keeping in mind.

4. Think through in advance what you will say when people ask you: What are you doing here? Who sent you? Who's funding you? What good is your research and who will it benefit? Why do you want to learn about people here? How long will you be here? How do I know you aren't a spy for _____ ? (where the blank is filled in by whoever people are afraid of). The rules for presentation of self are simple: Be honest, be brief, and be consistent. In participant observation, if you try to play any role other than yourself, you'll just get worn out (D. Jones, 1973).

5. Spend time getting to know the physical and social layout of your field site. If you are working in a village, or an urban enclave, or a hospital, then walk it and map it. If you are working in a large area, you may not be able to map it, but you should walk as much of it as possible, as early as possible in your fieldwork. If you are studying a group that has no physical location (such as a social movement), it still pays to spend time "mapping the social scene" (Schatzman & Strauss, 1973). This means getting down the names of the key players and charting their relationships.

Similarly, it is a good idea to make a kinship chart of a village, and to take a census as soon as you can. Be careful, though. Taking a census can be a way to gain rapport in a community (walking around and visiting every household can have the effect of giving you credibility), but it can also backfire if people are afraid you might be a spy. Agar (1980) was branded as a Pakistani spy when he went to India, so his village census was useless.

The Skills of a Participant Observer

To a certain extent, participant observation must be learned in the field. The strength of participant observation is that you, as a researcher, become the instrument for both data collection and analysis through your own experience. Consequently, you have to experience participant observation to get good at it. Nevertheless, there are a number of skills that you can develop before you go into the field.

Learning the Language

Unless you are a full participant in the culture you're studying, being a participant observer makes you a freak. Here's how anthropologists looked to Vine Deloria (1969), a Sioux writer:

> Anthropologists can readily be identified on the reservations. Go into any crowd of people. Pick out a tall gaunt white man wearing Bermuda shorts, a World War II Army Air Force flying jacket, an Australian bush hat, tennis shoes, and packing a large knapsack incorrectly strapped on his back. He will invariably have a thin, sexy wife with stringy hair, an I.Q. of 191, and a vocabulary in which even the prepositions have eleven syllables. . . . This creature is an anthropologist. (p. 78)

Now, 25 years later, it may be the anthropologist's husband who has the stringy hair, but the point remains: The most important thing you can do to stop being a freak is to speak the language of the people you're studying—and speak it well. Over 30 years ago, Raoul Naroll (1962:89-90) surveyed ethnographies and found that anthropologists who speak the local language are statistically more likely to report witchcraft than those who don't. His interpretation was that local language fluency improves your rapport, and this, in turn, increases the probability that people will tell you about witchcraft.

Does the credibility of our data depend on control of the local language? In 1933 Paul Radin, one of Franz Boas's students, complained that Margaret Mead's work on Samoa was superficial because she wasn't fluent in Samoan (1966, orig. 1933:179). Fifty years later, Derek Freeman (1983) claimed that Mead had been duped by her informants because she didn't know the local language.

According to Brislin et al. (1973:70), Samoa is one of those cultures where "it is considered acceptable to deceive and to 'put on' outsiders. Interviewers are likely to hear ridiculous answers, not given in a spirit of hostility but rather sport." Brislin et al. call this the "sucker bias" and warn field workers to watch out for it. Presumably, knowing the local language fluently is one way to become alert to and avoid this problem.

How to Learn a New Language

In my experience, the way to learn a new language is to learn a few words and to say them brilliantly. Yes, you should study the grammar and vocabulary and so on, but the key to learning a new language is saying things right, even just a handful of things. This means capturing not just the pronunciation of words, but also the intonation, the use of your hands, and other nonverbal cues that show you are really, really serious about the language and are trying to look and sound as much like a native as possible.

When you say "hey, hiya doin'" or its equivalent in !Khosa or Aymara with just the right intonation, people will think you know more than you do. They'll come right back at you with a flurry of words, and you'll be lost. That's just fine. Tell them to slow down—again, in that great accent you're cultivating. Consider the alternative: You announce to people, with the first, badly accented word out of your mouth, that you know next to nothing about the language and that they should therefore speak to you with that in mind.

When you talk to someone who is not a native speaker of your language, you make an automatic assessment of how large their vocabulary is and how fluent they are. You adjust both the speed of your speech and your vocabulary to ensure comprehension. That's what !Khosa and Aymara speakers will do with you, too. So, the trick is to act in a way that gets people into pushing your limits of fluency and into teaching you cultural insider phrases.

As you articulate more and more of those phrases like a native, people will increase the rate at which they teach you by raising the level of their discourse with you. They may even compete to teach you the subtleties of their language and culture. When I was learning Greek on Greek merchant vessels, the sailors took delight in seeing to it that my vocabulary of obscenities was up to their standards and that my usage of that vocabulary was suitably robust.

Try to find an intensive summer course in the country where your field language is spoken. Not only will you learn the language, you'll make personal contacts, find out what the problems are in selecting a research site, and discover how to tie your study to the interests of local scholars.

If you can't go to the country where the language is spoken, then study the language at your university. Today, there are university and self-study courses available in Ulithi, Aymara, Quechua, Nahuatl, Swahili, Turkish, Amharic, Basque, Eskimo, Navaho, Zulu, Hausa, Amoy, and many other languages. If the language you need is not offered in a formal course, then try to find an individual scholar of the language who would be willing to tutor you in a self-paced course.

When Not to Mimic

My rule about mimicking pronunciation changes when you are studying an ethnic or occupational subculture in your own society and the people in that subculture speak a different dialect of your native language. In this situation, mimicking the local pronunciation will just make you look silly. Even worse, people may think you're ridiculing them.

The key to understanding the culture of loggers, lawyers, bureaucrats, schoolteachers, or ethnic groups, however, is to become intimately familiar with their vocabulary. Words are where the cultural action is. (For lots of good hints about learning a field language, see Burling, 1984.)

Building Explicit Awareness

Another important skill in participant observation is what Spradley (1980:5) called "explicit awareness" of the little details in life. Try this experiment: The next time you see someone look at their watch, go right up to them and ask them the time. Chances are they'll look again because when they looked the first time they were not *explicitly aware* of what they saw. Tell them that you are a student conducting a study and ask them to chat with you for a few minutes about how they tell time.

Many people who wear analog watches look at the *relative positions* of the hands, and not at the numbers on the dial. They subtract the current time (the position of the hands now) from the time they have to be somewhere (the image of what the position of the hands will look like at some time in the future), and calculate whether the difference is anything to worry about. They never have to become explicitly aware of the fact that it is 3:10 p.m. People who wear digital watches may be handling the process somewhat differently.

Kronenfeld et al. (1972) report an experiment in which informants leaving several different restaurants were asked what the waiters and waitresses were wearing and what kind of music was playing. Informants agreed much more about what the waiters were wearing than about what the waitresses were wearing. The hitch: None of the restaurants had waiters at all, only waitresses.

Informants also provided more detail about the kind of music in restaurants that did not have music than they provided for restaurants that did have music. Kronenfeld speculated that, in the absence of real memories about things they'd seen or heard, informants turned to cultural norms for what must have been there, i.e., "what goes with what" (D'Andrade, 1973).

You can test this yourself. Pick out a large lecture hall where a male professor is not wearing a tie. Ask a group of students on their way out of a lecture hall what color tie their professor was wearing. Or observe a busy store clerk for an hour and count the number of sales she rings up. Then ask her to estimate the number of sales she handled during that hour.

You can build your skills at becoming explicitly aware of ordinary things. Get a group of colleagues together and write separate, detailed descriptions of the most mundane, ordinary things you can think of: making a bed, doing laundry, building a sandwich, shaving (face, legs, underarms), picking out produce at the supermarket, and so on. Then discuss one another's descriptions and see how many details others saw that you didn't and vice versa. If you work carefully at this exercise you'll develop a lot of respect for how complex, and how important, the details of ordinary life are.

Building Memory

Even when we are explicitly aware of things we see, there is no guarantee that we'll remember them long enough to write them down. Building your ability to remember things you see and hear is crucial to successful participant observation research.

Try this exercise: Walk past a store window at a normal pace. When you get beyond it and can't see it any longer, write down all the things that were in the window. Go back and check. Do it again with another window. You'll notice an improvement in your ability to remember little things almost immediately. You'll become acutely aware of how much you don't see unless you concentrate, and you'll start immediately to create mnemonic devices for remembering more of what you do see. Keep up this exercise until you are satisfied that you can't get any better at it.

Here's another one. Go to a church service, other than one you're used to. Take along two colleagues. When you leave, write up what you each think you saw, in as much detail as you can muster, and compare what you've written. Go back to the church and keep doing this exercise until all of you are satisfied that (a) you are all seeing and writing down the same things, and (b) you have reached the limits of your ability to recall complex behavioral scenes.

Try this same exercise by going to a church service with which you *are* familiar and take along several colleagues who are *not*. Again, compare your notes with theirs and keep going back and taking notes until you and they are seeing and noting the same things. You can do this with any repeated scene that's familiar to you: a bowling alley, a fast-food restaurant, etc. Remember, training your ability to see things reliably does not guarantee that you'll see thing accurately. But unless you become at least a reliable instrument of data gathering, you don't stand much of a chance of making valid conclusions.

Bogdan (1972:41) offers some practical suggestions for remembering details in participant observation. If for some reason you can't take notes during an interview or at some event, and you are trying to remember what was said, *don't talk to anyone* before you get your thoughts down on paper. Talking to people reinforces some things you heard and saw at the expense of other things.

Also, when you sit down to write, try to remember things in historical sequence, as they occurred throughout the day. As you write up your notes you will invariably remember some particularly important detail that just pops into memory out of sequence. When that happens, jot it down on a separate piece of paper (or tuck it away in a separate little note file on your word processor) and come back to it later, when your notes reach that point in the sequence of the day.

Another useful device is to draw a map of the physical space where you have spent time observing. As you move around the map, you will dredge up details of events and conversations. In essence, let yourself walk through your experience. You can practice all these memory-building skills now, while you are preparing for long-term fieldwork.

Maintaining Naiveté

Try also to develop your skill at being a novice—at being someone who genuinely wants to learn a new culture. This may mean working hard at suspending judgment about some things. David Fetterman made a trip across the Sinai desert with a group of Bedouins. One of the Bedouins, says Fetterman (1989),

> shared his jacket with me to protect me from the heat. I thanked him, of course, because I appreciated the gesture and did not want to insult him. But I smelled like a camel for the rest of the day in the dry desert heat. I thought I didn't need the jacket. . . . I later learned that without his jacket I would have suffered from sunstroke. . . . An inexperienced traveler does not always notice when the temperature climbs above 130 degrees Fahrenheit. By slowing down the evaporation rate, the jacket helped me retain water. (p. 330)

Maintaining your naiveté will come naturally in a culture that's unfamiliar to you, but it's a bit harder to do in your own culture. Most of what you do "naturally" is so automatic that you don't know how to intellectualize it.

These days, if you are like many middle-class Americans, your eating habits can be characterized by the word "grazing"—that is, eating small amounts of food at many irregular times during the course of a typical day, rather than sitting down for meals at fixed times. Would you have used that kind of word to describe your own eating behavior? Other members of your own culture are often better informants than you are about that culture, and if you really let people teach you, they will.

If you look carefully, though, you'll be surprised at how heterogeneous your culture is and how many parts of it you really know nothing about. For example, I'm a "ham" (amateur) radio operator. When CB radio buffs start learning to be hams they make a lot of mistakes. They think that their experience with CB radios will transfer to ham radio and are usually surprised at how little they know about all the etiquette for over-the-air interaction that ham operators take for granted.

The CBers feel awkward at first. Their jargon isn't right, and they don't share any of the ham lore. Try studying to become a ham operator and see for yourself what it takes to learn to act properly in that culture. Or find some other part of your own culture that you don't control and try to learn it. That's what you did as a child, of course. Only this time, try to intellectualize the experience. Take notes on what you learn about *how to learn*, on what it's like being a novice, and how you think you can best take advantage of the learner's role. Your imagination will suggest a lot of other nooks and crannies of our culture that you can explore as a thoroughly untutored novice.

The role of naive novice is not *always* the best one to play. Humility is inappropriate is when you are dealing with a culture whose members stand a lot to lose by your incompetence. Michael Agar (1973, 1980) did field research on the life of heroin addicts in New York City. His informants made it plain that Agar's ignorance of their lives wasn't cute or interesting to them.

Even with the best of intentions, Agar could have given his informants away to the police by just being stupid. Under such circumstances, you shouldn't expect your informants to take you under their wing and teach you how to appreciate their customs. Agar had to learn a lot, and very quickly, to gain credibility with his informants.

There are situations where your expertise is just what's required to build rapport with people. Anthropologists have typed documents for illiterate people in the field and have used other skills (from coaching basketball to dispensing antibiotics) to help people and to gain their confidence and respect. If you are studying highly educated people, you may have to prove that you know a fair amount about research methods before they will deal with you. Agar (1980:58) once studied an alternative lifestyle commune and was asked by a biochemist who was living there: "Who are you going to use as a control group?" In my study of ocean scientists (1974), several informants asked me what computer programs I was going to use to do a factor analysis of my data.

Under the best conditions, it takes at least 3 months to achieve reasonable intellectualized competence in another culture and be accepted as a participant observer, that is, as someone who has learned enough to learn.

Building Writing Skills

The ability to write comfortably and clearly is one of the most important skills you can develop as a participant observer. Ethnographers who are not comfortable as writers produce few field notes and little published work. If you have any doubts about your ability to sit down at a typewriter or word processor and pound out thousands of words, day in and day out, then try to build that skill now, before you go into the field for an extended period.

The way to build that skill is to team up with one or more colleagues who are also trying to build their expository writing ability. Set concrete and regular writing tasks for yourselves, and criticize one another's work on matters of clarity and style. There is nothing "Mickey-Mouse" about this kind of exercise. If you think you need it, do it.

Good writing skills will carry you through participant observation fieldwork, writing a dissertation, and, finally, writing for publication. Don't be afraid to write clearly and compellingly. The worst that can happen is that someone will criticize you for "popularizing" your material. I think ethnographers should be criticized if they take the exciting material of real people's lives and turn it into deadly dull reading.

Hanging Out

It may sound silly, but just hanging out is a skill, and until you learn it you can't do your best work as a participant observer. Remember what I said at the beginning of this chapter. Participant observation is a strategic method that lets you learn what you want to learn and apply all the data collection methods that you may want to apply.

When you enter a new field situation, the temptation is to ask a lot of questions in order to learn as much as possible as quickly as possible. There are many things that people can't or won't tell you in answer to questions. If you ask people too quickly about the sources of their wealth, you are likely to get incomplete data. If you ask about sexual liaisons directly, you may get thoroughly unreliable responses.

Hanging out builds trust, and trust results in ordinary conversation and ordinary behavior in your presence. Once you know, from hanging out, exactly what you want to know more about, and once people trust you not to betray their confidence, you'll be surprised at the direct questions you can ask.

In his study of Cornerville, William Foote Whyte (1989) wondered whether "just hanging on the street corner was an active enough process to be dignified by the term 'research.' Perhaps I should ask these men questions," he thought. He soon realized that "one has to learn when to question and when not to question as well as what questions to ask" (p. 78).

Philip Kilbride studied child abuse in Kenya. He did a survey and focused ethnographic interviews, but "by far the most significant event in my research happened as a byproduct of participatory 'hanging out,' being always in search of case material." While visiting informants one day, Kilbride and his wife saw a crowd gathering at a local secondary school. It turned out that a young mother had thrown her baby into a pit latrine at the school. The Kilbrides offered financial assistance to the young mother and her family in exchange for "involving ourselves in their . . . misfortune." The event that the Kilbrides had witnessed became the focus for a lot of their research activities in the succeeding months (Kilbride, 1992:190).

Objectivity

Finally, objectivity is a skill, like language fluency, and you can build it if you work at it. Some people build more of it, others less. More is better.

An objective measurement is one made by a robot, that is, a machine that is not prone to the kind of measurement error that comes from having opinions and memories. Using this criterion, no human being can ever be completely objective. We can't rid ourselves of our experiences, and I don't know anyone who thinks it would be a good idea even to try.

We can, however, become aware of our experiences, our opinions, our values. We can hold our field observations up to a cold light and ask whether we've seen what we wanted to see, or what is really out there. The goal is not for us, as humans, to become objective machines; it is for us to achieve objective—that is, accurate—knowledge by transcending our biases.

Laurie Krieger, an American woman doing fieldwork in Cairo, studied physical punishment against women. She learned that wife beatings were less violent than she had imagined and that the act still sickened her. Her reaction brought out a lot of information from women who were recent recipients of their husbands' wrath. "I found out," she says, "that the biased outlook of an American woman and a trained anthropologist was not always disadvantageous, as long as I was aware of and able to control the expression of my biases" (Krieger, 1986:120).

Colin Turnbull held objective knowledge as something to be pulled from the thicket of subjective experience. Fieldwork, said Turnbull, involves a self-conscious review of one's own ideas and values—one's *self*, for want of any more descriptive term. During fieldwork you "reach inside," he observed, and give up the "old, narrow, limited self, discovering the new self that is right and proper in the new context." We use the field experience, he said, "to know ourselves more deeply by conscious subjectivity." In this way, he concluded, "the ultimate goal of objectivity is much more likely to be reached and our understanding of other cultures that much more profound" (Turnbull, 1986:27).

Many phenomenologists see objective knowledge as the goal of participant observation. Danny Jorgensen, for example, advocates complete immersion and "becoming the phenomenon" you study. "Becoming the phenomenon," Jorgensen says, "is a participant observational strategy for penetrating to and gaining experience of a form of human life. It is an objective approach insofar as it results in the accurate, detailed description of the insiders' experience of life" (Jorgensen, 1989:63).

If you use this strategy of full immersion, Jorgensen says, you must be able to switch back and forth between the insiders' view and that of an analyst. To do that—to maintain your objective, analytic abilities—Jorgensen suggests finding a colleague with whom you can talk things over regularly. That is, give yourself an outlet for discussing the theoretical, methodological, and emotional issues that inevitably come up in full participation field research. It's good advice.

Objectivity and Neutrality

Objectivity does not mean (and has never meant) value neutrality. No one asks Cultural Survival, Inc. to be neutral in documenting the violent obscenities against indigenous peoples of the world. No one asks Amnesty International to be neutral in its effort to document state-sanctioned torture. We recognize that the power of the documentation is in its objectivity, in its chilling irrefutability, not in its neutrality.

Claire Sterk, an ethnographer from the Netherlands, has studied prostitutes and intravenous drug users in mostly African-American communities in New York City and Newark, New Jersey. Sterk was a trusted friend and counselor to many of the women with whom she worked. In one 2-month period in the late 1980s, she attended the funerals of seven women she knew who had died of AIDS. She felt that "every researcher is affected by the work he or she does. One cannot remain neutral and uninvolved; even as an outsider, the researcher is part of the community" (Sterk, 1989:99).

Objectivity and Indigenous Anthropology

Objectivity gets its biggest test when you study your own culture. Barbara Meyerhoff worked in Mexico when she was a graduate student. Later, in the early 1970s, when she became interested in ethnicity and aging, she decided to study elderly Chicanos. The people she approached kept putting her off, asking her "Why work with us? Why don't you study your own kind?" Meyerhoff was Jewish. She had never thought about studying her own kind, but she launched a study of poor, elderly Jews who were on public assistance. She agonized about what she was doing and, as she tells it, never resolved whether it was anthropology or a personal quest.

Many of the people she studied were survivors of the Holocaust. "How, then, could anyone look at them dispassionately? How could I feel anything but awe and appreciation for their mere presence? . . . Since neutrality was impossible and idealization undesirable, I decided on striving for balance" (Meyerhoff, 1989:90).

There is no final answer on whether it's good or bad to study your own culture. Plenty of people have done it and plenty of people have written about what it's like to do it. On the plus side, you'll know the language and you'll be less likely to suffer from culture shock. On the minus side, it's harder to recognize cultural patterns that you live every day and you're likely to take a lot of things for granted that an outsider would pick up right away.

If you are going to study your own culture, start by reading the experiences of others who have done it so you'll know what you're facing in the field (Messerschmidt, 1981; Stephenson & Greer, 1981; Fahim, 1982; Altorki & El-Solh, 1988).

Gender, Parenting, and Other Personal Characteristics

By the 1930s, Margaret Mead had already made clear the importance of gender as a variable in data collection (see Mead, 1986). Gender has at least two consequences: It limits your access to certain information; it influences how you perceive others.

In all cultures, you can't ask people certain questions because you're a [woman] [man]. You can't go into certain areas and situations because you're a [woman] [man]. You can't watch this or report on that because you're a [woman] [man]. Even the culture of anthropologists is affected: Your credibility is diminished or enhanced with your colleagues when you talk about a certain subject because you're a [woman] [man] (see Scheper-Hughes, 1983; Golde, 1986; Whitehead & Conaway, 1986; Altorki & El-Solh, 1988; Warren, 1988).

On the other hand, feminist scholars recently have made it clear that gender is a negotiated idea. What you can and can't do if you are a man or a woman is more fixed in some cultures than in others, and in all cultures there is lots of individual variation in gender roles. While men or women may be expected to be this way or that way in any given place, the variation in male and female attitudes and behaviors within a culture can be tremendous.

All participant observers confront their personal limitations and the limitations imposed on them by the culture they study. When she worked at the Thule relocation camp for Japanese-Americans during World War II, Rosalie Wax did not join any of the women's groups or organizations. Looking back after more than 40 years, Wax concluded that this was just poor judgment:

> I was a university student and a researcher. I was not yet ready to accept myself as a total person, and this limited my perspective and my understanding. Those of us who instruct future field workers should encourage them to understand and value their full range of being, because only then can they cope intelligently with the range of experience they will encounter in the field. (1986:148)

Besides gender, we have learned that being a parent helps you talk to people about certain areas of life and get more information than if you were not a parent. My wife and I arrived on the island of Kalymnos, Greece, in 1964 with a 2-month-old baby. As Joan Cassell says, children are a "guarantee of good intentions" (1987:260), and wherever we went the baby was the conversation opener. But be warned: Taking children into the field can place them at risk. More on this later.

Being divorced has its costs. Nancie González found that being a divorced mother of two young sons in the Dominican Republic was just too much. "Had I to do it again," she says, "I would invent widowhood with appropriate rings and photographs" (1986:92). Even height may make a difference: Alan Jacobs once told me he thought he did better fieldwork with the Maasai because he's 6'5" than he would have if he'd been, say, an average-sized 5'10".

Personal characteristics do make a difference in fieldwork. Being old or young lets you into certain things and shuts you out of others. Being wealthy lets you talk to certain people about certain subjects and makes others avoid you. Being gregarious makes some people open up to you and makes others shy away. There is no way to eliminate the personal equation—the influence of the observer on the data—in anthropological fieldwork, or in any other scientific data-gathering exercise for that matter without sending robots out to do the work. Of course, the robots would have their own problems (Romney, 1989).

Sex and Fieldwork

It is unreasonable to assume that single, adult field workers are all celibate, yet the literature on field methods is nearly silent on this topic. When E. E. Evans-Pritchard was a student, just about to head off for central Africa, he asked his major professor for advice. "Seligman told me to take 10 grains of quinine every night and keep off women" (1973:1). As far as I know, that's the last we heard from Evans-Pritchard on the subject.

Colin Turnbull (1986) tells us about his affair with a young Mbuti woman and Dona Davis (1986) discusses her relationship with an engineer who visited the Newfoundland village where she was doing research on menopause. In Turnbull's case, he had graduated from being an asexual child in Mbuti culture to being a youth and was expected to have sexual relations. In Davis's case, she was expected not to have sexual relations, but she also learned that she was not bound by the expectation. In fact, Davis says that "being paired off" made women more comfortable with her because she was "simply breaking a rule everyone else broke" (1986:54).

The rule on sexual behavior in the field is this: Do nothing that you can't live with, both professionally and personally. Be even more conscious of the possible fallout, for you and for your partner, than you would in your own community. Eventually, you will be going home. Will that affect your partner negatively? Proscriptions against sex in fieldwork are silly, because they don't work. But understand that this is one area that people everywhere may take very seriously.

Surviving Fieldwork

The title of this section is the title of an important book by Nancy Howell (1990). All anthropologists should read Howell's book, especially those who expect to do fieldwork in developing nations. Howell surveyed 204 anthropologists about illnesses and accidents in the field, and the results are sobering. The maxim that "anthropologists are otherwise sensible people who don't believe in the germ theory of disease" is apparently correct (Rappaport, 1990).

One hundred percent of anthropologists who do fieldwork in South Asia report being exposed to malaria, and 41% report contracting the disease. Eighty-seven percent of anthropologists who work in Africa report exposure, and 31% report having had malaria. Seventy percent of anthropologists who work in South Asia report having had some liver disease.

Among all anthropologists, 13% report having hepatitis A. I was hospitalized for 6 weeks for hepatitis in 1968 and spent most of another year recovering. Glynn Isaac died of hepatitis B at age 47 in 1985 after a long career of archeological fieldwork in Africa. Typhoid fever is also common among anthropologists, as are amoebic dysentery, giardia, ascariasis, hookworm, and other infectious diseases.

Accidents have injured or killed many anthropologists. Fei Xiaotong, a student of Malinowski's, was caught in a tiger trap in China in 1935. The injury left him an invalid for 6 months. His wife died in her attempt to go for help. Michelle Zimbalist Rosaldo was killed in a fall in the Philippines in 1981. Thomas Zwickler, a graduate student at the University of Pennsylvania, was killed by a bus on a rural road in India in 1985. He was riding a bicycle when he was struck. Kim Hill was accidentally hit by an arrow while out with an Ache hunting party in Paraguay in 1982 (Howell, 1990:passim).

What can you do about the risks? Get every inoculation you need before you leave, not just the ones that are required by the country you are entering. Check your county health office for the latest information from the Centers for Disease Control about illnesses prevalent in the area you're going to. If you go into an area that is known to be malarial, take a full supply of antimalarial drugs with you so you don't run out while you're out in the field.

When people pass around a gourd full of chicha or pulque or palm wine, decline politely and explain yourself if you have to. You'll probably insult a few people, and your protests won't always get you off the hook, but even lowering the number of times you are exposed to disease lowers your risk of contracting disease.

After being very sick in the field, I've learned to carry a supply of bottled beer with me when I go to visit a house where I'm sure to be given a gourd full of local brew. The gift of bottled beer is generally appreciated and heads off the embarrassment of having to turn down a drink I'd rather not have. It also makes plain that I'm not a teetotaler. Of course, if you *are* a teetotaler, you've got a ready-made get-out.

If you do fieldwork in a remote area, consult with physicians at your university hospital for information on the latest blood-substitute technology. If you are in an accident in a remote area and need blood, a nonperishable blood substitute can buy you time. Some field workers carry a supply of sealed hypodermic needles with them in case they need an injection. Don't go anywhere without medical insurance and consider whether you need evacuation insurance. It can cost about $60,000 to evacuate a person by jet from central Africa to Paris or Frankfurt. It costs relatively little for insurance that will cover it.

The Stages of Participant Observation

In what follows, I draw on three sources of data: (a) literature that deals with field research; (b) 5 years of work, with the late Michael Kenny, directing National Science Foundation field schools in cultural anthropology and linguistics; and (c) conversations with colleagues during the last 30 years specifically about their experiences in the field.

During our work with the field schools (1967-1971), Kenny and I developed an outline of *researcher response* in participant observation fieldwork. Here are what we thought were the stages of participant observation fieldwork: (a) Initial Contact; (b) Shock; (c) Discovering the Obvious; (d) The Break; (e) Focusing; (f) Exhaustion, the Second Break, and Frantic Activity; (g) Leaving.

There is no guarantee, of course, but from Kenny's and my data, the chances are good that you will experience many of these well-defined stages at some point in your field research. If you know what's coming, you're better able to cope with it.

1. Initial Contact

During the initial contact period, many anthropologists report experiencing a kind of euphoria and excitement as they begin to move about in a new culture. People who become cultural anthropologists in the first place are attracted to the idea of living in a new culture. They are often delighted when they begin to do so.

But not always. Here is Napoleon Chagnon's recollection of his first encounter with the Yanomami: "I looked up and gasped when I saw a dozen burly, naked, sweaty, hideous men staring at us down the shafts of their drawn arrows! . . . Had there been a diplomatic way out, I would have ended my fieldwork then and there" (Chagnon, 1983:10-11).

The desire to bolt and run is more common than we have admitted in the past. Charles Wagley, who would become one of our discipline's most accomplished ethnographers, made his first field trip in 1937. A local political chief in Totonicapán, Guatemala, invited Wagley to tea in a parlor overlooking the town square. The chief's wife and two daughters joined them. In the middle of the tea, two of the chief's aides came in and hustled everyone off to another room. The chief explained the hurried move to Wagley:

> He had forgotten that an execution by firing squad of two Indians, "nothing but vagrants who had robbed in the market," was to take place at 5 p.m. just below the parlor. He knew that I would understand the feelings of ladies and the grave problem of trying to keep order among brutes. I returned to my ugly pensión in shock and spent a night without sleep. I would have liked to have returned as fast as possible to New York. (Wagley, 1983:6)

Finally, listen to Rosalie Wax describe her encounter with the Arizona Japanese internment camp that she studied during World War II (1971). When she arrived in Phoenix it was 110°. Later that day, after a bus ride and a 20-mile ride in a GI truck, across a dusty landscape that "looked like the skin of some cosmic reptile," with a Japanese-American who wouldn't talk to her, Wax arrived at the Gila camp. By then it was 120°. She was driven to staff quarters, which was an army barracks divided into tiny cells, and abandoned to find her cell by a process of elimination.

> It contained four dingy and dilapidated articles of furniture: an iron double bedstead, a dirty mattress (which took up half the room), a chest of drawers, and a tiny writing table—and it was hotter than the hinges of Hades. . . . I sat down on the hot mattress, took a deep breath, and cried. . . . Like some lost two-year-old, I only knew that I was miserable. After a while, I found the room at the end of the barrack that contained two toilets and a couple of wash basins. I washed my face and told myself I would feel better the next day. I was wrong. (p. 67)

2. Shock

Even among those anthropologists who have a pleasant experience during their initial contact period (and many do), almost all report experiencing some form of depression and shock soon thereafter (within a week or two). One kind of shock comes as the novelty of the field site wears off and there is this nasty feeling that anthropology has to get done. Some researchers (especially those on their first field trip) may also experience feelings of anxiety about their ability to collect good data.

A good response is to do highly task-oriented work. making maps, taking censuses, doing household inventories, collecting genealogies, and so on. Another useful response is to make clinical, methodological field notes about your feelings and responses in doing participant observation fieldwork.

Another kind of shock is to the culture itself. Culture shock is an uncomfortable stress response and must be taken very seriously. In severe cases of culture shock, nothing seems right. Local eating habits and child-rearing practices may upset you. A lack of clean toilet facilities may make you angry. The prospect of having to put up with certain local foods for a year or more may become frightening. You find yourself focusing on little annoyances—something as simple as the fact that light switches go side to side rather than up and down can irritate you.

This last example is not fanciful, by the way. It happened to a colleague of mine, and I once became infuriated with the fact that men didn't shake hands the way "they're supposed to." You may find yourself blaming everyone in the culture, or the culture itself, for the fact that your informants don't keep appointments for interviews.

Culture shock commonly involves a feeling that people really don't want you around (this may, in fact, be the case). You feel lonely and wish you could find someone with whom to speak your native language. Even with a spouse in the field, the strain of using another language day after day, and concentrating hard so that you can collect data in that language, can be emotionally wearing.

In any long-term field study, be prepared for some serious tests of your ability to remain a dispassionate observer. Powdermaker (1966) was once confronted with the problem of knowing that a lynch mob was preparing to go after a particular black man. She was powerless to stop the mob and was fearful for her own safety.

I have never grown accustomed to seeing people ridicule the handicapped, although I see it every time I'm in Mexico and Greece, and I recall with horror the death of a young man on one of the sponge diving boats I sailed with in Greece. I knew the rules of safe diving that could have prevented that death; so did all the divers and the captains of the vessels. They ignored those rules at terrible cost. I wanted desperately to *do* something, but there was nothing I *could* do except watch—or be told to leave for interfering.

The most common personal problem for anthropologists in the field is not being able to get any privacy. Many people find the Anglo-Saxon notion of privacy grotesque. When we first went out to the island of Kalymnos in Greece in 1964, my wife and I rented quarters with a family. The idea was that we'd be better able to learn about family dynamics. Women of the household were annoyed and hurt whenever my wife asked for a little time to be alone. When I came home at the end of each day's work I could never just go to my family's room, shut the door, and talk to my wife about my day, or hers, or our new baby's. If I didn't share everything during waking hours with the family we lived with, they felt rejected.

After about two months of this, we finally had to move out and find a house of our own. My access to data about intimate family dynamics was cut off. But it was worth it to me because I felt that I would have had to abort the whole trip if I'd had to continue living in what my wife and I felt was a glass bowl all the time. As it turns out, there is no word for the concept of privacy in Greek. The closest gloss translates as "being alone," and connotes loneliness.

M. N. Srinivas, an anthropologist from India, also felt this need for privacy. Here's what he wrote about his work in the rural village of Ramapura, near Mysore (1979):

> I was never left alone. I had to fight hard even to get two or three hours absolutely to myself in a week or two. My favorite recreation was walking to the nearby village of Kere where I had some old friends, or to Hogur which had a weekly market. But my friends in Ramapura wanted to accompany me on my walks. They were puzzled by my liking for solitary walks. Why should one walk when one could catch a bus, or ride on bicycles with friends. I had to plan and plot to give them the slip to go out by myself. On my return, however, I was certain to be asked why I had not taken them with me. They would have put off their work and joined me. (They meant it.) I suffered from social claustrophobia as long as I was in the village and sometimes the feeling became so intense that I just had to get out. (p. 23)

Culture shock subsides as researchers settle in to the business of gathering data on a daily basis, but it doesn't go away because the sources of annoyance don't go away.

Unless you are one of the very rare people who truly "go native" in another culture (in which case it will be very difficult for you to intellectualize your experience), you will cope with culture shock, not eliminate it. You will remain conscious of things annoying you, but you won't feel like they are crippling your ability to work. Like Srinivas, when things get too intense, you'll have the good sense to leave the field site for a bit rather than try to stick it out.

3. Discovering the Obvious

In the next phase of participant observation, researchers settle into collecting data on a more or less systematic basis (see Kirk & Miller, 1986). This is sometimes accompanied by an interesting personal response, a sense of discovery where you feel as if informants are finally letting you in on the "good stuff" about their culture. Much of this good stuff will later turn out to be commonplace. You may "discover," for example, that women have more power in the community than meets the eye, or that there are two systems for dispute settlement—one embodied in formal law and one that works through informal mechanisms.

A concomitant to this feeling of discovery is sometimes a feeling of being in control of dangerous information and a sense of urgency about protecting informants' identities. You may find yourself going back over your field notes, looking for places that you might have lapsed and identified an informant, and making appropriate changes. You may worry about those copies of field notes you have already sent home and even become a little concerned about how well you can trust your major professor to maintain the privacy of those notes.

This is the stage of fieldwork when anthropologists start talking about "their" village, and how people are, at last, "letting them in" to the secrets of the culture. This feeling often spurs researchers to collect more and more data; to accept every invitation, by every informant, to every event; to fill the days with observation and the nights with writing up field notes. Days off become unthinkable, and the sense of discovery becomes more and more intense. This is the time to take a serious break.

4. The Break

The midfieldwork break, which usually comes after three or four months, is a crucial part of the overall participant observation experience. It's an opportunity to get some distance, both physical and emotional, from the field site. It gives you a chance to put things into perspective, think about what you've got so far, and what you need to get in the time remaining. Use this time to collect data from regional or national statistical services; to visit with colleagues at the local university and discuss your findings; or to visit other communities in other parts of the country. And be sure to leave some time to just take a vacation, without thinking about research at all.

Your informants also need a break from you. "Anthropologists are uncomfortable intruders no matter how close their rapport," noted Charles Wagley. "A short respite is mutually beneficial. One returns with objectivity and human warmth restored. The anthropologist returns as an old friend," who has gone away and returned, and has thereby demonstrated his or her genuine interest in a community (Wagley, 1983:13).

5. Focusing

After the break, you will have a better idea of exactly what kinds of data you are lacking, and your sense of problem will also come more sharply into focus. The reason to have a formally prepared design statement *before* you go to the field, of course, is to tell you what you should be looking for. Nevertheless, even the most focused research design will have to be modified in the field. In some cases, you may find yourself making radical changes in your design, based on what you find when you get to the field and spend several months actually collecting data.

There is nothing wrong or unusual about this, but new researchers sometimes experience anxiety over making any major changes. The important thing at this stage is to focus the research and use your time effectively rather than agonizing over how to save components of your original design.

6. Exhaustion, the Second Break, and Frantic Activity

After 7 or 8 months, some participant observers start to think that they have exhausted their informants, both literally and figuratively. That is, they may become embarrassed about continuing to ask their informants for more information. Or they may make the supreme mistake of believing that their informants have no more to tell them. The reason this is such a mistake, of course, is that the store of cultural knowledge in any culturally competent person is enormous—far more than anyone could hope to extract in a year or two.

At this point, another break is usually a good idea. You'll get another opportunity to take stock, order your priorities for the time remaining, and see both how much you've done and how little. The realization that, in fact, informants have a great deal more to teach them, and that they themselves have precious little time left in the field, sends many investigators into a frenetic burst of activity during this stage.

7. Leaving the Field

The last stage of participant observation is leaving the field. When should you leave the field? Steven Taylor says that when he starts to get bored writing field notes, he knows it's time to close down and go home (1991:243). Taylor recognizes that writing field notes is time consuming and tedious; but it's exciting, too, when you're chasing down information that plugs directly into your research effort. When it stops being exciting, it's time to leave.

Don't neglect this part of the process. Let people know that you are going and tell them how much you appreciate their help. The ritual of leaving a place in a culturally appropriate way will make it possible for you to go back, and even to send others.

Participant observation is an intensely intimate and personal experience. People who began as your informants may become your friends as well. In the best of cases, you come to trust that they will not deceive you about their culture, and they come to trust you not to betray them—that is, not to use your intimate knowledge of their lives to hurt them. (You can imagine the worst of cases.) There is often a legitimate expectation on both sides that the relationship may be permanent, not just a one-year fling.

In some ways, no anthropologist ever really leaves the field. I've been working with some people, on and off, for 30 years. Like many anthropologists who work in Latin America, I'm godparent to the children of my closest research collaborators. From time to time, people from Mexico or from Greece will call us on the phone, just to say "hi" and to keep the relationship going.

Many anthropologists have been called on to help the children of their informants get into a college or university. This is the sort of thing that happens 20 years after you've "left" the field. The fact is, participant observation fieldwork can be a lifetime commitment. As in all aspects of ordinary life, you have to learn to choose your relationships well. Don't be surprised if you make a few mistakes.

8

Informants

When we conduct questionnaire surveys we know exactly how to choose informants—randomly. In any large aggregate of people (even in a community of just 30 people), there are bound to be serious differences of opinion and behavior. A truly random sample ensures that these differences (even if you don't know what they might be) are represented in your data. (The logic for this was explored thoroughly in Chapter 4.) Ethnography, on the other hand, relies on a few key informants rather than on a representative sample.

An important question for ethnography then, is: Are a few informants really capable of providing adequate information about a culture? The answer is: Yes, but it depends on two things: choosing good informants and asking them things they know about. In other words, we must select informants for their *competence* rather than just for their representativeness.

Key Informants

Key informant interviewing is an integral part of ethnographic research. Good informants are people who you can talk to easily, who understand the information you need, and who are glad to give it to you or get it for you. Pelto and Pelto (1978:72) advocate training informants "to conceptualize cultural data in the frame of reference employed by the anthropologist."

Some anthropologists disagree with this approach, but I think it's just fine. In some cases, you may want to just listen. But when you run into a really great informant, I see no reason to hold back. Teach the informant about the analytic categories you're developing and ask whether the categories are correct. If you let yourself become the student, really good informants will educate you.

I've worked with Jesús Salinas for 32 years. In 1971, I was about to write an ethnography of his culture, the Otomí of central Mexico (they're now called the Ñähñu), when he mentioned that he'd be interested in writing an ethnography himself. I dropped my project and taught him to read and write Otomí.

Over the next 15 years, Salinas produced four volumes about the Otomí people—volumes that I translated and from which I learned many things that I'd never have learned had I done the ethnography myself. For example, Otomí men engage in rhyming duels, much like the "dozens" of African-Americans. I could not have asked the questions in Otomí that would have retrieved the information about those rhyming duels in Salinas's work (see Bernard & Salinas, 1989).

Just as Salinas has influenced my thinking about Mexican Indian life, Salinas's ethnography was heavily influenced by his association with me. We've discussed analytic categories over the years and have argued over interpretation of observed facts. If it seems somehow insulting to call Salinas my informant, then consider that I've been his informant as well, telling him what he wanted to know about anthropology and about how anthropologists look at data about cultures.

Finding Key Informants

One of the most famous key informants in the ethnographic literature is Doc in William Foote Whyte's *Street Corner Society* (1955). Whyte studied "Cornerville," an Italian-American slum neighborhood in a place he called "Eastern City." Whyte asked some social workers if they knew anyone who could help him with his study. One social worker told Whyte to come to her office and meet a man whom she thought could do the job. When Whyte showed up, the social worker introduced him to Doc and then left the room. Whyte nervously explained his predicament and Doc asked him "Do you want to see the high life or the low life?" (Whyte, 1989:72).

Whyte couldn't believe his luck. He told Doc he wanted to see all he could, learn as much as possible about life in the neighborhood. Doc told him

> Any nights you want to see anything, I'll take you around. I can take you to the joints—the gambling joints. I can take you around to the street corners. Just remember that you're my friend. That's all they need to know. I know these places and if I tell them you're my friend, nobody will bother you. You just tell me what you want to see, and we'll arrange it. . . . When you want some information, I'll ask for it, and you listen. When you want to find out their philosophy of life, I'll start an argument and get it for you. (ibid.)

Doc was straight up; he told Whyte to rely on him and to ask him anything, and Doc was good to his word all through Whyte's 3 years of fieldwork. Doc introduced Whyte to the boys on the corner; Doc hung out with Whyte and spoke up for Whyte when people questioned Whyte's presence. Doc was just spectacular. (See also Whyte, 1984, for a wonderful retrospective by Whyte about his fieldwork).

Doc may be famous, but he's not unique. He's not even that rare. All successful ethnographers will tell you that they eventually came to rely on one or two key people in their fieldwork. What was rare about Doc is how quickly and easily Whyte teamed up with him. It's not easy to find informants like Doc. When Jeffrey Johnson began fieldwork in a North Carolina fishing community, he went to the local marine extension agent and asked for the agent's help. The agent, happy to oblige, told Johnson about a fisherman whom he thought could help Johnson get off on the right foot.

It turned out that the fisherman was a transplanted northerner; he had a pension from the Navy; he was an activist Republican in a thoroughly Democratic community; and he kept his fishing boat in an isolated moorage, far from the village harbor. He was, in fact, maximally different from the typical local fisherman. The agent had meant well, of course (J. Johnson, 1990:56).

In fact, the first informants with whom you develop a working relationship in the field may be "deviant" members of their culture. Agar (1980:86) reports that during his fieldwork in India, he was taken on by the *naik*, or headman of the village. The naik, it turned out, had *inherited* the role, but he was not respected in the village and did not preside over village meetings. This did not mean that the naik knew nothing about village affairs and customs; he was what Agar called a "solid insider," and yet somewhat of an outcast—a "marginal native," just like the anthropologist was trying to be (Freilich, 1977). If you think about it, Agar said, you should wonder about the kind of person who would befriend an ethnographer.

In my own fieldwork (at sea, in Mexican villages, on Greek islands, in rural communities in the United States, and in modern American bureaucracies) I have consistently found the best informants to be people who are cynical about their own culture. They may not be outcasts (in fact, they are always solid insiders), but they claim to *feel* somewhat marginal to their culture, by virtue of their intellectualizing of and disenchantment with their culture. They are always observant, reflective, and articulate—all the qualities that I'd like to have myself.

Don't choose key ethnographic informants too quickly. Allow yourself to go awash in data for a while, and play the field. When you have several prospects, check on their roles and statuses in the community. Be sure that the informants you select don't prevent you from gaining access to other important informants, i.e., people who won't talk to you when they find out you're so-and-so's friend. Since good ethnography is, at its best, a good story, find trustworthy informants who are observant, reflective, and articulate—who know how to tell good stories—and stay with them. In the end, ethnographic fieldwork stands or falls on building mutually supportive relations with a few key people.

Informants Sometimes Lie

Don't be surprised if informants lie to you. Jeffrey Johnson, a skilled boat builder, worked in an Alaskan boat yard as part of his field study of a fishing community. At one point in his fieldwork, two other anthropologists showed up, both women, to conduct some interviews with the men in the boat yard. "The two anthropologists had no idea I was one of *them*" Johnson reports, "since I was dressed in carpenter's overalls, with all the official paraphernalia—hammer, tape measure, etc. I was sufficiently close to overhear the interview and, knowing the men being interviewed, recognized quite a few blatant lies. In fact, during the course of one interview, a captain would occasionally wink at me as he told a whopper of a lie" (personal communication).

This is not an isolated incident. A Comox Indian woman spent 2 hours narrating a text for Franz Boas. The text turned out to be nothing but a string of questions and answers. Boas didn't speak Comox well enough to know that he was being duped, but when he found out he noted it in his diary (Rohner, 1969:61). Nachman (1984), drawing on his own experience with the Nissan of New Guinea, offers interesting insights into the problem of informants lying to anthropologists.

Selecting Informants

The search for ways to select key informants has been going on for some time. In 1957, Tremblay reported in the *American Anthropologist* on how he selected key informants to help him design a good questionnaire. "In using key informants," Tremblay said, "one chooses them strategically, considering the structure of the society and the content of the inquiry. . . . When we use key informants, we are not randomly sampling from the universe of characteristics under study. Rather, we are selectively sampling specialized knowledge of the characteristics" (1957:689).

Tremblay was involved in a Cornell University survey research project on poverty in Nova Scotia and wanted to use key informants to help the researchers design a useful questionnaire. He made a list of some roles in the community he was studying—things like sawmill owners, doctors, farmers, bankers—and chose informants who could talk to him knowledgeably about things in their area of expertise. He had no external test to tell him whether the informants he selected were, in fact, the most competent in their areas of expertise, but he felt that on-the-spot clues made the selection of informants valid.

Robbins et al. (1969) studied acculturation and modernization among the Baganda of Uganda. They used a more formal method to select informants who might be competent on this topic. They did a survey of households in a rural sector, asking about things that would indicate respondents' exposure to Western culture. They had 80 variables in the survey that had something to do with acculturation and they ran a factor analysis to find out which variables package together.

We'll look more closely at factor analysis in Chapter 20. For now, think of factor analysis as a way to reduce those 80 variables to just a handful of underlying variables around which individual variables cluster. It turned out that 14 of the original 80 variables clustered together in one factor. Among those original variables were: being under 40 years of age, drinking European beer, speaking and reading English, having a Western job, and living in a house that has concrete floors and walls.

Robbins called this cluster the "acculturation factor." He chose informants who had high scores on this factor and interviewed them about

TABLE 8.1

Agreement Between Informants and Survey Data in Seven Villages

Question Asked of Informants	Correlation with Questionnaire Data
Number of men from this town who are workers in Ciudad Industrial	.90
Percentage of houses made of adobe	.71
Percentage of households that have radios	.52
Percentage of people who eat eggs regularly	.33
Percentage of people who would *like* to live in Ciudad Industrial	.23
Percentage of people who eat bread daily	.14
Percentage of people who sleep in beds	.05

SOURCE: "Toward Control in Key Informant Data," by J. J. Poggie, in *Human Organization* (1972). Reprinted with permission.

acculturation. Robbins reversed Tremblay's method. Tremblay used key informants to help him build a survey instrument; Robbins used a survey to find key informants,

In 1972, John Poggie reported an important early study of informant competence. Poggie selected a key informant in each of seven Mexican communities. The communities ranged in size from 350 to 3,000 inhabitants. The informants were village or town presidents, or judges, or (in the case of agricultural communities), the local commissioners of communal land. Poggie asked these knowledgeable informants questions about life in the communities, and he compared the answers with data from a high-quality social survey.

For example, Poggie asked informants "How many men in this town are workers in Ciudad Industrial?" The survey asked whether the respondent had ever worked in Ciudad Industrial. (Ciudad Industrial is a fictitious name of a city that attracted many labor migrants from the communities that Poggie studied.) The correlation between the answers given by Poggie's expert informants and the data obtained from the survey was .90.

Poggie also asked "What percentage of the houses here are made of adobe?" This time the correlation between the informants and the survey was only .71. Table 8.1 shows the seven questions Poggie asked, and how well his informants did when their answers were compared to the survey.

Overall, informants produce answers most like those in the survey when they are asked to respond to questions about things that are publicly observable. The survey data are not necessarily more *accurate* than the informants' data. But as the questions require informants to talk about things inside people's homes (such as what percentage of the people eat eggs), or about what people think (what percentage of people would *like* to work in Ciudad Industrial), informants' answers look less and less like those of the survey. Poggie concluded that "there is little reason to believe that trust and rapport would improve the reliability and precision concerning what percentage sleep in beds, who would like to live in the new industrial city, or what percentage eat bread daily" (1972:29).

The Cultural Consensus Model of Informant Competence

In any given domain of culture, some people are more competent than others. In our culture, some people know a lot about the history of baseball; some people can name the actors in every sitcom from the 1950s. Some people are experts on medicinal plants, while others are experts on cars and trucks. Romney et al. (1986) developed a way to test informants for competence *within specific cultural domains*. The cultural consensus model is not a test of general competence, only of particular competence.

Romney et al.'s theory is based on a simple and powerful insight: Informants who agree with one another about some items of cultural knowledge know more about the domain those items belong to (are more competent in that domain) than informants who disagree with each other.

This insight is illustrated by an ingenious experiment conducted by Boster (1985, 1986). Boster walked 58 Aguaruna Jívaro women through a manioc garden, in which he had planted 61 varieties of manioc. He asked the women *waji mama aita?* ("What kind of manioc is this?") and calculated the likelihood that all possible pairs of women agreed on the name of a particular plant. Since Boster had planted the garden himself, he knew the true identification of each plant. Sure enough, the more that women agreed on the identification of a plant, the more they were likely to know what the plant actually was. In other words, as cultural consensus increased, so did cultural competence.

Suppose you give a test about the rules of baseball to two groups of people: a group of baseball fans and another group of Americans who never watch the game. You'd expect that (a) the baseball fans would agree more among themselves about the answers to your test questions than would the nonfans, and (b) they would get the answers right more often than the nonfans. Again, there would be a relationship between cultural consensus and cultural competence.

Boster's experiment and the hypothetical baseball experiment are pretty much like any test you might take in a class. The instructor makes up both the test and an answer key with the (supposedly) correct answers. Your job is to match your answers with those on the answer key.

But what if there were no answer key? That's exactly what happens when we ask informants to tell us the uses of various plants, or to list the sacred sites in a village, or to rate the social status of others in a community. We are not asking people for their opinions, attitudes, beliefs, or values. We ask informants to list the sacred sites in a region because we want to *know* the list of sacred sites. The problem is, we don't have an answer key to tell whether informants are accurate in their reporting of information.

How the Consensus Model Works

Romney et al. (1986) formulated a way to test informant competence *without having an answer key*. The theory behind the technique makes three critical assumptions:

1. You test only those informants who share a common culture. Any variation you find among informants is the result of *individual* differences in their knowledge, not the result of their being members of subcultures.
2. Informants give their answers to your test questions independently of one another.
3. All the questions in your test come from the same domain. A test that asked about kinship and football and diseases would be a poor test. Informants might be competent in one domain and incompetent in another. The cultural consensus method should be used only for finding informants who are knowledgeable in a particular domain.

To use the consensus technique, simply give a sample of informants a test that asks them to make some judgments about a list of items in a cultural domain. To keep things simple for the moment, just to explain the model, I'm going to use true-false and yes-no questions. An example of a true-false question in fieldwork might be: "You can get [pneumonia] [diarrhea] [*susto*] from [being overweight] [tired] [scared] [in the room with a sick person]."

Other typical test questions might be: "The bear clan is the one with the most medicine"; or "A field goal is worth 7 points." (If you have the ANTHROPAC program with you in the field, however, you can use multiple-choice questions or even open-ended, fill-in-the-blank questions. See Appendix G.)

For the test to reliably distinguish cultural competence among informants, you should have about 40 test items and about 40 informants.

Next, compute the number of agreements between all pairs of informants on the set of questions. Table 8.2 shows the answers of four informants to a 40-question true-false test. The 1's are items to which an informant answered "true" (or "yes," etc.), and the 0's are items to which an informant answered "false" (or "no," etc.).

Table 8.3 shows the *number* of matches between informants, the *proportion of matches* (the number of matches divided by the number of items in the test), and the proportion of matches *corrected for guessing*. This correction is necessary because an informant can guess the answers to any true-false test item half the time.

The formula for correcting the proportion of matches in order to take guessing on true-false questions into account is

$$(\text{Proportion of Raw Matches} \times 2) - 1$$

The formula is more complicated for multiple-choice questions, but that's where computer programs like ANTHROPAC come in handy.

The three matrices in Table 8.3 are called *similarity matrices* because the entries in each matrix gives some direct estimate of how similar any pair of informants is (see chapters 19 and 20 for more on similarity matrices). Look at the matrix called "proportion of corrected matches." Informants 1 and 2 are .35 alike, while informants 2 and 3 are .70 alike. Informants 2 and 3 are twice as similar to one another as informants 1 and 2 are to one another. Look down the last column of the matrix. Informant 4 is not like any other informant. That is, informant 4's answers to the 40 questions were practically idiosyncratic compared to the answers that other informants gave.

We can use this information to compute a competency score for each informant. To do this, run a factor analysis on the matrix of corrected matches. (The ANTHROPAC program does all this automatically. You do not need to understand factor analysis to read the rest of this section. For an introduction to factor analysis, see Chapter 20.) If the three conditions I've listed for the model have been met, then the first factor in the solution should be at least three times the size of the second factor.

Recall that a factor is an underlying variable that accounts for some portion of the variation in a matrix of data. In the example above, there is just one factor, and it accounts for all the variation in the matrix. (There are, after all, only four informants). Here are the factor loadings (the scores) for each informant:

TABLE 8.2
Answers by 40 Students to a 40-Question True-False General Knowledge Test

```
1 1 1 0 0 1 0 0 0 0 1 1 0 0 0 0 1 1 0 0 1 0 0 1 1 0 1 0 1 1 1 0 1 1 0 1 1 0 1 0 1
0 1 1 0 0 1 0 0 1 1 1 0 1 1 0 0 1 1 1 0 1 1 1 0 0 1 1 1 1 0 0 0 1 0 0 0 1 0 1 0 1
0 1 0 0 0 1 0 0 1 1 1 0 1 1 0 1 1 0 0 1 1 1 0 0 0 1 0 0 1 1 1 0 1 0 1 0 0 1 0 0 0
0 1 1 1 0 0 0 1 0 0 0 0 0 0 0 0 0 1 0 0 0 0 0 0 1 0 1 1 0 1 1 0 1 1 0 C 1 0 0
```

SOURCE: Romney et al. (1986). Reproduced by permission of the American Anthropological Association from *American Anthropologist* 88: 2, 1986. Not for further reproduction.
NOTE: 1 represents "True"; 0 represents "False."

TABLE 8.3
Matches, Proportion of Matches, Proportion of Corrected Matches, and Competency Scores for the Data in Table 8.2

	Number of Matches				Proportion of Matches				Proportion of Corrected Matches				Competency Score for Student	
	1	2	3	4	1	2	3	4	1	2	3	4		
1	–	27	25	22	–	.675	.625	.550	–	.35	.25	.10	1	.48
2	27	–	34	21	.675	–	.850	.525	.35	–	.70	.05	2	.61
3	25	34	–	23	.625	.850	–	.575	.25	.70	–	.15	3	.61
4	22	21	23	–	.550	.525	.575	–	.10	.05	.15	–	4	.32

SOURCE: Romney et al. (1986). Reproduced by permission of the American Anthropological Association, from *American Anthropologist* 88:2, 1986. Not for further reproduction.

Informant 1	.37
Informant 2	.91
Informant 3	.76
Informant 4	.13

Thus, informant 2 is the most competent of the four informants for this particular cultural domain.

If you don't have a computer with you in the field, you can get a rough approximation of the results of a factor analysis by taking the square root of the mean of each row of the corrected match scores. In Table 8.3, the competency score for informant number 1 is then:

$$\sqrt{(.35 + .25 + .10)/3} = .48$$

The last column of Table 8.3 shows the rough competency score for each of the four informants. Clearly, these scores are not the same as you get from a factor analysis, but the rough scores place informants in *roughly the same order of competency* as they would be ranked by the full statistical treatment. The last column of Table 8.3 tells you (just as the factor analysis does) to use informants 2 and 3 for further exploration of the cultural domain represented by your test. Those informants are the most "culturally competent." If you ask them a series of questions about the domain, they are most likely to get the answers "right."

You can use the consensus test on any group of informants, for any cultural domain, so long as you have a way to generate a similarity matrix of informants. Pile sorts, triad tests, paired comparisons, ratings, and rankings all produce data that can be subjected to consensus analysis. I'll explain how to use these techniques in Chapter 11.

How Many Informants for the Consensus Model?

How many informants must be tested in order to select the most competent informants? Table 8.4 shows that, assuming a true-false (or yes-no) test, and a pool of informants who are more or less equal in their competence, just 10 informants, with an average competence of .7, have a 99% probability of answering each question on a test correctly, with a confidence level of .95. Only 13 informants, with a relatively low competency level of .5 are needed if you want a 90% probability of answering each question on a test correctly, with a confidence level of .95.

TABLE 8.4

Minimal Number of Informants Needed to Classify a Desired Proportion
of Questions with a Specified Confidence Level When the Average
Cultural Competence is Known

Proportion	Average Level of Cultural Competence				
of Questions	.5	.6	.7	.8	.9
.90 Confidence level					
.80	9	4	4	4	4
.85	11	6	4	4	4
.90	13	6	6	4	4
.95	17	10	6	6	4
.99	25	16	10	8	4
.95 Confidence level					
.80	9	7	4	4	4
.85	11	7	4	4	4
.90	13	9	6	4	4
.95	17	11	6	6	4
.99	29	19	10	8	4

SOURCE: Romney et al. (1986). Reproduced by permission of the American
Anthropological Association, from *American Anthropologist 88*:2, 1986. Not for
further reproduction.
NOTE: Confidence levels of .9, .95, .99, and .999 are included.

The problem is, when you start out you don't have any idea of whether
your informants are more or less equally competent in cultural domain. In
fact, that's what you want to find out so you can select the most competent
for in-depth interviews. That's why, if you can get them, it's good to have
about 40 informants when you run a consensus test.

A study by Boster et al. (1987), though, shows that the consensus model
can, indeed, be used on small groups. They studied how much the people
in a university administrative office knew about the social structure of the
office. There were 16 people in the office, including 4 professional staff,
5 support staff, 2 graduate student workers, and 5 undergraduate workers.
Each of the 16 office personnel were given a deck of cards with the names
of all the office members. The informants were asked to sort the names
into piles, according to how similar the informants thought the people in
the office were to one another in the social structure.

When all 16 informants had done this, Boster et al. had all the data they
needed to produce a similarity matrix of their informants. If there are 16
names to sort, then there are (16 × 15)/2, or 120 pairs of names. Any
informant can put any of the pairs together in a pile. The similarity between

TABLE 8.5

Competency Scores for the 16 People in Boster et al.'s 1987 Study

Person	Score	Position
1	0.856	professional staff
2	0.625	support staff
3	0.563	support staff
4	0.901	graduate student worker
5	0.830	support staff
6	0.871	support staff
7	0.630	professional staff
8	0.757	graduate student worker
9	0.700	undergraduate worker
10	0.291	undergraduate worker
11	0.775	support staff
12	0.217	undergraduate worker
13	0.689	undergraduate worker
14	0.522	undergraduate worker
15	0.700	professional staff
16	0.895	professional staff

SOURCE: J. Johnson (1990:84).

any two informants, then, is the number of pairs they put together in common. If you and I sort the 16 names in exactly the same way, we get a similarity score of 1.0. If we put just half of the 120 pairs of names in the same piles, then we get a similarity score of .50, and so on.

Boster et al. didn't run the consensus test in their original study, but Jeffrey Johnson (1990:84) did, and the results are very clear. Table 8.5 shows the competency scores for the 16 people in the group. The professional staff agreed with one another more and knew a lot more about the structure of the group than did the undergraduate workers.

If you are doing work in cognitive anthropology, then the cultural consensus test should definitely be part of your tool kit. But if you are doing general descriptive ethnography, and looking for all-around good informants, the cultural consensus technique is *not* a substitute for the time-honored way that ethnographers have always chosen key informants: luck, intuition, and hard work by both parties to achieve a working relationship based on trust.

Paying Informants

Should you pay informants? It all depends. If you are studying elites in your own culture, then payment is inappropriate. If you are studying elites in an African village, then payment may be mandatory. Be sensitive to the situation and be prepared to pay people a reasonable, negotiated fee for their time and information if circumstances require it.

William Foote Whyte was a colleague of Allan Holmberg's at Cornell University during the 1950s when Holmberg was conducting action research at Hacienda Vicos in the Peruvian highlands. Holmberg took over the hacienda when the local patrón failed to pay his government fees. Holmberg immediately declared the Indian serfs on the hacienda free of their obligations to the patrón and then studied what happened.

According to Whyte, "Holmberg did not pay Indian informants, but he was most generous in allowing other researchers access to his field site. "One summer," Whyte tells us, "a group of well-financed psychologists and psychoanalysts moved in and paid informants willing to tell their life stories and describe their dreams. Having discovered that their information had a commercial value," Whyte said, "naturally Vicosinos thereafter sought to charge researchers the going rate" (1984:109).

Whyte did not recommend paying informants in general, but felt that "if the informant is not wealthy and has to make a financial sacrifice to talk with us, then clearly some material compensation is needed" (ibid.).

In today's market-oriented economy, information is a commodity and often has a price. Personally, I think anthropologists should pay for information whenever they can and whenever it's appropriate. If we pay informants nothing (or almost nothing) and then sell the information at a value-added price when we return from the field, we deny our informants a fair share of the value of the information. The problem, of course, is to decide what a fair price should be. Obviously, it will vary with circumstances—yours and your informant's. As a student, you can afford to pay less than when you are a paid professional. Don't be surprised if your informants know that and charge you more as your own wealth increases.

Note that I've taken it for granted that you'll be going back to your field sites during your professional career. Paying informants a just, negotiated fee when you're a student will only make it easier for you to go back later. Professional anthropologists get paid for what they know—for their culture, in other words. If we sell our culture, we should not expect others to give it away, particularly in the Third World where people need all the material support they can get.

9

Field Notes: How to Take, Code, and Manage Them

"Those who want to use qualitative methods because they seem easier than statistics are in for a rude awakening" (Taylor & Bogdan, 1984:53).

Anthropologists collect many kinds of qualitative data. These include audio tapes (of musical performances and of recitations of folktales and myths), videotapes (of ceremonies, dances, and everyday activities), photographs, newspaper clippings, transcriptions of formal interviews, notes from formal interviews, caches of personal letters, texts written by native people about their own lives and, of course, field notes.

In this chapter, I focus on field notes—how to *write* them, how to *code* them, and how to *manage* them. The lessons about coding and managing field notes apply just as well to transcripts of interviews and to other textual data.

The method I present here for making and coding field notes was developed and tested by the late Michael Kenny and me, between 1967 and

1971, when we ran those NSF-supported field schools in cultural anthropology I described in Chapter 7. Kenny and I relied initially on our own experience with field notes and we borrowed freely from the experience of many colleagues. The method we developed—involving jottings, a diary, a daily log, and three kinds of formal notes—was used by 40 field-school participants in the United States and in Mexico and by others since then. Some years later, after microcomputers came on the scene, my students and I began to think about using machines to help manage textual data (Bernard & Evans, 1983).

Two things can be said about the method I'm going to lay out here: (a) It works, and (b) it's not the only way to do things. You'll develop your own style of writing field notes and add your own little tricks as you go along. Still, the method described in this chapter will help you work systematically at taking field notes, and it will allow you to search through them quickly and easily to look for relationships in your data. I wish I had used this method when I was doing my own MA and Ph.D fieldwork—and I wish microcomputers had been available then, too.

The Four Types of Field Notes:
Jottings, the Diary, the Log, and the Notes

Jottings

Field *jottings*—or what Roger Sanjek calls "scratch notes" (1990:96)—are what get you through the day. Human memory is a very poor recording device, especially for the kind of details that make the difference between good and so-so anthropological research. Keep a note pad with you at all times and make field jottings on the spot. This applies to both formal and informal interviews that you conduct with people, in bars and cafés, in homes, and on the street.

It also applies to things that just strike you as you are walking along. Jottings will provide you with the trigger you need to recall a lot of details that you don't have time to write down while you're observing events or listening to an informant. Even a few key words will jog your memory later. Remember: If you don't write it down, it's gone.

Of course, there are times when you just can't take notes. Morris Freilich did research with the Mohawks in Brooklyn, New York, and on the Caughnanaga reservation, 10 miles south of Montreal, in the 1950s. He did a lot of participant observation in a bar and, as Freilich tells it, every time he pulled out a notebook his audience became hostile. So, Freilich kept a small notebook in his hip pocket and would periodically duck into the men's room at the bar to scribble a few jottings (Freilich, 1977:159).

William Sturtevant used stubby little pencils to take furtive notes (1959). When Hortense Powdermaker did her research on race relations in Mississippi in 1932, she took surreptitious notes on sermons at African-American churches. "My pocketbook was large," she said, "and the notebook in it was small" (1966:175).

Every anthropologist runs into situations where it's impossible to take notes. It is always appropriate to be sensitive to the feelings of your informants, and it is sometimes a good idea to just listen attentively to an informant and leave your notebook in your pocket. You'd be surprised, however, how few of these situations there are. Don't talk yourself into not jotting down a few notes by *assuming* that informants won't like it if you do.

The key is to take the role of researcher immediately when you arrive at your field site, whether that site is a peasant village or a corporate office. Let people know from the very first day you arrive that you are there to study their way of life. Don't try to become an inconspicuous participant rather than what you really are: an observer who wants to participate as much as possible. Participant observation means that you try to *experience* the life of your informants to the extent possible; it doesn't mean that you try to melt into the background and *become* a fully accepted member of a culture other than your own.

It's usually impossible to do anyway. After three decades of coming and going in Indian villages in Mexico, I still stick out like a sore thumb and have yet to become the slightest bit inconspicuous. Be honest with people, and keep your note pad out as much of the time as possible. Ask your informants for their permission to take notes while you are talking with them. If people don't want you to take notes, they'll tell you.

Or they may ask to see your notes. A student researcher in one of our field schools worked in a logging camp in Idaho. He would write up his notes at night from the jottings he took all day. Each morning at 6 a.m. he nailed the day's sheaf of notes (along with a pen on a string) to a tree for everyone to look at. Some of the men took the time to scribble helpful (or amusing) comments on the notes. If you use this technique, watch out for the TV-news effect. That's when people tell you things they want to tell everyone because they know you're going to broadcast whatever they say.

The Diary

Notes are based on observations that will form the basis of your publications. A diary, on the other hand, is personal. It's a place where you can run and hide when things get tough. You absolutely need a diary in the field. It will help you deal with loneliness, fear, and other emotions that make fieldwork difficult.

A diary chronicles how you feel and how you perceive your relations with others around you. If you are really angry at someone in the field, you should write about it—in your diary. Jot down emotional highs and lows while they're happening, if you can, and write them up in your diary at the end of the day. Try to spend at least half an hour each day pouring out your soul to a diary. Later on, during data analysis, your diary will become an important professional document. It will give you information that will help you interpret your field notes, and will make you aware of your personal biases.

The important thing about a diary is just to have one, and to keep it separate from your other field notes. Franz Boas was engaged to Marie Krackowizer in May 1883, just 3 weeks before beginning his first field trip. It was a grueling 15 months on Baffin Island and at sea. Boas missed German society terribly, and though he couldn't mail the letters, he wrote about 500 pages to his fiancée. Here is an excerpt from this extraordinary diary:

> December 16, north of Pangnirtung. My dear sweetheart. . . . Do you know how I pass these long evenings? I have a copy of Kant with me, which I am studying, so that I shall not be so completely uneducated when I return. Life here really makes one dull and stupid. . . . I have to blush when I remember that during our meal tonight I thought how good a pudding with plum sauce would taste. But you have no idea what an effect privations and hunger, real hunger, have on a person. Maybe Mr. Kant is a good antidote! The contrast is almost unbelievable when I remember that a year ago I was in society and observed all the rules of good taste, and tonight I sit in this snow hut with Wilhelm and an Eskimo eating a piece of raw, frozen seal meat which had first to be hacked up with an axe, and greedily gulping my coffee. Is that not as great a contradiction as one can think of? (Cole, 1983:29)

> February 16. Anarnitung. . . . I long for sensible conversation and for someone who really understands me! Unfortunately, this time I did not bring a book to read, so I cannot help myself. I read all the advertisements and everything else on one page of the Kolnische Zeitung [a magazine]. In four days I shall have been away eight months. I have heard from none of you for four and a half months. (ibid.:42)

Bronislaw Malinowski spent much of World War I trapped in the Trobriand Islands. He, too, missed his fiancée and European society and occasionally lashed out at the Trobrianders in his diary (Malinowski, 1967):

Monday, 4.16 . . . I took a walk through the little villages—11 huts and a couple of *bwaymas* [storehouses] scattered pell-mell on the sand. . . . For the first time deep regret that E. R. M. is not Polish. [E. R. M. was Elsie R. Masson, Malinowski's first wife.] But I rejected the idea that perhaps our engagement is not definitive. I shall go back to Poland and my children will be Poles.

Tuesday, 4.24. . . . Last night and this morning looked in vain for fellows for my boat. This drives me to a state of white rage and hatred for bronze-colored skin, combined with depression, a desire to "sit down and cry," and a furious longing "to get out of this." For all that, I decide to resist and work today—"business as usual," despite everything.

6.27. Cold day, sky overcast. Worked to the point of complete exhaustion. . . . In the morning Tokulubakiki and Tokaka'u from Tilakaywa. Then Tokaka'u alone. After lunch, short talk with Towese'i, then went to observe construction of big *gugula,* [a display of food] and to Kwaybwaga, where they were roasting *bulukwa* [a European type of pig]. . . . I felt rotten and wondered whether I should risk a long walk or lie down and sleep. I went to M'tava, and this did me a great deal of good. When I came back I wrote down *wosi* [songs] . . . During my walk I thought that some day I'd like to meet Anatole France. (From "A Day in the Strict Sense of the Term" by Bronislaw Malinowski. Reprinted by permission of John Hawkins & Associates, Inc., pp. 253-254, 261, 293-294)

Fieldwork is an intense experience that will test your ability to function as a scientist under sometimes stressful conditions. Your diary will give you an outlet for writing things that you don't want to become part of a public record. Publication of Malinowski's and Boas's diaries have helped make all field workers aware that they are not alone in their frailties and self-doubts.

The Log

A log is a running account of how you plan to spend your time, how you actually spend your time, and how much money you spent. A good log is the key to doing systematic fieldwork and to collecting both qualitative and quantitative data on a systematic basis.

A field log should be kept in bound books of blank, lined pages. There are schedule-planning computer programs, of course, but I suspect they will never take the place of a big, clunky logbook for anthropological fieldwork. Don't use a skimpy little notebook for your log, like the kind you might keep in your pocket for jottings. Use a book around 6" × 8" in size, or one even larger.

Each day you are in the field should be represented by a double page of the log. The pages on the left should list what you *plan* to do on any given day. The facing pages will recount what you *actually* do each day.

Begin your log on pages 2 and 3. Put the date on the top of the even-numbered page to the left. Then, go through the entire notebook and put the successive dates on the even-numbered pages. By doing this in advance, even the days on which you "do nothing," or are away from your field site, will have double log pages devoted to them.

The first day or two that you make a log you will use only the right-hand pages where you keep track of where you go, who you see, and what you spend. Some people like to carry their log around with them. Others prefer to jot down the names of the people they run into or interview, and enter the information into their logs when they write up their notes in the evening. Keep an alphabetized file of 25-word profiles on as many people you meet as you can. It will make it much easier to remember who you're dealing with.

For the first few weeks, at least, and then for 2-week periods at various times in your field trip, jot down the times that you eat and what you eat, especially if you are doing fieldwork in another culture. Also, write down who you eat with and how much you spend on all meals away from your house. You are likely to be surprised at the results you get from this.

After a day or two, you will begin to use the left-hand sheets of the log. As you go through any given day, you will think of many things that you want to know but can't resolve on the spot. Write those things down in your jot book or in your log. When you write up your field notes, think about who you need to interview, or what you need to observe, regarding each of the things you wondered about that day.

Right then and there, open your log and commit yourself to finding each thing out at a particular time on a particular day. If finding something out requires that you talk to a particular person, then put that person's name in the log, too. If you don't know the person to talk to, then put down the name of someone whom you think can steer you to the right person.

Suppose you're studying a local educational system. It's April 5 and you are talking with an informant called MJR. She tells you that since the military government took over, children have to study politics for 2 hours every day and she doesn't like it. Write a note to yourself in your log to ask other mothers about this issue and to interview the school principal.

Later on, when you are writing up your notes, you may decide not to interview the principal until after you have accumulated more data about how mothers in the community feel about the new curriculum. On the left-hand page for April 23 you note: "target date for interview with school principal." On the left-hand page of April 10th you note: "make appointment for interview on 23rd with school principal." For April 6 you note, "need more interviews with mothers about new curriculum."

As soon as you think that you need to know how many kilowatt hours of electricity were burned in a village, or the difference in price between fish sold off a boat and the same fish sold in the local market, commit yourself in your log to a specific time when you will try to resolve the questions. Whether the question you think of requires a formal appoint ment, or a personal observation, or an informal interview in a bar, write it down in one of the left-hand pages of your log.

Don't worry if the planned activity log you create for yourself winds up looking nothing like the activities you actually engage in from day to day. Frankly, you'll be lucky to do half the things you want to do, much less do them when you want to. The important thing is to fill those left-hand pages, as far out into the future as you can, with specific information that you need, and specific tasks you need to perform to get that information.

This is not just because you want to use your time effectively, but because the process of building a log forces you to think hard about the questions you really want to answer in your research and the data you really need. You will start any field research project knowing some of the questions you are interested in. But those questions may change; you may add some, and drop others—or your entire emphasis may shift.

The right-hand pages of the log are for recording what you actually accomplish each day. As I said, you'll be appalled at first at how little resemblance the left-hand and the right-hand pages have to one another. Remember that good field notes do not depend on the punctuality of inform- ants or your ability to do all the things you want to do. They depend on your systematic work over a period of time. If some informants do not show up for appointments (and often they won't), you can evaluate whether or not you really need the data you thought you were going to get from them. If you do, then put a note on the left-hand page for that same day, or for the next day, to contact the informant and reschedule the appointment.

If you still have no luck, you may have to decide whether it's worth more of your time to track down a particular informant or a particular piece of informa- tion. Your log will tell you how much time you've spent on it already and will make the decision easier. There's plenty of time for everything when you think you've got months stretching ahead of you. But you only have a finite amount of time in fieldwork to get useful data, and the time goes very quickly.

Field Notes

There are three kinds of notes: notes on method and technique; ethno- graphic, or descriptive notes; and notes that discuss issues or provide an analysis of social situations.

Methodological Notes

Methodological notes deal with technique in collecting data. If you work out a better way to keep a log than I've described here, don't just *use* your new technique; write it up in your field notes and publish a paper about your technique so others can benefit from your experience. If you find yourself spending too much time with marginal people in the culture, make a note of it, and discuss how that came to be. You'll discover little tricks of the trade, like the "uh-huh" technique, discussed in Chapter 10, in which you learn how and when to grunt encouragingly to keep an interview going. Write up notes about your discoveries. Mark all these notes with an "M" at the top—M for "method."

Methodological notes are also about your own growth as an instrument of data collection. Collecting data is always awkward when you begin a field project, but gets easier as you become more comfortable in a new culture. During this critical period of adjustment you should intellectualize what you're learning about doing fieldwork by taking methodological notes.

When I first arrived in Greece in 1960, I was invited to dinner at "around 7 p.m." When I arrived at around 7:15 (what I thought was a polite 15 minutes late), I was embarrassed to find that my host was still taking a bath. I should have known that he really meant "around 8 p.m." when he said "around 7." My methodological note for the occasion simply stated that I should not show up for dinner before 8 p.m. in the future. Some weeks later, I figured out the general rules for timing of evening activities, including cocktails, dinner, and late-night desserts in the open squares.

When I began fieldwork with the Otomí people of central Mexico in 1962 I was offered *pulque* everywhere I went. Pulque is fermented nectar from the maguey cactus. I tried to refuse politely; I couldn't stand the stuff. But people were very insistent and seemed offended if I didn't accept the drink. Things were particularly awkward when I showed up at someone's house and there were other guests there. Everyone enjoyed pulque but me, and most of the time people were too poor to have beer around to offer me.

At that time, I wrote a note that people "felt obliged by custom to offer pulque to guests." I was dead wrong. As I eventually learned, people were testing me to see if I was affiliated with the Summer Institute of Linguistics, an evangelical missionary group that had its regional headquarters in the area where I was working.

The SIL is comprised mostly of excellent linguists whose major output is translations of the Bible into the various nonwritten languages of the world. There was, and is, serious friction between the Indians who had converted to Protestantism and those who remained Catholic. It was important for me to disassociate myself from the SIL, so my methodological note discussed the importance of conspicuously consuming alcohol and tobacco in order to identify myself as an anthropologist and not as an evangelical missionary.

Nine years later I wrote:

> After all this time, I still don't like pulque. I'm sure it's unhealthy to drink out of the gourds that are passed around. I've taken to carrying a couple of six-packs of beer in the car and telling people that I just don't like pulque, and telling people that I'd be pleased to have them join me in a beer. If they don't offer me beer, I offer it to them. This works just fine, and keeps my reputation of independence from the SIL intact.

Eight years later, in 1979, I read that William Partridge had a similar predicament during his work in Colombia (Kimball & Partridge, 1979:55). Everywhere he went, it seems, people offered him beer, even at 7 a.m. He needed an acceptable excuse, he said, to avoid spending all his waking hours getting drunk.

After a few months in the field, Partridge found that telling people *"Estoy tomando una pastilla"* ("I'm taking a pill") did the trick. Locally, the pill referred to in this phrase was used in treating venereal disease. Everyone knew that you didn't drink alcohol while you were taking this pill, and the excuse was perfect for adding a little virility boost to Partridge's reputation. Add this to your file of methods notes.

Methodological notes, then, have to do with the conduct of field inquiry itself. You will want to make methodological notes especially when you do something silly that breaks a cultural norm. If you are feeling particularly sheepish, you might want to write those feelings into your diary where no one else will see what you've written; but you don't want to waste the opportunity to make a straightforward methodological note on such occasions, as well.

Descriptive Notes

Descriptive notes are the meat and potatoes of fieldwork. Most notes are descriptive and are from two sources: watching and listening. Interviews with informants produce acres of notes, especially if you use a tape recorder and later write down large chunks of what people say. Observations of processes, like making beer, skinning animals, feeding children, hoeing, house building, and so on, also produce a lot of notes. Descriptive field notes may contain birth records that you've copied out of a church registry; or they may consist of summary descriptions of a village plaza, or an urban shopping mall, or any environmental characteristics that you think are important.

The best way to learn to write descriptive field notes is to practice doing it with others who are also trying to learn. Get together with one or more partners and observe a process that's unfamiliar to all of you. It could be a church service other than one you've seen before, or it could be an occupational process that you've not witnessed. (Until recently, I had never seen plasterers hang ceilings. They do it on stilts.)

Whatever you observe, try to capture in field notes the details of the behavior and the environment. Try to get down "what's going on." Then ask informants who are watching the ceremony or process to explain what's going on and try to get notes down on their explanation. Later, get together with your research partner(s) and discuss your notes with one another. You'll find that two or three people see much more than just one sees. You might also find that you and your partners saw the same things but wrote down different subsets of the same information.

Gene Shelley studied people who suffer from end-stage kidney disease. Most patients are on hemodialysis. Some are on peritoneal dialysis. The "hemo" patients go to a dialysis center, several times a week, while the "pero" patients perform a dialysis (called CAPD) on themselves several times a day. Here are four descriptive notes from Shelley's research. (The numbers at the top of each note are topical codes. More on topical codes in a bit. And ignore the dollar sign. We'll get back to that, too.)

$ 81689: 757.3; Dr. H

Dr. H explains that in peritoneal dialysis you exchange 2 liters of fluid several times a day (based on body size). Women do it about 3 times and men about 4 times because of larger body size. People mostly do a "dwell" for about 8 hours overnight while they sleep (fluid is inflowed into peritoneal cavity and allowed to sit there overnight). Then they do peritoneal dialysis when they wake up and another time or two during the day. Peritoneal dialysis patients are pretty close to being healthy. They have to take medication but you can not tell them from healthy people, he says.

$ 83089: 57.3, 757.5; Nurse Ralph B.

CAPD training takes about a week to 10 days. During this time, the patient comes in every day and receives training. Ralph thinks that when the whole family comes in for the training, the patients do better. They have about 20 CAPD patients right now. Ralph said there are 3 types of CAPD patients: (1) those patients who are already on hemo and in pretty good shape, usually well-motivated, (2) those who are late getting started and are in trouble (medically) and are hurriedly trying to learn the procedure (It takes 2 weeks to get a catheter inserted and then have it heal. Since this surgery is viewed as "elective surgery," it can be bumped and rescheduled. Only after surgery and healing can the training take place.), and (3) those who have lost a kidney which was transplanted. They are just waiting for another kidney and they view CAPD as temporary and are not that motivated to learn it because they think they won't be on it long.

$ 9589: 57; 572; 752.2; 76; 157; Inf. #2

She says the social network is important, in her opinion. It is important to have a person to support you (emotionally and physically). Her friends and school children (she was a teacher for deaf students for a short time), called her to see how she was doing and they still get in touch with her now. However, her friends cry and say what a brave person she is and she doesn't like them to cry. "People get upset, so I don't talk to them about it." She also doesn't like to talk to people for another reason. She started dialysis in 1972. Since then, all others who started with her (in her cohort) are dead. She doesn't want to meet new people. She doesn't want to talk to other patients about personal stuff because she will get attached to them and they will die (or suffer horribly with another disease like diabetes). Even with people who are not sick, she doesn't always tell everyone about CAPD. She would rather talk to them about normal things, not her disease.

$ 12689: Waiting Room 571; 580; 580.7; 580.1; 264; 12

While waiting to talk to Dr. H, I sat in the hemodialysis waiting room. I watched and listened to patients (and waiting family) who were waiting to get on the dialysis machines. They were talking about how sometimes the staff is rough with them when putting the needles in to get the vein access. One guy said the needle went once "right into my bone." Another guy said "the girl had to try 7 times" to get his blood and he was about to hit her. (The nurse said at the time, "I know this hurts.") Another woman threatened physical harm to technicians who draw blood roughly. One patient mentioned that sometimes they have to get different vein access sites (i.e., the groin or the top of the foot). They were all talking, not always to anyone in particular (but sometimes they were). They were talking in a way so that everyone in the room could be in the conversation if they wanted to. (Gene A. Shelley, 1993, by permission)

Analytic Notes

You will write up fewer analytic notes than any other kind. This is where you lay out your ideas about how you think the culture you are studying is organized. Analytic notes can be about relatively minor things. When I finally figured out the rules for showing up on time for evening functions in Greece, that was worth an analytic note. And when I understood the rules that governed the naming of children, that was worth an analytic note, too.

As I said in Chapter 2, in the section on theory, it took me almost a year to figure out why the casualty rate among Kalymnian sponge divers was going up while the worldwide demand for natural sponges was going down. When it finally made sense, I sat down and wrote a long, long analytic field note about it. Recently, after thinking about the problem for some years, I finally understood why bilingual education in Mexico does not result in the preservation of Indian languages (it's a long story; see Bernard, 1992a). As the ideas developed, I wrote them up in a series of notes.

In her research on kidney patients, Shelley noticed that African-Americans were far more likely to be on hemodialysis than on peritoneal dialysis, or CAPD. In her analytic notes, she explains that white physicians tend to assign African-American patients to hemodialysis because CAPD is very demanding and the physicians don't trust black patients to handle properly the chores involved.

Analytic notes are the product of a lot of time and effort and may go on for several pages. They are often the basis for published papers, or for chapters in dissertations and books. They will be the product of your understanding, and that will come about through your organizing and working with descriptive and methodological notes over a period of time. Don't expect to write a great many analytic notes, but write them all your life, even (especially) after you are out of the field.

Writing Field Notes

The difference between field*work* and field *experience* is field *notes*.

Plan on spending 2 to 3 hours, every working day, writing up field jottings into field notes, working on your diary, and coding interviews and notes. Ralph Bolton asked 34 anthropologists about their field note practices; they reported spending anywhere from an hour and a half to 7 hours a day on write-up (1984:132).

Set aside a time each day for working on your notes. I tried to "squeeze in" the time to work on notes and it was a disaster. Don't sleep on your notes, either. That is, don't write up notes in the morning from the previous day's jottings. You'll forget a lot of what you would like to have in your notes if you don't write them up in the afternoon or evening each day. The same goes for your own thoughts and impressions of events. If you don't write them up every day, while they are fresh, you'll forget them.

This means that you shouldn't get embroiled in a lot of activities that prevent you from spending time writing up your day's jottings. Of course, when an informant calls at your house and tells you to come quickly because there is an important event going on, well, that's another matter. But you can easily let this become the norm rather than the exception, and your research will suffer for it if you do.

Create many small notes rather than one long, running commentary. If you write your notes on a computer, make many separate files—one for each day is fine—rather than adding to the same humongous file day after day. The advantage is that you can name your notes by their date of creation. That way, the computer will present the notes to you in chronological order so you can always find a particular day's (or week's) notes. Many small files are also easier to handle when you get to text management and retrieval programs.

Plan on spending twice as long writing up notes about tape-recorded interviews as you spend conducting the interviews in the first place. You have to listen to a recorded interview at least once before you can write up the essential notes from it, and then it takes as long again to get the notes down. Actually *transcribing* a tape takes about six to eight hours for each hour of interview.

Coding Field Notes

Start each note with a number, beginning with 00001. Next, put in the date and place; then add the name of informant, if any. Use codes for places and informant names and keep the codebook of names and locations physically separate from your field notes. William Partridge studied cannabis use in highland Colombia. He recorded interviews with cannabis growers separately from all his other notes and kept the only copy of those notes in a locked trunk. The interview texts were identified only by a letter code (Kimball & Partridge, 1979:174).

Under the circumstances, it's pretty obvious why he did this. But it's a good idea to use a code for informant names on *all* your data. You just never know what would embarrass or hurt someone if your data fall into the wrong hands.

After the informant name and place, leave room for topical codes and finish writing up the contents of the note. When you are finished writing up your notes for the day, go back and fill in the topical codes. Code field notes as you go along. Miles and Huberman are right: "Coding is hard, obsessive work. It is not nearly as much fun as getting the good stuff in the field" (1994:63). As the pile of uncoded field notes grows, it gets harder and harder to be obsessive.

Furthermore, as I'll have occasion to say a few more times, most of what qualitative data analysis really is—is coding. By the time you've coded your field notes, you've established the themes that need to be indexed and the patterns that need to be located and thought about. Spending a lot of time coding notes is not Mickey-Mouse work. It's analysis.

Coding Versus Indexing

Before considering topical codes, I want to make clear the different meanings of the word "code" and stress the difference between coding and indexing. When I say "use codes for places and informant names," the word "code" means an *encryption device*. The object is to hide information, not dispense it. When I say: "after the informant name and place, leave room for topical codes," the word "code" means an *indexing device*. The object is to identify the existence of a variable. The third meaning of the word "code" is a *measurement device*. Here's the difference.

Suppose you are going to do 200 interviews with young mothers about their experiences in childbirth. One of the things you want to know, for each woman, is whether she recalls her birthing experience as stressful and if so, how stressful. You put together a formal interview booklet and question 27 is: "How would you describe your birthing experience?"

This is a formal interview, but you've left a lot of space in the booklet for answers to this question and you encourage each informant to ramble on for a bit about the experience. In this case, you'll have no problem locating the qualitative data on the topic. They're right after question 27 on the interview form.

But suppose you don't ask the straightforward question. Suppose you only figure out that you want to know this piece of information for each mother after you've completed your research (this happens all the time). You comb through all the interview material and look for verbal clues about the birthing experience. Every time you find a sentence or phrase in the corpus that deals with this topic, you stick a code, say STRESS, at the top of or next to the paragraph. Strictly speaking, the word STRESS is an *index*, not a true code.

Next, for each indexed phrase or sentence, you evaluate the content. Suppose, in one case, the sentence reads "KW says that the pain was so intense during childbirth she wanted to die." You decide to code KW's experience as "very stressful." The word "very" implies an ordinal measure and is a *true code*. The phrases "not stressful," "somewhat stressful," and "very stressful" are all true codes, just as the numbers 1, 2, and 3 are true codes.

Index words (or numbers) are indicators of the *presence* of a variable. Code words (or numbers) are indicators of *measurement* of a variable: presence-absence, more or less, amount, frequency, and so on. The word "code" gets used as a flag for all three concepts: the presence of a variable; the measurement of a variable; and the encryption of information. Remember the differences. Now, on to topical codes.

Topical Codes 1: The OCM and Johnson's Checklist

The OCM

The *Outline of Cultural Materials*, or OCM, was developed by George Peter Murdock (1971) as a tool for coding (indexing) information from ethnographies about cultures of the world. The OCM is thorough and flexible and can be applied (with some adaptation) to almost any project. There are codes for childbirth, for example (844), divorce (586), homosexuality (838), accumulation of wealth (556), military organization (701), crime (674), and so on. The full list of index numbers and phrases in the OCM is in Appendix C.

The OCM has been used by researchers at the Human Relations Area Files (HRAF) for 45 years. HRAF comprises about 900,000 pages of primary ethnographic materials (articles and books) dealing with 350 cultures. The primary materials are edge coded, or indexed. Figure 9.1 is a typical edge-coded page from the HRAF.

The OCM is not the only coding scheme you can use, and it appears to have fallen out of favor in recent years, but it has been used by many illustrious anthropologists in the past and I still recommend it. George Foster used the OCM to code his notes about Tzintzuntzan; John Honigman used it in his fieldwork on Canadian Indians; the 37 field researchers in Clyde Kluckhohn's Comparative Study of Values in Five Cultures Project all used the OCM to code their notes, as did the field workers on the Cornell University team project studying a village in India (Sanjek, 1990:108, 232, 331).

Every project is unique and you'll need some (perhaps many) codes that aren't in this list, but you can add decimals and extend the codes forever. Shelley used the OCM in her study of kidney patients. Here is her adaptation of the OCM code 757 (medical therapy):

Hiroa—Samoan Material Culture

up through on the other. The *'ofu* package is thus neatly and deftly folded and 252
securely fastened.

When the food is placed on the prepared oven, the *talo* leaf packages are placed round the circumference. They require less heat to cook and must not have fish or flesh placed above them lest the distinctive flavor of the vegetable be affected.

On cooking, the *talo* leaf pulps into a soft mass mixed with the coconut cream. In serving, attendants remove the outer breadfruit leaf covering but the banana leaf is left as a receptacle which the guest opens out himself.

1. *Potoa.* The *lu'au* leaves are cooked without any coconut cream. They are folded in a package and may be covered merely with a large piece of *talo* leaf, as the impervious banana loaf is unnecessary where no liquid is used.

2. *Lu.* A larger package than usual is formed of *lu'au*, coconut cream as treated above, and banana and breadfruit leaf covers. Kramer (18, vol. 2, p. 147) gives the name of *fa'afatupa'o* for this preparation.

3. *Palu sami.* This favorite preparation is made exactly like *lu* but in smaller packages while sea water is added to the prepared coconut cream to give it a salty taste. The sea water may be added to the grated nut before the cream is expressed. A metaphorical name is *'oto ma le sau* (plucked with the dew) inferring that the leaves were plucked while the dew was on them.

4. *Lu'au fui.* Coconut cream is not used but a little sea water is poured into the cupped *lu'au* before wrapping with the two leaves.

5. *Fa.* The stalks (*fa*) of the *talo* leaves are peeled and wrapped in a package without the addition of the coconut cream or sea water. The preparation may be made more palatable for sick people by adding coconut cream with sea water, which Kramer's informant referred to as *sua palusami*.

No meal is complete without a preparation of *talo* leaf. Of these, *palu sami*, is 262
easily the most in demand. In recent times salt is often added to the *talo* leaves in 263
place of sea water. The use of sea water dates from a period when other forms of
salt could not be procured. The *lu*, with coconut cream alone, is used more in inland villages where sea water is not available.

In Manua, the pinching off of the tips of the *talo* leaves is said to commemorate a historical incident that occurred between Tangaloa and Pava in a kava-drinking ceremony. (See p. 153.)

The breadfruit (*'ulu, Artocarpus incisa*). The breadfruit stands next in 262
importance as a food to *talo*. The name *'ulu,* with dialectical letter changes as *'uru,* [17]
kuru, is found throughout Polynesia. It occurs in Maori traditional history as *kuru*
and formed one of the causes of strife in the Society group before the Maori left for 245
New Zealand. The tree is grown round the villages and in the plantations. The fruit is picked with a long pole picker. The Samoans do not care for the ripe or over mature fruit. When so eaten, it is from force of circumstances and not preference. 252
The outer rind is scraped off with an *'asi* scraper before cooking. Medium sized
fruit is cooked whole, but large ones are split in two or in thirds with a characteristic wooden splitter (*to'i pua*). Of the food preparation, *taufolo* ranks high. In abun-

Figure 9.1. Sample page of data fom the Human Relations Area Files.

SOURCE: Buck (1930). Used with permission.

757.1   transplantation

757.2   hemodialysis

757.3   CAPD (peritoneal dialysis)

757.4   home dialysis

757.5   adjustment to dialysis

757.6   compliance with medical regime

757.7   machinery involved in dialysis

757.8   medicines

757.9   medical test results

757.91 HIV test results

Code 759 refers to "medical personnel." You can create 759.1 for midwives, 759.2 for physicians, 759.3 for acupuncturists, and the like. Code 231 is for practices relating to the keeping of livestock. If you are studying the use of livestock in a peasant community, you might use 231.1 to refer to data on the keeping of goats and 231.2 to refer to data about pigs. If you need totally new categories, use the numbers from 890 and above, with as many decimal places as you need.

Don't be put off by the lengthiness of the OCM coding list. That's its strength. You'll only use a fraction of the codes on any given project, and once you start using it in the field, you'll quickly find yourself building supplemental coding schemes to fit your particular needs.

Here are two descriptive field notes coded with the OCM. The first is from fieldwork I did in Tarpon Springs, Florida (Bernard, 1965); the second is from a study of an ocean-going research vessel (Bernard & Killworth, 1974).

> #118 7/15/64 Coffee house EK D 177, 185, 528, 887 K
>
> EK made a recent trip to K [Kalymnos, an island in Greece] and went back to the village where he was born. He hadn't been back in 22 years, and he is very ambivalent about things. On the one hand, he feels that he should be planning to retire to K. "That's what everybody around here talks about doing when they retire," he says. On the other hand, he doesn't want to do that, and he feels a bit trapped by custom. "I really didn't feel like I belonged there any more—not to live, really. It was great to visit and to see all the people and like that, and I'd really like my kids to know the place, but I wouldn't want to live there permanently, you know?" He wonders if there is something wrong with him and then "And my wife? Forget it."

In this case, I have coded the note for assimilation, cultural goals, vacations, and retirement. I have also added a code, K, which refers to people's relations to Kalymnos, the island in Greece where they, or their parents were born.

> #81 7/28/73 R/V TW PJ D 571.1
>
> Although the mess is open, I rarely see any of the crew eating with the scientists on this cruise. This was the case on the other cruise, too. The crew takes a lot less time to eat than the scientists who sit around "shooting the science" after dinner, as PJ says. There is a shortage of mess seats, and people have to eat in shifts. PJ says that it annoys him to see the scientific personnel just sitting around and lingering over coffee after dinner when they could be letting others sit down. "That's just another example of how obtuse these guys are." As I was considering his use of the word "obtuse" he said "They're so wrapped up in themselves, they just don't think about other people."

Code 571 in the OCM refers to "social relationships and groups." I have expanded it here to include 571.1, which I've labeled "between-group conflict."

Johnson's Checklist

Allen Johnson, along with a group of students and colleagues, developed a thorough checklist for recording cultural data. The list was developed in conjunction with Johnson's Time Allocation Project (see Chapter 14 on direct observation methods). The cultural checklist can be used both as a reminder of the kinds of data you might want to collect in a general ethnographic research project and as a template for coding data collected during field research. Johnson's checklist is available from the Human Relations Area Files, Inc. See Johnson et al. (1987) and Appendix G for details.

Topical Codes 2: Making Up Your Own Mnemonics

Many people find the use of number codes distracting. Matthew Miles and Michael Huberman (1994), authors of an excellent book on qualitative data analysis, advocate the use of words or mnemonics that look like the original concept. Like many researchers, they find that mnemonic codes (like ECO for economics, DIV for divorce, and so on) are easier to remember than are numbers. Here's a piece of Miles and Huberman's code book for a study they did of innovations in a school system.

Short Description	Code
Adoption Process	AP
AP:Event chronology-official version	AP-chron/pub
AP:Event chronology subterranean	AP-chron/prov
AP:Inside/outside	AP-in/out
AP:Centrality	AP-cent
AP:Motives	AP-mot
AP:User fit	AP-fit
AP:Plan	AP-Plan
AP:Readiness	AP-Redi
AP:Critical events	AP-crit

SOURCE: Miles and Huberman (1994:59).

Another value of using your own codes is that they develop naturally from your study and you'll find it easy to remember them as you code your notes each day. Strauss and Corbin (1990:68) recommend using *in vivo* codes as names for things. In vivo codes are catchy phrases or words used by informants. In his study of Alaskan fishermen, Jeffrey Johnson heard people talking about a "clown." The word turned out to be a terrific label for a type of person found in many organizations. The term emerged in vivo from the mouths of Johnson's informants.

In making up your own codes, be careful not to get too picky. Coding is supposed to be data *reduction* not proliferation. Mathew Miles was involved in a major ethnographic project to evaluate six schools. The researchers each developed their own codes. The list of codes quickly grew to 202 categories of actors, processes, organizational forms, and efforts. Each of the six researchers insisted that his or her field site was unique and that the highly specialized codes were all necessary. It became impossible for anyone to use the unwieldy system and they just stopped coding altogether (Miles, 1983:123).

Private codes also tend to disappear from your memory quickly when you're not using them. If you use your own coding scheme, or if you modify an existing scheme (like the OCM), be sure to write up a codebook in case you forget what "A5" or "EMP" or whatever-abbreviations-you-dreamed-up-at-the-time-you-did-the-coding mean.

The important thing is not which coding scheme you use, it's that you code your notes and do it consistently. In most projects, the coding scheme takes shape as the notes are written. The scheme is revised a lot before it becomes stable. Some anthropologists, even those who use the OCM, wait a month or more, to see how their field notes are shaping up, before they think about how to code the notes.

The Mechanics of Coding

Put codes directly into the text of the field notes, either at the top of each note, or to the right or left side of each note. Here is an example of coding at the top, using mnemonic codes:

> 412 MA XOR 101290 MIG WOM ECO
>   This note is number 412. It's about an informant named MA in these notes, and she is from a village you label XOR. The date is October 12, 1990, and the note is about MA's migration from her village to the city in search of work. The note is coded in abbreviations as being about *migration* (MIG), about *women* (WOM), and about *economics* (ECO).

Here is the same note coded on the side:

412	This note is number 412. It's about an
MA	informant named MA in these notes, and
XOR	she is from a village you label XOR. The
101290	date is October 12, 1990, and the note is
MIG	about MA's migration from her village to the
WOM ECO	city in search of work. The note is coded in
	abbreviations as being about migration (MIG),
	about women (WOM), and about economics (ECO).

The choice of top coding or edge coding is really a matter of taste. Especially if you're using a computer, there's no advantage to one method over the other. All late-model word processors let you define columns that you can type into and edit on the screen. If you want to code your notes along the edge, just define a narrow column of, say, 15 or 20 spaces for the codes. You can put the notes either to the right or to the left of the text. Then define a broad column of, say, 50 or 55 columns for the body of text.

You can use inexpensive computer programs to count the number of times that words occur in your text (see Appendix G for a list of software). By looking at a list of words that are repeated often, you can get hints about themes in your notes. This will help you decide on a list of code words.

When you have a list of code words, use a word processor to grab the codes and put them into your notes wherever you want. Gery Ryan has developed a system of macros for WordPerfect 5.1 that lets you build the code list and insert your codes into your notes, either along the edge or across the top of each note (Ryan, 1993a, 1993b).

Using Computers

If at all possible, write your notes on a computer. As I said, the log needs to be a big, easy-to-scan book, and you need to be able to carry it around with you in your backpack or bag all day. Jottings are always going to be jottings (I still have some priceless bar napkins with jottings I'm rather fond of). The diary is your *personal* document and if, like me, there are some things you just like to write with a pen in your hand, well, that's what diaries are for.

But when it comes to writing up field notes, there isn't much to be said these days for using pre-word-processor technology. Computers are still pretty expensive for students, and a few anthropologists work in places where there is no way even to harness the energy from a jeep battery or from a set of solar cells to run a computer, but most anthropologists today use a word processor to type up their field notes.

This will not save paper. If you type field notes on a computer, you still need to print them out every day and keep a hard copy safe and sound. After all, what happens if the computer is stolen or if all your backup disks are destroyed in a fire? Make lots of paper backups and print everything in big type and double spaced so you can scan your notes easily. Trees are a renewable resource.

So if it's not to save paper, why use a computer? First, it makes writing notes less of a chore than it is with pen and paper and typewriters. Second, if you type your notes on a word processor, you can use a text management program.

Reducing the Chore Factor

Let's face it: After a hard day trekking all over [town] [the village] [the jungle] [the desert] interviewing people, hanging out, or recording nonverbal behavior, it's hard to sit down and write up field notes. Sometimes, it's downright intimidating. We know this much about field notes for sure: The faster you write up your observations, the more detail you can get down. More is better. Much more is much better (except, of course, when data are systematically biased, in which case more is decidedly worse). Word processors remove some of the intimidation. They make it easier to spend the extra time getting fresh thoughts into retrievable form.

Using a Text Management Program

Traditionally, searches of text are handled by the ocular scan method, also known as "eyeballing," in which you lay out your notes in piles on the floor, live with them, handle them and read them over and over again, tack bunches of them to a bulletin board, and eventually get a feel for what's in them. This is followed by the interocular percussion test where you wait for patterns to hit you between the eyes.

This may not seem like a very scientific way of doing things, but I don't know any way that's better. No single researcher working alone for less than 2 years can produce more field notes than she or he can grasp by pawing and shuffling through them. For sheer fun and analytic efficiency, nothing beats pawing and shuffling through your notes and thinking about them. As far as I'm concerned, there is still no substitute for handling paper when you're trying to understand the patterns of material in texts.

Using a text management (TM) program, though, makes the work more fun. It is not unusual for anthropologists to produce 10,000 words some weeks in field notes. That's the equivalent of a 40-page, double-spaced paper, or about 6 pages a day. This won't happen every week, but when you're doing fieldwork, bombarded all day long with new sensory experiences and interviewing informants about topics that really mean something to you, writing 40 pages of field notes is easy. Even at a more modest clip, you're likely to accumulate 500 to 1,000 pages of notes in a year.

How do you manage all that information? When you get intimidated by the size of the note pile, the next thing you know you're backing away from taking a lot of notes on the theory that fewer notes are easier to handle. I know; it happened to me, and it has happened to many of our colleagues. This is where text management software comes in.

TM programs are why thousands of previously dedicated compuphobes own computers. Word processors may be a godsend, but you can always pay someone else to type texts into a computer. TM programs are another matter. They help you do what only you can do—analyze field notes (or any other text material)—and they make it fun. TM programs treat every single word in a corpus of text as a keyword. With a TM program you can ask the computer to "find every note in which I used the word 'woman' but only if I also used the word 'migration' within three lines of the word 'woman'."

To Code or Not to Code

TM programs make it tempting to avoid coding field notes. Resist this temptation. You can watch a wedding ceremony for 3 hours, spend a day and a half writing up 22 pages of notes on your observations, and never use the words "marriage" or "affine" in your notes. If you use a text manager to find the word "marriage," you'll retrieve all the notes in which you did use that word. You won't find any of the 22 pages where you wrote about the wedding ceremony you attended.

Whether you code your notes with the OCM scheme or with your own mnemonics, the TM program treats the codes the same as it would treat any other words in your text. Suppose you want to find all the notes in which you dealt with rural-urban migration (166 in the OCM). You'd ask the computer to "find all the notes that have the code 166 (or the word 'migr')." Of course, this will dredge up notes that have the word "migraine" in addition to notes that contain the words "migration," "migrant," and "migratory."

If you want only those notes in which you dealt with migration *and* with network relations (572.1, a subcategory of friendship), you'd ask the computer to "find those notes that contain the numbers 166 and 572.1 on the same line." This presumes that you've put all your topical codes on one line. If you've left up to three lines at the top of each note for topical codes, you'd ask the computer to "find 166 and 572.1 if they occur within three lines of one another."

With edge-coded notes, of course, you need a different search strategy. If you have 33 lines of text on each double-spaced page of field notes or interview transcription, you could have indexing codes anywhere along the edge of the page from line 1 to line 66. To handle this problem, just decide on a marker to delineate the top and bottom of each field note. Then you can ask a TM program to look for a pair or a series of codes between consecutive markers. Here is one of Gene Shelley's notes coded along the edge. This is where the dollar sign comes in. It's called a *delimiter*. It tells the computer where a note begins and ends.

$

9589Inf#2   She says the social network is important, in her
               opinion. It is important to have a person to support
57   you (emotionally and physically). Her friends and school
               children (she was a teacher for deaf students
572   for a short time), called her to see how she was doing
               and they still get in touch with her now. However, her
               friends cry and say what a brave person she is and she
752.2   doesn't like them to cry. "People get upset, so I don't
               talk to them about it." She also doesn't like to talk to
               people for another reason. She started dialysis in 1972.
               Since then, all others who started with her (in

76	her cohort) are dead. She doesn't want to meet new people. She doesn't want to talk to other patients about personal stuff because she will get attached to them and they will dic (or suffer horribly with another
157	disease like diabetes). Even with people who are not sick, she doesn't always tell everyone about CAPD. She would rather talk to them about normal things, not her disease.
$	

If all you want to do is look for words or pairs of words in the text (including index words, or codes), like "nutrition" and "children," then a simple, inexpensive program like GoFer will do the job (Bernard, 1992b). If you want to specify a set of words that occur *between* a set of delimiters, you can use a program like *dtSearch*, or *TALLY*, or *The ETHNOGRAPH* (see Appendix G for information on these programs).

Gregory Truex (1993) uses dtSearch and marks off chunks of text using what he calls the "B-E convention." He marks the beginning of a chunk of related text with a code in angle brackets and tacks on the letter "B," for beginning. Then he uses the same code, again in angle brackets, with the letter "E" tacked on to mark the end of the chunk.

For example, Truex marks the beginning of any text about land use with ANDB and marks the end of the block with ANDE. Then he uses dtSearch to retrieve any chunk of text that begins with ANDB and ends with ANDE. He can also find just those chunks that begin with ANDB, end with ANDE, *and* contain some third code, like AGRICULTURE. Truex finds that this process of "tagging and tying," as he calls it, helps him understand his corpus of text.

Database Management for Paper Notes

But what do you do if you have a big pile of paper notes from projects gone by? The computer-aided solution to this problem is database management, or DBM.

If someone asks you to suggest a French restaurant that costs less than $50.00 per person, you search through the list of French restaurants you know (your database of French restaurants) and pull out only those that also satisfy the second criterion. You can handle this chore mentally, so long as the list that you have to search is not very long and the number of simultaneous criteria you're searching for is small.

When the list of things in the database gets long, like the list of books in a library, then a card catalog can be used as a DBM. Each card contains information (author, title, date of publication, etc.) about each thing in the database. The problem with card catalogs is that there is limited filing space in the world (you can file cards by author and by subject, for example, but not by publisher), and it takes a long time to search through the database by hand. If you are looking for a book on statistical methods in the social sciences, you might have to look through all the books filed under "statistics," and through all those filed under "social science, methods," and so on.

The human mind, then, is a fast, but limited database manager; card files are unlimited, but slow. A computer database manager is both fast and has unlimited capacity. It can handle enormous lists, and it doesn't care if you ask it to sort on a dozen criteria simultaneously. (See Stone et al., 1966, for the theory of DBM.)

DBM software, like *File Express* and *Wampum*, are available at low cost for all popular models of microcomputers (see Appendix G). You can use DBM software to manage paper field notes, photos and slides, collections of artifacts, collections of news clippings—in short, any collection of *things*.

To use a database manager, you need to understand two basic concepts: records and fields. A record is the unit whose characteristics you want to retrieve. The fields are the characteristics. For example, you can think of all the books in your personal library as the units. Each book then becomes a record. The descriptive fields for each record might be: author, title, publisher, date of publication, and a series of topics that tell what the book is about. If you have 1,000 books in your library, then you have 1,000 records in the database.

It should now be clear how you can use this system to do searches of paper field notes or other texts. Just number the notes, starting with 00001. Consider each note a record and create appropriate descriptive fields. As with all field notes, you'll have one for the name of the informant; another for the place; another for the date; and several for the topics covered in each note. Some notes may get one or two topical codes, others may need 10. Be sure to define enough topical codes when you design your database. Ten codes are usually enough.

Once you've defined the fields it takes two or three minutes per field note to enter the codes. That means only about 30 to 50 hours of work at the computer to enter codes for 1,000 pages of field notes. Once that's done, you can ask the same kinds of questions you can ask with a text manager. The difference is that with a database manager, you can only look for the codes that represent the fields, not every word in the text.

You can ask questions like "Which notes are about religion, and also about political factionalism, but not about generational conflict?" When you ask your DBM system for information like this, you'll get back answers like: "The information you want is on pages 113, 334, 376, 819, 820, and 1168." You simply flip through the database of field notes on your lap. As you do, you will see the entire page of each field note and you'll get a feel for the context.

Relational Database Management

Suppose you have 3,000 pages of field notes from open-ended interviews with 200 informants. Now suppose you want to ask this enormous database, "Which notes are about migration and about females who are under 30 years of age?" To answer this question with an ordinary DBM program, you have to code every note with the age and gender of the informant.

There's a better way, called *relational database management*. In a relational database, you'd have a separate file of informants. It would have 200 records, one for each informant, and as many fields of information as you need on each informant. You can put in the informants' incomes, their ages, whether their parents are living, whether they are married, and so on. When you ask "Which notes are about migration and about females under 30?" a relational DBM program finds all the notes that are coded for migration and makes a temporary list of them.

Then the program looks at each note in the temporary list. It finds the informant's name or code and looks up that informant in the informant file. If the informant is not female, or is not female under 30, the program drops the note from the temporary list. When the program finishes, it tells you whether any of the notes conform to all the criteria you listed in your question. Asking questions like this about 3,000 records takes a couple of seconds on any late-model home computer.

With relational DBM, you can handle projects where you may have several cohorts of informants. You can have one file on people who are in an experiment (like a health care intervention project) and another on people who are not in the experiment (the controls). Then you can ask tough questions, like: "What's the average difference in weight gain for children who were on the food supplement program in village A compared to the weight gain for children who were not on the program, and for children in village B who were on the program?"

The problem with relational DBM systems is that they are not for amateurs. It takes a lot of effort and know-how to develop the *structure* of a large, relational database with many components. That's what professional DBM programmers do. If you are working on a big team project, expect to have access to those professionals. When you talk to those people, and work with them to design the database structure, it helps a lot if you are familiar with ordinary database management. This is a good reason to get hold of one of the inexpensive programs listed in Appendix G and go through the tutorials.

Database Management for Things

Even if you use a computer to type and manage all your field notes and other textual data, you'll find database managers useful for handling other kinds of data. Anything you can list is a candidate for database management. You can code your photographs and make each one a record in a DBM program. Then ask the program "Which photos are about palm oil?" or "Which photos are about old men in the plaza?" or "Which are about market sellers *and* about meat *and* about servants making purchases for others?"

Local newspapers provide important information for ethnologists. Once you start clipping all the interesting stories, however, you soon wind up with hundreds of pieces. Just number them and code them for the topics that are germane to your research. Then, later, you can ask the database, "Which clippings are about property disputes between siblings?"

If you collect folk songs, you'll quickly develop a collection of several hundred, even several thousand. If you have the lyrics typed into a computer, you can use a text management program to look for recurrent words and themes. If you've got a collection of several hundred audio tapes, you can use a database manager. If you collect artifacts, you can catalog them, index them for variables, and manage the information in a DBM program. Once you get accustomed to setting up databases, you'll wonder how you ever got along without them.

Equipment

All anthropologists should invest in a computer that they can take with them to the field. You can use a computer as a word processor, as a database manager, and as a statistical processor for handling quantitative data on the spot. You can even use it for interviewing informants in some cases. There are programs available that allow you to build a questionnaire and have informants answer it at a computer. This cuts way down on coding errors and is a great time saver as well. Of course this particular use of computers in fieldwork assumes literate informants.

If you are going to a field site where there is no electricity, you will need a computer that can run off a car battery. When Gery Ryan did his fieldwork in Cameroon, he took two notebook computers, one for him and one for his field assistant. Having a backup computer is a good idea in any case. If you think the cost of taking two computers is high, consider the cost of your time if your one computer breaks down while you're away from repair facilities.

All machines break down sooner or later, and notebook computers, while wonderful for traveling, are practically unfixable in many developing countries. Desktop computers may be hard to lug with you to the field, but if they break down, you can get them repaired, particularly if they are fully compatible with the IBM-PC. (By the way, if you buy an IBM-PC-compatible machine, rather than the IBM brand, be sure the computer is both hardware- and software-compatible with the IBM-PC. That's what *fully* compatible means.)

There is no best answer to the question "Which brand of computer should I buy?" The first question in selecting a computer is: Does it run the software I want to use? Many special-purpose programs, like ANTHROPAC, are only available for PC-compatible machines. (ANTHROPAC is particularly useful in analyzing data from pile sorts and other systematic data collection methods that we'll explore in Chapter 11.) On the other hand, new models of the Macintosh will run programs written for the PC environment, and many people find the Macintosh easier to use than the PC.

A couple of other hints: Remember that diskettes are volatile. They lose data in high temperatures and have to be backed up more frequently if you are working in a desert or jungle environment. Some machines do not do well in hot climates. Check the manufacturer's specifications for the operating temperature range of any computer you are thinking of buying. Some brands are more rugged than others. A field computer should be able to take some punishment, but don't expect miracles.

Don't skimp on diskettes, even if you use a hard disk in the field. Back up your data frequently and send a copy out of the field to a safe storage place. Computers make the taking and managing of data much more enjoyable than these tasks used to be. But they do not diminish at all the need for all field scientists to be thoroughly paranoid about protecting their data.

10

Unstructured and Semistructured Interviewing

Unstructured interviewing is the most widely used method of data collection in cultural anthropology. We interview people informally during the course of an ordinary day of participant observation; we interview people on their boats and in their fields; and we interview people in our offices or theirs. There is a vast literature on how to conduct effective interviews: how to gain rapport, how to get informants to open up, how to introduce an interview, and how to end one.

Anthropologists have made relatively little contribution to this literature. I think that's because we do so *much* interviewing, we just take for granted that it's all a matter of on-the-job training. But precisely because so much of our primary data comes from unstructured interviews, I think we have to work as hard as we can on improving interviewing skills.

This chapter reviews some of what is known about interviewing. After you read this chapter, and practice some of the techniques described, you should be well on your way to becoming an effective interviewer. You should also have a pretty good idea of how much more there is to learn and be on your way to exploring the literature.

Interview Control

There is a continuum of interview situations based on the amount of *control* we try to exercise over the responses of informants (Dohrenwend & Richardson, 1965; Gorden, 1975; Spradley, 1979). For convenience, I divide the continuum into four large chunks.

1. At one end there is *informal interviewing*, characterized by a total lack of structure or control. The researcher just tries to remember conversations heard during the course of a day "in the field." This requires constant jotting and daily sessions in which you sit at a typewriter, unburden your memory, and develop your field notes. Informal interviewing is the method of choice during the first phase of participant observation, when you're just settling in and getting to know the lay of the land. It is also used throughout fieldwork to build greater rapport and to uncover new topics of interest that might have been overlooked.

2. Next comes *unstructured interviewing*, the focus of this chapter. There is nothing at all "informal" about unstructured interviewing. You sit down with an informant and hold an interview. Period. Both of you know what you're doing, and there is no shared feeling that you're just engaged in pleasant chit-chat. Unstructured interviews are based on a clear plan that you keep constantly in mind, but are also characterized by a minimum of control over the informant's responses.

The idea is to get people to open up and let them express themselves in their own terms, and at their own pace. A lot of what is called "ethnographic interviewing" is unstructured. Unstructured interviewing is used in situations where you have lots and lots of time—like when you are doing long-term fieldwork and can interview people on many separate occasions.

3. In situations where you won't get more than one chance to interview someone, *semistructured interviewing* is best. It has much of the freewheeling quality of unstructured interviewing, and requires all the same skills, but semistructured interviewing is based on the use of an *interview guide*. This is a written list of questions and topics that need to be covered in a particular order.

The interviewer still maintains discretion to follow leads, but the interview guide is a set of clear instructions—instructions like this: "Probe to see if informants who have daughters have different values about dowry and female sexuality than informants who only have sons." Interview guides are built up from informal and unstructured interview data.

Formal, written guides are mandatory if you are sending out several interviewers to collect data. But even if you do all the interviewing on a project yourself, you should build a guide and follow it if you want reliable, comparable qualitative data. Semistructured interviewing works very well in projects where you are dealing with managers, bureaucrats, and elite members of a community—people who are accustomed to efficient use of their time. It demonstrates that you are fully in control of what you *want* from an interview but leaves both you and your informant to follow new leads. It shows that you are prepared and competent but that you are not trying to exercise excessive control over the informant.

4. Finally, there are fully *structured interviews* in which all informants are asked to respond to as nearly identical a set of stimuli as possible. One variety of structured interview involves use of an *interview schedule*—an explicit set of instructions to interviewers who administer questionnaires orally. Instructions might read "If the informant says that she has at least one daughter over 10 years of age, then ask questions 26b and 26c. Otherwise, go on to question 27." Self-administered questionnaires are structured interviews. Other structured interviewing techniques include pile sorting, frame elicitation, triad sorting, and tasks that require informants to rate or rank order a list of things. I'll deal with structured interviews in Chapter 11 and with questionnaires in Chapter 12.

Starting an Unstructured Interview

There are some important steps to take when you start interviewing an informant for the first time. First of all, assure informants of anonymity. Explain that you simply want to know what *they* think, and what *their* observations are. If you are interviewing someone whom you have come to know over a period of time (what I mean by an *informant*), explain why you think their opinions and observations on a particular topic are important. If you are interviewing someone chosen from a random sample, and whom you are unlikely to see again (a *respondent*), explain how they were chosen and why it is important that you have their cooperation to maintain representativeness.

If informants say that they really don't know enough to be part of your study, assure them that their participation is crucial and that you are truly interested in what they have to say (and you'd better mean it, or you'll never pull it off). Tell everyone you interview that you are trying to learn from *them*. Encourage them to interrupt you during the interview with anything they think is important. Finally, ask informants for permission to record every interview and to take notes. This is vital. If you can't take notes, then, in most cases, the value of an interview plummets.

Always keep in mind that informants know that you are deliberately shopping for information. There is no point in trying to hide that fact. If you are open and honest about your intentions, and if you are genuinely interested in what your informants have to say, many people will help you.

This is not always true, of course. When Colin Turnbull went out to study the Ik in Uganda, he found a group of people who had seemingly lost interest in life and in exchanging human kindnesses. The Ik had been brutalized, decimated, and left by the government to fend for themselves on a barren reservation. They weren't impressed with the fact that Turnbull wanted to study their culture. In fact, they weren't much interested in anything Turnbull was up to, and were anything but friendly (Turnbull, 1972).

Letting the Informant Lead

The case of the Ik is extreme. In general, if you are really interested in learning about the lives of other people, some of them, at least, will be pleased to spend time with you, in unstructured or semistructured interviews, teaching you what you need to know. In order for them to do this, informants must understand your questions, they must have the information you are asking them for, and they must be willing to spend the time and energy required to sit and talk with you (Cannell & Kahn, 1968:574).

If you can carry on "unthreatening, self-controlled, supportive, polite, and cordial interaction in everyday life" then interviewing will come easy to you, and informants will feel comfortable responding to your questions (Lofland, 1976:90). No matter how supportive you are as a person, though, an interview is never really like a casual, unthreatening conversation in everyday life. In casual conversations, people take more or less balanced turns (Spradley, 1979), and there is no feeling that somehow the discussion has to stay on track or follow some theme (see also Merton et al., 1956; Hyman & Cobb, 1975). In unstructured interviewing, you keep the conversation focused on a topic, while giving the informant room to define the content of the discussion.

The rule is: Get an informant on to a topic of interest and get out of the way. Let the informant provide information that he or she thinks is important.

During my research on the Kalymnian sponge fishermen, I spent a lot of time at Procopis Kambouris's *taverna*. (A Greek taverna is a particular kind of restaurant.) Procopis's was a favorite of the sponge fishermen. Procopis was a superb cook, he made his own wine every year from grapes that he selected himself, and he was as good a teller of sea stories as he was a listener to those of his clientele. At Procopis's taverna I was able to collect the work histories of sponge fishermen—when they'd begun their careers, the training they'd gotten, the jobs they'd held, and so on. The atmosphere was relaxed (plenty of retsina wine and good things to eat), and conversation was easy.

As a participant observer I developed a sense of camaraderie with the regulars, and we exchanged sea stories with a lot of flourish. Still, no one at Procopis's ever made the mistake of thinking that I was there just for the camaraderie. They knew that I was writing a book about their lives and that I had lots of questions to ask. They also knew immediately when I switched from the role of participant observer to that of ethnographic interviewer.

One night, I slipped into such an interview/conversation with Savas Ergas. He was 64 years old at the time and was planning to make one last 6-month voyage as a sponge diver during the coming season in 1965. I began to interview Savas on his work history at about 7:30 p.m., and we closed Procopis's place at about 3 a.m. During the course of the evening, several other men joined and left the group at various times, as they would on any night of conversation at Procopis's. Savas had lots of stories to tell (he was a living legend and he played well to a crowd), and we had to continue the interview a few days later, over several more liters of retsina.

At one point on that second night, Savas told me (almost offhandedly) that he had spent more than a year of his life walking the bottom of the Mediterranean. I asked him how he knew this, and he challenged me to document it. Savas had decided that there was something important that I needed to know, and he maneuvered the interview around to make sure I learned it.

This led to about three hours of painstaking work. We counted the number of seasons he'd been to sea over a 46-year career (he remembered that he hadn't worked at all during 1943 because of "something to do with the war"). We figured conservatively the number of days he'd spent at sea, the average number of dives per trip, and the average depth and time per dive. We joked about the tendency of divers to exaggerate their exploits and about how fragile human memory is when it comes to this kind of detail.

It was difficult to stay on the subject, because Savas was such a good raconteur and a perceptive analyst of Kalymnian life. The interview meandered off on interesting tangents, but after a while, either Savas or I would steer it back to the issue at hand. In the end, discounting heavily for both exaggeration and faulty recall, we reckoned that he'd spent at least 10,000 hours under water—about a year and a fourth, counting each day as a full 24 hours—and had walked the distance between Alexandria and Tunis at least three times.

The exact numbers really didn't matter. What did matter was that Savas Ergas had a really good sense of what *he* thought I needed to know about the life of a sponge diver. It was I, the interviewer, who defined the focus of the interview; but it was Savas, the informant, who determined the content. And was I ever glad that he did.

The Uses of Unstructured Interviewing

Unstructured interviewing is very versatile. Many field researchers use it to develop formal guides for semistructured interviews, or to learn what questions to include, in the native language, on a questionnaire. (See Werner & Schoepfle, 1987, for a good discussion of this.) It is not always necessary to do this, however. I once asked a fisherman in Greece if I could have a few minutes of his time to discuss the economics of small-scale fishing. I was about five minutes into the interview, treading lightly, when he interrupted me and asked, "Why don't you just get to the point? You want to know how I decide where to fish, and whether I use a share system or a wage system to split the profits, and how I find buyers for my catch, and things like that, right?" He had heard from other fishermen that these were some of the topics I was interviewing people about. No unstructured interviews for him; he was a busy man and wanted to get right to it.

Unstructured interviewing is also excellent for building initial rapport with informants, before moving to more formal interviews, and it's useful for talking to informants who would not tolerate a more formal interview. The personal rapport you build with close informants in long-term fieldwork can make highly structured interviewing feel somehow unnatural. In fact, highly structured interviewing can get in the way of your ability to communicate freely with key informants.

Once you learn the art of *probing* (which I'll discuss next), unstructured interviewing can be used for studying sensitive issues, like sexuality, racial or ethnic prejudice, or hot political topics. I find it particularly useful in studying conflict. In 1972-1973, for example, I went to sea on two different oceanographic research vessels (Bernard & Killworth, 1973, 1974). In both cases, there was an almost palpable tension between the scientific personnel and the crew of the ship. Through both informal and unstructured interviewing on land between cruises, I was able to establish that the conflict was predictable and regular. Let me give you an idea of how complex the situation was.

In 1972-1973, it cost $5,000 a day to run a major research vessel, not including the cost of the science. (The cost is about four times that today.) The way oceanography works, at least in the United States, the chief scientist on a research cruise has to pay for both ship time and for the cost of any experiments he or she wants to run. To do this, ocean scientists compete for grants from institutions like the U.S. Office of Naval Research, NASA, and the National Science Foundation.

The spending of so much money is validated by publishing significant results in prominent journals. It's a tough, competitive game, and one that leads scientists to use every minute of their ship time. As one set of scientists comes ashore after a month at sea, the next set is on the dock waiting to set up their experiments and haul anchor.

The crew, consequently, might only get 24 or 48 hours shore leave between voyages. That can cause some pretty serious resentment by ships' crews against scientists. And that can lead to disaster. I found many documented instances of sabotage of expensive research by crew members who were, as one of them said, "sick and tired of being treated like goddamn bus drivers." In one incident, involving a British research vessel, a freezer filled with Antarctic shrimp, representing 2 years of data collection, went overboard during the night. In another, the crew and scientists from a U.S. Navy oceanographic research ship got into a brawl while in port (*Science*, 1972:489).

The structural problem I uncovered began at the top. Scientists whom I interviewed felt they had the right to take the vessels wherever they wanted to go, within prudence and reason, in search of answers to questions they had set up in their proposals. The captains of the ships believed (correctly) that *they* had the last word on maneuvering their ships at sea. They reported that scientists sometimes went beyond prudence and reason in what they demanded of the vessels.

For example, a scientist might ask the captain to take a ship out of port in dangerous weather because ship time is so precious. This conflict between crew and scientists was apparently mentioned by Charles Darwin in his diaries from HMS *Beagle*—and then promptly ignored. This problem will no doubt play a role in the productivity of long-term space station operations.

Unraveling this conflict at sea required participant observation and unstructured interviewing with many people. No other strategy for data collection would have worked. At sea, people live for long periods of time in close physical quarters, and there is a common need to maintain good relations for the organization to function well. It would have been inappropriate for me to have used highly structured interviews about the source of tension between the crew and the scientists. Better to steer the interviews around the issue of interest and to let informants teach me what I needed to know. In the end, no analysis was better than that offered by one engine room mechanic who told me "these scientist types are so damn hungry for data, they'd run the ship aground looking for interesting rocks if we let them."

Probing

The key to successful interviewing is learning how to probe effectively—that is, to stimulate an informant to produce more information, without injecting yourself so much into the interaction that you only get a reflection of yourself in the data. Suppose you ask, "Have you ever been away from the village to work?" and the informant says "Yes." The next question (the probe) is "Like where?" Suppose the answer is "Oh, several different places." The correct response is not "Pachuca? Querétaro? Mexico City?" but "Like where? Could you name some of the places where you've gone to get work?"

There are many kinds of probes that you can use in an interview. In what follows, I will draw on the important work by Kluckhohn (1945), Merton et al. (1956), Kahn and Cannell (1957), Whyte (1960, 1984), Dohrenwend and Richardson (1965), Gorden (1975), Hyman and Cobb (1975), Warwick and Lininger (1975), Reed and Stimson (1985), and on my own experience over the last 30 years.

The Silent Probe

The most difficult technique to learn is the *silent probe,* which consists of just remaining quiet and waiting for an informant to continue. The silence may be accompanied by a nod, or by a mumbled "uh-huh" as you focus on your note pad. The silent probe sometimes produces more information than does direct questioning. At least at the beginning of an interview, informants look to you for guidance as to whether or not they're on the right track. They want to know whether they're "giving you what you want." Most of the time, especially in unstructured interviews, you want the informant to define the relevant information

Some informants are more glib than others and require very little prodding to keep up the flow of information. Others are more reflective and take their time. Inexperienced interviewers tend to jump in with verbal probes as soon as an informant goes silent. Meanwhile, the informant may be just reflecting, gathering thoughts, and preparing to say something important. You can kill those moments (and there are a lot of them) with your interruptions.

Glibness can be a matter of *cultural*, not just personal style. Gordon Streib reports that he had to adjust his own interviewing style radically when he left New York City to study the Navaho in the 1950s. Streib, a New Yorker himself, had done studies based on semistructured interviews with subway workers in New York. Those workers uniformly maintained a fast, hard-driving pace during the interviews—a pace with which Streib, as member of the culture, was comfortable. But that style was entirely inappropriate with the Navaho, who were uniformly more reflective than the subway workers (Streib, personal communication). In other words, the silent probe is sometimes not a "probe" at all; being quiet and waiting for an informant to continue may simply be appropriate cultural behavior.

On the other hand, the silent probe is a risky technique to use, and that is why beginners avoid it. If an informant is genuinely at the end of a thought and you don't provide further guidance, your silence can become awkward. You may even lose your credibility as an interviewer. The silent probe takes a lot of practice to use effectively. But it's worth the effort.

The Echo Probe

Another kind of probe consists of simply repeating the last thing an informant has said and asking them to continue. This *echo probe* is particularly useful when an informant is describing a process, or an event. "I see. The goat's throat is cut and the blood is drained into a pan for cooking with the meat. Then what happens?" This probe is neutral and doesn't redirect the interview. It shows that you understand what's been said so far and encourages the informant to continue with the narrative. If you use the echo probe too often, though, you'll hear an annoyed informant asking you, "Why do you keep repeating what I just said?"

The Uh-huh Probe

You can encourage an informant to continue with a narrative by just making affirmative noises, like "uh-huh," or "yes, I see," or "right, uh-huh," and so on. Matarazzo (1964) showed how powerful this *neutral probe* can be. He did a series of identical, semistructured, 45-minute interviews with a group of informants. He broke each interview into three 15-minute chunks. During the second chunk, the interviewer was told to make affirmative noises, like "uh-huh," whenever the informant was speaking. Informant responses during those chunks were about a third longer than during the first and third periods.

The Long Question Probe

You can also create longer and more continuous responses by making your questions longer. Instead of asking "How do you plant a yam garden?" ask "What are all the things you have to do to actually get a yam garden going?" When I interviewed sponge divers on Kalymnos, instead of asking them "What is it like to make a dive into very deep water?" I said "Tell me about diving into really deep water. What do you do to get ready, and how do you descend and ascend? What's it like down there?" Later in the interview, of course, or on another occasion, I would home in on special topics. But to break the ice and get the interview flowing, there is nothing quite as useful as what Spradley (1979) called the "Grand Tour" question.

This does not mean that asking longer questions or asking neutral probes necessarily produces *better* responses. But they do produce more responses, and, in general, more is better. Furthermore, the more you can keep an informant talking, the more you can express interest in what they are saying and the more you build rapport. This is especially important in the first interview you do with someone whose trust you want to build (see ibid:80). There is still a lot to be learned about how various kinds of probes affect what informants tell us.

Probing by Leading

After all this, you may be cautious about being really directive in an interview. Don't be. Many researchers caution against *leading* an informant. Lofland (1976), for example, warns against questions like "Don't you think that . . ." and suggests asking "What do you think about. . . . " He is, of course, correct. On the other hand, any question an interviewer asks leads an informant. You might as well learn to do it well.

Consider this leading question that I asked an Otomí Indian informant: "Right. I understand. The *compadre* [co-godparent] is *supposed* to pay for the music for the baptism fiesta. But what happens if the compadre doesn't have the money? Who pays then?" This kind of question can stop the flow of an informant's narrative stone dead. It can also produce more information than the informant would otherwise have provided. At the time, I thought the informant was being overly "normative." That is, I thought he was stating an ideal behavioral custom (having a compadre pay for the music at a fiesta) as if it were never violated.

It turned out that all he was doing was relying on his own cultural competence—"abbreviating," as Spradley (1979:79) called it. The informant took for granted that the anthropologist knew the "obvious" answer: If the compadre didn't have enough money, well, then there might not be any music. My interruption reminded the informant that I just wasn't up to his level of cultural competence; I needed him to be more explicit. He went on to explain other things that he considered obvious but that I would not have even known to ask about. Someone who has committed himself to pay for the music at a fiesta might borrow money from *another* compadre to fulfill the obligation. In that case, he wouldn't tell the person who was throwing the fiesta. That might make the host feel bad, like he was forcing his compadre to go into debt.

In this interview, in fact, the informant eventually became irritated with me because I asked so many things that he considered obvious. He wanted to abbreviate a lot and to provide a more general summary; I wanted details. I backed off and asked a different informant for the details. I have since learned to start some probes with "This may seem obvious, but. . . . "

Directive probes (leading questions) may be based on what an informant has just finished saying or on something an informant told you an hour ago or a week ago. As you progress in long-term field research, you come to have a much greater appreciation for what you really want from an interview. It is perfectly legitimate to use the information you've already collected to focus your subsequent interviews.

This leads researchers from informal to unstructured to semistructured interviews, and even to completely structured interviews like questionnaires. When you feel like you've learned something valid about a culture, it's essential to test that knowledge by seeing if it can be reproduced in many informants, or if it is idiosyncratic to a particular informant or subgroup in the culture.

Verbal Informants

Some informants try to tell you *too much*. They are the kind of people who just love to have an audience. You ask them one little question and off they go on one tangent after another, until you become exasperated. New interviewers are sometimes reluctant to cut off informants, afraid that doing so is poor interviewing technique. In fact, as William Foote Whyte notes, informants who want to talk your ear off are probably used to being interrupted. It's the only way their friends get a word in edgewise. You do, however, need to learn to cut people off without rancor. "Don't interrupt *accidentally* . . . ," Whyte said, "learn to interrupt *gracefully*" (1960:353, italics his). Each situation is somewhat different; you learn as you go in this business.

Phased Assertion

A particularly effective probing technique is called *phased assertion* (Kirk & Miller, 1986), or *baiting* (Agar, 1980:94). This is when you act like you already know something in order to get people to open up. I used this technique in a study of how Otomí Indian parents felt about their children learning to read and write Otomí. Bilingual (Spanish-Indian) education in Mexico is a politically sensitive issue (S. Heath, 1972), and when I started the study people were reluctant to talk about it.

In the course of informal interviewing I learned from a schoolteacher in one village that some fathers had come to complain about the teacher trying to get the children to read and write Otomí. The fathers, it seems, were afraid that studying Otomí would get in the way of their children becoming fluent in Spanish. Once I heard this story, I began to drop hints that I knew the reason parents were against children learning to read and write Otomí. As I did this, the parents opened up and confirmed what I'd found out.

Every journalist (and gossip monger) knows this technique well. As you learn a piece of a puzzle from one informant, you use it with the next informant to get more information, and so on. The more you seem to know, the more comfortable people feel about talking to you, and the less people feel they are actually divulging anything. *They* are not the ones who are giving away the "secrets" of the group. Phased assertion also prompts some informants to jump in and correct you if they think you know a little, but that you've "got it all wrong." In some cases I've purposely made wrong assertions in order to provoke a correcting response.

The Ethics of Probing

Are these tricks of the trade ethical? I think they are, but using them creates some important responsibilities to your informants.

First, there is no ethical imperative in anthropology more important than seeing to it that you do not harm innocent informants who have provided you with information in good faith. The problem, of course, is that not all informants are innocents. Some informants commit wartime atrocities. Some practice infanticide. Some are HIV positive and, out of bitterness, are purposely infecting others. Do you protect them all?

Are any of these examples more troublesome to you than the others? These are not extreme cases, thrown in here to prepare you for the worst, "just in case." They are the sort of ethical dilemmas that field researchers confront all the time.

Second, the better you get at making informants "open up," the more responsible you become that they don't later suffer some emotional distress for having done so. Informants who divulge *too* quickly what they believe to be secret information can later come to have real regrets, even loss of self-esteem. They may suffer anxiety over how much they can trust you to protect them in the community.

It is sometimes better to stop an informant from divulging privileged information in the first or second interview and to wait until both of you have built a mutually trusting relationship. If you sense that an informant is uncomfortable with having spoken too quickly about a sensitive topic, end the interview with light conversation and reassurances about your discretion. Soon after, look up the informant and engage in light conversation again, with no probing or other interviewing techniques involved. This will also provide reassurance of trust.

Remember: The first ethical decision you make in research is whether to collect certain kinds of information at all. Once that decision is made, *you* are responsible for what is done with that information, and *you* must protect informants from becoming emotionally burdened for having talked to you.

Learning to Interview

It's impossible to eliminate reactivity and subjectivity in interviewing, but like any other craft, you will get better and better at interviewing the more you practice. It helps a lot to practice in front of others and to have an experienced interviewer monitor and criticize your performance. Even without such help, however, you can improve your interviewing technique just by paying attention to what you're doing.

Do *not* use your friends as practice informants. You can not learn to interview with friends because there are role expectations that will get in the way. Just when you're really rolling, and getting into probing deeply on some topic that you both know about, they are likely to laugh at you or tell you to knock it off. Practice interviews should *not* be just for practice. They should be done on topics you're really interested in and with informants who are likely to know a lot about those topics. Every interview you do should be conducted as professionally as possible and should produce useful data (with plenty of notes that you can code and file and cross file).

Most anthropology students do their fieldwork outside their own country. If possible, find persons from the culture you are going to study and conduct interviews on some topic of interest. If you are going to Turkey to study women's roles at the village level, then find Turkish students at your university and interview them on some related topic. It is often possible to employ the spouses of foreign students for these kinds of "practice" interviews. I put "practice" in quotes to emphasize again that these interviews should produce data of interest to you. If you are studying a language that you'll need for fieldwork, these practice interviews will help you sharpen your skills at interviewing in that language.

Even if you are going off to the interior of the Amazon, this does not let you off the hook. It is unlikely that you'll find native speakers of Yonomami on your campus, but you can not use this as an excuse to wait until you're out in the field to learn general interviewing skills. Interviewing skills are honed by practice, and one of the most constructive things you can do in preparing for fieldwork is to practice conducting unstructured and semistructured interviewing.

Among the biggest problems faced by researchers who rely heavily on semistructured interviews are boredom and fatigue. Even a small project requires 40 to 60 interviews to generate sufficient data to be worthwhile. Most anthropologists collect their own interview data, and asking the same questions over and over again can get pretty old. Gorden (1975) studied 30 interviewers who worked for 12 days doing about two tape-recorded interviews per day. Each interview was from 1 to 2 hours long.

The first interview on each day, over all interviewers, averaged about 30 pages of transcription. The second averaged only 25 pages. Furthermore, the first interviews, on average, got shorter and shorter during the 12-day period of the study. In other words, on any given day, boredom made the second interview shorter; and over the 12 days, boredom (and possibly fatigue) took its toll on the first interviews of each day.

Of course, anthropologists don't have to conduct their interviews in 12 days. Nevertheless, the lesson is clear. Plan each project in advance and calculate the number of interviews you are going to get. Pace yourself. Don't try to bring in all your interview data in a short time. Spread the project out, if possible.

In sociology, where interviews are conducted to investigate people's reactions to current issues, spreading out a project over a long period of time raises a serious history confound (see Chapter 3). This may not be as big a problem in cultural anthropological fieldwork, especially if you are studying patterns of behavior that have been stable for some time.

Still, there is always a trade-off: The longer a project takes, the less likely that the first interviews and the last interviews will be valid indicators of the same things. In long-term participant observation fieldwork, I recommend going back to your early informants and interviewing them a second time. See whether their observations and attitudes have changed, and if so, why.

As you learn to interview, practice being nonjudgmental. You *usually* do better in interviews by not showing disapproval of your informants' beliefs and reported actions. But not always. In 1964, when we were working on the island of Kalymnos, my wife Carole would take our 2-month-old baby for daily walks in a carriage. Older women would peek into the baby carriage and make disapproving noises when they saw our daughter sleeping on her stomach. Then they would reach into the carriage and turn the baby over, explaining forcefully that the baby would get the evil eye if we continued to let her sleep on her stomach. Not wanting to offend anyone, Carole listened politely and tried to act nonjudgmental.

One day, enough was enough. Carole told off a woman who had intervened and that was that. From then on, women were more eager to discuss child-rearing practices, and the more we challenged them, the more they challenged us. There was no rancor involved, and we learned a lot more than if Carole had just listened politely and said nothing.

Using a Tape Recorder

Don't rely on your memory in interviewing; use a tape recorder in all cases except where informants specifically ask you not to. Tapes are a permanent record of primary information that can be archived and passed on to other researchers. If informants are self-conscious about the tape recorder, Holly Williams (personal communication) recommends asking them to hold the machine; explain that you don't want to miss anything they say and that you need both hands free to take notes.

For simple recording of interviews in a language you understand well, you can get away with a basic cassette machine for about $50. Buy two of them. The absolute rule is that if you don't have a spare, you'll need one at the most inconvenient moment.

If you are doing linguistic work, or if you are recording in a language that you are just learning, you need a cassette machine with a much better signal-to-noise ratio than the low-end cassette recorders. A very good field machine is the Sony WM-D6C. It weighs less than 2 pounds and was selling for $379 in 1993. When you are straining to hear phonemes or trying to understand a slurred phrase on tape, you'll be glad you spent that much. And, of course, if you're going to record a lot of music in the field, a good machine is a must.

Use really good tapes, too—the kind that are put together with screws. You can open those cassettes and fix the tape when it (inevitably) jams or tangles. Don't use thin (120-minute) tape. Transcribing involves listening, stopping, and rewinding—often hundreds of times per tape. Thin tape just won't stand up to this kind of use.

Bruce Jackson (1987:145), a very experienced field worker in folklore, recommends taking brand new tapes to a studio and getting them bulk erased before recording on them for the first time. This cuts down the magnetic field noise on the new tape. Jackson also recommends running each tape through your machine three or four times on fast forward and fast reverse. All tapes stretch a bit, even the best of them, and this will get the stretch out of the way.

Test your tape recorder before every interview. And do the testing at home. There's only one thing worse than a recorder that doesn't run at all: It's one that runs but doesn't record. Then your informant is sure to say at the end of the interview: "Let's run that back and see how it came out!" (Yes, that happened to me. But just once. And it needn't happen to anyone who reads this.)

Good tape recorders have battery indicators. Want a foolproof way to kill an exciting interview? Ask the informant to "please hold that thought" while you change batteries. When batteries are slightly low, throw them out. To ensure recording fidelity, it's better to rely on batteries than on house current—unless you are sure that the current is stable and is the same as you have at home.

Good tape recorders also come with voice activation. When you're in VA mode, the recorder only turns on if there is noise to record. During long pauses (while an informant is thinking, for example), the recorder shuts off, saving tape. Holly Williams (personal communication) recommends against using the VA mode. It doesn't save much tape, and she finds that the long breaks without any sound make transcribing tapes much easier. You don't have to shut the machine off and turn it on as many times while you're typing.

It can take from 6 to 8 hours to transcribe 1 hour of tape, depending on how closely you transcribe, how clear the tape is, and how proficient you are in the language. It may not be necessary to fully transcribe interviews. If you are using life histories to describe how families in some community deal with prolonged absence of fathers, then you *must* have full transcriptions to work with. And you can't study cultural *themes*, either, without full transcriptions. But if you want to know how many informants said they had helped their brothers with bride price, you may be able to get away with only partial transcription. You may even be as well off using an interview guide and taking notes.

If you transcribe your interview tapes, invest in a transcription machine. These machines cost around $400. You use a foot pedal to start and stop the machine, to back up and to fast forward, and even to slow down the tape so you can listen carefully to a phrase or a word. A transcription machine and a good set of earphones will save you many hours of work because you can keep both hands on your keyboard all the time.

Whether you do full transcriptions or just take notes during interviews, you should try to tape your interviews anyway. You may need to go back and fill in details in your notes.

Finally, never substitute tape for note taking. A lot of very bad things can happen to tape, and if you haven't got back-up notes, you're out of luck. Don't wait until you get home to take notes, either. Take notes during the interview *about* the interview. Did the informant seem nervous or evasive? Were there a lot of interruptions? What were the physical surroundings like? How much probing did you have to do? Take notes on the contents of the interview, even though you get every word on tape.

A few informants, of course, will let you use a tape recorder but will balk at your taking notes. Don't assume, however, that informants will be offended if you take notes. Ask them. Most of the time, all you do by avoiding note taking is lose a lot of data. Informants are under no illusions about what you're doing. You're interviewing them. You might as well take notes and get people used to it, if you can.

Focus Groups

Focus groups are recruited to discuss a particular topic—like people's reaction to a television commercial or their attitudes toward a social service program. The method derives from work by Paul Lazarsfeld and Robert Merton in 1941 at Columbia University's Office of Radio Research. A group of people listened to a recorded radio program that was supposed to raise public morale prior to America's entry into World War II.

The listeners were told to push a red button whenever they heard something that made them react negatively. When they heard something that made them react positively, they were to push a green button. The reactions were recorded automatically by a primitive polygraphlike apparatus. When the program was over, an interviewer talked to the group of listeners to find out why they had felt positively or negatively about each message they'd reacted to (Merton, 1987).

The commercial potential of Lazarsfeld and Merton's pioneering work was immediately clear. The method of real-time recording of people's reactions, combined with focused interviewing of a group, is today a mainstay in advertising research. Whole companies now specialize in focus group research, and there are manuals on how to recruit participants and how to conduct a focus group session (Goldman & McDonald, 1987; Greenbaum, 1987; Templeton, 1987; Kreuger, 1988; Morgan, 1993; Stewart & Shamdasani, 1990).

Focus groups typically have 6 to 12 members, plus a moderator. Eight people is a popular size. If a group is too small, it can be dominated by 1 or 2 loudmouths, and if it gets beyond 10 or 12, it gets tough to manage. The participants in a focus group should be more or less homogeneous and, in general, should not know one another.

The group moderator gets people talking about whatever issue is under discussion. Leading a focus group requires the combined skills of an ethnographer, a survey researcher, and a therapist. In a focus group about sensitive issues like abortion or drug use, the leader works at getting the group to gel and getting members to feel that they are part of an understanding cohort of people. If the group is run by an accomplished leader, one or more members will eventually feel comfortable about divulging sensitive information about themselves. Once the ice is broken, others will feel less threatened and will join in.

In the hands of a skilled moderator, focus groups produce remarkable results. MCI, the long-distance phone company, used focus groups to develop their initial advertising. They found that customers didn't blame AT&T for the high cost of long-distance phone bills; they blamed *themselves* for talking too long on long-distance calls. MCI came out with the advertising slogan: "You're not talking too much, just spending too much." The campaign worked, of course (Kreuger, 1988:33).

While the focus group method was a commercial success from the 1950s on, it lay dormant in academic circles for more than 20 years. This is probably because the method is virtually devoid of statistics. Since the late 1970s, however, interest among social researchers of all kinds has boomed as researchers have become more comfortable with combining qualitative and quantitative methods.

Focus groups are less expensive to conduct than questionnaire surveys and they yield insights on *why* people feels as they do about a particular product or issue or behavior. Knodel et al. (1984), for example, used focus groups to study the fertility transition in Thailand. They held separate group sessions for married men under 35 and married women under 30 who wanted three or fewer children. They also held separate sessions for men and women over 50 who had at least five children. This gave them four separate groups. In all cases, the participants had no more than an elementary-school education.

Knodel et al. repeated this four-group design in six parts of Thailand to cover the religious and ethnic diversity of the country. The focus of each group discussion was on the number of children people wanted and why. Thailand has recently undergone fertility transition, and the focus group clearly study illuminated the reasons for the transition. "Time and again," these researchers report, "when participants were asked why the younger generation wants smaller families than the older generation had, they responded that nowadays everything is expensive" (1984:302).

People also said that all children, girls as well as boys, needed education in order to get the jobs that would pay for the more expensive, monetized lifestyle to which people were becoming accustomed. It is, of course, easier to pay for the education of fewer children. These consistent responses are what you'd expect in a society undergoing fertility transition.

Ruth Wilson and her co-workers (1993) used focus groups in their study of acute respiratory illness (ARI) in Swaziland. They interviewed 33 individual mothers, 13 traditional healers, and 17 health care providers. They also ran 33 focus groups, 16 male groups and 17 female groups. The groups had from 4 to 15 participants, with an average of 7.

Each individual respondent and each group was presented with two hypothetical cases. Wilson et al. asked their respondents to diagnose each case and to suggest treatments. Here are the cases:

> Case 1. A mother has a 1-year-old baby girl with the following signs: coughing, fever, sore throat, running or blocked nose, and red or teary eyes. When you ask the mother, she tells you that the child can breast-feed well but is not actively playing.

> Case 2. A 10-month-old baby was brought to a health center with the following signs: rapid/difficult breathing, chest indrawing, fever for one day, sunken

eyes, coughing for three days. The mother tells you that the child does not have diarrhea but has a poor appetite.

Many useful comparisons were possible with the data from this study. For example, mothers attributed the illness in Case 2 mostly to the weather, heredity, or the child's home environment. The male focus groups diagnosed the child in Case 2 as having asthma, or as having fever, indigestion, malnutrition, or worms.

Wilson et al. (1993) acknowledge that a large number of individual interviews make it easier to estimate the degree of error in a set of interviews. However, they conclude that the focus groups provided valid data on the terminology and practices related to ARI in Swaziland. Wilson and her co-workers did, after all, have 240 respondents in their focus groups; they had data from in-depth interviews of all categories of persons involved in treating children's ARI; and they had plenty of participant observation in Swaziland to back them up.

Paul Nkwi (1992), an anthropologist at the University of Yaounde, Cameroon, studied people's perceptions of family planning in his country. He and his team worked in four communities, using participant observation, in-depth interviews, a questionnaire and focus groups. In each community, the team conducted nine focus groups on community development concerns, causes of resistance to family planning, cultural and economic factors that can be used to promote family planning, community problems with health and family-planning services, how services could be improved to meet the needs of communities, and how much (if at all) people would pay for improved health care services.

The focus groups, conducted in the local language of each community, lasted from an hour and a half to 2 hours and were conducted in the homes of influential men of the communities. This helped ensure that the discussions would produce useful information. The groups were stratified by age and sex. One group was exclusively young men 12 to 19 years of age; another group was exclusively young women of that age. Then there were male and female groups 20 to 35, 36 to 49, and 50 and over. Finally, Nkwi and his team did a single focus group with mixed ages and sexes in each community.

The focus groups were taped and transcribed for analysis. It turned out that the information from the focus groups duplicated much of the information gathered by the other methods used in the study. Nkwi's study shows clearly the value of using several data-gathering methods in one study. When several methods produce the same results, you can be a lot more secure in the validity of the findings. Nkwi's study also shows the potential for focus group interviewing in assessing public policy issues (Paul Nkwi, personal communication).

Focus groups do not replace surveys, but rather complement them. Krenger (1988:35) recommends testing survey instruments on focus groups to find out if people understand the questions. Ward et al. (1991) compared focus group and survey data from three studies of voluntary sterilization (tubal ligation or vasectomy) in Guatemala, Honduras, and Zaire. Overall, for 87% of the variables the results were similar in the focus group and survey data (1991:273). For some variables, however, the focus groups provided more detail, while for others the survey provided richer data.

For example, 10% of the women surveyed reported having had a tubal ligation for health reasons. In the focus groups, too, just a few women reported health factors in their decision to have the operation, but they provided more detail and context, citing such things as complications from previous pregnancies. Thus, on this variable, the focus group provided more detail. Data from the focus groups and the survey confirm that women heard about the operation from similar sources, but the survey showed that 40% of the women heard about it from a sterilized woman, 26% heard about it from a health professional, and so on. Here, the survey provides more detail.

The focus group method is now widely used in basic and in applied research. Morgan (1989) ran focus groups with widows to find the factors that made it easier for some to cope with bereavement than others; Morgan and Spanish (1985) studied what people thought were the risk factors in heart attacks; Shariff (1991) reports on the use of focus groups to assess primary health care and family-planning facilities in Gujerat State, India; and Pramualratana et al. (1985) used focus groups to explore ideal marriage age among men and women in Thailand.

Running a Focus Group

To conduct focus group research, you have to decide on and recruit the population you want to study. The study by Knodel et al. covered all of Thailand; Nkwi's study covered both Francophone and Anglophone areas of Cameroon. You can do a focus group study in one village, but the method is always at its best when you compare the reactions of at least two groups (men and women, for example).

You also have to decide on the properties of the population you want to study. Focus groups should be homogeneous, but homogeneity depends on what you are studying. For some topics, it is inappropriate to mix men and women, or older and younger people, in a focus group. For other topics, these criteria may not make a difference.

Tape record (or videotape) the full content of any focus group you conduct. If you are just trying to confirm some ideas or to get a general notion of the how people feel about a topic, you can simply take notes from the tapes and work with your notes. Most focus groups, however, are transcribed. The real power of focus groups is that they produce ethnographically rich data. Only transcription captures all the richness.

In running a focus group, remember that people will disclose more in groups that are supportive and nonjudgmental. Tell people that there are no right or wrong answers to the questions you will ask and emphasize that you've invited people who are similar in their backgrounds and social characteristics. This, too, helps people open up (Kreuger, 1988:10).

Above all, don't lead too much and don't put words in people's mouths. In studying nutritional habits, don't ask people in a focus group why they don't eat certain foods; ask them to talk about what kinds of foods they like and dislike, and why. In studying sexual practices, don't ask, "Why don't you use condoms?" Ask people to explain what they like or dislike about various methods of birth control. Your job is to keep the discussion on the topic. Eventually, people will focus on the nutritional habits or the sexual practices that interest you.

You can analyze focus group data with the same techniques you would use on field notes, life histories, open-ended interviews, or any other corpus of text. As with all large chunks of text, you have two choices for very different kinds of analysis. You can do formal content analysis, or you can do qualitative analysis based on intensive text management. See Chapter 9 (on field notes) for more on how to use computer software to do the text management and see Chapter 15 for more on how to do content analysis.

Response Effects

Response effects refers to measurable differences in interview data that are predictable from characteristics of informants, interviewers, and environments. As early as 1929, Rice showed that the political orientation of interviewers can have a substantial effect on what they report their respondents told them. Rice was doing a study of derelicts in flop houses and he noticed that the men contacted by one interviewer consistently said that their down-and-out status was the result of alcohol; the men contacted by the other interviewer blamed social and economic conditions and lack of jobs. It turned out that the first interviewer was a prohibitionist and the second was a socialist (cited in Cannell & Kahn, 1968:549).

Since Rice's pioneering work, hundreds of studies have been conducted on the impact of things like race, sex, age, and accent of both the interviewer and the informant; the source of funding for a project; the level of experience respondents have with interview situations; whether there is a cultural norm that encourages or discourages talking to strangers; whether the question being investigated is controversial or neutral (Bradburn, 1983).

Katz (1942) found that middle-class interviewers got more conservative answers in general from lower-class respondents than did lower-class interviewers, and Robinson and Rhode (1946) found that interviewers who looked non-Jewish and had non-Jewish-sounding names were almost *four times more likely* to get anti-Semitic answers to questions about Jews than were interviewers who were Jewish looking and who had Jewish-sounding names.

Hyman and Cobb (1975) found that female interviewers who took their cars in for repairs themselves (as opposed to having their husbands do it), were more likely to have female respondents who report getting their own cars repaired. And Zehner (1970) found that when women in the United States were asked by women interviewers about premarital sex, they were more inhibited than if they were asked by men. Male respondents' answers were not affected by the gender of the interviewer.

By contrast, Axinn (1989) found that women in Nepal were better than men as interviewers. In the Tamang Family Research Project, the female interviewers had significantly fewer "don't know" responses than did the male interviewers. Axinn supposes this might be because the survey dealt with marital and fertility histories.

Robert Aunger (1992) studied three groups of people in the Ituri forest of Zaire. The Lese and Budu are horticultural, while the Efe are foragers. Aunger wanted to know if they shared the same food avoidances. He and three assistants, two Lese men and one Budu man, interviewed a total of 65 informants. Each of the informants was interviewed twice and asked the same 140 questions about a list of foods.

Aunger identified two types of errors in his data: forgetting and mistakes. If informants said in the first interview that they did not avoid a particular food but said in the second interview that they did avoid the food, Aunger counted the error as forgetfulness. If informants reported in interview 2 a different type of avoidance for a food than they'd reported in interview 1, Aunger counted this as a mistake.

Even with some missing data, Aunger had over 8,000 pairs of responses in his data (65 *pairs* of interviews, each with up to 140 responses), so he was able to look for the causes of discrepancies between interviews 1 and 2. About 67% of the forgetfulness errors and about 79% of the mistake errors were correlated with characteristics of informants (gender, ethnic group, age, and so on). However, about a quarter of the variability in what informants answered to the same question at two different times was due to characteristics of the interviewers (ethnic group, gender, native language, etc.).

And get this: About 12% of variability in forgetting was explained by interviewer experience. As the interviewers interviewed more and more informants, the informants were less likely to report "no avoidance" on interview 1 and some avoidance on interview 2 for a specific food. In other words, interviewers got better and better with practice at drawing out informants on their food avoidances.

Of the four interviewers, though, the two Lese and the Budu got much better, while the anthropologist made very little progress. Was this because of Aunger's interviewing style, or because informants generally told the anthropologist different things than they told local interviewers, or because there is something special about informants in the Ituri forest? We'll know when we add variables to Aunger's important study and repeat it in many cultures.

The Deference Effect

When informants tell you what they think you want to know, in order not to offend you, that's called the *deference effect*. Aunger may have experienced this in Zaire. In the United States, the answers you get to questions about race depend a lot on the race of the interviewer and the respondent. In 1989, Douglas Wilder, an African-American, ran against Marshall Coleman, who is white, for the governorship of Virginia. Preelection polls showed that Wilder was way ahead, but in the end, he won by a slim margin. Research by Finkel et al. (1991) showed that Wilder's big lead was due to the deference effect.

Thus, when white voters were asked whom they would vote for, they were more likely to claim Wilder as their choice if the interviewer was African-American than if the interviewer was white. This effect accounted for as much as 11 percentage points of Wilder's support. The finding has serious consequences for the future of election polls in the United States, as more and more elections involve white and African-American candidates.

Reese et al. (1986:563) tested the deference effect in a survey of Anglo and Mexican-American respondents. When asked specifically about their cultural preference, 58% of Hispanic respondents said they preferred Mexican-American culture over other cultures, irrespective of whether the interviewer was Anglo or Hispanic. Just 9% of Anglo respondents said they preferred Mexican-American culture when asked by Anglo interviewers, but 23% said they preferred Mexican-American culture when asked by Hispanic interviewers.

Cotter et al. (1982) found the deference effect in telephone interviews, too. White respondents are systematically more sympathetic toward African-Americans if they are interviewed by a person who *sounds* to them like an African-American. (The same effect is not found when African-American respondents are interviewed by whites, however.)

Questions that aren't race related are not affected much by the race or the ethnicity of either the interviewer or the respondent. The Center for Applied Linguistics conducted a study of 1,472 bilingual children in the United States. The children were interviewed by whites, Cuban-Americans, Chicanos, Native Americans, or Chinese-Americans. Weeks and Moore (1981) compared the scores obtained by white interviewers with those obtained by various ethnic interviewers, and it turned out that the ethnicity of the interviewer didn't have a significant effect.

In general, if you are asking someone a nonthreatening question, slight changes in wording of the question won't make much difference in the answers you get. Peterson (1984) asked 1,324 people one of the following questions: (a) How old are you? (b) What is your age? (c) In what year were you born? (d) Are you 18 to 24 years of age, 25 to 34, 35 to 49, 50 to 64, 65 or older? Then Peterson got the true ages for all the respondents from reliable records.

There was no significant difference in the accuracy of the answers obtained with the four questions. (However, almost 10% of respondents refused to answer the first question, while only 1% refused to answer the fourth, and this difference *is* significant.) On the other hand, if you ask people about their alcohol consumption, or whether they ever shoplifted when they were children, or whether they have family members who have had mental illness, then expect even small changes in the wording to have significant effects on informants' responses.

The Expectancy Effect

In 1966, Robert Rosenthal conducted an experiment. At the beginning of the school year, he told some teachers at a school that the children they were about to get had tested out as "spurters." That is, according to tests, he said, those particular children were expected to make significant gains in their academic scores during the coming year. The children did, in fact, improve dramatically. The only problem was, Rosenthal had matched the "spurter" children and teachers at random.

The results, published in a widely read book called *Pygmalian in the Classroom* (Rosenthal & Jacobson, 1968) established once and for all what experimental researchers across the sciences had long suspected. There is an *expectancy effect*. The expectancy effect is "the tendency for experimenters to obtain results they expect, not simply because they have correctly anticipated nature's response but rather because they have helped to shape that response through their expectations" (Rosenthal & Rubin, 1978:377).

In 1978, Rosenthal and Rubin reported on the "first 345 studies" that were generated by the discovery of the expectancy effect. The effect is largest in animal studies (perhaps because there is no danger that animals will go into print rejecting findings from experiments on them), but it is likely in all experiments on people. As Rosenthal's first study proved, the effect extends to teachers, managers, therapists—anyone who makes a living creating changes in the behavior of others.

Expectancy is different from distortion. The *distortion effect* comes from seeing what you want to see, even when it's not there. The expectancy effect involves creating the objective results we want to see. We don't distort results to conform to our expectations as much as we make the expectations come true. Strictly speaking, then, the expectancy effect is not a response effect at all. But for field workers, it is an important effect to keep in mind. If you are in a village for a year or more, interacting daily with a few key informants, your own behavior can affect theirs in subtle (and not so subtle) ways.

Accuracy

Perhaps the most important response issue concerns the accuracy of data obtained from interviews. The problem was articulated clearly in 1934 by Richard La Pierre who was interested in the relationship between attitude and behavior. Accompanied by a Chinese couple, La Pierre traveled a total of 10,000 miles by car, crossing the United States twice between 1930 and 1932.

The three travelers were served in 184 restaurants (refused in none), and were refused accommodation in only one out of 66 hotels. Six months after the experiment ended, La Pierre sent a questionnaire to each of the 250 establishments where the threesome had stopped. One of the things he asked was, "Will you accept members of the Chinese race as guests?" Ninety-two percent replied no.

By today's standards, La Pierre's experiment was crude. There was no control group. La Pierre might have surveyed another 250 establishments from the towns they had visited, but which they did not patronize. There was attrition in response. La Pierre might have used a "two-wave" survey approach to increase the response rate. There was no way to tell whether the people who answered the survey (and claimed that they wouldn't serve Chinese) were the same ones who had actually served the threesome. And La Pierre did not mention in his survey that the Chinese would be accompanied by a white man.

Still, La Pierre's experiment was terrific for its time. It established a major focus of research on the relationship between attitudes and behavior (see Deutscher, 1973) and on informant accuracy in reporting behavior. A long list of studies now shows that a fourth to a half of what informants say about their behavior is inaccurate (Killworth & Bernard, 1976; Bernard et al., 1984).

This finding shows up in studies of what people say they eat, who they say they talked to on the phone, how often they claim to have gone to the doctor. . . . It shows up in the most unlikely (we would have thought) places: In the 1961 census of Addis Ababa, 23% of the women underreported the number of their children. Apparently, people don't *count* babies who die before reaching the age of 2 (Pausewang, 1973:65).

There are many reasons why informants report inaccurate data about matters of externally verifiable fact—like whether they were hospitalized in the last year, as opposed to, say, whether they think that ancestor worship should be abolished. Here are five:

1. Informants may report what they suppose happened, rather than what they actually saw.
2. Informants may distort what they see to conform to their own prejudices.
3. Informants' memories simply fail them.
4. Informants will usually try to answer all your questions, once they agree to be interviewed—even if they don't remember what happened, or don't want to tell you, or don't understand what you're after, or don't know.
5. Informants sometimes lie simply because they want to mislead you.

Progress is being made. Thirty years ago, Cancian (1963) showed how informant errors conformed to expected patterns in prestige rankings in a

Mexican village. D'Andrade showed in 1974 that there is a general pressure to think in terms of "what goes with what," even if this creates errors in reporting factual events. (Also see Shweder and D'Andrade, 1980.) Freeman et al. (1987) asked people in their department to report on who attended a particular colloquium. People who were *usually* at the department colloquium were mentioned as having attended the particular colloquium—even those who hadn't attended.

People round off, in other words, and report behavior according to rules of central tendency. This may go for informants' reports of their own behavior as well as for their reports of the behavior of others. (Cognitive psychologists, of course, have done careful investigations of how people store and retrieve information.)

Cannell et al. (1961) found that people's ability to remember their stays in the hospital was related to the length of time since their discharge, the length of their stay, the level of threat of the illness that put them in the hospital, and whether or not they had surgery. Cannell and Fowler (1965) found, however, that people report accurately 90% of all overnight hospital stays that happened 6 months or less prior to being interviewed.

Following in this research tradition, Means et al. (1989) tried to increase informant accuracy in recall of hospitalizations and other health-related events. They asked informants first to recall landmark events in their lives going back 18 months from the time of the interview. Once the list of personal landmark events was established, informants were better able to recall other events in relation to the landmarks.

Jogging Informants' Memories

Sudman and Bradburn (1974) distinguish two types of memory errors. The first is simply forgetting things, whether a visit to the city, the purchase of a product, attendance at an event, etc. The second type is called *forward telescoping*. An informant reports that something happened 1 month ago when it really happened 2 months ago. (Backward telescoping is relatively rare.)

Loftus and Marburger (1983) found that giving informants landmark events, against which to recall incidents of crime in their lives, led to recall of *fewer* incidents. This was, they said, because landmarks help reduce forward telescoping.

Besides giving informants landmarks, three techniques are commonly used to deal with memory errors: (a) Informants are asked to consult records, such as bank statements, telephone bills, college transcripts, and so on; (b) informants are given a list of possible answers to a question and asked to choose among them (this is *aided recall*); and (c) informants are interviewed periodically, reminded what they said last time in answer to a question, and asked about their behavior since their last report (this is *bounded recall*).

Having informants consult their records does not always produce the results you might expect. Horn (1960) asked people to report their bank balance. Of those who did not consult their records, 31% reported correctly. Those who consulted their records did better, but not by much. Only 47% reported correctly (reported in Bradburn, 1983:309).

Aided recall appears to increase the number of events recalled, but also appears to increase the telescoping effect (ibid.). Bounded recall corrects for telescoping but does not increase the number of events recalled, and in any event is only useful in studies where the same informants are interviewed again and again. The problem of informant accuracy remains an important issue and a fruitful area for research in social science methodology. For more on this problem, see Neter and Waksberg (1964), Linton (1975), Moss and Goldstein (1979), Bernard et al. (1984), Bradburn et al. (1987), Freeman and Romney (1987), and McNabb (1990).

11

Structured Interviewing

S tructured interviewing involves exposing every informant in a sample to the same stimuli. The stimuli may be a set of questions or they may be a list of names, a set of photographs, a table full of artifacts, a garden full of plants, etc. The idea is to control the input that triggers each informant's responses so that the output can be reliably compared.

The most common form of structured interviewing is the questionnaire. A questionnaire may be self-administered, or it may be administered over the phone or in person, but in all cases the questions posed to informants are the same. I'll deal with the building and administering of question-naires in the next chapter. This chapter is an introduction to some exciting new systematic interviewing techniques that are being used in *cultural domain analysis*.

Two things make these methods very productive for anthropological fieldwork. First, they are fun to use and informants find them fun to respond to. Second, the ANTHROPAC computer software (Borgatti, 1992a) has made it much easier than it was just a few years ago to collect and analyze data using these techniques.

Cognitive Anthropology and Cultural Domains

Cognitive anthropology is the study of how peoples of different cultures acquire information about the world (cultural transmission), how they process that information and reach decisions, and how they act on that information in ways that other members of their culture consider appropriate.

Modern cognitive anthropology traces its roots to 1956 with Ward Goodenough's application of the *emic* and *etic* principle from linguistics to other areas of culture. The emic-etic principle in linguistics was named by the linguist Kenneth Pike (1956, 1967). It illustrates the fact that human beings distinguish phon*emes* (the basic set of underlying constructs that generate the sounds of a language) from their phon*etic* representations (what we actually hear). Many phonetic outcomes might be accepted by native speakers of a language as being representative of a single underlying phoneme.

In English, for example, we have an aspirated *t*, as in "tough," and an unaspirated *t*, as in "spit." (You can distinguish the aspiration by putting your hand up to your mouth and feeling the breath of air that the *t* in "tough" makes as you say it. The *t* in "sit" doesn't do that.) There are no contexts in English in which the acoustical feature of aspiration changes the meaning of a word.

Suppose, though, that in another language the *t* in "tough" and the *t* in "spit" were the *only* difference in the two words "t^{h}ao" and "tao," where the first meant "one million" and the second meant "the axle of an oxcart." (The raised *h* is for the aspiration.) In that case, the *distinctive feature* of aspiration would be meaningful in that particular language.

Goodenough's insight was that this principle could be applied to areas of culture other than phonology. An adequate ethnographic description of the named category "cousin," for example, would consist of stating the emic rules that people use when they decide whether two people are cousins (1956:195).

Etically, you have eight kinds of cousins: The male and female offspring of the male or female siblings of your male or female parents are all your "cousins" in English. In other cultures, the male and female offspring of the male or female siblings of your father are one kind of relative, while the male or female offspring of the male or female siblings of your mother are another kind of relative.

By emic rules, there are many different possible packages of cousins that might be defined. The general research strategy that grew from this insight was dubbed *ethnoscience*—the search for the grammars of behavior in the cultures of the world, and the underlying principles that govern how those grammars differ.

Grammars consist of rules that people carry around in their heads—rules that let them understand brand new sentences they've never heard before and make up new ones that other people understand. This fundamental idea continues to capture the imagination of many ethnographers. The messy, noisy cultural behavior at the observable surface is treated as being driven by a relatively clean set of underlying rules, just as the infinite number of grammatical utterances can be accounted for by a large, but finite set of grammatical rules.

Soon after this principle was articulated, anthropologists began to apply it to what was called "cultural domains"—kinship terms, plants, animals, occupations, and so on—anything that could be listed by informants (Tyler, 1969).

The spectrum of colors, for example, has a single etic reality (you can see the spectrum on a machine) and many emic realities. Several American Indian peoples identify a color we gloss as "grue." The word covers all the colors across the etic spectrum of green and blue.

This does not mean that people who use a word like "grue" fail to see the difference between things that are the color of grass and things that are the color of a clear blue sky. They just label different chunks of the etic spectrum of colors than we do. If this seems exotic to you, get a list of, say, 100 lipstick colors and ask college women and men to describe all those colors. You may find that, on average, women recognize many more colors than do men.

Today, anthropologists are studying many interesting domains—things people do on weekends, ways people believe they can succeed in business, traits that people think of when they think of particular ethnic groups, categories of fast foods, and more. The goal is to understand what people think, how they think it, and how they organize the material. The challenge is to devise methods that get at these things and that produce data that can be checked for their reliability and validity. The most common techniques for gathering data in cognitive anthropology are: free listings, frame elicitations, triad tests, pile sorts, paired comparisons, and rank order tests (Weller & Romney, 1988).

Free Listing

Free listing is a deceptively simple but powerful technique. It is generally used to study a cultural domain. The list of the days in a week is a cultural domain, with no intracultural variation. Everyone knows the same list. "Things to do on vacation" is a much richer domain, with lots of intracultural variation. Common domains studied by anthropologists are things like diseases, plants, occupations, and animals. But you can just as easily study how people classify names of movie stars, brands of computers, types of machines, or titles of anthropology articles.

In free listing, you tell informants: "Please list all the X you know about" or ask them "What kinds of X are there?"

Henley (1969) asked 21 adult Americans (students at Johns Hopkins University) to name as many animals as they could in 10 minutes. You'd be surprised at how much Henley learned from this simple experiment. First of all, there is an enormous variety of expertise in the culture when it comes to naming animals. In just this small group of informants (which didn't even represent the population of Johns Hopkins University, much less that of Baltimore or of the United States), the lists ranged in length from 21 to 110, with a median of 55.

In fact, those 21 people named 423 different animals, and 175 were mentioned just once. The most popular animals for this group of informants were: dog, lion, cat, horse, and tiger, all of which were named by more than 90% of informants. Only 29 animals were listed by more than half the informants, but 90% of those were mammals. By contrast, among the 175 animals named only once, just 27% were mammals.

But there's more. Previous research had shown that the 12 most commonly talked about animals in U.S. speech are: bear, cat, cow, deer, dog, goat, horse, lion, tiger, mouse, pig, and rabbit. There are N $(N - 1)/2$, or 66 possible unique pairs of 12 animals (dog-cat, dog-deer, horse-lion, mouse-pig, etc.). Henley examined each informant's list of animals, and for each of the 66 pairs found the difference in order of listing.

That is, if an informant mentioned goats 12th on her list and bears 32nd, then the distance between goats and bears, for that informant, was $32 - 12$ $= 20$. This distance was standardized: It was divided by the length of the informant's list and multiplied by 100. Then Henley calculated the mean distance, over all the informants, for each of the 66 pairs of animals.

The lowest mean distance was between sheep and goats (1.8), and the highest was between cats and deer (56.1). Deer are related to all the other animals on the list by at least 40 units of distance, except for rabbits, which are only 20 units away from deer. Cats and dogs are only 2 units apart, while mice and sheep are nearly 52 units from each other. This experiment, too, needs to be replicated in other components of American culture and in other cultures.

Robert Trotter (1981) reports on 378 Mexican-Americans who were asked to name the *remedios caseros* (home remedies) they knew, and what illnesses the remedies were for. Informants listed a total of 510 remedies for treating 198 illnesses. However, the 25 most frequently mentioned remedies (about 5% of the total) constituted about 41% of all the cases, and the 70 most frequently mentioned illnesses (about 36%) constituted 84% of the cases.

Trotter's free-list data reveal a lot about Mexican-American perceptions of illness and home cures. He was able to count which ailments were reported more frequently by men and which by women; which ailments were reported more frequently by older people and by younger people; which by those born in Mexico and those born in the United States; and so on.

Free listing is often a prelude to cluster analysis and multidimensional scaling, which we'll get to in Chapter 20. But you can learn an awful lot from *just* a free list. Gatewood (1983a) asked 40 adult Pennsylvanians to name all the trees they could think of. Then he asked them to check the trees on their list that they thought they could recognize in the wild. Thirty-seven people (out of 40) listed "oak," 34 listed "pine," 33 listed "maple," and 31 listed "birch." I suspect that the list of trees and what people say they could recognize would look rather different in, say Wyoming or Mississippi. We could test that.

Thirty-one of the 34 who listed "pine" said they could recognize a pine. Twenty-seven people listed "orange," but only four people said they could recognize an orange tree (without oranges hanging all over it, of course). On average, the Pennsylvanians in Gatewood's sample said they could recognize about 50% of the trees they listed. Gatewood calls this the *loose talk* phenomenon. He thinks that many Americans can name a lot more things than they can recognize in nature.

Does this loose-talk phenomenon vary by gender? Suppose, Gatewood says, we ask Americans from a variety of subcultures and occupations to list other things besides trees. Would the 50% recognition rate hold?

Gatewood and a group of students at Lehigh University interviewed 54 informants—27 men and 27 women, all university students. The informants free listed all the musical instruments, fabrics, hand tools, and trees they could think of. Then the informants were asked to check off the items in each of their lists that they thought they would recognize in a natural setting.

All of Gatewood's hypotheses were supported: Men and women named about the same number of musical instruments; women named more fabrics; men named more hand tools; and both men and women named more trees than they could identify (Gatewood, 1984).

Romney and D'Andrade asked 105 U.S. high school students to "list all the names for kinds of relatives and family members you can think of in

English" (1964:155). They were able to do a large number of analyses on these data. For example, they studied the order and frequency of recall of certain terms and the productiveness of modifiers, such as "step-," "half-," "-in-law," "grand-," "great," and so on. They assumed that the nearer to the beginning of a list that a kin term occurs, the more salient it is for that particular informant. By taking the average position in all the lists for each kin term, they were able to derive a rank order list of kin terms, according to the variable's saliency.

They also assumed that more salient terms occur more frequently. So, for example, "mother" occurs in 93% of all lists and is the first term mentioned on most lists. At the other end of the spectrum is "grandson," which was only mentioned by 17% of the 105 informants, and was, on average, the 15th, or last term to be listed. They found that the terms "son" and "daughter" occur on only about 30% of the lists. But remember, these informants were all high school students. It would be interesting to repeat Romney and D'Andrade's experiment on many different U.S. populations. We could then test the saliency of English kin terms on the many subpopulations.

Finally, free listing can be used to find out where to concentrate effort in applied research—that is, as part of a rapid assessment approach. In a recent project, a team of anthropologists and sociologists studied how people on the North Carolina coast viewed the possibility of offshore oil drilling. During regular interviews, the field researchers asked people "What are the things that make life good around here?"

The researchers decided to ask this question after preliminary ethnographic research (hanging out, talking informally to a lot of people) in seven small, seaside towns. People kept saying what a "nice little town this is" and "What a shame it would be if things changed around here." Informants had no difficulty with the question, and after just 20 interviews, the researchers had a list of over 50 "things that make life good around here." The researchers chose the 20 items mentioned by at least 12 informants and explored the meaning of those items further (ICMR et al., 1993).

The humble free list has many uses. Use it a lot.

The True-False/Yes-No and Sentence Frame Techniques

Another common technique in cultural domain analysis is called the *sentence frame* or *frame elicitation* method (see also Chapter 16 on qualitative analysis and native taxonomies). The method produces true-false, or yes-no, data.

The frame elicitation method has been used extensively in anthropology to study the distribution of beliefs about the causes of and cures for illnesses (Fabrega, 1970; D'Andrade et al., 1972).

Linda Garro (1986) used the frame elicitation method to compare the knowledge of curers and noncurers in Pichátaro, Mexico. She used a list of 18 illness terms and 22 causes, based on prior research in Pichátaro (Young, 1978). The frames were questions, like "Can _____ come from _____ ?" Garro substituted names of illnesses in the first blank, and things like "anger," "cold," "overeating," and so on in the second blank. (ANTHROPAC has a routine for building questionnaires of this type.) This produced an 18×22 yes-no matrix for each of the informants. The matrices could then be added together and submitted to analysis by multidimensional scaling (see Chapter 20).

James Boster and Jeffrey Johnson (1989) used the frame substitution method in their study of how recreational fishermen in the United States categorize ocean fish. They asked 120 fishermen to consider 62 belief frames, scan down a list of 43 fish (tarpon, silver perch, Spanish mackerel, etc.), and pick out the fish that fit each frame. Here are a few of the belief frames:

The meat from _____ is oily tasting.
It is hard to clean _____ .
I prefer to catch _____ .

That's $43 \times 62 = 2,666$ judgments by each of 120 informants, but informants were usually able to do the task in less than half an hour (Jeffrey Johnson, personal communication). The 62 frames, by the way, came straight out of ethnographic interviews where informants were asked to list fish and to talk about the characteristics of those fish.

Gillian Sankoff (1971) studied land tenure and kinship among the Buang, a mountain people of northeastern New Guinea. The most important unit of social organization among the Buang is the *dgwa*, a kind of descent group, like a clan. Sankoff wanted to figure out the very complicated system by which men in the village of Mambump identified with various dgwa and with various named garden plots.

The Buang system was apparently too complex for bureaucrats to fathom, so in order to save administrators a lot of trouble, the men of Mambump had years earlier devised a simplified system that they presented to outsiders. Instead of claiming that they had ties with one or more of five different dgwa, they each decided which of the two largest dgwa they would belong to, and that was that as far as the New Guinea administration knew.

To unravel the complex system of land tenure and descent, Sankoff made a list of all 47 men in the village and all 140 yam plots that they had used over the recent past. Sankoff asked each man to go through the list of men and identify which dgwa each man belonged to. If a man belonged to more than one, then Sankoff got that information, too. She also asked her informants to identify which dgwa each of the 140 garden plots belonged to.

As you might imagine, there was considerable variability in the data. Only a few men were uniformly placed into one of the five dgwa by their peers. But by analyzing the matrices of dgwa membership and land use, Sankoff was able to determine the core members and peripheral members of the various dgwa.

She was also able to ask important questions about intracultural variability. She looked at the variation in cognitive models among the Buang for how land use and membership in descent groups were related. Sankoff's analysis was an important milestone in our understanding of the measurable differences between individual culture versus shared culture. It supported Goodenough's notion (1965) that cognitive models are based on shared assumptions, but that ultimately they are best construed as properties of individuals.

True-false and yes-no tests that generate nominal data are easy to construct (especially with computer programs) and can be administered to a large number of informants. Frame elicitation in general, however, can be quite boring, both to the informant and to the researcher alike. Imagine, for example, a list of 25 animals (mice, dogs, antelopes . . .), and 25 attributes (ferocious, edible, nocturnal . . .).

The structured interview that results from such a test involves a total of 625 (25 × 25) questions to which an informant must respond—questions like "Is an antelope edible?" "Is a dog nocturnal?" "Is a mouse ferocious?" Informants can get pretty exasperated with this kind of silliness. Be careful, therefore, about cultural relevance when doing frame elicitations and true-false tests. It is essential to have a good ethnographic grounding in the local culture in order to select domains, items, and attributes that make sense to people.

Triad Tests

In a *triad test*, you show informants three things and tell them to "choose the one that doesn't fit" or "choose the two that seem to go together best," or "choose the two that are the same." The "things" can be photographs, actual plants, 3 × 5 cards with names of people on them, or whatever. (Informants often ask "what do you mean by things being 'the same' or 'fitting together'?" Tell them that you are interested in what *they* think that means.) By doing this for all triples from a list of things or concepts, you can explore differences in cognition among individuals, and among cultures and subcultures.

Suppose you ask a group of Americans to "choose the item that is least like the other two" in each of the following triads:

WHALE DOLPHIN MOOSE

SHARK DOLPHIN MOOSE

All three items in the first triad are mammals, but two of them are sea mammals. A few people would choose "dolphin" as the odd item because "whales and moose are both big mammals and the dolphin is smaller." Most people I know, however, would choose "moose" as the most different. In the second triad, many of the same people who chose "moose" in triad 1 will choose "shark" because moose and dolphins are both mammals, and a shark is not.

But some people who chose "moose" in triad 1 will choose "moose" again in triad 2 because sharks and dolphins are sea creatures, while moose are not. Giving informants a judiciously chosen set of triad stimuli can help you understand interindividual similarities and differences in how people think about the items in a cultural domain.

The triads test was developed in psychology (see Kelly, 1955; Torgerson, 1958) and was introduced into anthropology by Romney and D'Andrade (1964). They presented informants with triads of U.S. kinship terms and asked them to choose the term that was most dissimilar in each triad. For example, when they presented informants with the triad "father, son, nephew," 67% selected "nephew" as the most different of the three items. Twenty-two percent chose "father," and only 2% chose "son."

They also interviewed informants and asked them about their reasons for choosing an item on a triad test. For the triad "grandson, brother, father," for example, one informant said that a "grandson is most different because he is moved down further" (Romney & D'Andrade, 1964:161). There's a lot of ethnographic wisdom in that statement.

By studying which pairs of kinship terms their informants chose most often as being similar, Romney and D'Andrade were able to isolate some of the salient components of the American kinship system (components such as male versus female, ascending versus descending generation, etc.).

They were able to do this, at least, for the group of informants they used. Repeating their tests on other populations of Americans, or on the same population over time, would yield interesting comparisons of anthropological significance.

Lieberman and Dressler (1977) used triad tests to examine intracultural variation in ethnomedical beliefs on the Caribbean island of St. Lucia. They wanted to know if cognition of disease terms varied with bilingual proficiency. They used 52 bilingual English-Patois speakers and 10 monolingual Patois speakers. From ethnographic interviewing and cross-checking against various informants, they isolated nine disease terms that were important to St. Lucians.

Here's the formula for finding the number of triads in a list of N items:

$$\text{The number of triads in } N \text{ items} = \frac{N(N-1)(N-2)}{6}$$

In this case, N is nine, so there are 84 possible triads.

Lieberman and Dressler gave each of the 52 bilingual informants two triad tests, a week apart: one in Patois and one in English. (Naturally, they randomized the order of the items within each triad and also randomized the order of presentation of the triads to informants.) They also measured how bilingual their informants were, using a standard test. The 10 monolingual Patois informants were simply given the triad test.

The researchers counted the number of times that each possible pair of terms was chosen as most alike among the 84 triads. (There are $N(N-1)/2$ pairs or $(9 \times 8)/2 = 36$ pairs). They divided the total by seven (the maximum number of times that any pair appears in the 84 triads). This produced a similarity coefficient, varying between 0.0 and 1.0, for each possible pair of disease terms. The larger the coefficient for a pair of terms, the closer in meaning are the two terms. They were then able to analyze these data among English-dominant, Patois-dominant, and monolingual Patois speakers.

It turned out that when Patois-dominant and English-dominant informants took the triad test in English, their cognitive models of similarities among diseases was similar. When Patois-dominant speakers took the Patois-language triad test, however, their cognitive model was similar to that of monolingual Patois informants.

This is a very interesting finding. It means that Patois-dominant bilinguals manage to hold on to two distinct psychological models about diseases, and that they switch back and forth between them, depending on what language they are speaking. By contrast, the English-dominant group displayed a similar cognitive model of disease terms, irrespective of the language in which they are tested.

The Balanced Incomplete Block Design for Triad Tests

Anthropologists have used the triad test to study occupations (Burton, 1972), personality traits (Kirk & Burton, 1977), and other domains of culture. Typically, the terms that go into a triad test are generated by a free list, and typically the list is much too long for a triad test. There are 84 stimuli in a triad test containing 9 items. But with just 6 more items the number of decisions an informant has to make jumps to 455. At 20 items, it's a mind-numbing 1,140.

Free lists of illnesses, ways to prevent pregnancy, advantages of breast-feeding, places to go on vacation, and so on easily produce 60 items or more. Even a selected, abbreviated list may be 20 items.

This led Burton and Nerlove (1976) to develop the *balanced incomplete block* design, or BIB, for the triad test. BIBs take advantage of the fact that there is a lot of redundancy in a triad test. Suppose you have just four items, 1, 2, 3, 4, and you ask informants to tell you something about *pairs* of these items (e.g., if the items were vegetables, you might ask "Which of these two is less expensive?" or "Which of these two is more nutritious?" or whatever). There are exactly six pairs of four items (1-2, 1-3, 1-4, 2-3, 2-4, 3-4), and the informant sees each pair just once.

But suppose that instead of pairs you show the informant triads and ask which two out of each triple are most similar. There are just four triads in four items (1-2-3, 1-2-4, 2-3-4, 1-3-4), but each item appears $(N - 1)(N - 2)/2$ times, and each pair appears $N - 2$ times. For four items, there are $N(N - 1)/2$ = six pairs; each pair appears twice in four triads, and each item on the list appears three times.

It is all this redundancy that reduces the number of triads needed in a triads test. If you want each pair to appear just once (called a *lambda 1* design), instead of seven times in a triads test involving nine items, then, instead of 84 triads, only 12 are needed. If you want each pair to appear just twice (a *lambda 2* design), then 24 triads are needed. For analysis, lambda 2 designs are much better than lambda 1's. Table 11.1 shows the lambda 2 design for 9 and 10 items.

For 10 items, a lambda 2 design requires 30 triads; for 13 items, it requires 52 triads; for 19 items, 114 triads; and for 25 items, 200 triads. In literate societies, most informants can respond to 200 triads in less than 15 minutes.

TABLE 11.1

Balanced Incomplete Block Designs for Triad Tests
Involving 9 and 10 Items

For 9 items, 24 triads are needed, as follows;

Items:	1, 5, 9	1, 2, 3
	2, 3, 8	4, 5, 6
	4, 6, 7	7, 8, 9
	2, 6, 9	1, 4, 7
	1, 3, 4	2, 5, 9
	5, 7, 8	3, 6, 8
	3, 7, 9	1, 6, 9
	2, 4, 5	2, 4, 8
	1, 6, 8	3, 5, 7
	4, 8, 9	1, 5, 8
	3, 5, 6	2, 6, 8
	1, 2, 7	3, 4, 9

For 10 items, 30 triads are needed, as follows:

1, 2, 3	9, 3, 10	7, 10, 3	5, 6, 3
2, 5, 8	10, 6, 5	8, 1, 10	6, 1, 8
3, 7, 4	1, 2, 4	9, 5, 2	7, 9, 2
4, 1, 6	2, 3, 6	10, 6, 7	8, 4, 7
5, 8, 7	2, 4, 8	1, 3, 5	9, 10, 1
6, 4, 9	4, 9, 5	2, 7, 6	10, 5, 4
7, 9, 1	5, 7, 1	3, 8, 9	
8, 10, 2	6, 8, 9	4, 2, 10	

SOURCE: Burton and Nerlove (1976).
NOTE: These are lambda 2 designs. See text for explanation.

Unfortunately, there is no easy formula for choosing *which* triads in a large set to select for a BIB. Fortunately, Burton and Nerlove (1976) worked out various lambda BIB designs for up to 21 items, and Stephen Borgatti has incorporated BIB designs into ANTHROPAC (1992a). You simply tell AN-THROPAC the list of items you have, select a design, and tell it the number of informants you want to interview. ANTHROPAC then prints out a randomized triad test, one for each informant. (Randomizing the order in which the triads appear to informants eliminates *order-effects*—possible biases that come from responding to a list of stimuli in a particular order.)

Boster et al. (1987) used a triad test and a pile sort in their study of the social network of an office. There were 16 employees, so there were 16 "items" in the cultural domain ("the list of all the people who work here" is a perfectly good domain). A lambda 2 test with 16 items has 80 distinct triads. Informants were asked to "judge which of three actors was the most different from the other two."

Triad tests are easy to create with ANTHROPAC, easy to administer, and easy to score, but they can only be used when you have relatively few items in a cultural domain. Also, informants sometimes find triad tests to be boring. Use the triad test method when you have just a few items in a domain. Use the pile sort method to look at the cognitive organization of a large cultural domain. I find that informants easily handle lambda 2 triad tests with 9 to 15 items, and pile sorts with 40 to 60 items.

Pile Sorts

Typically, pile sorts are done with cards or slips of paper. Each card has the name of a thing or a concept written on it. Once again, the items are gleaned from a free list that defines a cultural domain. Informants are asked to "sort these cards into piles, putting things that are similar together in a pile."

Two questions that informants often ask are: "What do you mean by 'similar'?" and "Can I put something in more than one pile?" The answer to the first question is "Well, whatever you think is similar. We want to learn what you think about these things. There are no right or wrong answers."

The easy answer to the second question is "no," just because there is one card per item and a card can only be in one pile at a time. This answer cuts off a lot of information, however, because informants can think of items in a cultural domain along several dimensions at once. For example, in a pile sort of consumer electronics, an informant might want to put a VCR in one pile with TVs (for the obvious association) and in another pile with camcorders (for another obvious association) but might not want to put camcorders and TVs in the same pile. You can make up a duplicate card on the spot if you want and, fortunately, the ANTHROPAC software makes easy work of handling this during analysis. An alternative is to ask the informant to do *multiple pile sorts* of the same object.

Free Pile Sorts and the Lumper and Splitter Problem

Most researchers use the *free* or *unconstrained* pile sort method, where informants are told that they can make as many piles as they want, so long as they don't make a separate pile for each item or lump the items into one pile. Like the triad test, the free pile sort presents a common set of stimuli to informants. But here, the informants manage the information and put the items together as they see fit. The result is that some informants will make many piles, others will make few. This is known as the *lumper-splitter problem* (Weller & Romney, 1988:22).

In a pile sort of animals, for example, some informants will put all the following together: giraffe, elephant, rhinoceros, zebra, wildebeest. They'll explain that these are the "African animals." Others will put giraffe, elephant, and rhino in one pile, and the zebra and wildebeest in another, explaining that one is the "large African animal" pile and the other is the "medium-sized African animal" pile.

Some informants will have singleton piles, explaining that each singleton is unique and doesn't go with the others. It's fine to ask informants why they made each pile of items, but wait until they finish the sorting task so you don't interfere with their concentration. And don't hover over informants. Find an excuse to walk away for a couple of minutes after they get the hang of it.

Pile Sorts with Objects

Although pile sorts are typically done with cards or slips of paper, they can also be done with objects. James Boster (1987) studied the structure of the domain of birds among the Aguaruna Jívaro of Peru. He paid people to bring him specimens of birds and he had the birds stuffed. He built a huge table out in the open, laid the birds on the table, and asked the Aguaruna to sort the birds into groups.

Carl Kendall led a team project in El Progreso, Honduras, to study beliefs about dengue fever (Kendall et al., 1990). Part of their study involved a pile sort of the nine most common flying insects in the region. They mounted specimens of the insects in little boxes and asked people to group the insects in terms of "those that are similar." Some anthropologists have used photographs of objects as stimuli for a pile sort.

Borgatti (1992b:6) points out that asking an informant to sort photographs of objects (or actual objects) rather than cards with the names of object can produce different results. Imagine sorting 30 photographs of automobiles—sports cars, pickup trucks, minivans, etc. Seeing the photos, you might classify the vehicles on the basis of physical form or function. If you sorted cards with stimuli like "Alpha Romeo coupe," "Dodge minivan," "Mercedes sedan," and so on, you might do the sort on other criteria, like price, prestige, desirability. "If you are after shared cultural beliefs," says Borgatti, "I recommend keeping the stimulus as abstract as possible" (ibid.).

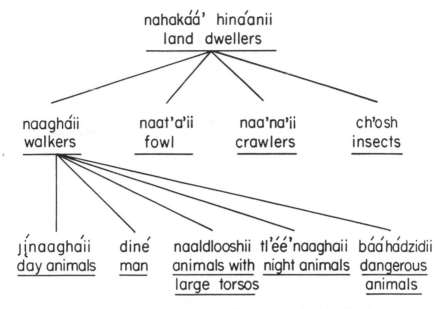

Figure 11.1. Part of the Navaho animal kingdom, derived by Perchonock and Werner (1969) from a pile sort.

SOURCE: "Navaho Systems of Classification" by N. Perchonock and O. Werner, 1969, *Ethnology, 8*, 229-242. Reprinted by permission.

Pile Sorts and Taxonomic Trees

Pile sorting is a an efficient method for generating taxonomic trees (Werner & Fenton, 1973). Simply hand informants the familiar pack of cards, each of which contains some term in a cultural domain. Informants sort the cards into piles, according to whatever criterion makes sense to them. After the first sorting, informants are handed each pile and asked to go through the exercise again. They keep doing this until they say that they can not subdivide piles any further. At each sorting level, informants are asked if there is a word or phrase that describes each pile.

Perchonock and Werner (1969) used this technique in their study of Navaho animal categories. After an informant finished doing a pile sort of animal terms, Perchonock and Werner built a branching tree diagram (such as that shown in Figure 11.1) from the data. They would ask the informant to make up sentences or phrases that expressed some relationship between the nodes. They found that informants intuitively grasped the idea of tree representations for taxonomies.

Pile Sorts and Networks

I've used pile sorts to study the social structure of institutions such as prisons, ships at sea, and bureaucracies, and also to map the cognitively defined social organization of small communities. I simply hand people a deck of cards, each of which contains the name of one of the people in the institution, and ask informants to sort the cards into piles, according to their own criteria. The results tell me how various components of an organization (managers, production workers, advertising people; or guards, counselors, prisoners; or seamen, deck officers, engine room personnel; or men and women in a small Greek village) think about the social structure of the group. Instead of "what goes with what," I learn "who goes with who."

Informants usually find pile sorting fun to do. Asking informants to explain *why* people appear in the same pile produces a wealth of information about the cognitively defined social structure of a group.

Rankings

Rank ordering produces interval-level data, though not all behaviors or concepts are easy to rank. Hammel (1962) asked people in a Peruvian village to rank order the people they knew in terms of prestige. By comparing the lists from different informants, Hammel was able to determine that the men he tested all had a similar view of the social hierarchy. Occupations can easily be rank ordered on the basis of prestige or lucrativeness.

Or even accessibility. The instructions to informants would be "Here is a list of occupations. Please rank them in order, from most likely to least likely that your son will have this occupation." Then ask informants to do the same thing for their daughters. (Be sure to assign informants randomly to doing the task for sons or daughters first.) Then compare the average ranking of accessibility against some independent variables and test for intracultural differences among ethnic groups, genders, age groups, and income groups.

Weller and Dungy (1986) studied breast-feeding among Hispanic and Anglo women in southern California. They asked 55 informants for a free list of positive and negative aspects of breast-feeding and bottle-feeding. Then they selected the 20 most frequently mentioned items in this domain and converted the items to neutral, similarly worded statements. A few examples: "a way that doesn't tie you down, so you are free to do more things"; "a way that your baby feels full and satisfied"; "a way that allows you to feel closer to your baby."

Next, Weller and Dungy asked 195 women to rank the 20 statements. The women were asked which statement was most important to them in selecting a method of feeding their baby; which was the next most important to them; and so on. In the analysis, Weller and Dungy were able to relate the average rank order for Hispanics and for Anglos to independent variables like age and education.

Paired Comparisons

The method of paired comparisons is an alternative way to get rank orderings of a list of items in a domain. If you have a list of 14 items, there are $N (N - 1)/2$, or $14(13)/2 = 91$ pairs of items. You write out a list of all the pairs (A and B, A and C . . . B and C . . . F and J . . ., etc.). Show informants each pair and ask them to circle the item that conforms to some criterion. You might say: "Here are two animals. Which one is the more _____ ?" where the blank is filled in by "vicious," or "wild," or whatever. You could ask informants to choose the "illness in this pair that is more life threatening" or "the food in this pair that is better for you."

In a list of 14 items, each item appears 13 times (A and B, A and C, A and D, etc., down through A and N). To find the rank order of the list for each informant, you simply count up how many times each item "wins"— that is, how many times each item was circled. If cancer is on a list of illnesses and the criterion is "life threatening" you expect to find it circled each time it is paired with another illness—except, perhaps, when it is paired with AIDS. By contrast, the rank ordering of diabetes and high blood pressure on the life-threatening criterion is not so predictable, especially across cultures and ethnic groups.

The paired comparison technique has a lot going for it. Informants make one judgment at a time, so it's much easier on them than asking them to do a rank ordering of a list of items. Also, you can use paired comparisons with nonliterate informants by reading the list of pairs to them, one at a time and recording their answers. Weller and Dungy (1986) did that in their study of breast-feeding.

Like triad tests, paired comparisons can only be used with a relatively limited number of items in a domain. With 20 items, for example, informants have to make 190 judgments. Fortunately, there are BIB designs for paired comparisons, just as there are for triad tests (see above), and ANTHROPAC has a routine for producing individual paired comparison tests.

Ratings

Rating scales produce ordinal data and are easy to administer. Combined with pile sorts and unstructured interviews, ratings are powerful data generators. In a series of papers, John Roberts and his co-workers used pile sorts and rating tasks to study how people perceive various kinds of behaviors in games (see, e.g., Roberts & Chick, 1979; Roberts & Nattrass, 1980).

One "game," studied by Roberts et al. (1981) is pretty serious: searching for foreign submarines in a P3 airplane. The P3 is a four-engine, turboprop, low-wing aircraft that can stay in the air for long periods of time and cover large patches of ocean. It is also used for search-and-rescue missions. Making errors in flying the P3 can result in death or injury at worst, and career damage and embarrassment at least.

Roberts et al. (ibid.) isolated 60 named pilot errors, through extensive unstructured interviews with Navy pilots of the P3. Here are a few of the errors: flying into a known thunderstorm area; taking off with the trim tabs set improperly; allowing the prop wash to cause damage to other aircraft; inducing an autofeather by rapid movement of power level controls. (This is the equivalent of extracting a "free list" from your interviews.) The researchers asked 52 pilots to do an unrestricted pile sort of the 60 errors and to rate each error on a 7-point scale of "seriousness."

They also asked their informants to rank a subset of 13 errors on four criteria that were chosen on the basis of unstructured interviews: (a) how much each error would "rattle" a pilot; (b) how badly each error would damage a pilot's career; (c) how embarrassing each error would be to commit; and (d) how much "fun" it would be to commit each error.

Flying into a thunderstorm on purpose, for example, could be very damaging to a pilot's career, and extremely embarrassing if he had to abort the mission and turn back in the middle. But if the mission turned out to be successful, then taking the risk of committing a very dangerous error would be a lot of fun for pilots who are "high self-testers" (Roberts, personal communication).

Inexperienced pilots rated "inducing an autofeather" as more serious than did highly experienced pilots. Inducing an autofeather is more embarrassing than it is dangerous, and is the sort of error that experienced pilots just don't make. On the other hand, as the number of air hours increased, so did pilots' view of the seriousness of "failure to use all available navigational aids to determine position." Roberts et al. (1981) suggested that inexperienced pilots might not have had enough training to assess the seriousness of this error correctly.

Sydel Silverman (1966) used a pile sort as a rating device to study prestige rankings in an Italian village. During the first few months of her fieldwork, she noticed that people showed deference to one another. She learned that the term *rispetto* (respect) was the important quantity to measure, and that some people had more rispetto than others. The more someone had, the more deference they could expect from others who had less. Everyone in the village was expected to know, more or less, how much rispetto each person had, so that proper interpersonal relations could be maintained.

Occupation didn't predict people's deference to one another, so Silverman worked intensively with three key informants, adult men between 43 and 65 years of age. All three were lifelong residents of the village and had expert knowledge of all families in the village. Silverman gave each key informant a deck of 175 cards containing the names of the families in the village and asked them to sort the cards into piles, according to how much rispetto each family had.

The three informants produced seven, six, and four piles respectively. Silverman asked them to look at a number of paired comparisons between cards in one pile and cards in another. Informants did this exercise until they were satisfied that they had produced a set of internally consistent piles—that each family in a pile belonged in that pile with other families that had the same amount of rispetto.

When the pile-sorting task was done, each informant had created a 3-point, or 6-point, or 7-point ordinal scale, depending on how many piles he wound up creating. Silverman was then able to ask her informants about the sizes of the gaps between the piles. In other words, she tried to understand the intervals between the ordinal ranks. Silverman did not do a statistical analysis of these data. Instead, she used the results of her rating exercise to create a working hypothesis concerning the relative prestige of persons in the village—a model that she could (and did) check against behavioral observations and reports of behavior from informants.

As I said at the beginning of this chapter, I consider the techniques reviewed here to be among the most fun and most productive in the repertoire of anthropological method. They can be used in both applied and basic research; they are attractive to informants; and they produce a wealth of information that can be compared across informants and across cultures. Thirty years in development, the field of cognitive anthropology is becoming increasingly important in anthropology. For further reading, consult Werner and Schoepfle (1987) and Weller and Romney (1988); for handling the actual chores of data collection and analysis, consult the ANTHROPAC manual (Borgatti, 1992a).

12

Questionnaires and
Survey Research

S urvey research is a major industry in the United States. Ten years ago, it employed around 50,000 people, including 4,000 to 6,000 professional social scientists (Rossi et al., 1983:10). It is also an accepted part of many other cultures of the world. Japan developed a survey research industry soon after World War II (see Passin, 1951, for a discussion of this fascinating story). India, South Korea, Jamaica, Greece, Mexico, and many other countries have since developed their own survey research capabilities, either in universities or in the private sector, or both.

The industry began its modern development in the mid-1930s when quota sampling was first applied to voting behavior studies and to determining the characteristics of listeners to various radio programs, readers of various magazines, and purchasers of various products. Then, as now, survey research helped advertisers target their messages more profitably.

Studies of U.S. soldiers in World War II provided massive opportunities for social scientists to refine their skills in taking samples and in collecting and analyzing survey data (Stouffer et al., 1947-1950). The continued need for consumer behavior data in the private sector and the developing need by government agencies for information about various "target populations" (poor people, black people, Hispanic people, users of public housing, users of private health care, etc.) have provided impetus for the growth of the survey research industry.

We have learned a lot over the past 60 years about how to collect reliable and valid data using questionnaires. In this chapter I review some of the important lessons concerning the wording of questions, the format of questionnaires, the management of survey projects, the maximizing of response rates, and the minimizing of response effects.

Survey Research in Non-Western Societies

Is survey research really feasible everywhere? Perhaps not. But Gordon Streib did survey research among the Navaho in 1950 and had only a 2% refusal rate. Streib says that this was because the Navaho were able to put his role as a survey researcher into meaningful perspective. The Navaho had, of course, been studied by many anthropologists, but when Streib (a sociologist) began his survey they said to him "We wondered what you were doing around here. Now we know that you have a job to do like other people" (Streib, personal communication; see also Streib, 1952).

This refusal rate of 2% is identical to that experienced by Stycos in five different surveys he did on fertility patterns in the Caribbean in the 1950s (1960:377; see also Stycos, 1955). By contrast, typical refusal rates for face-to-face, personal interviews in the United States and Britain run between 5% and 20%. Refusal to be interviewed is linked to several factors, including the perceived threat of the questions being asked, the length of the interview, and the education level of the respondents (respondents with low education refuse more).

The Caribbean fertility studies reported by Stycos contained questions of a very intimate nature—dealing, for example, with sexual experiences in and out of marriage. The questionnaires took from one and a half to 6 hours to administer in person, and the average education of Stycos's Caribbean respondents was much lower than the typical educational level of U.S. and British respondents.

Personal Interviews, Mail, and Telephone

There are three methods for collecting survey questionnaire data: (a) personal, face-to-face interviews, (b) self-administered questionnaires, and (c) telephone interviews. Self-administered questionnaires are usually mailed to respondents, but they may also be dropped off and picked up later or they may be given to people in a group all at once.

Each of the data collection methods has its own advantages and disadvantages. There is no conclusive evidence that one method of administering questionnaires is better, overall, than the others. Your choice of a method will depend on your own calculus of things like cost, convenience, and the nature of the questions you are asking. (Consult Kahn and Cannell, 1957, Gorden, 1975, Dillman, 1983, and Fowler, 1984, for more information on this and other topics in this chapter. Also consult the journal *Public Opinion Quarterly* for the latest research on how to improve the results of survey research. POQ covers such topics as the costs and benefits of various types of surveys, the advantages and disadvantages of various ways of asking the same question, and so on.)

Personal Interviews

Face-to-face administration of questionnaires offers some important advantages.

1. They can be used with informants who could not otherwise provide information—informants who are nonliterate, blind, bedridden, or very old, for example.

2. If a respondent doesn't understand a question in a personal interview, you can fill in and, if you sense that the respondent is not answering fully, you can probe for more complete data.

3. You can use several different data collection techniques with the same respondent in a face-to-face survey interview. Part of the interview can consist of open-ended questions; another part may require the use of visual aids, such as graphs or cue cards; and in still another, you might hand the respondent a self-administered questionnaire booklet and stand by to help clarify potentially ambiguous items. This is a particularly useful technique if you want to ask really sensitive questions in a face-to-face interview.

4. Personal interviews can be much longer than telephone or self-administered questionnaires. An hour-long personal interview is relatively easy, and even 2-hour and 3-hour interviews are common. It is next to impossible to get respondents to devote 2 hours to filling out a questionnaire that

shows up in the mail, unless you are prepared to pay well for their time; and it requires exceptional skill to keep a telephone interview going for more than 20 minutes, unless respondents are personally interested in the topic.

5. Face-to-face respondents get one question at a time and can't flip through the questionnaire to see what's coming. If you design an interview to start with general questions (how farmers feel about using new technologies, for example) and move on to specific questions (how farmers feel about a particular new technique), then you really don't want people flipping ahead.

6. With face-to-face interviews you know who answers the questions.

But personal interviews have their disadvantages, as well.

1. They are intrusive and reactive in ways that we are only beginning to understand. It takes a lot of skill to administer a questionnaire without subtly telling the respondent how you hope he or she will answer your questions. Other methods of administration of questionnaires may be impersonal, but that's not necessarily bad. Furthermore, the problem of reactivity increases when more than one interviewer is involved in a project.

2. Personal interviews are costly in both time and money. In addition to the time spent in interviewing people, locating respondents in a representative sample may require going back several times. In urban research especially, count on making up to half a dozen callbacks to get the really hard-to-find respondents.

By the way, it's really important to keep going back and back in order to land those hard-to-get interviews. Survey researchers sometimes use the "sampling-by-convenient-replacement" technique—which just means going next door or down the block and picking up a replacement for an interviewee who happens not to be home when you show up. This keeps the sample size honest, but as I mentioned in Chapter 4 on sampling, it can produce some deadly bias. This is because, as you replace nonresponders with conveniently available respondents, you tend to homogenize your sample and make it less and less representative of all the variation in the population you're studying (T. Smith, 1989).

3. The number of people whom you can contact personally in a year's ethnographic field research appears to be around 400. With mailed and telephone questionnaires you can survey thousands of respondents.

4. Personal interview surveys conducted by lone anthropologists over a long period of time run the risk of being overtaken by events. A war may

break out, a volcano may erupt, or the government may decide to distribute free food to people in a village you are studying. Even lesser events can make the responses of the last 100 people you interview radically different from those of the first 100 to the same questions. If you conduct a questionnaire survey over a long period of time in the field, it is a good idea to reinterview your first few respondents and check the stability (reliability) of their reports.

Self-Administered Questionnaires

Self-administered questionnaires also have some clear advantages and disadvantages.

1. Mailed questionnaires put the post office to work for you in finding respondents. If you can not use the mail (because sampling frames are unavailable, or because you can not expect people to respond, or because mail service is unreliable), you can use cluster and area sampling (see Chapter 4), combined with the drop-and-collect technique. This involves leaving a questionnaire with an informant and going back later to pick it up. In either case, self-administered questionnaires allow a single researcher to gather data from a large, representative sample of respondents, at relatively low cost per datum.

2. All respondents get the same questions with a self-administered questionnaire. There is no worry about interviewer bias.

3. You can ask more complex questions with a self-administered questionnaire than you can in a personal interview. Questions that involve a long list of response categories, or that require a lot of background data, are hard to follow orally, but are often challenging to respondents if worded right.

4. You can ask long batteries of otherwise boring questions on self-administered questionnaires that you just couldn't get away with in a personal interview. Look at Figure 12.1. Imagine trying to ask an informant to sit still while you recited, say, 30 items and asked for the informant's response.

5. Respondents report socially undesirable behaviors and traits more willingly (and presumably more accurately) in self-administered questionnaires (and in telephone interviews) than they do in face-to-face interviews. They aren't trying to impress interviewers, and anonymity gives people a sense of security, which produces more reports of things like premarital sexual experiences, constipation, arrest records, alcohol dependency, interpersonal violence, and so on (Hochstim, 1967; Bradburn, 1983).

Here is a list of things that people like to see in their community.
For each item check how you feel this community is doing:

This community is doing

	WELL	REASONABLY WELL	POORLY
Drinking water	____	____	____
Water for Irrigation	____	____	____
School Buildings	____	____	____
School Teachers	____	____	____
Cooperativeness on Community Work Projects	____	____	____

- •
- •
- •
- •
- •

Figure 12.1. A battery item in a questionnaire. Batteries can consist of many items.

This does *not* mean that *more* reporting of behavior means more *accurate* reporting. We know better than that now. But more is usually better than less. If Chicanos report spending 12 hours per week in conversation with their families at home, while Anglos report spending 4 hours, I wouldn't want to bet that Chicanos *really* spend 12 hours, on average, or that Anglos *really* spend 4 hours, on average, talking to their families. But I'd find the fact that Chicanos reported spending three times as much time talking with their families of some interest.

Despite these advantages, there are some hefty disadvantages to self-administered questionnaires.

1. You have no control over how people interpret questions on a self-administered instrument. There is always the danger that, no matter how much

ethnographic background work you do, respondents will be forced into making culturally inappropriate choices in closed-ended questionnaires.

2. If you are not working in a highly industrialized nation, and if you are not prepared to use Dillman's Total Design Method (discussed below), you are likely to see response rates of 20% to 30% from mailed questionnaires. This is unacceptable for drawing conclusions about populations. With such low response rates, you'd be better off doing ethnographic research and semistructured interviews with several good informants.

3. Even if a questionnaire is returned, you can't be sure that the respondent who received it is the person who filled it out.

4. Mailed questionnaires are prone to serious sampling problems. Sampling frames of addresses are almost always flawed, sometimes very badly. For example, if you use a phone book to select a sample, you miss all those people who don't have phones or who choose not to list their numbers. Face-to-face administration of questionnaires is usually based on an area cluster sample, with random selection of households within each cluster. This is a much more powerful sampling design than most mailed questionnaire surveys can muster.

5. In some cases, you may want a respondent to answer a question without their knowing what's coming next. This is impossible in a self-administered questionnaire.

6. Self-administered questionnaires are simply not useful for studying nonliterate or illiterate populations, or for studying people who can't see.

Telephone Interviews

Telephone interviewing has become an important method of gathering survey data in recent years, particularly in the industrialized nations where so many households have their own phones. In the United States, 95% of all households have one or more telephone lines (Lavrakas, 1987:14).

Administering questionnaires by phone has some very important advantages.

1. Research has shown that, in the United States at least, answers to questionnaires given by phone are as valid as those to questionnaires given in person or through the mail (Dillman, 1978).

2. Phone interviews have the impersonal quality of self-administered questionnaires and the personal quality of face-to-face interviews. Hence, telephone surveys are unintimidating (like questionnaires), but allow interviewers to probe or to answer questions dealing with ambiguity of items (like personal interviews).

3. Telephone interviewing is inexpensive and convenient to conduct.

4. Using random digit dialing, you can sample everyone who has a phone.

5. Unless you do all your own interviewing, interviewer bias is an ever-present problem in survey research. It is relatively easy to monitor the quality of telephone interviewers' work by having them come to a central place to conduct their operation.

6. There is no reaction to the appearance of the interviewer in telephone surveys, although respondents *do* react to accents and speech patterns of interviewers. Oskenberg et al. (1986) found that telephone interviewers who had the lowest refusal rates had higher-pitched, louder, and clearer voices.

7. Telephone interviewing is safe: You can talk to people on the phone who live in certain urban neighborhoods where professional interviewers (most of whom are women) prefer not to go.

The disadvantages of telephone surveys, especially for anthropologists, are obvious.

1. Even in highly industrialized nations, everyone does not have a telephone, so sampling frames are automatically biased. If you are studying a poor population, the chance that a household has no phone is much higher. While 95% of all households in the United States have telephones, the state by state penetration of phones is uneven. In Arkansas, Nevada, Mississippi, and West Virginia, telephone saturation is 85% or less. In California, New Jersey, and Vermont, it's 100% (Lavrakas, 1987:15). In the Third World, telephone surveys are out of the question, except for some urban centers, and then only if your study requires a sample of relatively well-off people.

2. Telephone interviews must be relatively short, or people will hang up. There is some evidence that once people agree to give you their time in a telephone interview, you can keep them on the line for a remarkably long time (up to an hour) by developing special "phone personality" traits. Generally, however, you should not plan a telephone interview that lasts for more than 20 minutes.

The technology of telephone interviewing has become quite sophisticated. There are several companies that sell telephone numbers for surveys. The numbers are chosen to represent businesses or residences and to represent the varying saturation of phone service in different calling areas. For step-by-step instructions on planning and conducting telephone interview studies, consult Lavrakas (1987) and Frey (1989).

Remember, though, that all these sampling aids are of little value if the population you want to reach is hard to find. A needs assessment survey of Florida's elderly took 72,000 calls for 1,647 interviews (about 43 calls per interview) (Henry, 1990:88). That's because the elderly are just 6.5% of Florida's population, so a random call to a Florida household is pretty unlikely to turn up an elderly respondent. By contrast, the monthly Florida survey of 600 representative consumers takes about 5,000 calls (about 8 per interview). That's because just about everyone in the state 18 and older is a consumer and is eligible for the survey (Christopher McCarty, personal communication).

When to Use What

There is no perfect data collection method. However, self-administered questionnaires are preferable to personal interviews when three conditions are met: (a) You are dealing with literate respondents; (b) you are confident of getting a high response rate (which I put at 70%, minimum); and (c) the nature of the questions you want to ask does not require a face-to-face interview and the use of visual aids such as cue cards, charts, and the like.

Under these circumstances, you get much more information for your time and money than from the other methods of questionnaire administration. If you are working in a highly industrialized country, and if a very high proportion (at least 80%) of the population you are studying has its own telephones, then consider doing a phone survey whenever a self-administered questionnaire would otherwise be appropriate.

The best method of survey data collection for anthropologists who are working alone in the field, or who are working in places where the mails and the phone system are inefficient vehicles for data collection, is the drop-and-collect technique. You simply leave a self-administered questionnaire with a respondent at his or her workplace or home and then retrieve it later. A response rate similar to that for a face-to-face survey can usually be achieved with this technique, although you may have to drop off two, three, or four survey instruments to some households before they come through.

Using Interviewers

There are several advantages to using multiple interviewers in survey research. The most obvious is that you can increase the size of the sample.

Another is that interviewers who are native speakers of the local language in which you are working are always better equipped to answer respondents' questions about ambiguous items. Multiple interviewers, however, introduce several disadvantages, and whatever problems are associated with interviewer bias are increased with more than one interviewer.

Just as important, multiple interviewers increase the cost of survey research. If you can collect 400 interviews yourself and maintain careful quality control in your interview technique, then hiring one more interviewer would probably not improve your research by enough to warrant both spending the extra money and worrying about quality control. Recall that for dichotomous questions (like yes-no polls), you'd have to quadruple the sample size to halve the sampling error. If you can't afford to hire three more interviewers (besides yourself), and to train them carefully so that they at least introduce the *same* bias to every interview as you do, you're better off running the survey yourself and saving the money for other things.

Training Interviewers

If you do hire interviewers, be sure to train them—and monitor them throughout the research. A colleague used a doctoral student as an interviewer in a project in Atlanta. The senior researcher trained the student, but listened to the interview tapes that came in. At one point, the interviewer asked an informant: "How many years of education do you have?" "Four," said the informant. "Oh," said the student researcher, "you mean you have four years of education?" "No," said the informant, bristling and insulted, "I've had four years of education beyond high school." The informant was affluent; the interview was conducted in his upper-middle-class house; he had already told the interviewer that he was in a high-tech occupation. So monitor interviewers.

If you hire a *team* of interviewers, you have one extra chore besides monitoring their work. You need to get them to act as a team. Be sure, for example, that they all use the same probes to the various questions on the interview schedule. Especially with open-ended questions, do random spot checks *during the survey* of how interviewers are coding the answers they get. The act of spot checking keeps coders alert. When you find discrepancies in the way interviewers code responses, bring the group together and discuss the problem openly.

Billiet and Loosveldt (1988) found that asking interviewers to tape all their interviews produces a higher response rate, particularly to sensitive questions about things like sexual behavior. Apparently, when interviewers know that their work can be scrutinized (from the tapes) they probe more and get informants to open up more.

William Axinn ran the Tamang Family Research Project, a comparative study of villages in Nepal (Axinn, 1989; Axinn et al., 1991). Axinn and some co-workers trained a group of interviewers using the *Interviewer's Manual* from the Survey Research Center at the University of Michigan (1976). That manual contains the distilled wisdom of hundreds of interviewer training exercises in the United States, and Axinn found the manual useful in training Nepalese interviewers, too.

Axinn recruited 32 potential interviewers. After a week of training (5 days at 8 hours a day, and 2 days of supervised field practice), the 16 best interviewers were selected, 10 men and 6 women. The researchers hired more interviewers than they needed, and after 3 months 4 of the interviewers were fired. "The firing of interviewers who clearly failed to follow protocols," said Axinn et al., "had a considerable positive effect on the morale of interviewers who had worked hard to follow our rules" (ibid.:200). No one has accused Axinn of overstatement.

In general, when hiring interviewers, look for professionals first. Next, look for people who are high school graduates and who are mature enough to handle being trained and to work as part of a team. Look for interviewers who can handle the possibility of going into some rough neighborhoods and who can answer the many questions that respondents will come up with in the course of the survey.

In the Third World, consider hiring college students, and even college graduates, in the social sciences. "Social sciences," by the way, does not mean humanities. In Peru, Warwick and Lininger (1975) found that "some students from the humanities . . . were reluctant to accept the 'rigidities' of survey interviewing." Those students felt that "as educated individuals, they should be allowed to administer the questionnaire as they saw fit in each situation" (p. 222).

Students from sociology, however, are likely to be experienced interviewers and will have a lot to contribute to the design and content of questionnaires. It is very important in those situations to remember that you are dealing with colleagues who will be justly resentful if you treat them as simply employees of your study. By the same token, college students in the Third World are almost certain to be members of the elite who may find it tough to establish rapport with subsistence farmers or the urban poor (Hursh-César & Roy, 1976:308).

If you use interviewers, be sure to make the questionnaire booklet easy to use. Leave enough space for interviewers to write in the answers to open-ended questions—but not too much space. Big spaces are an invitation to some interviewers to develop needlessly long answers (Warwick & Lininger, 1975:152).

Also, use two different type faces for questions and answers; put instructions to interviewers in capital letters and questions for respondents in normal type. Figure 12.2 is an example.

5. INTERVIEWER: CHECK ONE OF THE FOLLOWING

☐ **R HAS BEEN IN NAIROBI MORE THAN FIVE YEARS. SKIP TO Q.7**

☐ **R IN NAIROBI LESS THAN 5 YEARS. ASK Q.6 AND CONTINUE WITH QUESTION 7.**

6. Could you tell me where you were living five years ago?

7. Where were you born?

Figure 12.2. Using two different type faces in a survey instrument.
Adapted from Warwick and Lininger (1975:153).

Closed Versus Open-Ended: The Problem of Threatening Questions

The most often-asked question about survey research is whether forced-choice (also called "closed") or open-ended items are better. Schuman and Presser (1979) tested this. They asked one sample of people this question: "Please look at this card and tell me which thing you would most prefer in a job." The card had five items listed: (a) high income, (b) no danger of being fired, (c) working hours are short—lots of free time, (d) chances for advancement, and (e) the work is important and gives a feeling of accomplishment. Then they asked another sample the open-ended question: "What would you most prefer in a job?"

About 17% of the respondents to the closed-ended question chose "chances for advancement," and over 59% chose "important work." Under 2% of the respondents who were asked the open-ended question mentioned "chances for advancement," and just 21% said anything about "important" or "challenging" or "fulfilling" work.

When the questions get really threatening, the problem gets worse. In surveys done in the industrialized nations, instances of masturbation, alcohol consumption, and drug use are reported with 50% to 100% greater frequency in response to open-ended questions (Bradburn, 1983:299). For reporting this kind of behavior, people are apparently least threatened when they can offer their own answers on a self-administered question- naire, rather than being forced to choose among a set of fixed alternatives (e.g., once a month, once a week, once a day, several times a day), and are most threatened by a face-to-face interviewer (Blair et al., 1977).

Still, since closed-ended items are so efficient, most survey researchers prefer them to open-ended questions and use them whenever possible. There is no rule that prevents you from mixing question types, however. Use the open-ended format for intimidating questions and the fixed-choice format for everything else. It is also a good idea to put a few open-ended items in what would otherwise be a completely fixed-choice questionnaire. The open-ended questions break the monotony for the respondent, as do tasks that require referring to visual aids (like a graph).

The responses to fixed-choice questions are unambiguous for purposes of analysis. Be sure to take full advantage of this and *precode* fixed-choice items on a questionnaire. Put the codes right on the instrument so that computer input of the data is made as easy (and as error free) as possible.

Question Wording and Format

There are some well-understood rules that all survey researchers follow in constructing questionnaire items. Here are 15 of them.

1. Be unambiguous. If respondents can interpret a question differently from the meaning you have in mind, they will. In my view, this is the source of most response error in closed-ended questionnaires.

The problem is not easy to solve. A simple question like "How often do you visit a doctor?" can be very ambiguous. Are native curers, herbalists, acupuncturists, chiropractors, chiropodists, and public clinics staffed by nurses "doctors"? Does a friendly chat at a neighborhood doctor's house count as a "visit"? What about "How long have you lived in Mexico City?" Does "Mexico City" include the 18 million people who live in the urban sprawl, or just the 9 million who are residents of the Federal District? And how "near" is "near Nairobi"?

Words like "lunch," "village," "community," "people," and hundreds of other innocent lexical items have lurking ambiguities associated with them, and phrases like "family planning" will cause all kinds of mischief. Even the word "you," can be ambiguous, as Payne pointed out more than 40 years ago (1951). Ask a nurse at the clinic "How many patients did you see last week?" and you might get a response like "Who do you mean, me or the clinic?" Of course, if nurses fill out self-administered questionnaires, they'll have to decide for themselves what you had in mind. Maybe they'll get it right; maybe they won't.

2. Use a vocabulary that your respondents will understand, but don't be condescending. This is a difficult balance to achieve. If you are studying a narrow population (maize farmers, midwives, race car drivers), then proper ethnography and pretesting with a few respondents will help you ensure appropriate wording of questions. But if you are studying a more general population, even in a village of just 3,000 people, then things are very different.

Some respondents will require a low-level vocabulary; others will find that vocabulary insulting. This is one of the reasons often cited for doing personal interviews in rural anthropological field research: You want the opportunity to phrase your questions differently for different segments of the population. Realize, however, that this poses risks in terms of reliability of response data.

3. Remember that your respondents must *know* enough to respond to your questions. You'd be surprised at how often questionnaires are distributed to people who are totally unequipped to answer them. I get questionnaires in the mail all the time asking for information I simply don't have.

Many people can't recall with any acceptable accuracy how often they went to church last year, how many miles they drive each week, or whether they've cut back on their use of electricity. They *can* recall whether they own a television, have *ever* been to Cairo, or voted in last year's election, and they can tell you whether they *think* they are well paid, or *believe* the rebel government is better than the previous regime. Don't confuse these reports of feelings with reports of behavior.

4. Try to make a questionnaire look well planned. Don't lengthen questionnaires with items that appear thrown in for no apparent reason. And once you're on a topic, stay on it and finish it. Respondents can get frustrated, confused, and annoyed at the tactic of topic switching and of coming back to a topic that they've already dealt with on a questionnaire. Some researchers do this in order to ask the same question in more than one way and to check respondent reliability. This underestimates the intelligence of respondents and is asking for trouble—I have known respondents to sabotage questionnaires that they found insulting to their intelligence.

You can (and should) ask questions that are related to one another at different places in a questionnaire, so long as each question makes sense in terms of its placement in the overall instrument. For example, in a section on employment history, you might ask where a respondent has worked as a labor migrant. Later, in a section on family economics, you might ask whether a respondent has ever sent remittances and from where.

As you move from one topic to another, put in a transition paragraph that makes each shift logical to the respondent. For example, you might say: "Now that we have learned something about the kinds of food you like, we'd like to know about. . . ." The exact wording of these transition paragraphs should be varied throughout a questionnaire.

5. Pay careful attention to contingencies and *filter questions*. Many question topics contain several contingencies. Suppose you ask someone if they are married. If they answer "no," then you probably want to ask whether they've ever been married. You may want to know whether they have children, irrespective of whether they are married or have ever been married. You may want to know what people think is the ideal family size, irrespective of whether they've been married, plan to be married, have children, or plan to have children. You can see that the contingencies can get very complex. The best way to ensure that all contingencies are accounted for is to build a contingency flow chart like that shown in Figure 12.3 (Sirken, 1972; Sudman & Bradburn, 1982).

6. Use clear scales. There are some commonly used scales in survey research—things like: Excellent-Good-Fair-Poor; Approve-Disapprove; Oppose-Favor; For-Against; Good-Bad; Agree-Disagree; Better-Worse-About the Same; etc. Just because these are well known, however, does not mean that they are clear and unambiguous to respondents.

To cut down on the ambiguities associated with these kinds of scales, explain the meaning of each potentially ambiguous scale when you introduce it. Also, use five points rather than three, whenever possible. For example, use Strongly Approve, Approve, Neutral, Disapprove, Strongly Disapprove, rather than Approve, Neutral, Disapprove. This will at least give respondents the opportunity to make finer-grained choices.

If your sample is large enough, you can distinguish during analysis among respondents who answer, say, "strongly approve" versus "approve" on some item. For smaller samples, you'll have to aggregate the data into three categories for analysis. Self-administered questionnaires allow the use of 7-point scales, like the semantic differential scale shown in Figure

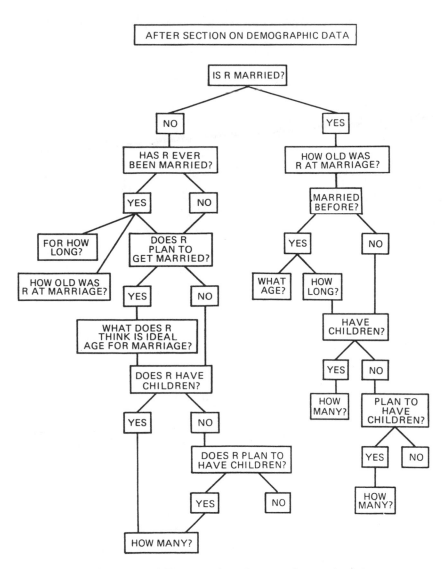

Figure 12.3. Flow chart of filter questions for part of a questionnaire.

12.4. Telephone interviews usually require 3-point scales. (See Chapter 13 for more on how to construct scales and see Figure 13.1 for another example of a semantic differential scale.)

CHECK HOW YOU FEEL ABOUT EACH OF THE FOLLOWING

DAUGHTERS

GOOD	—	—	—	—	—	—	—	BAD
	1	2	3	4	5	6	7	
WEAK	—	—	—	—	—	—	—	STRONG
	1	2	3	4	5	6	7	
ACTIVE	—	—	—	—	—	—	—	PASSIVE
	1	2	3	4	5	6	7	

etc.   etc.

MOMBASA

GOOD	—	—	—	—	—	—	—	BAD
	1	2	3	4	5	6	7	
WEAK	—	—	—	—	—	—	—	STRONG
	1	2	3	4	5	6	7	
ACTIVE	—	—	—	—	—	—	—	PASSIVE
	1	2	3	4	5	6	7	

etc.   etc.

Figure 12.4. A 7-point semantic differential scale.

7. Try to "package" questions in self-administered questionnaires, as shown earlier in Figure 12.1. This is a way to get a lot of data quickly and easily, and, if done properly, will prevent respondents from getting bored with a survey. For example, you might say "Please indicate how close you feel to each of the persons on this chart," and provide the respondent with a list of relatives (mother, father, sister, brother, etc.) and a scale (very close, close, neutral, distant, very distant, etc.).

Be sure to make scales unambiguous (if you are asking how often people think they do something, don't say "regularly" when you mean "more than once a month"), and limit the list of activities to no more than seven. Then introduce a question with a totally different format, to break up the monotony and to keep the respondent interested.

Packaging is best done in self-administered questionnaires. If you use these kinds of lists in a personal interview, you'll have to repeat the scale for at least the first three items or activities you name, or until the respondent gets the pattern down. This can get very tiring for both interviewers and respondents.

8. Make the possible responses to a question exhaustive and exclusive, particularly if you want respondents to check just one response. Here is an example (taken from a questionnaire I got in the mail) of what *not* to do:

How do you perceive communication between your department and other
departments in the university?

There is much communication . . . .
There is sufficient communication . . . .
There is little communication . . . .
There is no communication . . . .
No basis for perception . . . .

The problem is that I wanted to check both "little communication" and "sufficient communication." These two categories are not mutually exclusive.

Partly to make questionnaire items mutually exhaustive, give respondents the option of saying "don't know" as an answer to a question. Some researchers feel that this just gives respondents a lazy way out—that respondents need to be made to work a bit. Furthermore, the "don't know" option doesn't always work; the "no basis for perception" alternative on the item above, for example, doesn't achieve exhaustiveness.

On balance, though, I think the "don't know" option is too important to leave out. No matter how hard you try to make your questionnaire relevant to respondents' concerns and knowledge, many of them simply will not know the answer to some of your questions. It is better, in my view, to risk getting less data and to maximize the likelihood that the data are honest reflections of respondents' views and memories.

9. Keep unthreatening questions short. Questions that are likely to intimidate respondents should have long preambles to lessen the intimidation effect. The questions themselves, however, should contain as few words as possible.

10. Always provide alternatives, if appropriate. Suppose people are being moved off their land to make way for a dam. The government offers to compensate people for the land, but people are suspicious that the government won't evaluate fairly how much compensation landowners are entitled to. If you take a survey and ask "Should the government offer people compensation for their land?" respondents can answer yes or no for very different reasons. Instead, let people check whether they agree or disagree with a set of alternatives, like: "The government should offer

people compensation for their land" and "An independent board should determine how much people get for their land."

11. Avoid loaded questions. Any question that begins "Don't you agree that . . ." is a loaded question. Sheatsley (1983) points out, however, that asking loaded questions is a technique you can use to your advantage, on occasion, just as leading or baiting informants can be used in unstructured interviewing. A famous example comes from Kinsey's landmark study of sexual behavior of American men (Kinsey et al., 1948). Kinsey asked men "How old were you the first time you masturbated?" This made respondents feel that the interviewer already *knew* about the fact of masturbation and was only in search of additional information.

12. Don't use double-barreled questions. Here is one I found on a questionnaire once: "When did you leave home and go to work on your own for the first time?" There is no reason to assume, of course, that someone had to leave home in order to go to work, or that they necessarily went to work if they left home.

13. Don't put false premises into questions. I once formulated the following question for a survey in Greece: "Is it better for a woman to have a house and cash as a dowry, or for her to have an education and a job that she can bring to the marriage?" This question was based on a lot of ethnographic work in a community, during which I learned that many families were sinking their resources into getting women educated and into jobs and offering this to eligible bachelors as a substitute for traditional material dowries.

My question, however, was based on the false premise that all families respected the custom of dowry, and did not allow respondents to state a third alternative—namely, that they didn't think dowry was a custom that ought to be maintained in any form, traditional or modern. In fact, many families were deciding to reject the dowry custom altogether—a fact that I missed for some time because I failed to pretest the item (see Pretesting, below).

14. Don't take emotional stands in the wording of questions. Here's an example of the sort of question you see on surveys all the time, and that you should never ask: "Should the legislature raise the drinking age to 21 in order to reduce the carnage among teens on our highways?" Another example of a bad question is: "Do you agree with the president when he says? . . . "

15. When asking for opinions on controversial issues, specify the referent situation as much as possible. Instead of asking "Do you approve of abortion?" ask "Under what conditions do you approve of abortion?" Then

give the respondent as exhaustive a list of circumstances as possible to check. If the circumstances are not exclusive (rape and incest are not necessarily exclusive, for example), then let respondents check as many circumstances as they think appropriate. And don't forget to include "under no condition" as one of the options for respondents to check.

Translation and Back Translation

All the tips given here about writing good survey questions continue to apply when you are working in another culture. They are just a lot more difficult to implement because you have to deal with phrasing questions properly in another language as well. The best way to deal with this is through *back translation*.

First, write any questionnaire in *your* native language, paying attention to all the lessons of this chapter. Then have the questionnaire translated by a bilingual person who is a native speaker of the language you are working in. Work closely with the translator, so that he or she can fully understand the subtleties you want to convey in your questionnaire items.

Next, ask another bilingual person, who is a native speaker of *your* language, to translate the questionnaire back into that language. This back translation should be almost identical to the original questionnaire you wrote. If it isn't, then something was lost in one of the two translations. You'd better find out which one it was and correct the problem. This is what Axinn et al. (1991) did in their study of fertility in Nepal. In fact, they cross-checked the meaning of each question in the back translation against the original and went through the whole exercise several times until they were satisfied that questions in Nepalese were sensible.

The Response Rate Problem

The biggest problem with mailed questionnaires is getting them back from enough respondents to make the exercise worthwhile. In 1936, the *Literary Digest* sent out 10 million straw poll ballots in an attempt to predict the winner of the presidential election. It got back 2.3 million ballots and predicted Alf Landon over Franklin Delano Roosevelt in a landslide. Roosevelt got 61% of the vote.

Two things caused the *Digest* debacle. First, it selected its sample from automobile registries and telephone books. In 1936, this favored richer people who tend to be Republican. Second, the low response rate biased the results in favor of the Republican challenger (Squire, 1988).

Skip to 1991. The American Anthropological Association sent question-naires to a sample of 1,229 members. The sample was stratified into several cohorts who had received their Ph.D degrees beginning in 1971-1972 and 1989-1990. The 1989-1990 cohort sample comprised 306 recent Ph.Ds. The idea was to find out what kinds of jobs those anthropologists had.

The AAA got back 840 completed questionnaires, or 68% of the 1,229, and the results of the survey were reported in the *Anthropology Newsletter* for May 1991. The response rate may seem high, but the U.S. Office of Management and Budget demands a minimum 75% response rate from survey contract researchers (Fowler, 1984:48).

Now, 41% of those responding from the 1989-1990 cohort, said they had academic jobs. The *Newsletter* didn't report the response rate by cohort, but suppose that 68% of the 1989-1990 cohort—the same percent-age as applies to the overall survey—sent back their questionnaires. That's 208 out of 306 responses. The 41% who said they had academic jobs would be 85 of the 208 respondents; the other 123 had nonacademic jobs.

Suppose that everyone who didn't respond (32%, or 98 out of 306) got nonacademic jobs. (Maybe that's why they didn't bother to respond.) In that case, 98 + 123 = 221 out of the 306 people in the cohort, or 72%, got nonacademic jobs that year.

It's unlikely, of course, that *all* the nonresponders were in nonacademic jobs. To handle the problem of nonresponse, the AAA might have run down a random grab of 10 of the nonresponders and interviewed them by telephone. Suppose that 7 said they had nonacademic jobs. You'll recall from Chapter 4 (on sampling) that the standard error of the mean is

$$\sqrt{\frac{p(1-p)}{N}\left(1-\frac{n}{N}\right)}$$

which means that

$$\sqrt{\frac{(0.7)(0.3)}{10}\left(1-\frac{10}{98}\right)} = 0.14$$

The probable answer for the 10 holdouts is .70 ± .14. Somewhere between 56% and 84% of the nonresponders had nonacademic jobs. Be conservative and take the higher value. (Being conservative in data analy-sis means making the weakest case for your hypothesis, not the strongest. If the weakest case is convincing, you're on solid ground.) We guess that 84%, or 82 of the 98 nonresponders had nonacademic jobs. We can now make a reasonable guess: 123 of the responders and 82 of the nonresponders (205 of the 306 people in the cohort, or 67%) had nonacademic jobs.

Low response rate can be a disaster. People who are quick to fill out and return mailed questionnaires tend to have higher incomes, and consequently tend to be more educated than the later respondents. Any dependent variables that covary with income and education, then, will be seriously distorted if you get back only 50% of your questionnaires. And what's worse, there is no accurate way to measure nonresponse bias. With a lot of nonresponse, all you know is that you've got bias but you don't know how to take it into account.

Improving Response Rates: Dillman's Total Design Method

Fortunately, a lot of research has been done on increasing response rates to mailed questionnaires. Don Dillman, of the Survey Research Laboratory at Washington State University, has synthesized the research and has developed the "Total Design Method" of mail and telephone surveying.

Professional surveys done in the United States, following Dillman's Total Design Method, achieve an *average* return rate of around 73%, with many surveys reaching 85% to 90% response. In Canada and Europe, around 79% of personal interviews are completed, and the response rate for mailed questionnaires is closer to 75% (Dillman, 1978, 1983). In The Netherlands, Nederhof (1985) tested Dillman's method by conducting a mail survey on a very threatening topic—attitudes toward suicide—and achieved a 65% response rate.

The average response rate for face-to-face interviews in the United States was between 80% and 85% during the 1960s, but fell to less than 70% in the early 1970s (American Statistical Association, 1974) and has not recovered (Goyder, 1985). Thus, with the work of Dillman and others, the gap between the response rate to personal interviews and mailed questionnaires is now insignificant. If anything, mailed questionnaires have the edge on response rates, at least in the United States.

This does not in any way reduce the value of personal interviews, especially for anthropologists working in developing nations. It does mean, however, that if you *are* conducting survey research in the United States, Canada, Western Europe, Australia, New Zealand, or Japan you should use Dillman's method.

1. Type mailed questionnaires onto standard letter-sized paper. This is 8.5" × 11" in the United States, and slightly longer, A4 paper, in the rest

of the world. Several researchers have found that green paper produces a higher response rate than white paper (Fox et al., 1988).

When the questionnaire is complete, reduce it into a booklet of about 6.25" × 8.5". This is an odd size, but the booklet format, as well as the size and color are designed *not* to look like advertising literature, to be less intimidating than a stack of letter-size paper, and to be sent in a small envelope for one unit of first-class postage in the United States.

2. Don't put any questions on either the front or back covers of the booklet. The front cover should contain a title that provokes the respondent's interest, some kind of eye-catching illustration, and instructions. The back cover should contain a note thanking the respondent and inviting open-ended comments about the questionnaire.

3. Pay careful attention to question order. Be sure that the first question is directly related to the topic of the study (as determined from the title on the front of the booklet); that it is interesting and easy to answer; and that it is nonthreatening. Once someone starts a questionnaire or an interview, they are very likely to finish it. Introduce threatening questions well into the instrument, but don't cluster them all together.

Put general socioeconomic and demographic questions at the end of a questionnaire. These seemingly innocuous questions are threatening to many respondents who fear being identified (Sudman & Bradburn, 1982). Once someone has filled out a questionnaire, they are unlikely to balk at stating their age, income, religion, occupation, etc.

4. Construct the pages of the questionnaire according to standard conventions. Use capital letters for instructions to respondents and mixed upper and lower case for the questions themselves. Never allow a question to break at the end of a page and continue on another page. Use plenty of paper; don't make the instrument appear cramped. Line answers up vertically rather than horizontally, if possible.

It pays to spend time on the physical format of a questionnaire. The general appearance, the number of pages, the type of introduction, and the amount of white (or green) space—all can affect how people respond, or whether they respond at all. Once you've gone to the expense of printing up hundreds of survey instruments, you're pretty much stuck with what you've got.

Use lots of open space in building schedules for personal interviews, too. Artificially short, crowded instruments only result in interviewers missing items and possibly in annoying respondents (imagine yourself sitting for 15 minutes in an interview before the interviewer flips the first page.)

5. Keep mailed questionnaires down to 10 to 12 pages, with no more than 125 questions. Beyond that, response rates drop (Dillman, 1978). Herzog and Bachman (1981) recommend splitting questionnaires in half and alternating the order of presentation of the halves to different respondents in order to test for response effects of questionnaire length.

It is tempting to save printing and mailing costs, and to get more questions into a few pages by reducing the amount of white space in a self-administered questionnaire. Don't do it. Respondents are never fooled into thinking that a thin-but-crowded questionnaire is anything other than what it seems to be: a long questionnaire that has been forced into fewer pages and is going to be hard to work through.

6. Send out the questionnaire with a one-page cover letter. The cover letter is very important. It should explain, in the briefest possible terms, the nature of the study, how the respondent was selected, who should fill out the questionnaire (the respondent or the members of the household), who is funding the survey, and why it is important for the respondent to send back the questionnaire. The cover letter must also guarantee confidentiality, and must explain the presence of an identification number on the questionnaire.

Some survey topics are so sensitive that respondents will balk at seeing an identification number on the questionnaire, even if you guarantee anonymity. In this case, Fowler (1984) recommends eliminating the identification number (thus making the questionnaire truly anonymous) and telling the respondents that they simply can not be identified. Enclose a printed postcard, with the respondent's name on it, and ask the respondent to mail back the postcard *separately* from the questionnaire. Explain that this will notify you that the respondent has sent in the questionnaire so that you won't have to send the respondent any reminders later on. Fowler (1984) found that respondents hardly ever send back the postcard without the questionnaire.

The cover letter is a very important part of Dillman's method. The letter must be individually typed (not photocopied or mimeographed); the respondent's name and address must be individually typed; the researcher must sign the letter personally, using a blue ball point pen (ball points make an indentation that respondents can see, and this marks the letter as having been individually signed).

7. Package the questionnaire, cover letter, and reply envelope in another envelope for mailing to the respondent. The respondent's name and address must be typed on the mailing envelope. Never use mailing labels. Use first-class postage on both the mailing envelope and the reply envelope. Hansley (1974) found that using bright commemorative stamps increased response rate.

Mizes et al. (1984) found that offering respondents $1 to complete and return a questionnaire resulted in significantly increased returns; but offering respondents $5 did not produce a sufficiently greater return to warrant using this tactic. This is because $5 is getting close to the value of many respondents' time for filling out a questionnaire. "The closer the monetary incentive comes to the value of the service performed," says Dillman (1978:16), the more the transaction becomes a strictly economic exchange and the easier it is for people to turn it down.

First-class postage and monetary incentives may seem expensive but they are cost effective because they increase the response rate. Whenever you think about cutting corners in a survey, remember that all your work in designing a representative sample goes for nothing if your response rate is low. Random samples cease to be representative unless the people in it respond. Also remember that small monetary incentives may be insulting to some people. This is a cultural and socioeconomic class variable that only you can evaluate in your specific research situation.

8. Pay careful attention to contact procedures. Send a letter to each respondent explaining the survey and informing the respondent that a questionnaire will be coming along soon. Send a postcard reminder out to all potential respondents a week after sending out the questionnaire. Don't wait until the response rate drops before sending out reminders. Many respondents hold onto a questionnaire for a while before deciding to fill it out or throw it away. A reminder after a week stimulates response among this segment of respondents.

Send a second cover letter and questionnaire to everyone who has not responded 2 weeks later. Finally, 4 weeks later, send another cover letter and questionnaire, along with an additional note explaining that you have not yet received the respondent's questionnaire, and stating how important it is that the respondent participate in the study. This time, send the packet by certified mail. House et al. (1977) showed that certified mail made a big difference in return rate for the second follow-up.

The one thing that increases response rate more than any other is university sponsorship (Fox et al., 1988). University sponsorship, though, is not enough. If you want a response rate that is not subject to bias, don't send out "Dear Respondent" cover letters, and don't send a reminder letter without a second questionnaire. Heberlein and Baumgartner (1978, 1981) found that sending a second copy of the questionnaire increases response rate 1% to 9%. Since there does not appear to be any way to predict whether the increase will be 1% or 9%, the best bet is to send the extra questionnaire.

In face-to-face interviewing, you'll find that the first people you contact will be easy to find and easy to interview. As the study wears on, it will get harder and harder to find those last few people. You may spend 6 hours getting a 1-hour interview. That's just the price of collecting data. The same holds for mailed questionnaires; the last few may cost five times per respondent what the first few cost to collect. If you really care about representative data, you won't think of this as a nuisance but rather as a necessary and important expense of data collection, and you'll prepare for it in advance by establishing a realistic budget of both time and money.

Pretesting and Learning from Mistakes

There is no way to emphasize sufficiently the importance of pretesting any survey instrument you prepare. No matter how much ethnography you do to prepare a culturally relevant questionnaire, it is absolutely guaranteed that you will have forgotten something important or that you will have poorly worded one or more vital elements. These glitches can only be identified by pretesting. If you are building a self-administered questionnaire, bring in at least 6 to 10 pretest respondents and sit with them as they fill out the entire instrument. Encourage them to ask questions about each item. Your pretest respondents will make you painfully aware of just how much you took for granted, no matter how much ethnographic research you did before making up a questionnaire.

For face-to-face interviews, do your pretesting under the conditions you will experience when the survey is underway for real. If respondents are going to come to your office, then pretest the instrument in your office. If you are going to respondents' homes, then go to their homes for the pretest.

Never use any of the respondents in a pretest for the main survey. If you are working in a small community, where each respondent is precious (and you don't want to use up any of them on a pretest), take the survey instrument to another community and pretest it there. This will also prevent the pretest respondents in a small community from gossiping about the survey before it actually gets underway.

Use all your interviewers in any pretest of a face-to-face interview schedule and be sure to do some of the pretesting yourself. After the interviewers have done the pretests, bring them together to discuss how to improve the survey instrument. As you conduct the actual survey, ask respondents to tell you what they think of the study and of the interview they've just been through. At the end of the study, bring all the interviewers back together for an evaluation of the project. If it is wise to learn from your mistakes, then the first thing you've got to do is find out what the mistakes are. If you give them a chance, your respondents and interviewers will tell you.

Cross-Sectional and Longitudinal Surveys

Most surveys are *cross-sectional*. The idea is to measure some variables at a single time. Of course, people's attitudes and reported behaviors change over time, and you never know if a single sample is truly representative of the population. Many surveys are conducted again and again to monitor changes and to ensure against picking a bad sample. Multiple cross-sectional polls use what's called a *longitudinal design*. The daily tracking polls in presidential elections are an extreme example.

Multiple cross-sectional surveys have their own problems. If the results from two successive samples are very different, you don't know if it's because people's attitudes or reported behaviors have changed, or the two samples are very different, or both. To deal with this problem, survey researchers may use the powerful *panel design*. In a panel study, you interview the exact same people over again.

There are things that only a panel design can uncover. In Malawi, the Agricultural Development Division runs annual surveys of farmers. According to Art Hansen (1988:113), the cross-sectional surveys indicated consistently that about 20% of agricultural household heads were women. Local extension agents made the original paper survey forms available to Hansen in 1982, and he was able to interview many of the previous year's respondents. Hansen found that, as women marry and divorce and their husbands emigrate for wage labor, women may become heads of agricultural households at different times in their lives.

From a policy perspective, the number of households headed by women at any given time may not be an important statistic. More important, says Hansen, is the percentage of women who will ever be heads of households. "Recognizing that more women cycle through this phase increases the importance of working with women who are not now heads of households but who might occupy that decision-making status in the future" (ibid.). Hansen points out that many government agencies in developing countries counduct annual surveys as part of the policy and planning process. Those surveys are a terrific source of data, especially if you can locate the same respondents to reinterview them.

Panel studies may suffer from what's called the *respondent mortality* problem. This is where people drop out between successive waves of the panel survey. If this happens, and the results of successive waves are very different, you can't tell if that's because of (a) the special character of the drop-out population, or (b) real changes in the variables you're studying, or (c) both.

Hansen did another panel study that illustrates how much you can learn even when respondents disappear between waves of the survey. In 1972, he interviewed a representative sample of 1,223 people in three Zambian villages. The sample was stratified to include resettled refugees from Angola and their Zambian host villagers (people who had lived in the villages all along). In 1989, Hansen went back to the area to interview a random sample of 300 of the original 1,223: 75 male and 75 female refugees, and 75 male and 75 female hosts.

Only 78 of the original 300 were available to be interviewed, but this panel design produced important results because Hansen (1990) was able to determine what had happened to each of the other 222. Forty percent of the original sample had died, but the death rate was the same for men and women, hosts and refugees alike. Another important finding was that just 23% of the host villagers had emigrated, but 39% of the refugees had left the area.

Some Specialized Survey Techniques

Factorial Surveys

In a *factorial survey*, respondents are presented with vignettes that describe hypothetical social situations and are asked for their judgments about those situations. Here is a typical vignette from a survey conducted by the developer of the method, Peter Rossi:

> You find yourself discussing [your personal life] with a [black] [male] who is [younger] than you. He is [working class] and is someone who [shares your general religious beliefs]. He is someone who [works where you do] and [generally doesn't vote].
> How likely is this to happen to you (circle one)?
>
> HIGHLY LIKELY   1   2   3   4   5   6   7   HIGHLY UNLIKELY

You can make substitutions for each of the bracketed phrases in the vignette. So, another vignette might hypothesize that you are "discussing [business problems] with a [Hispanic] [female] who is [wealthy], [the same age as you], [an atheist], [unemployed], and who [generally votes Republican]."

Obviously, each dimension in this situation (socioeconomic class, age, religion, etc.) can have several alternatives. Several thousand vignettes would be needed to cover all the possible combinations, and no survey respondent could deal with all of them. In a factorial survey, however, vignettes like these are created by randomly combining the criteria and giving each respondent a unique questionnaire to deal with.

Over many respondents, all the possible combinations in a complex social situation are dealt with many times. If 400 respondents each respond to 100 vignettes, you get 40,000 unique judgments to analyze. This technique combines the internal validity features of a randomized experiment with the external validity features of a sample survey. It reduces the size of samples needed for investigating multidimensional phenomena by sampling both situations and people (Rossi & Nock, 1982).

Miller et al. (1991) used the factorial survey method to measure perceptions of appropriate prison sentences for convicted felons. Here is one of the vignettes:

> Victor J., a white, employed sewing machine operator, was convicted of intentionally shooting his friend, Laura L., a housewife. The victim required two weeks' hospitalization. In the last 5 years, the offender has not been arrested or convicted. The offender claims to have been taking drugs at the time. Victor J. was sentenced to 10 years in prison.

The sentence given was . . .

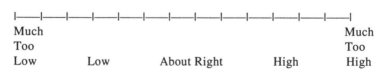

Much				
Too				
Low	Low	About Right	High	Too High

The independent variables in this study combined to form 61,025 vignettes, but each respondent only needed to see 50 randomly selected vignettes.

Randomized Response

Randomized response is a technique for measuring directly the amount of some socially negative behavior in a population—things like shoplifting, using cocaine, being hospitalized for emotional problems, extramarital sex, and so on. It was introduced by Stanley Warner in 1965. Abernathy and Greenberg (1970), in a pre-Roe v. Wade study, used the technique to estimate the rate of abortion among African-American and white women in urban North Carolina and since then there have been dozens of studies using randomized response, or RR (For a review of RR studies, see Fox & Tracy, 1991.)

I am not aware of the randomized response technique having been used by anthropologists, but it is a simple, fun, and interesting tool that should find wide acceptance in the social sciences in the future. The technique is well described by Williams (1978:73). Here's how it works.

First, you formulate two questions, A and B, that can be answered "yes" or "no." One question (A) is the question of interest (say, "Do you use cocaine on a regular basis, that is, more than once a week?"). The possible answers to this question (either "yes" or "no") do not have known probabilities of occurring. That is what you want to find out.

The other question (B) must be innocuous and the possible answers (again "yes" or "no") must have known probabilities of occurring. For example, if you ask a respondent to toss a fair coin and ask "Did you toss a heads?" then the probability of the respondent answering "yes" or "no" is 50%. If the chances of being born in any given month were equal, then you could ask respondents "Were you born in April?" and the probability of getting a "yes" would be 8%. Unfortunately, births are seasonal, so the coin-toss question is preferable.

Let's assume you use the coin toss for question B. You ask the respondent to toss the coin and to note the result *without letting you see it*. Next, have the respondent pick a card, from a deck of 10 cards, where each card is marked with a single integer from 1 to 10. The respondent does not tell you what number he or she picked, either. The secrecy associated with this procedure makes respondents feel secure about answering question A (the sensitive question) truthfully.

Next, hand respondents a card with the two questions, marked A and B, written out. Tell respondents that if they picked a number between 1 and 4, they should answer question A. If they picked a number between 5 and 10, they should answer question B.

That's all there is to it. You now have the following: (a) Each respondent knows they answered "yes" or "no" and which question they answered; and (b) you know *only* that a respondent said "yes" or "no" but not which question, A or B, was being answered.

If you perform this procedure with a sufficiently large, representative sample of a population, and if respondents cooperate and answer all questions truthfully, then you can calculate the percentage of the population that answered "yes" to question A.

The percentage of people who answer "yes" to *either* A or B = (the percentage of people who answer "yes" to question A) (the percentage of times that question A is asked) + (the percentage of people who answered "yes" to question B) (the percentage of times question B is asked).

Now, the only unknown in this equation is the percentage of people who answered "yes" to question A. We know from our data the percentages of "yes" answers to *either* question. Suppose that 33% of all respondents said "yes" to *something*. Since respondents answered question A only if they chose a number from 1 to 4, then A was answered 40% of the time and B was answered 60% of the time. Whenever B was answered, there was a 50% chance of it being answered "yes" because that's the chance of getting a heads on the toss of a fair coin. The problem now reads:

$$.33 = X(.4) + (.50)(.6) \text{ or}$$

$$.33 = .4X + .30$$

which means that $X = .08$. That is, given the parameters specified in this experiment, if 33% of the sample says "yes" to either question, then 8% of the sample answered "yes" to question A.

There are two problems associated with this technique. First of all, no matter what you say or do, some informants will not believe that you can't identify them and will therefore not tell the truth. Bradburn et al. (1979) report that 35% of known offenders would not admit to having been convicted of drunken driving in a randomized response survey. Second, like all survey techniques, RR depends on large, representative samples. The RR technique is time consuming to administer, and this makes getting large, representative samples difficult.

Still, the evidence is mounting that for some sensitive questions, when you want the truth, the randomized response method is worth the effort. Scheers and Dayton (1987) gave a standard questionnaire to 194 undergraduates in a large university. The students were asked if they'd ever lied to avoid an exam, lied to avoid a term paper, purchased a term paper, obtained an illegal copy of an exam, or copied answers on an exam. Scheers and Dayton asked 184 other students the same questions, but with the second sample they used the RR method. Across all GPAs, more students admitted to these behaviors in the RR test than in the questionnaire. A lot more. The difference in the rate of admission was as high as 83% (for purchasing a term paper).

Combining Ethnographic and Survey Research

No method of data collection is perfect. Unstructured interviews and questionnaires produce different *kinds* of data, and it is up to you to decide which method, or combination of methods, is best. Survey research is generally better suited to policy research than participant observation. If you were among the scientists consulted about whether to continue the 55 MPH speed limit or the federal Head Start Program in the United States, you would hardly expect to appear before Congress armed *only* with ethnographic data from a few informants.

On the other hand, qualitative data can be a powerful asset, too. The testimony of mothers who had lost their children in traffic accidents involving alcohol was certainly instrumental in raising the legal drinking age from 18 to 21—perhaps more instrumental than the horrifying mortality statistics among teenage drivers.

Many anthropologists and sociologists combine questionnaires and ethnographic interviews in their research—and there's nothing new about doing this, either. Raymond Firth did a survey census in his work among the Tikopia in the 1930s (Firth, 1954), and M. G. Smith (1962) did a major survey study of family patterns in West Indian society. Vidich and Shapiro (1955) used participant observation and questionnaire research in their study of prestige in a small town in the United States, and Schwab conducted sample surveys during his ethnographic research on a Yoruba community in Nigeria (1954). William Foote Whyte combined both forms of data collection in his study of villages in highland Peru (Whyte & Alberti, 1983).

Recently, William Axinn and his colleagues conducted the Tamang Family Research Project about fertility, family life, and cultural change among the Tamang of Nepal (Axinn et al., 1991). They studied two communities: a remote settlement of subsistence farmers that remains self-contained and a village near Kathmandu, where education and wage labor are prevalent and where the economy is highly monetized.

The team did ethnography before developing their questionnaires and *during* the survey research part of the study. A good thing, too. In one community, they learned about a unit of social organization called the *memekhor* after launching their surveys. The memekhor defined eligible marriage partners. The memekhor of each respondent was a critical variable in this fertility study, so the researchers ran a supplemental page on aspects of the marriage process and recanvassed their respondents.

In the other community there is a local project called the Small Farmers Development Program, or SFDP. Besides giving credit to poor farmers, the SFDP also has programs that affect the use of contraceptives. Not knowing who belonged to the SFDP leads to the conclusion that wage labor has no effect on the use of contraceptives. Statistical models that include this one extra piece of data lead to exactly the opposite conclusion (ibid.:209). Once again, after the survey was launched, only ongoing ethnography led Axinn and his colleagues to understand the importance of this variable.

The combination of ethnography and survey research is hard to beat when it comes to improving the description of complex human behavior patterns and unraveling important questions about how variables interact to produce those patterns. Good survey research often depends on the development of scales. This is the subject of the next chapter.

13

Scales and Scaling

This chapter is about building and using scales. I'll focus on four kinds: (a) indexes, (b) Guttman scales, (c) Likert scales, and (d) semantic differential scales. There are other kinds of scales (Thurstone scales, direct magnitude scales), but the first four that I've listed are the most commonly used in social research today, particularly in anthropology. First, though, some basic concepts of scaling.

Scales with Single Indicators

A scale is a device for assigning units of analysis to categories of a variable. The assignment is usually done with numbers, and questions are used a lot as scaling devices. Here are three typical scaling questions:

1. "How old are you?"

You can use this question to assign individuals to categories of the variable "age." In other words, you can *scale* people by age. The number that this first question produces has ratio properties (someone who is 50 is twice as old as someone who is 25).

2. "How satisfied are you with your classes this semester? Are you satisfied, neutral, or unsatisfied?"

You can use *this* question to assign people to one of three categories of the variable "satisfied." That is, you can *scale* them according to how satisfied they are with their classes. Let satisfied = 3, neutral = 2, and unsatisfied = 1. Then, someone who is assigned the number 3 is *more* satisfied than someone who is assigned the number 1. We don't know if that means 3 times more satisfied, or 10 times, or just marginally more satisfied, so this scaling device produces numbers that have ordinal properties.

3. "Do you consider yourself to be heterosexual, bisexual, homosexual, or asexual?"

This scaling device lets you assign individuals to (scale them by) categories of the variable "sexual orientation." Let heterosexual = 1, bisexual = 2, homosexual = 3, and asexual = 4. The numbers produced by *this* device have nominal properties. You can't add them up and find the "average sexual orientation."

These three questions have different content (they tap different concepts) and they produce numbers with different properties, but they have two very important things in common. All three questions are devices for scaling people, and in all three cases the informant is the principal source of measurement error.

The units of analysis could be Girl Scout troops or court cases or cultures, and the principal source of measurement error could be you. If you do a survey and assign people by observation to the category "male" or "female," then *you* are the principal source of measurement error, and similarly if you are scaling cultures.

Suppose you have a list of 100 cultures and your job is to assign each a number that signifies whether the predominant form of postmarital residence is patrilocal, matrilocal, neolocal, bilocal, etc. For each culture you have an ethnography—a pile of 100 books. You read each book, look for clues about postmarital residence, and assign a number (1, 2, 3, etc.) to each culture. In this case, each culture is a unit of analysis and is scaled on the nominal variable called "postmarital residence."

Scales with Multiple Indicators

You can see that even a single question on a questionnaire acts like a scale if it lets you assign the people (or groups or artifacts) you're studying to categories of a variable. The problem is, many of the most interesting variables in social science are complex and can't easily be assessed with single indicators. We try to measure complex variables with complex instruments—that is, instruments that are made up of several indicators.

These instruments are what we usually call scales. A classic social science concept is *socioeconomic status* or SES. It is often measured by combining measures of income, education and occupational prestige. Each of these measures is an operationalization of the concept SES, but none of the measures, by itself, captures the complexity of the idea of socioeconomic status. Each indicator captures a piece of the concept, and together the indicators produce a single measurement of SES.

Now, by Ockham's razor, we would never use a complex scale to measure something when a simple scale will do. Suppose you ask people some questions designed to find out how they feel about growing old. If their income alone predicts their responses to the growing-old attitude questions, then there's no point in making the scale more complex. Often, though, a complex measure of SES predicts attitudes better than single indicators do.

One more time, then: The function of *single-indicator measures* is to assign units of analysis to categories of a variable. The function of *composite measures* (complex scales) is exactly the same, but they are used when single indicators won't do the job.

Indexes

The simplest composite measure is a *cumulative index*. These are made up of several items, all of which count the same. Multiple-choice exams are cumulative indexes. The idea is that asking just one question about the material in a course would not be a good indicator of students' knowledge of the material. Instead, students are typically asked 50 or 60 or more multiple-choice questions.

Taken together, the reasoning goes, all the questions measure how well a student has mastered the body of material. If you take a test that has 60 multiple-choice questions and you get 45 correct, you get 45 points, 1 for each correct answer. That number, 45 (or 75%), is a cumulative index of how well you did on the test.

Note that in a cumulative index, it makes no difference *which* items are assigned to you. In a test of 6 questions, for example, there are 6 ways to get 1 right, but there are 15 ways to get 2 right, 20 ways to get 3 right, and so on. Students can get the same score of 80% on a test of 100 questions and miss entirely different sets of 20 questions. On the one hand, this makes cumulative indexes robust; they provide many ways to get at an underlying variable (in the case of an exam, the underlying variable is competence.) On the other hand, this is also the weakness of cumulative indexes. Here's why.

Suppose you're studying acculturation among Bolivian Indians. If you think that Indians who speak Spanish are more acculturated than those who don't, you'd give them one point for speaking the dominant language. If you think that Indians who wear Western-style clothing are more acculturated than those who wear traditional dress, you'd give them another acculturation point.

If you think that Indians who live in modern houses are more acculturated than those living in traditional houses, you'd give them still another. You can make up indexes with observational variables (like seeing what kind of clothing people wear or whether they speak a particular language), or with attitudinal ones (like asking people whether they agree or disagree with some statement).

Just stringing together a series of items to form an index, however, does not mean that the composite measure will be useful, any more than stringing together a series of multiple-choice questions will fairly test a student's knowledge of anthropology. Is an Indian who dresses in Western clothing and who lives in a Western-type house but doesn't speak Spanish more or less acculturated than one who speaks Spanish and dresses in Western clothing but lives in a traditional house? One way to tell is to see if the data to form a *Guttman scale*.

Guttman Scales

In a Guttman scale, as compared to a cumulative index, the measurements for the items have a distinct pattern. To understand the pattern we're looking for, consider the following three questions.

TABLE 13.1

An Example of an Index that Scales with a Guttman Coefficient of
Reproducibility Greater Than 0.90

Informant	Western-Type House	Speak Spanish	Western-Style Clothing
1	+	+	+
2	+	+	+
3	+	+	+
4	+	+	+
5	−	+	+
6	−	+	+
7	−	+	+
8	−	−	+
9	−	−	+
10	−	−	+
11	−	−	−
12	−	−	−
13	−	+	(−) error
14	−	+	(−) error
15	+	+	(−) error
16	+	+	(−) error

NOTE: An example of an index that scales with a Guttman coefficient of reproducibility greater than .90. There are 4 scaling errors out of a possible 48 entries (16 informants $\times$ 3 index items = 48). The coefficient of reproducibility is .92 $(1 - 4/48 = .92)$.

1. How much is 124 plus 14?
2. How much is $\frac{1}{2} + \frac{1}{3} + \frac{1}{5} + \frac{2}{11}$?
3. If $3X = 133$, then how much is X?

If you know the answer to question 3, you probably know the answer to questions 1 and 2. If you know the answer to question 2, but not to 3, it's still safe to assume that you know the answer to question 1.

Similarly, if *all* informants in a Bolivian village who occupy modern houses also speak Spanish and dress in Western-style clothes, you need only determine the kind of house an Indian informant lives in and you can fill in the data for the other two variables. Table 13.1 shows visually what the pattern looks like for data on 16 informants regarding the three items in the hypothetical index of acculturation.

The data for the first 12 informants in Table 13.1 form a perfect scale. Informants 1, 2, 3, and 4 score positive on all three items. The next three informants speak Spanish and wear Western-style clothing but live in traditional houses. The next three wear Western-style clothing but speak only their Indian language and live in traditional houses. Informants 11 and 12 are totally unacculturated according to this index: They wear traditional dress, speak only their Indian language, and live in traditional houses.

From these data, it is apparent that living in a Western-style house is the most difficult item to achieve in the index. By the time someone can afford to build such a house, they must already speak Spanish and wear Western clothing. By contrast, it is easy for someone to adopt Western clothing without learning Spanish or living in a Western-style house.

There are four informants who break the pattern. Informants 13 and 14 speak Spanish but wear traditional clothing and live in traditional houses. Perhaps they learned Spanish in the markets but otherwise live unacculturated lives. Informants 15 and 16 are affluent; they live in modern houses, and speak Spanish but wear traditional clothing. Perhaps they have achieved sufficient wealth to build modern houses but want to make a statement about their Indianness by wearing traditional costume.

Whatever the reasons, informants 13, 14, 15, and 16 do not conform to the pattern seen in the majority of cases. These informants cause "errors" in the sense that their data diminish the extent to which the index of acculturation forms a perfect scale. You can test how closely any set of index data reproduces a perfect scale by applying Guttman's *coefficient of reproducibility*, or CR.

$$1 - (\text{No. Errors/No. Entries})$$

Given the pattern in Table 13.1, we don't expect to see those minus signs in column 3 for informants 13, 14, 15, and 16, so we count them as errors in the attempt to reproduce a perfect scale. For Table 13.1 the CR is

$$1 - (4/48) = .92$$

which is to say that the data come within 8% of scaling perfectly. By convention, a coefficient of reproducibility of .90 or greater is accepted as a significant approximation of a perfect scale (Guttman, 1950).

How to Test for a Guttman Scale

Robert Carneiro (1962, 1970) had an idea that cultural evolution is orderly and cumulative. If Carneiro is right, then cultures evolve by adding certain traits in an orderly way and should show a Guttman-scale-like pattern. Carneiro coded 100 cultures for 354 traits and looked at the pattern. Here is a sample of 12 societies and 11 traits.

TABLE 13.2(a)

Carneiro's Matrix Showing the Presence (+) or Absence (−)
of 11 Culture Traits Among 12 Societies.
The Order of Both the Traits and the Societies is Random

	Iroquois	Marquesans	Tasmanians	Yahgan	Dahomey	Mundurucú	Ao Naga	Inca	Semang	Tanala	Vedda	Bontoc
Political leader has considerable authority	+	+	−	−	+	−	−	+	−	+	−	−
Sumptuary laws	−	−	−	−	+	−	−	+	−	−	−	−
Headman, chief, or king	+	+	−	−	+	+	+	+	−	+	+	+
Surplus of food regularly produced	+	+	−	−	+	−	−	+	−	+	−	+
Trade between communities	+	+	−	+	+	+	+	+	−	+	+	+
Ruler grants audiences	−	+	−	−	+	−	−	+	−	+	−	−
Special religious practitioners	+	+	−	+	+	+	+	+	+	+	+	+
Paved streets	−	−	−	−	−	−	−	+	−	−	−	−
Agriculture provides 75% + of subsistence	+	+	−	−	+	−	+	+	−	+	−	+
Full-time service specialists	−	+	−	−	+	−	−	+	−	−	−	−
Settlements of 100+ persons	+	+	−	−	+	+	+	+	−	+	−	+

SOURCE: Carneiro R. C. (1970), Scale analysis, evolutionary sequences, and the rating of cultures. In R. Naroll & R. Cohen (Eds.), *A handbook of method in cultural anthropology,* p. 830. Reprinted with permission of Doubleday, a division of Bantam, Doubleday, Dell Publishing Group, Inc.

TABLE 13.2(b)

The Data in Table 13.2(a) Rearranged.
The Data Form a Perfect Guttman Scale

	Tasmanians	Semang	Yahgan	Vedda	Mundurucú	Ao Naga	Bontoc	Iroquois	Tanala	Marquesans	Dahomey	Inca
Paved streets	−	−	−	−	−	−	−	−	−	−	−	+
Sumptuary laws	−	−	−	−	−	−	−	−	−	−	+	+
Full-time service specialists	−	−	−	−	−	−	−	−	−	+	+	+
Ruler grants audiences	−	−	−	−	−	−	−	−	+	+	+	+
Political leader has considerable authority	−	−	−	−	−	−	−	+	+	+	+	+
Surplus of food regularly produced	−	−	−	−	−	−	+	+	+	+	+	+
Agriculture provides 75% + of subsistence	−	−	−	−	−	+	+	+	+	+	+	+
Settlements of 100+ persons	−	−	−	−	+	+	+	+	+	+	+	+
Headman, chief, or king	−	−	−	+	+	+	+	+	+	+	+	+
Trade between communities	−	−	+	+	+	+	+	+	+	+	+	+
Special religious practitioners	−	+	+	+	+	+	+	+	+	+	+	+

SOURCE: Carneiro R. C. (1970), Scale analysis, evolutionary sequences, and the rating of cultures. In R. Naroll & R. Cohen (Eds.), *A handbook of method in cultural anthropology,* p. 830. Reprinted with permission of Doubleday, a division of Bantam, Doubleday, Dell Publishing Group, Inc.

When you collect data on cases, you don't know what (if any) pattern will emerge, so you pretty much grab cases and code them for traits in random order. The 12 societies and traits in Table 13.2(a) are in random order.

The first thing to do is arrange the pluses and minuses in their "best" possible order—the order that conforms most to the perfect Guttman scale—and compute the CR. We look for the trait that occurs most frequently (the one with the most pluses across the row) and place that one at the bottom of the matrix. The most frequently occurring trait is the existence of special religious practitioners. Then we look for the next-most-frequent trait and put it on the next-to-the-bottom row of the matrix.

We keep doing this until we rearrange the data to take advantage of whatever underlying pattern is hiding in the matrix. The best arrangement of the pluses and minuses is shown in Table 13.2(b). Now we can count up the "errors" in the matrix and compute Guttman's coefficient of reproducibility. For these 12 societies and 11 traits, the coefficient is a perfect 1.0.

Of course, it's one thing to find this kind of blatant pattern in a matrix of 12 societies and 11 traits. Carneiro, you'll recall, coded 100 societies for 354 traits and then went looking for subsets of the data that showed the desired pattern. When Carneiro did this in the 1960s, it was rather heroic work. Today, ANTHROPAC (Borgatti, 1992a) has a routine for looking at big matrices of pluses and minuses, rearranging the entries into the best pattern, calculating the CR, and showing you which units of analysis and traits to drop in order to find the optimal solution to the problem.

De Walt (1979) used Guttman scaling to test his index of material style of life in a Mexican farming community. He scored 54 informants on whether they possessed eight material items (a radio, a stove, a sewing machine, etc.) and achieved a remarkable CR of .95. This means that, *for his data*, the index of material style of life is highly reliable and differentiates among informants.

An index must be checked for its Guttman scalability each time it is used on a population. My hunch is that De Walt's material-style-of-life scale has its analog in nearly all societies. The particular list of items that De Walt used in Mexico may not scale in a village in Cameroon, but *some* list of material items *will* scale there. You just have to find them.

The way to do this is to code every household for the presence or absence of a list of material items. The particular list will emerge from participant observation and from informal interviews. Then use a program like AN-THROPAC to sort out the matrix, drop some material items, and build the material index that has a CR of 0.90 or better.

Indexes That Don't Scale

Indexes that do not scale can still be useful in comparing populations. Dennis Werner (1985) studied psychosomatic stress among Brazilian farmers who were facing the uncertainty of having their lands flooded by a major dam. He used a 20-item stress index developed by Berry (1976).

Since the index did not constitute a scale, Werner could not differentiate among his informants (in terms of the amount of stress they were under) as precisely as De Walt could differentiate among *his* informants (in terms of their quality of life). But farmers in Werner's sample gave a stress response to an average of 9.13 questions on the 20-item test, while Berry found that Canadian farmers gave stress responses on an average of 1.79 questions. It is very unlikely that a difference of such magnitude between two *populations* would occur by chance.

Unidimensionality

If the items in a cumulative index form a Guttman scale with 0.90 CR or better, we can say that, for the sample we've tested, the concept measured by the index is *unidimensional*. That is, the items are a composite measure of one, and only one, underlying concept. Carneiro's index shows that, for the 12 cultures he studied, cultural evolution is a unidimensional concept (at least as it's operationalized by the indicators that Carneiro chose). De Walt's data show that, for the informants he studied, the concept of "material style of life" is unidimensional (at least for the indicators he used).

I want to make it absolutely clear that the unidimensionality of an index is sample dependent. The Guttman technique is a way to test whether unidimensionality holds for a particular set of data.

Likert Scales

Perhaps the most commonly used form of scaling is attributed to Renis Likert (1932). Likert introduced the ever-popular 5-point scale that we talked about in Chapter 12 on questionnaire construction. Recall that a typical question might read as follows: "Please consider the following statements carefully. After each statement, circle the answer that most reflects your opinion. Would you say you agree a lot with the statement, agree a little, are neutral, disagree a little, or disagree a lot with each statement?"

The 5-point scale might become 3 points or 7 points, and the agree-disagree scale might become approve-disapprove, favor-oppose, or excellent-bad, but the principle is the same. These are all Likert scales.

Likert did more than just introduce a format. He was interested in measuring internal states of people attitudes, emotions, and orientations, and he realized that most inner states are multidimensional. He wanted a way to tease apart the various dimensions. "Political orientation," for example, is anything but unidimensional. It has an economic dimension, a domestic policy dimension, a foreign policy dimension, and what we might label a "personal behavior" dimension.

A person who is fiscally liberal on matters of domestic policy (favoring government-supported health care, for example) may be quite conservative on matters of foreign policy (against involvement in foreign military actions under almost any circumstances). Someone who is liberal on matters of foreign policy (favoring economic aid for all democracies that ask for it) may be quite conservative on matters of personal behavior (against equal protection under the law for homosexuals).

Furthermore, even an underlying dimension like "attitude on matters of personal behavior" is complicated. We could not assign people to a category of this variable by asking one question. We might have to ask where people stand on sexual preference, on abortion, on divorce, on extramarital sex. Taken all together, the indicators may be a better measure of the variable "attitude toward matters of personal behavior."

Of course, there are tendencies and packaging effects. People who are conservative on one dimension of political orientation are *likely* to be conservative on other dimensions, and people who are liberal on one kind of personal behavior are likely to be liberal on others. Still, no single question lets you scale people in general on a variable as complex as "attitude toward personal behavior," let alone "political orientation."

Steps in Building a Likert Scale

Likert's method was to take a long list of possible scaling items for a concept and find the subsets that measured the various dimensions. If the concept were unidimensional, then one subset would do. If it were multidimensional, then several subsets would be needed. Here are the steps in building and testing a Likert scale.

1. Identify and label the variable you want to measure. This is generally done by induction from your own experience (Spector, 1992:13). After you work in a community for a while, you'll develop some ideas about the

variables you want to measure. Your informants may impress you with the idea that "people are afraid of crime," and you decide to scale people on the variable "fear of crime."

You may observe that some people seem very modern while others seem traditional. The task is then to scale (measure) people on the variable "traditional" with all its multidimensionality. (The other way to identify variables is by deduction. This generally involves analyzing similarity matrices, about which more in Chapter 19.)

2. Write a long list of indicator questions or statements. This is another exercise in induction. Ideas for the indicators can come from ethnography, from reading newspapers, or from interviews with expert informants.

They can also come from a free-listing exercise. If you want to build a scaling device for the concept of "attitudes toward growing old," you might start by asking a large group of people to "list things that you associate with growing old." You could build the questions or statements in a Likert scale around the items in the list.

If you've been doing ethnography in a community for several months, you'll have plenty of intuition to guide you in writing indicator items for a Likert scale. Be sure to use both negative and positive indicators. If you have a statement like "Life in Xakalornga has improved since the missionaries came," then you need a negatively worded statement for balance, like "The missionaries have caused a lot of problems in our community."

And don't make the indicator items extreme. Here's a badly worded item: "The coming of the missionaries is the most terrible thing that has ever happened here." The idea is to let your informants tell *you* where they stand by giving them a range of response choices (strongly agree— strongly disagree). Don't bludgeon informants with such strongly worded items that they feel forced to reduce the strength of their response.

In wording items, all the cautions from Chapter 12 on questionnaire design apply: Remember who your informants are and use *their* language. Make the items as short and as uncomplicated as possible. No double negatives. No double-barreled items. "People should speak Spanish and give up their native language" is a terrible item. An informant can agree with both parts, or agree with one and disagree with the other.

When you get through, you should have four or five times the number of items as you think you'll need in your final scale. If you want a scale of, say, 6 items, use 25 or 30 items in the first test (DeVellis, 1991:57).

3. Determine the type and number of response categories. Some popular response categories are agree-disagree, favor-oppose, helpful-not helpful,

many-none, like me-not like me, true-untrue, suitable-unsuitable, always-never, and so on. Most Likert scale items have an odd number of response choices: three, five, or seven. The idea is to give people a range of choices that includes a midpoint. The midpoint usually carries the idea of neutrality—neither agree nor disagree, for example. An even number of response choices forces informants to "take a stand," while an odd number of choices lets informants "sit on the fence." There is no best format. The choice of either format has its own consequences.

4. Test your item pool on some informants. Ideally, you need at least 100 respondents to test an initial pool of items. In fact, anthropologists working in rural communities often make do with just 20 or 30 respondents, but this is certainly not ideal because you can't be sure you've tapped the range of responses with so few informants.

If you are working in an urban area and if your resources permit, get the 100 or even 200 respondents that you need for the initial test (Spector, 1992:29). This will ensure that you capture the full variation in responses to all your items. If you can select 100 to 200 respondents at random, you'll also ensure that the response variability represents the variability in the general population to which you eventually want to apply your scale.

5. Conduct an item analysis to find the items that form a unidimensional scale of the variable you're trying to measure.

6. Use your scale in your study and run the item analysis again to make sure that the scale is holding up. If it does, then look for relationships between the scale scores and the scores of other variables for persons in your study.

Item Analysis

This is the key to building scales. The idea is to find out which, among the many items you're testing, need to be kept and which should be thrown away. The set of items that you keep should tap a single social or psychological dimension. In other words, the scale should be unidimensional.

In the next few pages, I'm going to walk through the logic of building scales that are unidimensional. Read these pages very carefully. At the end of this section, I'll advocate using factor analysis to do the item analysis quickly, easily, and reliably. No fair, though, using factor analysis for scale construction until you understand the logic of scale construction itself.

There are three steps to doing an item analysis and finding a subset of items that constitute a unidimensional scale: (a) scoring the items, (b) taking the interitem correlation, and (c) taking the item-total correlation.

1. Scoring the Responses

The first thing to do is make sure that all the items are properly scored. Assume that we're trying to find items for a scale that measures the strength of support for formal training in research methods among anthropology students. Here are two potential scale items:

Training in statistics should be required for all students of anthropology.

1	2	3	4	5
Strongly disagree	Disagree	Neutral	Agree	Strongly agree

Anthropologists do not need training in statistics.

1	2	3	4	5
Strongly disagree	Disagree	Neutral	Agree	Strongly agree

When you go to score informants' responses, you need to remember that a 1 on the first item is a 5 on the second, and vice versa. Informants who circle "strongly agree" on the first item get a 5 for that item. Informants who circle "strongly agree" on the second item get scored as 1. You can let the big and small numbers stand for any direction you want, but you must be consistent. In this case, I've decided to let the bigger numbers (4 and 5) represent support for training in formal research methods and the smaller numbers (1 and 2) represent lack of support for that concept.

2. Taking the Interitem Correlation and Cronbach's Alpha

Next, test to see which items contribute to measuring the construct you're trying to get at, and which don't. This involves two calculations: the intercorrelation of the items and the correlation of the item scores with the total scores for each informant. Here are the scores for three people on three items, where the items are scored from 1-5.

	item 1	item 2	item 3
person 1	1	3	5
person 2	5	2	2
person 3	4	1	3

To find the interitem correlation, we would look at all pairs of columns. There are three possible pairs of columns for a three-item matrix:

item 1	item 2	item 1	item 3	item 2	item 3
1	3	1	5	3	5
5	2	5	2	2	2
4	1	4	3	1	3

A simple measure of how much these pairs of numbers are alike or unalike is to add up their differences. In the first pair, the difference between 1 and 3 is 2; the difference between 5 and 2 is 3; the difference between 4 and 1 is 3. The sum of the differences is $2 + 3 + 3 = 8$. For each item, there could be as much as a 4-point difference—someone could have answered 1 to item 1 and 5 to item 2, for example.

For three items, the total possible difference would be $4 \times 3 = 12$. The actual difference is $8/12 = 0.67$, which means that these two items are 0.33 alike. Items 1 and 3 are also 0.33 alike, and items 2 and 3 are 0.67 alike.

Items that measure the same underlying construct should be related to one another. If I answer "strongly agree" to the statement "training in statistics should be required for all students of anthropology," then (if I'm consistent in my attitude and if the items that tap my attitude are properly worded) I should strongly disagree with the statement that "anthropologists do not need training in statistics." If everyone who answers "strongly agree" to the first statement answers "strongly disagree" to the second, then the items are perfectly correlated.

Cronbach's alpha is a statistical test of how well the items in a scale are correlated with one another. One of the methods for testing the unidimensionality of a scale is called the split-half reliability test. If a scale of, say, 10 items, were undimensional, all the items would be measuring parts of the same underlying concept. In that case any 5 items should produce scores that are more or less like the scores of any other 5 items. Like this:

	score on items 1-5	score on items 6-10
person 1	X_1	Y_1
person 2	X_2	Y_2

person 3	X_3	Y_3
.		
.		
.		
person N	X_n	Y_n
Total	A	B

There are many ways to split a group of items into halves, and each split will give you a different set of totals. On average, though, the totals for all possible split-half tests should be fairly similar. Cronbach's coefficient alpha tests this.

The formula for Cronbach's alpha is

$$\alpha = N\rho/[1 + \rho(N - 1)]$$

where ρ is the mean interitem correlation. The Greek letter ρ (called rho) in the formula stands for the average correlation among all pairs of items being tested.

By convention, a good set of scale items should have a Cronbach's alpha of 0.80 or higher. Be warned, though, that if you have a long list of scale items, the chances are good of getting a high alpha coefficient. An interitem correlation of just .14 produces an alpha of .80 in a set of 25 items (DeVellis, 1991:92).

Eventually, you want an alpha coefficient of 0.80 or higher for a *short* list of items, all of which hang together and measure the same thing. Cronbach's alpha will tell you if your scale hangs together, but it won't tell you which items to throw away and which to keep. To do that, you need to identify the items that do not discriminate between people who score high and people who score low on the total set of items.

3. Finding the Item-Total Correlation

First, find the total score for each person. Add up each respondent's scores across all the items. Suppose there are 50 items in your item pool, and you test those items on 200 people. Your data will look like this:

	item 1	item 2	item 3	. . .	item 50
person 1	x	x	x		x
person 2	x	x	x		x
person 3	x	x	x		x
.	.	.	.		.
.	.	.	.		.
.	.	.	.		.
person 200	x	x	x		x

where the x's are the scores for each person on each item. For 50 items, scored from 1 to 5, each person could get a score as low as 50 (by getting a score of 1 on each item) or as high as 250 (by getting a score of 5 on each item). In practice, of course, each respondent in a survey will get a total score somewhere in between.

A rough and ready way to find the items that discriminate well among respondents is to divide the respondents into two groups, the 25% with the highest total scores and the 25% with the lowest total scores. Look for the items that the two groups have in common. Those items are not discriminating among informants with regard to the concept being tested. Items that fail, for example, to discriminate between people who strongly favor training in methods (the top 25%) and people who don't (the bottom 25%) are not good items for scaling people in this construct. Throw them out.

There is a more formal way to find the items that discriminate well among respondents and the items that don't. This is the item-total correlation. Here are the data you need for this:

	total score	item 1	item 2	item 3	...
person 1					
person 2					
person 3					
.					
.					
.					

With 50 items, the total score gives you an idea of where each person stands on the concept you're trying to measure. If the interitem correlation were perfect, then every item would be contributing equally to our understanding of where each respondent stands. Of course, some items do better than others. The ones that don't contribute a lot will correlate poorly with the total score for each person. Keep the items that have the highest correlation with the total scores.

You can use any statistical analysis package to find the interitem correlations, the alpha coefficient, and the item-total correlations for a set of preliminary scale items. Your goal is to get rid of items that detract from a high interitem correlation and to keep the alpha coefficient above 0.80. For an excellent, step-by-step explanation of item analysis on a real social research scale, see Spector (1992:43-46).

Testing for Unidimensionality with Factor Analysis

Factor analysis is a technique for data reduction. (See Chapter 20 for a brief introduction to factor analysis, and Comrey, 1992, for more coverage.) If you have 30 items in a pool of potential scale items, and responses from a sample of people to those pool items, factor analysis lets you reduce the 30 items to a smaller set—say, 2 or 3 or 4. Each item is given a score, called its factor loading. This tells you how much each item "belongs" to each of the underlying factors.

Many professional scale developers today routinely use factor analysis to test for unidimensionality in Likert scales. If a scale is unidimensional, there will be a single, overwhelming factor that underlies all the variables (items) and all the items will "load high" on that single factor. Scale developers get a large pool of potential scale items (at least 40), ask a lot of people (at least 200) to respond to the items, run the factor analysis, and select those items that load high on the factor (the underlying concept) they are trying to understand.

I expect that with easy-to-use computer programs now making light work of factor analysis, most scale development in the future will use this and similar methods. You can use any full-featured statistical package to factor analyze a matrix of responses to a set of scale items. ANTHROPAC (Borgatti, 1992a) contains a program for testing the unidimensionality of a set of Likert scale items.

If you want to see what professional scale developers do, consult any of the following recent articles: Koeske and Koeske (1989) (a scale for measuring job burnout), Morris et al. (1990) (a scale for self-assessment by old people on seven dimensions), Gatz and Hurwicz (1990) (a scale that measures depression in old people), Heatherton and Polivy (1991) (a scale that measures self-esteem), Simpson and Gangstad (1991) (a scale that measures willingness to engage in uncommitted sexual relations), and Handwerker (1994) (a scale developed in Barbados for measuring family violence).

Margo-Lea Hurwicz and Penn Handwerker (two of the authors listed above) are anthropologists, by the way. Most anthropologists won't develop major scales for others to use. What they *will* do (and should do), is test the unidimensionality of the measures in their own field data, using the techniques of scale development that I've laid out here.

Semantic Differential

I've always liked the semantic differential scaling method. It was developed in the 1950s by Charles Osgood and his associates at the University of Illinois and has become an important research tool in psychology (Osgood et al., 1957; Snider & Osgood, 1969). I counted 377 articles and book chapters where the method was used in 1992.

The semantic differential is particularly suited for anthropological research: It's easy to construct a semantic differential test for any culture; the test is easy to administer, even to marginally literate informants; and the results are intuitively easy to interpret.

Osgood was interested in how people interpreted things—inanimate things (like artifacts or monuments), animate things (like persons, or the self), behaviors (like incest, or buying a new car or shooting a deer), and intangible concepts (like gun control or literacy). Of course, this is exactly what Likert scales are designed to test. Osgood's tested people's feelings by giving them a target item and a list of paired adjectives about the target. The adjective pairs could come from ethnographic interviews.

Figure 13.1 is an example of a semantic differential test. The target is the concept of "statistics in anthropology." If you were taking this test right now, you'd be asked to place a check on each line, depending on your reaction to each pair of adjectives.

Statistics in anthropology:

Good	├──┼──┼──┼──┼──┼──┼──┤	Bad
	1 2 3 4 5 6 7	
Active	├──┼──┼──┼──┼──┼──┼──┤	Passive
Difficult	├──┼──┼──┼──┼──┼──┼──┤	Easy
Permanent	├──┼──┼──┼──┼──┼──┼──┤	Impermanent
Warm	├──┼──┼──┼──┼──┼──┼──┤	Cold
Ethical	├──┼──┼──┼──┼──┼──┼──┤	Corrupt
Beautiful	├──┼──┼──┼──┼──┼──┼──┤	Ugly
Strong	├──┼──┼──┼──┼──┼──┼──┤	Weak
Reassuring	├──┼──┼──┼──┼──┼──┼──┤	Unsettling
Important	├──┼──┼──┼──┼──┼──┼──┤	Trivial
Fast	├──┼──┼──┼──┼──┼──┼──┤	Slow
Clean	├──┼──┼──┼──┼──┼──┼──┤	Dirty
Exciting	├──┼──┼──┼──┼──┼──┼──┤	Boring
Useful	├──┼──┼──┼──┼──┼──┼──┤	Useless

Figure 13.1. A semantic differential scale to test how anthropologists feel about statistics. The dimensions in this scale are useful for measuring how people in various cultures feel about many different things.

With a Likert scale, you ask informants a series of questions that get at the target concept. In a semantic differential scale, you name the target concept and ask informants to rate their feelings toward it on a series of variables. The semantic differential is usually a 7-point scale, as I've indicated in the first adjective pair above. You can leave out the numbers and let informants respond to the visual form of the scale. Your score on this test would be the sum of all your answers to the 14 adjective pairs.

Osgood and his associates did hundreds of replications of this test, using hundreds of adjective pairs, in 26 different cultures. Their factor analyses showed that in every culture there are three major kinds of adjectives. The most important (the ones that account for most of the variation in people's responses) are adjectives of evaluation (good-bad, difficult-easy), followed by adjectives of potency (strong-weak, dominant-submissive, etc.), and of activity (fast-slow, active-inactive, sedentary-mobile, etc.).

In the semantic differential test above, you could substitute the phrase "late twentieth-century America," or "like me," or "abortion on demand," or "land reform" for "statistics in anthropology." As the target changes, of course, you have to make sure that the adjective pairs make sense. The adjective pair indoor-outdoor works for lots of targets (kinds of music, hobbies, even famous persons), but it may not be appropriate for others (like the concept of statistics in anthropology.).

Other Scales

There are many interesting variations in the construction of scales. Hadley Cantril (1965) devised a 10-rung *ladder of life,* shown in Figure 13.2. Informants are asked to name their concerns in life (financial success, healthy children, freedom from war, and so on). They are told that the bottom rung of the ladder represents the worst possible situation, while the top rung represents the best. For each of their concerns they are asked to point out where they are on the ladder right now, where they were 5 years ago, and where they think they'll be 5 years from now.

The ladder of life is a self-anchoring scale. Respondents are asked to explain, in their own terms, what the top and bottom rungs of the ladder mean—that is, what the worst and best outcomes in life might be.

Art Hansen and Lucia McSpadden (1993) used this technique in their studies of Zambian and Ethiopian refugees. In Zambia, Hansen actually constructed a small wooden ladder to use as a prop and found that the method worked well, even with nonliterate informants. McSpadden used several methods to explore how Ethiopian refugees adjusted to life in the

Figure 13.2. The ladder of life.

SOURCE: From *The Pattern of Human Concerns* by Hadley Cantril. Copyright © 1965 by Rutgers, The State University. Reprinted by permission of Rutgers University Press.

United States. Even when other methods failed, McSpadden found that the ladder of life method got people to talk about their experiences, fears, and hopes (ibid.).

Another interesting device is Andrews and Withey's faces scale (1976), shown in Figure 13.3. It's a 7-point scale with stylized faces that change from joy to gloom. Informants are told: "Here are some faces expressing various feelings. Which face comes closest to how you feel about _____?" You can give informants a list of items for this scale. Try using this scale with a list of well-known political figures as the cues, just to get a feel for how interesting it is.

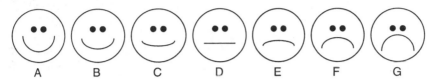

Figure 13.3. The faces scale.
SOURCE: Andrews and Withey (1976:Appendix A, p. 13). Used with permission.

There are thousands of published scales. Whatever you're interested in, the chances are good that someone has developed and tested a scale to measure it. Of course, scales are not automatically portable. A scale that measures emotional stress among Barbadian women may not measure emotional stress among Ghanaian men.

Still, it makes sense to seek out any published scales on variables you're studying. You may be able to adapt the scales to your needs, or you may get ideas for building and testing an alternative scale. Just because scales are not perfectly transportable across time and cultures doesn't mean those scales are useless to you. For a start on looking for scales that you can adapt, consult Delbert Miller's *Handbook of Research Design and Social Measurement* (D. Miller, 1991).

14

Direct, Reactive Observation

Interviewing people gets at information about their attitudes and values and what they think they do. When you want to know what people actually *do*, however, there is no substitute for watching them or studying the traces their behavior leaves behind.

There are two general strategies for observing behavior: (a) You can be obvious and reactive, or (b) you can be unobtrusive and nonreactive. In reactive observation, people know that you are watching them and may play to their audience—you. Thus, there is always a danger in reactive observation that you will record what people want you to see, and not the behavior that goes on when you're not there.

This is one reason why participant observation is so important; once you've built up rapport and trust in a field situation, people are less likely to change their behavior when you're around. Even if they do change their behavior, you're more likely to notice the change and take that fact into account.

Nonreactive, or *unobtrusive observation* is a strategy for studying people's behavior without their knowing it. This eliminates the problem of informants playing to the audience, but it can involve serious ethical problems. I will discuss these ethics issues at length in the next chapter. In this chapter I will focus on direct, reactive observation, including *continuous monitoring* and *spot sampling* of behavior.

Continuous Monitoring

In continuous monitoring, or CM, you watch a subject, or group of subjects and record their behavior as faithfully as possible. The technique was developed in the field of management and is widely used today in all the behavioral sciences, including anthropology. The earliest example of continuous monitoring is attributed to Charles Babbage, the nineteenth-century mathematician who invented the computer. He studied the behavior of workers in a factory and determined that a pound of number 11 pins (5,546 of them) should take exactly 7.6892 hours to make (Niebel, 1982:4).

In 1911, F. B. Gilbreth studied bricklayers. He looked at things like where masons set up their pile of bricks and how far they had to reach in order to retrieve each brick. From these studies, he was able to make recommendations on how to lessen worker fatigue, increase morale, and raise productivity through conservation of motion. Before Gilbreth, the standard in the trade was 120 bricks per hour. After Gilbreth published, the standard reached 350 bricks per hour (ibid.:24).

CM is still used in assessing work situations (Chadsey-Rusch & Gonzalez, 1988) and has become a common method of data collection in many fields. It is used in clinical psychology for evaluating behavioral disorders (Cone & Foster, 1982; Fassnacht, 1982; Foster & Cone, 1986; Hartmann & Wood, 1990). Organizational researchers use CM to evaluate the performance of professionals such as teachers and lawyers in actual classroom and courtroom settings (Everton & Green, 1986; Mileski, 1971; Rosenshine & Furst, 1973), and for assessing employee-employer interactions (Sproull, 1981; Weick, 1985).

Educational researchers use CM to study teacher-pupil interaction (Guilmet, 1979) and children's behavior (Raver & Peterson, 1988), and it is at the core of animal ethology studies (Hutt & Hutt, 1970; Lehner, 1979; Sullivan, 1990). In sociology and social psychology, continuous monitoring in the field has been used to study police-civilian interactions (Black & Reiss, 1967; Reiss, 1971; McCall, 1978; Sykes & Brent, 1983), how people eat (Stunkard & Kaplan, 1977), and how people use architectural space (Bechtel, 1977).

Direct, continuous observation of people is hard, often boring work, but when you want to know what people do, and won't settle for what they say they do, it's worth the effort. I don't want to give the impression that direct observation data are automatically accurate. Lots of things can clobber the accuracy of directly observed behavior. Observers may be biased by their own expectations of what they are looking for or by expectations about the behavior of women or men or any ethnic group (Kent et al., 1977; Repp et al., 1988).

While it may be impossible to eliminate observer bias entirely, there is lots and lots of evidence that training helps make people better—more reliable and more accurate—observers (Kent et al., 1977; Hartmann & Wood, 1990). We do the best we can. Just because a "perfectly aseptic environment is impossible," said Clifford Geertz, doesn't mean we "might as well conduct surgery in a sewer" (1973:30).

Many researchers record their observations on tape. This has a lot of advantages: It's a lot less tedious than writing; it lets you focus your eyes on what's going on; it lets you record a lot of detail that might be left out of a written description; it avoids the limitations of a check list; and it lets you get information on about context as well as about the behavior you're studying ("Alex is chopping wood; the dog gets in his way and he gives it a gentle kick; it's about 20 degrees outside but Alex has taken his coat off and is sweating from the heavy labor. . . .")

CM, especially using a tape recorder, generates a *lot* of data, much of it qualitative and contextual. I mentioned in Chapter 7 that John Roberts and a native Zuni interpreter studied three Zuni households and one Zuni sheep camp over a period of 5 days in 1951. Roberts and his assistant took turns sitting in one of the rooms, dictating their observations into a tape recorder. That recorder was the size of a suitcase and weighed 30 pounds (Roberts, personal communication). But 5 days of observation produced over 75,000 words of description, enough for an entire book (Roberts, 1965). Figure 14.1 shows excerpts from Roberts's work.

Coding Continuous Monitoring Data

Go to a shopping mall and record the interaction behavior of 30 mother-child pairs for 5 minutes each. Record carefully the number of children each mother has and her interaction with each child. Try to find out whether interaction patterns are predictable from (a) the number of children a mother has to cope with, (b) the ages of the children, (c) the socioeconomic class or ethnicity of the family, or (d) some other factors.

0940

E1DaE1So9 is dressed in blue denim overalls and blue denim shirt. FaSiSoSo is wearing a cotton shirt, heavy trousers, jacket and oxfords. The girls are wearing dresses, socks, and shoes. 2Da24 has on a blouse, skirt, green socks, and oxfords.

0941-(FaSiSo37D)

YoDaSo1 came into SCR from ESCR carrying a little toy in his hand.

0945-(FaSiSo37d)

I intended going to the buck herd today to take out my bucks (rams). I was going to bring them down to Zuni to feed them to get them in good shape – but there is no time to go over there today. I think I will go tomorrow.

AdE1So27A went into ESCR, ENCR, and SER, but he had nothing to report.

Mo61 is still in SER shelling corn.

0950

Mo61 walks back into WNCR to build a fire in the WNCR cooking stove.

AdE1So27A says that she is going to make hominy with the stew.

3Da22 is mounting turquoise on sticks for grinding.

YoDaSo1 came into SCR a few moments ago with a homemade cardboard horse which had been cut out by YoDaHu22.

2Da2Da3 followed YoDaSo1.

This house is full of activity and the children are running back and forth. They are not playing outside today because the weather is poor.

E1Da28 is mounting turquoise on sticks in preparation for grinding. She has a fire going in WR, which is a very large room to heat.

Figure 14.1. Excerpts from Roberts's observations of a Zuni household. Persons and things are identified by shorthand notation. For example, 2Da2Da3 is the family's second daughter who is 3 years old. Sequence begins at 9:40 a.m. and ends at 10:00 a.m.

SOURCE: Roberts (1965); reproduced with permission.

This exercise is instructive, if not humbling. It's a real challenge to code for socioeconomic class and ethnicity when you can't talk to the people you observe. Do this with at least one colleague so you can both check the reliability of your coding.

In hypothesis-testing research, where you already know a lot about the people you are studying, you go out to the field armed with a coding scheme worked out in advance. The idea is to record any instances of behavior that conform to the items in the scheme. This allows you to see if your hunches are correct about conditions under which certain behaviors occur. In some studies you might be interested in noting instances of aggressive versus submissive behavior. In other cases, those variables might be irrelevant.

Problem areas

Observation categories

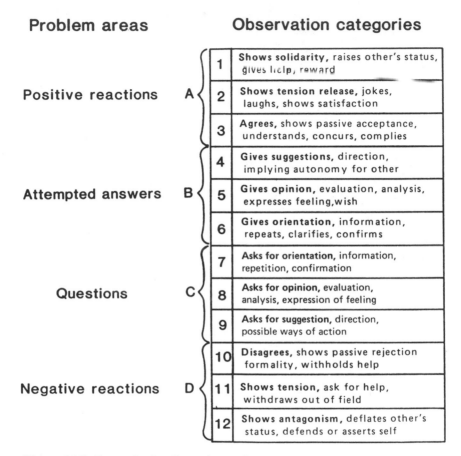

Positive reactions	A	1 — Shows solidarity, raises other's status, gives help, reward
		2 — Shows tension release, jokes, laughs, shows satisfaction
		3 — Agrees, shows passive acceptance, understands, concurs, complies
Attempted answers	B	4 — Gives suggestions, direction, implying autonomy for other
		5 — Gives opinion, evaluation, analysis, expresses feeling, wish
		6 — Gives orientation, information, repeats, clarifies, confirms
Questions	C	7 — Asks for orientation, information, repetition, confirmation
		8 — Asks for opinion, evaluation, analysis, expression of feeling
		9 — Asks for suggestion, direction, possible ways of action
Negative reactions	D	10 — Disagrees, shows passive rejection formality, withholds help
		11 — Shows tension, ask for help, withdraws out of field
		12 — Shows antagonism, deflates other's status, defends or asserts self

Figure 14.2. Categories for direct observation.

SOURCE: Adapted from *Readings in Social Psychology,* Revised Edition by G. E. Swanson, T. M. Newcomb, & E. L. Hartley, copyright 1952 and renewed 1980 by Holt, Rinehart and Winston, Inc., reproduced by permission of the publisher.

If you were studying police-civilian interactions, and you had already done a lot of participant observation, you might decide to ride in a squad car and monitor occurrences of specific behaviors that show respect or disdain for civilians. If you had not done the participant observation, you would monitor the entire stream of behavior during your time in the car and look for clues as to what behaviors are important.

It is often possible to use a coding scheme that has been developed and tested by other researchers. This will allow you to make direct comparisons between your data and those of other researchers. Figure 14.2 shows the basic coding scheme developed over 40 years ago by Bales (1952) in his research on communications in small groups.

Although the Bales scheme was worked out in laboratory research, the 12 behavioral categories are considered universal and exhaustive by many researchers. They are recognizable in all cultures and any act of communication can be identified as being one of the 12 categories in the Bales scheme. A highly detailed scheme for coding interpersonal relations was developed by Bales and Cohen (1979). A complete course on how to use their system is available in their book, aptly titled *SYMLOG*, which stands for "a system of multiple level observation of groups."

Broad, general coding schemes like this are useful for cross-cultural field studies. John and Beatrice Whiting found that all children's behavior could be coded with 12 labels: seeks help, seeks attention, seeks dominance, suggests, offers support, offers help, acts socially, touches, reprimands, assaults sociably, assaults not sociably, symbolic aggression (frightens, insults, threatens with gesture, challenges to compete). Full details on the use of the Whiting scheme are published in Whiting et al. (1966). Other schemes are published for studies of interpersonal exchange behavior (Longabaugh, 1963), nonverbal behavior (Birdwhistle, 1952), subsistence activities (D. Werner, 1980), and other arenas of human action.

Continuous Monitoring in Anthropology

Darna Dufour (1983) spent 3 weeks assessing the caloric intake and expenditures of Yapú villagers in the Colombian Amazon. The 3 weeks that Dufour devoted to this assessment came after an *entire year* of fieldwork. During her 21 days of direct observation, Dufour monitored the food intake and caloric expenditure of just four families. Getting really good data about "simple" things, like what people eat, is tough work, but the effort is vital for a cross-cultural science of human behavior.

Dufour weighed all food harvested, gathered, fished, hunted, or received as gifts and used standard tables for calculating the caloric values of foods (Leung & Flores, 1961). For energy expenditure in major subsistence activities, Dufour used direct calorimetry on a sample of 10 village women. (Direct calorimetry measures calories used in performing a task from the volume of oxygen consumed. See Stein et al., 1988, and Huss-Ashmore et al., 1989, for details on a new technique called the doubly labeled water method of measuring energy expenditure in the field.)

Richard Lee used CM in his study of !Kung Bushman (1968). Lee followed a band of Bushmen around on their hunts and interviewed them to record their work and leisure activities. Prior to Lee's work, it was commonly held that technologically primitive peoples did not have much leisure time—they were too busy, it was reasoned, extracting a living from the environment with their simple tools. Lee's observations showed that the !Kung could meet their basic food requirements with an average of less than 2.5 hours per day per food producer, and consequently have *more* leisure than so-called advanced peoples (see also Draper, 1975).

Pearson (1990) studied the energy expenditure of 145 Samoan men and women in Western Samoa, in American Samoa, and in Honolulu. He wanted to know if urbanization changed the Samoans' lifestyle as measured by their energy intake and expenditure. He interviewed his informants and asked them to recall their activities over the past 24 hours, noting each activity and probing during the interview to help people remember their activities.

To check the 24-hour recall data, he did continuous monitoring of 47 men, while a female assistant monitored 43 women. They accumulated a total of 825 hours of observation with their subjects in direct view 92% of the time. The estimates of active energy expenditure from direct observation data of men were 33% to 80% lower than the estimates from the recall data. The estimates for women were 27% to 53% lower. Women did better than men did in recalling their activities, but both men and women were way off the mark, particularly in recalling their light-to-moderate work of the previous day. Pearson's work makes it clear that recall is not a good substitute for observation.

Michael Murtagh (1985) used continuous monitoring to understand how people use arithmetic in grocery shopping. He recruited 24 adults in Orange County, California, for his study. Each informant wore a tape recorder while shopping at a supermarket, and was accompanied by two researchers. As the informants went about their shopping, they talked into the tape recorder about how they were deciding which product to buy, what size to choose, and so on.

One observer mapped the shopper's route through the store and recorded the prices and amounts of everything purchased. The other researcher kept up a running interview with the shopper, probing for details. Murtagh was aware of the potential for reactivity in his study. But he was interested in understanding the way people thought through ordinary, everyday arithmetic problems, and his experiment was a good way to generate those problems under natural conditions.

Finally, Ryutaro Ohtsuka (1989) studied the hunting efficiency of Gidra Papuans. For 38 days in 1971-1972, Ohtsuka monitored 26 Gidra hunters. He recorded the time of departure and time of return to the village for each of the hunters each day, and weighed all the game they brought back. He checked the method of kill in each instance (bow and arrow or shotgun) and determined the kilogram/hour efficiency of each hunter and each method.

Ohtsuka repeated the observation regime for 14 days in 1981 and was then able to determine how the efficiency of each hunter had grown or declined with age. Moreover, Ohtsuka was able to compare his observations with those of Hames (1979) for the Yanomami and Ye'kwana of the Upper Orinoco on the efficiency of the bow and arrow versus the shotgun among tropical forest hunters. (See O'Connell and Hawkes, 1984, for an example of continuous monitoring of hunters in central Australia.)

Technology and Continuous Monitoring

Even with a fixed coding scheme, an observer in a continuous monitoring situation has to decide among alternatives when noting behavior—whether someone is acting aggressively, or just engaging in rough play, for example. Recording behavior on tape or film or video lets several analysts study the behavior stream and decide at leisure how to code it.

In 1958, William Soskin, a psychologist, and Vera John, an anthropologist, got several pairs of people—young married couples at a resort—to wear voice transmitters 14 to 16 hours a day for 2 weeks. This was before spy-size transmitters. The contraptions were 1.5" x 2.5" x 5", and were worn on a shoulder strap. A 1'-long antenna, attached to the strap, stuck up from the shoulder blade, and the couples carried a battery pack that was changed daily. The couples' conversations were recorded on tape.

The couples weren't meant to be inconspicuous, and (incredibly) the resort manager not only gave permission for the experiment, he announced at dinner one night why the couples were wearing the apparatus. The data from this experiment make clear how much we miss when we take notes of real conversations. There is a violent argument in the data and moments of joy and tenderness (Soskin, 1963; Soskin & John 1963).

In the 1930s, Margaret Mead and Gregory Bateson filmed lengthy sequences of Balinese dancers for later close analysis (Belo, 1960). See Kendon (1979) for a review of methodological issues in the use of film for the close study of human social interaction.

Videotape has made CM easier. In the 1970s, Marvin Harris and his students installed videotape cameras in the public rooms of several households in New York City. Families gave their permission, of course, and were guaranteed legal control over the cameras during the study and of the videotapes after the cameras were removed. Teams of observers monitored the equipment from remote locations. Later, the continuous verbal and nonverbal data were coded to study regularities in interpersonal relationships in families.

Dehavenon (1978), for example, studied two black and two white families for 3 weeks and coded their nonverbal behavior for such things as compliance with requests and the distribution and consumption of foods in the households. Dehavenon's data showed that the amount of authoritarianism in the four families correlated perfectly with income differences. The lower the family income, the more superordinate behavior in the home (p. 3).

One would hypothesize, from participant observation alone, that this was the case. But *testing* this kind of hypothesis requires the sort of quantified data that straightforward, direct observation provides. (See Sharff, 1979, and Reiss, 1985, for two more studies of households using the Harris videotapes.)

As video cameras get smaller, easier to use, and less expensive, more field researchers will use this technology for close examination of behavior streams. C. Heath (1986), for example, studied interactions between patients and physicians, and Brigitte Jordan has used videotape to study birthing events across cultures (1992; also Jordan & Henderson, 1993).

Anthropology and Advertising

Anthropologists are putting continuous observation of behavior to work in commercial applications. Steven Barnett formed a group of five anthropologists within the consulting firm of Planmetrics in New York. The team of anthropologists uses direct observation of behavior, in combination with in-depth ethnographic interviews. In one study, researchers videotaped 70 volunteer parents, for over 200 total hours, as the volunteers diapered their babies. (The research was done on contract with Kimberly-Clark, manufacturer of "Huggies" brand disposable diapers.) The cameras were not hidden, and after a while people just went about their business as usual, according to Barnett.

Close observation showed that many parents could not tell whether their babies needed a diaper change. So the anthropologists recommended that the diapers contain an exterior chemical strip that changed color when the baby was wet. The researchers also noticed that parents were powdering their babies' legs. Parents were treating the red marks left by the diaper gathers as if the marks were diaper rash. The anthropologists recommended that the gathers be redesigned so that there would be no more red marks (Associated Press, 1985; *Wall Street Journal*, 1986:29).

The Six Culture Project

Continuous monitoring is particularly useful in studying children (N. Jones, 1972; McGrew, 1972). Self-administered questionnaire surveys are practically useless with children: the young ones can't read them or fill them out, and the older ones won't put up with questionnaires. Personal interviews are useful but don't tell you what children actually do with their time.

You can do participant observation with children (see Fine & Sandstrom, 1988, for tips on how to do this), but the attractive thing about studying children by CM is that, unlike adults, children seem not to be bothered by the presence of researchers. Children don't usually change their behavior when they're being studied, and when they do, they're pretty obvious about it. Most researchers report that, after a time, children go about their business and ignore researchers, note pads, stopwatches, video cameras, and other gadgets. (See Longabaugh, 1980, for a review of the uses of direct observation in cross-cultural psychology.)

The most important cross-cultural study of children was coordinated by Beatrice and John Whiting between 1954 and 1956. In the Six Culture Project, field researchers spent from 6 to 14 months in Okinawa, Kenya, Mexico, the Philippines, New England, and India. They made a total of some 3,000 5-minute (continuous monitoring) observations on 67 girls and 67 boys between the ages of 3 and 11.

Observations were limited to just 5 minutes because they were so intense, produced so much data, and required so much concentration and effort that researchers would have become fatigued and lost a lot of data in longer sessions. The investigators wrote out, in clear sentences, everything they saw children doing during the observation periods and also recorded data about the physical environment and others with whom children were interacting.

The data were sent from the field to Harvard University for coding according to a scheme of 12 behavior categories that had been worked out in research going back some 15 years before the Six Culture Study began. The behavioral categories included things like "seeks help," "assaults," "offers support," and so on. (See Whiting et al., 1966, for a complete description of the coding scheme; see Whiting & Whiting, 1973, for a discussion of their methods for observing and recording behavior.)

On average, every 10th observation was coded by two people, and these pairs of *coding partners* were rotated so that coders could not slip into a comfortable pattern with one another. Coders achieved 87% agreement on childrens' actions; that is, given a list of 12 kinds of things a child might be doing, coders agreed 87% of the time. They agreed 75% of the time on the act that precipitated a child's actions, and 80% of the time on the effects of a child's actions (Whiting & Whiting, 1975:55).

The database from the Six Culture Study consists of approximately 20,000 recorded acts, for 134 children, or about 150 acts per child, on average. Very strong conclusions can be drawn from such a robust database. For example, Whiting and Whiting note that nurturance, responsibility, success, authority, and casual intimacy "are types of behavior that are differentially preferred by different cultures." They conclude that "these values are apparently transmitted to the child before the age of six" (ibid.:179). They found no difference in amount of nurturant behavior among boys and girls 3 to 5 years of age. After that, however, nurturant behavior by girls increases rapidly with age, while boys' scores on this trait remain stable.

By contrast, reprimanding behavior starts out low for both boys and girls and increases with age equally for both sexes, across six cultures. Whiting and Whiting also found that the older children get, the more likely they are to reprimand anyone who deviates from newly learned cultural rules. "Throughout the world," the Whitings conclude, "two of the dominant personality traits of children between 7 and 11 are self-righteousness and bossiness" (ibid.:184). Anyone who grew up with an older sibling already knows that, but the Whiting's demonstration of this cross-cultural fact is a major scientific achievement.

The Zapotec Children Study

Douglas Fry used continuous monitoring to study aggressive play among Zapotec children. In 1981-1983, Fry did 18 months of participant observation fieldwork in La Paz and San Andrés, two small Zapotec villages just 4 miles apart in the Valley of Oaxaca. During the last 5 months of his research, Fry did direct, continuous monitoring of 24 children (3 to 8 years old) in each village. Before that, he visited almost all the households in the villages several times so that children had become accustomed to him when he began his intensive observation.

Fry (1990) describes his data collection procedures clearly:

The formal focal sampling observations were conducted between May and September of 1983. They represent each day of the week and encompass the daylight hour. Most observations (84%) were conducted within family compounds, although children were also observed in the streets, town squares, school yards, fields, and hills. I alternated sampling between the two communities on a weekly to biweekly basis. A total of 588 observations were conducted, resulting in an average of approximately 12 observations for each focal child (M=12.25, SD=6.21). On average, each focal child was observed for just over 3 hours (M=3.13 hours, SD=1.39 hours), resulting in a total of 150 hours of observation time for the entire sample. [It is common in scientific papers to report means and standard deviations; hence the M and SD figures in this paragraph. HRB]

Focal observation were narrated into a tape recorder carried in a small backpack or recorded on paper using a shorthand system. I recorded a running commentary of the behaviors engaged in by the focal child, using behavior elements defined in the previously developed ethogram. I moved with a focal child in order to maintain continuous visual contact (Altmann, 1974), but did not remain so close as to interfere with actions or unduly attract the child's attention. Whenever a focal child engaged in any type of antagonistic behavior, the specifics of the interaction were noted, including identity of the interactant(s) and any facial expressions or gestures. For instance, interactions such as the following were recorded: focal boy punches, pushes sister of 3 year old while laughing (sister does nothing in response). (From "Play aggression among Zapotec children: Implications for the practice hypothesis," by D. P. Fry. *Aggressive Behavior, 16,* 326-327. Copyright © 1990 by Wiley-Liss. Reprinted by permission of Wiley-Liss, a division of John Wiley and Sons, Inc.)

It is standard practice in ethology to develop an *ethogram*, or list of behaviors, for a species being studied. Fry developed his ethogram of Zapotec children by watching them in public places before beginning his study of focal individuals. Based on 150 hours of focal child observation, Fry's data contain 764 episodes of what he calls "play aggression" and 85 episodes of "serious aggression."

Play aggression is a punch, kick, tackle, etc., accompanied by smiles, laughs, and playfaces. Serious aggression are episodes accompanied by low frowns, bared teeth, fixated gazes, and crying. Fry found that when girls initiated serious aggression, it was almost always with other girls (93% of cases). But when boys initiated serious aggression, it was just as likely to be with girls as with other boys.

Spot Sampling and Time Allocation Studies

Time allocation (TA) studies are based on *spot sampling,* a technique in which a researcher simply appears at randomly selected places, and at

randomly selected times, and records what people are doing when they are
first encountered (Gross, 1984). There is usually no attempt at continuous
monitoring of a behavior stream, although Pederson (1987) combined
random spot sampling with 15-minute continuous monitoring of behavior.

The idea behind spot sampling is simple and appealing: If you sample
a sufficiently large number of representative acts, you can use the percentage of *times* people are seen doing things (working, playing, resting,
eating) as a proxy for the percentage of *time* they spend in those activities.

Time sampling was pioneered by behavioral psychologists in the 1920s.
Influenced by John B. Watson's (then) revolutionary behaviorist approach
to psychology, W. C. Olson (1929) sought to measure the behavior of
nervous habits in normal children by taking repeated short samples under
the most natural conditions possible.

Charles Erasmus used time sampling in his study of a Mayo Indian
community in northern Mexico (1955). As Erasmus and his wife went
about the village, investigating "various topics of ethnographic interest,"
they took notes on what people were doing at the moment they encountered
them. They did not use a representative sampling strategy, but they were
very systematic in their recording of data.

> Individual charts were made for each man, woman, and child in the village,
> and on those charts were noted the page numbers from the field log where the
> activity descriptions were to be found. These page numbers were recorded on
> the charts according to the hours of the day when the observations were made.
> Thus, the individual charts served as indexes to the field log as well as a means
> of making sure that equal attention was being given to all families at all hours
> of the day. Periodic examination of the charts showed which households and
> which hours of the day were being neglected, so that visits about the commu-
> nity could be planned to compensate for these discrepancies. (p. 325)

It's difficult to top this research for sheer elegance of design and the
power of the data it produced. In the 3 months from July to September
1948, the Erasmuses made about 5,000 observations on 2,500 active
adults, 2,000 children, and 500 aged persons in the community. From those
observations, Erasmus demonstrated that men in the village he studied
spent about the same time at work each day as did semiskilled workers in
Washington, DC. At the time, Melville Herskovits was trying to combat
the racist notion that primitive and peasant peoples are lazy and unwilling
to exert themselves. Herskovits's assertion was vindicated by Erasmus's
TA research.

Reactivity in TA Research

Since TA research is reactive, the trick is to catch a glimpse of people in their natural activities before they see you coming on the scene—before they have a chance to modify their behavior. Richard Scaglion (1986) did a TA survey of the residents of Upper Neligum, a Samakundi Abelam village in the Prince Alexander mountains of East Sepik Province in Papua New Guinea. "It is not easy," he says, "for an anthropologist in the field to come upon an Abelam unawares. Since I did not want to record 'greeting anthropologist' as a frequent activity when people were first observed, I often had to reconstruct what they were doing immediately before I arrived" (p. 540).

Borgerhoff-Mulder and Caro (1985) coded the observer's judgment of whether subjects saw the observer first, or vice versa, and compared that to whether the Kipsigis they were studying were observed to be active or idle. Subjects were idle significantly more often when they spied the observer coming upon them before the observer saw them.

Did subjects become idle when they saw an anthropologist approaching? Or was it easier for idle subjects to see an anthropologist before the anthropologist saw them? Borgerhoff-Mulder and Caro found that idle subjects were sitting or lying down much more often than active subjects. People at rest may be more attentive to their surroundings than working people, and would be judged more often to have seen the anthropologist approaching.

Sampling Problems

There are five questions to ask when drawing a sample for a TA study: (a) Who do I watch? (b) Where do I go to watch them? (c) When do I go there? (d) How often do I go there? (e) How long do I spend watching people when I get there? (Gross, 1984). Allen Johnson's study (1975) of the Machiguenga is instructive.

The Machiguenga are horticulturists in the Peruvian Amazon. They live along streams in small groups of related families, with each group comprised of from about 10 to 30 people, and they subsist primarily from slash-and-burn gardens. They supplement their diet with fish, grubs, wild fruits, and occasional monkeys from the surrounding tropical forest. Johnson spent 14 months studying the Machiguenga in the community of Shimaa.

Johnson's strategy for selecting people to study was simple: Because all travel was on foot, he decided to sample all the households within 45 minutes of his own residence. This produced a convenience sample of 13 households totaling 105 persons. Since the Machiguenga live along streams, each time Johnson went out he walked either upstream or downstream, stopping at a selected household along the route. Which hour of the day to go out and which houses to stop at were determined by using a table of random numbers, like the one in Appendix B of this book.

Thus, Johnson used a nonrandom sample of all Machiguenga households, but he randomized the times that he visited any household in his sample. This sampling strategy sacrificed some external validity, but it was high on internal validity. Johnson could not claim that his sample of households *statistically* represented all Machiguenga households. His 14 months' worth of experience in the field, however, makes his claim for the representativeness of his data credible.

That is, if Johnson's data on time allocation in those 13 households seem to *him* to reflect TA in Machiguenga households generally, then they probably do. But we can't be sure. Fortunately, randomizing his visits to the 13 households and making a lot of observations (3,945 of them, over 134 different days during the 14-month fieldwork period), gives Johnson's results a lot of *internal* validity. So, even if you're skeptical of the external validity of Johnson's study, you could repeat it (in Shimaa or in some other Machiguenga community) and see whether you got the same results.

Regina Smith Oboler (1985) did a TA study among the Nandi of Kenya. She was interested in differences in the activities of adult men and women. The Nandi, Smith Oboler said, "conceptualize the division of labor as sex segregated. Is this true in practice as well? Do men and women spend their time in substantially different or similar types of activities?" (p. 203).

Oboler selected 11 households, comprising 117 people, for her TA study. Her sample was not random. "Selecting a random sample," she said, ". . . even for one *kokwet* [neighborhood] would have made observations impossibly difficult in terms of travel time" (ibid.:204). Instead, Oboler chose a sample of households that were matched to social and demographic characteristics of the total population and which were within half an hour's walking distance from the compound where she lived.

Oboler divided the daylight hours of the week into 175 equal time periods and gave each period (about two hours) a unique three-digit number. Then, using a table of random numbers, she chose time periods to visit each household. She visited each household four times a week (on different days of the week) during 2 weeks each month and made nearly 1,500 observations on those households during her 9 months in the field.

Oboler found that, for her sample of observations, adult men spend around 38% of their time "in activities that might reasonably be considered 'work' by most commonly used definitions of that term" (ibid.:205). Women in her sample spent over 60% of their time working.

Table 14.1 shows the number of spot observations necessary to estimate the frequency f of an activity to within a fractional accuracy. It also tells you how many observations you need if you want to compare time estimates. (For the formula used to derive the numbers in Table 14.1, see Bernard & Killworth, 1993.) Here's how to read the table.

Suppose people spend about 5% of their time eating. This is shown in the first column as a frequency, f of 0.05. If you want to estimate the frequency of the activity to within 20%, look across to the column in the center part of the table under 0.20. If you have 1,825 observations, and your data say that people eat 5% of the time, then you can safely say that the true percentage of time spent eating is between 4% and 6%. (Twenty percent of 5% is 1%. Five percent, plus or minus 1%, is 4% to 6%.)

Suppose your data show that men eat 4% of the time while women eat 6% of the time. If you have 300 observations, then the *error bounds* of the two estimates overlap considerably (about .02 to .06 for the men and .04 to .08 for the women). You need about 1,800 observations to tell whether 0.06 is really bigger than 0.04 comparing across groups. It's the same for activities: If women are seen gardening 20% of their time and caring for children 25% of their time, then 1,066 observations are required in order to tell if women really spend more time caring for children than they do gardening.

Oboler had 1,500 observations. It is clear from Table 14.1 that her findings about men's and women's leisure and work time are not accidents. An activity seen in a sample of just 256 observations to occur 40% of the time can be estimated actually to occur between 40%, plus or minus 15% of 40%, or between 34% and 46%. Since men are seen working 38% of the time, and about half of Oboler's 1,500 observations were of men, her finding is solid.

Nighttime Sampling

Virtually all spot sampling studies of behavior are done during the daylight hours, between 6 a.m. and 7 p.m. In Johnson's case, this was explicitly because "travel after dark is hazardous and because visiting at night is not encouraged by the Machiguenga" (A. Johnson, 1975:303). Recently, however, Scaglion (1986) showed the importance of nighttime observations in TA studies.

When Scaglion did his TA study of the Abelam in 1983, there were 350 people in the village, living in 100 households. Scaglion randomly selected 2 households each day and visited them at randomly selected times, through-

TABLE 14.1

Number of Observations to Estimate the Frequency of an Activity
to Within a Fractional Accuracy

True Frequency of Activity	Number of Observations Needed							
f	0.05	0.10	0.15	0.20	0.30	0.40	0.50	to see activities at least once with 95% probability
0.01	152127	38032	16903	9508	4226	2377	1521	299
0.02	75295	18824	8366	4706	2092	1176	753	149
0.03	49685	12421	5521	3105	1380	776	497	99
0.04	36879	9220	4098	2305	1024	576	369	74
0.05	29196	7299	3244	1825	811	456	292	59
0.06	24074	6019	2675	1505	669	376	241	49
0.07	20415	5104	2268	1276	567	319	204	42
0.08	17671	4418	1963	1104	491	276	177	36
0.09	15537	3884	1726	971	432	243	155	32
0.10	13830	3457	1537	864	384	216	138	29
0.15	8708	2177	968	544	242	136	87	19
0.20	6147	1537	683	384	171	96	61	14
0.25	4610	1152	512	288	128	72	46	11
0.30	3585	896	398	224	100	56	36	9
0.40	2305	576	256	144	64	36	23	6
0.50	1537	384	171	96	43	24	15	5

SOURCE: Bernard and Killworth (1993), Sampling in time allocation research, *Ethnology 32*, 211. Reprinted with permission.

out the day *and night*. Now, if your sampling strategy demands that you be somewhere at 3 a.m., this will cut down considerably on the number of observations you can make. You have to sleep sometime! Nevertheless, Scaglion managed to make 153 observations in one month of work.

Scaglion used a recording scheme composed of 13 categories of activities: sleeping, gardening, idle, cooking and food preparation, ritual, visiting, eating, hunting, construction, personal hygiene, child care, cleansing and washing, and craftswork. Among his findings were that only 74% of Abelam activities during nighttime hours were coded as "sleeping." Seven of the nine observations that he coded as "ritual" occurred after dark. Half of all observations coded as "hunting" occurred at night, and six out of eight observations coded as "visiting" were nocturnal.

Had he done his TA study only during the day, Scaglion would have overestimated the amount of time that Abelam people spend gardening by about a fourth. His data show that gardening takes up about 26% of the Abelam's daylight hours, but only 20% of their total waking time in each 24-hour period.

Of course, it may not always be possible to conduct TA studies at night. Johnson, you'll remember, made a point of the fact that the Machiguenga discourage nighttime visiting. Scaglion, on the other hand, worked among a people who "go visiting at unusual hours, even when their prospective host is likely to be sleeping." Scaglion, in fact, rather enjoyed showing up at odd hours in 1983 to observe households in Neligum village. "In 1974 to '75," he said, "when I was still quite a novelty . . . I was frequently awakened by hearing *"Minoa, mine kwak?"* ("Hey, you, are you sleeping?"). This study allowed me to return old favors by visiting people in the late night hours to be sure *they* were sleeping" (p. 539).

Coding and Recording Time Allocation Data

Sampling is one of two problems in TA research. The other is measurement. How do we know that when Oboler recorded that someone was "working," we would have recorded the same thing? If you were with Johnson when he recorded that someone was engaged in "hygiene behavior," would you have agreed with his assessment? Every time? You can see the problem.

It gets even more thorny. Suppose you work out a coding scheme that everyone agrees with. And suppose you train other observers to see just what you see (Rogoff, 1978, achieved a phenomenal 98% interobserver agreement in her study of 9-year-olds in Guatemala). Or, if you are doing the research all by yourself, suppose you are absolutely consistent in recording behaviors (i.e., you never code someone lying in a hammock as sleeping when they're just lounging around awake).

Even if all these reliability problems are taken care of, what about observation validity? What do you do, for example, when you see people engaged in multiple behaviors? A woman might be holding a baby and stirring a pot at the same time (Gross, 1984:542). If someone saw that you were lying down reading, and you were studying for an exam, should they record that you were working or relaxing?

Do you record all behaviors? Do you mark one behavior as primary? This last question has important implications for data analysis. There are only so many minutes in a day, and the percentage of people's time that they allocate to activities has to add up to just 100%. If you code multiple activities as equally important, then there will be more than 100% of the day accounted for. Most TA researchers use their intuition, *based on partici-pant observation*, to decide which of the multiple simultaneous activities they witness to record as the primary one, and which as secondary.

The best solution is to record *all* possible behaviors you observe in the order of their primacy, according to your best judgment at the time of observation. This may be difficult to do in longhand, but new technology makes the work easy. The "Observer" is a hardware and software system that lets you use a hand-held computer to record up to code up to 90 different kinds of behaviors as you observe them (Whiten & Barton, 1988; Hile, 1991).

Many anthropologists will continue to find check sheets handy for record-ing spot sample data. Figure 14.3 is a modified version of the check sheet recommended by Borgerhoff-Mulder and Caro (1985) for collecting spot sample data. You should use a separate 8.5" × 11" sheet for each observation you make (or A4 size outside the United States), even if it means printing up 1,000 sheets for a TA study and hauling them home later.

An alternative to carrying check sheets around every day is to record your observations of behavior on audio tape and to fill in the data sheets at night. We have no evidence, however, on whether audio recording or check sheets produces more reliable or more valid observational data.

As you can see from Table 14.1, 1,000 spot observations is enough for most TA studies. If you have a microcomputer in the field you can enter all the quantitative data from 1,000 sheets like those in Figure 14.3 onto one floppy disk and mail several copies to friends for safekeeping. If you don't have a microcomputer in the field you can still code the data onto 100 code sheets of 10 lines each. It is a good idea to code your TA data in the field, as you go, just as a precaution against loss of the original data sheets. Be paranoid about data. The horror stories you've heard about lost data are true.

Medical Anthropology and Direct Observation

A lot of data about health care delivery are gathered by standing around in rural clinics and counting the number of children who get vaccinated or the number of women who come for advice about the treatment of their children's illnesses. One of the most common forms of direct observation in medical anthropology is assessment of children's nutritional status. This involves measuring children's height and weight and comparing the results to international standards for children of each age. Here is Jean Brainard's

(1) Date
(2) Time
(3) Weather
(4) Location
(5) Subject code
(6) Observer sees subject first
(7) Subject sees observer first
(8) Physical description of activity

(9) Subject report on purpose and content of activity

(10) Other activities going on at the same time and place

(11) Comments: Observer's judgments as to truthfulness of subject.
Observer's judgment as to which of several behaviors is primary.

Figure 14.3. Checksheet for collecting spot sample data.

SOURCE: Adapted from "The use of quantitative observational techniques in anthropology" by Burgerhoff-Mulder and Caro, 1985, *Current Anthropology,* 326. Copyright © 1985 by Wenner-Gren Foundation for Anthro- pological Research. Used with permission of The University of Chicago Press.

(1990) description of how she did this for 236 Nakwamoru children (ages 1 to 10) in the Turkana district of Kenya:

> Height was measured using a Harpenden anthropometer with subjects stand-ing on a level concrete floor in bare feet and recorded to the nearest mm. Supine length was measured, also to the nearest mm, on a level table to which a cloth tape had been affixed, with a stationary foot board and adjustable head board. Weight was measured to the nearest tenth of a kg with a commercial beam balance scale, except for weights of infants under 12 months, which were taken with a fabric-sling baby scale. Nude weights were estimated by subtracting weights of clothing and ornaments that could not be removed without jeopardizing subject compliance. (p. 156)

Brainard compared the weight-for-age, weight-for-height, and height-for-weight data of the Turkana children against standards published by the National Center for Health Statistics in the United States. (See United States Public Health Service, 1976, if you want to take a copy of the height-for-weight standards with you to your field research site.)

She also took triceps skinfold and arm circumference measurements. The triceps skinfold is measured with a special skinfold calipers that allows measurement to the nearest tenth of a millimeter. Arm circumference is measured with a cloth tape to the nearest millimeter. Both measurements are made in the middle of the upper arm.

With these measures you can calculate the percentage of fat and muscle in the upper arm—another indicator of nutritional status. (See Frisancho, 1981, World Health Organization, 1983, WHO Working Group, 1986, and J. B. M., 1990, for standards on muscle and fat and on measuring children.) One of the problems in this area of research, of course, is that different populations have different body shapes, so the standards are not as "standard" as they might otherwise be. Brainard compared her findings with the findings of other studies of Turkana children.

A Few Final Words on Reactive Observation

Where does all this leave us? If you are unfamiliar with the direct, reactive-observation approach to data gathering, you may find it a bit alien to traditional anthropological work. You may feel awkward about walking around with a clipboard (and perhaps a stopwatch) and writing down what people are doing. This is a reasonable concern, and direct observation is not for everyone. It is not a "friendly" technique. Hanging out, participating in normal daily activities with informants, and writing up field notes at night is more enjoyable than monitoring and recording what people are doing.

But many field workers today find that direct observation allows them to address issues that are not easily studied by any other method. Grace Marquis (1990) studied a shantytown in Lima, Peru. Children in households that kept chickens were at higher risk for getting diarrhea than were other children. The chickens left feces in the homes, and the feces contained an organism that causes diarrhea. Continuous monitoring showed that children touched the chicken droppings and, inevitably, touched their mouths with their hands.

Direct observation may also seem overly time consuming. Actually, random spot checking of behavior is a cost-effective and productive way to use *some* of your time in the field. In small villages, you can get very fine-grained data about people's behavior from a TA study, based on random spot checks. More importantly, as you can see from Table 14.1, with proper sampling you can generalize to a very large population (even a city) from spot checks of behavior, in ways that no other method allows.

You may be concerned that a strictly behavioristic approach to gathering anthropological data, while appropriate to the study of nonhuman primates, fails to capture the *meaning* of data about human behavior. This, too, is a legitimate concern; people can engage in the same behavior for a variety of reasons, so knowing the meaning of behavior is essential to understanding it. On the other hand, keep in mind that one of our most important goals in science is to challenge our own ideas (and those of our informants, as well) about what things mean.

Finally, you may have some qualms about the ethics of obtrusive observation. It can never be said too often that *every single data collection act* in the field has an ethical component, and a field worker is obliged every single time to think through the ethical implications of data collection acts. Personally, I have less difficulty with the potential ethical problems of obtrusive, reactive observation than I do with any other data collection method, including participant observation. In obtrusive observation, people actually *see* you (or a camera) taking down their behavior and they can ask you to stop. Nothing is hidden.

In participant observation (the method we usually think of as the least problematic from an ethical perspective), we try to put people at ease, make them forget we're really listening hard to what they're telling us, and get them to open up. I'm constantly aware when I do ethnographic fieldwork that people are taking me into their confidence, and I'm always a bit nervous about the responsibility that puts on me not to abuse their confidence.

The method that presents the *most* ethical problems, however, is unobtrusive, *non*reactive observation. That is the subject of the next chapter.

15

Unobtrusive Observation

U nobtrusive observation includes all methods for studying behavior where informants don't know that they're being studied. The methods of unobtrusive observation include *behavior trace studies*, *archival research*, *content analysis*, *disguised observation*, and *naturalistic field experiments*. Disguised observation and naturalistic field experiments pose serious ethical problems, which I will address at some length in this chapter. Trace studies, content analysis, and archival research are more limited in scope, but are almost always politically and ethically aseptic because they are so indirect. Each method has its pluses and minuses and each has something to offer when you do long-term fieldwork.

Behavior Trace Studies

Human behavior often leaves traces, and the study of those traces can tell us a lot. Sechrest and Flores (1969), for example, recorded and analyzed bathroom graffiti in a sample of men's public toilets in Manila and Chicago. They wanted to examine attitudes toward sexuality in the two cultures. The results were striking. There was no difference in the percentage of graffiti in the two cities that dealt with heterosexual themes. But fully 42% of the Chicago graffiti dealt with homosexuality, while only 2% of the Manila graffiti did, showing a clear difference in the two cultures regarding level of concern with homosexuality.

Gould and Potter (1984) did a survey of used-up (not smashed up) automobiles in five Providence, Rhode Island, junkyards. They calculated that the average use-life of American-made cars is 10.56 years, irrespective of how many times cars change hands. This is a good deal longer than most Americans would guess. Gould also compared use-life against initial cost and found that paying more for a car doesn't affect how long it will last. Interesting and useful findings.

Webb et al. (1966) identified a class of unobtrusive measures based on "erosion." Administrators of Chicago's Museum of Science and Industry had found that the vinyl tiles around an exhibit showing live, hatching chicks needed to be replaced about every 6 weeks. The tiles around other exhibits lasted for years without having to be replaced. Webb et al. (p. 37) suggested that this erosion measure (the rate of wear on vinyl tiles) might be a proxy for a direct measure of the popularity of exhibits. The faster the tiles wear out, the more popular the exhibit.

Weighing the Evidence

Dean Archer and Lynn Erlich (1985) report a method for studying confidential records when you want to know only aggregate outcomes and don't need data about individuals. They had a hypothesis that sensational crimes (with a lot of press coverage) result in increased sales of handguns. The police would not allow them to see the handgun applications, so they asked a member of the police staff to put the permits into envelopes, by month, for 3 months prior to and 3 months after a particular sensational crime. Then they weighed the envelopes and converted the weight to handgun applications. To do this, they got a chunk of blank applications and found out how many applications there were per ounce.

The technique is very reliable. The correlation between the estimates of researchers and the actual weights of the envelopes was .99, and in a controlled experiment, researchers were able to tell the difference of just one sheet of paper in 15 out of 18 tries. Real data can be messy, though. Lots of handgun applications have addenda attached, for example. Still, the correlation between researchers' estimates and the true number of handgun applications across 6 months was .94.

Archer and Erlich suggest that literally *weighing-the-evidence* can be used to study things like drunk driving arrests, the influx of psychiatric patients to a clinic, the number of grievance filings in a company, the number of abortion referrals, and the number of complaints against agencies.

The Garbage Project

The most important trace measure research ever attempted is the ongoing Garbage Project, headed by archeologist William Rathje at the University of Arizona. Since 1973, Rathje and his associates have studied the consumer behavior patterns of Tucson, Arizona (and, in 1978-1979, Milwaukee, Wisconsin), by analyzing the garbage from a representative sample of residents. In order to prevent reactivity, residents are *not told* that their refuse is being sorted and analyzed. (See Hughes, 1984, for a detailed review of the methodology of the Garbage Project.)

By studying the detritus of ordinary people, researchers on the Garbage Project, cultural anthropologists and archeologists alike, have learned interesting things about food consumption and waste among Americans. Squash is the favored baby food among Hispanics in the United States, and 35% of all food from chicken take-out restaurants is thrown away (Rathje, 1992). The researchers also learned that they could accurately estimate the population of an area by weighing only the plastic trash. Children, it turns out, generate as much plastic trash as adults do (Edmonson, 1988).

Early in the Garbage Project, researchers expected that people would not waste much beef during a shortage, but exactly the opposite happened in 1973. Two things were shown to be responsible for this finding.

First, as the shortage took hold, the price of beef rose, and people started buying cheaper cuts. Some residents did not know how to prepare those cuts properly, and this created more waste; others found that they didn't like the cheaper cuts and threw out more than they usually would have; and cheaper cuts have more waste fat to throw out to begin with.

Second, as the price continued to rise, people started buying greater quantities of beef, perhaps as a hedge against further price hikes. Inevitably, some of the increased purchases spoiled from lack of proper storage (Rathje, 1984:17).

Rathje found the same pattern of consumer behavior during the sugar shortage of 1975 (ibid.). He reasoned that whenever people changed their food buying and consuming habits drastically, there would be at least a short-term increase in food loss. Conversely, when people use foods and ingredients that are familiar to them, they waste less in both preparation and consumption.

This led Rathje to compare the food loss rate among Mexican-Americans and Anglos. "The final results of Mexican-American cooking," Rathje said, "can be extremely varied—chimichangas, burros, enchiladas, tacos, and more—but the basic set of ingredients are very few compared to standard Anglo fare. Thus, Mexican-American households should throw out less food than Anglo households" (ibid.:18). In fact, this is exactly what Rathje found in both Tucson and Milwaukee.

Pros and Cons of Trace Studies

The most important advantage of trace studies is that they are nonreactive, so long as informants are kept in the dark about what you are doing. What happens when informants are told that their garbage is being monitored? Rittenbaugh and Harrison (1984) compared data from an experimental group (people who were told that their garbage was being monitored) and a control group (people who were not told). There was no difference in the refuse disposal behavior of the experimental and control groups—with one important exception. The number of empty bottles of alcoholic drinks that showed up was significantly lower when people knew that their garbage was being monitored. Where did the extra bottles go? Buried in the back yard? Stuffed in the trash cans of neighbors who were not in the sample? It remains a mystery.

In addition to being nonreactive, behavioral trace studies yield enormous amounts of data that can be standardized, quantified, and compared across groups and over time (Rathje, 1979). Moreover, traces reflect some behaviors more accurately than informant reports of those behaviors. If you want to know what informants eat, for instance, you're better off examining their garbage than asking them what they eat, and if you want to know about their long-distance calling behavior, you're better off looking at their phone bills than asking them (Bernard et al., 1984; see D'Andrade, 1973, 1974, Romney et al., 1986, and Freeman et al., 1987, for work on the causes of inaccuracy.)

Trace studies have plenty of problems, however. Early in the Garbage Project, it became apparent that garbage disposals were going to be a serious problem. The researchers constructed a subsample of 32 households, some of which had disposals, some of which did not. They studied these 32 households for 5 weeks and developed a "garbage disposal correction factor" (Rathje, 1984:16).

As the project went on, researchers learned that some families were recycling all their aluminum cans, while others were throwing theirs in the trash. This made it difficult to compare households regarding their consumption of soft drinks and beer. Some families had compost heaps that they used as fertilizer for their vegetable gardens. This distorted the refuse count for those families. Garbage Project researchers had to develop correction factors for all of these biases, too (see Harrison, 1976).

As with all unobtrusive research, the Garbage Project raised some difficult ethical problems. To protect the privacy of the households in the study, no addresses or names of household members are recorded. All personal items, such as photographs and letters, are thrown out without being examined. The hundreds of student sorters who have worked on the project have signed pledges not to save anything from the refuse they examine. All the sampling, sorting, and data analysis procedures are approved by the Human Subjects Research Committee of the University of Arizona.

The Garbage Project receives consistent coverage in the press, both nationally and locally in Tucson. In 1984, after 10 years of work, Hughes (1984) reported that "no public concern over the issue of personal privacy has been expressed, and community response has been supportive" (p. 42). With proper safeguards, trace measures can be used in cultural anthropology to generate useful data about human behavior.

Archival Research

The great advantage of archival research is that it is truly nonreactive. After all, if you are studying documentary records of births, migrations, visits to a hospital, or purchases made of hybrid seed, the informants can hardly change their behavior after the fact. On the other hand, while *your* examination of archival data has no reactive effect, there is no guarantee that the data were collected nonreactively in the first place.

Another advantage is that it's possible to study things using archival data that would be too politically "hot" to study any other way. Archival research is inexpensive, too. I see no reason to collect new data in the field if there are documentary resources already available that address some of your research questions. Be on the lookout for archival materials: government reports, newspaper archives, personal diaries or photo collections, industrial data, medical records, school records, wills, deeds, records of court cases, tax rolls, and land-holding records.

Cultural Processes

Archival resources can be particularly useful in studying cultural processes through time. June Helm (1980) found that between 1829 and 1891, traders at the Hudson's Bay Company posts of the upper Mackenzie Delta had surveyed the Indians who traded at their stores. On the basis of those data, Helm concluded that, before 1850, the Indians of the area had practiced female infanticide. After 1850, missionaries were successful in stopping infanticide. Nancy Howell (1981), a demographer, subjected Helm's data to a sophisticated statistical analysis and corroborated Helm's conclusion.

Daniel Swan and Gregory Campbell (1989) studied the population records of 1877 to 1907 for the Osage reserve. They were able to show that from 1877 to 1887 the full bloods declined at 6.4% a year, while the mixed bloods increased at 7.3% a year. This had great consequences for the Osage because the full bloods and mixed bloods had formed voting blocs on economic issues. In particular, the full bloods resisted turning the reserve land into private property. Whites who married into the tribe fraudulently claimed tribal mixed-blood status. The mixed bloods were in favor of the private property measures.

Perhaps the best-known study of cultural process using archival sources is Alfred Kroeber's research on long-term trends and cycles of behavior in civilization (Kroeber, 1919). He studied women's fashions and made eight separate measurements, including diameter of skirt at hem, diameter of waist, depth of decolletage (measured from the mouth to the middle of the corsage edge in front), and so on. His study became a classic in anthropology. Where did he get his data?

> I began the measurements with the year 1844 for the reason that that was the first volume of a fashion journal which I happened to know to be accessible in New York City, where I then was. The journal was the *Petit Courrier des Dames* in the Avery Library of Columbia University. The broken set ended in 1868, and I was driven to the Public Library for continuation. . . . The Parisian journal contained beautiful lithographs, the American exponent of fashion woodcuts of a horribly crude kind; and I feared at first that the difference in mode of illustration would vitiate comparison, and render wasted the work already done. The American waists seemed at least a quarter thicker, and all of the proportions clumsier. Juxtaposition of the percentages for adjacent years however proved at once that the difference was only in artistic execution. . . .
>
> [More recently] half-toned photographs of living models suddenly made their appearance, and again I was disconcerted. Surely no dress worn on an actual human frame could be as extreme as the stylistically idealized pictures that had preceded. But again alarm was in vain. . . .
>
> It is surprising how poorly equipped in fashion journals the greater institutional libraries of our largest cities are. For those interested in similar researches, I would recommend inquiry at theatrical organizations for data on dress, and files of manufacturers' catalogues for industrial products. (pp. 243-245)

Kroeber did a thorough quantitative analysis of his data and concluded that he had demonstrated "an underlying pulsation in the width of civilized women's skirts, which is symmetrical and extends in its up and down beat over a full century; and an analogous rhythm in skirt length, but with a period of only about a third the duration" (ibid.:257).

Allport and Hartman (1931) criticized Kroeber for having been insufficiently critical of his sources.

> Upon inspection of the raw data, however, it becomes apparent that little assurance can be attached to the year-percentage averages [of skirt dimensions] upon which [Kroeber] bases his conclusions. . . . Consider for example, the figures on the length of the waist for the year 1859. There are nine actual measurements and one estimate. Reducing the raw data to ratios based on the length of the entire figure . . . we find a total range of 2.41.
>
> This range within the individual measurements for the year 1859 is greater than that within the yearly averages that the author assigns for the years 1859-1864. The range within the year 1886 in the width of the skirt . . . is greater than the range of year-percentage averages between the years 1870 and 1908. . . . Considering the small number of cases and the wide variability within a given year, we question whether the reliability of the averages, and consequently of the plotted curves [the regularities Kroeber claimed to have found], is adequate. (pp. 342-343)

This criticism led to Richardson's expanding Kroeber's database, and *this* time the archives of fashion plates were simply scoured (Richardson & Kroeber, 1940). There were still problems with the data, but Richardson found plates going back to 1605! And before making measurements for all the new years included in the study, Richardson redid Kroeber's measurements for 1844-1846 and for 1919 and assured herself that she had attained what we would call today "high interrater reliability" with Kroeber. In other words, she checked to see if she was independently coding each plate the same way Kroeber had done in 1919 (ibid.).

The data in Richardson and Kroeber's study were reanalyzed by Lowe and Lowe (1982), using all the firepower of modern statistics and computers. You'll be pleased to know that Kroeber was vindicated: Stylistic change in women's dress is probabilistic in nature, is in stable equilibrium (changing with patterned regularity), and is driven by "inertia, cultural continuity, a rule system of aesthetic proportions, and an inherently unpredictable element" (p. 521). Nevertheless, Allport and Hartman's critique was right on target in 1931. You can't be too critical of your sources.

The Problem with Archival Data

A word of caution about archival data: They may appear "clean"—especially if they come from modern data banks and are already packaged on computer disks or tape, coded, and ready to be analyzed—but they may be riddled with error. This makes it all the more important to consider carefully all the possible sources of bias (informant error, observer error, etc.) that might have been at work in the setting down of the data. Ask how, why, and under what conditions a particular set of archival data was collected. Ask who collected it and what biases he or she might have had.

No data are free of error. In some parts of Mexico, the number of consensual unions is greater than the number of formal marriages, making court records about marriages problematic. In the United States, on the other hand, crime statistics are notoriously untrustworthy. Many crimes go unreported, and those that are reported may not be recorded at all, or may be recorded in the wrong category. In other countries, records of births and deaths may be biased. Rural people may wait as long as 6 months to report a birth, and a significant fraction of their children may die within that period. (See Naroll, 1962, and Handlin, 1979, for discussions of data quality control in archival research.) It is almost always better to understand distortion in data than to throw them out.

Content Analysis

Content analysis is a catch-all term covering a variety of techniques for making inferences from "texts." The texts can be any chunk of qualitative data—fiction, nonfiction, recorded folktales, newspaper editorials, advertisements, films and videos, photographs, songs. The idea is to reduce the information in a text to a series of variables that can then be examined for correlations.

Elizabeth Hirschman (1987), for example, selected 100 personal ads placed by men and 100 placed by women in *New York Magazine* and *The Washingtonian.* She coded the ads for the kind of resources that people sought and the kind they offered. On average, men sought physical attractiveness more than twice as often as women did; women offered physical attractiveness about 50% more often than men did. Men offered monetary resources three times more often than women did, and women sought monetary resources eight times more often than men did.

I like content analysis. It's a blend of qualitative and quantitative, positivistic and interpretive methods—perfect for anthropologists. You start with text (qualitative data), make formal hypotheses about what you think is "in there," do systematic coding and statistical analysis, and interpret the results in the light of historical or ethnographic information.

Content Dictionaries

The real power of computers for content analysis is in the building of analytic dictionaries. A content-analysis dictionary is a list of words that are all indexed with the same code word. Karen Jehn and Oswald Werner (1993) studied the effect of intragroup conflict on group task effectiveness in a large transportation company. Their content analysis dictionary contains the following entry:

> performance: efficiency, effectiveness, efficacy, skill,
> capability, ability, adeptness, competence,
> expertise, know-how, proficiency, prowess,
> capability, resourcefulness, productivity

All the words on the right are coded as having something to do with performance. Content analysis programs, then, can go through many documents (like interviews or transcripts of taped conversations), look for examples of the synonym words (shown here on the right), and tag them with the code word (shown on the left).

Some content analysis programs let you compare two documents. According to Tesch (1990:191), TEXTPACK makes a list of all the words in one document and counts how often each word occurs. Then it does the same thing for a second document and compares the lists. You can also do this with some word processors and with grammar-checking software.

Simple, Effective Content Analysis: Margolis's Study

Content analysis can be elegant and uncomplicated. Maxine Margolis (1984) did ethnohistorical research on the changing images of women in the United States. She used the *Ladies Home Journal*, from 1889 to 1980, as an archival database and asked a simple question: Do ads in the *Ladies Home Journal* for household products show homemakers or servants using those products (Margolis, personal communication)?

From historical data, Margolis knew that the large pool of cheap servant labor in U.S. cities—labor that had been driven there by the Industrial Revolution—was in decline by about 1900. The readers of the *Ladies Home Journal* in those days were middle-class women who were accustomed to employing household servants. Margolis's counts showed clearly the transformation of the middle-class homemaker from an employer of servants to a direct user of household products.

Margolis took a random sample of her database (2 years per decade of the magazine, and 2 months per year, for a total of 36 magazines), but she did not have to devise a complex tagging scheme. She simply looked for the presence or absence of a single, major message. It is very unlikely that Margolis could have made a mistake in coding the ads she examined. Servants are either portrayed in the ad, or they aren't. So, by defining a nominal variable, one that is easily recognized, Margolis was able to do a content analysis that added an interesting dimension to her historical ethnographic work on changing images of middle-class urban women.

Complex Content Analysis: Springle's Study

Most content analysis is considerably more complex and requires a lot of judgments to be made in coding text. Susan Springle (1986) was interested in the distribution of materialism as a value in American society. She felt that this distribution would be apparent in the symbolic content of mainstream comic strips and underground comics, known as "comix." The underground comix began publishing in the early 1960s, just as what became known as the counterculture movement got underway. Springle felt that support for materialism would be manifest in the mainstream Sunday comic strips, while rejection of materialism would show up in the comix.

To test her idea, Springle selected 55 panels from underground comix and 55 from popular Sunday comic strips in 1971-1972 and 1981-1982. The first year, 1971-1972, was the height of the counterculture era. It was near the end of the Vietnam War and was a time of intense activism on college campuses in the United States. By contrast, 1981-1982 was the beginning of the Reagan era—the beginning of what came to be known as the "decade of greed."

The 220 representative panels from the two media (Sunday comics and underground comix) contained references to 257 products and 137 retail establishments by name. Two coders went through all the strip panels and, for each product or establishment named, judged the artist's intent (to arouse laughter, to do a nonhumorous social critique, to portray social reality); the central character's orientation toward the product (negative or positive); the artist's representation of the product (positive or negative); and so on. Coders made 1,920 judgments in all and disagreed on just 154.

It turned out that, over time, the heroes of the comix were three times as likely as their counterparts in the mainstream comics to be portrayed pursuing wealth and material comfort. Moreover, consumer products were about six times more likely to show up in the comix than in the comics. Springle thought that this might have been because the artists who draw comix like to poke fun at consumer products. But the mainstream comics characters were three times more likely to be portrayed as negative to consumer products as were the comix characters.

Springle's interpretation: The counterculture, she says, embraced materialism in the early 1970s even as they were denouncing it. They were in their 20s at the time and had come from families that had enjoyed material abundance. They were on college campuses, had the time and the intellectual tools for protest, and had the civil rights movement of the 1960s as their model.

As the Vietnam War ended, however, the counterculturalists simply grew up and moved on. Over the next decade, they increased their acceptance of their deeply rooted materialism while their protest against it withered away. "Neither their consumption behavior nor their comic art," said Springle, "reflected a rejection of materialism" (1986:111). They accepted and consumed jeans, stereo systems, drugs, cars, and certain fashions that their parents had rejected. Acquisitiveness, Springle concluded, is a core value in America, one that provides "cultural integration through the national diffusion of symbols and meanings by the multibillion dollar advertising industry" (ibid.).

Springle's and Margolis's studies are clever uses of interesting, naturally occurring databases. These studies show how people lay down archeological traces of their values in their popular literature.

Problems with Content Analysis

Nevertheless, content analysis is full of methodological pitfalls, many of which Colby documented in his pioneering work in 1966. Colby studied folktales from around the world. He tagged each content word with labels that reflected concepts like "competition," "achievement," "aggression," "compliance," "affection," and so on. The idea was to determine the likelihood of one concept, like "aggression," appearing in the same paragraph as another, like "masculine."

But who makes up the codes? If it is done by a single researcher, then construct validity may be low. Even if constructs are developed by multiple researchers, the actual coding of text is critical. If one person does all the coding, then there is no check on reliability. A single coder may tag words *consistently* with the same concept, but may also make systematic errors in deciding which concepts to use in tagging certain words. Using multiple coders, developing high intercoder reliability, and training coders to use the correct concept when tagging words are required.

Another problem involves the database itself. Anthropologists and folklorists have presumed that folktales were more or less standardized artifacts—that variations in the telling of such stories are minor compared to their similarities. Mathews (1985) showed how one of the most popular folktales in rural Mexico (the story of *La Llorona*, or the "weeping woman") varied radically, and systematically, in a single village, depending on whether the teller was a man or a woman. This is not the fault of the method of content analysis, of course, but it points up how important intracultural variability is, and how it can affect content analysis.

Cross-Cultural Content Analysis: The Human Relations Area Files

The most important archive of ethnographic materials is the Human Relations Area Files. HRAF is a 900,000-page database, collected from more than 7,000 books and articles, on 350 cultural groups around the world. As shown in Chapter 9 on fieldnotes, each page of the HRAF is coded along the right-hand margin using a coding scheme, called the *Outline of Cultural Materials* (OCM) (Murdock, 1971). The archive is growing at about 25,000 coded pages a year.

The coding is done by professionals at HRAF, Inc. in New Haven, Connecticut. Every 10th page that a coder handles is recoded by someone else, so that they maintain an interrater reliability of 75%. This means that no more than 25% of the codes on any given page would be different if different coders at HRAF handled that page. Furthermore, the coders are 90% reliable within one digit of the third figure in each code. That is, if a coder labels a sentence 765 (mourning), then 90% of the time other coders would label the same sentence 765, or 764 (funerals) or 766 (deviant mortuary practices).

Each page of the HRAF is duplicated and filed under each code appearing on that page. On average, each page contains five different codes. Since there are around 900,000 pages of primary materials, there are about 4.5 million pages of material in the HRAF archive.

The whole archive is on microfiche. You can search fairly quickly for every reference to any of the 350 cultures, or you search for every reference to particular OCM codes—things like 177 (culture contact), 266 (cannibalism), 294 (clothing manufacture), 579 (brawls, riots, and banditry), 757 (medical therapy), 854 (infant care), and so on.

Since 1990, HRAF has been digitizing this gargantuan ethnographic database and publishing it piece by piece on CD-ROM. So far, the archive on a sample of 60 cultures from around the world has been published on CD-ROM. For those 60 cultures, you can use text management software, like the programs I discussed in Chapter 9, to search for co-occurrences of words on the same page, or within, say, 2, or 5, or 10 lines of one another.

HRAF turns the ethnographic literature into a database for content analysis and cross-cultural tests of hypotheses. There are five steps in doing an HRAF study (Otterbein, 1969):

1. State a hypothesis that requires cross-cultural data.
2. Draw a representative sample of the world's cultures from the 350 in the files.
3. Look for the appropriate OCM codes in the sample.
4. Code the variables according to whatever conceptual scheme you've developed in forming your hypothesis.
5. Run the appropriate statistical tests and examine the outcome to see if your hypothesis is confirmed.

Choosing a good sample is a problem. You must ensure that societies (a) are independent of one another, (b) represent the range of social evolutionary complexity, and (c) represent the geographic distribution of cultures in the world. Many researchers use either of two standard samples, one of 60 societies (developed at HRAF), and one of 186 societies (developed by Murdock and White, 1969). Both samples are comprised of societies for which ample ethnographic materials are available.

Fewer topics are covered in the literature on the 60-society sample than in the literature in the 186-society sample. On the other hand, the 60-society sample is based on material in the HRAF archive, while about a fourth of the societies in the 186-society sample are not represented in the HRAF archive.

Suppose you are interested in the relationship of the use of hallucinogens and certain types of religious practices. Many of the societies in the 60-society sample will lack coded materials on hallucinogens. The 186-society sample, however, will have more representatives of societies with data on this topic, but you'll have a harder time finding the material than if you could just look it up in the archive.

Note that steps 3 and 4 refer to different kinds of codes. If an HRAF analyst codes a particular paragraph as 591, this means only that the paragraph is about residence. The code 591 does not tell you what the residence is. You have to read the paragraph and convert the primary ethnographic material into usable codes for statistical analysis. You might use 1=patrilocal, 2=matrilocal, 3=neolocal, and so on.

Of course, many researchers have used residence as a variable in previous studies. Reliable numeric codes have been published for residence and for hundreds of other variables as well. Suppose you want to study Native American vision quests, however, and your hypothesis requires data on the variable "level of personal involvement in religious experiences." In that case, you'd have to do your own coding of the archive. You'd look through the archive for paragraphs marked 781, which refers to religious experiences, and decide exactly how to code each paragraph. You might use a simple scale, like high versus low involvement, or you might find sufficient data to code involvement from 1 to 5. In the end, in content analysis as in all research, you have to make the measurements.

Most researchers today use the 186-society Murdock-White (1969) sample. Over the last 25 years, codes for perhaps 500 variables have been published for all the societies in that sample. *Ethnology* and *Behavior Science Research* print the variable codes used by cross-cultural researchers who publish papers in those journals. Barry and Schlegel (1980) published codes for several hundred variables. Codes for 300 variables have been published on IBM-compatible diskette by HRAF Press for the 60-society sample.

The *World Cultures Journal* (WCJ), which comes on an IBM-compatible diskette, has published most of the codes from Barry and Schlegel's book (1980), and more besides. Cross-cultural researchers are constantly coding up new materials themselves and sending in their raw codes to WCJ. (See Appendix G for information on WCJ.)

Besides sampling and coding, there are other problems to keep in mind when using HRAF. You may not always find information where you expect it to be. David Levinson has been doing cross-cultural research on family violence. He asked the coders at HRAF how they would code family violence (which is not one of the categories in the OCM). They said that they would classify it under code 593 (family relationships) or code 578 (in-group antagonisms).

Levinson scoured the files for references to those codes and found quite a lot of useful information. He coded whether or not a society was reported to exhibit family violence, what kind of violence was reported (child abuse, abuse of the elderly, etc.), and how severe the violence was. Later, however, just by browsing through the files, Levinson noticed that wife beating was usually coded under 684, sex and marital offenses (personal communication).

Many societies, it turns out, only exhibit (or are reported to have) wife beating in cases of adultery or suspicion of adultery. The lesson for conducting a cross-cultural study is pretty clear: There is no substitute for reading the ethnographies and looking for new clues on how to code variables.

Finally, there is the problem of data quality control. Archival research in HRAF may be nonreactive, but the ethnographer who made the original observations may have been awfully obtrusive. He or she may have used inadequate informants (or informants who lied). Or the ethnographer may have been biased in recording data. These problems were brought to the attention of anthropologists in a pioneering work by Raoul Naroll in 1962. Cross-cultural researchers have since done many studies on this issue (see Levinson, 1978; Rohner et al., 1973).

Divale (1976) tested the long-standing notion that female status increases with societal complexity. He used two independent measures of female status, compared against a measure of societal complexity and found a relationship between these two variables—in the opposite direction from what everyone expected. According to the data, the higher the complexity of the society, the *lower* the status of women.

Divale then controlled for the effects of data quality control variables. He limited his database to ethnographies written by investigators who had spent at least a year in the field and who spoke the native language fluently. When he controlled for these factors, the unexpected inverse relationship between female status and societal complexity vanished. In these ethnographies, high female status is reported at all levels of societal complexity, while low status is reported primarily among less complex societies.

Despite some problems, however, research using HRAF continues to illuminate theoretically interesting problems. Candice Bradley (1986), for example, investigated the division of labor and the value of children in society. She found that where large animals are present, men, rather than women, engage in animal husbandry, and boys are particularly valued. Melvin Ember (1984-1985) showed that either high male mortality in warfare or delayed age of marriage for men produces an excess of marriageable women, and that both of these factors are strongly associated with the presence of polygyny in cultures of the world. Ferguson (1983:185) found that cultures with benevolent gods have "fewer, better defined, and more accessible, but less visible shrines than cultures with primarily malevolent gods."

Carol Ember (1975, 1978) learned that 62% of hunter-gatherers are patrilocal, 16% are matrilocal, and 16% are bilocal (the rest show a variety of rare postmarital residence types). The tendency of hunter-gatherers to be bilocal was predicted by three factors: level of depopulation, size of community, and stability of rainfall in their area.

Ember offered a theory that accounted for her statistical findings. Fluctuating rainfall leads to fluctuations in the presence of fauna. This, in turn, does not support rigid postmarital residence rules. If you have a protein resource problem, you have to keep the group size down. To do this, you have to able to move males and females around in a flexible fashion.

In other words, you have to go where the meat is and not insist on following marriage residence rules. Furthermore, in small communities, there is a statistically greater chance that at any moment there will be too few men or too few women available for marriage according to a rigid residence rule. If, for example, you insisted that women leave the group, then in extreme cases this might lead to a group becoming so small that it was no longer viable.

Ember was able to identify an important statistical relationship by her cross-cultural study. But even more importantly, she was able to show how that relationship came about. Cross-cultural research will doubtless become much more important as CD-ROM and other technologies make it easier and easier to use the HRAF archive expands, as fieldwork becomes more expensive, and as anthropologists become more skilled at quantitative analysis of qualitative data.

See Pool (1959), Holsti (1968), Carney (1972), Krippendorf (1980), and Weber (1990) for more examples of how content analysis has been used in the social sciences. For more on how to do cross-cultural archival research, see the special issue of *Behavior Science Research*, published in 1991 (Volume 25, 1-4), entitled "Cross-Cultural and Comparative Research: Theory and Method."

Disguised Field Observation

In disguised field observation, a researcher pretends to actually join a group and proceeds to record data about people in the group. It is the ultimate in participant observation—where the participation is so complete that informants do not know that the ethnographer is watching them. This presumes, of course, that the ethnographer can blend in physically and linguistically to the group he or she is studying.

In 1960, John H. Griffin, a white journalist underwent drug treatment to temporarily turn his skin black. He traveled the southern United States for about a month, taking notes on how he was treated and received. His book, *Black Like Me* (1961) was a real shocker. It galvanized a lot of white support in the north for the then-fledgling civil rights movement. Clearly, Griffin engaged in premeditated deception in gathering the data for his book. But Griffin was a journalist; social scientists don't deceive their informants, right?

The Tearoom Trade Study

Wrong. Without telling his subjects that he was doing research, Laud Humphreys (1975) observed hundreds of homosexual acts among men in St. Louis. Humphreys's study produced very important results. The men involved in this "tearoom trade," as it is called, came from all walks of life, and many were married and living otherwise "straight" lives. Humphreys made it clear that he did not engage in homosexual acts himself, but played the role of the "watch queen," or lookout, warning his informants when someone approached the rest room. This deception and unobtrusive observation, however, did not cause the storm of criticism that accompanied the first publication of Humphreys's work in 1970.

That was caused by Humphreys having taken his research a step further. He jotted down the license plate numbers of the men who used the rest room for quick, impersonal sex, and got their names and addresses from motor vehicle records. He waited a year after doing his observational work, and then, on the pretext that they had been randomly selected for inclusion in a general health survey, he interviewed 100 of his research subjects in their homes.

Humphreys was careful to change his car, his hair style, and his dress, and according to him, his informants did not recognize him as the man who had once played watch queen for them in public toilets. *This* is what made Humphreys's research the focus of another debate, that is still going on, about the ethics of nonreactive field observation.

Five years after the initial study was published, Humphreys himself said that he had made a mistake. He had endangered the social, emotional, and economic lives of his research subjects. Had his files been subpoenaed, he could not have claimed immunity. He decided at the time that he would go to jail rather than hurt his informants (Humphreys, 1975).

Everyone associated with Humphreys agreed that he was totally committed to protecting his informants. He was very concerned with the ethics of his research, as any reader of his monograph can tell. Humphreys was an ordained Episcopal priest who had held a parish for more than a decade before going to graduate school. He was active in the civil rights movement in the early 1960s and spent time in jail for committing crimes of conscience. His credentials as an ethical person, conscious of his responsibilities to others, were in good order. But listen to what Arlene Kaplan Daniels had to say about all this, in a letter to Myron Glazer, one of the most respected ethnographers in sociology.

In my opinion, no one in the society deserves to be trusted with hot, incriminating data. Let me repeat, *no one.* . . . We should not have to rely on the individual strength of conscience which may be required. Psychiatrists, for example, are notorious gossipers [about their patients]. . . . O. K., so they mainly just tell one another. But they *sometimes* tell wives, people at parties, you and me. [Daniels had done participant observation research on psychiatrists.] And few of them would hold up under systematic pressure from government or whatever to get them to tell. . . . The issue is not that a few brave souls *do* resist. The issue is rather what to do about the few who will not. . . . There is *nothing* in our training—any more than in the training of psychiatrists, no matter what they say—to prepare us to take up these burdens. (quoted in Glazer, 1975:219-220; emphasis in original)

Researchers who conduct the kinds of studies that Humphreys did, invoke several arguments to justify their use of deception. First of all, they say, it is impossible to study such things as homosexual encounters in public rest rooms in any other way. Second, they point out that disguised field observation is a technique that is available only to researchers who are physically and linguistically indistinguishable from the people they are studying.

In other words, to use this technique, you must be a member of the larger culture, and thus, they say, there is no real ethical question involved, other than whether you, as an individual, feel comfortable doing this kind of research. Third, public places, like rest rooms, are, simply, public. The counter argument is that people have a right to expect that their behavior in public toilets will not be recorded, period (Koocher, 1977).

Sechrest and Phillips (1979) take a middle ground. They say that "public behavior should be observable by any means that protect what might be called 'assumed' privacy, the privacy that one might expect from being at a distance from others or of being screened from usual views" (p. 14). This would make the use of binoculars, listening devices, peepholes, and periscopes unethical. Casual observation, on the other hand, would be within ethical bounds.

Some ethnographers (Erikson, 1967) take the stand that disguised observation should never be used as a data-gathering technique by social scientists. My own position is that the decision to use deception is up to you, provided that the *risks of detection are your own risks and no one else's.* If detection risks harm to others, then don't even consider disguised participant observation. Recognize, too, that it may not be possible to foresee the potential harm that you might do using disguised observation. This is what leads scholars like Erikson to the conclusion that the technique is never justified.

Grades of Deception

But is all deception equally deceitful? Aren't there grades of deception? In the 1960s, Edward Hall and other anthropologists (Hall, 1963, 1966, Watson & Graves, 1966) showed how people in different cultures use different "body language" to communicate—that is, they stand at different angles to one another, or at different distances when engaging in serious versus casual conversation. Hall called this different use of space *proxemics*. He noted that people learn this proxemic behavior as part of their early cultural learning and he hypothesized that subcultural variations in spatial orientation often leads to breakdowns in communication, isolation of minorities, and so on.

This seminal observation by an anthropologist set off a flurry of research by social psychologists. Aiello and Jones (1971) studied the proxemic behavior of middle-class white and lower-class Puerto Rican and black schoolchildren. They trained a group of elementary schoolteachers to observe and code the distance and orientation of pairs of children to one another during recess periods.

Sure enough, there were clear cultural and gender differences. White children stand much farther apart in ordinary interaction than do either black or Puerto Rican children. The point here is that the teachers were natural participants in the system. The researchers trained these natural participants to be observers, in order to cut out any reactivity that outsiders might have caused in doing the observation.

Scherer (1974) studied pairs of children in a schoolyard in Toronto. He used only lower-class black and lower-class white children in his study, in order to control for socioeconomic effects. Scherer adapted techniques from photogrammetry (making surveys by using photographs). He mounted a camera in a park adjacent to the schoolyard. Using a telephoto lens, he took unobtrusive shots of pairs of children who were at least 30 meters away.

This got rid of the reactivity problem. Then Scherer devised a clever way to measure the average distance between two children and did his analysis on the quantitative data. He found no significant differences in the distance between pairs of white or black children.

I don't consider any of these studies of children's proxemic behavior to have been unethical. The children were observed in the course of their ordinary activities, out in the open, in truly public places. Despite the training of teachers to make observations, or the taking of surreptitious pictures, the deception involved was passive—it didn't involve "taking in" the informants, making them believe one thing in order to get them to do another. I don't think that any real invasion of privacy occurred.

Contrast these studies with the work of Middlemist et al. (1976). They wanted to measure the length of time it takes for men to begin urinating, how long men continue to urinate, and whether these things are affected by how close men stand to each other in public toilets.

At first, the investigators simply pretended to be grooming themselves at the sink in a public toilet at a university. They tracked the time between the sound of a fly being unzipped and urine hitting the water in the urinal as the time for onset; they also noted how long it took for the sound of urine to stop hitting the water in the urinal and counted this as the duration of each event. They noted whether subjects were standing alone, next to someone, or one or two urinals away from someone.

In general, the closer a man stood to another man, the longer it took him to begin urinating and the shorter the duration of the event. This confirmed laboratory research showing that social stress inhibits relaxation of the urethral sphincter in men, thus inhibiting flow of urine.

Middlemist et al. decided to control the independent variable—how far away another man was from each subject. They placed "BEING CLEANED" signs on some urinals, and forced unsuspecting men to use a particular urinal in a public toilet. Then a confederate stood next to the subject, or one urinal away, or did not appear at all. The observer hid in a toilet stall next to the urinals and made the measurements. But then the observer couldn't hear flies unzipping and urine hitting the water from inside the stall—so the researchers used a periscopic prism, trained on the area of interest, to make the observations directly.

Personally, I doubt that many people would have objected to the study if Middlemist and his colleagues had just lurked in the rest room and done simple, unobtrusive observation. But when they contrived to make men urinate in a specific place; when they contrived to manipulate the dependent variable (urination time); and, above all, when they got that periscope into the act, that changed matters. This is a clear case of invasion of privacy by researchers, in my view.

In a severe critique of the research, Koocher (1977:120) said that "at the very least, the design seems laughable and trivial." Middlemist et al. (1977:123) defended themselves, saying that "we believe . . . that the pilot observation and the experiment together constitute an example of well-controlled field research, adequate to test the null hypothesis that closeness has no effect" on the duration of urination among males in public rest rooms. Actually, Middlemist et al.'s study *design* was anything but trivial. In fact, it was quite elegant. But is knowing what they found out worth using the method they chose?

Passive Deception

Passive deception involves no experimental manipulation of informants in order to get them to act in certain ways. Humphreys's first observational study (1975) involved passive deception. He made his observations in public places where he had every right to be in the first place. He took no names down, and there were no data that could be traced to any particular individual. Humphreys observed felonies, and that fact makes the case more complex. But in my mind, at least, he had the right to observe others in public places, irrespective of whether those observed believed that they would or would not be observed.

Many anthropologists use passive deception in their fieldwork, observation, and ethnography. I have spent hours pretending to be a shopper in a large department store and have observed mothers who are disciplining their children. I have played the role of a strolling tourist on Mexican beaches (an easy role to play, since that was exactly what I was), and recorded how American and Mexican families occupied beach space. I have surreptitiously clocked the time it takes for people who were walking along the streets of Athens (Greece), New York City, Gainesville (Florida), and Ixmiquilpan (Mexico) to cover 10 meters of sidewalk at various times of the day. I have stood in crowded outdoor bazaars in Mexico, watching and recording differences between Indians and non-Indians in the amount of produce purchased.

Personally, I have never felt the slightest ethical qualm about having made these observations. In my opinion, passive deception is ethically aseptic. Ultimately, however, the responsibility for the choice of method, and for the practical, human consequences of using a particular method, rests with you, the individual researcher. You can't foist off that responsibility on "the profession," or on some "code of ethics." Are you disturbed by the fact that Humphreys did his research at all, or only by the fact that he came close to compromising his informants? As you answer that question for yourself, you'll have a better idea of where *you* stand on the issue of disguised field observation.

Naturalistic Field Experiments

As I made clear in Chapter 3, *natural* experiments are going on around you all the time. They are the result of people making decisions about the allocation of their time, money, and human capital resources. All you have to do is figure out how to cleverly monitor them and evaluate their outcomes. A *naturalistic* experiment, on the other hand, has to be contrived. You *create* situations that result in behaviors that can be counted and measured.

The Lost-Letter Technique

Milgram et al. (1965) devised a naturalistic experiment for doing unobtrusive surveys of political opinion. The method is called the "lost-letter technique" and consists of "losing" a lot of letters that have addresses and stamps on them.

The technique is based on two assumptions. First, people in many societies believe that they ought to mail a letter if they find one, especially if it has a stamp on it. Second, people will be less likely to drop a lost letter in the mail if it is addressed to someone or some organization that they don't like.

Milgram et al. (1965) tested these ideas in New Haven, Connecticut. They lost 400 letters in 10 districts of the city. They dropped the letters on the street; they left them in phone booths; they left them on counters at shops; and they tucked them under windshield wipers (after penciling "found near car" on the back of the envelope). Over 70% of the letters addressed to an individual or to a medical research company were returned. Only 25% of the letters addressed to either "Friends of the Communist Party" or "Friends of the Nazi Party" were returned. (The addresses were all the same mailbox that had been rented for the experiment.)

By losing letters in a sample of communities, then, and by counting the differential rates at which they are returned, you can test variations in sentiment. Two of Milgram's students distributed anti-Nazi letters in Munich. The letters did not come back as much from some neighborhoods as from others, and the students were thus able to pinpoint the areas of strongest neo-Nazi sentiment (Milgram, 1969:68). The lost-letter technique has sampling problems and validity problems galore associated with it. But you can see just how intuitively powerful the results can be.

Three More Field Experiments

In a classic experiment, elegant in its simplicity of design, Doob and Gross (1968) had a car stop at a red light and wait for 15 seconds after the light turned green before moving again. In one experimental condition, they used a new car and a well-dressed driver. In another condition, they used an old, beat-up car and a shabbily dressed driver. They repeated the experiment many times and measured the time it took for people in the car behind the experimental car to start honking their horns. It won't surprise you to learn that people were quicker to vent their frustration at apparently low-status cars and drivers.

Piliavin et al. (1969) contrived an experiment to test what is called the "good Samaritan" problem. Students in the project rode a particular subway train in New York City. This particular express train made a 7.5 minute run; at 70 seconds into the run, a researcher pitched forward and collapsed. The team used four experimental conditions: the "stricken" person was either black or white and was either carrying a cane or a liquor bottle. Observers noted how long it took for people in the subway car to come to the aid of the supposedly stricken person, the total population of the car, whether bystanders were black or white, and so on. (You can conjure up the results. There were no surprises.)

In a theatrical field experiment (done by psychologists and drama majors at a university) Harari et al. (1985) tested whether men on a college campus would come to the aid of a woman being raped. These investigators staged the rape scenes and found that there was a significant difference in the helping reaction of male passersby if those men were alone or in groups.

Are Field Experiments Ethical?

Field experiments come in a range of ethical varieties, from innocuous to borderline to downright ugly. I see no ethical problems with the lost-letter technique. When people mail one of the lost letters, they don't know that they are taking part in a social science experiment, but that doesn't bother me. No real harm, either, in the experiment to test whether people vent their anger by honking their car horns more quickly at people they think are lower socioeconomic class.

Randomized field experiments, used mostly in evaluation research, can be problematic. Suppose you wanted to know whether fines or jail sentences are better at changing the behavior of drunk drivers. One way to do that would be to randomly assign people who were convicted of the offense to one or the other condition and watch the results. Suppose one of the subjects whom you didn't put in jail kills an innocent person? Similarly, is it fair to randomly deny some people the benefits of a new drug just to study the effects of not having it? These kinds of studies are done all the time.

The experiments by Piliavin et al. and Harari et al. on whether people will come to the aid of a stricken person or a woman being raped are ethically very problematic. Experiments like those can endanger the emotional health of the subjects. People do not like to find out that they have been duped into being part of an experiment, and some people may suffer a terrible loss of self-esteem if they do find out and conclude that they acted badly. That's one reason why most researchers who conduct field experiments debrief their subjects thoroughly. In the guerrilla theater experiment conducted by Piliavin et al., however, no debriefing is possible.

On the other hand, I'm not so sure that debriefing is always good, either. How would you feel if you were one of the people who failed to respond to a rape victim, and then were told that you were just part of an experiment—that no real rape ever took place, and thank you very much for your help? But if you think *these* cases are borderline, consider the study by West et al. (1975) on whether there is a little larceny in us all.

The Watergate Experiment

In the Watergate affair, men loyal to then President Richard Nixon broke into the headquarters of the Democratic party at the Watergate Hotel in Washington, DC, to photograph documents pertinent to the 1972 election campaign. Their bungling of the job, and the subsequent cover-up by Nixon and his staff at the White House, led to the unprecedented resignation of the president of the United States from office in 1974. Soon thereafter, West et al. (1975) conducted their experiment.

They confronted 80 different students with a proposition to burglarize a local advertising firm. Subjects were randomly assigned to one of four conditions. In the first condition, subjects were told that the job was to be committed for the Internal Revenue Service. The IRS, it seemed, needed to get the goods on this company in order to bring them to trial for tax evasion. If the subjects were caught in the act, then the government would guarantee immunity from prosecution. In the second condition, subjects were told that there was no immunity from prosecution.

In the third condition, subjects were told that another advertising agency had paid $8,000 for the job, and that they (the subjects) would get $2,000 for their part in it. (Remember, that was $2,000 in 1979—a lot of money.) Finally, in the fourth condition, subjects were told that the burglary was being committed just to see if the plan would work. Nothing would be taken from the office.

Understand that this was not a "let's pretend" exercise. Subjects were not brought into a laboratory and told to imagine that they were being asked to commit a crime. This was for real. Subjects met the experimenter at his home or at a restaurant. They were all criminology students at a university and knew the experimenter to be an actual local private investigator. The private eye arranged an elaborate and convincing plan for the burglary, including data on the comings and goings of police patrol cars, aerial photographs, blueprints of the building—the works.

The subjects really believed that they were being solicited to commit a crime. Just as predicted by the researchers, a lot of the subjects agreed to do it in the first condition, where they thought the crime was for a government agency and that they'd be free of danger from prosecution if caught. What do you suppose would happen to *your* sense of self-worth when you were finally debriefed and told that you were one of the 36 out of 80 (45%) who agreed to participate in the burglary in the first condition? (See Cook, 1975, for a critical comment on the ethics of this experiment.)

Field Experiments and Anthropology

Can field experiments provide data of interest to anthropologists? I'll discuss a few important examples of cross-cultural field experiments (also done by social psychologists), and let you be the judge.

Feldman (1968) did five field experiments in Paris, Boston, and Athens to test whether people in those cities respond more kindly to foreigners or to members of their own culture. In one experiment the researchers simply asked for directions and measured whether foreigners or natives got better treatment. Parisians and Athenians gave help significantly more often to fellow nationals than to foreigners. In Boston, there was no difference.

In the second experiment, foreigners and natives stood at major metro stops and asked total strangers to do them a favor. They explained that they were waiting for a friend, couldn't leave the spot they were on, and had to mail a letter. They asked people to mail the letters for them (the letters were addressed to the experiment headquarters) and simply counted how many letters they got back from the different metro stops in each city. Half the letters were unstamped.

In Boston and Paris, between 32% and 35% of the people refused to mail a letter for a fellow citizen. In Athens, 93% refused. Parisians treated Americans significantly better than Bostonians treated Frenchmen on this task. In fact, in the case where Parisians were asked to mail a letter that was stamped, they treated Americans significantly better than they treated other Parisians. (So much for *that* stereotype.)

In the third experiment, researchers approached informants and said "Excuse me, sir. Did you just drop this dollar bill?" (or other currency, depending on the city). It was easy to measure whether or not people falsely claimed the money more from foreigners than from natives. This experiment yielded meager results.

In the fourth experiment, foreigners and natives went to pastry shops in the three cities, bought a small item and gave the clerk 25% more than the item cost. Then they left the shop and recorded whether the clerk had offered to return the overpayment. This experiment also showed little difference among the cities, or between the way foreigners and locals are treated.

And in the fifth experiment, researchers took taxis from the same beginning points to the same destinations in all three cities. They measured whether foreigners or natives were charged more. In neither Boston nor Athens was a foreigner overcharged more than a local. In Paris, however, Feldman found that "the American foreigner was overcharged significantly more often than the French compatriot in a variety of ingenious ways" (1968:11).

Feldman collected data on more than 3,000 interactions and was able to draw conclusions about cultural differences in how various peoples respond to foreigners as opposed to other natives. Some stereotypes were confirmed, while others were crushed. Furthermore, using ethnographic data that had been collected by anthropologists in Greece, Feldman was able to interpret his findings and place them in a theoretically interesting context.

Bochner did a series of interesting experiments on the nature of Aboriginal-white relations in urban Australia (see Bochner, 1980:335-340, for a review). These experiments are clever, inexpensive, and illuminating, and Bochner's self-conscious critique of the limitations of his own work is a model for field experimentalists to follow. In one experiment, Bochner (1972) put two classified ads in a Sydney paper:

> Young couple, no children, want to rent small unfurnished flat up to $25 per week. Saturday only. 759-6000.
> Young Aboriginal couple, no children, want to rent small unfurnished flat up to $25 per week. Saturday only. 759-6161. (p. 335)

Different people were assigned to answer the two phones, to ensure that callers who responded to both ads would not hear the same voice. Note that the ads were identical in every respect, except for fact that in one of the ads the ethnicity of the couple was identified, while in the other it was not. There were 14 responses to the ethnically nonspecific ad and 2 responses to the ethnically specific ad (3 additional people responded to both ads).

In another experiment, Bochner exploited what he calls the *Fifi effect* (Bochner, 1980:336). The Fifi effect refers to the fact that urbanites acknowledge the presence of strangers who pass by while walking a dog and ignore others. Bochner sent a white woman and an Aboriginal woman, both in their early 20s, and similarly dressed, to a public park in Sydney. He had them walk a small dog through randomly assigned sectors of the park, for 10 minutes in each sector.

Each woman was followed by two observers, who gave the impression that they were just out for a stroll. The two observers *independently* recorded the interaction of the women with passersby. The observers recorded the frequency of smiles offered to the women, the number of times anyone said anything to the women, and the number of nonverbal recognition nods the women received. The white woman received 50 approaches, while the Aboriginal woman received only 18 (Bochner, 1971:111).

There are many elegant touches in this experiment. Note how the age and dress of the experimenters were controlled, so that only their ethnic identity remained as a dependent variable. Note how the time for each experimental trial (10 minutes in each sector) was controlled to ensure an equal opportunity for each woman to receive the same treatment by strangers. Bochner did preliminary observation in the park and divided it into sectors that had the same population density, so the chance for interaction with strangers would be about equal in each run of the experiment, and he used two independent observer-recorders.

As Bochner points out, however, there were still design flaws that threatened the internal validity of the experiment (1980:337). As it happens, the interrater reliability of the two observers in this experiment was nearly perfect. But suppose the two observers shared the same cultural expectations about Aboriginal-white relations in urban Australia. They might have quite reliably misrecorded the cues that they were observing.

Reactive and unobtrusive observation alike tell you *what* happened, not *why*. It is tempting to conclude that the Aboriginal woman was ignored because of active prejudice. But, says Bochner, "perhaps passersby ignored the Aboriginal . . . because they felt a personal approach might be misconstrued as patronizing" (ibid.:338).

In Bochner's third study, a young white or Aboriginal woman walked into a butcher's shop and asked for 10 cents' worth of bones for her pet dog. The dependent variables in the experiment were the weight and quality of the bones. (An independent dog fancier rated the bones on a 3-point scale, without knowing how the bones were obtained, or why.) Each woman visited seven shops in a single middle-class shopping district.

In both amount and quality of bones received, the white woman did better than the Aboriginal. But the differences were not statistically significant—the sample was just too small—and so, no conclusions could be drawn from that study alone.

Remember Feldman's research? He could draw stronger conclusion from his five cross-cultural experiments on cooperation with foreigners and natives than he could if he had done only one experiment. And, *taken all together*, the three studies done by Bochner and his students constitute a powerful set of information about Aboriginal-white relations in Sydney. Naturalistic experiments have their limitations; they lack the sort of context and texture that anthropologists correctly insist on. But if they are done carefully, and in concert with ethnography, they can be an important form of data collection in cultural anthropology.

16

Analysis of Qualitative Data

Q ualitative analysis—in fact, all analysis—is the search for patterns in data and for ideas that help explain the existence of those patterns. It starts even before you go to the field and continues throughout the research effort. As you develop ideas, you test them against your observations; your observations may then modify your ideas, which then need to be tested again; and so on. Don't look for closure in the process. If you're doing it right, it never stops.

Don't worry about getting ideas, either; if you've prepared for research by reading the relevant literature, and if you collect data of your own, your hardest job will be to sort through all the ideas and decide which ones to test. And don't worry about seeing patterns in your data, or about not being able to come up with causal explanations for things you see in fieldwork. It can happen very fast, often in a matter of hours or days, so be suspicious of your pet ideas and continually check yourself to make sure you're not embellishing or even inventing patterns. Early in fieldwork, eagerness and observer expectations can lead to seeing patterns that aren't there. If you are highly self-critical, then as fieldwork progresses your tendency to see patterns everywhere will diminish. But the problem can also get worse as research progresses if you accept uncritically the folk analyses of articulate or prestigious informants. It is important from a humanistic standpoint to seek the emic perspective and to document folk analyses (Lofland, 1971). In some cases, those analyses may be correct. But it is equally important to remain skeptical, to retain an etic perspective, not to "go native" (Miles & Huberman, 1994:216).

The Constant Validity Check

As field research progresses, try consciously to switch back and forth between these two perspectives, the emic and the etic, and to check yourself from either buying into the folk explanations or rejecting them without considering their possible validity. Checking yourself during fieldwork is not hard to do; it's just hard to remember to do it systematically. Here are some guidelines.

1. Look for consistencies and inconsistencies among knowledgeable informants and find out why informants disagree about important things.
2. Whenever possible, check informants' reports of behavior or of environmental conditions against more objective evidence (see Chapter 7).
3. Be open to negative evidence rather than annoyed when it pops up. When you encounter a case that doesn't fit your theory (middle-class suburban teenagers who don't like malls, for example), ask yourself whether it's the result of: (a) normal intracultural variation, (b) your lack of knowledge about the range of appropriate behavior, or (c) a genuinely unusual case.
4. As you come to understand how something works, seek out alternative explanations from informants and from colleagues, and listen to them carefully. American folk culture, for example, holds that women left the home for the work force because of something called "feminism" and "women's liberation." An alternative explanation is that feminist values and orientations are supported, if not caused, by women being *driven* out of their homes and into the work force as a result of inflation and the declining value of their husbands' incomes (Margolis, 1984). Both the emic, folk explanation and the etic, materialist explanation are interesting for different reasons.
5. Try to fit extreme cases into your theory, and if the cases won't fit, don't be too quick to throw them out. It is always easier to throw out cases than it is

TABLE 16.1

Chart for Checking the Shared Character
of a Perspective Offered by Informants

		Volunteered	Directed by Observer	Total
Statements	to observer alone	I	V	
	to others in everyday conversation	II	VI	
Activities	individual	III	VII	
	group	IV	VIII	
Total				

SOURCE: "Participant observation: The analysis of qualitative field data," by H. S. Becker & B. Geer in *Human Organization Research* (R. N. Adams & J. J. Preiss, Eds.), p. 287. © 1960 by The Dorsey Press. Used with permission.

to reexamine one's ideas, and the easy way out is hardly ever the right way in research.

Table 16.1 was developed by Becker and Geer (1960:287) and is still a great device for checking the patterns you think you see in qualitative data—patterns in things informants said or did. The idea is to understand how much a particular pattern of ideas or behavior is shared by members of a culture, how collective it is, and how legitimate (proper) they think it is. For each pattern, or hypothesis, go through your notes and extract the relevant informant statements and your observations of informants' behaviors.

For each *statement* made by an informant, ask whether it was made to others in everyday conversation or whether it was something you (or another observer in a multiresearcher project) extracted in an interview, alone with the informant. For each of those two conditions, ask whether the informant volunteered the statement, or if it was engineered by an observer. Cell VIII of Table 16.1 covers situations in which a participant observer maneuvers the conversation around to a topic he or she is interested in.

For each *behavior* or activity observed, ask whether it occurred when the researcher was alone with the informant or in a group, and for each of those conditions, ask whether the informant acted spontaneously or was directed to act by the observer. Public statements and behaviors are more likely to be legitimate, shared components of a culture than are statements and behaviors produced in private.

Similarly, statements and behaviors that are volunteered by informants are more likely to be part of the shared, collective culture than statements and behaviors that are engineered by a researcher. Intracultural variation, an important component of any culture, is more likely to emerge from field notes about spontaneously generated rather than researcher-generated statements and behavior.

Over time, two things should happen: The proportion of volunteered statements in your notes should increase, and the proportion of notes about behavior displayed only to you should decrease as you become less conspicuous in the culture. These are excellent checks on the credibility of both your data and your theoretical hunches. Also, presenting data on the number and proportion of volunteered versus directed statements and behaviors gives others a chance to judge for themselves whether your explanations are plausible.

Presenting Qualitative Data: Using Quotes

Qualitative data analysis depends heavily on the presentation of selected anecdotes and comments from informants—quotes that lead the reader to understand quickly what it took you months or years to figure out. This technique looks easy, but it's not. You have to avoid what Lofland (1971) called the two great sins of qualitative analysis in order to use the informant quote technique effectively.

The first sin, excessive analysis, involves the all-too-familiar practice of avoiding plain English to say plain things. If you analyze a batch of data and conclude that something simple is going on (like "The more generations that people are removed from their ethnic origins, the less anxiety they feel about their ethnic identity and roots"), don't be afraid to say so. There is absolutely nothing of scientific value to be gained from making straightforward things complicated.

The second sin consists of avoiding doing *any* analysis—being so gun-shy of theory and jargon that you simply fill up your papers and books with lengthy quotes from informants and offer no analysis at all. Data do not speak for themselves. You have to develop your ideas (your analysis) about what's going on, state those ideas clearly, and *illustrate* them with selected quotes from your informants.

Katherine Newman (1986), for example, collected life history material from 30 white, middle-class American women, ages 26 to 57, who had suffered severe losses of income as a result of divorce. Newman discovered and labeled two groups of women, according to her informants' own accounts of which period in their lives had the greatest effect on how they viewed the world. Women whose adolescent and early married years were in the 1960s and early 1970s seemed to be very different from "women of the Depression" who were born between 1930 and 1940.

These women had grown up in two very different socioeconomic and political environments; the differences in those environments had a profound effect on the shaping of people's subjective, interpretive, symbolic view of the world; and, according to Newman's analysis, this accounted for differences in how her informants responded to the economic loss of divorce. Newman illustrated her analytic finding with quotes from her informants.

One woman said:

> I grew up in the '30s on a farm in Minnesota, but my family lost the farm during the Depression. Dad became a mechanic for the WPA, after that, but we moved around a lot. I remember that we never had any fresh fruits or vegetables during that whole time. At school there were soup lines and food handouts. . . . You know, I've been there. I've seen some hard times and it wasn't pleasant. Sometimes when I get low on money now, I get very nervous remembering those times.

By contrast, "women of the '60s" felt the economic loss of divorce but tended to stress the value of having to be more self-reliant, and the importance of friends, education, and personal autonomy over dependence on material things. Newman illustrated this sentiment with quotes like the following:

> Money destroyed my marriage. All my husband wanted was to accumulate more real estate. We had no emotional relationship. Everything was bent toward things. Money to me now is this ugly thing.

Newman found differences in the way women in the two age cohorts dealt with kin support after divorce, the way they related to men in general, and a number of other things that emerged as patterns in her data. For each observation of a patterned difference in response to life after divorce, Newman used selected quotes from her informants to make the point.

Here's another example, from the study I did with Ashton-Vouyoucalos (1976) on Greek labor migrants. Everyone in the population we were studying had spent 5 years or more in West Germany and had returned to Greece to reestablish their lives. We were interested in how these returned migrants felt about the Greece they returned to, compared with the Germany they left.

Before doing a survey, however, we collected life histories from 15 persons, selected because of their range of experiences. Those 15 returned migrants were certainly no random sample, but the consistency of their volunteered observations of differences between the two cultures was striking. Once we noticed the pattern emerging, we laid out the data in tabular form, as shown in Table 16.2. The survey instrument that we eventually built reflected the concerns of our informants.

In reporting our findings, Ashton-Vouyoucalos and I referred to the summary table and illustrated each component with selected quotes from our informants. The issue of gossip, for example (under "negative aspects of Greece" in Table 16.2), was addressed by Despina, a 28-year-old woman from Thrace. Despina was happy to be back in Greece, but she said:

> Look, here you have a friend you visit. Sooner or later you'll wear or do something she doesn't like. We have this habit of gossiping. She'll gossip behind your back. Even if it's your sister. In Germany, they don't have that, at least. Not about what you wear or what you eat. Nothing like that. That's what I liked.

By the way, the translation of Despina's comment has been doctored to make it sound a bit more seamless than it did in the original. I've seen thousands of really interesting quotes in ethnographic reports, and common sense says that most of them were fixed up a bit. I don't see anything wrong with this. In fact, I'm grateful to writers who do it. Unexpurgated speech is terrible to read. It's full of false starts, run-ons, fragments, pauses, filler syllables (like "uh" and "y'know") and whole sentences whose sole purpose is to give speakers a second or two while they think of what to say next. If you don't edit that stuff, you'll bore your readers to death.

Presenting Qualitative Data: Matrices and Tables

An important part of qualitative analysis is the production of visual displays. Laying out your data in table or matrix form, and drawing your theories out in the form of a flow chart, or map, helps you understand what you have, and is also a potent way to communicate your ideas to others (Miles & Huberman, 1994). Learning to build and use qualitative data matrices and flow charts requires practice, but you can get started by studying examples published in research journals.

Van Maanen et al. (1982), for example, compared a traditional commercial fishing operation in Gloucester, Massachusetts, with a modern operation

TABLE 16.2

Summary of Repatriates' Ambivalent Statements About Greece

Negative Aspects of Greece

Economic

(1) Wages are low.

(2) Few jobs are available, especially for persons with specialized skills.

(3) Working conditions are poor.

(4) Inflation is high, especially in the prices of imported goods.

Sociocultural

(1) People in general (but especially public servants) are abrupt and rude.

(2) The roads are littered with rubbish.

(3) Everyone, even friends and relatives, gossips about each other and tries to keep each other down.

(4) People of the opposite sex cannot interact easily and comfortably.

Political

(1) The government is insecure and might collapse with ensuing chaos or a return to dictatorship.

(2) Fear of or actual war with Turkey creates a climate of insecurity.

Negative Aspects of Germany

Economic

(1) Economic opportunities are limited because a foreigner cannot easily open up a private business.

(2) People are reluctant to rent good housing at decent prices to migrant workers.

Sociocultural

(1)   One feels in exile from one's home and kin.

(2) Life is limited to house and factory.

(3) The weather seems bitterly cold and this furthers the sense of isolation.

(4) Migrants are viewed as second-class citizens.

(5) Children may be left behind in Greece, to the sometimes inadequate care of grandparents.

(6) Lack of fluency in German puts Greek workers at a disadvantage.

(7) Parents must eventually choose between sending their children to German schools (where they will grow away from their parents) or to inadequate Greek schools in German cities.

(8) Factory routines are rigid, monotonous, and inhuman and sometimes the machinery is dangerous.

Political

(1) Migrants have no political voice in Germany or in their home country while they are abroad.

SOURCE: "Return migration to Greece," by H. R. Bernard and S. Ashton-Vouyoucalos, 1976, *Journal of Steward Anthropological Society,* 8(1), 31-51. Used with permission.

in Bristol Bay, Alaska. Table 16.3 shows what they found in the analysis of their qualitative field notes. Simple inspection of Table 16.3 gives you an immediate feel for the results of Van Maanen et al.'s descriptive analysis.

The social organization of the traditional fishing operation is more homogeneous, more expressive, and more collegial than that of the modern operation, but profits are lower. Based on the qualitative analysis, Van Maanen et al. were able to state some general, theoretical hypotheses regarding the weakening of personal relations in technology-based fishing operations. This is the kind of general proposition that can be tested by using fishing operations as units of analysis and their technologies as the independent variable.

Donna Birdwell-Pheasant (1984) wanted to understand how differences in interpersonal relationships change over time in the village of Chunox, Belize. She questioned 216 informants about their relationships with members of their families over the years and simulated a longitudinal study with data from a cross-sectional sample. She checked the retrospective data with other information gathered by questionnaires, direct observations, and semistructured interviews. Table 16.4 shows the analytic framework that emerged from Birdwell-Pheasant's work.

Birdwell-Pheasant identified five kinds of relationships: absent, attenuated, coordinate, subordinate, and superordinate. These represent the rows of the matrix in Table 16.4. The columns in the matrix are the four major types of family relationships: ascending generation (parents, aunts, uncles, etc.), siblings, spouse, and descending generation (children, nephews, nieces, etc.).

Birdwell-Pheasant then went through her data and "examined all the available data on Juana Fulana and decided whether, in 1971, she had a coordinate or subordinate relationship with her mother (e.g., did she have her own kitchen? her own wash house?)." (In Latin America, Juan Fulano and Juana Fulana are the male and female equivalents of "so-and-so"—as in "Is so-and-so married?").

Birdwell-Pheasant repeated the process, for *each* of her 216 informants, for *each* of the four relationships in Table 16.4, and for *each* of the years 1965, 1971, 1973, 1975, and 1977. This required 216×4×5 = 4,320 decisions. Birdwell-Pheasant didn't have data on all possible informant-by-year-by-relationship combinations, but, by the time she was through, she had a database of 742 "power readings" of family relationships over time and was able to make some very strong statements about patterns of domestic structure over time in Chunox. This is an excellent example of the use of qualitative data to develop a theory and the conversion of qualitative data to a set of numbers for testing that theory.

TABLE 16.3

Contemporary Forms of Commercial Fishing

	Traditional Fishing (e.g., Gloucester, MA)	Modern Fishing (e.g., Bristol Bay, AK)
Social Organization		
backgrounds of fishermen	homogeneous	heterogen
ties among fishermen	multiple	single
boundaries to entry	social	economic
number of participants	stable	variable
social uncertainty	low	high
relations with competitors	collegial & individualistic	antagonistic & categorical
relations with port	permanent with ties to community	temporary with no local ties
mobility	low	high
relation to fishing	expressive (fishing as lifestyle)	instrumental (fishing as a job)
orientation to work	long-term, optimizing (survival)	short-term, maximizing (seasonal)
tolerance for diversity	low	high
nature of disputes	intra-occupational	transoccupational
Economic Organization		
relations of boats to buyers	personalized (long-term, informal)	contractual (short-term, formal)
information exchange	restrictive & private	open & public
economic uncertainty	low (long-term)	high (long-term)
capital investment range	small	large
profit margins	low	high
rate of innovation	low	high
specialization	low	high
regulatory mechanisms	informal & few	formal & many
stance toward authority	combative	compliant

SOURCE: Van Maanen et al. (1982: 209).

368

TABLE 16.4

Birdwell-Pheasant's Matrix of Criteria for Assigning Values to Major Relationships Between People in Her Study

Values of Relationships	Major Types of Relationships			
	Ascending Generation	Siblings	Spouse	Descending Generation
Absent	parents deceased, migrated permanently, or estranged	only child; siblings deceased, migrated permanently, or estranged	single or widowed; spouse migrated permanently or estranged	no mature offspring; all offspring deceased, migrated permanently, or estranged
Attenuated	does not live with parents or participate in work group with parent; does visit and/or exchange food	does not live with siblings or participate in work group with them; does visit and/or exchange food	separation, but without final termination of union; e.g., temporary migration	offspring do not live with parents or participate in work group with them; do visit and/or exchange food
Coordinate	participates in work group with parents, sharing decision-making authority	participates in work group with siblings under parents' authority; or works with siblings only, sharing decision making	married; in charge of own sex-specific domain with minimal interference from partner	participates in a work group with offspring, sharing decision-making authority
Subordinate	participates in work group with parent; parent makes decisions	participates in work group of siblings; other sibling(s) make decisions	individual's normal control within sex-specific domain is interfered with by spouse	dependent, elderly parent, unable to work
Superordinate	makes decisions for dependent, elderly parent who is unable to work	participates in work group with siblings; makes decisions for group	interferes with spouse's normal controls within sex-specific domain	heads work group that includes one or more mature offspring; makes decisions for group

SOURCE: Birdwell-Pheasant (1984: 702). Reproduced by permission of the American Anthropological Association, from *American Ethnologist* 11:4, 1984. Not for further reproduction.

TABLE 16.5

Family History of Haitian Migrants to Miami

	Jeanne	Anna (mother)	Lucie (sister)	Charles (brother)	Marc (Adopted son)	Helen (Aunt)	Hughes & Valerie (cousins)	# in house- hold
1968	+							1
1971	+	+	+	+				4
1975	+	+	+	+	+			5
1976	+	+	-	-	+			3
1978	+	+	-	+	+		*	4
1979	+	+	-	+	+	+	*	5
1982	+	+	-	-	+	-	*	4

SOURCE: "Haitian family patterns of migration to South Florida," by S. M. Fjellman and H. Gladwin, 1985. *Human Organization, 44,* 307. Reprinted by permission of the Society for Applied Anthropology.

Stephen Fjellman and Hugh Gladwin (1985) studied the family histories of Haitian migrants to the United States. Fjellman and Gladwin found an elegant way to present a lot of information about those histories in a simple chart. Table 16.5 shows one chart for a family of four people in 1982.

This Haitian-American family began in 1968 when Jeanne's father sent her to Brooklyn, New York, to go to high school. The single plus sign for 1968 shows the founding of the family by Jeanne. Jeanne's father died in 1971, and her mother, sister, and brother joined her in New York. Jeanne adopted Marc in 1975, and in 1976 she and her mother moved with Marc to Miami. Lucie and Charles remained in New York together. The two minus signs in the row for 1976 indicate that Jeanne's sister and brother were no longer part of the household founded by Jeanne.

Two years later, in 1978, Lucie got married and Charles joined Jeanne's household in Miami. Also in 1978, Jeanne began saving money and applying for visas to bring her cousins Hughes and Valerie to Miami. The asterisks show that these two people are in the process of joining the household. In 1979, Anna's sister, Helen joined the family and in 1982 Charles went back to New York to live again with Lucie.

There is a lot of information in this chart, but the ethnographic detail is gone. We don't know *why* Jeanne went to the United States in 1968; we don't know *why* Charles left Jeanne's household in 1976 or why he rejoined the group in 1978. Fjellman and Gladwin present seven of these family history charts in their article and they provide the historical detail in vignettes below each chart. Their purpose in reducing all the historical detail to a set of pluses and minuses, however, is to allow us to see the *patterns* of family growth, development, and decay.

Presenting Qualitative Data: Causal Flow Charts

Causal maps represent theories about how things work. They are visual representations of ideas that emerge from studying data, seeing patterns, and coming to conclusions about what causes-what. Causal maps do not have to have numbers attached to them, although that is where causal modeling eventually leads. After all, it is better to know *how much* one thing causes another than to know simply that one thing *does* cause another. With or without numbers, though, causal models are best expressed as a flow chart, or causal map.

A causal flow chart consists of a set of boxes connected by a set of arrows. The boxes contain descriptions of states (like being the youngest child, or owning a tractor, or being Catholic, or feeling angry), and the arrows tell you how one state leads to another. The simplest causal map is a visual representation of the relationship between two variables

$$A \longrightarrow B$$

which reads: "A leads to or causes B."

Of course, real life is usually much, much more complicated than that. Look at Figure 16.1. It is Stuart Plattner's algorithm, based on intensive interviews and participant observation at produce markets in St. Louis, for how merchants decide what stock to buy (1982). An algorithm is a set of ordered rules that tell you how to solve a problem—like "find the average of a list of numbers," or, in this case, "determine the decisions of produce merchants."

Read the flow chart from top to bottom and left to right, following the arrows. At the beginning of each week, the merchants seek information on the supply and cost of produce items. After that, the algorithm gets complicated. Plattner notes that the model may seem "too complex to represent the decision process of plain folks at the marketplace." However, Plattner says, the chart "still omits consideration of an enormous amount of knowledge pertaining to qualities of produce at various seasons from various shipping areas" (ibid.:405).

Ethnographic Decision Models

Ethnographic decision models (EDMs) are qualitative, causal analyses that predict what kinds of choices people will make under specific circumstances.

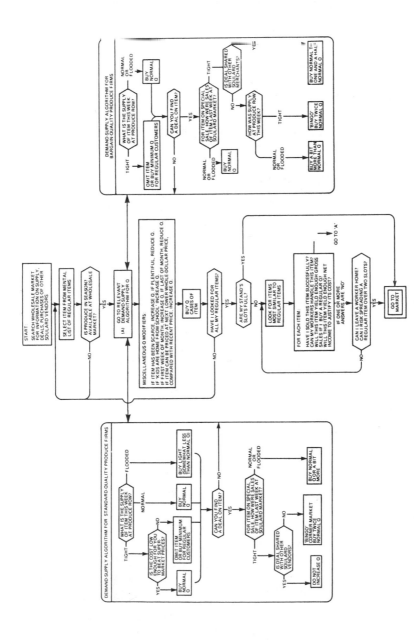

Figure 16.1. Plattner's model for how merchants in the Soulard Market in St. Louis decide what and how much produce to buy. Q = quantity

SOURCE: Plattner (1982). Reprinted by permission of the American Anthropological Association from *American Ethnologist, 9:2*, May 1982. Not for further reproduction.

They have been used to study how fishermen decide where to fish (Gatewood, 1983b), what price to place on their products (H. Gladwin, 1971; Quinn, 1978), and how people decide on which treatment to use for an illness (Young, 1980).

Here's the idea behind decision models. Suppose I could ask a farmer some questions, none of which is "What did you plant last year?" When I'm done, I make a prediction about what the farmer planted. *Then* I ask the farmer what crop he or she planted and I get it right most of the time. In fact, Christina Galdwin has modeled the planting and credit-seeking decisions of farmers in Malawi, Guatemala, the United States, Mexico, and Peru and typically predicts with 80% to 90% accuracy (C. H. Gladwin, 1976, 1980, 1983, 1989, and personal communication).

As with all cognitive research methods, there is a question as to whether decision models simply predict behavior, or whether they also reflect the way people think about things. The jury is still out on that one. But even if an EDM "simply" predicts behavior, that would make it a very important part of the field worker's tool kit.

Prediction of a dependent variable (like planting maize instead of some other crop) from some independent variables (like a farmer's financial condition, family size, or whatever) is the goal of statistical analysis, which is the subject of the next four chapters. But ethnographic decision modeling is based on asking questions, sorting out some logical rules about how the questions have to be ordered, and laying out the order in a picture (like a tree diagram) or in writing. It is, in other words, entirely qualitative.

How to Build an EDM

C. Gladwin (1989) lays out the steps to building an ethnographic decision tree model. The first thing to do is decide which decision you are studying and what the alternatives are in that decision. Let's use the decision "to make your 8 a.m. class or not" as an example.

A grand tour ethnographic probe like "Tell me about why people go to class or skip 8 a.m. classes" will get you a lot of information about the alternatives and the reasons for the alternatives, especially from expert informants. The major alternatives are: Get up and go to class, get up and do something else, sleep in. The "get up and do something else" alternative consists of a list: Lounge around, watch old soaps on the tube, study for an exam later in the day, and so on.

To make your ethnographic knowledge about the decision more formal—that is, to build an EDM—track down Alex, an informant who has

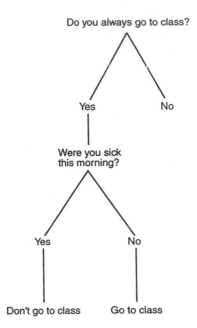

Figure 16.2. An ethnographic decision model after interviewing one informant (Alex).

an 8 a.m. class and ask "Did you make your 8 a.m. class today?" When he answers, ask him "Why [did you] [didn't you] go to that class?" Suppose he says "I went to class today because I *always* go to class unless I'm sick." Ask him: "Were you sick this morning?" Record his answer and draw a tree diagram like the one in Figure 16.2, to represent his decision.

Figure 16.2 accounts perfectly for Alex's decision. It has to; it contains nothing more than the information from the ethnographic interview with Alex.

Now go to your second informant, Sheila, who says that yes, she went to her 8 a.m. class. Why? "It's a really tough class," she says. "If I miss one of those classes, I'll never catch up."

Every reason for your informants' decisions becomes a question you can ask. Use what you learned from your interview with Alex and ask Sheila: "Do you *always* go to class?" Sheila says that she sometimes skips early "cake" classes if she needs to study for an exam in another class later in the day. Ask her: "Were you sick this morning?" If she says "no," draw the diagram in Figure 16.3.

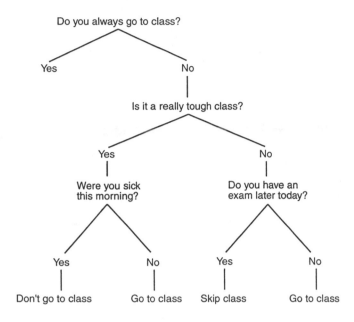

Figure 16.3. An ethnographic decision model after interviewing two informants (Alex and Sheila).

Your third informant, Brad, says that no, he didn't go to class this morning; no, he doesn't always go to class; yes, he skips class when he's sick; no, he wasn't sick this morning; no, he didn't have an exam later in the day; no, his 8 a.m. class isn't tough; but he was out very late last night and just didn't feel like going to class this morning. Figure 16.4 combines all the information we have for Alex, Sheila, and Brad.

In fact, we don't know if Sheila was out late last night, and if she had been, whether that would have affected her decision to go to class early this morning. We can find out by going back and asking Sheila the new question. We could also go back and ask Alex if he had an exam later in the day and if he'd been out late last night.

But we won't. In practice, it's difficult to go back to informants and ask them all the questions you accumulate from EDM interviews. Instead, a common practice is to build a composite diagram, like the one in Figure 16.4, and push on. We also won't ask Brad what he *would* have done if he'd had a really tough 8:00 a.m. class and had been out late the night before. In building EDMs, we deal only with people's reports of their behavior.

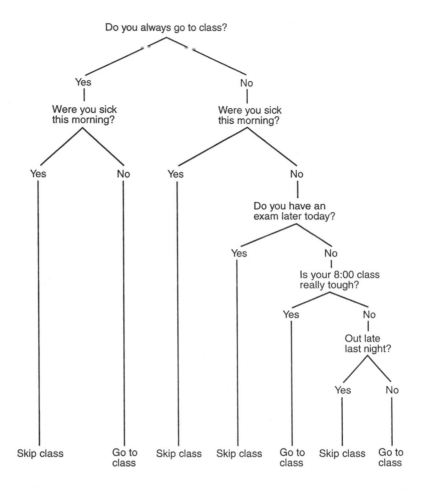

Figure 16.4. An ethnographic decision model after interviewing three informants (Alex, Sheila, and Brad).

Eventually, you'll stop getting new decisions, reasons, and constraints. In a homogeneous culture, this should not require more than about 20 informants. In a heterogeneous culture, you may have to interview 100 informants before you stop getting lots of new information (C. Gladwin, 1989:26). What's a homogeneous culture? That's an empirical question, but building a model for the decision on your campus to go to early classes will probably not require more than 20 informants.

Building an EDM that accounts for this particular decision at small, private schools and at gigantic state schools in the United States may take twice that many informants. As the student culture gets more complex (heterogeneous), the sample size needed in order to find a stable decision model goes up and up. Accounting for the decisions of students in New York City and Sussex, England, will require more interviews. Add Mexico City and the number may double again. Add Cameroon. . . .

Testing an EDM

Figure 16.4 may account for all the decisions of your next several informants, but eventually you'll run into an informant who says she doesn't always go to class, she wasn't sick this morning, she doesn't have a tough class at 8 a.m., she wasn't out late last night, and she *still* didn't make her early class today. Why? Because she just didn't feel like it.

Now, you can always build a model complex enough to account for every decision of every informant. A model with 20 different sets of ordered reasons can (trivially) account for the decisions of 20 informants. But suppose you can model the decisions of 18 out of 20 informants with just a handful of ordered rules. That's 90% prediction. Is it worth building a complicated model, with a long list of rules in order to account for the last 10%?

The whole idea of models is to make them parsimonious and to test them. You want to account for many outcomes with just a few rules. So, when you stop getting new reasons or constraints from EDM interviews, try to build a model that accounts for at least 80% of the decisions with the fewest number of rules. Then—and here's the important part—test your model against an entirely new group of informants.

The interview for the second group of informants is rather different. You ask them all the questions in your model (that is, you probe for all the reasons and constraints for the decision that your first group taught you), and then you guess what their decision was. In our example, you'd interview 20 or 30 new informants, all of whom have 8 a.m. classes, and you'd ask each one: Do you always go to class? Were you sick this morning? Were you out late last night? and so on, exhausting all the questions from your model. If your model works, you'll be able to *predict* the decisions of the second group from their answers to the model's questions.

Representing Complicated Models With Tables
and IF-THEN charts

James Young's EDM

James Young (1980) studied how Tarascan people in Pichátaro, Michoacán, Mexico, choose one of four possible ways to treat an illness: Use a home remedy, go to a native curer, see a *practicante* (a local, nonphysician practitioner of modern medicine), or go to a physician. From his ethnographic work, Young believed that the decision to use one or another of these treatments depended on four factors:

1. how serious an illness was perceived to be (gravity);
2. whether a home remedy for the illness was known;
3. whether the informant had faith in the general efficacy of a mode of treatment for a particular illness; and
4. the accessibility (in terms of cost and transportation) of a particular mode of treatment.

The choice situations emerged from structured interviews with eight men and seven women who were asked:

> If you or another person in your household were ill, when—for what reasons—would you (consult) (use) _____ instead of (consulting) (using) _____ ?

Young used this question frame to elicit responses about all six possible pairs of treatment alternatives: home remedy versus a physician, curer versus home remedy, etc. To check the validity of the statements made in the interviews, Young collected case histories of actual illnesses and their treatments from each of the 15 informants.

Next, Young completed interviews with 20 informants using a series of "what if . . ." questions to generate decisions, under various combinations of circumstances, regarding the selection of treatments for illnesses. For example, informants were asked:

> Let's say there is a person who has a very grave illness. In this family, money is scarce—sure, they're eating, but there is just not anything left over. They have had this illness in the family before, and they now know of the remedy that benefited the illness on the previous occasion. What do you think they are going to do?

TABLE 16.6

Young's Decision Table for How Pichatareños Choose an Initial Method
of Treating an Illness

Rules		1	2	3	4	5	6	7	8	9
Conditions										
1	gravity	1	1	1	2	2	2	3	3	3
2	known home remedy	Y	N	N	Y	N				
3	"faith"		F	M	(F)	F	M	F	M	(M)
4	accessibility								N	Y
Choices										
a	self-treatment	X			X					
b	curer		X			X		X		
c	*practicante*			X			X		X	
d	physician									X

Key:	1 Gravity	3 "Faith"
Y = yes	1 = nonserious	F = favors folk treatment
N = no	2 = moderately serious	M = favors medical treatment
	3 = grave	

4 Accessibility

Y = money and transportation available
N = either money or transportation not available

SOURCE: Young (1980: 116). Reproduced by permission of the American Anthropological Association, from *American Ethnologist* 7:1, 1980. Not for further reproduction.

This vignette combines the condition of a serious illness (level 3 on gravity in Tables 16.6 and 16.7), with lack of accessibility (no money), and a known remedy that can be applied at home. Young used the three levels of gravity, two possible conditions of knowing a remedy (yes and no), and two possible conditions of accessibility (yes and no) in making up his vignettes, which meant that he had to make up eight of them. Each vignette was presented to each informant for a response.

From these qualitative data, collected in structured interviews, Young developed his decision model, for the initial choice of treatment. The model, containing nine decision rules, is shown in Table 16.6. Rule number 1, for example, says that if the illness is not serious and there is a known home remedy, then treat the illness yourself. Rule number 9 says that for grave illnesses, there is an implicit understanding that physicians are better (hence the M in parentheses), so if there is money, then go to a physician.

TABLE 16.7

Young's Decision Table Showing How Pichatareños Choose a Method of Treating an Illness When Their First Choice Doesn't Work

Rules	1	2	3	4	5	6	7	8	9	10	11
Conditions											
0 preceding choice	ST	ST	ST	ST	C-P	C-P	C	P	Dr	Dr	Dr
1 current gravity		1-2	3	3	1	2-3	2-3	2-3			
3 "faith"	F	M	M	(M)					F		M
4 accessibility			N	Y		Y	N	N		N	Y
Choices											
a self-treatment	X										
b curer		X							X	X	
c practicante			X				X	X	X		
d physician				X	X	X					X

Key

0 Preceding choice
ST = self-treatment
C = curer
P = practicante
Dr = physician

1 Current gravity
1 = nonserious
2 = moderately serious
3 = grave

3 "Faith"
F = favors folk treatment
M = favors medical treatment

4 Accessibility
Y = money and transportation available
N = either money or transportation not currently available

SOURCE: Young (1980: 118). Reproduced by permission from the American Anthropological Association, from *American Ethnologist* 7:1, 1980. Not for further reproduction.

Rule number 9 also says that for the few cases of very grave illnesses where physicians are commonly thought not to be effective, apply rule number 7 and go to a curer. The blank spaces in the top part of Table 16.6 indicate irrelevant conditions. In rule number 1, for example, there is no question about accessibility for home remedies because they cost little or nothing, and everyone has access to them.

Sometimes, of course, the treatment selected for an illness doesn't work, and another decision has to be made. Table 16.7, with 11 decision rules, shows Young's analysis of this second stage of decision making. Young's entire 2-stage model is based on his sense of emerging patterns in the data he collected about decision making. The question, of course, is: Does it work?

Young tested his model against 489 treatment choices gathered from 62 households over a 6-month period. To make the test fair, none of the informants in the test were among those whose data were used in developing the model. Table 16.8 shows the results of the test. There were 157 cases covered by rule number 1 from Table 16.6 (first-stage decision), and in every single case informants did what the rule predicted. Informants did what rule number 6 of the first-stage decision model predicted 20 out of 29 times.

Overall, for the first stage, Young's decision rules predict about 95% of informants' reported behavior. After removing the cases covered by rules 1 and 4 (which account for half the cases in the data, but which could be dismissed as common-sense, routine decisions and not in need of any pretentious "analysis"), Young's model still predicts almost 83% of reported behavior. Even for the second stage, after first-stage decisions fail to result in a cure and decisions get more complex and tougher to predict, the model predicts an impressive 84% of reported behavior.

Ryan and Martínez's EDM

Gery Ryan and Homero Martínez (1993) studied how mothers in San José, Mexico, decide what treatment to use when their children have diarrhea. They built an EDM on interviews with 17 mothers who had children under 5, asking each mother what she did the last time her child had diarrhea. Then they asked why she had used this treatment or series of treatments.

Ryan and Martínez knew from living in San José that mothers in the village used seven different treatments. These included manipulating the child's body (massaging the child's body, pinching the child's back), taking the child to the doctor, and giving the child one or more of the

TABLE 16.8

Test Results of Young's Decision Model of How Pichatareños Choose a Treatment Method When They Are Il[l]

Table	Rule	Self-Treatment	Curer	Practicante	Physician	Totals	Percentage Correct
4	1	157				157	
	2		4			4	
	3			5		5	
	4	67			(1)	68	
	5		8			8	
	6	(2)		20	(7)	29	
	7		8			8	
	8		(2)	4	(2)	8	
	9			(2)	11	13 = 300	94.7%
5	1		19			19	
	2		(1)	28	(6)	35	
	3		(3)	6		9	
	4			(2)	22	24	
	5	3	(1)			4	
	6	(2)	(2)	(1)	24	29	
	7	(1)		3	(2)	6	
	8		2	(1)		3	
	9	(1)	7			8	
	10					0	
	11				7	7 = 144	84.0%
						444	91.2% (overall)

Not covered = 18
Insufficient data = 27
Total = 489

SOURCE: Young (1980: 123). Reproduced by permission from the American Anthropological Association, from *American Ethnologist* 7:1, 1980. Not for further reproduction.

following: tea, homemade rice water, medication from the pharmacy (their informants told them "if you can say it you can buy it"), a carbonated beverage, or commercially produced oral rehydration solution. Ryan and Martínez went systematically through the treatments, asking each mother why she had used X instead of A, X instead of B, X instead of C, and so on down through the list.

Mothers in San José listed the following factors for choosing one treatment modality over another.

Duration of the episode
Perceived cause (from worms, from *empacho*, from food, etc.)
Whether there was mucous in the stool
Whether there was blood in the stool
Whether the stools smelled bad
Whether the stools were frequent or not
Whether the stools were loose or not
Whether the child had fever
Color of the stool
Whether the child had a dry mouth
Whether the child had dry eyes
Whether the child was vomiting
Whether the child had swollen glands

Table 16.9 shows the data from the 17 women in Ryan and Martínez's original sample and the decision to take the child to the doctor (the eighth treatment modality). Read the table like this: Mother #1 said that her child's last episode of diarrhea lasted 2 days and was caused by bad food. The stools contained mucous, but did not contain blood. The stools smelled bad, were frequent and loose. The child had fever, the stools were yellow. The child had dry mouth and dry eyes, but was not vomiting and did not have swollen glands.

Table 16.9 makes it clear that mothers took their children to the doctor if the child had blood in the stool, had swollen glands, or was vomiting, or if the diarrhea had lasted *more than* 7 days. None of the other factors played a part in the final decision to take the child to the doctor.

But remember: There were seven different treatments, and mothers would try several treatments in any given episode. Ryan and Martínez looked at the pattern of circumstances for all seven treatments and built a model that accounted for all the treatment decisions made by the 17 mothers. Their model had just six rules and three constraints.

TABLE 16.9

Decision to Take the Child to the Doctor

Mother	Doctor	Days	Cause	Muc.	Blood	Smell	Freq.	Loose	Fever	Color	Mouth	Eyes	Vomit	Gland
1	N	2	C	Y	N	Y	Y	Y	Y	A	Y	Y	N	N
2	N	20	E	Y	N	Y	Y	Y	N	A	Y	Y	N	N
3	Y	8	T	N	N	Y	Y	Y	Y	N	Y	Y	N	N
4	Y	8	C	Y	N	Y	N	Y	Y	V	.	.	Y	Y
5	N	3	P	Y	N	Y	Y	Y	Y	A	Y	Y	N	Y
6	N	3	L	N	N	Y	Y	Y	N	B	Y	Y	N	N
7	Y	8	D	Y	N	Y	Y	Y	N	A	Y	Y	N	N
8	N	1	D	N	N	Y	Y	Y	N	A	.	.	N	N
9	N	.	C	Y	N	N	Y	Y	N	B	Y	Y	N	N
10	N	3	O	N	N	Y	Y	Y	N	A	Y	Y	N	N
11	N	2	C	N	N	N	N	N	N	A	.	.	N	N
12	N	.	C	N	N	Y	Y	Y	N	A	Y	Y	N	N
13	N	4	C	N	N	Y	N	N	N	A	Y	Y	N	N
14	Y	4	E	N	N	Y	Y	Y	Y	V	Y	.	N	N
15	Y	3	I	Y	Y	Y	Y	Y	Y	A	Y	Y	Y	N
16	N	2	C	Y	N	N	Y	Y	N	V	Y	Y	N	N
17	N	7	E	N	N	N	Y	Y	N	A	N	N	N	N

Cause

C = Food
L = Worms
E = Empacho
I = Indigestion
D = Teething
T = Dirt
P = Parasites
O = Other

Color

A = Yellow
V = Green
B = White
D = Don't Know
N = Black

SOURCE: Ryan and Martínez (1993). Used with permission.

Figure 16.5 shows their model as a series of IF-THEN statements. Notice the constraints: In order for a woman to choose a modern medication, she had to know about it and it had to be cheap and easy to obtain. The constraints to the rules are derived from ethnographic interviews. So was the observation that mothers distinguished between curative and palliative treatments—things that stopped the diarrhea and things that just made the child feel better during the episode. The model accounted for (postdicted) 89% of the treatments that the 17 mothers had reported.

Ryan and Martínez interviewed 20 more women. This time they asked the women all the questions inherent in the model. That is, they asked each of the 20 women: "In your child's last episode of diarrhea, did the stools have blood in them? Did the child have swollen glands? What caused the diarrhea?" and so on. The model in Figure 16.5 accounted for 84% of the second group's treatment decisions.

Rule 1

IF	child has blood stools OR
	child has swollen glands OR
	child is vomiting
THEN	take child to doctor.

Rule 2

IF	diarrhea is caused by empacho
THEN	give physical treatment.

Rule 3

IF	previous rules do not apply OR
	there is no cure with the empacho treatment
THEN	give the highest preferred curing treatment that meets constraints.

Rule 4

IF	previous treatment did not stop diarrhea
THEN	compare the two highest treatments of remaining options.

4.1

IF	one is a curing remedy AND
	meets its constraints
THEN	give this treatment.

4.2

IF	both or neither are curing remedies AND
	each meets its respective constraints
THEN	give the highest ranked preference.

Rule 5

IF	the previous treatment did not stop the diarrhea AND
	the episode is less than 1 week long
THEN	repeat rule 4.

Rule 6

IF	the episode has lasted more than 1 week
THEN	take the child to a doctor.

Constraints

IF	you know how to make ORS (oral rehydration solution) AND
	your child will drink ORS
THEN	give ORS.
IF	you know a medication that works for diarrhea AND
	you have it in the house
THEN	give the pill or liquid medication.
IF	you know a medication that works for diarrhea AND
	it is cheap AND
	it is easy to obtain
THEN	give the pill or liquid medication.

Figure 16.5. Ryan and Martínez's decision model as a series of IF-THEN rules.
SOURCE: Ryan and Martínez, 1993.

Taxonomies

One of the most commonly used techniques in qualitative analysis is the production of *native taxonomies*, or *folk taxonomies*, a method pioneered by Berlin et al. (1974). A native taxonomy is a description of how people divide up domains of culture, and how the pieces of a domain are connected. By "domain" I mean simply a list of words in a language that somehow belong together.

Some domains are very large and inclusive, while others are small and narrow; some lists are known to all speakers of a language, while others represent highly specialized knowledge. The names of all the plants found in Arkansas constitutes a very large domain, requiring highly specialized knowledge. The names of carpenters' tools is a relatively short list, but only a few people, with highly specialized knowledge, control it.

By contrast, the list of kinship terms in Spanish is short and doesn't require much specialized knowledge. Indeed, all native speakers of Spanish know the list, and although there are some specialized uses of terms that vary from one Spanish-speaking country to another, no student of any Spanish-speaking culture could avoid learning that domain.

We use folk taxonomies all the time to order our experience and guide our behavior. Walk into any large supermarket in the United States and note how the merchandise is assembled and laid out. There are frozen foods, meats, dairy products, canned vegetables, soaps and cleansers, household gadgets, and so on. Take an informant to a supermarket where they haven't shopped before and ask them to find peanut butter (without asking anyone where it is, of course). As they make their way around the store, get informants to talk about what they think they're doing. A typical response goes like this:

> Well, let's see, milk and eggs are over there by that wall, and the meat's usually next to that, and the canned goods are kind of in the middle, with the soaps and paper towels and stuff on the other side, so we'll go right in here, in the middle. No, this is the soap aisle, so let's go over to the right. Sure, here's the coffee, so it's got to be on this aisle or the next, with cans of things like ravioli and stuff you can eat for lunch right out of the can.

It isn't very long before any competent member of this culture will find the peanut butter. Not everything is equally clear. Shredded coconut and walnuts are often shelved with flour because they are used in baking. Other nuts may be shelved separately. Matzohs (unleavened bread boards eaten primarily by Jews) and litchi nuts (a Chinese dessert food) are sometimes shelved together under "ethnic foods," but may be shelved in separate

"Jewish foods" and "Oriental foods" sections if local populations of those groups are sufficiently large.

Spradley (1979) reported that he once called the St. Paul, Minnesota, police department and said he needed to find the case number of a robbery that had been committed at his house. Two bicycles had been stolen from his garage in the middle of the night, while he was asleep. The police had investigated, but Spradley's insurance company needed the case number to process the claim. When Spradley told the police that he needed the case number for a "robbery," they quite naturally transferred his call to the robbery unit. But they couldn't help him because, according to their rules, robberies are acts committed with a gun and where there is a face-to-face encounter between the criminal and the victim.

Spradley was transferred to burglary, but after another frustrating conversation he was transferred to the juvenile division. It seems that any theft of bicycles is handled by that division in St. Paul, and Spradley got his case number. Spradley observed that if he had understood the police culture he "would have begun with a simple question: What part of the police department has records of bicycles stolen from a garage when no one is present?" (ibid.:142). If he'd known the native (police) taxonomy of crimes, he'd have asked the right question and gotten taken care of right away.

Folk taxonomies are constructed from data collected with the *frame elicitation* technique developed by Frake (1964), Metzger and Williams (1966), and D'Andrade et al. (1972). (See also Chapter 11 on structured interviewing.) Once you have identified a domain of interest to you, the next step is to construct a list of terms that signify parts of the domain. This is done by using the frame:

What kinds of _____ are there?

where the blank is "cars," "trees," "saddles," "snow," "soldiers"—whatever you're interested in understanding. This frame is used again and again, until an informant says that the question is silly. For example, suppose you asked a professor of anthropology: "What kinds of courses are there in anthropology?" You might get a list like: courses in cultural anthropology, archeology, physical anthropology, and linguistics. Some anthropologists would add "applied anthropology" and some wouldn't. That's part of the intracultural variation in this particular group of people.

Now suppose you asked: "What kinds of cultural anthropology courses are there?" The answer might be: methods courses, theory courses, and area courses. You would ask the same question about each of the other fields (archeology, etc.). Then you would ask: "What kinds of area (methods) (theory) courses are there in cultural anthropology?" For area courses, the answer might be something like: peoples and cultures of Latin America, peoples and cultures of Africa, peoples and cultures of Asia, and so on.

Next, for each area named, you would ask: "What kinds of people and cultures of Latin America (Asia, Africa, . . .) courses are there?" For Latin America, the answer might be: peoples and cultures of Mesoamerica, and peoples and cultures of South America. The South America courses might be broken down into peoples and cultures of the Amazon, and peoples and cultures of the Andes; or it might be divided into chunks like peoples and cultures of Peru, peoples and cultures of Brazil, and so on.

Finally, when you asked: "What kinds of peoples and cultures of the Amazon courses are there?" you might be told: "There are no kinds; they are just courses about cultures of the Amazon" or, if you are dealing with a specialist, you might be told about a course dealing specifically with the Yanomami.

Once you have a list of lexical items in a domain, and once you've got the basic divisions down, the next step is to find out about overlaps. A course about hunters and gatherers includes material about the Amazon, and thus has an area component, but it may also be categorized as a theory course. Some anthropologists may distinguish theory, method, and ethnography courses and then include a course on hunters and gatherers in ethnography, along with courses on cultural areas.

The point is, there is no codified set of rules for dividing the domain of anthropology courses. The only way to map this is to construct folk taxonomies from information provided by a number of informants and to get an idea of the range of variation and areas of consistency in how people think about this domain. You can learn about the possible overlaps in folk taxonomies by using the substitution frames:

Is _____ a kind of _____ ?
Is _____ a part of _____ ?

Once you have a list of terms in a domain, and a list of categories, you can use this substitution frame for all possible combinations. Is a course on peoples and cultures of the Amazon a kind of ethnography course? A kind of theory course? A kind of methods course? Is a course on kinship a kind of theory course? As you can imagine, this can be tedious, but discovering how people categorize their worlds can also be a fascinating exercise, for informants as well as for anthropologists.

A common way to display folk taxonomies is with a branching tree diagram. Figure 16.6 shows a tree diagram for part of a folk taxonomy of passenger cars.

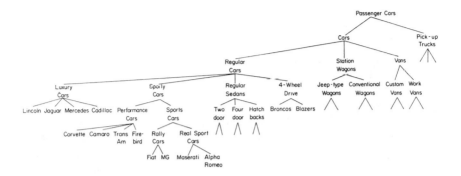

Figure 16.6. Part of Jack's taxonomy of cars and trucks.

To elicit a similar taxonomy, pick up a copy of any automobile buyer's guide and make a list of the currently available cars in the United States. Write the name of each car and model on a card and ask an informant to sort the cards into as many piles as he or she thought were necessary to reflect "kinds of cars." Next, ask the informant to try and name each pile, then use the frame elicitation technique to refine the taxonomy and get at the links between the categories. There are four important points to make about the taxonomy shown in Figure 16.6:

1. Interinformant variation is common in folk taxonomies. That is, different informants may use different words to refer to the same category of things. Sometimes, in fact, terms can be almost idiosyncratic. Jack, the informant whose taxonomy is displayed here, distinguishes among what he calls "regular cars," "station wagons," and "vans." The term "regular cars" is not one you'll see in automobile advertisements or hear from a salesperson on a car lot.

2. Category labels do not necessarily have to be simple lexical items, but may be complex phrases. The category labeled "4-wheel drive" vehicles in Figure 16.6 is sometimes called "off-road vehicles." I've heard it referred to as "vehicles you can go camping in or tow a horse trailer with."

3. There are categories for which informants have no label at all—at least not one that they find easily accessible. Some informants insist that Corvettes, Camaros, Maseratis, and MGs are contained in a single category, which they find difficult to name. (One informant recently suggested "sporty cars" as a label.) Others, like Jack, separate "performance cars" from "sports cars" and even subdivide sports cars into "true sports cars" and "rally cars." Be on the lookout for unlabeled categories (nodes in a branching tree diagram) in all folk taxonomies.

4. Even when there are consistent labels for categories, the categories themselves may not be "clean." There may be overlap and indeterminacy in

categories. For example, many informants recognize a category of "foreign cars" that cuts across the taxonomy in Figure 16.6. There are foreign sports cars, foreign luxury cars, and foreign regular cars.

The category "station wagon" is not completely clean in Figure 16.6. Jack recognizes Jeep station wagons as both wagons and as 4-wheel-drive cars you can go camping in. Folk taxonomies can be very, very complex. One way to get at the complexity is through a technique known as componential analysis. (Another is multidimensional scaling, which we'll take up in Chapter 20.)

Componential Analysis

Componential analysis is a formal, qualitative technique for studying meaning. There are two objectives: (a) to specify the conditions under which a native speaker of a language will call something (a plant, a kinswoman, a car) by a particular term; and (b) to understand the cognitive process by which native speakers decide which of several possible terms they should apply to a particular thing.

The first objective falls under what I have called "descriptive analysis" earlier in this chapter. The second is closer to being "causal analysis" and was the objective envisioned by the developers of the technique in the 1950s and 1960s (see Conklin, 1955; Goodenough, 1956; Frake, 1962; Wallace, 1962). Charles Frake, for example, described componential analysis as a step toward an "operationally explicit methodology for discovering how people construe their world of experience from the way they talk about it."

Componential analysis is based on the principle of *distinctive features*. The principle was well known in phonology, the branch of linguistics devoted to the study of the sounds of a language, and was adapted for use in studying other domains of culture. To understand the principle, think about the difference in the sounds represented by *p* and *b* in English. Both are made by twisting your mouth into the same shape. This is a *feature* of the *p* and *b* sounds called "bilabial" or "two-lipped."

Another feature is that they are both "stops." That is, they are made by stopping the flow of air for an instant as it moves up from your lungs, and releasing the flow suddenly. An *s* sound, by contrast, also requires that you restrict the air flow, but not completely. You kind of let the air slip by in a hiss. The only difference between a *p* and a *b* sound is that the *p* is voiceless, and the *b* is voiced—you vibrate your vocal cords while making a *p*.

You can think of the feature of voicing as something that can change *meaning* in English. If you add up all the phonological features of the

TABLE 16.10

A Componential Analysis of Four Things With Two Features

	Feature 1	Feature 2
Thing 1	+	+
Thing 2	+	−
Thing 3	−	+
Thing 4	−	−

words "bit" and "pit" the only feature that differentiates them is voicing on the first sound in each word. The "pitness" of a pit and the "bitness" of a bit are clearly not in the voicelessness or voicedness of the sounds p and b, but any native speaker of English will distinguish the two words, and their meanings, and can trace the difference between them to that little feature of voicing if you push them a bit. There is a unique little bundle of features that define each of the consonantal sounds in English. The only difference between the words "mad" and "bad" is that the bilabial sound m is nasal, and not a stop.

Any two "things" (sounds, kinship terms, names of plants, names of animals, etc.) can be distinguished by exactly one binary feature that either occurs (+) or doesn't occur (−). Table 16.10 shows that with two features you can distinguish four things: Thing 1 can be ++, thing 2 can be +−, thing 3 can be −+, and thing 4 can be −−. Each bundle of features is different and defines each of the four things. With three binary features you can distinguish eight things; with four, 16; with five, 32; and so on.

When componential analysis was introduced into cultural anthropology it was applied to the set of English kinship terms (Goodenough, 1956), and it continues to be used for understanding kinship systems (Rushforth, 1982). A "daughter" in English, for example, is a consanguineal, female, descending generation person. So is a niece, but a niece is kin through a sibling or a spouse.

Componential analysis can be applied to any domain of a language where you are interested in understanding the semantic features that make up the domain. Table 16.11 shows a componential analysis of seven cars, using three features elicited from Jack. A Corvette is an expensive car, not very practical, and not foreign; a Mercedes is an expensive, practical, foreign car; and so on. Each of the seven cars is uniquely defined by the three features Jack mentioned.

There are two problems with componential analysis. First of all, it seems a bit shallow to say that a Corvette is an expensive, impractical, American

TABLE 16.11

Minimal Componential Analysis for Seven Cars, According to Jack

	1 Expensive	2 Practical	3 Foreign
Corvette	+	−	−
Firebird	−	−	−
MG	−	−	+
Maserati	+	−	+
Mercedes	+	+	+
Jeep	−	+	−
Dodge Van	+	+	−

car and nothing more, or that a Mercedes is an expensive, practical, foreign car and nothing more. You can get so caught up in finding the minimal analytic combination of features in this type of analysis that you forget you're interested in the meaning that informants assign to different objects in a domain. Still, you certainly want to find the most parsimonious set of distinctive features. That way, you can predict how informants are likely to label new things they haven't encountered before.

The second problem with componential analysis is the same one we run into with all cognitive research methods: We have no idea if it reflects how people actually think. This problem was raised early in the development of cognitive anthropology by Robbins Burling (1964), who noted that, in a folk taxonomy of trees, he could not tell the essential cognitive difference between hemlock and spruce. "Is it gross size, type of needle, form of bark, or what?" If an ethnographer could not answer this question, Burling observed, then no componential analysis could claim to be "more than an exercise of the analyst's imagination" (p. 27).

Of course, this same critique could apply to most of anthropology "whenever it refers to values, orientations, attitudes, beliefs, or any notion which imputes the presence of something inside people," and must be balanced with a positive perspective on what *can* be done (Hymes, 1964:119).

In fact, what can be done is impressive, intuitively compelling analysis of the meanings that people attach to terms in their languages: Decision analysis allows us to predict which of several behavioral options people will take, under specific circumstances; taxonomic analysis lets us predict which class of things some new thing will be assigned to; componential analysis lets us predict what classification label will be assigned to some object. These are all important achievements of qualitative analysis in the science of anthropology.

17

Coding and Codebooks for Quantitative Data

The next few chapters are about *quantitative* data processing and analysis. Quantitative data processing depends crucially on having a useful *codebook*. A codebook for quantitative data spells out exactly how to transform observations into numbers that can be manipulated statistically and searched for patterns.

Coding data is not a major *stage* of research, like design, or data collection, or analysis and write up. Coding is just a chore, but a very important one. A good codebook is worth a lot in data analysis, and it gets worth more every year. It tells you (and others) what you have in your data—what variables you've studied, what you've called those variables, and how you've stored information about them. You simply can't analyze quantitative data without a good, clear codebook.

Just as important, neither can anyone else. You can't share your data with other researchers unless you give them a codebook they can use. Six months after you finish anything but the simplest projects (those with only half a dozen or fewer variables), even *you* won't recognize your own data without a codebook. Should you want to reanalyze your data several years after a project has ended, or compare 1990 data with current data, you won't be able to do so unless you have built and filed away a good codebook.

Coding

The key to coding is detail. Make your codes as verbose as possible and don't try to analyze your data while you're coding. The rule is exactly the opposite rule that applies to coding qualitative data. Most of the analysis of qualitative data is done in the act of coding. The rule for quantitative data is: *Don't do data analysis until you've got data*, and "data" in this case means numbers.

By contrast, text *is* data. Coding text is an act of data reduction—thinking about it, extracting meaning from it, developing hypotheses about the people described in it, boiling it down to a series of mnemonics. The mnemonics can be numbers, as with the HRAF codes, but those numbers are categories of nominal variables; the numbers contain no information about quantity. In content analysis, variables that are described in text are extracted and codified as numbers that *do* contain information about quantity.

To understand the rule about not analyzing quantitative data until you've got the data, consider the variable "age." It is one of the most commonly collected pieces of information in all the social sciences. If you ask 400 randomly selected informants, age 20 to 70, how old they are, you could get as many as 51 different ages. You will probably get at least 25 different ages.

I've seen many researchers code such data into four or five categories, such as 20 to 29, 30 to 39, 40 to 49, 50 and older, before seeing what they've got. Recall from Chapter 2 that this only succeeds in throwing away the interval level power of data about age. You can always instruct the computer to package data about age (or income, or any interval level variable) into a set of ordinal chunks. But if you code the data in ordinal chunks to begin with, you can never go back.

Here's a concrete example of something that's a little more complex than age. Gene Shelley studied the strength of ties between friends and acquaintances (Shelley et al., 1990). Every other day for a month, she asked 20 informants to think about things they'd learned in the previous 2 days about their friends and acquaintances. People mentioned things like "so-and-so told me she was pregnant," "so-and-so's father called and told me my friend made his first jump in parachute school," and so on. Informants were also asked to estimate how long it had been between the time something happened to one of their friends/acquaintances and the time they (the informants) heard about it. This estimated time was the major dependent variable in the research.

There were 20 informants, who submitted to 15 interviews each, and in each interview almost every informant was able to name several events of interest. Thus, there were over 1,000 data records (1 for each event remembered by an informant). The length of time estimated by informants between an event happening to someone they knew and their hearing about it ranged from "immediately," to "10 years," with dozens of different time periods in between ("about five minutes," "two-and-a-half months," etc.).

The temptation was to make up about five codes, like 1=5 minutes or less, 2=6 minutes to 19 minutes, 3=20 minutes to an hour, and so on. But how do you decide what the right breaks are? In the end, Shelley decided to code everything in *days*. (1 minute is .0007 days; 10 years is 3,650 days, without worrying about leap years) (ibid.).

Here's another example, using a nominal variable. Suppose you are studying the personal histories of 200 Mexican men who have had experience as illegal labor migrants to the United States. If you ask them to name the towns in which they have worked, you might get a list of 300 communities—100 more than you have informants! The temptation would be to collapse the list of 300 communities into a shorter list, using some kind of scheme. You might code them as Southeast, Southwest, California, Midwest, Northwest, mid-Atlantic, and so on. Once again, you'd be making the error of doing your analysis in the coding.

After all your data are in the machine, you can print them, lay them out, stare at them, and start making some decisions about how to "package" them for statistical analysis. You might decide to label each of the 300 communities in the list according to its population size; or according to its ethnic and racial composition (more than 20% Spanish surname, for example); or its distance in kilometers from the Mexico-United States border. All those pieces of information are available from the U.S. census or from road atlases. If you collapse the list into a set of categories during coding, then your option to add codes about the communities is closed off.

Building Codebooks

Figure 17.1 displays the codebook for a network study I conducted in Mexico City. It contains four essential pieces of information:

1. The line number and column number(s) in which each variable is coded, for each unit of analysis.

2. A full, clear description of each variable.

3. A coded name for each variable, preferably containing no more than eight characters.

4. A list of the possible values that each variable can take.

I will discuss these in turn.

1. Data are collected for each unit of analysis, whether those are informants, songs, or judicial outcomes. Some studies consist of just a few variables; others may contain hundreds. Data are stored in lines of 80 spaces, or columns, but one line may not be sufficient to record all the data for one unit of analysis in any particular study.

We distinguish, therefore, between data *records* and data *lines*. A data record contains all the information collected about one unit of analysis— say, an informant. The data record may consist of 1, 2, or 10 lines, depending on how many variables are involved, and how they are coded.

Each variable requires a certain number of columns. The line and columns that each variable occupies are specified in a codebook. Don't try to conserve lines or columns. There is nothing magical about getting all your data about one informant to fit into a single line of 80 spaces. The computer won't care at all if you use 1.5 lines, or whatever. Use as many columns as you think you'll *ever* need for each variable. An example will make this clear.

It is customary to begin each data record with a unique identifier, and to list that identifier as the first variable in a codebook. This usually means the "informant number" in a project. If you have fewer than 100 informants, then the identifier variable can consist of just two digits, beginning with 01, 02, 03, etc. Note, however, that if you ever repeat the research in order to do comparative analysis, and if your next study has 100 or more informants, then your entire codebook becomes useless. More to the point, your original *data*, as they are coded in the computer, will be useless for comparative purposes (the codebook merely reflects the data). Here's why.

In the original data on fewer than 100 informants, the variables begin in column 3, after a two-digit identifier; in the new data, on 100 or more informants, the variables begin in column 4, after a three-digit identifier (001, 002, 003, etc.). The two data sets will not be comparable. One will be one little space off from the other—enough so that the computer, idiot that it is, can not make direct comparisons between data sets on variables. One of the data sets will have to be rewritten to conform to the other. While

Column	Variable Name	Variable Description
1-4	INT.NO	Interview number, from 0001-2400.
5-7	ZONE	Number of the zone, from 1-120 in Mexico City where interview was conducted.
8	CLAZONE	Socioeconomic class of the zone, as determined by the interviewer. 1 = lower class. 2 = middle class. 3 = upper class.
9	SEX	The gender of the respondent. 1 = male. 2 = female.
10	CLASRESP	Socioeconomic class of the respondent, as determined by the interviewer. 1 = lower class. 2 = middle class. 3 = upper class.
11-12	AGE	Age of respondent, in years.
13-14	SCHOOL	Number of years respondent spent in school.
15-16	DFLIVE	Number of years respondent has lived in Mexico City (D.F. or Distrito Federal).
17	OCCN	Occupation. 1 = Housewife. 2 = Regular employment. 3 = Retired. 4 = Unemployed. 5 = Other.
18	DOC	Does the respondent know a physician who works in the public hospitals? 1 = Yes. 2 = No.
19	YESDOC	Does the interviewer think the respondent really does know a physician who works in the public hospitals, given that the respondent answered "yes" to DOC? 1 = Yes. 2 = No.
20	QUAKE	Does the respondent know a person who died in the 1985 earthquake? 1 = Yes. 2 = No.
21	YESQUAKE	Same as YESDOC, Column 19, for QUAKE.
22	HOWLONG	How many days did it take before the respondent learned that someone he or she knew had died in the quake? 1 – 0-15 days. 2 = 15-30 days. 3 = 30-45 days. 4 = 45-60 days. 5 = 60+ days.
23	MAIL	Does the respondent know someone who works for the postal authority? 1 = Yes. 2 = No.
24	YESMAIL	Same as YESDOC, Column 19, for MAIL.
25	ROBBED	Does the respondent know someone who was robbed in the street during 1986? 1 = Yes. 2 = No.
26	YESROB	Same as YESDOC, Column 19, for ROBBED.
27	BUS.100	Does the respondent know someone who is a bus driver on Route 100? (This is the name of the job of public bus driver in Mexico City.) 1 = Yes. 2 = No.
28	YESBUS	Same as YESDOC, Column 19, for BUS. 100.
29	PESERO	Does the respondent know someone who drives a pesero in Mexico City? (These are private cars and Volkswagen minibuses that operate along established licensed routes as privately owned, public conveyances). 1 = Yes. 2 = No.

Continued

Figure 17.1. Codebook for Mexico City network study, January 15, 1987.

Column	Variable Name	Variable Description
30	YESPES	Same as YESDOC, Column 19, for PESERO.
31	PRIEST	Does the respondent know a Catholic Priest in Mexico City? 1 = Yes 2 = No.
32	YESPRIES	Same as YESDOC, Column 19, for PRIEST.
33	VENDOR	Does the respondent know someone who is a street vendor in the underground economy? 1 = Yes. 2 = No.
34	YESVEND	Same as YESDOC, Column 19, for VENDOR.
35	TV	Does the respondent know someone who works for Televisa, the television company in Mexico City? 1 = Yes. 2 = No.
36	YESTV	Same as YESDOC, Column 19, for TV.
37	WIND	Does the respondent know someone who makes his living cleaning car windshields at stoplights in Mexico City, and asking for tips? 1 = Yes. 2 = No.
38	YESWIND	Same as YESDOC, Column 19, for WIND.
39	RAPE	Does the respondent know someone who was raped in Mexico City during 1986? 1 = Yes. 2 = No.
40	YESRAPE	Same as YESDOC, Column 19, for RAPE.
41	INTID	Identity of interviewer. 1 = Norma. 2 = Yolanda. 3 = Alejandro. 4 = Miguel Angel. 5 = Mari Carmen. 6 = Patricio.
42	KNOW	How many people does the respondent think he or she knows? 1 = 0-100. 2 = 100-500. 3 = 500-1000. 4 = 1000-1500. 5 = 1500+.

Figure 17.1. Continued

this is not the worst thing that can happen in research, it is one nuisance you can avoid simply by using identifiers with more digits than you need.

One more example to make the point that this problem can occur anywhere in your data, not just in something like the identifier. If you are studying juveniles, you can obviously get away with using two columns for age since, by definition, no one in your study will ever be over 100 years old. If you are studying a general population, however, then use three columns for age. Hardly anyone lives to be 100 or more, but you never know. All the informants in your present study may be less than 100 years old, but if you repeat the study and you run into a centenarian, then you're in big trouble.

Either you have to list all such persons as "99" in the second study, or you have to rewrite your entire first set of data to show three columns for age instead of two. Both solutions are less than ideal. Remember: Every time you have to transform your data, you run the risk of introducing errors through carelessness. In addition, overspecified data are less attractive to others who might want to do comparative work, using your research as a baseline. Make your data entry, and your codebooks, as general as possible.

2. *Always* provide a full, discursive description of each variable in your study. There is no rule that says codebooks have to be terse. On the contrary, nothing is to be gained by being telegraphic in describing your variables. Even a variable like "age" should be described as fully as possible. Leave nothing to the imagination of the user of a codebook (and that includes you). For example, "age of informant, to the nearest year, and reported by the informant," is much better than "age of informant."

Some variables require a lot of description. Consider this helpful codebook description of a variable: "Perceived Quality of Life. This was measured using an index consisting of the six items which follow. Each item is scored separately, but the items can be added to form an index. Since each item is scored from 1 to 5, the index of perceived quality of life can vary from 6 to 30 for any informant."

If you are using an established index or scale, or data collection technique, then you should name the technique (i.e., "the Bogardus social distance scale") and provide a citation to the source (Bogardus, 1933). If you have adapted a published technique to meet your particular needs, then you should mention that, too, in your codebook. For example, "I have used the Fischer method of generating social networks (Fischer, 1982), but have adapted it in translation for use with the Kipsigis."

Later, either you or another researcher can compare the relevant items on your survey instrument with those in the published index, if that seems necessary. The rule to remember is: Don't skimp on paper in building a codebook; be verbose and descriptive. And always file a copy of any survey instrument with your codebook.

3. Make variable names as obvious as possible, and keep them down to no more than 8 characters. Some computer programs for data analysis allow variable names up to 12 characters, while others require 8. It's just as easy to make up short variable names as long ones. Here are some examples of variable names commonly seen in social research: AGE, INCOME, EDUC, HOUSETYP (house type), OWNCAR (does the informant own a car?), MIGRATE (does the informant have plans to migrate?), PQOL (perceived quality of life). (It is customary to use all capital letters when referring to variable names in print.)

Of course, each project is different and will contain many variables that are specific to the research. Some examples that I've seen recently are VISKAB (has the informant ever visited Kabul?), BIRTHCON (what is the informant's position on birth control?), and DISTH20 (how far is the household from potable water?). You can be as clever as you like with variable names; just keep them short and be sure that you include a good, verbose description of each variable in the codebook so that you'll know what all those clever names mean a year later.

4. You must specify carefully in a codebook the values that each variable can take and what each value means. Age, for example, typically takes a three-digit number, occupying three columns in a record. Marital status, on the other hand, typically takes up just one column in a record.

Suppose marital status is coded as 1=married, 2=divorced, 3=separated, 4=widowed, 5=never married, 6=unknown. These six categories are mutually exclusive and exhaustive for this nominal variable, but there are, after all is said and done, just six possible categories. The values 1 to 6 each take up one column. Similarly, religion might be coded as 1=Shintoist, 2=Buddhist, 3=Hindu, 4=Tribal, 5=Unknown.

If you have any questions about how to build a codebook, go back over this section carefully and keep referring to Figure 17.1. If you follow the steps outlined here, you will produce effective codebooks and your data will be much more useful, to you and to others, than if you just try to "get by" without a highly detailed codebook.

A Few Final Words About Data

I should warn you, though, that just making a good codebook is not good enough: You have to use it. I once failed to follow my own advice and the results were painful. In 1981, Peter Killworth, Christopher McCarty, and I did the data analysis on a large project in social network analysis (Killworth et al., 1984).

In this ongoing series of studies, we give informants some information about other people (called "targets") whom the informants do not know. Informants are asked to select, from among their own friends and acquaintances, a person who could act as an intermediary to the target—someone who the informant believes has a chance of knowing the target, or who might know someone who knows the target, and so on. Informants are allowed to ask as many questions as they like about each target, until they feel comfortable about making a choice of intermediary. Then they tell us about the intermediary, and why that person is a good link to the target.

We do this for 50 targets for each informant, and from this we learn what people need to know about others in order to establish a link to strangers through their friends and acquaintances. Then we build a survey instrument made up of 500 targets from around the world, along with a collection of information about each target based on what informants in the particular culture told us they needed to know.

In the 1981 study, we determined that, at least for informants in Gainesville, Florida, people needed to know seven things about other people in order to choose an intermediary: the target's location, occupation, age, sex, marital status, hobbies, and organizational affiliations. We designed and administered the main survey instrument, analyzed the data, and wrote up the results. We built a good codebook for our data, and after the analysis was finished, we tucked the codebook away. We took all the usual precautions: We kept a printed copy of the data; we made *two* magnetic tape backups; we stored the tapes in physically separate places (one in the United States, the other in England) in order to ensure the safety of the data.

In 1986, we replicated the study among three other groups: white Mormons in Utah, Paiute Indians in Arizona, and Micronesians on the island of Ponape (Bernard et al., 1987). When I went to code the data from those comparative studies, I did not pay close attention to the codebook from 1981. In the three studies done in 1986, it turns out, Paiute and Ponapean informants only needed the targets' occupation and location in order to make a choice of an intermediary. The white Mormon group needed the targets' location, occupation, and religion.

Now, all the programs that we had developed for data analysis in 1981 were based on data formats that conformed to the 1981 codebook. We had left seven spaces open under the variable "information informants need to know." But when I went to code the 1986 data, I left only three spaces: for location, occupation, and religion.

Had this variable been at the very end of each data record, this wouldn't have mattered. But it was smack in the middle of each record. All the programs had been designed to look for seven pieces of information (about whether or not the informant needed to know location, occupation, age, sex, etc.), but I had only coded up to three. We wound up having to rewrite the data (we determined that it was cheaper than rewriting the programs). Fortunately, the computer was able to do the rewriting, but this took time, money, and effort, and caused a lot of needless aggravation.

The lessons are clear: Make good, clear codebooks; make them as general as possible so that you (or others) can use them to replicate research; file codebooks away with your original data; and be sure to drag them out and follow them if you do decide to replicate your research. Even experienced researchers sometimes ignore these basic lessons, and when they do, the result is always costly.

Cleaning Data

You know from several earlier chapters how measurement error and sampling error can creep into data collection. There is one more source of error to watch out for: errors in coding and data entry. Believe me, it's easy to make mistakes. Everyone does. The trick is to catch the mistakes.

The best way to catch coding and data entry errors is with a professional data editor, like KEDIT (see Appendix G). These programs are like word processors with terrific search and block control. Suppose you have a variable "number of children" in columns 16 and 17 of a data record. You suspect that none of your informants have more than 10 children. You can tell a program like KEDIT to "find the cases in columns 16-17 where the entry is greater than 10." If the program finds such cases, you can decide whether the entry is an error or if it just means the informant has a lot of kids. Similarly, if an informant says that she has never had children, you want to make sure that the variable for number of grandchildren is also 0.

You can move columns of numbers around with a data editor. When you enter data, you often don't know what variables to put together. Later, as you become more familiar with your data, you'll want to move columns around so you can eyeball the data matrix and look for mistakes and incompatibilities.

Once you have your data into the computer and cleaned, you're ready to start statistical analysis. That's the subject of the next three chapters.

18

Univariate Statistics: Describing a Variable

U nivariate analysis is the first step in data analysis. Before you conduct any fancy statistical operations on your data, lay them out and get a "feel" for them. How many cases are there of people over 80? How many people report that they never go to church anymore? What is the average number of children in each household? Once you've done the univariate work, you can go on to asking about relationships between and among variables.

Raw Data

Table 18.1 shows the raw data for six variables on 30 Thai rice farmers. The first two variables are nominal or qualitative variables. Either a farmer owns his land or he doesn't; he either participates in the government-

TABLE 18.1

Data From a Study of 30 Thai Rice Farmers

	Nominal				Ordinal						Interval	
	Owns Land		Participates in Agricultural Credit Program		Social Class			Attitude Toward Daughters			Family Size	Productivity Per Hectare in Kilograms
	Y	N	Y	N	H	M	L	U	N	H		
1	x		x			x		x			8	1800-1899
2	x			x	x					x	12	2000-2099
3		x	x			x		x			7	1500-1599
4	x		x		x			x			9	1600-1699
5	x			x			x	x			5	1400-1499
6		x	x			x			x		5	1500-1599
7	x		x		x			x			6	2200-2299
8	x		x				x		x		9	1400-1499
9	x			x		x		x			10	1600-1699
10		x	x			x			x		10	1400-1499
11		x	x			x		x			4	1600-1699
12	x		x		x					x	11	1900-1999
13	x		x				x	x			6	1400-1499
14	x		x			x			x		8	1600-1699
15		x		x		x			x		8	1700-1799
16		x	x				x	x			8	1500-1499
17	x		x			x			x		9	1800-1899
18	x		x			x			x		10	2000-2099
19		x		x			x	x			7	1600-1699
20	x		x			x		x			5	2100-2199
21	x		x			x		x			9	1700-1799
22		x	x			x				x	9	1700-1799
23		x		x		x				x	6	1600-1699
24	x		x				x	x			8	1600-1699
25	x			x			x	x			7	1500-1599
26		x	x			x		x			5	1700-1799
27	x		x		x			x			12	2100-2199
28	x		x		x				x		8	1900-1999
29	x		x			x			x		9	1700-1799
30	x			x		x		x			8	1600-1699

supported agricultural credit program or he doesn't. In statistics, qualitative description entails identifying and tagging classes of behaviors, ideas, objects, or persons. It also involves assigning numbers to classes of things, like 1 for owning land and 0 for not owning land. Those numbers, though, are still just names, not quantities. You can count the number of 1's and 0's, but you can't add the numbers up and take their average.

The second two variables are ordinal. In the first, each of the 30 farmers has been classified as being in the upper, middle, or lower socioeconomic class in the village. In the second ordinal variable, each farmer is coded as unhappy, neutral, or happy with the idea of having more daughters than sons. This ordinal variable is extracted from ethnographic field notes and from unstructured interviews. This item is like most attitudinal questions on questionnaires.

Variables 5 and 6 are interval level. (They are really ratio variables, but recall from Chapter 2 that ratio variables are conventionally referred to as "interval.") The first is a measure of the number of mouths that must be fed by each farmer. This can vary from 4 to as many as 12 in these data. The second interval variable is an estimate of the number of kilograms of rice per hectare that each farmer produces.

These last are *grouped data*, with intervals of 100 kilograms in each group. Recall the rule: Never aggregate data when you collect it unless it's absolutely necessary to do so. In this case, you should assume that it was necessary because whatever method was used to make the estimates was not very precise. It could only give results to within 100 kilograms per hectare.

Frequency Distributions

Table 18.2 shows the raw data from Table 18.1 transformed into a set of *frequency distributions*. These distributions were produced using MYSTAT, but any program will do (see Appendix G).

Note how the variables in Table 18.1 were coded as they went into the computer. The variable called LAND in Table 18.2 refers to the data on whether a farmer owns his land or not. *By convention, variable names are in capital letters*. In this case, all the "yes" answers were coded 1 and all the "no" answers were coded 2. The values for the variable are shown directly under the variable name. LAND has two values: 1.000 and 2.000.

Table 18.2 shows that 20 farmers were coded with 1 for LAND—that is, they own their land. Ten farmers were coded with 2. The variable CREDIT has been coded the same way. The ordinal variable called SEC in Table 18.2 (for socioeconomic class) was coded as 1 (for lower class), 2 (for middle class) and 3 (for upper class). The ordinal variable called DAUGHTER was coded 1 (for unhappy with more daughters than sons), 2 (neutral on the subject), and 3 (happy with more daughters than sons).

The two interval variables are called PRODUCT (for rice productivity in kilos per hectare) and FAMSIZE (for family size). (Programs like

TABLE 18.2
Frequency Distribution for Raw Data in Table 18.1

Count	Cum Count	Pct	Cum Pct	Variable LAND
20	10	66.7	66.7	1.000 = Y
10	30	33.3	100.0	2.000 = N

Count	Cum Count	Pct	Cum Pct	CREDIT
19	19	63.3	63.3	1.000 = Y
11	30	36.7	100.0	2.000 = N

Count	Cum Count	Pct	Cum Pct	SEC
8	8	26.7	26.7	1.000 = L
16	24	53.3	80.0	2.000 = M
6	30	20.0	100.0	3.000 = H

Count	Cum Count	Pct	Cum Pct	DAUGHTER
17	17	56.7	56.7	1.000 = U
9	26	30.0	86.7	2.000 = N
4	30	13.3	100.0	3.000 = H

Count	Cum Count	Pct	Cum Pct	FAMSIZE
1	1	3.3	3.3	4.000
4	5	13.3	16.7	5.000
3	8	10.0	26.7	6.000
3	11	10.0	36.7	7.000
7	18	23.3	60.0	8.000
6	24	20.0	80.0	9.000
3	27	10.0	90.0	10.000
1	28	3.3	93.3	11.000
2	30	6.7	100.0	12.000

Count	Cum Count	Pct	Cum Pct	PRODUCT
4	4	13.3	13.3	1400.000
4	8	13.3	26.7	1500.000
8	16	26.7	53.3	1600.000
5	21	16.7	70.0	1700.000
2	23	6.7	76.7	1800.000
2	25	6.7	83.3	1900.000
2	27	6.7	90.0	2000.000
2	29	6.7	96.7	2100.000
1	30	3.3	100.0	2200.000

MYSTAT allow you eight characters with no spaces for names of variables, so family size becomes FAMSIZE.) Four farmers produced at least 1,400 kilograms of rice per hectare, but less than 1,500 kilograms. Just one farmer had 4 people in his family. Three farmers had 10 people in their families.

Table 18.2 also shows the *cumulative frequency* distribution (labeled CUM COUNT) and *cumulative percentage* distribution (labeled CUM PCT) for each variable. Look at the distribution for FAMSIZE. One farmer has four people in his family. The cumulative count is 1, and this case is 3.3% of the 30 cases. Four farmers have five people in their families. These four cases are 13.3% of the 30 cases. The cumulative count is now 5 (= 4 + 1), and the cumulative percentage is 16.7% (= 3.3% + 13.3%).

Using a Distribution Table

The first thing to look for is variability. If a variable has none, then it is simply not of any further interest for analysis. There are 8 lower-class farmers in these data, 16 are middle class, and 6 are upper class. But suppose that every single farmer in these data were middle class. That would be an interesting fact to report, but variation in socioeconomic class can't predict anything else if socioeconomic class doesn't vary. We wouldn't use SEC in any further analysis.

What if 26 of the 30 farmers were middle class and two each were upper and lower class? That still wouldn't be enough variation to be helpful in analysis of correlations among variables. Looking carefully at the frequency distribution is your first line of defense against wasting a lot of time on variables that don't vary.

Frequency distributions also tell you how to collapse variables that vary *too much*. Suppose you ask 50 people this question: "On a scale of 1-5, please tell me how you feel about your children's future. Are you very positive? Somewhat positive? Neutral? Somewhat negative? Very negative?" With so few respondents, you're likely to get a frequency distribution like this:

Very negative	4
Somewhat negative	26
Neutral	9
Somewhat positive	5
Very positive	6

The frequency distribution tells you to collapse these data into three categories: positive (with 11 respondents), negative (with 30) and neutral (with 9).

Central Tendency, Dispersion, and Shape

There are three things you want to know next about each variable in your data. First, you want some overall measure of the typical value; this is called a measure of *central tendency*. Second, you want a measure of how much *variation* or *dispersion* there is, so you can interpret the measure of central tendency. Third, you want to know the *shape* of the distribution of the variable. We will take up measures of central tendency first.

There are three basic measures of central tendency: the *mode*, the *median*, and the *mean* (the average). Each carries important information about the values of a variable.

The Mode

Although we use the word "average" as a synonym for "mode" in everyday speech, we have to be more precise in statistics. All variables (nominal, ordinal, and interval) have modal values, but nominal variables can *only* have modal values. Suppose you have a list of 100 people in a village, and for each of them you know their religion. There are 65 Muslims and 35 Christians. If you assigned the number 1 to being a Muslim and the number 2 to being a Christian, then the "average" religion would be

$$(65 \times 1 + 35 \times 2)/100 = 1.35$$

Clearly, this is a meaningless statistic. For nominal variables, like religious affiliation, the mode is the appropriate measure of central tendency.

The mode is the attribute of a variable that occurs most frequently. It is found by simply scanning the data and seeing which attribute of a nominal variable occurs the most. Looking at Table 18.2, we see that the modal value for the variable "land ownership" is 1, or "yes."

The mode is the weakest measure of central tendency, but then nominals are the weakest kind of variables. The mode is very useful, however, when you want to make a statement about a prominent qualitative attribute of a group. "More people are self-proclaimed Shintoists in this group than any other religion," is such a statement. The mode is also useful as a common-sense alternative to the sometimes unrealistic quality of the mean. Saying that "the modal family size is 5 people" adds a lot of easily interpreted information to the statement that the "average family size is 5.43 people."

The Median

The median is the point in a distribution above and below which there are an equal number of scores in a distribution. It can be used with data that are ranked—that is, with data that are at least ordinal level, or with interval level data. For an odd number of unique observations on a variable, the median score is simply $(N + 1)/2$, where N is the number of cases. For example, in the following distribution of 7 family sizes, 6 is the median observation

3 4 5 6 7 8 9

because there are exactly three scores below and three scores above it.

Of course, many data distributions are much larger than this one, and it is more difficult to find the median by inspection. Often as not, as in the data on those 30 Thai farmers, you'll have an even number of cases. In this event, the median is the average of $N/2$ and $(N/2) + 1$, or the midpoint between the *two* middle observations (unless, of course, the middle two observations are the same).

To calculate the median, use the formula for finding *percentiles*. The percentile concept is very useful. Ten percent of scores in a list are below the 10th percentile, and 90% are above it. The 25th percentile is also known as the first *quartile*; similarly, the 75th percentile is the third quartile. The difference between the values for the 25th and 75th percentiles is known as the *interquartile range* and is a simple measure of dispersion for ordinal and interval level variables.

The general formula for finding any percentile in a distribution of observed scores is

$$P = L + \frac{i(PN - C)}{f}$$

where P is the percentile you want to calculate, L is the lower limit of the interval in which the percentile lies, N is the number of cases, C is the cumulative frequency of the cases up to the interval *before* the one in which the percentile lies, i is the interval size, and f is the frequency of the interval in which the median lies.

Calculate the median for productivity (the variable called PRODUCT) in Table 18.2. Conveniently, the median is the 50th percentile. Substituting in the formula, we get

$$P = 1,600 + \frac{100[(.50)(30) - 8]}{16} = 1,643.75$$

The data are only accurate to the nearest 100 kilograms, so we would report that "the median rice production is approximately 1,600 kilograms per hectare."

Box-and-Whisker Plots

I've given you this grand tour of the median because I want you to understand the conceptual basis for this statistic. I'm going to do the same thing for all the statistical procedures I introduce here and in the next chapter. You only need to work through these detailed examples once, though. When you understand the concepts behind the median, the standard deviation, z-scores, chi-square, t-tests, and regression, you need never again calculate these statistics by hand. Once you understand a statistic, you can do all the calculations by computer.

In fact, even for small data sets, it's best to use a computer to handle statistical chores. It's not just easier to do the calculations. It's easier than it is by hand to get the numbers down right, to find mistakes when you get them down wrong, and to fix mistakes as you find them. Just as it's easy to check your spelling and grammar in a word-processed document, it's easy to find data-entry errors if you put your data into a computer to start with.

Here are some data collected by Allyn Stearman (1989:224). She measured the amount of game meat taken, over 56 days, by 16 Yuquí hunters in the Bolivian Amazon.

Box-and-whisker plots (which you can generate with programs like MYSTAT and KWIKSTAT) let you *see* how data are distributed. Figure 18.1 (generated with MYSTAT) shows the box-and-whisker plots for the two variables in Table 18.3.

The boxes show you the middle 50% of the cases. This is the interquartile range. The vertical line inside the box is the median, or the 50th percentile. Twenty-five percent of the cases in the distribution fall to the right of the median line and 25% fall to the left. The vertical line that marks

TABLE 18.3

Ranking of Yuquí Hunters by Game Take

Name	Kilos of Meat	Kilos of Fish
1. Alejandro	226.00	53.75
2. Jaime	185.50	101.00
3. Leonardo	152.50	8.50
4. Humberto	144.75	120.50
5. Daniel	78.00	119.50
6. Joel	74.50	34.25
7. Jorge	59.50	23.00
8. Timoteo	51.00	1.50
9. Tomás	51.00	123.80
10. Lucas	46.00	107.50
11. Guillermo	45.75	199.25
12. Victor	29.50	38.25
13. Manuel	14.50	28.50
14. Benjamín	10.00	128.00
15. Jonatan	0.00	198.00
16. Lorenzo	0.00	279.60

SOURCE: From "Yuquí foragers in the Bolivian Amazon: Subsistence strategies, prestige and leadership in an acculturating society" by A. M. Stearman, 1989, *Journal of Anthropological Research, 45,* 219-244. Used with permission.

BOX PLOT OF VARIABLE: MEAT, *N* = 16

0.00   226.00
MINIMUM   MAXIMUM

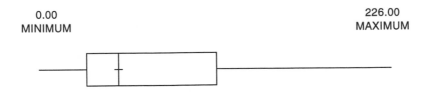

BOX PLOT OF VARIABLE: FISH, *N* = 16

1.50   279.60
MINIMUM   MAXIMUM

Figure 18.1. Box-and-whisker plots for Stearman's data on Yuquí hunters.

off the box at the left is the 25th percentile. It is called the *lower hinge* on a box-and-whisker plot. The vertical line that marks off the box at the right is the 75th percentile and is called the *upper hinge*.

The median number of kilograms of meat produced by the 16 Yuquí hunters is 51; the lower hinge is 22 kilograms, and the upper hinge is 111.375 kilograms. This means that 50% of the Yuquí hunters bagged between 22 and 111.375 kilos of meat during the 56 days that Stearman observed them.

The median for fish was 104.25 kilos; the 25th percentile was 31 kilos, and the 75th percentile was 125.9 kilos. Comparing the two box plots, we see that the distribution for meat is slightly skewed to the left, while the distribution for fish is slightly skewed to the right.

The whiskers on these plots show the top 25% and the bottom 25% of scores. The whisker on the left goes from the 25th percentile to the smallest value that is within one-and-a-half times the interquartile range. The whisker on the left goes from the 25th percentile to the largest value that is within one-and-a-half times the interquartile range. The length of the whiskers tells you graphically how far the upper and lower values in the distribution extend away from the median.

The asterisk to the right of the plot is a case that is more than one-and-a-half times the interquartile range away from the median. If there were two such cases, there would be two asterisks, and so on. Box-and-whisker plots are very useful. They're full of information and by comparing plots, you get a good feel for the distributions in your data.

Stem-and-Leaf Plots

Another way to get a feel for the distribution characteristics of your data is to produce stem-and-leaf plots for all your ordinal and interval variables. Here is a stem-and-leaf plot for the variable on family size in Table 18.1. (This plot was also created with MYSTAT.)

The values for the variables (4 children, 5 children ... 12 children) are the stem on this plot. The cases (indicated by a string of zeros) are the leaves. Thus, in Table 18.1 there was one case of a family with 4 children, four cases of families with 5 children, and so on. The 25th and 75 percentiles, or lower and upper hinges, are indicated with an H. The median is indicated by an M.

STEM-AND-LEAF PLOT OF VARIABLE: FAMSIZE, $N = 30$

MINIMUM IS:	4.000
LOWER HINGE IS:	6.000
MEDIAN IS:	8.000
UPPER HINGE IS:	9.000
MAXIMUM IS:	12.000

4		0
5		0000
6	H	000
7		000
8	M	0000000
9	H	000000
10		000
11		0
12		00

The Mean

The arithmetic mean is simply the average of the scores for a variable. The formula is

$$\bar{X} = \frac{\sum fX}{N}$$

where the symbol $\sum$ is a summation of scores and f is the frequency of a score, X. Here is the mean calculated for the data on family size in Table 18.1.

Family Size (X)	Frequency (f)	fX
4	1	4
5	4	20
6	3	18
7	3	21
8	7	56
9	6	54
10	3	30
11	1	11
12	2	24
$N = 30$	$\sum fX = 238$	$\bar{X} = 238/30 = 7.933$

The average amount of meat and fish caught by the 16 Yuquí hunters is
73.06 kilograms; the average amount of fish caught is 97.81 kilograms.

Dispersion and Shape

Once you have a measure of central tendency for your raw variable
scores, the next thing you need is a measure of *dispersion* for each set of
scores. The concept of dispersion (or variation) is easily seen in the
following example. Here are the ages of two groups of five people:

Group 1:	35	35	35	35	35
Group 2:	35	75	15	15	35

Both groups have an average age of 35, but one of them obviously has a
lot more variation than the other.

Consider the data for family size in Table 18.2. Notice how close the
mode (8), the median (8), and the mean (7.93) are to one another for those
data. This is not always the case. While the mean is generally considered
to be the most useful measure of central tendency, it is easily *skewed* by a
few extreme scores.

In Stearman's lopsided distribution (Table 18.3), the mean for game meat
is 73, but the median is just 51. Lorenzo and Jonatan had no meat, while the
four men at the top of the list had over 177 kilos apiece, on average.

Different kinds and amounts of dispersion in data cause distributions to take
on different *shapes*. Look at Figure 18.2 and get a feel for the various shapes of
distributions. You can see that the mean is easily affected by a few very large
or very small scores in a distribution, whereas the median is more stable.

Some distributions are *bimodal*—that is, their shape looks like Figure
18.2(d). This shape is quite common in data about the real world. In a village
that has experienced a lot of out-migration, for example, the age structure is
likely to be bimodal—a lot of young people who aren't old enough to leave,
and a lot of old people who can't find work in the city because of their age.

Notice what happens when you take the mean of a bimodal distribution:
Instead of giving you a realistic idea of the central tendency in your data,
it distorts what's going on. Always be on the lookout for bimodal distributions. This is easy to do by simply examining the frequency distribution
for each of your variables and by examining box-and-whisker plots for
interval variables to see if the distributions around the median are symmetrical. If the distributions *are* symmetrical, then the mean is the measure
of choice for central tendency.

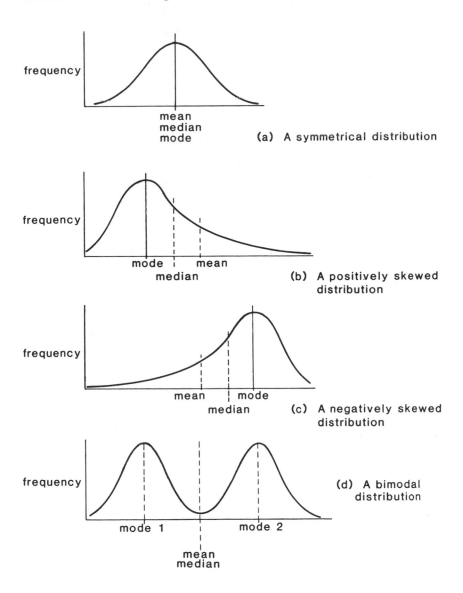

Figure 18.2. Shapes of distributions.

The Variance and Standard Deviation

The best-known and most useful measure of dispersion, at least for interval data, is the *standard deviation*, usually written as just *s* or SD. We use *s* or SD for the standard deviation of a *sample*, and the small Greek sigma, σ, for the standard deviation of a population.

In the example above of two groups of age scores, there is no variation in group 1, and a lot of variation in group 2. A statistic that told you *how much* variation there was in the two groups would be very useful.

SD is just such a statistic. It is a measure of how much the scores in a distribution vary from—that is, deviate from—the mean score. It is gives you a feel for how homogeneous or heterogeneous a population is, and this is especially important for understanding intracultural variation.

SD is calculated from the *variance*, which is the *average squared deviation from the mean* of the measures in a set of data. To find the variance in a distribution, subtract each observation from the mean of the set of observations, then square the difference (thus getting rid of negative numbers), then sum the differences. Divide that sum by the sample size to get the variance. Here is the formula for calculating the variance in a set of interval data.

$$s^2 = \frac{\sum (X - \overline{X})^2}{N}$$

where s^2 is the variance, X represents the raw scores in a distribution of interval level observations, $\overline{X}$ is the mean of the distribution of raw scores, and N is the total number of observations. *The standard deviation, s, is the square root of the variance,* s^2. We need to square the difference of each observation from the mean and then take the square root later because $\sum(X - \overline{X}) = 0$.

Variance is an important concept in statistics. Study the formula carefully and think about what it's doing. Be sure that you understand the difference between variation and variance. Variation refers only to the individual differences between the scores in a distribution and the mean score. Variance is an aggregate measure; it is the average of these variations. It describes in a single statistic just how homogeneous or heterogeneous a set of data is, and, by extension, how similar or different are the people described by those data.

There is some debate about this, but many researchers see variance as the thing you want to explain when you do statistical analysis of data. If you can explain 100% of the variance in a distribution, that means you can

TABLE 18.4

Data Needed for Calculating the Standard Deviation

Family Size	Frequency (f)	x^2	fx^2
4	1	16	16
5	4	25	100
6	3	36	108
7	3	49	147
8	7	64	448
9	6	81	486
10	3	100	300
11	1	121	121
12	2	144	288
	N = 30 $\bar{x}$ = 7.93		Σfx^2 = 2014

$$S = \sqrt{\frac{\Sigma fx^2}{N} - \bar{x}^2} = \sqrt{\frac{2014}{30} - 62.88} = 2.06$$

predict 100% of the scores on a dependent variable by knowing the scores on some independent variable.

Consider the original set of scores in Table 18.1 on farmers' attitudes toward having more daughters than sons. Suppose that for each change in family size you could predict the change in attitudes toward having daughters. If you could do this in 100% of all cases, then you would speak of "explaining all the variance" in the dependent variable.

I've never encountered this strength of association between two variables, but the principle is important. One goal of multivariate analysis is to explain a piece of the variance in a dependent variable with one independent variable, another piece with another independent variable, and so on. We'll look more closely at this in Chapter 20 on multivariate analysis.

In practice, the standard deviation is calculated from the formula

$$s = \sqrt{\frac{\Sigma fX^2}{N} - \bar{X}^2}$$

where the quantity under the square root can be shown to be another way of writing variance, as defined previously. Table 18.4 shows how to calculate the standard deviation for the data on family size in Table 18.1.

Substituting in the formula for standard deviation we get

TABLE 18.5

Calculating the Standard Deviation for Grouped Data

Interval	y	fx	x^2	fx^2
2200-2299	2,250	1	5,062,500	5,062,500
2100-2199	2,150	2	4,622,500	9,245,000
2000-2099	2,050	2	4,202,500	8,405,000
1900-1999	1,950	2	3,802,500	7,605,000
1800-1899	1,850	2	3,422,500	6,845,000
1700-1799	1,750	5	3,062,500	15,312,500
1600-1699	1,650	8	2,722,500	21,780,000
1500-1599	1,550	4	2,402,500	9,610,000
1400-1499	1,450	4	2,102,500	8,410,000
				92,275,000

$$\bar{x} = 1740 \qquad S = \sqrt{\frac{\Sigma fx^2}{N} - \bar{x}^2} = 219.62$$

$$s = \sqrt{\frac{2,014}{30} - 62.88} = 2.06$$

and if we were reporting these data we would say that "the average family size is 7.93, with SD 2.06."

For grouped data we take the midpoint of each interval as the raw score. Table 18.5 shows the procedure for calculating the standard deviation for the grouped data in Table 18.1.

Substituting in the formula for SD we get

$$s = \sqrt{\frac{92,275,000}{30} - 3,027,600} = 219.62$$

and we report that "the mean number of kilograms of rice per hectare produced by these farmers is 1,740, SD 219.62."

Are these numbers describing family size and the productivity of farmers and hunters large, or small, or about normal? As you do research, and as you read the research reports of others, you will come to have a comparative under-standing of the numbers that describe variables in which you are interested.

If you study demography, you will eventually get a feel for the distribution of mean family sizes and the standard deviations of those means around the world. If you study agricultural productivity, you will come to understand whether a group of people is producing a "high" or a "low" number of bushels per hectare of some crop.

TABLE 18.6
z-Scores for the Meat and Fish Data in Table 18.3

	Meat	Fish
Alejandro	2.238	−0.559
Jaime	1.645	0.040
Leonardo	1.162	−1.133
Humberto	1.049	0.288
Daniel	0.072	0.275
Joel	0.021	−0.806
Jorge	−0.198	−0.949
Timoteo	−0.323	−1.222
Tomás	−0.323	0.330
Lucas	−0.396	0.123
Guillermo	−0.400	1.287
Victor	−0.637	−0.755
Manuel	−0.857	−0.879
Benjamín	−0.915	0.383
Jonatan	−1.069	1.271
Lorenzo	−1.069	2.306

SOURCE: Adapted from Stearman (1989:224).

By themselves, numbers such as means and standard deviations simply describe a set of data. But in comparative perspective they help us make qualitative judgments as well.

z-Scores

Every real score in a distribution has a *z-score*, also called a *standard score*. A z-score tells you how far, in standard deviations, a real score is from the mean of the distribution. The formula for finding a z-score is

$$(\text{raw score} - \overline{X})/\text{standard deviation}$$

The mean for the meat data in Table 18.3 is 73.06, and the standard deviation is 68.34. To find the z-scores of the meat data in Table 18.3, subtract 73.06 from each raw score and divide the result by 68.34. To find the z-scores for the fish data in Table 18.3, subtract 97.81 (the mean) from each score and divide the result by 78.84 (the standard deviation). Table 18.6 is the list of z-scores for the data in Table 18.3.

```
                         x x
                        x x x x
                       x x x x x x
                      x x x x x x x x
                      x x x x x x x x
                     x x x x x x x x x x
                    x x x x x x x x x x x x
                   x x x x x x x x x x x x x x
                  x x x x x x x x x x x x x x x x
                 x x x x x x x x x x x x x x x x x x
```

```
           .         .           .       .
         -2sd      -1sd     0    1sd    2sd
```

Figure 18.3. 100 *x*'s distributed normally.
SOURCE: After Fitz-Gibbon and Morris (1987:35).

Raw scores are always in specialized units: kilos of meat, hours of time, and the like. Standard scores measure the difference, in standard deviations, between a raw score and the mean of the set of scores. A *z*-score close to zero means that the raw score was close to the average. A *z*-score that is close to plus or minus one means that the raw score was about one standard deviation from the mean, and so on.

About 68% of raw scores in a set of *normally distributed* scores fall within one standard deviation of the mean—that's 34% within one SD *above* the mean and 34% within one SD *below* the mean. Figure 18.3 shows what a normal distribution looks like.

There are 100 *x*'s in Figure 18.3. If the *x*'s were, say, heights of adult men, and if the heights of adult men are distributed normally, then Figure 18.3 is more or less what 100 scores would look like. There would be a mean score, which is 0 standard deviations from the mean, by definition. Then, about 34% of the scores would fall 1 SD above the mean and 34% below the mean. (Count the *x*'s out from the mean.) About 96% of all scores would fall within 2 SD above and below the mean.

If you draw a nice smooth line around Figure 18.3, you'll get the familiar bell curve of a normal distribution. Notice the little hump where the seven *x*'s are stacked on both sides of the mean. That's the place where the normal curve flares outward.

We know from Table 18.3 that Alejandro brought in a lot of meat and that Lorenzo brought in a lot of fish during Stearman's 56-day observation period. Table 18.6 tells more about Alejandro's and Lorenzo's prowess. Their *z*-scores are more than 2 standard deviations from the mean. If the distribution of Stearman's data is normal (that is, if the 56-day data are representative of life in the Yuquí forest) then Lorenzo's and Alejandro's raw scores are no fluke. Those men are just spectacular foragers in their respective spheres of hunting and fishing.

Why Use Standard Scores?

The advantage of using standard scores over raw measurements is seen clearly in the research by Linda Hodge and Darna Dufour (1991) on the growth and development of Shipibo Indian children. They weighed and measured 149 infants, from newborns to those 36 months in age. By converting all measurements for height and weight to z-scores, they were able to compare their measurements of the Shipibo babies against standards set by the World Health Organization for healthy babies (see WHO Working Group, 1986).

The result: By the time Shipibo children are 12 months old, 77% of boys and 42% of girls have z-scores of -2 or more on length-for-age. In other words, by 1 year old, Shipibo babies are more than 2 standard deviations under the mean for healthy babies on this measure.

By contrast, only around 10% of Shipibo babies (both sexes) have z-scores of -2 or worse on weight-for-length. By a year, then, most Shipibo babies are clinically "stunted" but are not clinically "wasted." This does not mean that Shipibo babies are just small but healthy. Infant mortality is as high as 50% in some villages, and the z-scores on all three measures are similar to scores found in many developing countries where children suffer from malnutrition.

The *t*-Test: Comparing Two Means

You will be surprised at how much qualitative anthropological "feel" you can develop for your data just by looking at a set of means and standard deviations. Suppose you measure the size of land holdings in a sample of 68 households from a small Indian town of about 800 households. It turns out that there are 18 Muslim households in your sample and 50 Hindu households. The average size of land holding among the Muslims is 1.6 hectares (SD 3.2), while the average size for the Hindu families is 2.3 (SD 4.8). From the sample, it appears that the Hindu families in the town are wealthier, with respect to land holdings, than the Muslim families.

We can test whether this is true using the t-distribution. The t-test asks a simple question: Do two sample means $\overline{X}_1$ and $\overline{X}_2$ differ enough to make me believe that there are real differences between the two populations? In

other words, is the difference, in this case, between the average size of
land holdings by Muslims and Hindus statistically significant?

To know this, we need to look at how big $\overline{X}_1 - \overline{X}_2$ is in terms of the
standard deviation (σ) of the "parent population."

The parent population is the general population from which the two
samples were pulled. The problem, of course, is that we know the 2
standard deviations s_1 and s_2 for our samples, but these are not the same.
It turns out that if we pool the 2 sample standard deviations together, we
get the best guess at what σ is, represented by $\hat{\sigma}$. (This is called "sigma
hat." It is customary in statistics to put a little hat on estimates of quantities.) The formula for finding $\hat{\sigma}$ is

$$\hat{\sigma} = \sqrt{\frac{N_1 s_1^2 + N_2 s_2^2}{N_1 + N_2 - 2}}$$

We now have to allow for the fact that we are comparing *means* and not
individual readings. The standard deviation of the means is given by

$$\sigma = \hat{\sigma} \sqrt{\frac{N_1 + N_2}{N_1 N_2}}$$

$$= \sqrt{\frac{(N_1 s_1^2 + N_2 s_2^2)(N_1 + N_2)}{(N_1 + N_2 - 2)(N_1 N_2)}}$$

which is very messy, but just a lot of arithmetic. Then we get

$$t = \frac{\overline{X}_1 - \overline{X}_2}{\sigma}$$

Degrees of Freedom and Tails

You can test whether t is significant (i.e., whether two means are
significantly different) by referring to the t-table in Appendix D. In using
Appendix D you need to know two things: how many *degrees of freedom*
you have and whether you want a *one-tailed* or a *two-tailed* test.

You will encounter these concepts in using other statistical tables, too.
Suppose I give you a jar filled with thousands of beans numbered from 1

to 9 and ask you to pick two that sum to 10. If you pick a 4 on the first draw, then you must pick a 6 on the next; if you pick a 5 on the first draw, then you must pick another 5; and so on. After the first draw, then, you have no degrees of freedom.

By contrast, if I ask you to pick four beans that sum to 25, then no matter what you pick on the first draw, you have lots of combinations you could pick on the next three and still sum to 25. But if you pick a 6, a 9, and a 7 on the first three draws, then you must pick a 3 on the last draw. You've run out of degrees of freedom.

For this *t*-test, the number of degrees of freedom is

$$(N_1 + N_2 - 2)$$

To understand the concept of one-tailed and two-tailed tests, suppose you have a bell curve, like the one in Figure 18.2(a), that represents the distribution of means from many samples of a population. Sample means are like any other variable. Each sample has a mean, and if you took thousands of samples from a population you'd get a distribution of means. Some would be large, some small, and some exactly the same as the true mean of the population.

The unlikely means (the very large ones and the very small ones) show up in the narrow area under the tails of the curve, while the likely means (the ones closer to the true mean of the population) show up in the fat, middle part. In research, the question you want to answer is whether the means of variables from one particular sample (the one *you've* got) probably represent the tails or the middle part of the curve.

Hypothesis tests are one tailed when you know the direction in which variables covary. You are then only interested in whether the magnitude of some statistic is significant (i.e., whether you would have expected that magnitude by chance). When the direction is not important, then a two-tailed test is called for.

In other words, if you predict that one mean will be higher than another, you are entitled to use a one-tailed test. After all, you're only asking whether the mean was likely to fall in one tail of the distribution in Figure 18.2(a). If you don't predict that one mean will be higher than the other (if you're just shopping), then you have to use the two-tailed test. Look at Appendix D carefully. Scores significant at the .10 level for a two-tailed test are significant at the .05 level for a one-tailed test.

Testing *t*-Scores

To test whether the difference in mean land holding among the Hindu and Muslim families in our example is statistically significant, we proceed as follows. First, we take the difference between the two means

$$(\overline{X}_1 \overline{X}_2) = (1.6 - 2.3) = -0.70$$

Next, we calculate the approximate standard deviation for the parent population

$$\sigma = \sqrt{\frac{(18 \times 3.2^2 + 50 \times 4.8^2)(18 + 50)}{(18 + 50 - 2)18 \times 50}} = 1.24$$

and then we calculate *t*

$$t = \frac{-0.7}{1.24} = -0.56$$

You can see from Appendix D that *t* is not significant.

We use a two-tailed test because we are only interested in the magnitude of the difference between the means. The direction, or sign (plus or minus) of *t* also makes no difference. After all, who's to say that Hindus or Moslems get called set 1 or set 2 in our calculations? But the absolute size of *t* would have to reach nearly 2 for it to be significant at the 5% level on a two-tailed test with 66 degrees of freedom (18 Muslim households + 50 Hindu households − 2 = 66). Although the raw data in our sample show that the Hindu families in the village have larger land holdings than the Muslims, the *t*-test tells us that the difference is not significant.

The insignificant *t*-test score means that we can't generalize to the whole community from the test results on this variable in our sample. This is not a failure; it is a finding and needs to be interpreted. Perhaps one Muslim family had 30 times the average amount of land in the village but, as luck would have it, that family was not selected for the sample. In a small community, these kinds of things can make a big difference in how much faith you are willing to place in a particular statistical finding.

If you really believed in the hypothesis that the Hindus had more land, you'd test it with a larger sample and predict up front that Hindus have more land. Given the small size of the original sample, and the low value for the *t*-test, a larger sample might even reveal that the true situation is the reverse of what we thought it was: The Muslims might show up as having slightly more land.

The important thing is to produce findings and then to let all your data and your experience guide you in their interpretation. It is not always possible, however, to simply scan your data and use univariate, descriptive statistics like means and t-tests to understand the subtle relationships that they harbor. That will require more complex techniques that we'll take up in the next two chapters.

19

Bivariate Statistics:
Testing Relationships

This chapter is about finding and describing relationships between variables—*covariations*—and testing the significance of those relationships. We hear the concept of covariation used all the time in ordinary conversation, as when someone asserts that "If kids weren't exposed to so much TV violence, there would be less crime." Ethnographers also use the concept of covariation in statements like: "Most women said they really wanted fewer pregnancies, but claimed that this wasn't possible so long as the men required them to produce at least two fully grown sons to work the land." Here, the number of pregnancies is said to covary with the number of sons husbands say they need for agricultural labor.

The concept of statistical covariation is more precise than that used in ordinary conversation or in ethnographic writing. There are four things we want to know about a statistical relationship between two variables:

1. How big is it? In other words, how much better could we predict the score of a dependent variable in our sample if we knew the score of some independent variable?
2. Is the covariation due to chance, or does it exist in the overall population to which we want to generalize (is it significant)?
3. What is its direction? Is it positive or negative?
4. What is its shape? Is it linear or nonlinear?

Testing for significance is a mechanical affair—you look up in a table whether a statistic showing covariation between two variables is or is not significant. I'll discuss how to do this for several of the commonly used statistics that I introduce below. Interpreting the substantive importance of statistical significance, though, is anything but mechanical. Establishing the theoretical significance of covariations requires thinking, and that's *your* job.

Direction and Shape of Covariations

The concept of *direction* refers to whether a covariation is positive or negative. For example, the amount of cholesterol you have in your blood and the probability that you will die of a heart attack at any given age are positive covariants: the more cholesterol, the higher the probability. By contrast, if you are a native speaker of an Indian language in Mexico, and if you speak Spanish with a strong Indian accent, then the chances are better that you are poor than if you didn't have a strong accent. The higher your score on accent, the lower your wealth.

The various shapes of bivariate relationships are shown in Figure 19.1. Suppose that Figure 19.1(a) were a plot of the number of yams produced by men on a certain Melanesian island, and their height, in centimeters. As you can see, the dots are scattered haphazardly, and there is *no relationship* between the two variables. In Figure 19.1(b), comparing the number of yams produced and the number of wives supported, the relationship is *linear* and positive. The more yams the men produce, the more wives they support.

The third scattergram, Figure 19.1(c), lays out the amount of debt that men have with the amount that others have toward them. The relationship is linear and negative (the more they owe, the less others owe them).

Finally, in Figure 19.1(d), there is clearly a strong relationship (the data are not scattered around randomly), but it is just as clear that the relationship is *nonlinear*—that is, it's not in a single direction. The relationship

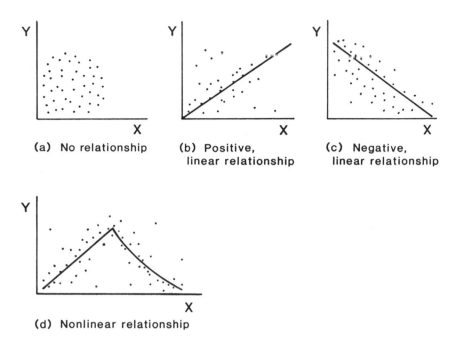

(a) No relationship

(b) Positive,
linear relationship

(c) Negative,
linear relationship

(d) Nonlinear relationship

Figure 19.1. Four scattergrams showing the common shapes of bivariate relationships.

between age and the number of people one knows is nonlinear. Early in
life the number of friends, kin, and acquaintances is small, but that number
grows as you get older. This relationship is linear and positive. The longer
you live, the more people you get to know.

Up to a point. If you live long enough, a lot of the people you know start
dying, and your network shrinks. There is a strong, negative relationship
between age and number of people in your network after age 70. It requires
a special kind of statistic, called eta, to test for nonlinear covariation, and
I'll discuss it at the end of this chapter when we deal with regression.

Tests for Bivariate Relationships and the PRE Principle

Table 19.1(a) is a hypothetical 2 × 2 (read: two-by-two) table showing
the breakdown, by gender, of monolingual Indians and bilingual Indian/
Spanish speakers in a Mexican village in 1962. A 2 × 2 table is also called
a four-fold table. Any table comparing data on two variables is called a

TABLE 19.1a

Bivariate Table Showing Monolingual and Bilingual Speakers by Gender
in a Mexican Village, 1962 (counts)

	Males	Females	
Bilingual	61 (82)	24 (36)	85
Monolingual	13 (18)	42 (64)	55
	74	66	140

old error = 55

new error = 13 + 24 = 37

$$\lambda = \frac{\text{old error} - \text{new error}}{\text{old error}} = .33$$

bivariate table, but not all bivariate tables are 2 × 2, since variables can take more than just two values.

TABLE 19.1b

Bivariate Table Showing Monolingual and Bilingual Speakers by Gender
in a Mexican Village, 1962 (percentages)

	Males	Females
Bilingual	82%	36%
Monolingual	18%	64%
	100%	100%
	N = 74	N = 66

$$\lambda = .33$$

NOTE: This table is set up according to the conventions generally followed in reporting data. Dependent variables on the rows, independent down the columns. Column percentages total to 100%, with N given for each column. Only column marginals are given. A statistic describing the table is provided.

In Table 19.1(a), the numbers in parentheses are the column percentages for each cell. Thus, 61 of 74 males, or 82%, are bilingual. Many researchers display only the column percentages in a bivariate table, along with the column totals, or N's, and a summary statistic that describes the table.

This convention is shown in Table 19.1(b). Tables are less cluttered this way, and you get a better understanding of what's going on from percentages than from raw numbers in a bivariate table. As long as the column N's are given, the interested reader can easily reconstruct the N's for each cell. Wherever appropriate, I will provide both the raw cell N's for the tables in this chapter, along with the column percentages for each cell in parentheses, so you can see how tables are constructed.

Numbers along the right side and below a table are called the *marginals*. The marginal in the lower right-hand corner of Table 19.1(a) is the total frequency of elements in the table. The sum of the marginals down the right-hand side and the sum of the marginals across the bottom are identical.

Note that the column percentages sum to 100% and that since we have percentaged the table down the columns it makes no sense to total the percentages in the right margin. In constructing bivariate tables, no matter what size (2×2, as in this case, or larger tables), the common convention is to put the dependent variable in the rows and the independent variable in the columns. Then we percentage down the columns and interpret the table across the rows.

Of course, you can switch the dependent and independent variables around if you like (this is usually done when the independent variable has too many categories to fit conveniently on a narrow page), but be sure to reverse the percentaging also and remember to be consistent. I will follow the convention followed by many scientific journals: *percentage down, read and compare across*.

Reading across Table 19.1(a), we see that 82% of the males were bilingual speakers, compared to 36% of the females. Clearly, gender is related to whether someone is a bilingual Indian/Spanish speaker, or whether they are monolingual in the Indian language only.

Suppose that for the 140 persons in Table 19.1(a) you were asked to guess whether they were bilingual or monolingual, but you didn't know their gender. What would you do? Since the mode for the dependent variable in this table is "bilingual" (85 bilinguals compared to 55 monolinguals), you should guess that everybody is bilingual. If you did that, you'd make 55 mistakes out of the 140 choices, for an error rate of 55/140, or 39%. We'll call this the *old error*.

Since both variables in Table 19.1(a) are nominal, the best measure of central tendency is their modes (recall from Chapter 18 that there is no way to calculate the average sex). Suppose you possessed the data in Table

19.1(a) and knew the mode for each independent variable (each column). The mode for males is bilingual, and the mode for females is monolingual. Knowing this, your best guess would be that every male is bilingual and every female is monolingual. You would still make some mistakes, but fewer than if you just guessed that everyone is bilingual.

Table 19.1(a) shows the aggregate result of this natural experiment on the recruitment of bilingual and monolingual people by gender. It tells you nothing about individual cases, but it contains all the data you need to find out how many fewer mistakes you'd make if you knew the modes of the independent variables.

When you guess that every male is bilingual, you make exactly 13 mistakes, and when you guess that every female is monolingual, you make 24 mistakes, for a total of 37 out of 140 or 37/140 = 26%. This is the *new error*. The difference between the old error (39%) and the new error (26%), divided by the old error is the *proportionate reduction of error*, or PRE. (The PRE principle is well described by Freeman, 1965, and by Mueller et al., 1970.) Thus,

$$PRE = \frac{55 - 37}{55} = .33 \quad \text{reduction in error, or}$$

$$PRE = \frac{39\% - 26\%}{39\%} = 33\% \quad \text{reduction in error}$$

This PRE measure of association for nominal variables is called lambda, written either L or λ. Like all PRE measures of association, lambda has the nice quality of being intuitively and directly interpretable. A lambda of .33 means that if you know the scores on an independent variable, you can guess the scores on the dependent variable 33% more of the time than if you didn't know anything about the independent variable.

The PRE principle is very powerful and is the basis for a large group of the most commonly used measures of association. PRE measures are all determined by calculating

$$PRE = \frac{\text{Old Error} - \text{New Error}}{\text{Old Error}}$$

Lambda can be used for tables larger than 2×2 and for analyzing relationships between nominal and ordinal variables. This is shown in Table 19.2.

TABLE 19.2

Calculating Lambda on a 3 × 3 Table for a Nominal
and an Ordinal Variable

| | Subsistence Type | | | |
	Hunters	Pastoralists	Agriculturalists	Total
Warfare				
often	(10%) 2	(40%) 8	(55%) 11	21
sometimes	(20%) 4	(45%) 9	(30%) 6	19
never or rarely	(70%) 14	(15%) 3	(15%) 3	20
	N = 20	N = 20	N = 20	

old error = 19 + 20 = 39

new error = (4 + 2) + (8 + 3) + (6 + 3) = 26

$$PRE = \frac{old\ error - new\ error}{old\ error} = \frac{39 - 26}{39} = .33$$

In this hypothetical example, 60 societies were selected from the Human Relations Area Files—20 hunting and gathering societies, 20 pastoral societies, and 20 irrigation agriculture societies. (I'm treating subsistence technology as a nominal variable here, although from a social evolutionary perspective hunters, pastoralists, and agriculturalists could form an ordinal scale.) Each society was graded on an ordinal scale as to how often it engaged in warfare with its neighbors. "Often" is once a year, or more; "sometimes" is at least once every 7 years, but less than once a year; and "never or rarely" is less often than once every 7 years.

If you didn't know the subsistence technology for each society, your best guess would be that all 60 societies engaged often in warfare—in which case you'd be correct on 21 guesses (35%) and wrong on 39 out of 60 guesses (65%). However, if you *knew* the subsistence technology, your best guess would be that hunters *rarely* engage in warfare (you'd be wrong 4 + 2 = 6 out of 20 times); that all pastoralist societies *sometimes* engage in warfare (you'd be wrong 8 + 3 = 11 out of 20 times); and that agriculturalists are *often* involved in war (you'd be wrong 6 + 3 = 9 out of 20 times).

Guessing this way, you'd make a total of 26 mistakes (a 43.3% error rate) instead of 39 (a 65% error rate). Making 21.7% fewer errors (65% − 43.3% = 21.7%) is a 33% improvement (21.7/65), and this is just what lambda shows in Table 19.2.

TABLE 19.3

Same as Table 19.1, but for 1987

	Males	Females	Total
Bilingual	63 (93)	46 (76)	109
Monolingual	5 (7)	14 (24)	19
	N = 68	N = 60	128

old error = 19

new error = 19

$$\lambda = \frac{19 - 19}{19} = \frac{0}{19} = 0$$

The Problems With Lambda

While lambda demonstrates the intuitively compelling PRE principle, there are three problems with lambda. First of all, there is no way to test whether any value of lambda shows a particularly strong or weak relationship between variables. Second, it is very awkward (even dangerous) to have a statistic that can take different values depending on whether you set up the dependent variable in the rows or the columns.

Third, lambda can be zero (indicating no relationship between the variables), even when there is clear and strong covariation between variables. This is especially likely in certain 2×2 tables, where more than 50% of the observations on the independent variable are contained in the cells for the same category of the dependent variable. Look at Table 19.3 to understand this.

These are the hypothetical follow-up data, 30 years later, from the Mexican Indian village study of bilingualism shown in Table 19.1. A new sample of 128 persons has been observed, consisting of 68 males and 60 females. A lot has changed in 30 years. There are hardly any monolingual males left (just 7% in the sample), and there has been a significant reduction in the proportion of monolingual females since a policy of universal, mandatory schooling for both boys and girls was implemented in the mid-1960s. Still, the relationship between gender and bilingualism continues to be obvious: There are many more monolingual females than males.

Despite this clear relationship in the variables, lambda is now zero. The mode for the dependent variable is still "bilingual," so you'd make 19 errors if you guessed that everyone in the sample was bilingual. But the mode for both columns of the independent variable, gender, is on the same row of the dependent variable. More than 50% of both the males and females are bilingual in Table 19.3. Having that table in front of you, then, you'd guess "bilingual" for males, making 5 errors, and "bilingual" for females, making 14 errors, for a total of 19 errors—and lambda would be zero.

Chi-Square

There are two ways to deal with this problem. One way is to play that trick of reversing the dependent and independent variables. The other way is to use a *non-PRE* measure of association for testing covariation between two nominal variables. The most popular of these measures is chi-square, written χ^2. It is very easy to compute, and there are standardized tables for determining whether a particular χ^2 value is significant.

Chi-square will tell you whether or not a relationship exists between or among variables. It will tell you what the probability is that a relationship is the result of chance. But it is *not* a PRE measure and won't tell you the *strength* of association among variables. It is very important to keep this in mind when interpreting this statistic. (You can use lambda as a way to get a better feel for what a particular χ^2 value means, and vice versa.)

The principal use of χ^2 is for testing the *null hypothesis*, i.e., that there is no relationship between two nominal variables. Say you suspect that there is a relationship between two variables in your data—variables like gender and bilingualism in Table 19.1. Using the null-hypothesis strategy, rather than trying to show the relationship, you would try as hard as you can to prove that you are dead wrong—that, in fact, no such relationship exists at all.

If, after a really good faith effort, you *fail to accept* the null hypothesis, you can reject it. Using this approach, you never prove anything; you just fail to disprove it.

Type I and Type II Errors

Chi-square is a particularly good statistic for this conservative, null-hypothesis approach to data analysis. It helps you avoid making either

Type I or Type II Errors—that is, either inferring that a relationship exists when it really doesn't, or inferring that a relationship doesn't exist when it really does. Both types of error are serious, but most researchers are more fearful of making a Type I error than a Type II error.

A Type II error is the result of caution and a conservative approach to data analysis—an approach that I fully endorse. When it comes to scientific data analysis, calling someone a "conservative" is to pay them a pretty strong compliment.

Type I errors are the result of what I call "buccaneer data analysis," of being too eager to find relationships, and of engaging in wishful thinking. On the other hand, all of science is based on making mistakes and learning from them. Expect to make a lot of mistakes; try to make more Type II mistakes than Type I, but be ready to engage in a little swashbuckling when you think you're on to something really important.

Calculating χ^2

The formula for χ^2 is

$$\chi^2 = \sum \frac{(O - E)^2}{E}$$

where O represents the observed number of cases in a particular cell of a bivariate table, and E represents the number of cases you'd expect for that cell *if there were no relationship* between the variables in that cell.

For each cell in a bivariate table, simply subtract the expected frequency from the observed and square the difference. Then divide by the expected frequency and sum the calculations for all the cells. Clearly, if all the observed frequencies equal all the expected frequencies, then chi-square will be zero; that is, there will be no relationship between the variables. While chi-square can be zero, it can never have a negative value. The more the O's differ from the E's (i.e., something nonrandom is going on), the bigger chi-square gets.

Finding the expected frequency for each cell is quite simple. As a first example, let's take a univariate distribution: the amount of land that people own. Suppose there are 14 families in a village and they own a total of 28 hectares of land. If the land were distributed equally among the 14 families, we'd expect each to own 2 hectares. Table 19.4 shows what we would expect, *ceteris paribus* (all other things being equal), compared to what we might find in an actual set of data. The χ^2 value for this distribution is 40.56.

TABLE 19.4
Chi-Square for a Univariate Distribution

Expected Land Holding, in Hectares per Family

Family #	1	2	3	4	5	6	7	8	9	10	11	12	13	14	
	2	2	2	2	2	2	2	2	2	2	2	2	2	2	= 28

Observed Land Holding, in Hectares per Family

Family #	1	2	3	4	5	6	7	8	9	10	11	12	13	14	
	.2	.4	6.6	1.2	2.1	5.1	.5	.4	.2	.4	.3	3.2	7.1	.3	= 28

(Observed-Expected)²

3.24	2.56	21.16	.64	.01	9.61	2.25	2.56	3.24	2.56	2.89	1.44	26.01	2.89

$$\frac{(Observed\text{-}Expected)^2}{E}$$

1.62	1.28	10.58	.32	.005	4.81	1.13	1.28	1.62	1.28	1.45	.72	13.01	1.45

$$\sum \frac{(O-E)^2}{E} = 1.62 + 1.28 + 10.58 + \ldots . \, 1.45 = 40.56$$

Finding the Significance of χ^2

To determine whether this value of χ^2 is significant, first calculate the *degrees of freedom* (abbreviated df) for the problem. For a univariate distribution

$$df = \text{number of cells} - 1$$

or $14 - 1 = 13$ in this case. For a 2×2 table, there is just one degree of freedom because you know the marginals and once you fill in one of the cells, all the other cell values are determined. The degrees of freedom for any size χ^2 table are calculated by

$$df = (r - 1)(c - 1)$$

That is, subtract 1 from the number of rows and columns and multiply the two numbers.

Next, go to Appendix E, which is the distribution for χ^2, and read down the left-hand margin to 13 degrees of freedom and across to find the *critical value* of chi-square for any given level of significance. The levels of significance are listed across the top of the table.

By custom (and only by custom) social researchers generally accept as *significant* any relationship that is not likely to occur by chance more than five times in 100 samples. This *p*-value (probability value) is called the .05 level of significance. A *p*-value of .01 level is usually considered *very significant*, and .001 is often labeled *highly significant*.

More and more social researchers are using asterisks instead of *p*-values in their writing. A single asterisk signifies a *p*-value of .05, a double asterisk signifies a value of .01 or less. If you read: "Men were more likely than women** to report dissatisfaction with local schoolteacher training," you'll know that the double asterisk means that the difference between men and women on this variable was significant at the .01 level or better.

The greater the significance of a chi-square value, the less likely it is that you'll make a Type I error. But remember: These customary levels of significance are simply artifacts of our culture. Whether to risk inferring the existence of a relationship that doesn't exist in the population is always a judgment call, for which *you*, not the χ^2 table, take responsibility.

In exploratory field research, you might be satisfied with a .10 level of significance. In evaluating the side effects of a medical treatment you might demand a .001 level. Considering the χ^2 value for the problem in

Table 19.4, I'd say we're on pretty safe ground. A χ^2 value of 34.528 is significant at the .001 level, with 13 degrees of freedom; with a χ^2 of 40.56 we can comfortably assert that inequality of land ownership in the village is significant.

If you are in the field, away from a table of χ^2 values, such as Appendix E, you can estimate the critical value of χ^2 at the 5% level of significance with the formula

$$\chi^2 \approx \text{(more or less equals)}$$

$$1.55(\text{df} + 2), \text{ for df} \leq \text{(equal to or less than) } 10$$

$$1.25(\text{df} + 5), \text{ for } 10 < \text{df} \leq 35$$

(for df greater than 10, but equal to or less than 35)

For a 3×3 table there are $2 \times 2 = 4$ degrees of freedom. As you can see from Appendix E, the critical value of χ^2 at the 5% level of significance for 4 df is actually 9.488. The rough field formula (Goodman, 1960) produces a critical value of $1.55(6) = 9.30$. It is very unusual to encounter a chi-square problem in anthropology with more than 35 degrees of freedom.

Calculating the Expected Frequencies for χ^2

The test for χ^2 can be applied to any size bivariate table. The expected frequencies are calculated *for each cell* with the formula

$$F_e = \frac{(R_t)(C_t)}{N}$$

where F_e is the expected frequency for a particular cell in a table; (R_t) is the frequency total for the row in which that cell is located; (C_t) is the frequency total for the column in which that cell is located; and N is the total sample size (the lower right-hand marginal). (It is inappropriate to use χ^2 if F_e is less than 5 for any cell.)

Chi-square can be used on bivariate tables comparing observations on nominal variables, or on observations comparing nominal and ordinal

TABLE 19.5

Observed and Expected Frequencies for Chi-Square

Observed Frequencies				
	Religion			
Tribe	1	2	3	Totals
1	150	104	86	340
2	175	268	316	759
3	197	118	206	521
4	68	214	109	391
	590	704	717	2,011

Expected Frequencies			
	Tribe		
Religion	1	2	3
1	99.75	119.03	121.22
2	222.68	265.71	270.61
3	152.85	182.39	185.76
4	114.71	136.88	139.41

$$\chi^2 = \sum \frac{(O - E)^2}{E} = \frac{(150 - 99.75)^2}{99.75}$$

$$+ \frac{(104 - 119.03)^2}{119.03} \ldots + \frac{(109 - 139.41)^2}{139.41} = 166.26$$

variables. Table 19.5 shows the observed adherents, in four Native American tribes, of three competing religions. Reading across the top of the table, in tribe #1, there are 150 Mormons, 104 Evangelical Protestants, and 86 members of the Native American Church. The lower half of Table 19.5 shows the expected frequency of each religion in each tribe. Chi-square is computed across the bottom of the table.

Unlike lambda, no matter how you set up a chi-square table (no matter which variable you make the independent one), the value of χ^2 will always be the same. In this case it's a walloping 166.26, with $(4 - 1 \text{ rows})(3 - 1 \text{ columns}) = 6$ degrees of freedom. In the field, you can trust χ^2 to tell you that something is going on, and you can trust Appendix E (or the rough-and-ready field formula above) to tell you whether a particular distribution of observations is likely to have occurred by chance. Once you have a significant χ^2, a PRE measure like lambda can tell you *how much* the variables are associated.

TABLE 19.6

Dobkin de Rios's (1981) Data on Experience With Witchcraft by Gender

	Personal Experience With Witchcraft, or Close Family With Personal Contact	No Personal Experience With Witchcraft	
Male clients	12	15	27
Female clients	63	5	68
Totals	75	20	95

SOURCE: Reprinted from *Social Science and Medicine, 15B,* M. Dobkin de Rios, "Personal experience of witchcraft and sex of adult interviewed," p. 61, © 1981, with kind permission from Pergamon Press Ltd, Headington Hill Hall, Oxford OX3 OBW, UK.

Cramer's *V*

Cramer's *V* is based on chi-square and is a direct test of the association of two variables. Once you know the χ^2 for a table, you can calculate Cramer's *V* easily. The formula is:

$$V = \sqrt{\frac{\chi^2}{N(k-1)}}$$

where *k* is the number of rows or columns in your table, whichever is less. If you have three rows and four columns, then *k* = 3 and *k* − 1 = 2. Multiply the number of cases in your sample by *k* − 1. Next, divide χ^2 by that number. Finally, take the square root of *that* number. It's that simple. Cramer's *V* is not a PRE measure, but it will give you an idea of how strong the association is between nominal variables.

Marlene Dobkin de Rios (1981) studied the clientele of a Peruvian folk healer. She suspected that women clients were more likely to have had personal experience with witchcraft (or to have a close family member who has had personal contact with witchcraft) than were men clients. Table 19.6 shows Dobkin de Rios's data.

The χ^2 for this table is 26.89. Consulting Appendix E, we see that, with one degree of freedom, this value of χ^2 is significant at the .001 level. We would not expect this distribution of cases by chance more than once in 1,000 tries.

Cramer's *V* for this χ^2 is the square root of 26.89/(95 × 1) = 0.28. Notice that when *k* = 2, the denominator in the formula for Cramer's *V* is simply *N*. Lambda for Dobkin de Rios's table is 0.47. Both Cramer's *V* and lambda show that there is a moderate association in these data between gender and having some personal experience with witchcraft.

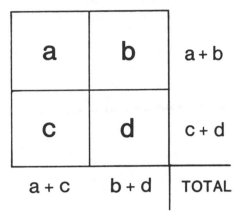

Figure 19.2. The cells in a 2 × 2 chi-square table.

The Special Case of the 2 × 2 Table

There is an easy-to-use formula that gives a good approximation of χ^2 for 2 × 2 tables. Since many of the bivariate tables you'll run in the field are of this variety, it pays to get comfortable with this formula:

$$\chi^2 = \frac{N(|ad - bc| - N/2)^2}{(a+b)(c+d) + (a+c) + (b+d)}$$

where a, b, c, and d are the individual cells shown in Figure 19.2, and N is the total of all the cells (the lower right-hand marginal).

The straight bars inside the parentheses mean that you take the absolute value of the operation $ad - bc$ (that is, you ignore a negative sign, if there is one), and you subtract $N/2$ from *it*. Then you square that number and multiply it by N and divide that by the denominator. It takes a little practice to keep track of all the numbers, but this formula is easy to implement in the field with just a simple calculator. Of course, if you have a computer with you in the field, any statistics program will calculate χ^2 for you.

As an example, I've used this formula to compute χ^2 for the data in Tables 19.1 and 19.3. The results are in Table 19.7.

As you'd expect, the χ^2 value for the 1962 data on the relationship between gender and bilingualism is much higher than the 1987 value.

Nevertheless, the 1987 value remains significant. Two-by-two tables have one degree of freedom. Any χ^2 value greater than 3.841 is significant

TABLE 19.7

Raw Frequency Data from Table 19.1 and Table 19.3 Computed for χ^2
Using the Formula for 2×2 Tables

	Male	Female	Total
Bilingual	61	24	85
Monolingual	13	42	55
	74	66	140

(a) 1962

	Male	Female	Total
Bilingual	63	46	109
Monolingual	5	14	19
	68	60	128

(b) 1987

$$\chi^2 \ (a) = \frac{140 \ (|(61) \ (42) - (24) \ (13)| - 70)^2}{(61 + 24) \ (13 + 42) \ (61 + 13) \ (24 + 42)} = 29.14$$

$$\chi^2 \ (b) = \frac{128 \ (|(63) \ (14) - (46) \ (5)| - 64)^2}{(63 + 46) \ (5 + 14) \ (63 + 5) \ (46 + 14)} = 5.24$$

at the .05 level, and any value over 6.635 is significant at the .01 level. We would expect to get the distribution of data in Table 19.7(b) less than 5 times in 100 tries. Not as good as the χ^2 for Table 19.7(a) (you'd expect *that* distribution less than once in 1,000 tries), but still pretty good.

Fisher's Exact Test

Fisher's exact probability test is used for 2×2 tables whenever the *expected* number of frequencies for any cell is less than 5. (With fewer than 5 expected occurrences in a cell, χ^2 values are generally not trustworthy.) Table 19.8 shows data from 20 rural women. After a year of working with these informants, your data show the following: When the 8 women who have equal to or less than 6 years of education need medical help, they rely mostly on traditional healers; when the 12 women who have at least 8 years of education need medical help, they rely on local clinics.

There are thousands of ways to throw 20 cases into four cells, but there are fewer ways to do it if you have to make the right-hand marginals add to 10 each and the bottom marginals add to 8 and 12. Fisher's exact test is based on the fact that, given the marginals for a 2×2 table, the number of configurations for achieving that table is fixed. The exact probability

TABLE 19.8

Hypothetical data on labor migration and education for Fisher's Exact Test

Medical Help	Education		Total
	≤ 6 Years	≥ 8 Years	
Healers	7	3	10
Clinics	1	9	10
Total	8	12	20

of getting the *particular* configuration in Table 19.8 is less than 1 in 100 ($p \leq .01$). It is quite safe to say that the women with more education rely on clinics rather than on traditional healers.

Fisher's test does not tell you *why* the distribution turned out the way it did. It could be that education directly influences the choice of medical help; or it could be that education leads to greater wealth and greater wealth leads to reliance on more costly medical services.

Fisher's exact test is handy for small samples (the kind anthropologists often work with), but it is very difficult to calculate by hand. To overcome this problem, Finney (1948) published a long set of tables, listing the exact probability of getting every possible 2 × 2 configuration for samples up to 30 in size. Those tables were extracted and republished by Siegel (1956), who also provided a plain English explanation on how to use them.

The best way to calculate Fisher's test, though, is with a computer program like SPSS, SAS, or SYSTAT. Those top-of-the-line programs automatically calculate Fisher's exact test along with chi-square.

Gamma: The All-Purpose PRE Measure of Association for Ordinal Variables

Once you understand the PRE principle, a lot of things in statistics fall into place. Suppose you test a group of men on how much knowledge they have about the use of wild plants. You rank them as having high, medium, or low knowledge, and you also rank them on a 3-point scale (high, medium, low) for the prestige they hold in their community. We'll assume that you've developed an appropriate index for each of these ordinal variables.

If the two variables are perfectly related, then every man who ranks high on knowledge will also rank high on prestige; every man who ranks low on knowledge will also rank low on prestige; and so on. Of course, things

TABLE 19.9

Plant Knowledge and Prestige Among Male Gardeners
in Amazonian Society

Prestige	Plant Knowledge			Total
	High	Medium	Low	
High	18	8	5	31
Medium	9	18	6	33
Low	7	12	12	31
	N = 34	N = 38	N = 23	95

Gamma = .41

never work out so neatly, but if you knew the *proportion of matching pairs* among your informants, you'd have a PRE measure of association for ordinal variables. The measure would tell you how much more correctly you could guess the rank of one ordinal variable for each informant if you knew the score for the other ordinal variable in a bivariate distribution. The raw frequency data for these two variables might look like those in Table 19.9.

What we would like is a PRE measure of association that tells us whether knowing the ranking of pairs of people on one variable increases our ability to predict their ranking on a second variable, and by how much. To do this, we need to understand the ways in which pairs of ranks can be distributed. This will not appear obvious at first, but bear with me.

The number of possible pairs of observations (on any given unit of analysis) is

$$\text{No. of Pairs of Observations} = N(N - 1)/2$$

where N is the sample size. There are $(95)(94)/2 = 4,465$ pairs of observations in Table 19.9.

There are several ways that pairs of observations can be distributed if they are ranked on two ordinal variables.

1. They can be ranked in the same order on *both* variables. We'll call these "same."
2. They can be ranked in the opposite order on both variables. We'll call these "opposite."

3. They can be tied on either the independent or dependent variables, or on both. We'll call these "ties."

In fact, in almost all bivariate tables comparing ordinal variables, there are going to be a lot of pairs with tied values on both variables. Gamma, written G, is a popular measure of association between two ordinal variables because it *ignores* all the tied pairs. The formula for gamma is

$$G = \frac{\text{No. of Same-Ranked Pairs} - \text{No. of Opposite-Ranked Pairs}}{\text{No. of Same-Ranked Pairs} + \text{No. of Opposite-Ranked Pairs}}$$

Gamma is an intuitive statistic; it ranges from -1 (for a perfect negative association) to $+1$ (for a perfect positive association), through 0 in the middle for complete independence of two variables. At best, the number of opposite-ranked pairs would be 0, in which case gamma would equal 1.

For example, suppose we measured income and education ordinally, such that anyone with less than a high school diploma is counted as having low education, and anyone with at least a high school diploma is counted as having high education. Similarly, anyone with an income of less than \$10,000 a year is counted as having low income, while anyone with at least \$10,000 a year is counted as having high income.

Now suppose that *no one* with at least a high school diploma earned less than \$10,000 dollars a year. There would be no pair of observations, then, in which low income and high education (an opposite pair) co-occurred.

In the worst case for gamma, the number of same-ranked pairs would be 0, in which case gamma would equal -1. For example, suppose that *no one* who had high education also had a high income. This would be a perfect negative association, and gamma would be -1.

The number of same-ranked pairs in a bivariate table is calculated by multiplying each cell by the sum of all cells *below it and to its right*. The number of opposite-ranked pairs is calculated by multiplying each cell by the sum of all cells *below it and to its left*. This is diagrammed in Figure 19.3.

In Table 19.9, the number of same-ranked pairs is

$$18(18 + 6 + 12 + 12) \quad = 864$$
$$+ 8(6 + 12) \quad\quad\quad\quad = 144$$
$$+ 9(12 + 12) \quad\quad\quad\; = 216$$
$$+ 18(12) \quad\quad\quad\quad\quad = 216$$
$$\text{Total} \quad \overline{1{,}440}$$

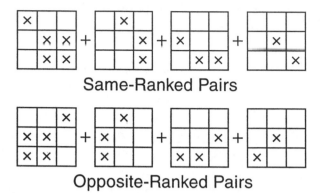

Figure 19.3. Calculating gamma. To calculate the same-ranked pairs in this 3 × 3 table, multiply each score by the sums of all scores below it and to the right. Then sum the totals. To calculate the opposite-ranked pairs, multiply each score by the sums of the scores below it and to the left. Then sum the totals.

The number of opposite-ranked pairs is

5(18 + 9 + 7 + 12)	= 230
+ 8(9 + 7)	= 128
+ 6(12 + 7)	= 114
+ 18(7)	= 126
Total	598

Gamma for Table 19.9, then, is

$$G = \frac{1,440 - 598}{1,440 + 598} = \frac{842}{2,038} = .41$$

So, plant knowledge and prestige are positively related.

Is Gamma Significant?

If you have more than 30 elements in your sample, you can test for the probability that gamma is due to sampling error using a procedure developed by Goodman and Kruskal (1963). A useful presentation of the procedure is given by Loether and McTavish (1974:552). First, the gamma value must be converted to a z-score, also called a "standard score." (I won't deal here with how z-scores are derived.) The formula for converting gamma to a z-score is

$$z = (G - \gamma)\sqrt{(N_s + N_o)/N(1 - G^2)}$$

where G is the *sample* gamma, γ is the gamma for the *population*, N is the size of your sample, N_s is the number of same-ranked pairs, and N_o is the number of opposite-ranked pairs.

As usual, we proceed from the null hypothesis, and assume that γ for the entire population is zero—that is, that there really is no association between the variables we are studying. If we can reject that hypothesis, then we can assume that the gamma value for our sample probably approximates the gamma value, γ, for the population. For the gamma value in Table 19.9,

$$z = (.41 - 0)\sqrt{(1{,}440 + 598)/95(1 - .41^2)} = 2.08$$

Appendix F is a z-score table. It lists the proportions of area under a normal curve that are described by various z-score values. To test the significance of gamma, look for the z-score in column 1 of the table. Column 2 shows the area under a normal curve between the mean (assumed to be zero for a normal curve) and the z-score. We're interested in column 3, which shows the area under the curve that is *not* accounted for by the z-score.

A z-score of 2.08 accounts for all but .0188 (1.88%) of the area under a normal curve. To be conservative, we'll round this up to 2%. Now we can reject the null hypothesis at about the 2% level, and we can presume that there is a real relationship between plant knowledge and prestige among the women in the general population from which we took our data. Chi-square for Table 19.8 confirms this finding. The value is $\chi^2 = 13.84$, with 4 degrees of freedom. Appendix E shows that, with 4 degrees of freedom, χ^2 has to exceed 13.277 to be significant at the 1% level.

Kendall's Tau-*b*

Because gamma ignores tied pairs in the data (and there might be a lot of them), some researchers prefer a statistic called Kendall's tau-*b* (written τb) for bivariate tables of ordinal data. The formula for τ_b is

$$\tau_b = \frac{N_s - N_o}{\sqrt{(N_s + N_o + N_{td})(N_s + N_o + N_{ti})}}$$

where N_s is the number of same-ranked pairs, N_o is the number of opposite-ranked pairs, N_{td} is the number of pairs tied on the dependent variable, and N_{ti} is the number of pairs tied on the independent variable. You can calculate the tied pairs as follows: For pairs tied on the dependent variable, multiply the first cell of the *row* of the table by the sum of the cells across the row. In Table 19.9

$$18(8 + 5) + 8(5)$$

$$+ 8(18 + 12) + 18(12)$$

$$+ 5(6 + 12) + 6(12) = 892$$

Pairs tied on the independent variable are calculated by multiplying the first cell of the *column* of the table by the sum of the cells down the columns. For Table 19.9

$$18(9 + 7) + 9(7)$$

$$+ 8(18 + 12) + 18(12)$$

$$+ 5(6 + 12) + 6(12) = 969$$

For Table 19.9, then,

$$\tau_b = \frac{1{,}440 - 598}{\sqrt{(1{,}440 + 598 + 892)(1{,}440 + 598 + 969)}} = .28$$

Kendall's τ_b will nearly always be smaller than gamma, because gamma ignores tied pairs while τ_b uses almost all the data (it ignores the relatively few pairs that are tied on both variables). Gamma is known as an intuitive, friendly statistic, easily interpreted as a PRE measure of association, and easy to evaluate using z-tables. On the other hand, many researchers like τ_b because it is a conservative statistic that doesn't inflate relationships between variables by ignoring data (tied pairs of observations). However, it is very difficult to test the significance of τ_b in the field—the formula is a beast, and there are no convenient tables that you can look up.

Yule's Q

A lot of work done by anthropologists in the field results in 2×2 tables of ordinal variables, like "high" versus "low" prestige, salary, education, hunting prowess, etc. In these cases, you can use a statistic called Yule's Q. This statistic is a modified, quick form of gamma (but without gamma's precise interpretation), and it can be calculated on frequencies or on percentages. Like the quick formula for χ^2, you can only use Yule's Q on 2×2 tables. The formula for Q is

$$Q = \frac{(ad) - (bc)}{(ad) + (bc)}$$

Yule's Q is a handy, easy-to-use statistic, and that's probably why it's so popular. Unlike a true gamma, however, you can not calculate its significance. A good rule of thumb for interpreting the significance of Q is given by James Davis (1971): When Q is 0, the interpretation is naturally that there is no association between the variables. When Q ranges from 0 to $-.29$, or from 0 to $+.29$, you can interpret this as a negligible or small association. Davis interprets a Q value of $\pm.30$ to $\pm.49$ as a "moderate" association; a value of $\pm.50$ to $\pm.69$ as a "substantial" association; and a value of $\pm.70$ or more as a "very strong" association.

What to Use for Ordinal Variables

My advice is this: Since Yule's Q is not easily interpreted, and since the significance of τ_b is very difficult to calculate, you should use these last two statistics only for special purposes. Specifically, Q is a useful statistic for getting a quick feel for the potential relationship of two ordinal variables in a 2×2 table. τ_b is a conservative statistic that lets you check how much stock to place in a marginally significant gamma.

In general, however, I recommend using chi-square and gamma on tables of nominal and ordinal data, respectively. Since 2×2 ordinal tables are usually chock full of tied pairs of ranked observations, try not to make up ordinal variables with only two ranks. This does *not* mean that you should make up artificial ranks just to fill out a variable. On the contrary, it means that you should work as hard as you can to *understand* the ordinal variables you are working with, so that you can make legitimate distinctions among at least three ranks.

For purposes of data analysis, an ordinal variable with seven legitimate ranks can be treated exactly as if it were an interval variable. Many researchers treat ordinals with just five ranks as if they were intervals, because association between interval-level variables can be analyzed by the most powerful statistics—which brings us to correlation and regression.

Correlation: The Powerhouse Statistic for Covariation

Where at least one of the variables in a bivariate relationship is interval or ratio level, we use either *Pearson's product moment correlation, written* simply as *r*, or a statistic called eta, written η, depending on the shape of the relationship. (Go back to the section on "shape of relationship" at the beginning of this chapter if you have any doubts about this concept.)

Pearson's *r*

Pearson's *r* is an intuitive PRE measure of association for linear relationships between lots of different types of variables. It is generally used to test for associations between interval variables, but it can also be used for an interval and an ordinal variable, or even for an interval and a nominal variable. It tells us how much better we could predict the scores of a dependent variable, if we knew the scores of some independent variable.

Consider two interval-level variables, like income (measured in some monetary unit like pesos or drachmas) and education (measured in years). Table 19.10 shows hypothetical data on 10 informants in a small village in Brazil. Now, suppose you had to predict the income level of each person in Table 19.10 *without knowing anything about their education*. Your best guess would be the mean, 45,600 escudos per month. If you have to make a wild guess on the particular scores of any interval-level variable, your prediction error will always be smallest if you pick the mean for each and every informant.

You can see this in Figure 19.4. I have plotted the distribution of income and education for the 10 informants shown in Table 19.10 and have drawn in the line for the mean (the dashed line).

Each dot is physically distant from the mean line by a certain amount. The sum of the squares of these distances to the mean line is the smallest sum possible (that is, the smallest cumulative prediction error you could make), given that you *only* know the mean of the dependent variable. The distances from the dots *above* the line to the mean are positive; the distances from the dots *below* the line to the mean are negative. The sum of the actual distances is zero. Squaring the distances gets rid of the negative numbers.

But suppose you *do* know the data in Table 19.10 regarding the education of your informants. Can you reduce the prediction error in guessing their income? Could you draw another line through Figure 19.4 that "fits" the dots better and reduces the sum of the distances from the dots to the line?

TABLE 19.10

Education and Income for Ten Rural Villagers in Brazil

Person	x Education in Years	y Income in Escudos per Month
1	0	32,000
2	0	42,000
3	3	35,000
4	4	38,000
5	6	43,000
6	6	37,000
7	6	39,000
8	8	54,000
9	12	58,000
10	12	78,000
	$\bar{x} = 5.7$	$\bar{y} = 45,600$

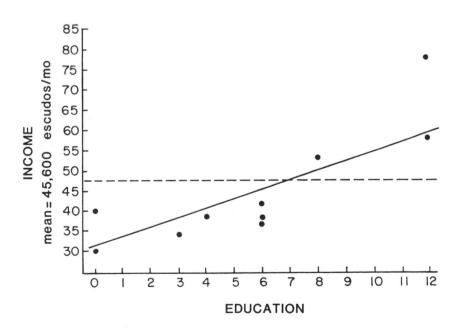

Figure 19.4. A plot of the data in Table 19.10. The dotted line is the mean. The solid line is drawn from the regression equation $Y = 30.10 + 2.72X$.

You bet you can. The solid line that runs diagonally through the graph minimizes the prediction error for these data. This line is called the *best-fitting* line, or the *least squares* line, or the *regression* line. When you understand how this regression line is derived, you'll understand how correlation works.

Regression

The formula for the regression line is

$$y = a + bx$$

where y is the variable value of the dependent variable, a and b are some constants (which you'll learn how to derive in a moment), and x is the variable value of the independent variable. The constant, a, is computed as

$$a = \bar{y} - b\bar{x}$$

and b is computed as

$$b = \frac{N\left(\sum xy\right) - \left(\sum x\right)\left(\sum y\right)}{N\left(\sum x^2\right) - \left(\sum x\right)^2}$$

Table 19.11 shows the data needed for finding the regression equation for the raw data in Table 19.10.

To reduce clutter, I have listed income in thousands of escudos/month. The constant b is

$$b = \frac{10(3,035) - (57)(456)}{10(485) - (57^2)} = \frac{4,358}{1,601} = 2.72$$

and the constant a is then

$$a = 45.65 - 2.72(5.7) = 30.10$$

The regression equation for any pair of scores on income (y) and education (x), then, is

TABLE 19.11
Computation of Pearson's r Directly From Data in Table 19.10

Person	x Education	y Income (in thousands)	xy	x^2	y^2
1	0	32	0	0	1024
2	0	42	0	0	1764
3	3	35	105	9	1225
4	4	38	152	16	1444
5	6	43	258	36	1849
6	6	37	222	36	1369
7	6	39	234	36	1521
8	8	54	432	64	2916
9	12	58	696	144	3364
10	12	78	936	144	6084
	$\Sigma x = 57$	$\Sigma y = 456$	$\Sigma xy = 3{,}035$	$\Sigma x^2 = 485$	$\Sigma y^2 = 22{,}560$
	$\bar{x} = 5.7$	$\bar{y} = 45.6$			

$$r = \frac{N\Sigma xy - \Sigma x\, \Sigma y}{\sqrt{\left[\, N\Sigma x^2 - (\Sigma x)^2 \,\right]\left[\, N\Sigma y^2 - (\Sigma y)^2 \,\right]}}$$

$$= \frac{10\,(3035) - (57)\,(456)}{\sqrt{\left[\, 10\,(485) - (57^2)\,\right]\left[\, 10\,(22{,}560) - (456)^2 \,\right]}} = .82$$

$$r^2 = (.82)^2 = .67$$

$$y = a + bx = 30.10 + 2.72x$$

Suppose we want to predict the dependent variable y (income) when the independent variable y (years of education) is 5. In that case,

$$y = 30.10 + 2.72(5) = 37.82$$

or 37,820 escudos a month. As you can see, the regression equation lets us estimate income for education levels that are not even represented in our sample.

The regression equation also lets us draw the solid line through Figure 19.4, such that the squared deviations (the distances from any dot to the line, squared) add up to less than they would for any other line we could draw through that graph. The mean is the least squares point for a *single* variable. The regression line is the least squares line for a plot of *two* variables. That's why the regression line is also called the "best-fitting" line.

Drawing the Regression Line

When you are doing data analysis in the field, I recommend that you actually plot out your data and draw in the regression lines on bivariate plots like Figure 19.4. There is no substitute for the "feel" that you get about covariation from looking at actual plots and regression lines.

To draw these lines, come up the y axis to the point where a (30.10 in Figure 19.4) intercepts it. This is called the "y intercept." Then, for every increment in x, simply apply the formula $y = a + bx$, and connect the dots. Actually, you only need to plot two points for the regression line, connect those points, and extend the line as far as you need to in both directions.

How Regression Works

To give you a clear idea of how the regression formula works, here are all the predictions along the regression line for the data in Table 19.10.

For person	whose education is	predict his or her income is
1	0 years	$30.1 + 2.72(0) = 30,100$
2	0	$30.1 + 2.72(0) = 30,100$
3	3	$30.1 + 2.72(3) = 38,260$
4	4	$30.1 + 2.72(4) = 40,980$
5	6	$30.1 + 2.72(6) = 46,420$
6	6	$30.1 + 2.72(6) = 46,420$
7	6	$30.1 + 2.72(6) = 46,420$
8	8	$30.1 + 2.72(8) = 51,860$
9	12	$30.1 + 2.72(12) = 62,740$
10	12	$30.1 + 2.72(12) = 62,740$

We now have two predictors of income: (a) the mean income, which is our best guess when we have no data about some independent variable like education; and (b) the values produced by the regression equation when we *do* have information about something like education. Each of these predictors produces a certain amount of error, or *variance*.

You'll recall from Chapter 18 that in the case of the mean, the total variance is the average of the squared deviations of the observations from the mean $(1/N)[\sum(x - \bar{x})^2]$. In the case of the regression line predictors, the variance is the sum of the squared deviations from the regression line. Table 19.12 compares these two sets of errors, or variances, for the data in Table 19.10.

We now have all the information we need for a true PRE measure of association between two interval variables. Recall the formula for a PRE measure: the old error minus the new error, divided by the old error. For our example in Table 19.12:

$$PRE = \frac{1,766.40 - 584.69}{1,766.40} = .67$$

In other words: The proportional reduction of error in guessing the income of someone in the sample displayed in Table 19.10, given that you know the distribution of education and can apply a regression equation, compared to just guessing the mean of income, is 67%.

This quantity is usually referred to as "r-squared" (written r^2), or the amount of variance accounted for by the independent variable. The Pearson product moment correlation, written as r, is the square root of this measure, or, in this instance, .82. Most researchers calculate Pearson's r directly from data, using the formula

$$r = \frac{N\sum xy - \sum x \sum y}{\sqrt{\left[N\sum x^2 - \left(\sum x\right)^2\right]\left[N\sum y^2 - \left(\sum y\right)^2\right]}}$$

Calculating r and r^2

Table 19.11 showed you the calculation of r and r^2 for the data in Table 19.10. As you can see, the procedure is simple and can be handled conveniently in the field without calculating y-intercepts, regression constants, and so on. But I've given you this grand tour of regression and correlation because I want you to see that Pearson's r is not a direct PRE measure of association; its *square* (written r^2) is.

There is a controversy in social statistics over whether Pearson's r or r^2 better describes the relationship between variables. Pearson's r is easy to

TABLE 19.12

Comparison of the Error Produced by Guessing the Mean Income for Each Informant in Table 19.10 and the Error Produced by Applying the Regression Equation for Each Guess

Person	x Education	y Income	Old Error $(y - \bar{y})^2$	Guess Using Regression Equation	New Error $\left[\begin{array}{c} y - \text{Guess Using} \\ \text{Regression Equation} \end{array}\right]^2$
1	0	32	184.96	30.10	3.61
2	0	42	12.96	30.10	141.61
3	3	35	112.36	38.26	10.63
4	4	38	57.36	40.98	8.88
5	6	43	6.76	46.42	11.70
6	6	37	73.96	46.42	88.74
7	6	39	43.56	46.42	59.60
8	8	54	70.56	51.86	4.58
9	12	58	153.76	62.74	22.47
10	12	78	1,049.76	62.74	232.87
		$\overline{y} = 45.6$	$\sum (y - \bar{y})^2 =$ 1,766.40		$\sum \left[\begin{array}{c} y - \text{guess using} \\ \text{regression equation} \end{array}\right]^2 = 584.69$

compute from raw data and it varies from −1 to +1, so it has direction and an intuitive interpretation of magnitude. It's also almost always bigger than r^2. By contrast, r^2 is a humbling statistic. A correlation of .30 looks impressive until you square it and see that it explains just 9% of the variance in what you're studying.

The good news is that if you double a correlation coefficient, you quadruple the variance accounted for. For example, if you get an r of .25, you've accounted for 6.25% of the variance, or error, in predicting the score of a dependent variable from a corresponding score on an independent variable. An r of .50 is twice as large as an r of .25, but four times as good, because .50r means that you've accounted for 25% of the variance.

Testing the Significance of *r*

Just as with gamma, it is possible to test whether or not any value of Pearson's r is the result of sampling error, or reflects a real covariation in the larger population. In the case of r, the null hypothesis is that, within certain confidence limits, we should predict that the real coefficient of correlation in the population of interest is actually zero. In other words, there is no relation between the two variables.

We must be particularly sensitive in anthropology to the possible lack of significance of sample statistics because we often deal with small samples. The procedure for testing the confidence limits of r is a bit complex. To simplify matters, I have constructed Table 19.13, which you can use in the field to get a ball-park reading on the significance of Pearson's r. The top half of Table 19.13 shows the 95% confidence limits for representative samples of 30, 50, 100, 400, and 1,000, where the Pearson's r values are .1, .2, .3, etc. The bottom half of Table 19.13 shows the 99% confidence limits.

Reading the top half of Table 19.13, we see that at the 95% level, the confidence limits for a correlation of .20 in a sample of 1,000 are .14 and .26. This means that in fewer than 5 tests in 100 would we expect to find the correlation smaller than .14 or larger than .26. In other words, we are 95% confident that the true r for the population (ρ, which is the Greek letter rho) is somewhere between .14 and .26.

By contrast, the 95% confidence limits for an r of .30 in a representative sample of 30 is not significant at all; the true correlation could be 0, and our sample statistic of .30 could be the result of sampling error.

The 95% confidence limits for an r of .40 in a representative sample of 30 is statistically significant. We can be 95% certain that the true correlation

TABLE 19.13

Confidence Limits for Pearson's *r* for Various Sample Sizes

Pearson's r	Sample Size				
	30	50	100	400	1,000
.1	ns	ns	ns	ns	.04−.16
.2	ns	ns	.004−.40	.10−.29	.14−.26
.3	ns	.02−.54	.11−.47	.21−.39	.24−.35
.4	.05−.67	.14−.61	.21−.55	.32−.48	.35−.45
.5	.17−.73	.25−.68	.31−.63	.42−.57	.45−.54
.6	.31−.79	.39−.75	.45−.71	.53−.66	.56−.64
.7	.45−.85	.52−.82	.59−.79	.65−.75	.67−.73
.8	.62−.90	.67−.88	.72−.86	.76−.83	.78−.82
.9	.80−.95	.83−.94	.85−.93	.88−.92	.89−.91
	(95% Confidence Limits)				
.1	ns	ns	ns	ns	.02−.18
.2	ns	ns	ns	.07−.32	.12−.27
.3	ns	ns	.05−.51	.18−.41	.23−.45
.4	ns	.05−.80	.16−.59	.28−.50	.33−.46
.5	.05−.75	.17−.72	.28−.67	.40−.59	.44−.56
.6	.20−.83	.31−.79	.41−.74	.51−.68	.55−.65
.7	.35−.88	.46−.85	.55−.81	.63−.76	.66−.74
.8	.54−.92	.62−.90	.69−.88	.75−.84	.77−.83
.9	.75−.96	.80−.95	.84−.94	.87−.92	.88−.91
	(99% Confidence Limits)				

in the population (ρ) is no less than .05 and no larger than .67. This is a significant finding, but not much to go on insofar as external validity is concerned. You'll notice that with very large samples (like 1,000), even very small correlations are significant at the .01 level. Just because a statistical value is significant doesn't mean that it's important or useful in understanding how the world works.

Looking at the lower half of Table 19.13, we see that even an *r* value of .40 is insignificant when the sample is as small as 30. If you look at the spread in the confidence limits for both halves of Table 19.13, you will notice something very interesting: A sample of 1,000 offers some advantage over a sample of 400 for bivariate tests, but the difference is small and the costs of the larger sample in the field are very high.

Recall from Chapter 4 that in order to halve the confidence interval you have to quadruple the sample size. Where the unit cost of data is high, as in research based on direct observation or personal interviews, the point of diminishing returns on sample size is reached quickly. Where the unit cost of data is low, as in much questionnaire research, a larger sample is worth trying for.

Nonlinear Relationships

All the examples I have used so far have been for linear relationships where the best-fitting "curve" on a bivariate scattergram is a straight line. Whenever long periods of time constitute one of the variables in a pair, however, there is a good chance that the relationship is nonlinear.

Consider political orientation over time. The Abraham Lincoln Brigade was a volunteer, battalion-strength unit of Americans who fought against the rightist forces of Francisco Franco during the Spanish Civil War, 1936-1939. The anti-Franco forces were supported by leftist groups and by the Soviet Union. On the 50th anniversary of the start of the Spanish Civil War, surviving members of the Lincoln Brigade gathered at Lincoln Center in New York City.

Covering the gathering for *The New York Times* (April 7, 1986:B3), R. Shepard noted that "While some veterans might still be inspired by their youthful Marxism, many, if not most, have broken with early orthodoxies" and had become critical of the (then) Soviet Union since their youth. There are many examples of leftist activists in modern society who are born into relatively conservative, middle-class homes, become radicals in their 20s, and become rather conservative after they "settle down" and acquire family and debt obligations. Later in life, when all these obligations are over, they may once again return to left-wing political activity. This back-and-forth swing in political orientation probably looks something like Figure 19.5.

Nonlinear relationships are everywhere, and you need to be on the lookout for them. Munroe et al. (1983) conducted four time allocation studies: two in horticultural peasant communities in Kenya, one in a highland community in Peru, and one on a sample of middle-class urbanites in the United States. They examined the relationship between the amount of time spent in productive labor and the technoeconomic level of the society.

The relationship between these two variables in their data is curvilinear. Labor inputs rise from moderate to very high levels as you go from hunter/gatherers and horticulturists to intensive agriculturalists. But labor inputs fall as you go from agricultural to industrial societies.

As I mentioned in Chapter 3, Lambros Comitas and I studied Greek labor migrants who had returned to Greece after more than 5 years in Germany. We found a nonlinear relationship between socioeconomic class and attitudes

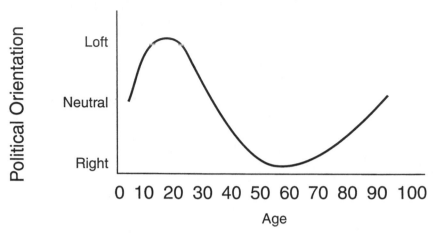

Figure 19.5. A nonlinear relationship. Political orientation through time.

toward dowry. Lower-class and upper-class men and women supported the traditional view that women need dowry in order to get married. Those in the middle class felt that dowry was an outmoded custom, that women should work outside the home, and that the income from that work should substitute for dowry.

If you get a very weak r or r^2 for two variables that you believe, from ethnographic evidence, are strongly related, then draw a scattergram (all statistical analysis packages produce scattergrams) and check out the relation more carefully. Scattergrams are packed with information. For sheer intuitive power, there is nothing like them. If a scattergram looks anything like either of the shapes in Figure 19.1(d) or Figure 19.5, or like any other complex curve, then r is not the right statistic to use because r is based on the concept of *linear* regression. An alternative is eta.

Calculating Eta

Eta, written η, is a very useful statistic. It is a PRE measure that tells you how much better you could do if you predicted the separate means for *chunks* of your data than if you predicted the mean for all your data. Figure 19.6 shows hypothetical data for a sample of 20 informants, ages 12 to 89, on the variable "number of friends and acquaintances." It is based on the data displayed in Table 19.14.

TABLE 19.14

Hypothetical Data on Number of Friends by Age

Person	Age	Number Friends	
1	12	40	
2	18	140	$\bar{y}_1 = 182.50$
3	21	300	
4	26	250	
5	27	560	
6	30	430	
7	36	610	
8	39	410	
9	42	820	$\bar{y}_2 = 570.0$
10	45	550	
11	47	700	
12	49	750	
13	51	410	
14	55	380	
15	61	650	
16	64	520	
17	70	220	
18	76	280	$\bar{y}_3 = 238.0$
19	80	110	
20	89	60	
		$\bar{y} = 409.5$	

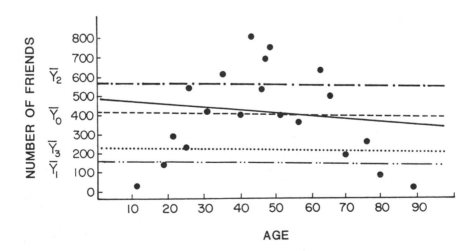

Figure 19.6. Number of friends by age.

In Figure 19.6, the large dots are the data points from Table 19.14. Informant #10, for example, is 45 years of age and was found to have approximately 550 friends and acquaintances. The horizontal dashed line marked $\overline{Y}_0$ is the global average for these data, 409.5. Clearly, (a) the global average is not of much use in predicting the dependent variable, (b) knowing an informant's age *is* helpful in predicting the size of his or her social network; but (c) the linear regression equation, $y = 451.45 - .89x$, is hardly any better than the global mean at reducing error in predicting the dependent variable. You can test this by comparing the mean line and the regression line (the slightly diagonal line running from upper left to lower right in Figure 19.6) and seeing how similar they are.

What that regression line depicts, of course, is the correlation between age and size of network, which is a puny .08. But if we inspect the data visually, we find that there are a couple of natural "breaks." It looks like there's a break in the late 20s, and another somewhere in the 60s. We'll break these data into three age chunks from 12 to 26, 27 to 61, and 64 to 89, take separate means for each chunk, and see what happens. I have marked the three chunks and their separate means on Table 19.14.

Unlike r, which must be squared to find the variance accounted for, eta is a direct measure of this and is calculated from the following formula:

$$\eta = 1 - \frac{\sum (y - \overline{y}_c)^2}{\sum (y - \overline{y})^2}$$

where $\overline{y}_c$ is the average for each chunk and $\overline{y}$ is the overall average for your dependent variable. For Table 19.14, eta is

$$\eta = 1 - \frac{395,355}{1,033,895} = .79$$

which shows a very strong relationship between the two variables, despite the very weak Pearson's r.

Eta varies between zero and one. It is a good statistic to use when you are testing covariation between an interval and a nominal variable—such as age and any yes-no variable like acculturated versus nonacculturated. (According to Freeman, 1965, eta is the *only* statistic to use in that case). It can also be used to compare interval and ordinal variables, and it allows you to test for nonlinear relationships between two interval variables. Eta is an all-around, varsity statistic.

Statistical Significance, the Shotgun Approach, and Other Issues

To finish this chapter, I want to deal with four thorny issues in social science data analysis: (a) measurement and statistical assumptions, (b) eliminating the outliers, (c) significance tests, and (d) the shotgun method of analysis.

Measurement and Statistical Assumptions

By now you are comfortable with the idea of nominal, ordinal, and interval-level measurement. This seminal notion was introduced into social science in a classic article by Stevens in 1946. Stevens said that statistics like *t* and *r*, because of certain assumptions that they made, required interval-level data, and this became an almost magical prescription.

Thirty-six years later, Gaito (1980) surveyed the (by then voluminous) mathematical statistics literature and found no support for the idea that measurement properties have anything to do with the selection of statistical procedures. Social scientists, says Gaito, confuse measurement (which focuses on the meaning of numbers) with statistics (which doesn't care about meaning at all) (p. 566). So, treating ordinal variables as if they were interval, for purposes of statistical analysis, is almost always a safe thing to do, especially with five or more ordinal categories (R. P. Boyle, 1970; Labovitz, 1971a).

The important thing is measurement, not statistics. As I pointed out in Chapter 2, many concepts, such as gender, race, and tribe, are much more subtle and complex than we give them credit for being. Instead of measuring them qualitatively (remember that assignment of something to a nominal category is a qualitative act of measurement), we ought to be thinking hard about how to measure them ordinally.

Durkheim was an astute theorist. He noted that division of labor became more complex as the complexity of social organization increased. But he, like other evolutionist theorists of his day, divided the world of social organization into a series of categories (gemeinschaft versus gesellschaft, or mechanical versus organic solidarity, or savagery, barbarism, and civilization).

When anthropologists rejected these simplistic schemes of social evolution, they did not substitute better measurement. Surely, what we really want to know is the *relationship* of the division of labor to social complexity in general. This requires some hard thinking about how to measure these two variables with more subtlety. The meaning of the measurements is crucial.

Eliminating the Outliers

Another controversial practice in data analysis is called "eliminating the outliers," that is, removing extreme values from data analysis. If there are clear indications of measurement error (a person with a score of 600 on a 300-point test turns up in your sample), you can throw out the data that are in error. If you decide to restrict the applicability of your sample, you can get rid of extreme cases—defining your population as "all cities in New York State under 2 million," for instance, eliminates New York City.

The problem is that outliers (so-called freak cases) are sometimes eliminated just to "smooth out" data and achieve better fits of regression lines to data. A single millionaire might be ignored in calculating the average net worth of a group of blue-collar workers on the theory that it's a "freak case." But what if it isn't a freak case? What if it represents a small proportion of cases in the population under study? Eliminating it only prevents the discovery of that fact.

Or suppose you counted the number of separate living quarters among five polygynous households, and found that one man had 11 wives, while the others had 2, 3, 2, and 4 wives, respectively. You might be tempted to eliminate the man with 11 wives from the data, at least for purposes of computing the average number of wives in the sample. But where do you stop? If the data were 2, 3, 4, 2, and 7, would you eliminate the man with 7 wives? On what basis would you make the decision?

Trivially, you can always achieve a perfect regression fit to a set of data if you reduce it to just two points. But is creating a good fit what you're after? Don't you really want to understand what makes the data messy in the first place? In general, you can not achieve understanding by eliminating outliers. Still, as in all aspects of research, be ready to break this rule, too, when you think you'll learn something by doing so.

Tests of Significance

This is one of the hottest topics in quantitative social science. Some researchers argue that statistical tests of significance are virtually useless (Labovitz, 1971b). I wouldn't go that far, but tests of significance aren't magical, either. If you do not have a representative sample, for example, then a test of statistical significance is not much evidence of support for a hypothesis—it doesn't allow you to generalize beyond your particular sample of data. On the other hand, if you get significant results on a nonrandom sample, at least you can rule out the operation of random properties *in your sample* (Blalock, 1979:239-242).

Nor are the .01 and .05 levels of significance sacred, either. These numbers are simply conventions that have developed for convenience over the years. If you want to be especially cautious in reporting correlations, you can apply a severe test known as the *Bonferroni adjustment*. Pick a level of significance for reporting findings in your data—say, .05. If you have 66 variables in your analysis, then there are $(66)(65)/2 = 2,145$ tests of covariations in your matrix. Simply divide .05 by 2,145 and look for correlations of .00002 in the matrix (these will be reported as .000 on most computer output).

The Bonferonni inequality states that if you report these correlations as significant at the 5% level (the level you chose originally), then your report will be valid (see Koopmans, 1981, and Kirk, 1982). This is a very, very conservative test, but it will prevent you from making those dreaded Type I errors and reporting significant relationships that aren't really there.

On the other hand, this will increase your chance of making Type II errors—rejecting some seemingly insignificant relationships when they really *are* important. You might fail to show, for example, that certain types of exposure are related to contracting a particular disease, and this would have negative public health consequences. There's no free lunch.

Consider the study by Dressler (1980). He examined a sample of 40 informants in St. Lucia, all of whom had high blood pressure, on nine variables having to do with their ethnomedical beliefs and their compliance with a physician-prescribed treatment regimen. He reported the entire matrix of $(9 \times 8)/2 = 36$ correlations, 13 of which were significant at the 5% level or better.

Dressler might have expected just $(36 \times .05) = 1.8$ such correlations by chance. Three of the 13 correlations were significant at the .001 level. According to the Bonferonni inequality, correlations at the $36/.05 = .0014$ level would be reportable at the .05 level as valid. Under the circumstances, however (13 significant correlations with only about 2 expected by chance), Dressler was quite justified in reporting all his findings, and not being overly conservative.

I feel that anthropologists who are doing fieldwork, and using small data sets, should be comfortable with tests of significance at the .10 level. On the other hand, you can always find significant covariations in your data if you lower the level of significance that you'll accept, so be careful. Remember, you're using statistics to get hints about things that are going on in your data. I can not repeat often enough the rule that real analysis (building explanations and suggesting plausible mechanisms that make sense out of covariations) is what you do *after* you do statistics.

The Shotgun Approach

A closely related issue concerns "shotgunning." This involves constructing a correlation matrix of all combinations of variables in a study and then relying on tests of significance to reach substantive conclusions. It is quite common for anthropologists to acquire measurements on as many variables as they have informants—and sometimes even *more* variables than informants.

There is nothing wrong with this. After a very short time in the field collecting ethnographic interview data, you will think up lots and lots of variables that appear potentially interesting to you. Include as many of them as you have time to ask on a survey without boring your informants.

The result of effective data collection is a large *matrix* of items-by-variables, like that in Figure 19.7(a). The items are the units of analysis. Most of the time, these units are people, but they could just as easily be cultures or schools. (If this is unfamiliar to you, see the section on units of analysis in Chapter 2.)

The matrix in Figure 19.7(a) is called a *profile matrix*. Each row is a profile of a single unit of analysis. In Figure 19.7(a), informant #1 is profiled by the following facts: She is 27 years old, is female (recorded as a 2 under the variable sex), has completed high school, has 1.5 hectares of land, comes from a household that had nine people in it, and is now part of a household that has six people in it.

For any profile matrix you can compare pairs of rows or pairs of columns to see how similar they are. If you compare rows, you find out how similar the units of analysis are to one another. If you compare columns, you find out how similar the variables are to one another.

Figure 19.7(b) shows a *similarity matrix* of variables. Imagine the list of variable names stretching several feet to the right, off the right-hand margin of the page, and several feet down, off the lower margin. That is what would happen if you had, say 100 variables about each of your informants. For each and every pair of variables in the matrix of data, you could ask: Are these variables related?

Now, if the matrix is symmetrical, then if x and y covary, so do y and x; that gets rid of half the pairs right there. Furthermore, no variable covaries with itself, so the entries in the diagonal have to be discounted. That still leaves $N(N-1)/2$ unique pairs of variables in a symmetric matrix. For 100 variables there are 4,950 pairs to consider.

Even a small matrix of 20 variables contains 190 unique pairs. It would take forever to go through each pair and: (a) decide whether it was worth spending the time to test for covariation in each case; (b) decide on the

Informant	Age	Sex	Education	Land Holding	Natal Household size	Current Household size
1	27	2	3	1.5	9	6
2	31	1	2	1.3	6	7
3	.	.	.	.	.	.
4	.	.	.	.	.	.
.	.	.	.	.	.	.
.	.	.	.	.	.	.
.	.	.	.	.	.	.
.	.	.	.	.	.	.

Figure 19.7(a). Profile matrix of persons by variables.

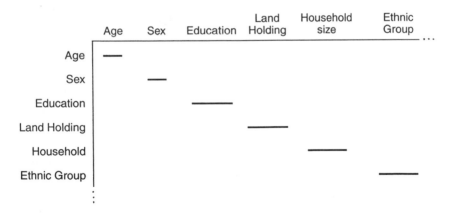

Figure 19.7(b). Similarity matrix of the variables (columns) in Figure 19.7(a).

proper test to run (depending on the level of measurement involved in each case); (c) run the test; and (d) inspect and interpret the results.

There are two ways out of this fix. One way is to think hard about data and ask only those questions about covariation that seem plausible on theoretical grounds. It may not be important, for example, to test whether an informant's rank in a sibling set (first child, second child, etc.) covaries with blood pressure. On the other hand, how can we be sure?

The other way out of the fix is the shotgun strategy. You simply use a computer to transform your data matrix into a correlation matrix in which each cell is occupied by a Pearson's r. Then you look through the correlation matrix in search of significant covariations.

Kunitz et al. (1981) studied the determinants of hospital utilization and surgery in 18 communities on the Navaho Indian Reservation during the 1970s. They measured 21 variables in each community, including 17 independent variables (the average education of adults, the percentage of men and women who worked full time, the average age of men and women, the percentage of income from welfare, the percentage of homes that had bathrooms, the percentage of families living in traditional hogans, etc.) and four dependent variables (the rate of hospital use and the rates for the three most common types of surgery). Table 19.15 shows the correlation matrix of all 21 variables in this study

Kunitz et al. (ibid.) point out in the footnote to their matrix that, for $N = 18$, the 0.05 level of probability corresponds to $r = 0.46$ and the 0.01 level corresponds to $r = 0.56$. They could have expected

$$21 \times (20/2) \times .05 = 10.5$$

correlations significant at the 0.05 level and

$$21 \times (20/2) \times .01 = 2.1$$

correlations significant at the 0.01 level by chance. There are 73 correlations significant at the 0.05 level in Table 19.15, and 42 of those correlations are significant at the 0.01 level.

Kunitz et al. (ibid.) examined these correlations and were struck by the strong association of the hysterectomy rate to all the variables that appear to measure acculturation. I'm struck by it, too. This interesting finding was not the result of deduction and testing; it was the result of shotgunning. The finding is not proof of anything, of course, but it sure seems like a strong clue to me about how acculturation affects the kind of medical care that Navaho women receive.

The Problem With the Shotgun Approach

The problem with shotgunning is that you might be fooled into thinking that *statistically* significant correlations are also *substantively* significant.

TABLE 19.15

Correlation Matrix of All 21 Variables in Kunitz et al.'s Study of Hospital Use on the Navaho Reservation

		1	2	3	4	5	6	7	8	9	10	11	12	13	14	15	16	17	18	19	20
1	Near hospital																				
2	Near surgery	0.67																			
3	Wage work	-0.24	-0.09																		
4	Welfare	0.52	0.46	-0.54																	
5	Education of men	-0.42	-0.43	0.73	-0.49																
6	Education of women	0.01	-0.21	0.67	-0.32	0.81															
7	Hogans	0.07	0.37	-0.26	0.72	-0.28	-0.40														
8	Bathrooms	-0.44	-0.57	0.63	-0.63	0.70	0.64	-0.47													
9	Household size	0.03	-0.16	-0.48	0.24	-0.34	-0.07	0.04	0.12												
10	Working women	-0.35	-0.36	0.68	-0.65	0.65	0.57	-0.48	0.62	-0.22											
11	Working men	-0.24	-0.18	0.73	-0.37	0.73	0.63	-0.16	0.41	-0.45	0.45										
12	Vehicles	0.34	-0.08	0.40	-0.17	0.22	0.52	-0.53	0.29	-0.06	0.31	0.40									
13	Median income	-0.45	-0.51	0.66	-0.60	0.67	0.60	-0.38	0.79	-0.07	0.83	0.48	0.27								
14	Per capita income	-0.25	-0.20	0.68	-0.46	0.61	0.40	-0.15	0.29	-0.68	0.48	0.51	0.30	0.47							
15	Age of women	-0.23	-0.03	-0.47	-0.15	-0.36	-0.66	-0.02	-0.46	-0.30	-0.37	-0.32	-0.56	-0.43	-0.04						
16	Age of men	0.28	0.15	-0.77	0.31	-0.60	-0.55	0.01	-0.67	0.06	-0.51	-0.68	-0.35	-0.63	-0.45	0.60					
17	Age of patients	0.13	0.47	0.13	-0.14	-0.21	-0.15	-0.18	-0.22	-0.36	-0.04	-0.26	-0.15	-0.26	-0.002	0.29	0.32				
18	Hysterectomies	-0.41	-0.48	0.62	-0.55	0.57	0.46	-0.23	0.75	-0.09	0.45	-0.04	0.39	-0.15	0.59	-0.31	-0.62	-0.28			
19	Appendectomies	-0.31	-0.40	0.32	-0.14	0.44	0.33	0.16	0.51	0.13	0.07	0.27	0.01	0.42	0.35	-0.49	-0.56	-0.62	0.70		
20	Cholecystectomies	-0.23	-0.70	0.15	-0.43	0.35	0.34	-0.46	0.68	0.22	0.19	0.12	0.31	0.40	0.14	-0.17	-0.17	-0.35	0.70	0.49	
21	Hospital rate	-0.49	-0.24	0.02	-0.26	0.02	-0.25	-0.09	0.16	-0.19	-0.04	-0.34	-0.33	0.01	0.22	0.43	0.16	0.45	0.17	0.10	0.18

$N = 18$
$0.46, P = 0.05$.
$0.56, P = 0.01$.

SOURCE: Reprinted from *Social Science and Medicine, 15B*, S. J. Kunitz, D. Temkin-Greener, D. Broudy, and M. Haffner, "Determinants of hospital utilization and surgery on the Navajo Indian Reservation, 1972-1978," p. 74, © 1981, with kind permission from Pergamon Press Ltd, Headington Hill Hall, Oxford OX3 OBW, UK.

This is a real danger, and it should not be minimized (Labovitz, 1972). It results from two problems.

1. First of all, it might not be appropriate to analyze some pairs of variables using Pearson's r. Some pairs of variables are more appropriately analyzed using gamma, or chi-square, or some other statistic. Any particular significant correlation in a matrix may be an artifact of the statistical technique employed and not of any substantive importance. Running a big correlation matrix of all your variables may produce some statistically significant results that would be insignificant if the proper test had been applied.

2. Second, there is a known probability that any correlation in a matrix might be the result of chance. The number of expected significant correlations in a matrix is equal to the level of significance you choose, times the number of variables. If you are looking for covariations that are significant at the 5% level, then you only need 20 tests of covariation to find one such covariation by chance. If you are looking for covariations that are significant at the 1% level, you should expect to find one, by chance, once in every 100 tries. In a matrix of 100 variables with 4,950 correlations, you might find around 50 significant correlations at the 1% level by chance.

This does not mean that 50 correlations at the 1% level in such a matrix *are* the result of chance. They just *might* be. There can easily be 300 or more significant correlations in a matrix of 100 variables. If 50 of them (4,950/100) might be the result of chance, then how can you decide which 50 they are? You can't. You can never know for sure whether any particular correlation is the result of chance. You simply have to be careful in your interpretation of *every* correlation in a matrix.

Use the shotgun. Be as cavalier as you can in looking for statistically significant covariations, but be very conservative in interpreting their substantive (as opposed to their statistical) importance. Correlations are hints to you that something is going on between two variables. Just keep in mind that the leap from correlation to cause is often across a wide chasm.

If you look at Table 19.13 again, you can see just how risky things can be. A correlation of .60 is significant at the 1% level of confidence with a sample as small as 30. Notice, however, that the correlation in the population is 99% certain to fall between .20 and .83, which is a pretty wide spread. You wouldn't want to build too big a theory around a correlation that just might be down around the .20 level, accounting for just 4% of the variance in what you're interested in.

Remember these rules:

1. Not all significant findings at the 5% level of confidence are equally important. A very weak correlation of .10 in a sample of a million persons would be statistically significant, even if it were substantively trivial. By contrast, in small samples, substantively important relations may show up as statistically insignificant.

2. Don't settle for just one correlation that supports a pet theory; insist on several, and be on the lookout for artifactual correlations.

Thirty years ago, when most of the current generation of senior anthropologists were trained, there were no easy-to-use statistical packages. It was a real pain to run statistical tests. It made a lot of sense to think hard about which of the thousands of possible tests one really wanted to run by hand on an adding machine.

Computers have eliminated the drudge work in data analysis, but *they haven't eliminated the need to think critically about your results.* If anything, computers have made it more important than ever to be self-conscious about the interpretation of statistical findings. But if you *are* self-conscious about this issue, and dedicated to thinking critically about your data, then I believe you should take full advantage of the power of the computer to produce a mountain of correlational hints that you can follow up.

Finally, by all means, use your intuition in interpreting correlations; common sense and your personal experience in the field are powerful tools for data analysis. If you find a correlation between the distance from an African farmer's house to credit agencies, and whether the farmer's family brews its own beer in the home, you might suspect that this is just a chance artifact.

On the other hand, maybe it isn't. There is just as much danger in relying slavishly on personal intuition and common sense as there is in placing ultimate faith in computers. What appears silly to you may, in fact, be an important signal in your data. The world is filled with self-evident truths that are not true, and self-evident falsehoods that are not false. The role of science, based on solid technique and the application of intuition, is to sort those things out.

20

Multivariate Analysis

M ost of the really interesting dependent variables in the social world—variables such as personality type, amount of risk-taking behavior, level of wealth accumulation, attitudes toward women or men—appear to be caused by a large number of independent variables, some of which are dependent variables themselves. The goal of multivariate analysis is to explain *how* variables are related and to develop a theory of causation that accounts for the fact that variables are related to one another.

There are two strategies for conducting multivariate analysis. One is called the *elaboration method*, developed by Paul Lazarsfeld and others at the Bureau of Applied Social Research at Columbia University (see Hyman, 1955; Rosenberg, 1968; Lazarsfeld et al., 1972; Zeisel, 1985). It involves nothing more than careful construction and inspection of percentage tables and the use of bivariate statistics.

The other kind of multivariate analysis involves an array of advanced statistical procedures. You will run into these procedures again and again as you read journal articles and monographs—things like multiple regression, partial regression, factor analysis, multidimensional scaling, analysis of variance, and so on. I'll discuss the elaboration method at length here and I'll just touch on the conceptual basis of the more complex procedures.

The Elaboration Method: Multivariate Percentage Tables

The elaboration method was popular in sociology up to about the mid-1970s but fell out of favor in some circles when computers became common. I still think that the method is excellent for use in anthropological fieldwork. This is not because elaboration analysis can be done without a computer. It *can* be done without a computer, but you know how I feel about that: Once you understand how any statistical method works, you should *only* do it by computer. The elaboration method is wonderful for field researchers because it keeps you close to your data.

It's going to take you a couple of hours to get through the next half-dozen pages on the elaboration method. The writing is clear and there's no heavy math, so they're not tough going; they're just plain tedious. But bear with me. If I give you 10 five-digit numbers to multiply, you'd probably use a calculator to make short work of the exercise, and quite properly, too. But in the fourth grade, you learned to do the operation by hand, with a pencil and paper, and it was an important learning experience.

The same applies here. Eventually, you'll simply give a computer a list of what you think are possible independent variables, specify a dependent variable, and let the machine do the rest. The next few pages will give you an appreciation of just what a multivariate analysis does. They will also give you the skills you need to conduct a multivariate analysis in the field, while your thoughts are fresh and you still have time to collect any data you find you need. So, be patient, pay close attention to the tables, and stay with it.

Building Tables

Suppose you are working in Peru and you suspect that Indians who move to Lima are no better off than Indians who remain in the villages. The Indians claim that they are seeking better jobs and better opportunities for

TABLE 20.1

Wealth by Residence for a Sample of 500 Peruvian Indians

Residence

Wealth	Rural	Urban	
Not poor	84 (34)	91 (36)	175
Poor	166 (66)	159 (64)	325
	250	250	500

x^2 = .56 NS (Not Significant)

their children, but you think that they are not getting what they came to the city to find. You conduct a survey of 250 village residents from a particular region and 250 migrants who have gone to the city from the same region. Table 20.1 shows the relation between residence and accumulated wealth status for your sample.

Chi-square for this table is not significant. Assuming that you have measured wealth status using an appropriate index for both the urban and village environments, residence appears to make no difference in wealth accumulation among these informants.

After 5 years or more in the city, 74% of the sample remained poor. On the other hand, 26% managed to rise out of poverty in that time. Table 20.2 shows that the correlation between time in the city and the chance of remaining poor is .83, but the chance of climbing out of poverty rises with each year spent in the urban environment, and using the regression formula introduced in the last chapter, the projected chance of still being poor after 10 years in the city is .50.

Given that time won't cure poverty at the village level, the Indians' perception that time *might* work in their favor in the cities is substantially correct from these data.

Just as a significant bivariate relation can be rendered spurious by a common third variable, so can an apparently trivial relation become significant when you control for the right intervening variable. From other studies, we know that education is related to both residence and wealth; urban people tend to be both more wealthy than rural people, and more educated.

TABLE 20.2

Wealth Status by Time in the City for 250 Indian Migrants

Wealth Status	Years in City			
	< 1	⩾ 1 < 3	⩾ 3 < 5	⩾ 5
Not poor	0	2	5	11
Poor	83	68	49	32

Time in City (in years)	Chance of Being Poor
1	83/83 = 1.0
2	68/70 = .97
4	49/54 = .91
5+	32/43 = .74
	r = .83

for 10 years, projected chance of remaining poor = .5

Tables 20.3 and 20.4 show the results of cross-tabulating wealth by education, and education by residence. Forty-four percent of those who completed the eighth grade have a family income above the poverty level, while just 26% of those who did not finish the eighth grade come from families whose income is above the poverty level. Chi-square for this table is highly significant.

TABLE 20.3

Wealth by Education for the Data in Table 20.1

Wealth	Education		
	Completed Eighth Grade	Did Not Complete	
Not poor	113 (44)	62 (26)	175
Poor	146 (56)	179 (74)	325
	259	241	500

$$\chi^2 = 17.28 \qquad Q = .38$$
$$p < .001$$

TABLE 20.4

Education by Residence for the Data in Table 20.1

Education	Residence Rural	Urban	
Completed 8th grade	100 (40)	159 (64)	259
Did not complete	150 (60)	91 (36)	241
	250	250	500

$$\chi^2 = 26.95 \qquad Q = .45$$
$$p < .001$$

These tables indicate that urban people receive more education, and that this leads to greater wealth. We test this hypothesis by *elaborating* the relationship (in Table 20.3) of wealth by education *controlling for* residence. This is done in Table 20.5, which really consists of two separate tables, each of which can be analyzed statistically. (Place the control variables above the independent variable when constructing multivariate tables.)

Things are a bit more complex than we imagined at first. Among rural people, those who had completed the eighth grade are more than twice as

TABLE 20.5

Wealth by Education, Controlling for Residence

Wealth	Residence Rural ≥ 8th-Grade Education	< 8th-Grade Education		Urban ≥ 8th-Grade Education	< 8th-Grade Education	
Not poor	50 (50)	34 (23)	84	63 (40)	28 (31)	91
Poor	50 (50)	116 (77)	166	96 (60)	63 (69)	159
	100	150	250	159	91	250

$$\chi^2 = 18.89 \qquad p < .001 \qquad\qquad \chi^2 = 1.60 \ \text{NS}$$
$$Q = .55$$

TABLE 20.6

Family Size by Education

Family Size	Education ≥ 8th Grade	< 8th Grade	
> 4 children	170 (66)	129 (54)	299
≤ 4 children	89 (34)	112 (46)	201
	259	241	500

$\chi^2 = 7.12$ $p = < .01$ $Q = .25$

likely (50% versus 23%) to have risen above poverty as those who had not finished school. Among urban people, by contrast, education doesn't make a significant difference in wealth status of poor migrant families. What's going on here? To find out, we continue to elaborate the analysis, looking at other variables and how they may be magnifying or suppressing relationships.

As you add variables, of course, (as you make the multivariate analysis more elaborate), the number of tables required goes up, *as does the required sample size*. Adding a third variable, residence, to the analysis of wealth by education, requires two additional tables: residence by wealth and residence by education. Adding family size to the model, we need *three* additional tables.

Tables 20.6, 20.7, and 20.8 show the breakdown for family size by education, wealth by family size, and family size by residence.

In Table 20.6 we see that people with more education tend to have smaller families. In Table 20.7 we see that smaller families are 17% more likely to be above the poverty line. And Table 20.8 shows that rural families tend to be larger than urban families. It appears from these tables that economic status is related to family size more strongly than to education or to residence.

To disentangle things we look at the original relationship between wealth and residence, controlling for family size. This is shown in Table 20.9.

Now things are becoming much clearer. When we control for family size, the effect of residence on economic status remains insignificant for rural people, but it makes a big difference for urban residents. We can elaborate further by looking at the relationship between wealth and education, controlling for family size. As Table 20.10 shows, the influence of education on wealth is insignificant for large families, but is highly significant for small families.

TABLE 20.7
Wealth by Family Size

Wealth	Family Size > 4 Children	≤ 4 Children	
Not poor	84 (28)	91 (45)	175
Poor	215 (72)	110 (55)	325
	299	201	500

$x^2 = 16.56$ $p < .001$ $Q = .36$

To get the full picture, we now produce Table 20.11, which shows the bivariate relationship between wealth status and education, now controlling for *both* family size and residence simultaneously. From Table 20.11, it is obvious why sample size is so crucial. The more cells you have in an elaboration table, the larger the sample you need if you want to ensure that you don't have empty cells.

Sample Size—Again

A good way to plan your sample size requirements is to mock up the analytic tables you intend to produce (without any numbers in them) and see how many control variables you intend to use simultaneously. The total

TABLE 20.8
Family Size by Residence

Family Size	Residence Rural	Urban	
> 4 Children	167 (67)	132 (53)	299
≤ 4 Children	83 (33)	118 (47)	201
	250	250	500

$x^2 = 9.62$ $p < .01$ $Q = .29$

TABLE 20.9

Wealth by Residence, Controlling for Family Size

Wealth	Family Size						
	Rural			Urban			
	> 4 Children	≤ 4 Children		> 4 Children	≤ 4 Children		
Not poor	54 (32)	30 (36)	84	30 (29)	61 (52)	91
Poor	113 (68)	53 (64)	166	102 (71)	57 (48)	159
	167	83	250	132	118	250

$$x^2 = .55 \text{ NS} \qquad x^2 = 23.85 \qquad Q = .57$$
$$p < .001$$

number of cells in a multivariate table depends on the number of control variables and the complexity of the variables. Dichotomous variables such as we're using here (e.g., large family versus small family) create fewer cells than do more complex variables (e.g., large, medium, small families).

Count the number of cells in the largest, most complex table you think you'll create in your analysis and, if you have the resources, make your sample large enough so that there are likely to be at least 20 values in each cell and 100 or more for each major control variable you intend to use. It

TABLE 20.10

Wealth by Education, Controlling for Family Size

Wealth	Family Size						
	> 4 Children			≤ 4 Children			
	≥ 8th-Grade Education	< 8th-Grade Education		≥ 8th-Grade Education	< 8th-Grade Education		
Not poor	54 (32)	30 (23)	84	59 (66)	32 (29)	91
Poor	116 (68)	99 (77)	215	30 (34)	80 (71)	110
	170	129	299	89	112	201

$$x^2 = 2.22 \text{ NS} \qquad x^2 = 26.98 \qquad p < .001$$
$$Q = .66$$

TABLE 20.11
Wealth by Education, Controlling for Family Size and Residence

Wealth	Rural Residence					Urban Residence				
	Family Size					Family Size				
	> 4 Children		≤ 4 Children			> 4 Children		≤ 4 Children		
	> 8th-Grade Education	< 8th-Grade Education	> 8th-Grade Education	< 8th-Grade Education		> 8th-Grade Education	< 8th-Grade Education	> 8th-Grade Education	< 8th-Grade Education	
Not poor	34 (49)	20 (21)	16 (53)	14 (36)	84	20 (20)	10 (31)	43 (73)	18 (31)	91
Poor	36 (51)	77 (79)	14 (47)	39 (64)	166	80 (80)	22 (69)	16 (27)	41 (69)	159
	70	97	30	53	250	100	32	59	59	250

$x^2 = 20.82$ $p < .01$ $x^2 = 46.78$ $p < .01$

480

is often impossible to achieve these numbers in field research. This only means that you'll have to either (a) avoid making your analysis too elaborate or (b) settle for lower significance levels in your test results (.10 instead of .05, or .05 instead of .01, for example).

Reading a Complex Table

Reading across Table 20.11, we see that among urban families with at least an eighth-grade education and four or fewer children, 73% are above the poverty line. Among urban families with at least an eighth-grade education and *more than* four children, only 20% are above the poverty line. Among rural families with at least an eighth-grade education and with four or fewer children, 53% are above the poverty line. Among rural people with at least an eighth-grade education and more than four children, 49% are above the poverty line.

In other words, for rural people, education is the key to rising above poverty. So long as they increase their education, they are about as likely (49% versus 53%) to increase their economic status, whether or not they limit natality. This is not true for urban migrants. Unless they limit their natality *and* increase their education, they are not likely to rise above poverty (20% versus 73%). However, if they *do* limit their family size, *and* increase their education, then urban migrants are 20% more likely (73% versus 53%) than their rural counterparts to rise above poverty.

Taking Stock: What Do We Know So Far?

The lesson from this elaboration is clear. We saw from Table 20.2 that the longer the urban migrants remained in the city, the greater the likelihood that they would rise above poverty. But now we know a lot more. Unless they are prepared to both lower their natality and increase their education, poverty-stricken villagers in our sample are probably better off staying home and not migrating to the city. If they remain in their villages and just increase their education, they stand about a 50-50 chance of rising above poverty. But if they migrate to the city and only increase their education level, then the chances are very great (80%) that they will remain poor.

It is true that people in the urban areas get more education. That much is clear from Table 20.4. But if the urban migrants in our sample (all of whom started out as poor villagers) fail to limit natality, they lose the

TABLE 20.12

Family Size by Education, Controlling for Residence

Family Size	Rural Residence			Urban Residence		
	≥ 8th-Grade Education	< 8th-Grade Education		≥ 8th-Grade Education	< 8th-Grade Education	
> 4 children	70 (70)	97 (65)	167	100 (63)	32 (35)	132
≤ 4 children	30 (30)	53 (35)	83	59 (37)	59 (65)	118
	100	150	250	159	91	250

$$x^2 = .55 \text{ NS} \qquad\qquad x^2 = 16.76 \quad p < .001$$
$$Q = .52$$

advantage that education would otherwise bring them. Rural people keep this advantage, irrespective of family size.

Explaining this finding, of course, is up to you. That's what theory is all about. A causal connection between variables requires a *mechanism* that explains how things work (see Chapter 2 if you need to go over the issue of covariation and causality). In this instance, we might conjecture that rural people have lower overall expenses, especially if they own their own land and homes. They usually have extended families that cut down the cost of child care and that provide no-interest loans during emergencies. They grow much of their own food, and having more children may help them farm more land and cut down on expenses.

Urban people get more education, and this gets them better paying jobs. But if they have many mouths to feed, and if they have to pay rent, and if they lack the financial support of kin close by, then these factors may vitiate any advantage their education might otherwise bring.

Taking the Elaboration Another Step

We can look for clues that support or challenge our theory by elaborating the model still further, this time using family size as the dependent variable. Table 20.12 shows the result of cross-tabulating family size by education, controlling for residence.

Chi-square for the left half of this table is insignificant, but for the right half it is highly significant. Rural informants with less than an eighth-grade education are almost twice as likely as urban informants with less than an eighth-grade education to have more than four children (65% versus 35%). Among rural informants, in fact, level of education has little or no effect on family size (70% of those with higher education have large families versus 65% of those with lower education).

Among urban informants, however, the effect of education on family size is dramatic. Highly educated urban informants are much more likely than less educated informants to have *large* families, from these data. This throws new light on the entire subject, and begs to be explained. We know that higher education without small families does not produce an increase in economic status for these poor migrants. We know, too, that most people, whether urban or rural, keep having large families, although large families are less prevalent among urbanites than among rural residents (132 out of 250 versus 167 out of 250).

To understand this case still further, consider Table 20.13, which cross-tabulates family size by wealth, controlling for both education and residence.

This table is illuminating. It shows that neither wealth nor education influences family size among rural informants. For urban residents, however, the story is quite different. As expected, those urban informants who have both increased their education and increased their wealth have small families.

Go through Table 20.13 carefully and make the appropriate comparisons across the rows and between the two halves. Compare also the results of this table with those of Table 20.11, in which wealth status was the dependent variable.

From these tables, we can now hazard a good guess about how these variables interact. A conceptual model of the process we've been looking at is shown in Figure 20.1. Most people in our sample are poor. Sixty-six percent of rural informants (166/250) and 64% of urban informants (159/250) are below the poverty line by our measurements. Among rural informants, education provides an edge in the struggle against poverty, irrespective of family size, but for urban migrants, education only provides an edge in the context of lowered family size.

Among those who remain in the villages, then, education may lead either to accumulation of wealth through better job opportunities, or it may have no effect. The chances are better that it leads to more favorable economic circumstances. Once this occurs, it leads to control of fertility. Among urban informants, education leads either to control of natality or not. If not, then education has practically no effect on the economic status of poor migrants. If it leads to lowered natality, then it may lead, over time, to a favorable change in economic status.

TABLE 20.13
Family Size by Wealth, Controlling for Education and Residence

Family Size	Rural Residence					Urban Residence				
	≥8th-Grade Education		<8th-Grade Education			≥8th-Grade Education		<8th-Grade Education		
	Poor	Not Poor	Poor	Not Poor		Poor	Not Poor	Poor	Not Poor	
>4 children	34	36	20	77	167	20	80	10	22	132
	(68)	(72)	(59)	(66)		(32)	(83)	(56)	(35)	
≤4 children	16	14	14	39	83	43	16	18	41	118
	(32)	(28)	(41)	(34)		(68)	(17)	(44)	(65)	
	50	50	34	116	250	63	96	28	63	250

$\chi^2 = 1.63$ NS $\chi^2 = 58.46$ $p < .001$

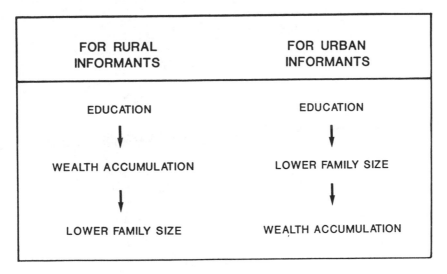

Figure 20.1. Model of how wealth, education, and family size interact in urban and rural environments for informants in Tables 20.11 and 20.13.

We can check this model by going back to our data on wealth status by number of years in the city to see if those migrants who are economically successful over time have both increased their education *and* lowered their natality. Plausible assumptions about time ordering of variables are crucial in building causal models. Knowing, for example, that wealthy villagers never move to the city, rules out some alternative explanations for the data presented here.

You get the picture. The elaboration method can produce subtle results, but it is quite straightforward to use and depends only on your imagination, on simple arithmetic (percentages), and on basic bivariate statistics. Using this method, you can actually get started on data analysis while you're still in the field.

A Recent Real Example

Keith and Wickrama (1990) studied how 136 female household heads in two rural Sri Lankan villages felt about the health care services in their district. Table 20.14 shows the results.

Try going over the data in Table 20.14. See if you can ferret out the key differences in reported use of the various medical facilities by women in

TABLE 20.14

An Elaboration Table Showing the Percentages of Reported Use and Opinion of Health Services Among Rural Sri Lankan Female Household Heads, by Age of Household Head

Use and opinion	Karametiya (N = 67)		Horawinna (N = 69)	
	Under 65 yr. (N = 44)	65 yr. or over (N = 23)	Under 65 yr. (N = 50)	65 yr. or over (N = 19)
Use of services				
Rarely				
Dispensary	38.6	60.9	24.0	57.9
Hospital	52.3	78.3	42.0	52.6
Ayuverda	45.5	60.9	20.0	10.5
Frequently or more often				
Dispensary	61.4	39.1	76.0	42.1
Hospital	47.7	21.7	48.0	47.4
Ayuverda	54.6	39.1	80.0	89.5
Opinion of services				
Poor				
Dispensary	29.5	39.1	48.0	47.4
Hospital	31.8	43.5	78.0	31.6
Ayuverda	45.5	56.5	6.0	—
Satisfactory or good				
Dispensary	71.5	60.9	52.0	52.6
Hospital	68.2	56.5	22.0	68.4
Ayuverda	54.6	43.5	94.0	100.0

SOURCE: From P. M. Keith and K. A. S. Wickrama, "Use and evaluation of health services by women in a developing country: Is age important?" *The Gerontologist, 30*, p. 267. Copyright © 1990 by The Gerontological Society of America. Used with permission.

the two villages, Karametiya and Horawinna. Which group uses the hospital more? Which group relies more on the *ayuverda* (traditional healer)?

Some General Advice on Data Analysis

How you actually conduct an elaboration analysis is up to you. There is no formula for deciding which variables to test. My advice is to follow every hunch you get. Other researchers insist that you have a good theoretical reason for including variables in your design and that you have a theory-driven reason to test for relationships among variables. They point out that anyone can make up an explanation for any relationship or lack of relationship after seeing a table of data or a correlation coefficient.

I consider this approach too restrictive, for three reasons.

1. First, I think that data analysis should be lots of fun, and it can't be unless it's based on following hunches. Most relationships are easy to explain, and peculiar relationships beg for theories to explain them. You just have to be very careful not to conjure up support for every significant relation, merely because it happens to turn up. There is a delicate balance between being clever enough to explain an unexpected finding and just plain reaching too far. As usual, there is no substitute for thinking hard about your data.

2. Second, it is really up to you during research design to be as clever as you can in thinking up variables to test. Just because you have no theory is no reason to avoid including variables in your design that you think might come in handy later on. Of course, you can overdo it. There is nothing more tedious than an interview that drones on for hours without any obvious point other than that the researcher is gathering data on as many variables as possible.

3. Third, the source of ideas has no necessary affect on their usefulness. You can get ideas from a prior theory or from browsing through data tables. The important thing is whether you can test your ideas and create plausible explanations for your findings. If others disagree with your explanations, then it is up to them to demonstrate that you are wrong, either by reanalyzing your data or by producing new data. Stumbling onto a significant relationship between some variables does nothing to invalidate the relationship.

So, when you design your research try to think about the kinds of variables that might be useful in testing your hunches. Use the principles in Chapter 5 and consider internal state variables (attitudes, values, beliefs); external state variables (age, height, gender, race, health status, occupation, wealth status, etc.); physical and cultural environmental variables (e.g., rainfall, socioeconomic class of a neighborhood); and time or space variables (Have attitudes changed over time? Do the people in one village behave differently from those in another otherwise similar community?).

In applied research, important variables are the ones that let you "target" a policy—that is, focus intervention efforts on subpopulations of interest (the rural elderly, victims of violent crime, overachieving third graders, etc.)—or that are more amenable to policy manipulation (knowledge is far more manipulable than attitudes, for example). No matter what the purposes of your research, or how you design it, the two principal rules of data analysis are:

1. If you have an idea, test it.
2. You can't test it if you don't have data on it.

Other Techniques for Multivariate Analysis

There are many multivariate techniques for finding subtle and complex relations in data. I will not deal with them at length in this book, but I do want to give you an idea of the range of tools available and enough information so you can read and understand research articles in which these techniques are used. I hope that this will arouse your curiosity enough so that you'll study these methods in more advanced classes.

Partial Correlation

Like the elaboration method, partial correlation allows you to control for the effects of a third (or fourth or fifth . . .) variable on a bivariate relationship. Making up cross-tabulated tables (cross-tabs, for short) is an intuitively satisfying way to go about data analysis, especially for a first cut where you're trying to get a "feel" for what's going on. The advantages of partial correlation are that it is a *direct* way to control for effects, and it can be applied even when your sample is very small. (Cross-tabs require larger samples in order to make sure that all the cells are adequately represented. Running chi-square on a table with empty cells will play havoc with your statistics.)

Suppose you have measured three variables for a sample of informants: Variable 1 is their perceived quality of life (PQOL), variable 2 is their score on a test of "locus of control," and variable 3 is their income. Locus of control refers to a well-known scale that measures the extent to which people feel they are in control of their own lives. A low score signals that the informant feels that the so-called locus of control for his or her life is "out there" in the hands of others.

The measurements for PQOL and locus of control show a correlation $r=.41$, which is to say that 17% $(.41^2)$ of the dependent variable (the score on the PQOL test) is accounted for by the independent variable (locus of control). What happens to this correlation when you control for income?

Suppose that PQOL and income have a correlation of .68 and that the correlation between locus of control and income is .31. The formula for partial correlation is

$$r_{12\cdot3} = \frac{r_{12} - (r_{13})(r_{32})}{\sqrt{(1 - r_{13}^2)(1 - r_{32}^2)}}$$

where $r_{12\cdot3}$ = means "the correlation between variable 1 (PQOL) and variable 2 (locus of control), *controlling* for variable 3 (income) is . . ." (Partial correlation can be done on ordinal variables by substituting a statistic like tau for r in the formula above.) Substituting in the formula, $r_{12\cdot3} = .29$. Thus, just 8% $(.29^2)$ of the variance in the mean PQOL is explained by locus of control, after removing the effect of income.

The test of significance for a partial correlation is based on the scores from the t-test table in Appendix D.

$$t = r_{12\cdot3}\sqrt{\frac{N-3}{(1 - r_{12\cdot3}^2)}}$$

You can use Appendix D to find the critical value of t with $N - 3$ degrees of freedom.

A simple correlation is referred to as a *zero-order* correlation. The formula above is for a *first-order* correlation. The formula for a *second-order correlation* (controlling for two variables at the same time) is

$$r_{12\cdot34} = \frac{r_{12\cdot3} - (r_{14\cdot3})(r_{24\cdot3})}{\sqrt{(1 - r_{14\cdot3}^2)(1 - r_{24\cdot3}^2)}}$$

For a thorough review of partial correlation, see Thorndike (1978) and Blalock (1979).

Multiple Regression

In simple regression, we derive an equation that expresses the relationship between the independent and dependent variable. On the left-hand side of the equation, we have the unknown score for y, the dependent variable. On the right-hand side, you'll remember, we have the y-intercept (the score for y if the dependent variable were zero), and a constant that tells by how much to multiply the score on the independent variable for each unit change in that variable. So, a regression equation like

Starting Annual Income = \$16,000 + \$2000 × Years of College

or

Dep. Var. y = Constant + (Another Constant) (Ind. Var. x)

predicts that, on average, people with a high school education will start out earning \$16,000 a year; people with a year of college will earn \$18,000; and so on. A person with a Ph.D and 9 years of university education would be predicted to start at \$34,000.

In multiple regression, we build more complex equations that tell us how much each of *several* independent variables contributes to predicting the score of a single dependent variable. In simple regression, if height and weight are related variables, we want to know "How accurately can we predict a person's weight if we know their height?" A typical question for a multiple regression analysis might be "How well can we predict a person's weight if we know their height, *and* their gender, *and* their age, *and* their ethnic background, *and* their parents' income?" Each of those independent variables contributes something to predicting a person's weight.

Many computer programs used today produce what is called a *stepwise multiple regression*. You specify a dependent variable and a series of independent variables that you suspect play some part in determining the scores of the dependent variable. The program looks for the independent variable that correlates best with the dependent variable. Then it adds in the variables one at a time, accounting for more and more variance, until all the specified variables are analyzed, or until variables fail to enter because incremental explained variance is lower than a preset value, e.g., 1%.

In stepwise multiple regression, the program prints out the correlation coefficient for each independent variable with the dependent variable and also prints out a multiple correlation coefficient, represented by a capital letter R. The square of *that* statistic, R-squared, is the amount of variance accounted for in the scores of the dependent variable, taking into account all the independent variables you specified. The programs will also print out the multiple regression equation. (If you are interested in learning how to derive multiple regression equations yourself, consult Blalock, 1979.)

Here are three examples of how multiple regression is actually used. John Poggie (1979) was interested in whether the beliefs of Puerto Rican fishermen about the causes of success in fishing were related to their actual success in fishing. He measured success by asking six key informants to rank 50 fishermen on this variable. Since his research was exploratory, he had a wide range of independent variables, three of which he guessed were related to fishing success: the fishermen's expressed orientation toward delaying gratification (measured with a standard scale), their boat size, and their years of experience at the trade.

The deferred gratification measure accounted for 15% of the variance in the dependent variable; years of experience accounted for another 10%; and boat size accounted for 8%. Together, these variables accounted for 33% of the variance in the success variable. Poggie's guess about which variables to test was pretty good.

Korsching et al. (1980) used a shotgun or shopping technique in their multivariate study of a group of families that were relocated when the land they lived on in Kentucky became part of a reservoir project. Their multiple regression found seven social and economic factors that accounted for at least some of the variance in relative satisfaction with new and old residences among those relocated. Those factors were: change in social activities (accounting for 18%); education (accounting for 4%); total family income before relocation (another 4%); change of financial situation (3%). Three other variables (satisfaction with resettlement payments, tenure status on the land, and length of residence in the old house) each accounted for 1% or less. All together, the seven independent variables accounted for 31% of the variance in satisfaction with the move.

Mwango (1986) studied small farming households in Malawi. He was interested in what made farmers decide to devote part of their land to growing new cash crops (tobacco and hybrid maize) rather than planting only the traditional crop, called "maize of the ancestors." His units of analysis were individual farms; his dependent variable was the ratio of land planted in tobacco and hybrid maize to the total land under plow.

Mwango's independent variables were (a) the total cultivated land area, in hectares; (b) the number of years a farmer was experienced in using fertilizers; (c) whether the farming household usually brewed maize beer for sale; (d) whether farmers owned any cattle at all; (e) whether farmers had had any training in animal husbandry practices from the local extension agents; (f) whether the family had an improved house (this required an index consisting of items such as a tin roof, cement floor, glass windows, and so on); (g) whether the farmer owned a bicycle; and (h) whether the farmer owned a plow and oxcart. All these independent variables together accounted for 48% of the variance in the dependent variable.

In social science research, multiple regression typically accounts for between 30% and 50% of the variance in any dependent variable, using between three and eight independent variables. In a list of six or eight independent variables accounting for, say, 40% of the variance, you will probably find that the first variable accounts for 10% to 20%. After that, the amount of variance in the dependent variable that is accounted for by any independent variable gets smaller and smaller. It is customary not to include independent variables that account for less than 1% of the variance in a multiple regression table (but there is no law against doing so).

If accounting for just 30% or 40% of the variance in what you're interested in seems puny, consider these two facts:

1. In 1983 the average white male had a life expectancy of 71.4 years in this country, or 26,061 days. The life expectancy for the average black male was 66.5 years, or 24,273 days. The *difference* is 1,788 days.

2. There were approximately 2.5 million births in Mexico in 1986 and around 47,500 infant deaths—that is, about 19 infant deaths per 1,000 live births. Compare these figures to the United States, where there were 3.7 million births and approximately 30,000 infant deaths, or about 8 per 1,000 live births. If the infant mortality rate in Mexico were the same as that in the United States, the number of infant deaths would be 20,000 instead of 47,500. The *difference* would be 27,500 infant deaths.

Suppose you could account for 10% of the *difference* in longevity among white and black males in the United States (179 days) or 10% of the *difference* between the United States and Mexico in infant deaths (2,750 children). Would that be worthwhile? How about 1%? To the extent that knowledge about phenomena leads to more effective control over those phenomena, I'd try to account for every percent I could.

Analysis of Variance

Analysis of variance, or ANOVA, is a statistical technique that applies to a set of averages. It is particularly popular in psychology and education

TABLE 20.15

A Typical Experiment in Which ANOVA Is Used in Educational Research

	Average Score on Pretest	Average Score on Posttest
Classes using new program	X_1	X_2
Classes not using new program	X_3	X_4

where groups of people are administered *tests* on which they get some kind of *score*. Each group, then, has an *average score* and these averages can be compared to see if they are significantly different.

For example, suppose educational researchers want to know whether a new method for teaching reading skills to fifth graders really makes a difference. They might divide the fifth-grade classes in a school district into two groups— one group that uses the new program and one group that does not. Both groups would be tested before the program is adopted and after the program is finished. (You'll recognize this method from Chapter 3 on experimental design.) Then the scores would be compared. Table 20.15 is a schematic of the scores that the researchers would be working with.

X_1, X_2, X_3, and X_4 are average scores. The question is: Are all the differences in these scores significant? Put another way (the null hypothesis), despite differences in the scores, are they really from identical populations? Does it make any real difference in their reading skills if fifth graders are exposed to the new program? There are four comparisons to make: between X_1 and X_2; X_3 and X_4; X_1 and X_3; and X_2 and X_4. Each of these comparisons can be done with a *t*-test, which is an analysis of the variance between two means.

But things can be much more complex. Suppose that each of the four cells in Table 20.15 is composed of several separate scores. That is, suppose that five classes are chosen for the new program and five are chosen not to participate, and that each of the groups of five classes is tested before and after the program. An analysis of the variance between more than two means requires the ANOVA technique.

Camilla Harshbarger (1986) investigated the relationship between the productivity of coffee farmers in one region of Costa Rica and their sources of credit. Her raw results are shown in Table 20.16.

Seven (16%) of the 44 farmers she interviewed did not use credit at all, and produced 21 *fanegas* of coffee per hectare (1 fanega = 1.58 bushels). Farmers who depended on commercial bank loans averaged 18.8 fanegas. Farmers who used one of the two cooperatives as credit sources averaged 26.6 and 17.6 fanegas. An analysis of variance showed that there was no

TABLE 20.16

Coffee Production by Credit Source for Four Costa Rican Farmers

	Beneficio	CSV	Bank	None
Number (%) of borrowers	3 (6.8)	12 (27)	22 (50)	7 (16)
Number of fanegas/ha	26.6	17.6	18.8	21

SOURCE: Harshbarger (1986).

significant difference in productivity among those farmers in Harshbarger's sample, no matter where they obtained credit, or even if they did not use credit.

Carole Jenkins (1981) surveyed 750 children in Belize for protein-calorie malnutrition (PCM). Her results are shown in Table 20.17.

An analysis of variance showed that there was a very strong relationship between ethnic group and the likelihood of suffering from childhood PCM.

Sokolovsky et al. (1978) compared the average number of "first-order relations" and the average number of "multiplex relations" among three groups of psychiatric patients who were released to live in a hotel in midtown New York City. (First-order relations are primary relations with others; multiplex relations contain more than one kind of content, such as relations based on visiting *and* borrowing money from, for example.)

One group of patients had a history of schizophrenia with residual symptoms; a second group had a history of schizophrenia without residual symptoms; and the third group had no psychotic history. An analysis of variance showed clearly that the average network size (both first-order and multiplex networks) was different among the three groups. From these data (and from field observation and in-depth interviews) Sokolovsky was able to draw strong conclusions about the ability of members of the three groups to cope with deinstitutionalization.

TABLE 20.17

PCM in Four Ethnic Groups in Belize

	Protein-Calorie Malnutrition		
	Yes	No	Total
Creole	28	170	198
Mestizo	43	184	227
Black Carib	38	144	182
Maya	47	96	143
Total			750

SOURCE: From Patterns of growth and malnutrition among preschoolers in Belize by C. L. Jenkins, *American Journal of Physical Anthropology, 56,* 175. Copyright © 1981 by Wiley-Liss. Reprinted by permission of Wiley-Liss, a division of John Wiley & Sons, Inc.

Whenever you observe three or more groups (age cohorts, members of different cultures or ethnic groups, people from different communities) and *count* anything (e.g., some behavior over a specific period of time, or the number of particular kinds of contacts they make, or the number of kilograms of fish they catch), then ANOVA is the analytic method of choice. If you are interested in the causes of morbidity, for example, you could collect data on the number of sick days among people in various social groups over a given period of time. Other dependent variables in which anthropologists are interested, and which are amenable to ANOVA, are things like blood pressure, number of minutes per day spent in various activities, number of grams of nutrients consumed per day, and scores on tests of knowledge about various cultural domains (plants, animals, diseases), to name just a few.

When there is one dependent variable (such as a test score) and one independent variable (a single intervention like the reading program), then no matter how many groups or tests are involved, a *one-way* analysis of variance is needed. If more than one independent variable is involved (say, several competing new housing programs, and several socioeconomic backgrounds), and there is a single dependent variable (a reading test score), then multiple-way ANOVA, or MANOVA, is called for. When two or more dependent variables are correlated with one another, then *analysis of covariance* (ANCOVA) techniques are used.

Multiple-way ANOVA allows you to determine if there are interaction effects among independent variables. Earlier in this chapter, we saw that independent nominal and ordinal variables (like level of education, family size, and residence) all *individually* affect wealth status, but that those independent variables also interacted with one another. The problem was that we could not tell *how much* they interacted. With interval-level scores on independent variables, we can use ANOVA to actually measure the interaction effects among variables—to determine if a variable has different effects under different conditions.

Like all popular multivariate techniques, ANOVA is available in the packaged computer programs that you are likely to deal with. Many research questions can be addressed using ANOVA in the field, especially these days with notebook computers and inexpensive statistical programs available. Consult Elifson et al. (1990) or Runyon and Haber (1991) for instructions on the fundamentals of analysis of variance.

Factor Analysis

Factor analysis is a technique for information packaging and data reduction. It has been around for about 60 years in the social sciences, although b.c. (before computers) it required truly Herculean efforts to use this technique. Factor analysis is based on complex statistics, but the principle behind the technique is simple and compelling. (For an introduction to factor analysis, see Rummel, 1970.)

In multiple regression, there is one dependent variable and several independent, or predictor variables. In factor analysis, all the variables in a matrix are considered together for their interdependence. The original, observed variables are thought of as reflections of (dependent on, in some way) some underlying dimensions (the so-called factors). The factors are thought to be reflections of the observed variables. The idea is to package and summarize the information contained in many variables (often dozens, or even hundreds) with a few underlying dimensions that covary with clumps of the variables in the original data. This reduces the original long list of variables to a shorter list that is easier to manipulate (e.g., to use in a regression analysis) and to interpret.

Since factors are extracted from a matrix of correlations among the variables in a study, they are really just new variables themselves. Factors consist of several "old" variables—variables in a correlation matrix that are closely related to one another. Some correlation matrices are very dispersed—they have very few significant correlations—while others are very dense. Dispersed matrices tend to have many factors, whereas dense matrices (where many variables are highly correlated with one another) tend to produce only a few factors.

The notion of variance is very important here. Factors account for chunks of variance—the amount of dispersion or correlation in a correlation matrix. Factors are extracted from a correlation matrix in the order of the amount of variance that they explain in the matrix. Some factors explain a lot of variance, while others may be very weak and are discarded by researchers as not being useful. In a dense matrix, then, only a few factors may be needed to account for a lot of variance; in a dispersed matrix, many factors may be needed.

The most common statistical solution for finding the underlying factors in a correlation matrix is called the *orthogonal solution*. In orthogonal factor analyses, factors are found that have as little correlation with each other as possible. Other solutions, which result in intercorrelated factors, are also possible (the various solutions are options that you can select in all the major statistical packages, like SAS and SPSS). Some researchers say that these solutions, although messier than orthogonal solutions, are more like real life.

So-called factor loadings are the correlations between the new factors and the old variables that are replaced by factors. All the old variables *load* on each new factor. The idea is to establish some cutoff (say, a correlation of 0.4) below which you would not feel comfortable accepting that an old variable "loaded onto" a factor. Then you simply go through the list of old variables and pick out those that load sufficiently high on each new factor. Finally, you look at the list of variables that constitute each factor and decide what the factor *means*.

As you saw in Chapter 13, factor analysis is widely used in building reliable, compact scales for measuring variables in the field. Typically, anthropologists find either: (a) that there are no existing, well-tested scales they can use in the field for the things in which they are interested, or (b) that if scales do exist, the instruments are not transportable to another culture.

Suppose, for example, that you are interested in attitudes about gender role changes among women. From ethnographic work you suspect that the underlying forces of role changes have to do with premarital sexuality, working outside the home, and development of an independent social and economic life among women. You make up 50 attitudinal items in the local language and collect data on those items from a sample of informants.

Factor analysis will help you decide whether the 50 items you made up really test for the underlying forces you think are at work. If they do, then you could use a few benchmark items (that load high on the factors), and this would save you (and others) from having to ask all informants about all 50 items you made up. You would still get the information you need—or much of it, anyway. The amount would depend on how much variance in the correlation matrix each of your factors accounted for. An example should make all this a lot clearer.

Marchione (1980) used factor analysis in his study of the nutritional status of 1-year-olds in Jamaica. He measured the height and weight of 132 children and compared these measurements with international standards to determine the nutritional status of the children in his sample. He also collected data on 31 measures relating to households. These included household size, income, and food expenditures; diet variety; presence of mother or father; mother's age; distance to piped water; and so on.

Nineteen of the 31 measures had some statistically significant relation with the height and weight measurements. Marchione reported that: "Although every possible bivariate . . . association was examined, a problem of interpretation remains—*the problem of interrelationships among the household measures themselves.* Examination of the matrix of interrelationships . . . displays a bewildering array of intercorrelations" (ibid.:242, italics added).

Marchione found that some household measures had no direct relationship with either height or weight, but were significantly correlated with other household measures that *were*. For example, employment history was related to both income and food expenditure. The latter two variables are significantly correlated with weight status of 1-year-old children, but the first variable is not.

Marchione wanted a way to use all his data on household measures, without risking throwing away potentially useful information. He factor analyzed the matrix of 132 households and the variables he had studied. Twelve factors emerged, of which 8 seemed to have some intuitive appeal. The first factor was composed of five variables, as follows:

Household Measure	Factor Loading
Father present	.87
Father support	.72
Mother present	.50
Mother's employment	−.30
Mother's age	.25

Marchione's task was to determine what this factor (this package of variables) represented. He decided that the variables in this factor were all related to family stability and integrity, and he labeled the factor "family cohesion." (The negative loading for mother's employment means that when fathers support the family, then mothers are less likely to.)

Marchione labeled the seven other factors he extracted "guardian maturity," "clinic case demand," "household diet," "age transition," "agricultural subsistence," "dependency stress," and "monetary wealth." Then he treated each factor as if it were a new independent variable and he looked at how they correlated with the two dependent variables in his study— weight status and height (or length) status of the 132 1-year-olds. Table 20.18 shows the results.

Overall, the eight factors accounted for about a quarter of the variation in weight or length status among the 1-year-olds studied. (The total variance is found by squaring the separate correlations and adding them together. The multiple correlation, R, is the square root of that result).

Factor analysis has become popular in anthropological research because it leaves a lot of room for interpretation by researchers (or informants) of the results. For example, Marchione noticed that there was a negative relationship between nutritional status of 1-year-olds and the degree to which households live off of subsistence agriculture. He explained this by the fact that plots are too small for household size.

Also, in Marchione's data, child growth was retarded as dependency stress increased. Dependency stress was what Marchione labeled a pack-

TABLE 20.18

Correlation Between Factors and Dependent Variables in Marchione's
Study of 1-Year-Olds in Jamaica

Factor	Nutritional Status	
	Weight Status N = 132	Length Status N = 114
1	−.25*	−.28*
2	−.22*	−.35*
3	.23*	.15
4	.22*	.11
5	−.08	−.14
6	−.03	−.14
7	.12	.07
8	.09	.03
Multiple R	.49	.53
Variance accounted for	24%	28%

SOURCE: Marchione (1980: 153).
*Correlation significant at the .05 level.

age of variables having to do with competition for resources among preschool children, and between them and older children in a household. Marchione also noticed that a child's weight-for-age improved as family cohesion improved. In each case, Marchione was led by the factor analysis to some insights about the phenomenon he was studying.

In some cases, a *lack* of correlation between factors and dependent variables may require an explanation and lead to insights. For example, Marchione found that neither the household diet factor nor the household wealth factor were significantly related to child growth. He interpreted this as a methodological problem. Diet was measured by a single 24-hour recall, which doesn't reflect any diversity and which is also highly unreliable and invalid. Wealth was measured by asking people about their income "last week." These unreliable self-reported data were too crude, according to Marchione, to provide a meaningful correlation with much of anything.

Multidimensional Scaling Analysis (MDS)

MDS is another multivariate data reduction technique. Like factor analysis, it is used to tease out underlying relationships among a set of observations. Also like factor analysis, MDS requires a matrix of measures of associations—

e.g., a correlation matrix based on things like r, tau, gamma, etc. But unlike factor analysis, MDS can handle *metric* and *nonmetric data.*

When you measure something like how strongly people feel about something, the numbers you assign to their feelings don't have the same meaning as, say, numbers that express distances in miles or kilograms of game meat killed per month. The latter numbers are metric because they are grounded in well-understood units of measurement. Most attitude and cognition data are nonmetric. MDS is particularly useful for anthropologists, since a lot of the measurements we make are nonmetric. Also, MDS produces a graphic display of the relationship among a set of items in a cultural domain and this, too, makes it really suited to the kinds of things anthropologists study. (See Romney et al., 1972, for an excellent introduction to the use of MDS in anthropology.)

How MDS Works

Suppose you measure three variables, A, B, and C, using Pearson's r. The association matrix for these three variables is in the *inside box* of Table 20.19.

TABLE 20.19

Matrix of Association among Four Variables

	A	B	C	D
A	x	.50	.80	.30
B		x	.40	.65
C			x	.35
				x

Clearly, variables A and C are more closely related to one another than are A and B, or B and C. You can represent this with a triangle, as in Figure 20.2(a).

In other words, we can place points A, B, and C on a plane in some position relative to each other. The distance between A and B is longer than that between A and C (reflecting the difference between .5 and .8); and the distance between B and C is longer than that between A and C (reflecting the difference between .4 and .8). The numbers in this graph are *similarities*: The lower the correlation, the longer the distance; the higher the correlation, the shorter the distance.

With just three variables, it is easy to plot these distances in proper proportion to one another. For example, the distance between B and C is

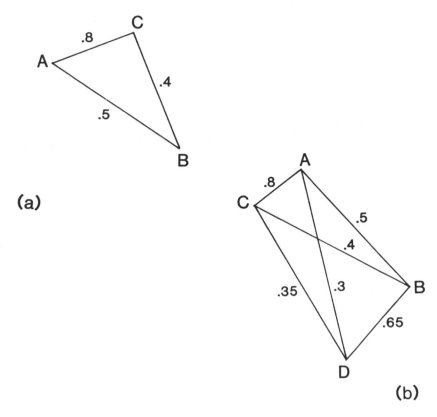

Figure 20.2. Two-dimensional plot of the relationship among three variables (a) and among four variables (b).

twice that of A and C in Figure 20.2(a). Figure 20.2(a) contains *precisely* the same information as the inside box of Table 20.19—but in graphic form.

With four variables, things get considerably more complicated. With four variables there are *six* relations to cope with. These relations are shown in the large box of Table 20.19. Only one two-dimensional graph (apart from rotations and enlargements) can represent the relative distances among the six relations in Table 20.19. The graph is shown in Figure 20.2(b).

Figure 20.2(b) is a two-dimensional graph of six relations in *almost* proper proportions. It is often impossible to achieve perfect proportionality in a graph of six relations if we have only two dimensions to work with. One way out of this is to depict the six relations in Table 20.19 in three dimensions, instead of only two. The extra dimension would give us plenty of room to move around, and we could better adjust the proportionality of the distances between the various pairs of variables.

In principle, you can perfectly represent the relative relations among N variables in $N -1$ dimensions, so that any graph of six variables can be perfectly represented in five dimensions. But even a three-dimensional graph is sometimes hard to read. What would you do with a five-dimensional graph?

Most researchers specify a two-dimensional solution when they run an MDS computer analysis, and hope for the best. MDS programs produce a statistic that measures the *stress* in the graph produced by the program. This is a measure of how far off the graph is from one that is perfectly proportional. The lower the stress, the better the solution. This means that a cluster of variables in an MDS graph with low stress is likely to reflect some reality about the cognitive world of the people being studied.

A Physical World Example

An example will make this clearer. Table 20.20 shows the actual distance in miles between all pairs of nine cities in the United States (this example is from Borgatti, 1992b).

TABLE 20.20

Distances Between Nine U.S. Cities, in Miles

	Boston	NY	DC	Miami	Chicago	Seattle	SF	LA	Denver
Boston	0								
NY	206	0							
DC	429	233	0						
Miami	1504	1308	1075	0					
Chicago	963	802	671	1329	0				
Seattle	2976	2815	2684	3273	2013	0			
SF	3095	2934	2799	3053	2142	808	0		
LA	2979	2786	2631	2687	2054	1131	379	0	
Denver	1949	1771	1616	2037	996	1037	1235	1059	0

SOURCE: Borgatti (1992a:24).

Note two things about the numbers in this table. First, the numbers are *dissimilarities*. Bigger numbers mean that things are farther apart—less like each other. Smaller numbers mean that things are more similar. Similarity and dissimilarity matrices are known collectively as *proximity* matrices because they tell you how close or far apart things are. Second, the numbers are reasonably accurate measures of a physical reality—distance between points on a map—so they are metric data.

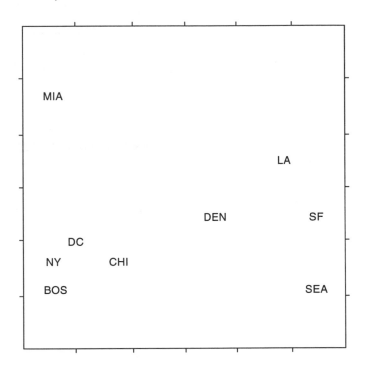

Figure 20.3. Two-dimensional MDS solution for the numbers in Table 20.20.

In principle, there should be a two-dimensional solution with low stress that fits the numbers in this table. I used ANTHROPAC (Borgatti, 1992a) to run MDS on these data, and the solution is shown in Figure 20.3.

Figure 20.3 looks suspiciously like a map of the United States. All nine cities are placed in proper juxtaposition to one another, but the map looks sort of upside-down and backward. If we could only flip the map over from left to right and from bottom to top. . . . Multidimensional scaling programs are notoriously unconcerned with details like this. So long as they get the juxtaposition right, they're finished. Figure 20.3 shows that the program got it right. You can rotate any MDS graph through 360° and it will still be the same graph.

A Cognitive World Example

Here's an example using nonmetric data. Susan Weller (1983) studied perceptions of illness among rural and urban Guatemalan women. She asked 20 women to list as many illnesses as they could think of. Then she took the 27 most frequently named illness, put each named illness on a card, and asked

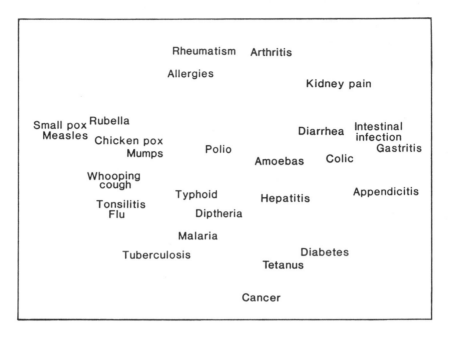

Figure 20.4. MDS representation of 27 illnesses for urban Guatemalan women.

SOURCE: From "New data on intracultural variability" by S. C. Weller, 1983, *Human Organization, 42*, p. 250, Copyright 1983. Reprinted with permission of the Society for Applied Anthropology.

24 other women to sort the cards into piles, according to similarity. The women were allowed to use any criteria they wished for making the piles.

Weller created a correlation matrix from the similarity data. That is, she produced a 27×27 illness-by-illness correlation matrix for the illnesses. The more any pair of illnesses had been placed in the same piles by the informants, the more similar the illnesses.

Then Weller did a multidimensional scaling analysis to represent how her informants collectively perceived the 27 illnesses. Weller said that "the two-dimensional solution was considered adequate because addition of a third dimension only decreased the stress from .142 to .081" (ibid.:249). There are no rules for deciding what "low" or "high" stress is in MDS. As with many things in research, it's a matter of judgment.

Figure 20.4 shows the graph solution that Weller found for her urban sample. As you can see, the MDS program converts similarities (correlations) into graphic distances. The illness terms that were judged to be similar, then, are closer together in Figure 20.4, and the terms judged to be dissimilar by informants are farther apart.

Try naming the clusters in Figure 20.4. There is a clump of illnesses on the right that might be called "gastrointestinal disorders." On the left there is a clump of "childhood disorders." Those, at least, are the "labels" that struck Weller as appropriate. I agree with her intuition about this. What do *you* think?

Remember: All I've done is *label* the group of illnesses on the right in Figure 20.4. The fact that I can come up with a label says absolutely nothing about whether I understand what is going on. It is possible to label anything, once you're confronted with the task. This means that you must be especially careful in the use of factor analysis, MDS, and other dredging techniques that present you with something to explain.

On the other hand, the mere fact that I might make a mistake in my interpretation of the results doesn't stop me from using these techniques. Use every technique you can think of in data analysis, and let your experience guide your interpretation. Interpretation of results is where data analysis in all science ultimately becomes a humanistic activity.

Cluster Analysis

Like factor analysis and MDS, cluster analysis is a descriptive tool for exploring relations among items in a matrix—for finding what goes with what. You start with a similarity matrix, like a matrix of Pearson correlation coefficients. If you factor the matrix, you find underlying variables that may encompass the variables in the original data. If you scale the matrix (MDS), you get a map that shows you graphically the relations among the items. Clustering tells you which items go together and in what order. Thus, in the MDS example from Weller (1983) above, a cluster analysis would let us check the guess about that chunk of illnesses labeled "gastrointestinal disorders."

I'm going to explain cluster analysis in some detail. It's a very important descriptive tool, but as we go through the next few paragraphs, keep in mind two things: First, clustering is just a technique for finding the similarity chunks. It doesn't label those chunks. That part is a Rorschach test, and *you* get to do it—just as you would name the factors in factor analysis or the clumps and dimensions in an MDS graph. Second, as with so many methods, different treatments of your data produce different outcomes. The next few pages will make it very clear just how much *you and only you* are responsible for every choice you make in data analysis.

How Cluster Analysis Works

Consider the following example from De Ghett (1978:121):

1   3   7   9   14   20   21   25

The distance between 1 and 3 is 2. The distance between 21 and 25 is 4. So, in a numerical sense, 1 and 3 are twice as similar to one another as 21 and 25 are to one another. Table 20.21 shows the dissimilarity matrix for these numbers.

TABLE 20.21
Dissimilarity Matrix for Clustering

	1	3	7	9	14	20	21	25
1	0							
3	2	0						
7	6	4	0					
9	8	6	2	0				
14	13	11	7	5	0			
20	19	17	13	11	6	0		
21	20	18	14	12	7	1	0	
25	24	22	18	16	11	5	4	0

SOURCE: From "Hierarchical cluster analysis" by V. J. De Ghett, in *Quantitative Ethology* (P. W. Colgan, Ed.), p. 123. Copyright © 1978. Reprinted by permission of John Wiley & Sons, Inc.

There are several ways to find clusters in this matrix. Two of them are called *single-link* or *closest-neighbor* analysis and *complete-link* or *farthest-neighbor* analysis (there are others, but I won't go into them here). In single-link clustering, we use only the numbers adjacent to the diagonal: 2, 4, 2, 5, 6, 1, 4. The two clustering solutions (again, done with ANTHROPAC) are shown in Figure 20.5.

In the single-link solution, the two closest neighbors are 20 and 21. They are exactly one unit of distance apart, and there is a 1 in the diagonal of the original matrix where 20 and 21 come together. In Figure 20.5(a), 20 and 21 are shown joined at level 1. The numbers 1, 3 and the numbers 7, 9 are the next closest neighbors. They are both two units apart. Figure 20.5(a) shows them joined at level 2.

Once a pair is joined, it is considered a unit. The pairs 1, 3 and 7, 9 are joined together at level 4 because they are four units apart (the nearest neighbor to the pair 1, 3 is 7, which is four units from 3). The pair 21, 25 are also four units apart. However, 20, 21 are already joined, so 25 joins this pair at level 4. The connections are built up to form a tree.

Figure 20.5(b) shows the complete-link (or farthest neighbor) clustering solution for the data in Table 20.21. In complete-link clustering, all the numbers in Table 20.21 are used. Once again, the pair 20, 21 is joined at level 1 because the pair is just one unit apart. The pairs 1, 3 and 7, 9 join at level 2.

(a) Single-Link Clustering

```
                    1   2   2   2
            1   3   7   9   4   0   1   5
Level   - - - -       - - - - - - - -
    1   .   .   .   .   .   XXX   .
    2   XXX  XXX   .   XXX   .
    4   XXXXXXX   .   XXXXX
    5   XXXXXXXXX  XXXXX
    6   XXXXXXXXXXXXXXX
```

(b) Complete-Link Clustering

```
                    1   2   2   2
            1   3   7   9   4   0   1   5
Level   - - - -       - - - - - - - -
    1   .   .   .   .   .   XXX   .
    2   XXX  XXX   .   XXX   .
    5   XXX  XXX   .   XXXXX
    7   XXX  XXXXX  XXXXX
   13   XXXXXXXXX  XXXXX
   24   XXXXXXXXXXXXXXX
```

Figure 20.5. Cluster analysis of data in Table 20.21.

At this point, the complete-link and single-link solutions are identical. At the next level, though, things change. The neighbors of 20, 21 are 14 and 25. The farthest neighbor from 14 to 20, 21 is 21. The distance is seven units. The farthest neighbor from 25 to 20, 21 is 20. The distance is five units. Since five is less than seven, 25 joins 20, 21 at level 5. But the two pairs 1, 3 and 7, 9 are not joined at this level.

The only number not yet joined to some other number is 14. It is compared to its farthest neighbors in the adjacent clusters: 14 is 11 units away from 25 (which is now part of the 20, 21, 25 cluster) and it is 7 units away from the 7, 9 cluster. So, at level 7, 14 is joined to 7, 9. The same game is played out with all the clusters to form the tree in Figure 20.5(b).

Clusters of Cities

The complete-link method tends to produce more clusters than the single-link method. The method you choose determines the results you get. Figure 20.6 shows what happens when we use the single-link and complete-link clustering methods on the data in Table 20.20.

To me, the complete-link method seems better with these data. Denver "belongs" with San Francisco and Los Angeles more than it belongs with

(a) Complete-Link

```
        M  B           C        S  D
        I  O  N  D  H  S  L  E  E
        A  S  Y  C  I  F  A  A  N
  Level 4  1  2  3  5  7  8  6  9
  ----    -  -  -  -  -  -  -  -  -
   206  .  XXX  .     .     .  .  .  .
   379  .  XXX  .     .  .  XXX  .
   429  .  XXXXX  .     .  XXX  .
   963  .  XXXXXXX  .  XXX  .
  1131  .  XXXXXXX  XXXXX  .
  1307  .  XXXXXXX  XXXXXXX
  1504  XXXXXXXXX  XXXXXXX
  3273  XXXXXXXXXXXXXXXXX
```

(b) Single-Link

```
        M  S           B           C  D
        I  E  S  L  O  N  D  H  E
        A  A  F  A  S  Y  C  I  N
  Level 4  6  7  8  1  2  3  5  9
  ----    -  -  -  -  -  -  -  -  -
   206  .     .     .     .  XXX  .     .  .
   233  .     .     .     .  XXXXX  .  .
   379  .     .  XXX  XXXXX  .  .
   671  .     .  XXX  XXXXXXX  .
   808  .  XXXXX  XXXXXXX  .
   996  .  XXXXX  XXXXXXXXX
  1059  .  XXXXXXXXXXXXXXX
  1075  XXXXXXXXXXXXXXXXX
```

Figure 20.6. Complete-link and single-link cluster solutions for the data in Table 20.20.

Boston and New York. But that may be my own bias. Coming from New York, I think of Denver as a western U.S. city. I've heard people from San Francisco talk about "going back east to Denver for the weekend."

Discriminant Function Analysis (DFA)

Discriminant function analysis (DFA) is used to predict membership in categorical (nominal) variables from ordinal and interval variables. For example, we may want to predict which of two (or more) groups an individual belongs to: male or female; those who have been labor migrants versus those who have not; those who are high, middle, or low income; those in favor of something and those who are not; and so on.

DFA is the technique developed for handling this problem. It has been around for a long time (Fisher, 1936) but, like most multivariate techniques, it is not feasible to do DFA on significant amounts of data without a computer.

DFA can be very useful for research in anthropology. Gans and Wood (1985) used this technique for predicting whether Samoan women informants were "traditional" or "modern" with respect to their ideal family size. (If informants stated that they wanted three or fewer children, then Gans and Wood placed those informants in a category they labeled "modern." Informants who said they wanted four or more children were labeled "traditional.") DFA showed that just six of the many variables that Gans and Wood had collected allowed them to predict correctly which category a woman belonged to in 75% of all cases. The variables were such things as age, owning a car, level of education, etc.

In another case, Lambros Comitas and I surveyed two groups of people in Athens, Greece: those who had returned from having spent at least 5 years in West Germany as labor migrants, and those who had never been out of Greece. We were trying to understand how the experience abroad might have affected the attitudes of Greek men and women about traditional gender roles (Bernard & Comitas, 1978). Our sample consisted of 400 persons: 100 male migrants, 100 female migrants, 100 male nonmigrants, and 100 female nonmigrants. Using DFA, we were able to predict with 70% accuracy whether an informant had been a migrant on the basis of just five variables.

There are some things you need to be careful about in using DFA, however. Notice that our sample in the Athens study consisted half of migrants and half of nonmigrants. That was because we used a disproportionate, stratified sampling design to ensure adequate representation of returned migrants in the study. Given our sample, we could have guessed whether one of our informants was a migrant with 50% accuracy, without any information about the informant at all.

Now, only a very small fraction of the population of Athens consists of former long-term labor migrants to West Germany. The chances of stopping an Athenian on the street and grabbing (at random) one of those returned labor migrants was less than 5% in 1977 when we did the study.

Suppose that, armed with the results of the DFA that Comitas and I did, I asked random Athenians five questions, the answers to which allow me to predict 70% of the time whether any respondent had been a long-term labor migrant to West Germany. No matter what the answers were to those questions, I'd be better off predicting that the random Athenian was *not* a returned migrant. I'd be right more than 95% of the time.

Furthermore, why not just ask the random survey respondent straight out: "Are you a returned long-term labor migrant from West Germany?" With such an innocuous question, presumably I'd have gotten a correct answer at least as often as our 70% prediction based on knowing five pieces of information.

The answer is that DFA can be a powerful descriptive device, even if you don't use it as a prediction technique. Gans and Wood, for example, felt that it was inappropriate to ask Samoan women directly whether they (the informants) were "traditional" or "modern." Combined with ethnography, the DFA gave them a good picture of the variables that go into Samoan women's desired family size.

Similarly, Comitas and I were able to describe the attitudinal components of gender role changes by using DFA. If you are careful about how you interpret a discriminant function analysis, then it can be a really important addition to your statistical tool kit.

Path Analysis

Path analysis is a technique for testing conceptual models of multivariate relationships. It was developed by the geneticist Sewall Wright in 1921, and has been popular in sociology since the 1960s (see Duncan, 1966). Path analysis has been used increasingly in anthropology since 1974, when Hadden and De Walt discussed it in an excellent review article. I expect that discriminant analysis and path analysis will become important multivariate techniques in anthropology.

In multiple regression, we know (a) which independent variables help to predict some dependent variable, and (b) how much variance in the dependent variable is explained by each independent variable. But multiple regression is an inductive technique: It does not tell us how *much* a particular independent variable influences the outcome of a dependent variable. And it doesn't tell us which are the antecedent variables, which are the intervening variables, and so on.

Those are things that researchers have to decide. Path analysis is a technique for deductive analysis. It allows us to test a model of how the independent variables in a multiple regression equation may be influencing each other—and how this ultimately leads to the dependent variable outcome.

In one sense, path analysis really doesn't add anything to a multiple regression analysis. It is simply a measure of the "direct influence along each separate path" in a system of multivariate relations, and a way to find "the degree to which variation of a given effect is determined by each particular cause" (Wright, 1921). Path analysis relies on knowing "the correlation among the variables in a system" and on any knowledge that the researcher happens to have about the causes of those correlations (ibid.).

In other words, path analysis is a statistical technique that depends crucially on the researcher's best guess about how a system of variables really works. It's a nice combination of quantitative and qualitative methods. Here's an example.

Thomas (1981) studied leadership in Niwan Witz, a Tojalabal Mayan village. He was interested in understanding what causes some people to emerge as leaders, while others remain followers. From existing theory, Thomas thought that there should be a relationship among leadership, material wealth, and social resources. He measured these complex variables for all the household heads in Niwan Witz (using well-established methods) and tested his hypothesis using Pearson's *r*. Pearson correlations showed that, indeed, in Niwan Witz, leadership is strongly and positively related to material wealth and control of social resources.

Since the initial hypothesis was supported, Thomas used multiple regression to look at the relationship of leadership to *both* types of resources. He found that 56% of the variance in leadership was explained by just three variables in his survey: wealth (accounting for 46%), family size (accounting for 6%), and number of close friends (accounting for 4%). But, since multiple regression does not "specify the causal structure among the independent variables" (ibid.:132), Thomas turned to path analysis.

From prior literature, Thomas conceptualized the relationship among these three variables as shown in Figure 20.7. He felt that leadership was caused by all three of the independent variables he had tested, that family size influenced both wealth and the size of one's friendship network, and that wealth was a factor in determining the number of one's friends.

I won't discuss here the mechanics of determining the value of the path coefficients. A computer program like SPSS or SAS will take care of that for you. If you are interested in learning more about path analysis, consult Heise (1975). Suffice to say here that the *path coefficients* in Figure 20.7 are standardized values: They show the influence of the independent variables on the dependent variables in terms of standard deviations. The path coefficients in Figure 20.7, then, show that "a one standard deviation increase in wealth produces a .662 standard deviation increase in leadership; a one standard deviation increase in family size results in a .468 standard deviation increase in leadership; and so on" (Thomas, 1981:133).

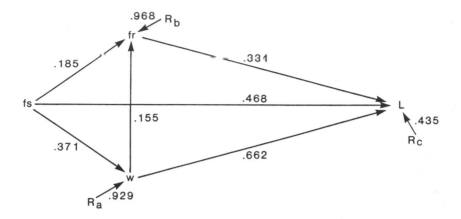

Figure 20.7. Path analysis of effects of wealth, friendship, and family size on leadership in Niwan Witz.

SOURCE: Thomas (1981); reproduced by permission of the American Anthropological Association from *American Ethnologist*, 8:1 (1981). Not for further reproduction.

Four things are clear from Figure 20.7. (a) Among the variables tested, wealth is the most important cause of leadership in individuals. (b) Family size has a moderate causal influence on wealth (making wealth a dependent, as well as an independent variable in this system). (c) The size of a person's friendship network is only weakly related to either family size or wealth. (d) The combined direct and indirect effects of family size, wealth, and friendship network on leadership account for 56% (1.435) of the variance in leadership scores for the household heads of Niwan Witz. Thomas concludes from this descriptive analysis that if one wants to become a leader in the Mayan village of Niwan Witz one needs wealth, and the best way to get that is to start by having a large family.

Path analysis is a tool for testing a particular theory about the relationships among a system of variables. Path analysis does *not* produce the theory; that's *your* job. In the case of Niwan Witz, for example, Thomas specified that he wanted his path analysis to test a particular model in which wealth causes leadership. The results were strong, leading Thomas to reject the null hypothesis that there really is no causal relation between wealth and leadership. Thomas noted, however, that despite the strength of the results, an alternative theory is plausible. It might be that leadership in individuals (wherever they get it from) causes them to get wealthy rather than the other way around. In fact, path analysis is often used to test which of several plausible theories is most powerful.

Conclusion

Once you have mastered the logic of multivariate analysis, you should seek out courses that take you more deeply into the use of these powerful tools. Most departments of sociology, psychology, education, and public health offer courses in multivariate analysis to their students. They often permit students from other disciplines to enroll. The examples used in those courses are usually not from research conducted by anthropologists. By now, however, you must have gathered that that doesn't make much difference.

All multivariate techniques require caution in their use. It is easy to be impressed with the elegance of multivariate analysis and to lose track of the theoretical issues that motivated your study in the first place. On the other hand, multivariate techniques are important aids to research, and I encourage you to experiment and learn to use them. Try out several of these techniques; learn to read the computer output they produce when used on your data.

And don't be afraid to play and have a good time. If you hang around social scientists who use complex statistical tools in their research, you'll hear people talk about "massaging" their data with this or that multivariate technique, of "teasing out signals" from their data, and of "separating the signals from the noise." These are not the sort of phrases used by people who are bored with what they're doing. Enjoy.

APPENDIX A
Table of Random Numbers

10097	32533	76520	13586	34673	54876	80959	09117	39292	74945
37542	04805	64894	74296	24805	24037	20636	10402	00822	91665
08422	68953	19645	09303	23209	02560	15953	34764	35080	33606
99019	02529	09376	70715	28311	31165	88676	74397	04436	27659
12807	99970	80157	36147	64032	36653	98951	16877	12171	76833
66065	74717	34072	76850	36697	36170	65813	39885	11199	29170
31060	10805	45571	82406	35303	42614	86799	07439	23403	09732
85269	77602	02051	65692	68665	74818	73053	85247	18623	88579
63573	32135	05325	47048	90553	57548	28468	28709	83491	25624
73796	45753	03529	64778	35808	34282	60935	20344	35273	88435
98520	17767	14905	68607	22109	40558	60970	93433	50500	73998
11805	05431	39808	27732	50725	68248	29405	24201	52775	67851
83452	99634	06288	98083	13746	70078	18475	40610	68711	77817
88685	40200	86507	58401	36766	67951	90364	76493	29609	11062
99594	67348	87517	64969	91826	08928	93785	61368	23478	34113
65481	17674	17468	50950	58047	76974	73039	57186	40218	16544
80124	35635	17727	08015	45318	22374	21115	78253	14385	53763
74350	99817	77402	77214	43236	00210	45521	64237	96286	02655
69916	26803	66252	29148	36936	87203	76621	13990	94400	56418
09893	20505	14225	68514	46427	56788	96297	78822	54382	14598
91499	14523	68479	27686	46162	83554	94750	89923	37089	20048
80336	94598	26940	36858	70297	34135	53140	33340	42050	82341
44104	81949	85157	47954	32979	26575	57600	40881	22222	06413
12550	73742	11100	02040	12860	74697	96644	89439	28707	25815
63606	49329	16505	34484	40219	52563	43651	77082	07207	31790
61196	90446	26457	47774	51924	33729	65394	59593	42582	60527
15474	45266	95270	79953	59367	83848	82396	10118	33211	59466
94557	28573	67897	54387	54622	44431	91190	42592	92927	45973
42481	16213	97344	08721	16868	48767	03071	12059	25701	46670
23523	78317	73208	89837	68935	91416	26252	29663	05522	82562
04493	52494	75246	33824	45862	51025	61962	79335	65337	12472
00549	97654	64051	88159	96119	63896	54692	82391	23287	29529
35963	15307	26898	09354	33351	35462	77974	50024	90103	39333
59808	08391	45427	26842	83609	49700	13021	24892	78565	20106
46058	85236	01390	92286	77281	44077	93910	83647	70617	42941
32179	00597	87379	25241	05567	07007	86743	17157	85394	11838
69234	61406	20117	45204	15956	60000	18743	92423	97118	96338
19565	41430	01758	75379	40419	21585	66674	36806	84962	85207
45155	14938	19476	07246	43667	94543	59047	90033	20826	69541
94864	31994	36168	10851	34888	81553	01540	35456	05014	51176
98086	24826	45240	28404	44999	08896	39094	73407	35441	31880
33185	16232	41941	50949	89435	48581	88695	41994	37548	73043
80951	00406	96382	70774	20151	23387	25016	25298	94624	61171
79752	49140	71961	28296	69861	02591	74852	20539	00387	59579
18633	32537	98145	06571	31010	24674	05455	61427	77938	91936

(continued)

514

APPENDIX A, Continued

74029	43902	77557	32270	97790	17119	52527	58021	80814	51748
54178	45611	80993	37143	05335	12969	56127	19255	36040	90324
11664	49883	52079	84827	59381	71539	09973	33440	88461	23356
48324	77928	31249	64710	02295	36870	32307	57546	15020	09994
69074	94138	87637	91976	35584	04401	10518	21615	01848	76938
90089	90249	62196	53754	61007	39513	71877	19088	94091	97084
70413	74646	24580	74929	94902	71143	01816	06557	74936	44506
17022	85475	76454	97145	31850	33650	75223	90607	15520	39823
24906	46977	78868	59973	61110	13047	84302	15982	72731	82300
50222	97585	15161	11327	66712	76500	81055	43716	93343	02797
60291	56491	75093	71017	92139	21562	67305	33066	60719	20033
31485	66220	71939	23182	44059	00289	17996	05268	97659	02611
16551	13457	83006	43096	71235	29381	93168	46668	30723	29437
90831	40282	48952	90899	87567	14411	31483	78232	52117	57484
19195	94881	99625	59598	33330	34405	45601	39005	65170	48419
06056	81764	46911	33370	35719	30207	61967	08086	40073	75215
46044	94342	04346	25157	73062	41921	82742	70481	83376	28856
03690	95581	83895	32069	94196	93097	97900	79905	79610	68639
23532	45828	02575	70187	64732	95799	20005	44543	08965	58907
81365	88745	79117	66599	32463	76925	70223	80849	48500	92536
57660	57584	14276	10166	82132	61861	63597	91025	76338	06878
13619	18065	33262	41774	33145	69671	14920	62061	42352	61546
07155	33924	34103	48785	28604	75023	46564	44875	07478	61678
19705	73768	44407	66609	00883	56229	50882	76601	50403	18003
04233	69951	33035	72878	61494	38754	63112	34005	82115	72073
79786	96081	42535	47848	84053	38522	55756	20382	67816	84693
76421	34950	98800	04822	57743	40616	73751	36521	34591	68549
28120	11330	46035	36097	93141	90483	83329	51529	94974	86242
45012	95348	64843	44570	26086	57925	52060	86496	44979	45833
45251	99242	98656	72488	35515	08968	46711	56846	29418	15329
97318	06337	19410	09936	28536	08458	90982	66566	30286	27797
55895	62683	25132	51771	70516	05063	69361	75727	48522	89141
80181	03112	21819	10421	35725	92004	36822	18679	51605	48064
39423	21649	18389	01344	36548	07702	85187	75037	89625	39524
37040	87608	46311	03712	42044	33852	52206	86204	99714	82241
72664	17872	02627	65809	17307	97355	60006	18166	51375	79461
71584	11935	87348	22204	93483	37555	31381	23640	31469	92988
87697	30854	25509	22665	31581	12507	53679	26381	48023	47916
73663	27869	40208	40672	83210	48573	22406	46286	46987	12017
51544	01914	17431	97024	09620	54225	44529	90758	11151	98314
82670	82296	96903	45286	85145	60329	27682	64892	75961	19800
30051	16942	17241	93593	75336	48698	48564	76832	29214	84972
23338	01489	39942	06609	14070	07351	28226	51996	31244	10725
08739	21034	57145	25526	58145	72334	87799	95132	70300	88277
76383	52236	07587	14161	82994	22829	72713	70265	88650	56335

(continued)

APPENDIX A, Continued

05933	81888	32534	56269	12889	05092	84159	40971	46430	86981
10347	07364	51963	31851	45463	41635	10195	18961	17515	34021
36102	55172	23170	81955	25621	25030	19781	48300	79319	34377
70791	56165	64310	28625	26760	82203	26535	99580	77676	91021
88525	67427	59554	42220	27202	18827	33362	90584	99516	72258
41221	71024	99746	77782	53452	52851	35104	20732	16072	72468
40771	10858	31707	46962	71427	85412	49561	93011	64079	38527
09913	14509	46399	82692	05526	19955	02385	85686	62040	39386
00420	06149	01688	72365	12603	83142	98814	66265	98583	93424
90748	19314	55032	64625	47855	32726	69744	54536	16494	33623

APPENDIX B

STATEMENT ON PROFESSIONAL
AND ETHICAL RESPONSIBILTIES
SOCIETY FOR APPLIED ANTHROPOLOGY

This statement is a guide to professional behavior for the members and fellows of the Society for Applied Anthropology. As members or fellows of the Society we shall act in ways that are consistent with the responsibilities stated below irrespective of the specific circumstances of our employment.

1. To the people we study we owe disclosure of our research goals, methods, and sponsorship. The participation of people in our research activities shall only be on a voluntary and informed basis. We shall provide a means throughout our research activities and in subsequent publications to maintain the confidentiality of those we study. The people we study must be made aware of the likely limits of confidentiality and must not be promised a greater degree of confidentiality than can be realistically expected under current legal circumstances in our respective nations. We shall, within the limits of our knowledge, disclose any significant risk to those we study that may result from our activities.

2. To the communities ultimately affected by our actions we owe respect for their dignity, integrity, and worth. We recognize that human survival is contingent upon the continued existence of a diversity of human communities, and guide our professional activities accordingly. We will avoid taking or recommending action on behalf of a sponsor which is harmful to the interests of a community.

3. To our social science colleagues we have the responsibility to not engage in actions that impede their reasonable professional activities. Among other things this means that, while respecting the needs, responsibilities, and legitimate proprietary interests of our sponsors we should not impede the flow of information about research outcomes and professional practice techniques. We shall accurately report the contributions of colleagues to our work. We shall not condone falsification or distortion by others. We should not prejudice communities or agencies against a colleague for reasons of personal gain.

4. To our students, interns, or trainees we owe nondiscriminatory access to our training services. We shall provide training which is

(continued)

APPENDIX B, Continued
---

informed, accurate, and relevant to the needs of the larger society. We recognize the need for continuing education so as to maintain our skill and knowledge at a high level. Our training should inform students as to their ethical responsibilities. Student contributions to our professional activities, including both research and publication, should be adequately recognized.

5. To our employers and other sponsors we owe accurate reporting of our qualifications and competent, efficient, and timely performance of the work we undertake for them. We shall establish a clear understanding with each employer or other sponsor as to the nature of our professional responsibilities. We shall report our research and other activities accurately. We have the obligation to attempt to prevent distortion or suppression of research results or policy recommendations by concerned agencies.

6. To society as a whole we owe the benefit of our special knowledge and skills in interpreting sociocultural systems. We should communicate our understanding of human life to the society at large.

Approved by SFAA, March 1983, superceding earlier published statements.

APPENDIX C
Codes From the Outline of Cultural Materials (Murdock, 1971)

000 MATERIAL NOT CATEGORIZED

10 ORIENTATION
- 101 Identification
- 102 Maps
- 103 Place Names
- 104 Glossary
- 105 Cultural Summary

11 BIBLIOGRAPHY
- 111 Sources Processed
- 112 Sources Consulted
- 113 Additional References
- 114 Comments
- 115 Informants
- 116 Texts
- 117 Field Data

12 METHODOLOGY
- 121 Theoretical Orientation
- 122 Practical Preparations
- 123 Observational Role
- 124 Interviewing
- 125 Tests and Schedules
- 126 Recording and Collecting
- 127 Historical Research
- 128 Organization and Analysis

13 GEOGRAPHY
- 131 Location
- 132 Climate
- 133 Topography and Geology
- 134 Soil
- 135 Mineral Resources
- 136 Fauna
- 137 Flora

14 HUMAN BIOLOGY
- 141 Anthropometry
- 142 Descriptive Somatology
- 143 Genetics
- 144 Racial Affinities
- 145 Ontogenetic Data

- 146 Nutrition
- 147 Physiological Data

15 BEHAVIOR PROCESSES AND PERSONALITY
- 151 Sensation and Perception
- 152 Drives and Emotions
- 153 Modification of Behavior
- 154 Adjustment Processes
- 155 Personality Development
- 156 Social Personality
- 157 Personality Traits
- 158 Personality Disorders
- 159 Life History Materials

16 DEMOGRAPHY
- 161 Population
- 162 Composition of Population
- 163 Birth Statistics
- 164 Morbidity
- 165 Mortality
- 166 Internal Migration
- 167 Immigration and Emigration
- 168 Population Policy

17 HISTORY AND CULTURE CHANGE
- 171 Distributional Evidence
- 172 Archeology
- 173 Traditional History
- 174 Historical Reconstruction
- 175 Recorded History
- 176 Innovation
- 177 Acculturation and Culture Contact
- 178 Sociocultural Trends

18 TOTAL CULTURE
- 181 Ethos
- 182 Function

(continued)

APPENDIX C, Continued

183   Norms
184   Cultural Participation
185   Cultural Goals
186   Ethnocentrism

19 LANGUAGE
191   Speech
192   Vocabulary
193   Grammar
194   Phonology
195   Stylistics
196   Semantics
197   Linguistic Identification
198   Special Languages

20 COMMUNICATION
201   Gestures and Signs
202   Transmission of Messages
203   Dissemination of News and
        Information
204   Press
205   Postal System
206   Telephone and Telegraph
207   Radio and Television
208   Public Opinion

21 RECORDS
211   Mnemonic Devices
212   Writing
213   Printing
214   Publishing
215   Photography
216   Sound Records
217   Archives
218   Writing and Printing Sup-
        plies

22 FOOD QUEST
221   Annual Cycle
222   Collecting
223   Fowling
224   Hunting and Trapping
225   Marine Hunting
226   Fishing
227   Fishing Gear

228   Marine Industries

23 ANIMAL HUSBANDRY
231   Domesticated Animals
232   Applied Animal Science
233   Pastoral Activities
234   Dairying
235   Poultry Raising
236   Wool Production
237   Animal By-Products

24 AGRICULTURE
241   Tillage
242   Agricultural Science
243   Cereal Agriculture
244   Vegetable Production
245   Arboriculture
246   Forage Crops
247   Floriculture
248   Textile Agriculture
249   Special Crops

25 FOOD PROCESSING
251   Preservation and Storage of
        Food
252   Food Preparation
253   Meat Packing Industry
254   Refrigeration Industry
255   Canning Industry
256   Cereal Industry
257   Confectionery Industries
258   Miscellaneous Food Pro-
        cessing and Packing In-
        dustries

26 FOOD CONSUMPTION
261   Gratification and Control
        of Hunger
262   Diet
263   Condiments
264   Eating
265   Food Service Industries
266   Cannibalism

(continued)

APPENDIX C, Continued

(continued)

APPENDIX C, Continued

35 EQUIPMENT AND MAINTE-
NANCE OF BUILDINGS
   351   Grounds
   352   Furniture
   353   Interior Decoration and
         Arrangement
   354   Heating and Lighting
         Equipment
   355   Miscellaneous Building
         Equipment
   356   Housekeeping
   357   Domestic Service
   358   Maintenance of Nondomes-
         tic Buildings

36 SETTLEMENTS
   361   Settlement Patterns
   362   Housing
   363   Streets and Traffic
   364   Sanitary Facilities
   365   Public Utilities
   366   Commercial Facilities
   367   Parks
   368   Miscellaneous Urban Fa-
         cilities
   369   Urban and Rural Life

37 ENERGY AND POWER
   371   Power Development
   372   Fire
   373   Light
   374   Heat
   375   Thermal Power
   376   Water Power
   377   Electric Power
   378   Atomic Energy
   379   Miscellaneous Power Pro-
         duction

38 CHEMICAL INDUSTRIES
   381   Chemical Engineering
   382   Petroleum and Coal Products
         Industries
   383   Rubber Industry

   384   Synthetics Industry
   385   Industrial Chemicals
   386   Paint and Dye Manufac-
         ture
   387   Fertilizer Industry
   388   Soap and Allied Products
   389   Manufacture of Explosives

39 CAPITAL GOODS INDUSTRIES
   391   Hardware Manufacture
   392   Machine Industries
   393   Electrical Supplies Indus-
         try
   394   Manufacture of Heating
         and Lighting Appliances
   395   Manufacture of Optical
         and Photographic Equip-
         ment
   396   Shipbuilding
   397   Railway Equipment In-
         dustry
   398   Manufacture of Vehicles
   399   Aircraft Industry

40 MACHINES
   401   Mechanics
   402   Industrial Machinery
   403   Electrical Machines and
         Appliances
   404   Household Machines and
         Appliances
   405   Weighing, Measuring, and
         Recording Machines
   406   Weight-Moving Machinery
   407   Agricultural Machinery

41 TOOLS AND APPLIANCES
   411   Weapons
   412   General Tools
   413   Special Tools
   414   Miscellaneous Hardware
   415   Utensils
   416   Appliances
   417   Apparatus

(continued)

APPENDIX C, Continued

(continued)

APPENDIX C, Continued

50 WATER AND AIR TRANSPORT
- 501 Boats
- 502 Navigation
- 503 Waterways Improvements
- 504 Port Facilities
- 505 Water Transport
- 506 Aircraft
- 507 Aviation
- 508 Airport Facilities
- 509 Air Transport

51 LIVING STANDARDS AND ROUTINES
- 511 Standard of Living
- 512 Daily Routine
- 513 Sleeping
- 514 Elimination
- 515 Personal Hygiene
- 516 Postures
- 517 Leisure Time Activities

52 RECREATION
- 521 Conversation
- 522 Humor
- 523 Hobbies
- 524 Games
- 525 Gambling
- 526 Athletic Sports
- 527 Rest Days and Holidays
- 528 Vacations
- 529 Recreational Facilities

53 FINE ARTS
- 531 Decorative Art
- 532 Representative Art
- 533 Music
- 534 Musical Instruments
- 535 Dancing
- 536 Drama
- 537 Oratory
- 538 Literature
- 539 Literary Texts

54 ENTERTAINMENT
- 541 Spectacles
- 542 Commercialized Sports

- 543 Exhibitions
- 544 Public Lectures
- 545 Musical and Theatrical Productions
- 546 Motion Picture Industry
- 547 Night Clubs and Cabarets
- 548 Organized Vice
- 549 Art and Recreational Supplies Industries

55 INDIVIDUATION AND MOBILITY
- 551 Personal Names
- 552 Names of Animals and Things
- 553 Naming
- 554 Status, Role, and Prestige
- 555 Talent Mobility
- 556 Accumulation of Wealth
- 557 Manipulative Mobility
- 558 Downward Mobility

56 SOCIAL STRATIFICATION
- 561 Age Stratification
- 562 Sex Status
- 563 Ethnic Stratification
- 564 Castes
- 565 Classes
- 566 Serfdom and Peonage
- 567 Slavery

57 INTERPERSONAL RELATIONS
- 571 Social Relationships and Groups
- 572 Friendships
- 573 Cliques
- 574 Visiting and Hospitality
- 575 Sodalities
- 576 Etiquette
- 577 Ethics
- 578 Ingroup Antagonisms
- 579 Brawls, Riots, and Banditry

(continued)

APPENDIX C, Continued

58 MARRIAGE
- 581 Basis of Marriage
- 582 Regulation of Marriage
- 583 Mode of Marriage
- 584 Arranging a Marriage
- 585 Nuptuals
- 586 Termination of Marriage
- 587 Secondary Marriages
- 588 Irregular Unions
- 589 Celibacy

59 FAMILY
- 591 Residence
- 592 Household
- 593 Family Relationships
- 594 Nuclear Family
- 595 Polygamy
- 596 Extended Families
- 597 Adoption

60 KINSHIP
- 601 Kinship Terminology
- 602 Kin Relationships
- 603 Grandparents and Grand-children
- 604 Avuncular and Nepotic Relatives
- 605 Cousins
- 606 Parents-in-Law and Children-in-Law
- 607 Siblings-in-Law
- 608 Artificial Kin Relationships
- 609 Behavior toward Nonrelatives

61 KIN GROUPS
- 611 Rule of Descent
- 612 Kindreds and Ramages
- 613 Lineages
- 614 Sibs
- 615 Phratries
- 616 Moieties
- 617 Bilinear Kin Groups
- 618 Clans
- 619 Tribe and Nation

62 COMMUNITY
- 621 Community Structure
- 622 Headmen
- 623 Councils
- 624 Local Officials
- 625 Police
- 626 Social Control
- 627 Informal Ingroup Justice
- 628 Intercommunity Relations

63 TERRITORIAL ORGANIZATION
- 631 Territorial Hierarchy
- 632 Towns
- 633 Cities
- 634 Districts
- 635 Provinces
- 636 Dependencies

64 STATE
- 641 Citizenship
- 642 Constitution
- 643 Chief Executive
- 644 Executive Household
- 645 Cabinet
- 646 Parliament
- 647 Administrative Agencies
- 648 International Relations

65 GOVERNMENT ACTIVITIES
- 651 Taxation and Public Income
- 652 Public Finance
- 653 Public Works
- 654 Research and Development
- 655 Government Enterprises
- 656 Government Regulation
- 657 Public Welfare
- 658 Public Education
- 659 Miscellaneous Government Activities

(continued)

APPENDIX C, Continued

66 POLITICAL BEHAVIOR
    661   Exploitation
    662   Political Image
    663   Public Service
    664   Pressure Politics
    665   Political Parties
    666   Elections
    667   Political Machines
    668   Political Movements
    669   Revolution

67 LAW
    671   Legal Norms
    672   Liability
    673   Wrongs
    674   Crime
    675   Contracts
    676   Agency

68 OFFENSES AND SANCTIONS
    681   Sanctions
    682   Offenses against Life
    683   Offenses against the Person
    684   Sex and Marital Offenses
    685   Property Offenses
    686   Nonfulfillment of Obliga-
           tions
    687   Offenses against the State
    688   Religious Offenses
    689   Social Offenses

69 JUSTICE
    691   Litigation
    692   Judicial Authority
    693   Legal and Judicial Person-
           nel
    694   Initiation of Judicial Pro-
           ceedings
    695   Trial Procedure
    696   Execution of Justice
    697   Prisons and Jails
    698   Special Courts

70 ARMED FORCES
    701   Military Organization
    702   Recruitment and Training
    703   Discipline and Morale
    704   Ground Combat Forces
    705   Supply and Commissariat
    706   Navy
    707   Air Forces
    708   Auxilliary Corps

71 MILITARY TECHNOLOGY
    711   Military Engineering
    712   Military Installations
    713   Ordnance
    714   Uniform and Accouter-
           ment
    715   Military Vehicles
    716   Naval Vessels
    717   Military Aircraft
    718   Special Military Equipment
    719   Munitions Industries

72 WAR
    721   Instigation of War
    722   Wartime Adjustments
    723   Strategy
    724   Logistics
    725   Tactics
    726   Warfare
    727   Aftermath of Combat
    728   Peacemaking
    729   War Veterans

73 SOCIAL PROBLEMS
    731   Disasters
    732   Defectives
    733   Alcoholism and Drug Ad-
           diction
    734   Invalidism
    735   Poverty
    736   Dependency
    737   Old Age Dependency
    738   Delinquency

(continued)

APPENDIX C, Continued

74 HEALTH AND WELFARE
- 741 Philanthropic Foundations
- 742 Medical Research
- 743 Hospitals and Clinics
- 744 Public Health and Sanitation
- 745 Social Insurance
- 746 Public Assistance
- 747 Private Welfare Agencies
- 748 Social Work

75 SICKNESS
- 751 Preventive Medicine
- 752 Bodily Injuries
- 753 Theory of Disease
- 754 Sorcery
- 755 Magical and Mental Therapy
- 756 Psychotherapists
- 757 Medical Therapy
- 758 Medical Care
- 759 Medical Personnel

76 DEATH
- 761 Life and Death
- 762 Suicide
- 763 Dying
- 764 Funeral
- 765 Mourning
- 766 Deviant Mortuary Practices
- 767 Mortuary Specialists
- 768 Social Readjustments to Death
- 769 Cult of the Dead

77 RELIGIOUS BELIEFS
- 771 General Character of Religion
- 772 Cosmology
- 773 Mythology
- 774 Animism
- 775 Eschatology
- 776 Spirits and Gods

- 777 Luck and Chance
- 778 Sacred Objects and Places
- 779 Theological Systems

78 RELIGIOUS PRACTICES
- 781 Religious Experience
- 782 Propitiation
- 783 Purification and Expiation
- 784 Avoidance and Taboo
- 785 Asceticism
- 786 Orgies
- 787 Revelation and Divination
- 788 Ritual
- 789 Magic

79 ECCLESIASTICAL ORGANIZATION
- 791 Magicians and Diviners
- 792 Holy Men
- 793 Priesthood
- 794 Congregations
- 795 Sects
- 796 Organized Ceremonial
- 797 Missions
- 798 Religious Intolerance

80 NUMBERS AND MEASURES
- 801 Numerology
- 802 Numeration
- 803 Mathematics
- 804 Weights and Measures
- 805 Ordering of Time

81 EXACT KNOWLEDGE
- 811 Logic
- 812 Philosophy
- 813 Scientific Method
- 814 Humanistic Studies
- 815 Pure Science
- 816 Applied Science

(continued)

APPENDIX C, Continued

82 IDEAS ABOUT NATURE AND
   MAN
   821   Ethnometeorology
   822   Ethnophysics
   823   Ethnogeography
   824   Ethnobotany
   825   Ethnozoology
   826   Ethnoanatomy
   827   Ethnophysiology
   828   Ethnopsychology
   829   Ethnosociology

83 SEX
   831   Sexuality
   832   Sexual Stimulation
   833   Sexual Intercourse
   834   General Sex Restrictions
   835   Kinship Regulation of Sex
   836   Premarital Sex Relations
   837   Extramarital Sex Relations
   838   Homosexuality
   839   Miscellaneous Sex Behavior

84 REPRODUCTION
   841   Menstruation
   842   Conception
   843   Pregnancy
   844   Childbirth
   845   Difficult and Unusual
          Births
   846   Postnatal Care
   847   Abortion and Infanticide
   848   Illegitimacy

85 INFANCY AND CHILDHOOD
   851   Social Placement
   852   Ceremonial During Infancy
          and Childhood
   853   Infant Feeding
   854   Infant Care
   855   Child Care
   856   Development and Matura-
          tion

857   Childhood Activities
858   Status of Children

86 SOCIALIZATION
   861   Techniques of Inculcation
   862   Weaning and Food Train-
          ing
   863   Cleanliness Training
   864   Sex Training
   865   Aggression Training
   866   Independence Training
   867   Transmission of Cultural
          Norms
   868   Transmission of Skills
   869   Transmission of Beliefs

87 EDUCATION
   871   Educational System
   872   Elementary Education
   873   Liberal Arts Education
   874   Vocational Education
   875   Teachers
   876   Educational Theory and
          Methods

88 ADOLESCENCE, ADULTHOOD,
   AND OLD AGE
   881   Puberty and Initiation
   882   Status of Adolescents
   883   Adolescent Activities
   884   Majority
   885   Adulthood
   886   Senescence
   887   Activities of the Aged
   888   Status and Treatment of
          the Aged

SOURCE: G. P. Murdock et al. *Outline of Cultural Materials* © 1961. Used with permission of Human Relations Area Files.

APPENDIX D

Student's *t*-Distribution

(compare absolute value of *t* to entries in this table)

df	Level of Significance for one-tailed test					
	.10	.05	.025	.01	.005	.0005
	Level of Significance for two-tailed test					
	.20	.10	.05	.02	.01	.001
1	3.078	6.314	12.706	31.821	63.657	636.619
2	1.886	2.920	4.303	6.965	9.925	31.598
3	1.638	2.353	3.182	4.541	5.841	12.941
4	1.533	2.132	2.776	3.747	4.604	8.610
5	1.476	2.015	2.571	3.365	4.032	6.859
6	1.440	1.943	2.447	3.143	3.707	5.959
7	1.415	1.895	2.365	2.998	3.499	5.405
8	1.397	1.860	2.306	2.896	3.355	5.041
9	1.383	1.833	2.262	2.821	3.250	4.781
10	1.372	1.812	2.228	2.764	3.169	4.587
11	1.363	1.796	2.201	2.718	3.106	4.437
12	1.356	1.782	2.179	2.681	3.055	4.318
13	1.350	1.771	2.160	2.650	3.012	4.221
14	1.345	1.761	2.145	2.624	2.977	4.140
15	1.341	1.753	2.131	2.602	2.947	4.073
16	1.337	1.746	2.120	2.583	2.921	4.015
17	1.333	1.740	2.110	2.567	2.898	3.965
18	1.330	1.734	2.101	2.552	2.878	3.922
19	1.328	1.729	2.093	2.539	2.861	3.883
20	1.325	1.725	2.086	2.528	2.845	3.850
21	1.323	1.721	2.080	2.518	2.831	3.819
22	1.321	1.717	2.074	2.508	2.819	3.792
23	1.319	1.714	2.069	2.500	2.807	3.767
24	1.318	1.711	2.064	2.492	2.797	3.745
25	1.316	1.708	2.060	2.485	2.787	3.725
26	1.315	1.706	2.056	2.479	2.779	3.707
27	1.314	1.703	2.052	2.473	2.771	3.690
28	1.313	1.701	2.048	2.467	2.763	3.674
29	1.311	1.699	2.045	2.462	2.756	3.659
30	1.310	1.697	2.042	2.457	2.750	3.646
40	1.303	1.684	2.021	2.423	2.704	3.551
60	1.296	1.671	2.000	2.390	2.660	3.460
120	1.289	1.658	1.980	2.358	2.617	3.373
∞	1.282	1.645	1.960	2.326	2.567	3.291

Appendix D is taken from Table III of R. A. Fisher and F. Yates' Statistical Tables for Biological, Agricultural and Medical Research, 6/e, 1974, published by Longman Group UK Ltd., London. Reprinted by permission of the authors and publishers.

APPENDIX E
The Chi-Square Distribution Table

			Probabilities			
df	.99	.95	.90	.80	.70	.50
1	.000157	.00393	.0158	.0642	.148	.455
2	.0201	.103	.211	.446	.713	1.386
3	.115	.352	.584	1.005	1.424	2.366
4	.297	.711	1.064	1.649	2.195	3.357
5	.554	1.145	1.610	2.343	3.000	4.351
6	.872	1.635	2.204	3.070	3.828	5.348
7	1.239	2.167	2.833	3.822	4.671	6.346
8	1.646	2.733	3.490	4.594	5.527	7.344
9	2.088	3.325	4.168	5.380	6.393	8.343
10	2.558	3.940	4.865	6.179	7.267	9.342
11	3.053	4.575	5.578	6.989	8.148	10.341
12	3.571	5.226	6.304	7.807	9.034	11.340
13	4.107	5.892	7.042	8.634	9.926	12.340
14	4.660	6.571	7.790	9.467	10.821	13.339
15	5.229	7.261	8.547	10.307	11.721	14.339
16	5.812	7.962	9.312	11.152	12.624	15.338
17	6.408	8.672	10.085	12.002	13.531	16.338
18	7.015	9.390	10.865	12.857	14.440	17.338
19	7.633	10.117	11.651	13.716	15.352	18.338
20	8.260	10.851	12.443	14.578	16.266	19.337
21	8.897	11.591	13.240	15.445	17.182	20.337
22	9.542	12.338	14.041	16.314	18.101	21.337
23	10.196	13.091	14.848	17.187	19.021	22.337
24	10.865	13.848	15.659	18.062	19.943	23.337
25	11.524	14.611	16.473	18.940	20.867	24.337
26	12.198	15.379	17.292	19.820	21.792	25.336
27	12.879	16.151	18.114	20.703	22.719	26.336
28	13.565	16.928	18.939	21.588	23.647	27.336
29	14.256	17.708	19.768	22.475	24.577	28.336
30	14.953	18.493	20.599	23.364	25.508	29.336

(continued)

APPENDIX E, Continued

				Probabilities			
df	.30	.20	.10	.05	.025	.01	.001
1	1.074	1.642	2.706	3.841	5.024	6.635	10.827
2	2.408	3.219	4.605	5.991	7.378	9.210	13.815
3	3.665	4.624	6.251	7.815	9.348	11.345	16.268
4	4.878	5.989	7.779	9.488	11.143	13.277	18.465
5	6.064	7.289	9.236	11.070	12.832	15.086	20.517
6	7.231	8.558	10.645	12.592	14.449	16.812	22.457
7	8.383	9.803	12.017	14.067	16.013	18.475	24.322
8	9.524	11.030	13.362	15.507	17.535	20.090	26.125
9	10.656	12.242	14.684	16.919	19.023	21.666	27.877
10	11.781	13.442	15.987	18.307	20.483	23.209	29.588
11	12.899	14.631	17.275	19.675	21.920	24.725	31.264
12	14.011	15.812	18.549	21.026	23.337	26.217	32.909
13	15.119	16.985	19.812	22.362	24.736	27.688	34.528
14	16.222	18.151	21.064	23.685	26.119	29.141	36.123
15	17.322	19.311	22.307	24.996	27.488	30.578	37.697
16	18.418	20.465	23.542	26.296	28.845	32.000	39.252
17	19.511	21.615	24.769	27.587	30.191	33.409	40.790
18	20.601	22.760	25.989	28.869	31.526	34.805	42.312
19	21.689	23.900	27.204	30.144	32.852	36.191	43.820
20	22.775	25.038	28.412	31.410	34.170	37.566	45.315
21	23.858	26.171	29.615	32.671	35.479	38.932	46.797
22	24.939	27.301	30.813	33.924	36.781	40.289	48.268
23	26.018	28.429	32.007	35.172	38.076	41.638	49.728
24	27.096	29.553	33.196	36.415	39.364	42.980	51.179
25	28.172	30.675	34.382	37.652	40.646	44.314	52.620
26	29.246	31.795	35.563	38.885	41.923	45.642	54.052
27	30.319	32.912	36.741	40.113	43.194	46.963	55.476
28	31.391	34.027	37.916	41.337	44.461	48.278	56.893
29	32.461	35.139	39.087	42.557	45.722	49.588	58.302
30	33.530	36.250	40.256	43.773	46.979	50.892	59.703

Appendix E is taken from Table IV of R. A. Fisher and F. Yates' Statistical Tables for Biological, Agricultural and Medical Research, 6/e, 1974, published by Longman Group UK Ltd., London. Reprinted by permission of the authors and publishers.

APPENDIX F
Table of Areas Under a Normal Curve

(A) z	(B) area between mean and z	(C) area beyond z	(A) z	(B) area between mean and z	(C) area beyond z	(A) z	(B) area between mean and z	(C) area beyond z
0.00	.0000	.5000	0.40	.1554	.3446	0.80	.2881	.2119
0.01	.0040	.4960	0.41	.1591	.3409	0.81	.2910	.2090
0.02	.0080	.4920	0.42	.1628	.3372	0.82	.2939	.2061
0.03	.0120	.4880	0.43	.1664	.3336	0.83	.2967	.2033
0.04	.0160	.4840	0.44	.1700	.3300	0.84	.2995	.2005
0.05	.0199	.4801	0.45	.1736	.3264	0.85	.3023	.1977
0.06	.0239	.4761	0.46	.1772	.3228	0.86	.3051	.1949
0.07	.0279	.4721	0.47	.1808	.3192	0.87	.3078	.1922
0.08	.0319	.4681	0.48	.1844	.3156	0.88	.3106	.1894
0.09	.0359	.4641	0.49	.1879	.3121	0.89	.3133	.1867
0.10	.0398	.4602	0.50	.1915	.3085	0.90	.3159	.1841
0.11	.0438	.4562	0.51	.1950	.3050	0.91	.3186	.1814
0.12	.0478	.4522	0.52	.1985	.3015	0.92	.3212	.1788
0.13	.0517	.4483	0.53	.2019	.2981	0.93	.3238	.1762
0.14	.0557	.4443	0.54	.2054	.2946	0.94	.3264	.1736
0.15	.0596	.4404	0.55	.2088	.2912	0.95	.3289	.1711
0.16	.0636	.4364	0.56	.2123	.2877	0.96	.3315	.1685
0.17	.0675	.4325	0.57	.2157	.2843	0.97	.3340	.1660
0.18	.0714	.4286	0.58	.2190	.2810	0.98	.3365	.1635
0.19	.0753	.4247	0.59	.2224	.2776	0.99	.3389	.1611
0.20	.0793	.4207	0.60	.2257	.2743	1.00	.3413	.1587
0.21	.0832	.4168	0.61	.2291	.2709	1.01	.3438	.1562
0.22	.0871	.4129	0.62	.2324	.2676	1.02	.3461	.1539
0.23	.0910	.4090	0.63	.2357	.2643	1.03	.3485	.1515
0.24	.0948	.4052	0.64	.2389	.2611	1.04	.3508	.1492
0.25	.0987	.4013	0.65	.2422	.2578	1.05	.3531	.1469
0.26	.1026	.3974	0.66	.2454	.2546	1.06	.3554	.1446
0.27	.1064	.3936	0.67	.2486	.2514	1.07	.3577	.1423
0.28	.1103	.3897	0.68	.2517	.2483	1.08	.3599	.1401
0.29	.1141	.3859	0.69	.2549	.2451	1.09	.3621	.1379
0.30	.1179	.3821	0.70	.2580	.2420	1.10	.3643	.1357
0.31	.1217	.3783	0.71	.2611	.2389	1.11	.3665	.1335
0.32	.1255	.3745	0.72	.2642	.2358	1.12	.3686	.1314
0.33	.1293	.3707	0.73	.2673	.2327	1.13	.3708	.1292
0.34	.1331	.3669	0.74	.2704	.2296	1.14	.3729	.1271
0.35	.1368	.3632	0.75	.2734	.2266	1.15	.3749	.1251
0.36	.1406	.3594	0.76	.2764	.2236	1.16	.3770	.1230
0.37	.1443	.3557	0.77	.2794	.2206	1.17	.3790	.1210
0.38	.1480	.3520	0.78	.2823	.2177	1.18	.3810	.1190
0.39	.1517	.3483	0.79	.2852	.2148	1.19	.3830	.1170

(continued)

APPENDIX F, Continued

(A) z	(B) area between mean and z	(C) area beyond z	(A) z	(B) area between mean and z	(C) area beyond z	(A) z	(B) area between mean and z	(C) area beyond z
1.20	.3849	.1151	1.61	.4463	.0537	2.02	.4783	.0217
1.21	.3869	.1131	1.62	.4474	.0526	2.03	.4788	.0212
1.22	.3888	.1112	1.63	.4484	.0516	2.04	.4793	.0207
1.23	.3907	.1093	1.64	.4495	.0505	2.05	.4798	.0202
1.24	.3925	.1075	1.65	.4505	.0495	2.06	.4803	.0197
1.25	.3944	.1056	1.66	.4515	.0485	2.07	.4808	.0192
1.26	.3962	.1038	1.67	.4525	.0475	2.08	.4812	.0188
1.27	.3980	.1020	1.68	.4535	.0465	2.09	.4817	.0183
1.28	.3997	.1003	1.69	.4545	.0455	2.10	.4821	.0179
1.29	.4015	.0985	1.70	.4554	.0446	2.11	.4826	.0174
1.30	.4032	.0968	1.71	.4564	.0436	2.12	.4830	.0170
1.31	.4049	.0951	1.72	.4573	.0427	2.13	.4834	.0166
1.32	.4066	.0934	1.73	.4582	.0418	2.14	.4838	.0162
1.33	.4082	.0918	1.74	.4591	.0409	2.15	.4842	.0158
1.34	.4099	.0901	1.75	.4599	.0401	2.16	.4846	.0154
1.35	.4115	.0885	1.76	.4608	.0392	2.17	.4850	.0150
1.36	.4131	.0869	1.77	.4616	.0384	2.18	.4854	.0146
1.37	.4147	.0853	1.78	.4625	.0375	2.19	.4857	.0143
1.38	.4162	.0838	1.79	.4633	.0367	2.20	.4861	.0139
1.39	.4177	.0823	1.80	.4641	.0359	2.21	.4864	.0136
1.40	.4192	.0808	1.81	.4649	.0351	2.22	.4868	.0132
1.41	.4207	.0793	1.82	.4656	.0344	2.23	.4871	.0129
1.42	.4222	.0778	1.83	.4664	.0336	2.24	.4875	.0125
1.43	.4236	.0764	1.84	.4671	.0329	2.25	.4878	.0122
1.44	.4251	.0749	1.85	.4678	.0322	2.26	.4881	.0119
1.45	.4265	.0735	1.86	.4686	.0314	2.27	.4884	.0116
1.46	.4279	.0721	1.87	.4693	.0307	2.28	.4887	.0113
1.47	.4292	.0708	1.88	.4699	.0301	2.29	.4890	.0110
1.48	.4306	.0694	1.89	.4706	.0294	2.30	.4893	.0107
1.49	.4319	.0681	1.90	.4713	.0287	2.31	.4896	.0104
1.50	.4332	.0668	1.91	.4719	.0281	2.32	.4898	.0102
1.51	.4345	.0655	1.92	.4726	.0274	2.33	.4901	.0099
1.52	.4357	.0643	1.93	.4732	.0268	2.34	.4904	.0096
1.53	.4370	.0630	1.94	.4738	.0262	2.35	.4906	.0094
1.54	.4382	.0618	1.95	.4744	.0256	2.36	.4909	.0091
1.55	.4394	.0606	1.96	.4750	.0250	2.37	.4911	.0089
1.56	.4406	.0594	1.97	.4756	.0244	2.38	.4913	.0087
1.57	.4418	.0582	1.98	.4761	.0239	2.39	.4916	.0084
1.58	.4429	.0571	1.99	.4767	.0233	2.40	.4918	.0082
1.59	.4441	.0559	2.00	.4772	.0228	2.41	.4920	.0080
1.60	.4452	.0548	2.01	.4778	.0222	2.42	.4922	.0078

(continued)

APPENDIX F, Continued

(A) z	(B) area between mean and z	(C) area beyond z	(A) z	(B) area between mean and z	(C) area beyond z	(A) z	(B) area between mean and z	(C) area beyond z
2.43	.4925	.0075	2.74	.4969	.0031	3.05	.4989	.0011
2.44	.4927	.0073	2.75	.4970	.0030	3.06	.4989	.0011
2.45	.4929	.0071	2.76	.4971	.0029	3.07	.4989	.0011
2.46	.4931	.0069	2.77	.4972	.0028	3.08	.4990	.0010
2.47	.4932	.0068	2.78	.4973	.0027	3.09	.4990	.0010
2.48	.4934	.0066	2.79	.4974	.0026	3.10	.4990	.0010
2.49	.4936	.0064	2.80	.4974	.0026	3.11	.4991	.0009
2.50	.4938	.0062	2.81	.4975	.0025	3.12	.4991	.0009
2.51	.4940	.0060	2.82	.4976	.0024	3.13	.4991	.0009
2.52	.4941	.0059	2.83	.4977	.0023	3.14	.4992	.0008
2.53	.4943	.0057	2.84	.4977	.0023	3.15	.4992	.0008
2.54	.4945	.0055	2.85	.4978	.0022	3.16	.4992	.0008
2.55	.4946	.0054	2.86	.4979	.0021	3.17	.4992	.0008
2.56	.4948	.0052	2.87	.4979	.0021	3.18	.4993	.0007
2.57	.4949	.0051	2.88	.4980	.0020	3.19	.4993	.0007
2.58	.4951	.0049	2.89	.4981	.0019	3.20	.4993	.0007
2.59	.4952	.0048	2.90	.4981	.0019	3.21	.4993	.0007
2.60	.4953	.0047	2.91	.4982	.0018	3.22	.4994	.0006
2.61	.4955	.0045	2.92	.4982	.0018	3.23	.4994	.0006
2.62	.4956	.0044	2.93	.4983	.0017	3.24	.4994	.0006
2.63	.4957	.0043	2.94	.4984	.0016	3.25	.4994	.0006
2.64	.4959	.0041	2.95	.4984	.0016	3.30	.4995	.0005
2.65	.4960	.0040	2.96	.4985	.0015	3.35	.4996	.0004
2.66	.4961	.0039	2.97	.4985	.0015	3.40	.4997	.0003
2.67	.4962	.0038	2.98	.4986	.0014	3.45	.4997	.0003
2.68	.4963	.0037	2.99	.4986	.0014	3.50	.4998	.0002
2.69	.4964	.0036	3.00	.4987	.0013	3.60	.4998	.0002
2.70	.4965	.0035	3.01	.4987	.0013	3.70	.4999	.0001
2.71	.4966	.0034	3.02	.4987	.0013	3.80	.4999	.0001
2.72	.4967	.0033	3.03	.4988	.0012	3.90	.49995	.00005
2.73	.4968	.0032	3.04	.4988	.0012	4.00	.49997	.00003

From Runyon and Haber (1984: 416-417); reproduced by permission.

APPENDIX G
Software and Other Resources

Statistics

If you're going to invest in a full-featured statistical package, I recommend SYSTAT. It's available for the MS-DOS, Windows, and Macintosh computing environments. Among the reasons I like SYSTAT is that SYSTAT, Inc. produces MYSTAT, an inexpensive program that handles most of the everyday statistical analysis you'll want to do while you're in the field. MYSTAT is easy to learn, and the commands are like those in SYSTAT.

For SYSTAT, contact SYSTAT, Inc., 1800 Sherman Ave., Evanston, IL 60201. Tel. 708-864-5670. For MYSTAT, see Hale, R. L., 1992, *MYSTAT Statistical Operations*. Cambridge, MA: Course Technology, Inc. Also see Bernard, H. R., and W. P. Handwerker, 1994, *Data Analysis With MYSTAT*. New York: McGraw-Hill. The Bernard and Handwerker volume is available with the purchase of statistics and research methods texts published by McGraw-Hill, Inc. The Bernard/Handwerker book accompanies the IBM and IBM-compatible version of MYSTAT. Hale's book is available for both MS-DOS and Macintosh versions.

Another excellent, easy-to-learn product for everyday statistical work is KwikStat. This program is available for IBM-compatible machines. Contact TexaSoft, P.O. Box 1169, Cedar Hill, TX 75104. Tel. 214-291-2115.

Text Management

For simple counts of words in a text, a program called WC is a treasure, although it only works on ASCII files. It provides a list of all unique words in a text and counts the number of times each word occurs. WC is available as shareware from Public Brand Software, P.O. Box 51325, Indianapolis, IN 46251, Tel. 800-426-3475, and from the distributer, The Software System, 3477 Westport Court, Cincinnati, OH 45248. Tel. 513-574-7523.

The ETHNOGRAPH was written expressly for qualitative social researchers and is a popular program for text management. It is distributed by Qualis Associates, P.O. Box 2240, Corvallis, OR 97339. Tel. 503-752-8619. For more on The ETHNOGRAPH, see Tesch (1990:251-269).

Three low-cost text management programs are: GOfer, dtSearch, and TALLY. For more information about these programs, see Bernard (1992b) (GOfer), Truex (1993) (dtSearch), and Trotter (1993) (TALLY).

GOfer is available for IBM, IBM-compatible, and Macintosh computers. Contact Microlytics, Inc., Two Tobey Village Office Park, Pittsford, NY 14534. Tel. 800-828-6293. dtSearch is distributed by DT Software, Inc., 2101 Crystal Plaza Arcade, Suite 231, Arlington, VA 22202. dtSearch is also available from The Public (software) Library, P.O. Box 35705, Houston, TX

77235. Tel. 800-242-4775. TALLY is distributed by William C. Brown Publishers, 2460 Kerper Blvd., Dubuque, IA. Tel. 800-338-5578.

ZyINDEX is an industrial-strength text management program. If you work with big data sets (thousands of pages of open-ended interviews from several sites in a multidisciplinary project, for example), then this is the sort of program you'll need. Contact ZyLAB Division, Information Dimensions, 100 Lexington Drive, Buffalo Grove, IL 60089. Tel. 708-459-8000. For more information on ZyINDEX, see Marshall (1993).

TEXTPACK, which I have not used, is reviewed thoroughly by Tesch (1990). According to Tesch, TEXTPACK is available from: Computer Dept., ZUMA, The Center for Surveys, Methods, and Analysis, B2,1, D6800, Mannheim, Germany.

ANTHROPAC is distributed by Analytic Technologies, 306 South Walker, Columbia, SC 29205. Tel. 803-771-7643. ANTHROPAC has routines for advanced statistical methods, such as factor analysis and log linear analysis. The program also does Guttman scaling, multidimensional scaling, and correspondence analysis.

Database Management

File Express is distributed by Expressware Corporation, P.O. Box 1800, Duvall, WA 98019. Tel. 206-788-0932.

Wampum is available as shareware (contact Public Brand Software, P.O. Box 51315, Indianapolis, IN 46251. Tel. 800-426-3475).

Other Resources

World Cultures Journal is published by Analytic Technologies, 306 S. Walker, Columbia, SC 29205. Tel. 803-771-7643. WCJ contains coded ethnographic information on disk. It is an essential resource for cross-cultural researchers who use the Human Relations Area Files.

The Cultural Context Checklist is an excellent checklist for field researchers. This list will tell you how to code information on local geographic landmarks, on household form, marriage type, forms of punishment, infant carrying practices, and on and on. This checklist was developed by a team of anthropologists at UCLA in connection with a major cross-cultural research project, led by Allen Johnson, on time allocation. The checklist comes with each volume of a series titled "Cross-Cultural Studies in Time Allocation," published by the Human Area Relations Files, P.O. Box 2015, Yale Station, New Haven, CT 06520. Tel. 203-777-2334.

Cultural Anthropology Methods is published by ECS-CAM, 2815 NW 38th Drive, Gainesville, FL 32605. CAM has how-to-do-it articles on both qualitative and quantitative research methods, plus articles on building bibliographies, on using electronic mail, and on writing grant proposals.

Data Editors

KEDIT is distributed by Mansfield Software Group, Inc., P.O. Box 532, Storrs, CT 06268. Tel. 203-429-8402.

References

Aaronson, E., & Mills, J. (1959). The effect of severity of initiation on liking for a group. *Journal of Abnormal and Social Psychology, 59*:177-181.

Abernathy, J. R., & Greenberg, B. G. (1970). Estimates of induced abortion in urban North Carolina. *Demography, 7*:29.

Adams, K. (1993). *Dowry as compensatory marriage payment.* Unpublished manuscript.

Agar, M. (1973). *Ripping and running.* New York: Academic Press.

Agar, M. (1980). *The professional stranger.* New York: Academic Press.

Agar, M. (1982). Toward an ethnographic language. *American Anthropologist, 84*:779-795.

Aiello, J. R., & Jones, S. E. (1971). Field study of the proxemic behavior of young school children in three subcultural groups. *Journal of Personality and Social Psychology, 19*:351-356.

Allport, F. H., & Hartman, D. A. (1931). The prediction of cultural change: A problem illustrated in studies by F. Stuart Chapin and A. L. Kroeber. In S. A. Rice (Ed.), *Methods in social science* (pp. 307-352). Chicago: University of Chicago Press.

Altmann, J. (1974). Observational study of behavior: Sampling methods. *Behaviour, 49*:227-267.

Altorki, S., & Fawzi El-Solh, C. (Eds.). (1988). *Arab women in the field: Studying your own society.* Syracuse, NY: Syracuse University Press.

American Statistical Association. (1974). Report on the ASA Conference on Surveys of Human Populations. *The American Statistician, 28* (February):30-34.

Anderson, A. B., & Anderson, E. S. (1983). People and the Palm Forest. (Contract 51-07-79-07 to John Ewel.) Final report to United States Dept. of Agriculture, Forest Service, Consortium for the Study of Man's Relationship with the Global Environment. Washington, DC: USDA. (Also available through NTIS.)

Andrews, F. M., & Withey, S. B. (1976). *Social indicators of well-being: Americans' perceptions of life quality.* New York: Plenum.

Archer, D., & Erlich, L. (1985). Weighing the evidence: A new method for research on restricted information. *Qualitative Sociology, 8*:345-358.

Associated Press. (1985, October 1).

Aunger, R. (1992). *Sources of variation in ethnographic interview data: The case of food avoidances in the Ituri forest, Zaire.* Paper presented at the annual meeting of the American Anthropological Association, San Francisco, CA.

Axinn, W. G. (1989). Interviewer and data quality in a less developed setting. *Journal of Official Statistics, 3*:265-280.

Axinn, W. G., Fricke, T. E., & Thornton, A. (1991). The microdemographic community-study approach. *Sociological Methods and Research, 20*(2):187-217.

Babbie, E. (1983). *The practice of social research* (3rd ed.). Belmont, CA: Wadsworth.

Bales, R. F. (1952). Some uniformities of behavior in small social systems. In G. Swanson, T. M. Newcomb, & E. L. Hartley (Eds.), *Readings in social psychology* (2nd ed., pp. 146-159). New York: Henry Holt.

Bales, R. F., & Cohen, S. P. (1979). *SYMLOG: A system for the multiple level observation of groups.* New York: Free Press.

Barry, H., III, & Schlegel, A. (1980). *Cross-cultural samples and codes.* Pittsburgh: University of Pittsburgh Press.

Bartlett, F. C. (1937). Psychological methods and anthropological problems. *Africa, 10*:401-419.

Bechtel, R. B. (1977). *Enclosing behavior.* Stroudsburg, PA: Dowden, Hutchinson, and Ross.

Becker, H. S., & Geer, B. (1960). Participant observation: The analysis of qualitative field data. In R. N. Adams & J. J. Preiss (Eds.), *Human organization research* (pp. 267-289). Homewood, IL: Dorsey (for the Society for Applied Anthropology).

Belk, R. W., Sherry, J. F., Jr., & Wallendorf, M. (1988). A naturalistic inquiry into buyer and seller behavior at a swap meet. *Journal of Consumer Research, 14*:449-469.

Belo, J. (1960). *Trance in Bali.* New York: Columbia University Press.

Bem, S. (1974). The measurement of psychological androgyny. *Journal of Consulting and Clinical Psychology, 42*:155-162.

Berlin, B., Breedlove, D. E., & Raven, P. H. (1974). *Principles of Tzeltal plant classification: An introduction to the botanical ethnography of a Mayan-speaking people of Highland Chiapas.* New York: Academic Press.

Berlin, B., & Kay, P. (1991). *Basic color terms: Their universality and evolution.* Berkeley: University of California Press.

Bermant, G. (1982). Justifying social research in terms of social benefit. In T. L. Beauchamp et al. (Eds.), *Ethical issues in social science research* (pp. 125-143). Baltimore: Johns Hopkins University Press.

Bernard, H. R. (1965). Greek sponge boats in Florida. *Anthropological Quarterly, 38*(2):41-54.

Bernard, H. R. (1967). Kalymnian sponge diving. *Human Biology, 39*:103-130.

Bernard, H. R. (1974). Scientists and policy makers: A case study in the ethnography of communications. *Human Organization, 33*(3):261-275.

Bernard, H. R. (1987). Sponge fishing and technological change in Greece. In H. R. Bernard & P. J. Pelto (Eds.), *Technology and social change* (2nd ed., pp. 167-206). Prospect Heights, IL: Waveland.

Bernard, H. R. (1992a). Preserving language diversity. *Human Organization 41*:82-88.

Bernard, H. R. (1992b). Managing text with GOfer. *Cultural Anthropology Methods, 4*(2): 9-10.

Bernard, H. R., & Ashton-Vouyoucalos, S. (1976). Return migration to Greece. *Journal of the Steward Anthropological Society, 8*(1):31-51.

Bernard, H. R., & Comitas, L. (1978). Greek return migration. *Current Anthropology, 19*:658-659.

Bernard, H. R., & Evans, M. J. (1983). New microcomputer techniques for anthropologists. *Human Organization, 42*:182-185.

Bernard, H. R., & Handwerker, W. P. (1994). *Data analysis with MYSTAT.* New York: McGraw-Hill.

Bernard, H. R., & Killworth, P. D. (1973). On the social structure of an ocean-going research vessel and other important things. *Social Science Research, 2*:145-184.

Bernard, H. R., & Killworth, P. D. (1974). Scientists and crew. *Maritime Studies and Management*, 2:112-125.

Bernard, H. R., & Killworth, P. D. (1993). Sampling in time allocation research. *Ethnology*, 32:207-215.

Bernard, H. R., Killworth, P. D., Evans, M. J., McCarty, C., & Shelley, G. A. (1987). Measuring patterns of acquaintanceship cross-culturally. *Ethnology*, 27:155-179.

Bernard, H. R., Killworth, P. D., Kronenfeld, D., & Sailer, L. (1984). The problem of informant accuracy: The validity of retrospective data. *Annual Review of Anthropology*, 13:495-517.

Bernard, H. R., & Salinas, J. P. (1989). *Native ethnography: A Mexican Indian describes his culture*. Newbury Park, CA: Sage.

Berry, J. (1976). *Human ecology and cognitive style*. New York: Wiley.

Biesele, M., & Tyler, S. A. (Eds.). (1986). The dialectic of oral and literary hermeneutics [Special issue]. *Cultural Anthropology*, 1(2).

Billiet, J., & Loosveldt, G. (1988). Improvement of the quality of responses to factual survey questions by interviewer training. *Public Opinion Quarterly*, 52:190-211.

Birdwell-Pheasant, D. (1984). Personal power careers and the development of domestic structure in a small community. *American Ethnologist*, 11:699-717.

Birdwhistle, R. L. (1952). *Introduction to kinesics*. Louisville: University of Kentucky Press.

Black, D., & Riess, A. J., Jr. (1967). Patterns of behavior in police and citizen transactions. In *Studies in Crime and Law Enforcement in Major Metropolitan Areas. Field Surveys III. U.S. President's Commission on Law Enforcement and Administration of Justice* Vol. 2, pp. 1-39. Washington, DC: U.S. Government Printing Office.

Blair, E., Sudman, S., Bradburn, N. M., & Stocking, C. B. (1977). How to ask questions about drinking and sex: Response effects in measuring consumer behavior. *Journal of Marketing Research*, 14:316-321.

Blalock, H. (1979). *Social Statistics* (2nd rev. ed.). New York: McGraw-Hill.

Bochner, S. (1971). The use of unobtrusive measures in cross-cultural attitudes research. In R. M. Berndt (Ed.), *A question of choice: An Australian Aboriginal dilemma* (pp. 107-115). Nedlands, Western Australia: University of Western Australia Press.

Bochner, S. (1972). An unobtrusive approach to the study of housing discrimination against Aborigines. *Australian Journal of Psychology*, 24:335-337.

Bochner, S. (1980). Unobtrusive observation in cross-cultural experimentation. In H. C. Triandis & J. W. Berry (Eds.), *Handbook of cross-cultural psychology: Vol. 2. Methodology* (pp. 319-388). Boston: Allyn and Bacon.

Bogardus, E. S. (1933). A social distance scale. *Sociology and Social Research*, 17(January-February):265:271.

Bogdan, R. (1972). *Participant observation in organizational settings*. Syracuse, NY: Syracuse University Press.

Bolton, R. (1984). We all do it, but how? A survey of contemporary fieldnote procedure. In *Final report: Computers in ethnographic research* (Grant NIE-G-78-0062). Washington, DC: National Institute of Education. (ERIC, No. ED 1. 310/2:248173)

Borgatti, S. (1992a). *ANTHROPAC 4.0*. Columbia, SC: Analytic Technologies.

Borgatti, S. (1992b). *ANTHROPAC 4.0 methods guide*. Columbia, SC: Analytic Technologies.

Borgerhoff-Mulder, M. B., & Caro, T. M. (1985). The use of quantitative observational techniques in anthropology. *Current Anthropology*, 26:323-336.

Boserup, E. (1970). *Women's role in economic development*. London: Allen and Unwin.

Boster, J. S. (1985). Requiem for the omniscient informant: There's life in the old girl yet. In J. Dougherty (Ed.), *Directions in cognitive anthropology* (pp. 177-198). Urbana: University of Illinois Press.

Boster, J. S. (1986). Exchange of varieties and information between Aguaruna manioc cultivators. *American Anthropologist, 88*:428-436.

Boster, J. S. (1987). Agreement between biological classification systems is not dependent on cultural transmission. *American Anthropologist, 89*:914-920.

Boster, J. S., & Johnson, J. C. (1989). Form or function: A comparison of expert and novice judgments of similarity among fish. *American Anthropologist, 91*:866-889.

Boster, J. S., Johnson, J. C., & Weller, S. C. (1987). Social position and shared knowledge: Actors' perceptions of status, role, and social structure. *Social Networks, 9*:375-387.

Boyle, E., Jr. (1970). Biological patterns in hypertension by race, sex, body weight, and skin color. *Journal of the American Medical Association, 213*(10):1637-1643.

Boyle, R. P. (1970). Path analysis and ordinal data. *American Journal of Sociology, 75*:461-480.

Bradburn, N. M. (1983). Response effects. In P. H. Rossi, J. D. Wright, & A. B. Anderson (Eds.), *Handbook of Survey Research* (pp. 289-328). New York: Academic Press.

Bradburn, N. M., Ripps, L. J., & Shevell, S. K. (1987). Answering autobiographical questions: The impact of memory and inference on surveys. *Science, 236*:157-161.

Bradburn, N. M., & Sudman, S. et al. (1979). *Improving interview method and questionnaire design: Response effects to threatening questions in survey research*. San Francisco: Jossey-Bass.

Bradley, C. (1986). The sexual division of labor and the value of children. *Behavior Science Research, 20*:159-185.

Brainard, J. (1990). Nutritional status and morbidity on an irrigation project in Turkana District, Kenya. *American Journal of Human Biology, 2*:153-163.

Bridgman, P. W. (1927). *The logic of modern physics*. New York: Macmillan. (Reprinted 1980, New York: Arno.)

Brislin, R. W., Lonner, W. J., & Thorndike, R. M. (1973). *Cross-cultural research methods*. New York: Wiley.

Burling, R. (1964). Cognition and componential analysis: God's truth or hocus-pocus? *American Anthropologist, 66*:20-28.

Burling, R. (1984). *Learning a field language*. Ann Arbor: University of Michigan Press.

Burnham, M. A., & Koegel, P. (1988). Methodology for obtaining a representative sample of homeless persons: The Los Angeles skid row study. *Evaluation Review, 12*:117-152.

Burton, M. L. (1972). Semantic dimensions of occupation names. In A. K. Romney, R. N. Shepard, & S. B. Nerlove (Eds.), *Multidimensional scaling: Applications in the behavioral sciences. Vol. 2. Applications* (pp. 55-72). New York: Seminar Press.

Burton, M. L., & Nerlove, S. B. (1976). Balanced design for triad tests. *Social Science Research, 5*:247-267.

Cahnman, W. J. (1948). A note on marriage announcements in the *New York Times. American Sociological Review, 13*:96-97.

Campbell, D. T. (1957). Factors relevant to the validity of experiments in social settings. *Psychological Bulletin, 54*:297-312.

Campbell, D. T. (1974). Evolutionary epistemology. In P. A. Schlipp (Ed.), *The Library of Living Philosophers: Vol. 14. The philosophy of Karl Popper. Book I* (pp. 413-463). La Salle, IL: Open Court Publishing.

Campbell, D. T. (1975). Degrees of freedom and the case study. *Comparative Political Studies, 8*:178-193.

Campbell, D. T. (1979). Degrees of freedom and the case study. In T. D. Cook & C. S. Reichart (Eds.), *Qualitative and quantitative methods in evaluation research* (pp. 49-67). Beverly Hills, CA: Sage.

Campbell, D. T., & Boruch, R. F. (1975). Making the case for randomized assignment to treatments by considering the alternatives: Six ways in which quasi-experimental evaluations tend to underestimate effects. In C. A. Bennett & A. A. Lumsdaine (Eds.), *Evaluation and experience: Some critical issues in assessing social programs*. New York: Academic Press.

Campbell, D. T., & Ross, H. L. (1968). The Connecticut crackdown on speeding: Time-series data in quasi-experimental analysis. *Law and Society Review, 3*:33-53.

Campbell, D. T., & Stanley, J. C. (1966). *Experimental and quasi-experimental designs for research*. Chicago: Rand McNally.

Cancian, F. (1963). Informant error and native prestige ranking in Zinacantán. *American Anthropologist, 65*:1068-1075.

Cannell, C. F., Fisher, G., & Bakker, T. (1961). Reporting of hospitalization in the Health Interview Survey. *Health Statistics* (Series D, No. 4. USDHEW, PHS). Washington, DC: U.S. Government Printing Office.

Cannell, C. F., & Fowler, F. J. (1965). Comparison of hospitalization reporting in three survey procedures. In *Vital and health statistics* (Series 2, No. 8). Washington, DC: U.S. Government Printing Office.

Cannell, C. F., & Kahn, R. L. (1968). Interviewing. In G. Lindzey & E. Aronson (Eds.), *The handbook of social psychology: Vol. 2. Research Methods* (2nd ed., pp. 526-595). Reading, MA: Addison-Wesley.

Cantril, H. (1965). *The pattern of human concerns*. New Brunswick, NJ: Rutgers University Press.

Carneiro, R. L. (1962). Scale analysis as an instrument for the study of cultural evolution. *Southwestern Journal of Anthropology, 18*:149-169.

Carneiro, R. L. (1973). Scale analysis, evolutionary sequences, and the rating of cultures. In R. Naroll & R. Cohen (Eds.), *A handbook of method in cultural anthropology* (pp. 834-871). New York: Columbia University Press.

Carney, T. F. (1972). *Content analysis: A technique for systematic inference from communications*. Winnipeg: University of Manitoba Press.

Cassell, J. (Ed.). (1987). *Children in the field*. Philadelphia: Temple University Press.

Chadsey-Rusch, J., & Gonzalez, P. (1988). Social ecology of the workplace: Employers' perceptions versus direct observations. *Research in Developmental Disabilities, 9*:229-245.

Chagnon, N. (1983). *Yanomamo. The fierce people* (3rd ed.). New York: Holt, Rinehart and Winston.

Chambers, R. (1991). Rapid (or relaxed) and participatory rural appraisal—notes on practical approaches and methods. *Qualitative Research Methods Newsletter* (Tata Institute of Social Research, Deonar, Bombay, India) (2), August:11-16.

Chomsky, N. (1972). *Language and mind*. New York: Harcourt, Brace, Jovanovich.

Christiansen, G. E. (1984). *In the presence of the creator: Isaac Newton and his times*. New York: Free Press.

Cialdini et al. (1976). Basking in reflected glory: Three (football) field studies. *Journal of Personality and Social Psychology 34*:366-375.

Claiborne, W. (1984, September 22). Dowry killings show social stress in India. *Washington Post*, p. A1.

Colby, B. (1966). The analysis of culture content and the patterning of narrative concern in texts. *American Anthropologist, 68*:374-388.

Cole, D. (1983). The value of a person lies in his herzenbildung: Franz Boas' Baffin Island letter-diary, 1883-1884. In G. W. Stocking, Jr. (Ed.), *Observers observed* (pp. 13-52). Madison: University of Wisconsin Press.

Comrey, A. L. (1992). *A first course in factor analysis* (2nd ed.). Hillsdale, NJ: Erlbaum.

Comte, A. (1974). *The essential Comte* (S. Andreski, Ed., M. Clarke, Trans.). New York: Barnes and Noble.

Cone, J. D., & Foster, S. L. (1982). Direct observation in clinical psychology. In P. C. Kendall & J. N. Butcher (Eds.), *Handbook of research methods in clinical psychology* (pp. 311-354). New York: Wiley.

Conklin, H. C. (1955). Hanunóo Color Categories. *Southwestern Journal of Anthropology, 11*:339-344.

Cook, S. W. (1975). A comment on the ethical issues involved in West, Gunn, and Chernicky's "Ubiquitous Watergate: An attributional analysis." *Journal of Personality and Social Psychology, 32*:66-68.

Cook, T., & Campbell, D. T. (1979). *Quasi-experimentation. Design and analysis for field settings.* Chicago: Rand McNally.

Cotter, P. R., Cohen, J., & Coulter, P. B. (1982). Race-of-interviewer effects in telephone interviews. *Public Opinion Quarterly, 48*:278-284.

D'Andrade, R. G. (1973). Cultural constructions of reality. In L. Nader & T. W. Maretzki (Eds.), *Cultural illness and health* (pp. 115-127). Washington, DC: American Anthropological Association.

D'Andrade, R. G. (1974). Memory and the assessment of behavior. In H. M. Blalock, Jr. (Ed.), *Measurement in the social sciences* (pp. 159-186). Chicago: Aldine.

D'Andrade, R. G., Quinn, N., Nerlove, S. B., & Romney, A. K. (1972). Categories of disease in American English and Mexican Spanish. In A. K. Romney, R. Shepard, & S. B. Nerlove (Eds.), *Multidimensional scaling: Vol. 2. Applications* (pp. 9-54). New York: Seminar Press.

Davis, D. (1986). Changing self-image: Studying menopausal women in a Newfoundland fishing village. In T. L. Whitehead and M. E. Conaway (Eds.), *Self, sex and gender in cross-cultural fieldwork* (pp. 240-262). Urbana: University of Illinois Press.

Davis, J. A. (1971). *Elementary survey analysis.* Englewood Cliffs, NJ: Prentice-Hall.

Davis, N. Z. (1981). Printing and the people. In H. J. Graf (Ed.), *Literacy and social development in the West* (pp. 69-95). Cambridge, England: Cambridge University Press.

De Ghett, V. J. (1978). Hierarchical cluster analysis. In P. W. Colgan (Ed.), *Quantitative ethology* (pp. 115-144). New Brunswick, NJ: Rutgers University Press.

De Santillana, G., & Zilsel, E. (1941). *The development of rationalism and empiricism.* Chicago: University of Chicago Press.

Dehavenon, A. L. (1978). *Superordinate behavior in urban homes: A video analysis of request-compliance and food control behavior in two black and two white families living in New York City.* Unpublished doctoral dissertation, Columbia University.

Dellino, D. (1984). *Tourism: Panacea or plight. Impacts on the quality of life on Exuma, Bahamas.* Unpublished masters thesis, University of Florida.

Deloria, V. (1969). *Custer died for your sins: An Indian manifesto.* New York: Macmillan.

Descartes, R. (1960, orig. 1637). *Discourse on method; and meditations.* New York: Liberal Arts Press.

Deutscher, I. (1973). *What we say, what we do.* Glenview, IL: Scott Foresman.

DeVellis, F. F. (1991). *Scale development: Theory and applications.* Newbury Park, CA: Sage.

De Walt, B. R. (1979). *Modernization in a Mexican ejido.* New York: Cambridge University Press.

Dillman, D. A. (1978). *Mail and telephone surveys: The total design method.* New York: Wiley.

Dillman, D. A. (1983). Mail and other self-administered questionnaires. In P. H. Rossi, J. D. Wright, & A. B. Anderson (Eds.), *Handbook of survey research* (pp. 359-378). New York: Academic Press.

Divale, W. T. (1976). Female status and cultural evolution. A study in ethnographic bias. *Behavior Science Research, 11*:169-212.

Dobkin de Rios, M. (1981). Socioeconomic characteristics of an Amazon urban healer's clientele. *Social Science and Medicine, 15B*:51-63.

Dohrenwend, B. S., & Richardson, S. A. (1965). Directiveness and nondirectiveness in research interviewing: A reformulation of the problem. *Psychology Bulletin, 63*:475-485.

Doob, A. N., & Gross, A. E. (1968). Status of frustrator as an inhibitor of horn honking responses. *Journal of Social Psychology, 76*:213-218.

Doughty, P. (1979). A Latin American specialty in the world context: Urban primacy and cultural colonialism in Peru. *Urban Anthropology, 8*(3/4):383-398.

Dow, J. (1986). Universal aspects of symbolic healing: A theoretical synthesis. *American Anthropologist, 88*:56-69.

Drake, S. (1978). *Galileo at work: His scientific biography*. Chicago: University of Chicago Press.

Draper, P. (1975). Cultural pressure on sex difference. *American Ethnologist, 4*:600-616.

Dressler, W. W. (1980). Ethnomedical beliefs and patient adherence to a treatment regimen: A St. Lucian example. *Human Organization, 39*:88-91.

Droessler, J. B., & Wilke, C. (1984). Physical anthropology literature: Online access. *Reference Services Review*, Summer:22-26.

Dufour, D. (1983). Nutrition in the Northwest Amazon: Household dietary intake and time-energy expenditure. In R. B. Hames & W. T. Vickers (Eds.), *Adaptive responses of native Amazonians* (pp. 329-355). New York: Academic Press.

Duncan, O. D. (1966). Path analysis: Sociological examples. *American Journal of Sociology, 72*:1-16.

Durkheim, E. (1958). *Socialism and Saint-Simon* (A. Gouldner, Ed., C. Sattler, Trans.). Yellow Springs, OH: Antioch Press.

Easlea, B. (1980). *Witch hunting, magic, and the new philosophy*. Atlantic Highlands, NJ: Humanities Press.

Edmonson, B. (1988). This survey is garbage. *American Demographics, 10*(6):13-15.

Eisenstein, E. (1979). *The printing press as an agent of change: Communications and cultural transformations in early modern Europe* (2 vols.). Cambridge, England: Cambridge University Press.

Elifson, K. W., Runyon, R. P., & Haber, A. (1990). *Fundamentals of social statistics*. New York: McGraw-Hill.

Ember, C. (1975). Residential variation among hunter-gatherers. *Behavior Science Research, 9*:199-207.

Ember, C. (1978). Myths about hunter-gatherers. *Ethnology, 17*:439-448.

Ember, M. (1974). Warfare, sex ratio, and polygyny. *Ethnology, 13*:197-06.

Ember, M. (1984-85). Alternative predictors of polygyny. *Behavior Science Research, 19*(1-4):1-23.

Erasmus, C. J. (1955). Work patterns in a Mayo village. *American Anthropologist, 57*:322-333.

Erikson, K. T. (1967). A comment on disguised observation in sociology. *Social Problems, 14*:366-373.

Euler, R. C. (1972). *The Paiute People*. Phoenix: The Indian Tribal Series.

Evans-Pritchard, E. E. (1973). Some reminiscences and reflections on fieldwork. *Journal of the Anthropological Society of Oxford*, 4(1):1-12.

Everton, C. M., and Green, J. L. (1986). Observation as inquiry and method. In M. C. Wittrock (Ed.), *Handbook of research on teaching*. New York: Macmillan.

Fabrega, H., Jr. (1970). On the specificity of folk illness. *Southwestern Journal of Anthropology*, 26:305-314.

Fahim, H. M. (1982). *Indigenous anthropology in non-Western societies: Proceedings of a Burg-Wartenstein symposium*. Durham: University of North Carolina Press.

Fassnacht, G. (1982). *Theory and practice of observing behavior*. New York: Academic Press.

Feigl, H. (1980). Positivism. In *Encyclopaedia Brittanica* (Vol. 14). Chicago: Encyclopaedia Brittanica, Inc.

Feigl, H., & Blumberg, A. (1931). Logical positivism: A new movement in European philosophy. *Journal of Philosophy*, 28:281-296.

Feldman, R. E. (1968). Response to compatriot and foreigner who seek assistance. *Journal of Personality and Social Psychology*, 10:202-214.

Ferguson, E. A. (1983). An investigation of the relationship between the physical organization of religious shrines and the perceived malevolence or benevolence of the gods. *Behavior Science Research*, 18:185-203.

Fermi, L., & Bernardin, B. (1961). *Galileo and the scientific revolution*. New York: Basic Books.

Festinger, L. A. (1957). *A theory of cognitive dissonance*. Stanford: Stanford University Press.

Fetterman, D. M. (1989). *Ethnography step by step*. Newbury Park, CA: Sage.

Fine, G. A., & Sandstrom, K. L. (1988). *Knowing children. Participant observation with minors*. Newbury Park, CA: Sage.

Finkel, S. E., Guterbock, T. M., & Borg, M. J. (1991). Race-of-interviewer effects in a preelection poll: Virginia 1989. *Public Opinion Quarterly*, 55:313-330.

Finkler, K. (1974). *Estudio comparativo de la economía de dos comunidades de México: El papel de la irrigación*. Mexico City: Instituto Nacional Indigenista.

Finney, D. J. (1948). The Fisher-Yates test of significance in 2 × 2 contingency tables. *Biometrika*, 35:144-156.

Firth, R. (1954). Census and sociology in a primitive island community. In Problems and Methods in Demographic Studies of Preliterate Peoples. *Proceedings of the World Population Conference*. New York: United Nations.

Fischer, C. (1982). *To dwell among friends: Personal networks in town and city*. Chicago: University of Chicago Press.

Fisher, R. A. (1936). The use of multiple measurements in taxonomic problems. *Annals of Eugenics*, 7:179-188.

Fitz-Gibbon, C. T., & Morris, L. L. (1987). *How to analyze data*. Newbury Park, CA: Sage.

Fjellman, S. M., & Gladwin, H. (1985). Haitian family patterns of migration to South Florida. *Human Organization*, 44:301-312.

Fleisher, M. (1989). *Warehousing violence*. Newbury Park, CA: Sage.

Fluehr-Lobban, C. (Ed.). (1991). *Ethics and the profession of anthropology: Dialog for a new era*. Phildelphia: University of Pennsylvania Press.

Foster, G. M., Scudder, T., Colson, E., & Kemper, R. V. (Eds.). (1979). *Long-term field research in social anthropology*. New York: Academic Press.

Foster, S. L., and Cone, J. D. 1986. Design and use of direct observation. In A. R. Ciminero, K. S. Calhoun, & H. E. Adams (Eds.), *Handbook of behavioral assessment* (2nd ed., pp. 253-324). New York: Wiley.

Fowler, F. J. (1984). *Survey research methods.* Newbury Park, CA: Sage.

Fox, J. A., & Tracy, P. E. (1991). *Randomized response—A method for sensitive surveys.* Newbury Park, CA: Sage.

Fox, R. J., Crask, M. R. & Kim, J. (1988). Mail survey response rate. *Public Opinion Quarterly,* 52:467-491.

Frake, C. O. (1962). The ethnographic study of cognitive systems. In T. Gladwin & W. C. Sturtevant (Eds.), *Anthropology and human behavior* (pp. 72-85). Washington, DC: Anthropological Society of Washington.

Frake, C. O. (1964). Notes on queries in anthropology. In A. K. Romney & R. G. D'Andrade (Eds.), Transcultural studies in cognition. *American Anthropologist,* 66(3):Part II.

Freeman, D. (1983). *Margaret Mead and Samoa: The making and unmaking of an anthropological myth.* Cambridge, MA: Harvard University Press.

Freeman, L. C. (1965). *Elementary applied statistics for students in behavioral science.* New York: Wiley.

Freeman, L. C., & Romney, A. K. (1987). Words, deeds and social structure: A preliminary study of the reliability of informants. *Human Organization,* 46:330-334.

Freeman, L. C., Romney, A. K., & Freeman, S. C. (1987). Cognitive structure and informant accuracy. *American Anthropologist,* 89:310-325.

Freilich, M. (Ed.). (1977). *Marginal natives at work: Anthropologists in the field* (2nd ed.). Cambridge, MA: Schenkman.

Frey, J. H. (1989). *Survey research by telephone* (2nd ed.). Newbury Park, CA: Sage.

Frisancho, A. R. (1981). New norms of upper limb fat and muscle areas for assessment of nutritional status. *American Journal of Clinical Nutrition,* 34:2540-2545.

Fry, D. P. (1990). Play aggression among Zapotec children: Implications for the practice hypothesis. *Aggressive Behavior,* 16:321-340.

Gaito, J. (1980). Measurement scales and statistics: Resurgence of an old misconception. *Psychological Bulletin,* 87:564-567.

Galilei, Galileo (1967, orig. 1632). *Dialogue concerning the two chief world systems, Ptolomaic and Copernican* (2nd ed., S. Drake., Trans.). Berkeley: University of California Press.

Gans, H. (1968). The participant observer as a human being: Observations on the personal aspects of fieldwork. In H. S. Becker, B. Greer, D. Reisman, & R. Weiss (Eds.), *Institutions and the person.* Chicago: Aldine.

Gans, L. P., & Wood, C. S. (1985). Discriminant analysis as a method for differentiating potential acceptors of family planning: Western Samoa. *Human Organization,* 44:228-233.

Garro, L. C. (1986). Intracultural variation in folk medical knowledge: A comparison between curers and noncurers. *American Anthropologist,* 88:351-370.

Gatewood, J. B. (1983a). Loose talk: Linguistic competence and recognition ability. *American Anthropologist,* 85:378-386.

Gatewood, J. B. (1983b). Deciding where to fish: The skipper's dilemma in southeast Alaska's salmon seining. *Coastal Zone Management Journal,* 10:347-367.

Gatewood, J. B. (1984). Familiarity, vocabulary size, and recognition ability in four semantic domains. *American Ethnologist,* 11:507-527.

Gatz, M., & Hurwicz, M. (1990). Are old people more depressed? Cross-sectional data on center for epidemiological studies depression scale factors. *Psychology and Aging* 5:284-290.

Gaulin, S. C., & Boster, J. S. (1990). Dowry as female competition. *American Anthropologist,* 92:994-1005.

Geertz, C. (1973). *The interpretation of cultures.* New York: Basic Books.

Gerard, H., & Mathewson, G. C. (1966). The effects of severity of initiation on liking for a group: A replication. *Journal of Experimental and Social Psychology*, 2:278-287.

Gilbreth, F. B. (1911). *Motion study*. New York: D. Van Nostrand. (Reprinted 1972 by Hive Publishing Co., Easton, PA.)

Gladwin, C. H. (1976). A view of plan puebla: An application of hierarchical decision models. *Journal of Agricultural Economics*, 59:881-887.

Gladwin, C. H. (1980). A theory of real life choice: Applications to agricultural decisions. In P. Barlett (Ed.), *Agricultural decision making*. New York: Academic Press.

Gladwin, C. H. (1983). Contributions of decision-tree methodology to a farming systems program. *Human Organization*, 42:146-157.

Gladwin, C. H. (1989). *Ethnographic decision tree modeling*. Newbury Park, CA: Sage.

Gladwin, H. (1971). *Decision making in the Cape Coast (Fante) fishing and fish marketing system*. Unpublished doctoral disssertation, Stanford University.

Glazer, M. (1975). Impersonal sex. In L. Humphreys (Ed.), *Tearoom trade: Impersonal sex in public places*. (Enlarged edition with a retrospect on ethical issues) (pp. 213-222). Chicago: Aldine.

Golde, P. (Ed.) (1986). Women in the field: Anthropological experiences (2nd ed.). Berkeley: University of California Press.

Goldman, A. E., & McDonald, S. S. (1987). *The group depth interview: Principles and practice*. Englewood Cliffs, NJ: Prentice-Hall.

Goldstein, M. C. (1971). Stratification, polyandry, and family structure in central Tibet. *Southwestern Journal of Anthropology*, 27:65-74.

Gonzalez, N. S. (1986). The anthropologist as female head of household. In T. L. Whitehead & M. E. Conaway (Eds.), *Self, sex and gender in cross-cultural fieldwork* (pp. 84-102). Urbana: University of Illinois Press.

Good, K. (with D. Chanoff). (1991). *Into the heart*. New York: Simon and Schuster.

Goode, W. J., & Hatt, P. K. (1952). *Methods in social research*. New York: McGraw-Hill.

Goodenough, W. (1956). Componential analysis and the study of meaning. *Language*, 32:195-216.

Goodenough, W. (1965). Rethinking "status" and "role": Toward a general model of the cultural organization of social relationships. In M. Banton (Ed.), *The relevance of models for social anthropology. Association of Social Anthropology Monographs I* (pp. 1-24). London: Tavistock.

Goodman, L., & Kruskal, W. (1963). Measures of association for cross classifications III: Approximate sampling theory. *Journal of the American Statistical Association*, 58:302-322.

Goodman, R. (1960). *Teach yourself statistics*. London: English Universities Press.

Gorden, R. L. (1975). *Interviewing: Strategy, techniques, and tactics*. Homewood, IL: Dorsey.

Gould, R. A., & Potter, P. B. (1984). Use-lives of automobiles in America: A preliminary archaeological view. In R. A. Gould (Ed.), *Toward an ethnoarchaeology of modern America* 69-93. Brown University: Department of Anthropology, Research Papers in Anthropology (No. 4).

Goyder, J. (1985). Face-to-face interviews and mailed questionnaires: The net difference in response rate. *Public Opinion Quarterly*, 49:234-252.

Greenbaum, T. L. (1987). *The practical handbook and guide to focus group research*. Lexington, MA: Heath.

Griffin, J. H. (1961). *Black like me* (1st ed.). Boston: Houghton-Mifflin.

Gross, D. R. (1984). Time allocation: A tool for the study of cultural behavior. *Annual Review of Anthropology*, 13:519-558.

Gross, D. R. (1992). *Discovering anthropology*. Mountain View, CA: Mayfield.

Guilmet, G. M. (1979). Instructor reaction to verbal and nonverbal-visual behavior in the urban classroom. *Anthropology and Education Quarterly, 10*:254-266.

Guttman, L. (1950). The basis for scalogram analysis. In S. A. Stouffer et al. (Eds.), *Studies in social psychology in World War II: Vol. 4. Measurement and prediction* (pp. 60-90). Princeton: Princeton University Press.

Hadden, K., & De Walt, B. (1974). Path analysis: Some anthropological examples. *Ethnology, 13*:105-128.

Hall, E. T. (1963). A system of notation of proxemic behavior. *American Anthropologist, 65*:1003-1026.

Hall, E. T. (1966). *The hidden dimension.* New York: Doubleday.

Hames, R. B. (1979). Comparison of the efficiencies of the shotgun and the bow in neotropical forest hunting. *Human Ecology, 7*:219-252.

Hammel, E. A. (1962). Social rank and evolutionary position in a coastal Peruvian village. *Southwestern Journal of Anthropology, 18*:199-215.

Handlin, O. (1979). *Truth in history.* Cambridge, MA: Harvard University Press.

Handwerker, W. P. (1993). Simple random samples of regional populations. *Cultural Anthropology Methods, 5*(1):12.

Handwerker, W. P. (1994). Short scales for family violence (exploitation) and affection (empowerment). *Cultural Anthropology Methods, 6*(2).

Hansen, A. (1988). Correcting the underestimated frequency of the head-of-household experience for women farmers. In S. V. Poats, M. Schmink, & A. Spring (Eds.), *Gender issues in farming systems research and extension* (pp. 111-126). Boulder, CO: Westview.

Hansen, A. (1990). *Refugee self-settlement versus settlement on government schemes: The long-term consequences for security, integration and economic development of Angolan refugees (1966-1989) in Zambia.* United Nations Research Institute for Social Development, Discussion Paper 17.

Hansen, A., & McSpadden, L. A. (1993). *Self-anchoring scale, or ladder of life: A method used with diverse refugee populations.* Unpublished manuscript.

Hansley, W. E. (1974). Increasing response rates by choice of postage stamps. *Public Opinion Quarterly, 38*:280-283.

Harari, H., Harari, O., & White, R. V. (1985). The reaction to rape by American male bystanders. *Journal of Social Psychology, 125*:653-658.

Harburg, E., Gleibermann, L., Roeper, P., Schork, M. A., & Schull, W. J. (1978). Skin color, ethnicity and blood pressure I: Detroit blacks. *American Journal of Public Health, 68*(12):1177-1183.

Harris, M. (1968). *The rise of anthropological theory.* New York: Thomas Crowell.

Harris, M. (1980). *Cultural materialism: The struggle for a science of culture.* New York: Vintage Books.

Harris, M. (in press). Who are the whites? Imposed census categories and the racial demography of Brazil. *Social Forces.*

Harrison, G. G. (1976). *Sociocultural correlates of food utilization and waste in a sample of urban households.* Unpublished doctoral dissertation, University of Arizona.

Harshbarger, C. (1986). *Agricultural credit in San Vito, Costa Rica.* Unpublished masters thesis, University of Florida.

Harshbarger, C. (1994). *Farmer-grazier conflict in Cameroon.* Unpublished doctoral dissertation, University of Florida.

Hartman, J. J. (1978). Social demographic characteristics of Wichita, Sedwick County. In G. Miller & J. Skaggs (Eds.), *Metropolitan Wichita—Past, present, and future* (pp. 22-37). Lawrence: Kansas Regents Press.

Hartman, J. J., & Hedblom, J. (1979). *Methods for the social sciences.* Westport, CT: Greenwood.

Hartmann, D. P., & Wood, D. D. (1990). Observational methods. In A. S. Bellack, M. Hersen, & A. E. Kazdin (Eds.), *International handbook of behavior modification therapy* (2nd ed., pp. 107-138). New York: Plenum.

Hatch, D., & Hatch M. (1947). Criteria of social status as derived from marriage announcements in the *New York Times. American Sociological Review, 12*:396-403.

Hay, F. (1992). Tozzer Library: How to access the world's largest anthropology bibliography. *Cultural Anthropology Methods, 4*(1):1-2.

Hay, F. (1993). OCLC: An essential database for anthropological documentation. *Cultural Anthropology Methods, 5*(1):6-7.

Heath, C. (1986). *Body movement and speech in medical interaction.* New York: Cambridge University Press.

Heath, S. B. (1972). *Telling tongues.* New York: Columbia University Press.

Heatherton, T. F., & Polivy, J. (1991). Development of a scale for measuring self-esteem. *Journal of Personality and Social Psychology, 60*:895-910.

Heberlein, T. A., & Baumgartner, R. (1978). Factors affecting response rates to mailed questionnaires: A quantitative analysis of the published literature. *American Sociological Review, 43*:447-462.

Heberlein, T. A., & Baumgartner, R. (1981). Is a questionnaire necessary in a second mailing? *Public Opinon Quarterly, 45*:102-108.

Heise, D. R. (1975). *Causal analysis.* New York: Wiley.

Helm, J. (1980). Female infanticide, European diseases, and population levels among the Mackenzie Dene. *American Ethnologist, 7*:259-285.

Henley, N. M. (1969). A psychological study of the semantics of animal terms. *Journal of Verbal Learning and Verbal Behavior, 8*:176-184.

Henry, G. T. (1990). *Practical sampling.* Newbury Park, CA: Sage.

Herzog, A. R., & Bachman, J. G. (1981). Effects of questionnaire length on response quality. *Public Opinion Quarterly, 45*:549-559.

Hiatt, L. R. (1980). Polyandry in Sri Lanka: A test case for parental investment theory. *Man, 15*:583-598.

Hile, M. G. (1991). Hand-held behavioral observations: The observer. *Behavioral Assessment, 13*:187-196.

Hirschman, E. C. (1987). People as producers. *Journal of Marketing, 51*(January):98-108.

Hochstim, J. R. (1967). A critical comparison of three strategies of collecting data from households. *Journal of the American Statistical Association, 62*:976-989.

Hodge, L. G., & Dufour, D. (1991). Cross-sectional growth of young Shipibo Indian children in eastern Peru. *American Journal of Physical Anthropology, 84*:35-41.

Holsti, O. (1968). Content analysis. In G. Lindzey & E. Aronson (Eds.), *Handbook of social psychology: Vol. 2. Research Methods* (2nd ed., pp. 596-692). Reading, MA: Addison-Wesley.

Horn, W. (1960). Reliability survey: A survey on the reliability of response to an interview survey. *Het PTT-Bedriff, 10*(October):105-156 (The Hague).

House, J. S., Gerber, W., & McMichael, A. J. (1977). Increasing mail questionnaire response: A controlled replication and extension. *Public Opinion Quarterly, 41*:95-99.

Howell, N. (1981). *Inferring infanticide from Hudson's Bay Company population data 1829-1934.* University of Toronto: Department of Sociology, Structural Analysis Programme, Working Paper No. 26.

Howell, N. (1990). *Surviving fieldwork.* Washington, DC: American Anthropological Association.

Hughes, W. W. (1984). The method to our madness: The garbage project methodology. In W. L. Rathje & C. K. Rittenbaugh (Eds.), *Household refuse analysis: Theory, method, and applications in social science. American Behavioral Scientist, 28*(1, entire issue):41-50.

Humphreys, L. (1975). *Tearoom trade: Impersonal sex in public places* (Enlarged edition with a retrospect on ethical issues). Chicago: Aldine.

Hunt, R. C. (1988). Size and structure of authority in canal irrigation systems. *Journal of Anthropological Research, 44*:335-351.

Hursh-César, G., & Roy, P. (Eds.). (1976). *Third World surveys: Survey research in developing nations.* Delhi: Macmillan.

Huss-Ashmore, R., Goodman, J. L., Sibiya, T. E., & Stein, T. P. (1989). Energy expenditure of young Swazi women as measured by the doubly-labeled water method. *European Journal of Clinical Nutrition, 43*:737-748.

Husserl, E. (1970). *Logical investigations* (J. N. Findlay, Trans.). New York: Humanities Press.

Hutt, S. J., & Hutt, C. (1970). *Direct observation and measurement of behavior.* Springfield, IL: C. C. Thomas.

Hyman, H. H. (1955). *Survey design and analysis.* New York: Free Press.

Hyman, H. H., & Cobb, W. J. (1975). *Interviewing in social research.* Chicago: University of Chicago Press.

Hymes, D. H. (1964). Discussion of Burling's paper. *American Anthropologist, 66*:116-119.

ICMR et. al. (1993). *Final technical report for the coastal North Carolina socioeconomic study.* Submitted to the U.S. Dept. of the Interior, Minerals Management Service, by the Institute for Coastal and Marine Resources and East Carolina University, Department of Sociology and Anthropology, in cooperation with Impact Assessment, Inc., La Jolla, CA.

Jackson, B. (1987). *Fieldwork.* Urbana: University of Illinois Press.

Jaeger, R. M. (1984). *Sampling in education and the social sciences.* New York: Longmans.

J. B. M. (1990). Measuring children. The uses of anthropometry. *SCN News,* No. 5. Washington, DC: Society for Culture and Nutrition (American Anthropological Association).

Jehn, K. A. & Werner, O. (1993). Hapax Legomenon II: Theory, a thesaurus, and word frequency. *Cultural Anthropology Methods, 5*(1):8-10.

Jenkins, C. (1981). Patterns of growth and malnutrition among preschoolers in Belize. *American Journal of Physical Anthropology, 56*:169-178.

Johnson, A. (1975). Time allocation in a Machiguenga community. *Ethnology, 14*:310-321.

Johnson, A. (1978). *Quantification in anthropology.* Stanford: Stanford University Press.

Johnson, A. et al. (1987). *The time allocation studies checklist.* Los Angeles: UCLA Time Allocation Project. (Also in Cross-Cultural Studies of Time Allocation. New Haven, CT: Human Relations Area Files.)

Johnson, J. C. (1990). *Selecting ethnographic informants.* Newbury Park, CA: Sage.

Jones, D. J. (1973). The results of role-playing in anthropological research. *Anthropological Quarterly 46*:30-37.

Jones, N. B. (Ed.). (1972). *Ethological studies of child behavior.* Cambridge, U.K.: Cambridge University Press.

Jones, W. T. (1965). *The sciences and the humanities; Conflict and reconciliation.* Berkeley: University of California Press.

Joravsky, D. (1970). *The Lysenko affair.* Cambridge, MA: Harvard University Press.

Jordan, B. (1992). *Birth in four cultures: A cross-cultural investigation of childbirth in Yucatan, Holland, Sweden, and the United States* (4th exp. ed., rev. by R. Davis-Floyd). Prospect Heights, IL: Waveland.

Jordan, B., & Henderson, A. (1993). *Interaction analysis: Foundations and practice.* Xerox Palo Alto Research Center and Institute for Research on Learning. Working paper.

Jorgensen, D. (1989). *Participant observation.* Newbury Park, CA: Sage.

Kahn, R. L., & Cannell, C. F. (1957). *The dynamics of interviewing.* New York: Wiley.

Katz, D. (1942). Do interviewers bias polls? *Public Opinion Quarterly, 6*:248-268.

Keegan, W. (1986). The optimal foraging analysis of horticultural production. *American Anthropologist, 88*:92-107.

Keil, J. E., Tyroler, H. A., Sandifer, S. H., & Boyle, E. Jr. (1977). Hypertension: Effects of social class and racial admixture. *American Journal of Public Health, 67*(7):634-639.

Keil, J. E., Sandifer, S. H., Loadholt, C. B., & Boyle, E., Jr. (1981). Skin color and education effects on blood pressure. *American Journal of Public Health, 71*(5):532-534.

Keith, P. M. , & Wickrama, K. A. S. (1990). Use and evaluation of health services by women in a developing country: Is age important? *The Gerontologist, 30*:262-268.

Kelly, G. A. (1955). *The psychology of personal constructs.* New York: Norton.

Kendall, C., Leontsini, E., Gil, E., Cruz, F., Hudelson, P., & Pelto, P. (1990). Exploratory ethnoentomology. *Cultural Anthropology Methods, 2*(2):11.

Kendon, A. (1979). Some methodological and theoretical aspects of the use of film in the study of social interaction. In G. P. Ginsburg (Ed.), *Emerging strategies in social psychological research* (pp. 67-92). New York: Wiley.

Kent, R. N., Kanowitz, J., O'Leary, K. D., & Cheiken, M. (1977). Observer reliability as a function of circumstances of assessment. *Journal of Applied Behavioral Analysis, 10*:317-324.

Kerlinger, F. N. (1973). *Foundations of behavioral research* (2nd ed.). New York: Holt, Rinehart and Winston.

Kilbride, P. L. (1992). Unwanted children as a consequence of delocalization in modern Kenya. In J. J. Poggie et al. (Eds.), *Anthropological research: Process and application* (pp. 185-206). Albany: State University of New York Press.

Killworth, P. D., & Bernard, H. R. (1974). CATIJ: A new sociometric technique and its application to a prison living unit. *Human Organization, 33*:335-350.

Killworth, P. D., & Bernard, H. R. (1976). Informant accuracy in social network data. *Human Organization, 35*:269-296.

Killworth, P. D., Bernard, H. R., & McCarty, C. (1984). Measuring patterns of acquaintanceship. *Current Anthropology, 25*:381-398.

Kimball, S. T., & Partridge, W. T. (1979). *The craft of community study: Fieldwork dialogues.* Gainesville: University of Florida Press.

Kinsey, A. C., Pomeroy, W. B., & Martin, C. E. (1948). *Sexual behavior in the human male.* Philadelphia: Saunders.

Kirk, J., & Miller, M. (1986). *Reliability and validity in qualitative research.* Newbury Park, CA: Sage.

Kirk, L., & Burton, M. l. (1977). Meaning and context: A study of contextual shifts in meaning of Maasai personality descriptors. *American Ethnologist, 4*:734-761.

Kirk, R. E. (1982). *Experimental design* (2nd ed.). Monterrey, CA: Brooks/Cole.

Kluckhohn, K. (1945). The personal document in anthropological science. In L. Gottschalk, C. Kluckhohn, & R. Angell (Eds.), *The use of personal documents in history, anthropology, and sociology* (pp. 79-176). New York: Social Science Research Council, Bulletin 53.

Knodel, J., Havanon, N., & Pramualratana, A. (1984). Fertility transition in Thailand: A qualitative analysis. *Population and Development Review, 10*:297-315.

Koeske, G. F., & Koeske, R. D. (1989). Construct validity of the Maslach Burnout Inventory: A critical review and reconceptualization. *Journal of Applied Behavioral Science, 25*:131-144.

Koocher, G. P. (1977). Bathroom behavior and human dignity. *Journal of Personality and Social Psychology, 35*:120-121.

Koopmans, L. H. (1981). *An introduction to contemporary statistics.* Boston: Duxbury.

Kornblum, W. (1989). Introduction. In C. D. Smith & W. Kornblum (Eds.). *In the field: Readings on the field research experience* (pp. 1-8). New York: Praeger.

Korsching, P., Donnermeyer, J., & Burdge, R. (1980). Perception of property settlement payments and replacement housing among displaced persons. *Human Organization, 39*:332-333.

Krejcie, R. V., & Morgan, D. W. (1970). Determining sample size for research activities. *Educational and Psychological Measurement, 30*:607-610.

Kreuger, R. A. (1988). *Focus groups: A practical guide for applied research.* Newbury Park, CA: Sage.

Krieger, L. (1986). Negotiating gender role expectations in Cairo. In T. L. Whitehead & M. E. Conaway (Eds.), *Self, sex and gender in cross-cultural fieldwork* (pp. 117-128). Urbana: University of Illinois Press.

Krippendorf, K. (1980). *Content analysis: An introduction to its methodology.* Newbury Park, CA: Sage.

Kroeber, A. L. (1919). On the principle of order in civilization as exemplified by changes in women's fashions. *American Anthropologist, 21*:235-263.

Kronenfeld, D. B., Kronenfeld, J., & Kronenfeld, J. E. (1972). Toward a science of design for successful food service. *Institutions and Volume Feeding, 70*(11), June 1:38-44.

Kunitz, S. J., Temkin-Greener, H., Broudy, D., & Haffner, M. (1981). Determinants of hospital utilization and surgery on the Navajo Indian Reservation, 1972-1978. *Social Science and Medicine, 15B*:71-79.

Labovitz, S. (1971a). The assignment of numbers to rank order categories. *American Sociological Review, 35*:515-524.

Labovitz, S. (1971b). The zone of rejection: Negative thoughts on statistical inference. *Pacific Sociological Review, 14*:373-381.

Labovitz, S. (1972). Statistical usage in sociology. *Sociological Methods and Research, 3*:14-37.

La Pierre, R. T. (1934). Attitudes versus actions. *Social Forces, 13*:230-237.

Lastrucci, C. L. (1963). *The scientific approach.* Cambridge, MA: Schenkman.

Latané, B., & Darley, J. M. (1968). Group inhibition of bystander intervention in emergencies. *Journal of Personality and Social Psychology, 10*:215-221.

Laumann, E. O., & Pappi, F. U. (1974). New directions in the study of community elites. *American Journal of Sociology, 38*:212-230.

Lavrakas, P. J. (1987). *Telephone survey methods.* Newbury Park, CA: Sage.

Lazarsfeld, P. F. (1954). *Mathematical thinking in the social sciences.* Glencoe, IL: Free Press.

Lazarsfeld, P. F. (1982). *The varied sociology of Paul F. Lazarsfeld: Writings.* New York: Columbia University Press.

Lazarsfeld, P., Pasanella, A., & Rosenberg, M. (Eds.). (1972). *Continuities in the language of social research.* New York: Free Press.

Lazarsfeld, P. F., & Rosenberg, M. (1955). *The language of social research.* Glencoe, IL: Free Press.

Lea, K. L. (1980). Francis Bacon. *Encyclopaedia Britannica* (Vol. 2). Chicago: Encyclopaedia Britannica, Inc.

Leach, E. (1967). An anthropologist's reflection on a social survey. In D. C. Jongmans & P. C. Gutkind (Eds.), *Anthropologists in the field* (pp. 75-88). Assen: Van Gorcum.

Le Compte, M. D., & Preissle, J. (with R. Tesch). (1993). *Ethnography and qualitative design in educational research* (2nd ed.). San Diego: Academic Press.

Lee, R. B. (1968). What hunters do for a living, or how to make out on scarce resources. In R. B. Lee & I. Devore (Eds.), *Man the hunter* (pp. 30-48). Chicago: Aldine.

Lehner, P. N. (1979). *Handbook of ethological methods.* New York: Garland STPM.

Leung, W., & Flores, M. (1961). *Food consumption table for use in Latin America.* Bethesda: INCAP-ICNND.

Levinson, D. (Ed.). (1978). *A guide to social theory: Worldwide cross-cultural tests.* New Haven, CT: HRAF Press.

Lewis, O. (1961). *The children of Sánchez.* New York: Random House.

Lewis, O. (1965). *La Vida: A Puerto Rican family in the culture of poverty—San Juan and New York.* New York: Random House.

Lieberman, D., & Dressler, W. W. (1977). Bilingualism and cognition of St. Lucian disease terms. *Medical Anthropology, 1*:81-110.

Likert, R. (1932). A technique for the measurement of attitudes. *Archives of Psychology,* Vol. 140.

Linton, M. (1975). Memory for real-world events. In D. A. Norman & D. E. Rumelhart (Eds.), *Explorations in cognition* (pp. 376-403). San Francisco: Freeman.

Loether, D., & McTavish, H. (1974). *Descriptive and inferential statistics: An introduction.* Boston: Allyn and Bacon.

Lofland, J. (1971). *Analyzing social settings. A guide to qualitative observation and analysis.* Belmont, CA: Wadsworth.

Lofland, J. (1976). *Doing social life.* New York: Wiley.

Loftus, E. F., & Marburger, W. (1983). Since the eruption of Mt. St. Helens, has anyone beaten you up? Improving the accuracy of retrospective reports with landmark events. *Memory and Cognition, 11*:114-120.

Longabaugh, R. (1963). A category system for coding interpersonal behavior as social exchange. *Sociometry, 26*:319-344.

Longabaugh, R. (1980). The systematic observation of behavior in naturalistic settings. In H. C. Triandis & J. W. Berry (Eds.), *Handbook of cross-cultural psychology: Vol. 2. Methodology* (pp. 57-126). Boston: Allyn and Bacon.

Lowe, J. W. G., & Lowe, E. D. (1982). Cultural pattern and process: A study of stylistic change in women's dress. *American Anthropologist, 84*:521-544.

Lowie, R. (1914). Social organization. *American Journal of Sociology, 20*:68-97.

Lundberg, G. A. (1964). *Foundations of sociology.* New York: David McKay.

Mach, E. (1976). *Knowledge and error: Sketches on the psychology of enquiry* (B. McGuiness, Ed., T. J. McCormack & P. Foulkes, Trans.). Boston: D. Reidel.

Malinowski, B. (1967). *A diary in the strict sense of the term.* New York: Harcourt, Brace & World.

Marchione, T. J. (1980). Factors associated with malnutrition in the children of Western Jamaica. In N. Jerome, R. Kandel & G. Pelto (Eds.), *Nutritional anthropology* (pp. 223-275). Pleasantville, NY: Redgrave.

Margolis, M. (1984). *Mothers and such.* Berkeley: University of California Press.

Markie, P. J. (1986). *Descartes' gambit.* Ithaca: Cornell University Press.

Marquis, G. S. (1990). Fecal contamination of shanty town toddlers in households with non-corralled poultry, Lima, Peru. *American Journal of Public Health, 80*:146-150.

Marriott, B. (1991). *The use of social networks by naval officers' wives.* Unpublished doctoral dissertation, University of Florida.

Marshall, P. (1993). ZY 5.0 for Windows. *InfoWorld, 15*(21), May 24:127.

Matarazzo, J. (1964). Interviewer mm-humm and interviewee speech duration. *Psychotherapy: Theory, Research and Practice, 1*:109-114.

Mathews, H. (1985). *The Weeping Woman: Variation and homogeneity in folk theories of gender in a Mexican community.* Paper read at the annual meetings of the American Anthropological Association, Washington, DC.

McCall, G. (1978). *Observing the law: Field methods in the study of crime and the criminal justice system.* New York: Free Press.

McGrew, W. C. (1972). *An ethological study of children's behavior.* New York: Academic Press.

McNabb, S. L. (1990). The uses of "inaccurate" data: A methodological critique and applications of Alaska Native data. *American Anthropologist, 92*:116-129.

Mead, M. (1986). Fieldwork in Pacific islands, 1925-1967. In P. Golde (Ed.), *Women in the field: Anthropological experiences* (2nd ed. pp. 293-332). Berkeley: University of California Press.

Means, B., Nigam, A., & Zarrow M. et al. (1989). *Autobiographical memory for health related events* (National Center for Health Statistics, Vital and Health Statistics, Series 6, No, 2). Washington, DC: U.S. Government Printing Office.

Merton, R. K. (1987). The focused interview and focus groups. *Public Opinion Quarterly, 51*:550-566.

Merton, R. K., Fiske, M., & Kendall, P. L. (1956). *The focused interview: A manual of problems and procedures.* Glencoe, IL: Free Press.

Messerschmidt, D. A. (Ed.). (1981). *Anthropologists at home in North America: Methods and issues in the study of one's own society.* New York: Cambridge University Press.

Metzger, D. G., & Williams, G. E. (1966). Procedures and results in the study of native categories: Tseltal firewood. *American Anthropologist, 68*:389-407.

Meyerhoff, B. (1989). So what do you want from us here? In C. D. Smith & W. Kornblum (Eds.), *In the field: Readings on the field research experience* (pp. 83-90). New York: Praeger.

Middlemist, R. D., Knowles, E. S., & Matter, C. F. (1976). Personal space invasion in the lavatory: Suggestive evidence for arousal. *Journal of Personality and Social Psychology, 33*:541-546.

Middlemist, R. D., Knowles, E. S., & Matter, C. F. (1977). What to do and what to report: A reply to Koocher. *Journal of Personality and Social Psychology, 35*:122-124.

Miles, M. B. (1983). *Qualitative data as an attractive nuisance: The problem of analysis.* Newbury Park, CA: Sage.

Miles, M. B., & Huberman, A. M. (1994). *Qualitative data analysis.* Newbury Park, CA: Sage.

Mileski, M. (1971). Courtroom encounters: An observation study of a lower criminal court. *Law and Society Review, 5*:473-538.

Milgram, S. (1963). Behavioral study of obedience. *Journal of Abnormal and Social Psychology, 67*:371-378.

Milgram, S. (1967). The small-world problem. *Psychology Today, 1*:60-67.

Milgram, S. (1969). The lost-letter technique. *Psychology Today, 3*:30-33, 66-68.

Milgram, S., Mann, L., & Harter, S. (1965). The lost-letter technique: A tool of social research. *Public Opinion Quarterly, 29*:437-438.

Mill, J. S. (1866). *Auguste Comte and positivism.* Philadelphia: Lippincott.

Miller, D. C. (1991). *Handbook of research design and social measurement* (5th ed.). Newbury Park, CA: Sage.

Miller, E. (1986). *Street women.* Philadelphia: Temple University Press.

Miller, J. L., Rossi, P. H., & Simpson, J. E. (1991). Felony punishments: A factorial survey of perceived justice in criminal sentencing. *Journal of Criminal Law and Criminology, 82*:396-422.

Milliman, R. (1986). The influence of background music on the behavior of restaurant patrons. *Journal of Consumer Research, 13*:286-289.

Minadeo, R. (1969). *The lyre of science: Form and meaning in Lucretius' De Rerum Natura.* Detroit: Wayne State University Press.

Mizes, J. S., Fleece, E. L., & Ross, C. (1984). Incentives for increasing return rates: Magnitude levels, response bias, and format. *Public Opinion Quarterly, 48*:794-800.

Morgan, D. L. (1988). *Successful focus groups.* Newbury Park, CA: Sage.

Morgan, D. L. (1989). Adjusting to widowhood: Do social networks make it easier? *The Gerontologist, 29*:101-107.

Morgan, D. L., & Spanish, M. T. (1985). Social interaction and the cognitive organization of health-relevant behavior. *Sociology of Health and Illness, 7*:401-422.

Morris, W. W., Buckwalter, K. C., Cleary, T. A., Gilmer, J. S., Hatz, D. L., & Studer, M. (1990). Refinement of the Iowa Self-Assessment Inventory. *The Gerontologist, 30*:243-248.

Moss, L., & Goldstein, H. (Eds.) 1979. *The Recall Method in Social Surveys.* London: University of London Institute of Education.

Mueller, J. H., Schuessler, K. F., & Costner, H. L. (1970). *Statistical reasoning in sociology* (2nd ed.). Boston: Houghton Mifflin.

Munroe, R. L., Munroe, R. H., Michelson, C., Koel, A., Bolton, R., & Bolton, C. (1983). Time allocation in four societies. *Ethnology, 22*:355-370.

Murdock, G. P. (1971). *Outline of cultural materials* (4th rev. ed., 5th printing, with modifications). New Haven, CT: Human Relations Area Files.

Murdock, G. P., & White, D. R. (1969). Standard cross-cultural sample. *Ethnology, 8*:329-369.

Murphy, G., Murphy, L. B., & Newcomb, T. M. (1937). *Experimental social psychology.* New York: Harper and Brothers.

Murtagh, M. (1985). The practice of arithmetic by American grocery shoppers. *Anthropology and Education Quarterly, 16*:186-192.

Mwango, E. (1986). *The sources of variation in farmer adoption of government recommended technologies in the Lilongwe rural development program area of Central Malawi.* Unpublished master's thesis, University of Florida.

Nachman, S. R. (1984). Lies my informants told me. *Journal of Anthropological Research, 40*:536-555.

Nachmias, D., & Nachmias, C. (1976). *Research methods in the social sciences.* New York: St. Martin's Press.

Naroll, R. (1962). *Data quality control.* New York: Free Press.

Nederhof, A. J. (1985). A survey on suicide: Using a mail survey to study a highly threatening topic. *Quality and Quantity, 19*:293-302.

Neter, J., & Waksberg, J. (1964). A study of response errors in expenditures data from household interviews. *Journal of the American Statistical Association, 59*:18-55.

Newman, K. S. (1986). Symbolic dialects and generations of women: Variations in the meaning of post-divorce downward mobility. *American Ethnologist, 13*:230-252.

New York Times. (1986, April 7). p. B3.

Niebel, B. W. (1982). *Motion and time study* (7th ed.). Homewood, IL: Irwin.

Nisbet, R. A. (1980). *The history of the idea of progress.* New York: Basic Books.

Nkwi, P. (1992). *Report to the Population Action Program for the Improvement of Quality of Life in Rural Communities.* Yaounde: World Bank, African Population Advisory Council.

Oboler, R. S. (1985). *Women, power, and economic change: The Nandi of Kenya.* Stanford: Stanford University Press.

O'Connell, J. F., & Hawkes, K. (1984). Food choice and foraging sites among the Alyawara. *Journal of Anthropological Research, 40*:504-535.

Ohtsuka, R. (1989). Hunting activity and aging among the Gidra Papuans: A biobehavioral analysis. *American Journal of Physical Anthropology, 80*.31-39.

Olson, W. C. (1929). *The measurement of nervous habits in normal children*. Minneapolis: University of Minnesota Press.

Osgood, C. E., Suci, D. J., & Tannenbaum, P. H. (1957). *The measurement of meaning*. Urbana: University of Illinois Press.

Oskenberg, L., Coleman, L., & Cannell, C. F. (1986). Interviewers' voices and refusal rates in telephone surveys. *Public Opinion Quarterly 50*:97-111.

Ostrander, S. A. (1980). Upper-class women: Class consciousness as conduct and meaning. In G. W. Domhoff (Ed.), *Power structure research* (pp. 73-96). Beverly Hills: Sage.

Otterbein, K. (1969). Basic steps in conducting a cross-cultural study. *Behavior Science Notes, 4*:221-236.

Paredes, J. A. (1974). The emergence of contemporary Eastern Creek Indian identity. In T. K. Fitzgerald (Ed.), Social and cultural identity: Problems of persistence and change. *Southern Anthropological Society Proceedings* (No. 8, pp. 63-80). Athens: University of Georgia Press.

Paredes, J. A. (1992)."Practical history" and the Poarch Creeks: A meeting ground for anthropologist and tribal leaders. In J. J. Poggie et al. (Eds.), *Anthropological research: Process and application* (pp. 211-226). Albany: State University of New York Press.

Passin, H. (1951). The development of public opinion research in Japan. *International Journal of Opinion and Attitude Research, 5*:20-30.

Paterson, A. M. (1973). *Francis Bacon and socialized science*. Springfield, IL: Charles C. Thomas.

Pausewang, S. (1973). *Methods and concepts of social research in a rural and developing society*. Munich: Weltforum Verlag.

Payne, S. L. (1951). *The art of asking questions*. Princeton: Princeton University Press.

Pearson, J. (1990). Estimation of energy expenditure in Western Samoa, American Samoa, and Honolulu by recall interviews and direct observation. *American Journal of Human Biology, 2*:313-326.

Pederson, J. (1987). Plantation women and children: Wage labor, adoption, and fertility in the Seychelles. *Ethnology, 26*:51-62.

Pelto, P. (1970). *Anthropological research: The structure of inquiry*. New York: Harper and Row.

Pelto, P., & Pelto, G. (1978). *Anthropological research: The structure of inquiry*. New York: Cambridge University Press.

Perchonock, N., & Werner, O. (1969). Navajo systems of classification: Some implications of food. *Ethnology, 8*:229-242.

Peterson, R. A. (1984). Asking the age question. *Public Opinon Quarterly, 48*:379-383.

Pike, K. (1956). Towards a theory of the structure of human behavior. In *Estudios antropológicos en homenaje al doctor Manuel Gamio*. Mexico City: Dirección General de Publicaciones, Universidad Nacional Autónoma de México.

Pike, K. (1967). *Language in relation to a unified theory of the structure of human behavior* (2nd. rev. ed.). The Hague: Mouton.

Piliavin, I. M., Rodin, J., & Piliavin, J. A. (1969). Good samaritanism: An underground phenomenon? *Journal of Personality and Social Psychology, 13*:289-299.

Plattner, S. (1982). Economic decision making in a public marketplace. *American Ethnologist, 9*:399-420.

Poggie, J., Jr. (1972). Toward quality control in key informant data. *Human Organization, 31*:23-30.

Poggie, J., Jr. (1979). Small-scale fishermen's beliefs about success and development: A Puerto Rican case. *Human Organization, 38*:6-11.

Pool, I. de S. (1959). *Trends in content analysis.* Urbana: University of Illinois Press.

Powdermaker, H. (1966). *Stranger and friend: The way of an anthropologist.* New York: Norton.

Pramualratana, A., Napaporn, H., & Knodel, J. (1985). Exploring the normative basis for age at marriage in Thailand: An example from focus group research. *Journal of Marriage and the Family, 47*:203-210.

Quételet, A. (1969, orig. 1842). *A treatise on man and the development of his faculties.* New York: Burt Franklin, Research Source Works Series, #247. Also Gainesville, FL: Scholars' Facsimiles and Reprints.

Quinn, N. (1978). Do Mfantse fish sellers estimate probabilities in their heads? *American Ethnologist, 5*:206-226.

Radin, P. (1966, orig. 1933). *The method and theory of ethnology.* New York: Basic Books.

Rand Corporation. (1965). *A million random digits with 100,000 normal deviates.* Glencoe, IL: Free Press.

Rappaport, R. (1990). Foreword. In N. Howell (Ed.), *Surviving fieldwork* (pp. vii-viii). Washington, DC: American Anthropological Association.

Rathje, W. L. (1979). Trace measures. Garbage and other traces. In L. Sechrest (Ed.), *Unobtrusive measurement today* (pp. 75-91). San Francisco: Jossey-Bass.

Rathje, W. L. (1984). The garbage decade. In W. L. Rathje & C. K. Rittenbaugh (Eds.), *Household Refuse Analysis: Theory, Method, and Applications in Social Science. American Behavioral Scientist, 28*(1, entire issue):9-29.

Rathje, W. L. (1992). Garbage demographics. *American Demographics, 14*(5):50-54.

Raver, S. A., & Peterson, A. M. (1988). Comparison of teacher estimates and direct observation of spontaneous language in preschool handicapped children. *Child Study Journal, 18*:277-284.

Reed, T. W., & Stimson, R. J. (Eds.). (1985). *Survey interviewing. Theory and techniques.* Sydney: Allen & Unwin.

Reese, S. D., Danielson, W. A., Shoemaker, P. J. et al. (1986). Ethnicity-of-interviewer effects among Mexican-American and Anglos. *Public Opinion Quarterly, 50*:563-572.

Reiss, A. J., Jr. (1971). *The police and the public.* New Haven, CT: Yale University Press.

Reiss, N. (1985). *Speech act taxonomy.* Philadelphia: John Benjamins.

Repp, A. C., Nieminen, G. S., Olinger, E., & Brusca, R. (1988). Direct observation: Factors affecting the accuracy of observers. *Exceptional Children, 55*:29-36.

Richardson, J., & Kroeber, A. L. (1940). Three centuries of women's dress fashions: A quantitative analysis. *Anthropological Records, 5*(2):111-153.

Rittenbaugh, C. K., & Harrison, G. G. (1984). Reactivity of garbage analysis. In W. L. Rathje & C. K. Rittenbaugh (Eds.), *Household refuse analysis: Theory, Method, and Applications in Social Science. American Behavioral Scientist, 28*(1, entire issue):51-70.

Robbins, M. C., Williams, A. V., Killbride, P. L., & Pollnac, R. B. (1969). Factor analysis and case selection in complex societies. *Human Organization, 28*:227-234.

Roberts, J. M. (1965, orig. 1956). *Zuni daily life.* Behavior Science Reprints. New Haven, CT: HRAF Press.

Roberts, J. M., & Chick, G. E. (1979). Butler County eight-ball: A behavioral space analysis. In J. H. Goldstein (Ed.), *Sports, games, and play: Social and psychological viewpoints* (pp. 65-100). Hillsdale, NJ: Erlbaum.

Roberts, J. M., Golder, T. V., & Chick, G. E. (1981). Judgment, oversight, and skill: A cultural analysis of P-3 pilot error. *Human Organization, 39*:5-21.

Roberts, J. M., & Nattrass, S. (1980). Women and trapshooting: Competence and expression in a game of physical skill with chance. In H. B. Schwartzman (Ed.), *Play and culture* (pp. 262-290). West Point, NY: Leisure Press.

Robinson, D., & Rhode, S. (1946). Two experiments with an anti-Semitism poll. *Journal of Abnormal and Social Psychology, 41*:136-144.

Robinson, W. S. (1950). Ecological correlations and the behavior of individuals. *American Sociological Review, 15*:351-357.

Rogoff, B. (1978). Spot observation: An introduction and examination. *Quarterly Newsletter of the Institute for Comparative Human Development, 2*(2), April:21-26.

Rohner, R. (1969). *The ethnography of Franz Boas.* Chicago: University of Chicago Press.

Rohner, R., De Walt, B. R., & Ness, R. C. (1973). Ethnographer bias in cross-cultural research. *Behavior Science Notes, 8*:275-317.

Romney, A. K. (1989). Quantitative models, science and cumulative knowledge. *Journal of Quantitative Anthropology, 1*:153-223.

Romney, A. K., & D'Andrade, R. G. (Eds.). (1964). Cognitive aspects of English kin terms. In *Transcultural Studies in Cognition. American Anthropologist, 66* (3, part 2, entire issue):146-170.

Romney, A. K., Shepard, R. N., & Nerlove, S. B. (Eds.). (1972). *Multidimensional scaling: Vol. 2. Applications.* New York: Seminar Press.

Romney, A. K., Weller, S. C., & Batchelder, W. H. (1986). Culture as consensus: A theory of culture and informant accuracy. *American Anthropologist 88*:313-338.

Rosenberg, M. (1968). *The logic of survey analysis.* New York: Basic Books.

Rosenshine, B., & Furst, N. (1973). The use of direct observation to study teaching. In R. W. Travers (Ed.), *Second handbook of research on teaching* (pp. 122-183). Chicago: Rand McNally.

Rosenthal, R., & Jacobson, L. (1968). *Pygmalion in the classroom.* New York: Holt, Rinehart and Winston.

Rosenthal, R., & Rubin, D. B. (1978). Interpersonal expectancy effects: The first 345 studies. *The Behavioral and Brain Sciences, 3*:377-415.

Rossi, P. H., & Nock, S. L. (1982). *Measuring social judgments: The factorial survey approach.* Newbury Park, CA: Sage.

Rossi, P. H., Wright, J. D., & Anderson, A. B. (1983). Sample surveys: History, current practice, and future prospects. In P. H. Rossi, J. D. Wright, & A. B. Anderson (Eds.), *Handbook of survey research* (pp. 1-20). New York: Wiley.

Rothschild, R. F. (1981). What happened in 1780? *Harvard Magazine, 83* (January-February): 20-27.

Rummel, R. J. (1970). *Applied factor analysis.* Evanston: Northwestern University Press.

Runyon, R. P., & Haber, A. (1991). *Fundamentals of behavioral statistics* (7th ed.). New York: McGraw-Hill.

Rushforth, S. (1982). A structural semantic analysis of Bear Lake Athapaskan kinship classification. *American Ethnologist, 9*:559-577.

Ryan, G. W. (1993a). Using WordPerfect to macros to handle field notes. *Cultural Anthropology Methods, 5*(1):10-11.

Ryan, G. W. (1993b). Using styles in WordPerfect as a template for your field notes. *Cultural Anthropology Methods, 5*(3):8-9.

Ryan, G. W., & Martínez, H. (1993). *Can we predict what mothers do? Modeling treatments for infantile diarrhea in rural Mexico.* Unpublished manuscript.

Sagar, H. A., & Schofield, J. W. (1980). Racial and behavioral cues in black and white children's perceptions of ambiguously aggressive acts. *Journal of Personality and Social Psychology, 39*:590-598.

Sanjek, R. (1978). A network method and its uses in urban ethnography. *Human Organization, 37*:257-268.

Sanjck, R. (1990). *Fieldnotes.* Ithaca: Corncll Univcrsity Prcss.

Sankoff, G. (1971). Quantitative analysis of sharing and variability in a cognitive model. *Ethnology, 10*:389-408.

Sapir, E. (1968, orig. 1916). *Time perspectives in aboriginal American culture.* New York: Johnson Reprint Corporation. (Originally published by Geological Survey of Canada, Anthropological Series, No. 13.)

Sarkar, N. K., & Tambiah, S. J. (1957). *The disintegrating village.* Colombo, Sri Lanka: Ceylon University Socio-Economic Survey of Pata Dumbara.

Sarton, G. (1935). Quételet (1796-1874). *Isis, 23*:6-24.

Scaglion, R. (1986). The importance of nighttime observations in time allocation studies. *American Ethnologist, 13*:537-545.

Schatzman, L., & Strauss, A. (1973). *Field research. Strategies for a natural sociology.* Englewood Cliffs, NJ: Prentice-Hall.

Scheers, N. J., & Dayton, C. M. (1987). Improved estimation of academic cheating behavior using the randomized response technique. *Research in Higher Education, 26*:61-69.

Scheper-Hughes, N. (1983). Introduction: The problem of bias in androcentric and feminist anthropology. In N. Scheper-Hughes (Ed.), Confronting problems of bias in feminist anthropology. *Women's Studies, 10*:109-116 (special issue).

Scherer, S. E. (1974). Proxemic behavior of primary-school children as a function of the socioeconomic class and subculture. *Journal of Personality and Social Psychology, 29*:800-805.

Schiller, F. C. S. (1969, orig. 1903). *Humanism: Philosophical essays.* Freeport, NY: Books for Libraries Press.

Schlegel, A., & Barry, H., III (1986). The consequences of female contribution to subsistence. *American Anthropologist, 88*:142-150.

Schofield, J. W., & Anderson, K. (1987). Combining quantitative and qualitative components of research on ethnic identity and intergroup relations. In J. S. Phinney & M. J. Rotheram (Eds.), *Children's ethnic socialization: Pluralism and development* (pp. 252-273). Newbury Park, CA: Sage.

Schuman, H., & Presser, S. (1979). The open and closed question. *American Sociological Review, 44*:692-712.

Schuster, J. A. (1977). *Descartes and the scientific revolution.* Princeton: Princeton University Press.

Schutz, A. (1962). *Collected papers I: The problem of social reality.* The Hague: Martinus Nijhoff.

Schwab, W. B. (1954). An experiment in methodology in a West African urban community. *Human Organization, 13*:13-19.

Science. (1972). The Brawling Bent. *Science, 175*(4028), March 24:1346-1347.

Scrimshaw, S. C. M., & Hurtado, E. (1987). *Rapid assessment procedures for nutrition and primary health care.* Los Angeles: University of California at Los Angeles, Latin American Center Publications.

Sechrest, L., & Flores, L. (1969). Homosexuality in the Philippines and the United States: The handwriting on the wall. *Journal of Social Psychology, 79*:3-12.

Sechrest, L., & Phillips, M. (1979). Unobtrusive measures: An overview. In L. Sechrest (Ed.), *Unobtrusive Measurement Today* (pp. 1-17). San Francisco: Jossey-Bass.

Shaner, W. W., Phillip, P. F., & Schmehl, W. R. (1982). *Farming systems research and development: Guidelines for developing countries.* Boulder: Westview Press.

Sharff, J. W. (1979). *Patterns of authority in two urban Puerto Rican households.* Unpublished doctoral dissertation, Columbia University.

Shariff, A. (1991). Focus group interviews: A research methodology for assessing the quality of primary health care and family planning programme. *Qualitative Research Methods Newsletter* (Tata Institute of Social Research, Deonar, Bombay, India) (3), December:12-19.

Sheatsley, P. B. (1983). Questionnaire construction and item wording. In P. H. Rossi, J. D. Wright & A. B. Anderson (Eds.), *Handbook of survey research* (pp. 195-230). New York: Wiley.

Shelley, G. A. (1992). *The social networks of people with end-stage renal disease: Comparing hemodialysis and peritoneal dialysis patients.* Unpublished doctoral dissertation, University of Florida.

Shelley, G. A., Bernard, H. R. & Killworth, P. D. (1990). Information flow in social networks *Journal of Quantitative Anthropology*, 2:201-225.

Shweder, R., & D'Andrade, R. (1980). The systematic distortion hypothesis. In R. Shweder (Ed.), *Fallible judgment in behavioral research* (pp. 37-58). San Francisco: Jossey-Bass.

Siegel, S. (1956). *Nonparametric statistics for the behavioral sciences.* New York: McGraw-Hill.

Silverman, S. F. (1966). An ethnographic approach to social stratification: Prestige in a Central Italian community. *American Anthropologist*, 68:899-921.

Simpson, J. A., & Gangstad, S. W. (1991). Individual differences in sociosexuality: Evidence for convergent and discriminant validity. *Journal of Personality and Social Psychology*, 60:870-883.

Sirken, M. G. (1972). *Designing forms for demographic surveys.* Chapel Hill: Laboratories for Population Statistics, University of North Carolina.

Skinner, B. F. (1957). *Verbal behavior.* New York: Appleton-Century-Crofts.

Smith, L. D. (1986). *Behaviorism and logical positivism.* Stanford: Stanford University Press.

Smith, M. E. (1986). The role of social stratification in the Aztec empire: A view from the provinces. *American Anthropologist*, 88:70-91.

Smith, M. G. (1962). *West Indian family structure.* Seattle: University of Washington Press.

Smith, T. W. (1989). The hidden 25 percent: An analysis of nonresponse on the 1980 General Social Survey. In E. Singer & S. Presser (Eds.), *Survey research methods* (pp. 50-68). Chicago: University of Chicago Press.

Snider, J. G., & Osgood, C. E. (Eds.). (1969). *Semantic differential technique.* Chicago: Aldine.

Snow, C. P. (1964). *The two cultures: And a second look.* Cambridge, U.K.: Cambridge University Press.

Sokolovsky, J., Cohen, C., Berger, D., & Geiger, J. (1978). Personal networks of ex-mental patients in a Manhattan SRO hotel. *Human Organization*, 37:5-15.

Soskin, W. F. (1963). *Verbal interaction in a young married couple.* University of Kansas Press.

Soskin, W. F., & John, V. (1963). The study of spontaneous talk. In R. G. Barker (Ed.), *The stream of behavior: Explorations of its structure and content* (pp. 228-282). New York: Appleton-Century-Crofts.

Spector, P. E. (1992). *Summated rating scale construction.* Newbury Park, CA: Sage.

Spradley, J. P. (1979). *The ethnographic interview*. New York: Holt, Rinehart and Winston.

Spradley, J. P. (1980). *Participant observation*. New York: Holt, Rinehart and Winston.

Springle, S. (1986). Measuring social values. *Journal of Consumer Research, 13*:100-113.

Sproull, L. S. (1981). Managing education programs: A micro-behavioral analysis. *Human Organization, 40*:113-122.

Squire, P. (1988). Why the 1936 "Literary Digest" poll failed. *Public Opinion Quarterly, 52*:125-133.

Srinivas, M. N. (1979). The fieldworker and the field: A village in Karnataka. In M. N. Srinivas, A. M. Shah, & E. A. Ramaswamy (Eds.), *The fieldworker and the field* (pp. 19-28). Delhi: Oxford University Press.

Stearman, A. M. (1989). Yuquí foragers in the Bolivian Amazon: Subsistence strategies, prestige, and leadership in an acculturating society. *Journal of Anthropological Research, 45*:219-244.

Stein, T. P., Johnston, F. E., & Greiner, L. (1988). Energy expenditure and socioeconomic status in Guatemala as measured by the doubly labelled water method. *American Journal of Clinical Nutrition, 47*:196-200.

Stemmer, N. (1990). Skinner's "Verbal Behavior," Chomsky's review, and mentalism. *Journal of the Experimental Analysis of Behavior, 54*:307-316.

Stephenson, J. B., & Greer, L. S. (1981). Ethnographers in their own cultures: Two Appalachian cases. *Human Organization, 30*:333-343.

Sterk, C. (1989). Prostitution, drug use, and AIDS. In C. D. Smith & W. Kornblum (Eds.), *In the field: Readings on the field research experience* (pp. 91-100). New York: Praeger.

Stevens, S. S. (1946). On the theory of measurement. *Science, 103*:677-680.

Stewart, D. W., & Shamdasani, P. N. (1990). *Focus groups: Theory and practice*. Newbury Park, CA: Sage.

Stone, P. J., Dunphy, D. C., Smith, M. S., & Ogilvie, D. M. (1966). *The general inquirer: A computer approach to content analysis*. Cambridge, MA: MIT Press.

Storer, N. W. (1966). *The social system of science*. New York: Holt, Rinehart and Winston.

Stouffer, S. A. et al. (1947-50). *Studies in social psychology in World War II* (4 vols). Princeton: Princeton University Press.

Strauss, A., & Corbin, J. (1990). *Basics of qualitative research*. Newbury Park, CA: Sage.

Streib, G. F. (1952). Use of survey methods among the Navaho. *American Anthropologist, 54*:30-40.

Stunkard, A., & Kaplan, D. (1977). Eating in public places: A review of reports of the direct observation of eating behavior. *International Journal of Obesity, 1*:89-101.

Sturtevant, W. C. (1959). A technique for ethnographic note-taking. *American Anthropologist, 61*:677-678.

Stycos, J. M. (1955). *Family and fertility in Puerto Rico*. New York: Columbia University Press.

Stycos, J. M. (1960). Sample surveys for social science in underdeveloped areas. In R. N. Adams & J. J. Preiss (Eds.), *Human organization research* (pp. 375-388). Homewood, IL: Dorsey.

Sudman, S. (1976). *Applied sampling*. New York: Academic Press.

Sudman, S., & Bradburn, N. M. (1974). *Response effects in surveys: Review and synthesis*. Chicago: Aldine.

Sudman, S., & Bradburn, N. M. (1982). *Asking questions*. San Francisco: Jossey-Bass.

Sullivan, K. A. (1990). Daily time allocation among adult and immature yellow-eyed juncos over the breeding season. *Animal Behaviour, 39*:380-388.

Survey Research Center. (1976). *Interviewer's manual*. Ann Arbor, MI: Institute for Social Research.

Swan, D. C., & Campbell, G. R. (1989). Differential reproduction rates and Osage population change 1877-1907. *Plains Anthropologist, 34*(124, Part 2):61-74.

Sykes, R. E., & Brent, E. E. (1983). *Policing: A social behaviorist perspective*. New Brunswick: Rutgers University Press.

Taylor, S. J. (1991). Leaving the field: Relationships and responsibilities. In W. B. Shaffir & R. A. Stebbins (Eds.), *Experiencing fieldwork: An inside view of qualitative research* (pp. 238-245). Newbury Park, CA: Sage.

Taylor, S. J., & Bogdan, R. (1984). *Introduction to qualitative research methods* (2nd ed.). New York: Wiley.

Templeton, J. F. (1987). *Focus groups: A guide for marketing and advertising professionals*. Chicago: Probus.

Tesch, R. (1990). *Qualitative research: Analysis and types of software tools*. New York: Falmer Press.

Thomas, J. S. (1981). The socioeconomic determinants of leadership in a Tojalabal Maya community. *American Ethnologist, 8*:127-138.

Thorndike, R. M. (1978). *Correlational procedures for research*. New York: Gardner Press.

Torgerson, W. (1958). *Theory and methods of scaling*. New York: Wiley.

Toulmin, S. E. (1980). Philosophy of science. *Encyclopaedia Brittanica* (Vol. 16). Chicago: Encyclopaedia Brittanica, Inc.

Tremblay, M. (1957). The key informant technique: A non-ethnographical application. *American Anthropologist, 59*:688-701.

Trotter, R. T., II (1981). Remedios caseros: Mexican-American home remedies and community health problems. *Social Science and Medicine, 15B*:107-114.

Trotter, R. T., II (1993) Review of TALLY 3.0. *Cultural Anthropology Methods, 5*(2):10-12.

Truex, G. (1993). Tagging and tying: Notes on codes in anthropology. *Cultural Anthropology Methods, 5*(1):3-5.

Turnbull, C. (1972). *The mountain people*. New York: Simon and Schuster.

Turnbull, C. (1986). Sex and gender: The role of subjectivity in field research. In: T. L. Whitehead & M. E. Conaway (Eds.), *Self, sex and gender in cross-cultural fieldwork* (pp. 17-29). Urbana: University of Illinois Press.

Tyler, S. A. (1969). *Cognitive anthropology*. New York: Holt, Rinehart and Winston.

United States Public Health Service. (1976). *National Center for Health Statistics growth charts*. Rockville, MD: USPHS Health Resources Administration.

Van Maanen, J., Miller, M., & Johnson, J. (1982). An occupation in transition: Traditional and modern forms of commercial fishing. *Work and Occupations, 9*(2):193-216.

Veatch, H. B. (1969). *Two logics: The conflict between classical and neoanalytic philosophy*. Evanston, IL: Northwestern University Press.

Vickers, B. (1978). *Francis Bacon*. Harlow, England: Published for the British Council by the Longman Group.

Vidich, A. J., & Shapiro, G. (1955). A comparison of participant observation and survey data. *American Sociological Review, 20*:28-33.

Wagley, C. (1983). Learning fieldwork: Guatemala. In R. Lawless, V. H. Sutlive & M. D. Zamora (Eds.), *Fieldwork: The human experience* (pp. 1-18). New York: Gordon and Breach.

Wall Street Journal. (1986, September 4), p. 29.

Wallace, A. F. C. (1962). Culture and cognition. *Science, 135*:351-357.

Ward, V. M., Bertrand, J. T., & Brown, L. F. (1991). The comparability of focus group and survey results. *Evaluation Review, 15*:266-283.

Warner, S. L. (1965). Randomized response: A survey technique for eliminating evasive answer bias. *Journal of the American Statistical Association, 60*:63-69.

Warren, C. A. B. (1988). *Gender issues in field research.* Newbury Park, CA: Sage.

Warwick, D. P., & Lininger, C. A. (1975). *The sample survey: Theory and practice.* New York: McGraw-Hill.

Watson, O. M., & Graves, T. D. (1966). Quantitative research in proxemic behavior. *American Anthropologist, 68*:971-985.

Wax, R. (1971). *Doing fieldwork: Warnings and advice.* Chicago: University of Chicago Press.

Wax, R. (1986). Gender and age in fieldwork and fieldwork education: "Not any good thing is done by one man alone." In T. L. Whitehead & M. E. Conaway (Eds.), *Self, sex and gender in cross-cultural fieldwork* (pp. 129-150). Urbana: University of Illinois Press.

Webb, E. J., Campbell, D. T., Schwartz, R. D., & Sechrest, L. (1966). *Unobtrusive measures: Nonreactive research in the social sciences.* Chicago: Rand McNally.

Webb, E. J., & Weick, K. E. (1983). Unobtrusive measures in operational theory: A reminder. In J. van Maanen (Ed.), *Qualitative methodology* (pp. 209-224). Newbury Park, CA: Sage.

Weber, R. P. (1990). *Basic content analysis* (2nd ed.). Newbury Park, CA: Sage.

Weeks, M. F., & Moore, R. P. (1981). Ethnicity-of-interviewer effects on ethnic respondents. *Public Opinion Quarterly, 45*:245-249.

Weick, K. E. (1985). Systematic observational methods. In G. Lindzey & E. Aronson (Eds.), *Handbook of social psychology: Vol. 2. Special fields and applications* (3rd ed., pp. 567-634). New York: Random House.

Weinberger, J. (1985). *Science, faith, and politics: Francis Bacon and the utopian roots of the modern age.* Ithaca, NY: Cornell University Press.

Weller, S. C. (1983). New data on intracultural variability: The hot-cold concept of medicine and illness. *Human Organization, 42*:249-257.

Weller, S. C., & Dungy, C. I. (1986). Personal preferences and ethnic variations among Anglo and Hispanic breast and bottle feeders. *Social Science and Medicine, 23*:539-548.

Weller, S. C., & Romney, A. K. (1988). *Structured interviewing.* Newbury Park, CA: Sage.

Werner, D. (1980). *The making of a Mekranoti chief: The psychological and social determinants of leadership in a Native South American community.* Unpublished doctoral dissertation, City University of New York.

Werner, D. (1985). Psycho-social stress and the construction of a flood-control dam in Santa Catarina, Brazil. *Human Organization, 44*:161-166.

Werner, O., & Fenton, J. (1973). Method and theory in ethnoscience or ethnoepistemology. In R. Naroll & R. Cohen (Eds.), *A handbook of method in cultural anthropology* (pp. 537-578). New York: Columbia University Press.

Werner, O., & Schoepfle, G. M. (1987). *Systematic fieldwork* (2 vols.). Newbury Park, CA: Sage.

West, S. G., Gunn, S. P., & Chernicky, P. (1975). Ubiquitous Watergate: An attributional analysis. *Journal of Personality and Social Psychology, 32*:55-65.

Westfall, R. S. (1980). *Never at rest: A biography of Isaac Newton.* Cambridge, U.K.: Cambridge University Press.

Whitehead, T. L., & Conaway, M. E. (Eds.). (1986). *Self, sex and gender in cross-cultural fieldwork.* Urbana: University of Illinois Press.

Whiten, A., & Barton, R. A. (1988). Demise of the checksheet: Using off-the-shelf miniature hand-held computers for remote fieldwork applications. *Trends in Ecology and Evolution, 3*:146-148.

Whiting, J. W. M., Child, I. L., Lambert, W. W. et al. (1966). *Field guide for a study of socialization.* New York: Wiley.

Whiting, B. W., & Whiting, J. W. M. (1973). Methods for observing and recording behavior. In R. Naroll & R. Cohen (Eds.), *Handbook of method in cultural anthropology* (pp. 282-315). New York: Columbia University Press.

Whiting, B. W., & Whiting, J. W. M. (with R. Longabaugh). (1975). *Children of six cultures. A psycho-cultural analysis.* Cambridge, MA: Harvard University Press.

WHO Working Group. (1986). Use and interpretation of anthropometric indicators of nutritional status. *World Health Organization Bulletin, 64*(6):929-941.

Whyte, W. F. (1955). *Street corner society: The social structure of an Italian slum.* Chicago: University of Chicago Press.

Whyte, W. F. (1960). Interviewing in field research. In R. W. Adams & J. J. Preiss (Eds.), *Human organization research* (pp. 299-314). Homewood, IL: Dorsey.

Whyte, W. F. (1984). *Learning from the field: A guide from experience.* Newbury Park, CA: Sage.

Whyte, W. F. (1989). Doing research in Cornerville. In C. D. Smith & W. Kornblum (Eds.), *In the field: Readings on the field research experience* (pp. 69-82). New York: Praeger.

Whyte, W. F., & Alberti, G. (1983). On the integration of research methods. In M. Bulmer & D. Warwick (Eds.), *Social research in developing countries* (pp. 352-374). New York: Wiley.

Wilke, J. R. (1992). Supercomputers manage holiday stock. *Wall Street Journal,* December 23, B1:8.

Williams, B. (1978). *A sampler on sampling.* New York: Wiley.

Wilson, R. P., Nxumalo, M., Magonga, B., Jr., Shelley, G. A., Parker, K. A., & Dlamini, Q. Q. (1993). *Diagnosis and management of acute respiratory infections by Swazi child caretakers, healers, and health providers, 1990-1991.* Office of Analysis and Technical Reports, United States Agency for International Development. Working Paper.

Winter, M. (1991). Interhousehold exchange of goods and services in the city of Oaxaca. *Urban Anthropology, 20:*67-86.

Winter, M., Morris, E. W., & Murphy, A. D. (1989). *Food expenditures, food purchases, and satisfaction with food in the city of Oaxaca.* Unpublished manuscript.

World Health Organization. (1983). *Measuring change in nutritional status: Guidelines for assessing the nutritional impact of supplementary feeding programmes for vulnerable groups.* Geneva: Author.

Wright, S. (1921). Correlation and causation. *Journal of Agricultural Research, 20:*557-585.

Young, J. C. (1978). Illness categories and action strategies in a Tarascan town. *American Ethnologist, 5:*81-97.

Young, J. C. (1980). A model of illness treatment decisions in a Tarascan town. *American Ethnologist, 7:*106-131.

Zehner, R. B. (1970). Sex effects in the interviewing of young adults. *Sociological Focus, 3:*75-84.

Zeisel, H. (1985). *Say it with figures* (6th ed.). New York: Harper & Row.

Zirkle, C. (1949). *The death of a science in Russia.* Philadelphia: University of Pennsylvania Press.

Author Index

Subject Index

About the Author

H. Russell Bernard is Professor of Anthropology at the University of Florida. He served two terms as editor of *American Anthropologist*, the official journal of the American Anthropological Association, and previously served as editor of *Human Organization*, journal of the Society for Applied Anthropology. Bernard's work has spanned the range of cultural anthropological concerns, from traditional ethnography and linguistics to applied work and statistics. His fieldwork settings include Greece, Mexico, and the United States and cover such diverse subjects as sponge divers, scientists, bureaucrats, and prisoners. He has developed, with a native speaker, a writing system for the Otomí people of Mexico and, through it, experimented with native-generated ethnographies. He is cofounder (with Alvin Wolfe) of the International Sunbelt Social Networks Conference. His books include *Technology and Social Change* (coedited with Pertti Pelto, two editions), *Introduction to Chicano Studies* (coedited with Livie Duran, two editions), *The Otomí* (with Jesús Salinas Pedraza), *The Human Way: Readings in Anthropology*, and *Native Ethnography* (with Jesús Salinas Pedraza).